QUICK CHANGE

QUICK CHANGE

28 THEATRE ESSAYS
4 PLAYS IN TRANSLATIONS

by

DANIEL GEROULD

MARTIN E. SEGAL THEATRE CENTER PUBLICATIONS
NEW YORK, ©2010

DANIEL GEROULD, DIRECTOR OF PUBLICATIONS
FRANK HENTSCHKER, EXECUTIVE DIRECTOR
JAN STENZEL, DIRECTOR OF ADMINISTRATION

Library of Congress Cataloging-in-Publication Data

Gerould, Daniel Charles, 1928-
Quick change : theatre essays and translations / by Daniel Gerould.
    p. cm.
ISBN 978-0-9790570-9-0
1. Drama--History and criticism. 2. Theater--History. I. Title.
PN1655.G46 2010
809.2--dc22
                        2010040057

Copy-editing and layout by
Kurt Taroff and Christopher Silsby

© 2010 Martin E. Segal Theatre Center
Daniel Gerould, Director of Publications
Frank Hentschker, Executive Director
Jan Stenzel, Director of Administration

QUICK CHANGE

THEATRE ESSAYS AND TRANSLATIONS

by

DANIEL GEROULD

MARTIN E. SEGAL
THEATRE CENTER

TABLE OF CONTENTS

QUICK CHANGE

FOREWORD

Daniel Gerould is having a long run—and this book is a sampling from 50 years from it. At first glance, Dan Gerould strikes me as unusual: his wide-eyes energetically alert, his trim body well-dressed and properly groomed, an elegant man in an epoch of slobs. Dan is thin, so he wears his clothes with a little room to spare, much as the widely divergent suite of writings that is *Quick Change* ranges freely across epochs, cultural areas, and genres. Dan is polite, he listens carefully; he responds to emails; he is someone to whom I have referred many scholars and students—and he has never to my knowledge turned any away. Dan speaks with a precision that is rare in these days of rampant blogs, twitters, YouTube splurges, and Facebook let-me-give-it-all-away. Care of dress, manners, speech, writing, and manners suits Dan, as does his unstinting generosity.

But this surface is not by any means all of who Gerould is. *Quick Change* is full of surprises. It is a nicely seasoned tossed-salad of a book concocted by an ironic cook-meister with a sometimes wild imagination. Gerould tells his readers that his book's title comes from his fascination with "sleight-of-hand artists" and that "transformation is the talisman or open-sesame of my entire output." And how many quick changes has he wrought in this book of 28 pieces. The writings range from translations of letters and plays to short commentaries to fully-developed essays. The topics bounce from Mayakovsky to Shakespeare, Kantor to Lunacharsky, Herodotus to Gerould's own play, *Candaules, Commissioner,* Gorky to Grotowski, Shaw to Mrożek, Briusov to Witkacy. From ancient Greeks to Renaissance and Enlightenment Europe, from pre-revolutionary Russia to the Soviet Union, from France and England to Poland. From an arcane discussion of medicine in theatre to a translation of Henry Monnier's *The Tart and the Student*, a "libertine" puppet play from 19th-century France.

Quick Change is a collection that both represents yet cannot fully comprehend Gerould's contribution to theatre studies and performance studies. That is because his work has been so varied and rich. In addition to the writings collected here, Gerould has translated twenty-two of Witkacy's plays, authored a study of Witkacy: *Ignacy Witkiewicz as an Imaginative Writer* (1981), and edited both the *Witkiewicz Reader* (1992) and the *Mrożek Reader* (2004). He co-edited with Saviana Stanescu *Romania After 2000: Five New Romanian Plays* (2007). His interest in popular forms is seen in his *Melodrama* (1980) and his co-edited *Comedy: a Bibliography of Critical Studies in English on the Theory and Practice of Comedy in Drama, Theatre, and Performance* (2006). He has also edited a book on basic theatre theory from Aristotle through Zeami to Havel (2000).

For all this breadth of scholarship and creativity, it will be no surprise to those who know Dan that there is a locus to his life's work: Eastern Europe. This region is not so easy to define as it might at first seem. Eastern Europe includes the former Soviet Union and its satellites, from the Czech Republic to Belarus and the Ukraine, from Estonia to Bulgaria; from Germany west to Russia and from the Baltic to the Black Seas. These are basically Christian territories, but with formerly large Jewish populations. There are anomalies, such as Muslim Albania and the former Yugoslavia now fractured into six nations, including Muslim Kosovo (whose independence Serbia and Russia refuse to recognize). Or where to put Armenia and Georgia which are south of the Caucasus Mountains demarking Asia from Europe, but whose peoples identify with Europe. Russia itself is bi-continental though most Russians think of themselves as Europeans.

The fact is that Eastern Europe is an in-between region often yearning Westward while fearing what may come from the East. The region is a complex conglomerate of cultural bridges and mixes, none more wrought than Poland—whose theatre is a favorite of Gerould's. Poland did not exist as a nation from 1795 to 1918. From 1939 to 1989 Poland was either divided between the Soviet Union and Germany, occupied by Germany, or a Soviet satellite. But throughout there was the imagined Polish nation, independent; a nation populated by people many of whom were illiterate peasants, many others living in ghettos speaking and writing Yiddish, and still others who preferred French which handled with elegance. As a group, Polish cultures were and are provincial and cosmopolitan; Slavic, Jewish, and Catholic; inflected/infected/invaded/liberated by the French, the Germans, and the Russians. Many of the essays in *Quick Change* start from and return to Poland. In Daniel Gerould's writings there is a Polish whimsy, fatalism, intellectual curiosity, irony, and virtuosity.

Enjoy.

— Richard Schechner

New York, September 2010

Daniel Gerould, The Graduate Center, City University of New York, Ph.D. Program in Theatre, at the defense of Kurt Taroff's thesis on Monodrama, 2005.

INTRODUCTION

The essays and translations in this volume, written over the past fifty years and previously uncollected, reflect my abiding interest in artistic creativity and the transformative power of the arts. They are for the most part devoted to individual theatre artists or to collective issues eliciting responses from different artists. Each essay is a separate inquiry about some aspect of the theory and practice of the arts of performance.

Theatre and drama find their natural place in the history of the arts. Theatre history, intellectual history, and history of the arts should, I am convinced, go hand in hand. Tadeusz Kantor, the subject of two of my essays, declared his goal to be "placing theatre within the realm of the totality of art." Could anything be simpler, and at the same time as all-embracing?

Quick Change is the title of the collection not only because it is the subject of one of the pivotal essays, but, more significantly, because the art of transformation is the talisman or open-sesame of my entire output. Theatre for me is the art of metamorphosis. Changing one's skin and shedding one's old self is fundamental to the dramatic impulse. "I want to be different, to begin again and again; to shed myself as a snake sheds its skin," says Shaw's Adam in *Back to Methuselah*.

Those artists like Villiers de l'Isle-Adam, Sologub, and Kantor, who believe deeply in the transformative powers of art are sorcerers and wizards. Reaching back to the buffoons and clowns of antiquity, Quick Change is the epitome of the theatrical— it existed in sixteenth-century commedia dell'arte, in seventeenth-century Kabuki as *hayagawari* (one actor sometimes playing six roles in a single act), and in nineteenth and twentieth-century variety theatre, home to the protean artist, transfigurator, or transformist.

A unifying motif behind all of the essays is the creation of forms, the pleasure we take in these, and our admiration for the skill of their artificers. Art lives by its dwelling in form. My fascination is for these artistic shapes: their fabrication, traditions, and histories. Forms are born, grow old, and die. Sometimes they are reborn—the recovery of old forms and the rediscovery of dead authors are crucial archeological activities. As Ludwik Flaszen, Grotowski's dramaturg, explains, "We do not wish to discover something new, but something forgotten."

Asserting the priority of form in no way denies the mutual attraction between art and life and their frequent cohabitation; it simply affirms that form is what makes art art. My exemplars along these lines of thought are the Russian Formalists, known for their belief in the artfulness of art and their curiosity about genres and the patterns, structures, and techniques of popular arts like melodrama. In his *Notebooks*, Chekhov writes, "Behind new forms in literature there always follow new forms of life."

My first contacts with theatre came about through magic, at which I dabbled as a child. I watched sleight-of-hand artists demonstrate tricks to one another at magicians' conventions, and I went to performances of master illusionists, like the Great Thurston, who staged spectacular acts with large casts, fancy props and costumes, and elaborate stunts dependent on complicated technology. At home I created a life-size dummy with a carved coconut head, who wore a hat, coat, shirt, tie, and trousers and had a concealed tube running from the basement up his left leg to his mouth that enabled me to carry on conversations and make jokes with my parents' guests at dinner parties.

I also regularly attended the circus, rodeos, and stunt car shows, since my father, a newspaperman, was the regular recipient of free tickets. At all of these spectacles, the self-extolled daring and skill of the performers were sources of wonder and delight, and I relished all the hyperbole, hoopla, and razzmatazz. I attended the stage shows accompanying the films at large movie houses and featuring big bands, such as Jimmy Dorsey, Bob Crosby, and Cab Calloway (the latter—constantly changing flamboyantly colored zoot suits—was himself a quick-change artist). I went to jazz concerts to hear James P. Johnson and Wild Bill Davison at Sunday matinees where teenagers were tolerated, although still the exception, not the rule.

By the late 1930s and early 40s I started attending the legitimate stage with my mother. At that time many Broadway-bound productions tried out first in Boston, and I remember Ethel Barrymore in *The Corn Is Green* by Emlyn Williams and *Arsenic and Old Lace* with Boris Karloff. I felt myself a seasoned spectator, was at home among audiences, and was always ready to applaud bravura displays of virtuoso acting. The seed had been planted, although it wasn't until the 1954–55 season in Paris (where I was an exchange student) that I again became an intensive spectator, followed by a similar stint in 1967 in Moscow (where I was on a faculty research grant).

These essays are addressed to friends, colleagues, and peers, who will perhaps have read some of them at the time of their original publication, but, beyond that limited circle of scholars, I now hope to reach a broader public of intellectually curious readers and theatregoers. To make the essays appealing to newer generations, I decided not simply to republish them verbatim as documents of historical value, but instead to revise and bring them up-to-date.

In a few cases revision meant only adding or updating the endnotes, but more often than not it has involved changing tenses, providing a present-day perspective, incorporating new materials previously inaccessible, and writing the endings that had not yet occurred at the time of composition because many of the stories I was telling were still ongoing. The fall of the Berlin Wall, the sudden collapse of communism in Eastern Europe, and the Soviet Union's quick demise were coups de théâtre radically altering the development of the theatre and modifying our assessments of its import. New materials have come out of archives, formerly censored authors have had their complete works published, and reviled and despised writers have been exalted. Given the opportunity to take into account all of these changes, I could not fail to revise the essays.

For the most part I have chosen to write about the underrated, the ignored, and the forgotten rather than the overexposed and universally celebrated. I have never been much concerned with whether an artist was a major or a minor figure, a canonical or non-canonical artist, since these valuations are constantly shifting and highly unreliable. Witkacy is a case in point, having gone from controversial outsider to classic of the avant-garde in three decades. My essays are open to writers of all provenance. Shakespeare and Molière, as well as Shaw and Ibsen, also put in frequent appearances.

I refuse to impose any hierarchy, and rather than ordering the essays chronologically or grouping thematically or by nationality (all Polish or Russian together), I have presented them seemingly at random as a variety show, at which the reader may pick and choose whatever looks interesting or amusing.

I consider these essays as part of a process of discovery and recovery, forays into murky and sometimes lurid areas, peopled by strange obsessive figures like Villiers de l'Isle-Adam, Tadeusz Miciński, Fyodor Sologub, and Alexander Scriabin, whose overheated imaginations gave birth to grandiose projects and the creation of myths of the future. The connections of the stage to the paranormal, to magic and alchemy, to the occult and esoteric, to the erotic and the macabre, are notorious and have often given the theatre a bad name as "sensational," and led its apologists to defend it as rational, instructive, and socially useful. The tensions between these two views of theatre—as metaphysical or as ethical—are at stake in a number of the essays, which consider the function of drama, particularly that of comedy. I endorse both views as equally valid, but express a personal preference for the sensational.

The functions of comedy and the qualities of different kinds of laughter have been at the forefront of my inquiries, which investigate how laughter can combat what is backward, and how it can dispel fear and even thrive in oppressive regimes. The relation of art to ideology, seen from the viewpoint of the artist, is a question that recurs in my essays, which are often situated against the background of life in Eastern Europe during the cold war.

My initial encounter with Eastern European drama came about thanks to Tom Lantos, then the director of overseas programs at San Francisco State College, who arranged for me to go to Poland for five weeks in the summer of 1965 as part of a faculty travel program underwritten by the State Department and paid for in counterpart funds. Tom was a Hungarian Jew who along with his young wife to be had been saved by Raoul Wallenberg in Budapest in 1944; he subsequently became an influential US congressman from 1981 until his death in 2008.

At that point modern Polish theatre was terra incognita in the United States and in most of the rest of the world. This was five years before Grotowski's theatre first appeared in New York and fourteen before Kantor brought *The Dead Class* to La MaMa. That I discovered Witkacy and got to meet many of the principal figures in the Polish theatre was a matter of good fortune. Witkacy was for me a found object that I came across by chance.

On my first full day in Poland, a meeting for me had been arranged with a bureaucrat in the theatre section at the Ministry of Culture in Warsaw, not far from the hotel where I was staying. I walked to the ministry and entered the office. Beneath a small picture of Lenin on the wall behind his desk, the official, Jerzy Sokolowski (later one of the editors of the journal *Teatr*), and I conversed in Russian because at that time I did not know Polish. After a few perfunctory remarks about the organization of the Polish theatre and its repertory, the official grew animated as he told me about a remarkable Polish playwright active during the 1920s and 30s who was in the process of being rediscovered, and he explained to me that the productions of his plays, many being staged for the first time, were the most exciting events taking place in the Polish theatre.

At that point he pulled open the bottom drawer of desk and drew out two compact gray volumes of plays (eight-by-five, more than five hundred pages each), which he proudly displayed. That was how I first became acquainted with Stanisław Ignacy Witkiewicz.

I took the volumes he handed me and looked at the covers: *Dramaty* at the top and the author's pen-name signature, Witkacy, across the lower left half. After that, the volumes went back into the desk drawer.

Later, I learned that this was the precious edition of all of Witkiewicz's plays that had recently been published (1962) in a drastically limited edition after several years of hard bargaining between the authorities and the editor, who had turned down the option offered by the censor, of a larger printing with some discrete cuts (of remarks that could be offensive to the Soviets), choosing instead an edition of only three thousand copies with no omissions. Eagerly awaited, this edition was sold out even before the day of its release; copies in bookstores were kept beneath the counter for those in the know who had the right contacts.

Within a few days after my first encounter with Witkiewicz, I met Konstanty Puzyna, the editor of that two volume edition, who suggested the idea of translating the playwright into English. That's how it all started. Now, some forty years later, I have translated nineteen of the twenty-one plays in those two compact volumes.

Living in the USSR in 1967 on a faculty exchange at Moscow State University and then spending two years in Poland as a Fulbright lecturer at Warsaw University from 1968 to 1970 enabled me observe firsthand how theatre functions in totalitarian regimes. As I became acquainted with writers and theatre artists in both Russia and Poland, I learned how their careers were shaped by ideology and saw the roles that they were forced to play. In Russia the novelist and playwright Vassily Aksyonov (1932–2009) was my guide. In Poland central to my understanding was my friendship with Zygmunt Hübner (1930–1989), director of the Teatr Stary in Cracow during its heyday in the 1960s and then director of the Teatr Powszechny in Warsaw and author of the essential book, *Theater and Politics*.

The position of the artist in twentieth-century totalitarian communist states has never ceased to fascinate. In the Soviet Union and its satellite Eastern bloc countries, which fostered, financed, and pampered its obedient musicians, painters, and poets as prize exhibits to be displayed to the world, the honored and decorated artist was expected, in return, to speak on behalf of the regime or at least refrain from criticizing it. Theatre artists in particular had to tread a delicate line in order to get their work produced without compromising their principles. Forced to co-exist with a hostile ideology that provided benefits and sets limits, the playwright, director, or actor, while seeming to subscribe to a rigid dogma, had to find ways to oppose and transcend it. Failure to play the game adroitly might result in loss of one's job and privileges or worse: loss of citizenship, expulsion, and exile (as happened to Aksyonov).

Finally, a few words about the craft of translation, to which I have devoted much time and thought. The translator is a medium at a séance, possessed by and speaking for the author. In my translations of Witkacy, I have tried to find a voice for a highly idiosyncratic playwright who was in search of a new autonomous stage language. Translation can also be a political weapon. A controversial and subversive author whose plays in performance were often subject to censorship in communist Poland, Witkacy gained posthumous prestige and security at home by being recognized abroad. Translation and subsequent foreign production and publication in the West helped assure the playwright's ultimate triumph over those who tried to suppress him.

There are four essays about Witkacy in *Quick Change*, but given the nature and scope of the collection, it was not possible to reprint any translation of his plays. Instead, I have included a selection of his letters and also translations that accompanied seven other essays as integral parts of the original publication. Five of these are theatrical—all miniatures in different dramatic idioms indicating the range of styles and forms that have attracted me as a translator: a lyrical Pierrot text by a mime, two naturalistic *comédies rosses*, a pornographic puppet play, and a surreal poetic evocation of post-revolutionary disenchantment. The other two examples are English renderings of theoretical texts—an important and undervalued aspect of the translator's work.

Of the many wise and clever things said about translation, two strike me as particularly incisive. Goethe writes, "People may say what they like of the inadequacy of translation, it is and remains one of the weightiest and worthiest of employments in the general life of the world." Struggling with intractable passages and full of self-doubts, the bedeviled translator can turn to this generous encomium for reassurance. In *Beyond Good and Evil*, II, 28, Nietzsche points out the greatest difficulty facing the translator, "That which translates worst from one language to another is the tempo of its style." This warning should be heeded. Quick Change demands fast rhythms. In his advice to potential future directors of his plays, Witkacy insists that the dialogue be spoken as rapidly as possible.

What has been the domain of these essays? Nothing vast, and yet, I hope, something substantive and coherent—the roughly one hundred years of modern European performance stretching from the founding of the Moscow Art Theatre to the death of Grotowski (with a few excursions back in time to antecedents and ancestors). This epoch saw the flowering of modern theatre—and its eventual end. My essays have touched on a few of the theatrical events and issues—both big and small—occurring within that panorama, and they have raised questions about the power of the theatrical arts which transcend the particular incidents that occasioned my inquiries.

This epoch is now over and complete—almost all its major practitioners are either dead or inactive. These essays are in praise of the art, and in remembrance of the artists, of that past time.

— Daniel Gerould

New York, August 2010

Acknowledgements

Of the many editors who have encouraged my work, I particularly wish to express my gratitude to Jeanine Plottel *(New York Literary Forum)*, Mel Gordon, Michael Kirby, and Richard Schechner *(TDR)*, Bonnie Marranca and Gautam Dasgupta *(PAJ, Performing Arts Journal; PAJ A Journal of Performance and Art)*, Joel Schechter, Erika Munk, and Elinor Fuchs *(yale/theater)*, Jill Levenson and Ruby Cohn *(Modern Drama)*, Darko Suvin *(Science-Fiction Studies)*, and Henry Salerno *(Drama and Theatre)*, who first published *Candaules Commissioner* and the earliest English translations of Witkiewicz.

The twenty-eight essays (sometimes with an accompanying play or theoretical text) appeared in the following fifteen journals or conference proceedings: *Assaph, Cahier Witkiewicz: Colloque de Bruxelles, Contemporary Russian and Polish Drama: Theatre Perspectives, Comparative Literature, Modern Drama, New York Literary Forum, PAJ, , Pamiętnik Teatralny, Sacred Theatre, Science-Fiction Studies, Slavic and East European Performance, Theatre Three, TDR, World Literature Today, yale/theatre (Theater)*. The source of each essay is acknowledged at the bottom of its first page.

I am pleased to be able to thank the many people and institutions who have contributed to the creation of *Quick Change*. First of all, my graduate students have played a key role in the genesis of these essays and translations, which have grown out of the seminars that I have taught at the Graduate Center over the past forty years. Many of these graduate students have worked directly on the preparation of *Quick Change*. I am particularly grateful to Kurt Taroff, the editor of origin, who set the project in motion, and to Christopher Silsby, the editor of destination, who brought the task to completion. Their work was complementary and essential, executed deftly and with zeal. Laura Hydak and Jake Hooker assisted in organizing the texts, and the index was ably prepared by Maria Mytilinaki.

The publication of the book was financed by the Lucille Lortel Chair in Theatre and sponsored by Marten E. Segal Center Publications. Frank Hentschker, executive director of the Segal Center, supervised the entire project in all its phases and was responsible for the book's design, typography, and cover art. Without his expert guidance and dedicated commitment, *Quick Change* could never have come into being. Jan Stenzel, director of administration at the Segal Center, has worked diligently on obtaining rights and permissions and on technical co-ordination. Anna Shulgat, a Segal Center intern now in Moscow, assisted with the illustrations.

Over the years I have made extensive use of the resources of the Library of the Graduate Center and the many other libraries of the City University of New York, as well as of the New York Public Library, its Slavonic Section and Performing Arts Library. I also did research in the British Library, Warsaw National Library, Bibliothèque Nationale Paris, Lenin Library, and Theatre Libraries in Moscow and in Leningrad.

My work has been supported by Fulbright Lectureships to Warsaw University, research grants to Poland and to the USSR from the International Research and Exchanges Board and from CUNY Research Grants.

Colleagues in Poland, Janusz Degler, Lech Sokół, Andrzej Wirth, and Anna Żakiewicz, have helped me for almost half a century in my research on Witkiewicz, for which I am very grateful.

It is my good fortune to have known several of the playwrights and theatre artists who are the subjects of these essays—Vassily Aksyonov, Jerzy Grotowski. Tadeusz Kantor, Sławomir Mrożek, and Tadeusz Różewicz among others; they are a source of inspiration and cause for celebration.

— Daniel Gerould, New York, 2010

Le Malade imaginaire frontispiece, 1682,
by Pierre Brissart, engraving by Jean Sauvé

IMAGINARY INVALIDS: A THEATRE OF SIMULATED PATIENTS

> In declining cultures, wherever the decision comes to rest with the masses, authenticity becomes superfluous, disadvantageous, a liability. Only the actor still arouses great enthusiasm.
>
> Nietzsche, *The Case of Wagner*[1]

> The most dangerous doctors are those born actors who imitate born doctors with perfect deceptive art.
>
> Nietzsche, *Human, All Too Human*[2]

I.

For a demonstration of diagnostic techniques in the analysis of symptoms and prescription of drugs, the examining doctor at a medical convention—appearing before an audience of doctors—may be interviewing a victim of arthritis played by an actress. In such settings physicians are discovering that the simulated patient is much more effective and convincing than the genuinely afflicted. For unlike the real sick person, who does not control his malady and cannot be counted on to give the correct responses, the actor/patient has complete mastery of his illness signs which he is able to produce and reproduce on demand. The simulator's uniform and typical symptoms can be played back as needed, his performance of the sick role is invariably satisfying. The skilled actor, not the true sufferer, is a willing guinea pig, ready to be interrogated in classes of medical schools and at promotional meetings of pharmaceutical companies, where simulations that always produce the requisite paradigms best serve educational and sales goals, in addition to providing entertainment in the form of live staged presentations. Hence there has arisen a market for specially trained performers who can accurately portray diseases, ranging from Alzheimer's to ulcers, in improvised scenes with real doctors conducting the examinations and diagnostic interviews.

When in 1986 I first learned of simulated patients from an article in the *New York Times* about a professional group based in New Jersey, called SIMULATIONS,[3] I felt that I had chanced upon extraordinary testimony to the power of the actor and his ability to play innovative extra-theatrical roles. Before looking in greater detail at SIMULATIONS and its cast of imaginary invalids and repertory of illnesses, I wish to place the phenomenon in the context of theatrical developments over several centuries and make some general reflections on the relations between doctors and the stage, patients and performers, medicine and drama. Theoretical issues raised by the simulated patient intersect with a number of motifs in the history of literature, and these questions have been for me a stimulus to speculation on diverse subjects.

In her study conducted among the Garinagu Indians of Belize, *Interpreting Signs of Illness: A Case Study in Medical Semiotics*, Kathryn Vance Staiano asserts that "the illness sign, its special communicative powers, its mythical and metaphorical qualities have through the centuries intrigued and provoked us." Semeiology has medical origins, and "the concept of interpretation of signs of illness (semeiotike) is at least as ancient as Greek medicine."[4] The illusory signs of sickness created by the actor or malingerer constitute a particularly intriguing problem in interpretation, with

—*Theater* 19, no. 1 (Fall/Winter 1987): 6–18.

mythical and metaphorical implications. According to Jean Baudrillard, every illness is simulatable, and medicine has been a favored terrain of simulations, where differences between true and false, the real and the imaginary, grow blurred.[5] Thomas Mann's Felix Krull carefully rehearsed the symptoms of psychic disorders found in textbooks, but when he appeared before the draft board, he gave an inspired Dionysian performance, as though possessed.

II.

First, some thoughts on the portrayal of the sick on stage. In the history of pre-modern theatre, illness, I should venture, is more often shown when it is counterfeit than when it is genuine. Rogues like Ben Jonson's Volpone, cunningly feign the symptoms of ailments from which they have never suffered, while dupes, like Molière's *malade imaginaire*, convince themselves that they are inwardly afflicted despite all appearances of good health. The fraudulent sick man is punished by being forced "to lie in prison, cramped with irons," (V, viii) until he actually has the diseases that he once affected. Volpone is doubly a medical impostor in that he also plays the role of a street mountebank selling quack medicine advertised to cure the simulated illnesses he has been feigning. In Jonson's archaic world view, inherited from the medieval morality play, the truth of real sickness is to triumph over the venal player's manipulation of man's body for gain.

In Molière's more modern universe, one sham is simply played against another. Argan's bourgeois affluence permits him to engage his own doctors and pharmacists, but their traditional medicine, based on scholastic erudition, is entirely ceremonial consisting of rhetoric, robes, and ritual instruments. Inflexible and backward looking (to Hippocrates and Galen), their system of diagnosis and therapy is unresponsive to Argan's self-generated symptoms and remains arrested in two useless cures, bleeding and purging.[6] The tyrannizing hypochondriac Argan is cleverly-manipulated, but ultimately humored by his commonsensical, skeptical household, who ceremoniously make him—through ritual use of language and gesture—a bogus doctor well qualified to minister to his own lovingly nurtured ailments. "Actors" (*les comédiens*), we are informed, have assisted in preparing the final show in which patient and practitioner are united in a single person in an apotheosis of medicine and illness as pure theatricality. Surrounded and protected by an army of doctors and now disguised like them, Argan imagines he can hold death at bay—by playing physician to his own complaints.[7] That the mortally sick author was stricken while performing the role of imaginary invalid and died shortly thereafter attests to the devious complexity confronting the interpreter of feigned illness signs in the theatre;[8] that the dead actor was denied extreme unction and at first refused burial in consecrated ground indicates in what official esteem the theatrical arts of simulation were then held.

The apparent exceptions to my rule (that pre-modern theatre prefers feigned disease) would seem to be madness and blindness, so often present in classical and Renaissance tragic drama as genuine afflictions. However, in such cases, madness is seen as a function of character and a consequence of moral choice, or as a punishment sent by the gods for past deeds; blindness is emblematic of spiritual states. Both afflict the upper head—brain and eyes—and appear intimately connected with man's individuality. Diseases of the lower body—mysterious in origin, arbitrarily inflicted—could only seem undramatic, unless they were simulated, deliberately chosen as roles to play. The sick body in pain could be replicated on stage by the actor as a ruse, but disease itself did not seem a fully human subject, nor constitute an appropriate antagonist. The struggle between man and his disordered body (unlike that between man and his disordered mind) was too little understood, too invisible, too private to be dramatizable in earlier ages.

It was not until the mid-nineteenth century, with the elevation of medicine to the rank of a serious science and doctors to social and professional respectability, that a new world of patients—mainly women and children—came into being[9] and for the first time the genuinely ill appeared on stage—with pale, emaciated faces, bulging eyes, and tell-tale coughs. Consumption was the preferred disease of the Victorian age, and Marguerite Gautier and Little Eva died of it before our eyes. But, as Susan Sontag points out, tuberculosis was viewed metaphorically as a disease of the soul.[10] In the nineteenth-century melodramas and tear-jerkers, disease still had moral equivalence, and the sick were perceived as pathetic objects of compassion, illustrating laws of divine justice. Little Eva died from an excess of goodness, the Lady of the Camellias from an insufficiency.

Zola and the Naturalists, on the other hand, looked to medicine for its cool objectivity and scientific methodology. Under the aegis of Dr. Claude Bernard (himself an unsuccessful playwright) and his *Introduction to the Study of Experimental Medicine*, Zola elaborated the case histories of his fictional characters. Artist and doctor were almost synonymous in their shared commitment to the experimental and the new.[11] Novelists and playwrights saw themselves as surgeons carrying out a dissection at an autopsy, and the patient was no more than a depersonalized body on the operating table. Now the ugly ravages of disease were for the first time shown on stage. In Zola's own adaptation of his novel, *Thérèse Raquin*, Mme Raquin suffers a stroke on stage and is shown throughout the rest of the play completely paralyzed in a wheelchair, but her affliction is plot-bound, caused by her learning of her son's murder, and it turns her into a mute figure of nemesis, serving to bring about the tragic denouement.

Under the influence of the experiments in hypnotism and suggestion then occurring in Paris, Strindberg in 1887 created *Vivisections*, a new form of psychological essay, and developed his idea of audience as a collective "subject," the performance as a hypnotic séance, and the actor as a medium in the hands of the author who put the performer into a trance and used him as his intermediary in affecting the public.[12]

By the fin de siècle, physicians had actually become playwrights (Chekhov, Schnitzler) and appear in dramas as *raisonneurs* (Dr. Relling in *The Wild Duck*, Dr. Astrov in *Uncle Vanya*), experts in reality and illusion, able to read the symptoms of private and public illness.

In the first half of the twentieth century, the medical world as it appeared in popular drama revolved around wise and courageous doctors, nobly conquering disease and discovering cures for mankind.[13] Only in the past generation has illness itself in its attacks on the human organism become a common theatrical subject. The patient, not the physician, is now the protagonist of a drama that confines its embattled hero to a hospital bed or sick room. Harold Pinter's *A Kind of Alaska* (1982), dealing with the amnesia produced by sleeping sickness, is directly based on a case history recounted by Dr. Oliver Sacks in his book *Awakenings*.

Pirandello's *Man with a Flower in His Mouth* of 1923, based on the author's earlier story "Caffe notturno," was a pioneering cancer play, its hero confronting his approaching death from epithelioma of the mouth as he talks with a stranger in an all-night cafe. Ronald Ribman's *Cold Storage* (1977) with its hospital setting is representative of clinical drama in which the struggle with death-threatening cancer replaces plot and becomes an extended agon. Some twenty years later, in Margaret Edson's *Wit* (1999), the nature of the conflict has changed markedly. The heroine Vivian Bearing—a brilliant professor and uncompromising intellectual—must battle not only her disease (ovarian cancer), but also, and above all, the radical experimental cure proposed by her research-oriented doctors who are more dedicated to the advancement of knowledge than to the spiritual well-being of the dying. The stoical, tough-minded professor of metaphysical poetry—in the hands of an antiseptic, soulless male medical establishment—loses every vestige of her identity as a human until at the moment of death she discovers in the simple compassion of a nurse and former teacher/mentor (both female) that neither science nor scholarship can touch the heart.

The stroke suffered by his father served Arthur Kopit as the starting point for his drama of aphasia, *Wings* (1978), whose heroine is closely modelled on two patients he met at the Burke Rehabilitation Center in White Plains, New York. Kopit then listened to tapes of the stroke victims in therapy and read medical literature on the subject, in order to achieve, as the author explains in his preface, "an absolutely solid clinical accuracy." The authenticity of rendering in *Wings* is such that doctors have found its portrayal of stroke symptoms and therapy exemplary. Kopit writes of his play's acclaim in the medical circles, "Neurologists who have seen it are anxious to use it as a teaching device because it does what textbooks don't do: it forces you to empathize with the victim."[14]

The personal case history drama, specialized by disease or impairment, and based on a particular patient's true story, appears to contain a higher theatrical truth that confers on its author and performers a special knowledge. On the basis of *Whose Life Is It Anyway?* (1972), about the rights of the terminally ill to time their own death, the playwright Brian Clark has been invited to medical conventions and asked to give expert testimony on euthanasia. Another stroke drama, Jean Claude van Itallie's *The Traveler* (1987) is a documentary account of the playwright's living through all the stages of Joe Chaikin's attack, subsequent aphasia, and painful efforts to relearn speech. A model of psychiatric authenticity in a historical setting was achieved earlier in Peter Brook's 1964 production of Weiss's *Marat/Sade*. To assure verisimilitude in the portrayals of mental aberrations, the director and actors visited English and French asylums, studied literature and art depicting madness and saw two films that graphically treated psychological disorders.[15] On stage were replicated the syphilis tubs at London's St. Bartholomew's Hospital (still in place, but no longer in use). The inventory of afflictions in contemporary medical drama is constantly expanding with each discovery of fresh symptoms of new diseases attacking man's body, as witness the many AIDS plays that have been written and performed since 1984. When the actor-impersonated patient leaves the stage world of illusion and appears outside the theatre in demonstration consultations with real doctors, we enter the world of simulations, or fictionalization assuming the guise of fact. The growing theatricalization of life and enhanced performance possibilities of modern medical practice are the preconditions of simulations, about which I must now say a few words.

III.

The dominance of theatre in the social and cultural life of late nineteenth-century France and the mania for actors and acting that accompanied it led certain writers to explore the hypnotic powers of the scenic arts and examine the proposition that, in a technological age of manipulatable appearances, artifice and imposture are more lifelike than reality. For example, in his *Cruel Tales* of 1883, the novelist and playwright Villiers de l'Isle-Adam portrays an inauthentic world in which illusion is rapidly replacing life, and genuine emotion has disappeared or has been driven inward to the realm of solitude and silence. Diminished natural feeling finds ready substitutes; everything can be faked, brilliantly staged, and given striking form through the use of appropriate signs. The theatre and its encroachments on life became key images of this fraudulent process for Villiers, an ardent playgoer who recognized the magic of the Parisian stage (with its cult of the actor and newly acquired technical means of producing dazzling illusions) and saw the implications for the creation of a performance society.

"I hope that there will soon be four or five hundred theatres in every capital, where the ordinary events of life are acted far better than in reality, so that nobody will take the trouble any more over living for himself," Villiers declares in one of his tales (*Sentimentality*), suggesting that whenever we feel a strong emotion we should hire an actor to express it for us, because only the performer can tell which words and gestures will be the most moving.[16]

In *Dr. Knock, or the Triumph of Medicine* (created by Louis Jouvet in 1923 and performed by him during the next twenty-five years more than 1,000 times on stage and twice in films), Jules Romains dramatizes the establishment of modern physician-patient relations in his hero's grasp of the theatricality of his calling and its power to mold a disparate group of individuals into a tightly controlled collective where each must play his assigned sick role. By giving the previously carefree and careless townspeople of St. Maurice a heightened consciousness of disease symptoms, Dr. Knock extends their sensitivity to illness and transforms them into patients, his motto (which he attributes to Dr. Claude Bernard) being: "Healthy people are sick people who don't know it."[17]

His genius resides in his ability to create a need where none existed before, by combining medicine and commerce and utilizing the techniques of advertising and propaganda. Dr. Knock, who learned his trade from reading medical announcements and pharmaceutical flyers, ushers in the era of "total medicine." His absolute patriarchal authority rests on the modern technology and rhetoric of the contemporary state.

It would be wrong to see Romains's super *homo medicus* as a quack or object of satire; he is simply such a consummate medical performer that he has become his own impenetrable mask. "My diagnostic machinery starts running by itself," Dr. Knock avows. In creating patients out of people and inaugurating "the medical existence"— which causes the stage to be illuminated by the bright light of Medical Science—the master diagnostician does exactly what modern medicine has been doing for the past one hundred years; he convinces a community to take seriously a whole range of illness signs, organs, and ailments that its members have previously disregarded.

In the ever-expanding process of disclosing new symptoms, diagnoses, and therapies, Dr. Knock sees as his indispensable ally the local pharmacist who will fill the prescriptions. The "pharmaco-medical spirit" that results from their dramaturgical cooperation is so pervasive that there are no longer any detached spectators (who, as in Molière's comedies, laugh at traditional medicine); we are all participants in the "life of medicine" and no longer remember a time without symptoms. Even Dr. Knock is afraid of looking in the mirror lest he should feel a diagnosis coming on.[18] *Homo medicus* cannot risk passing to the other side and joining the ranks of the sick.

Louis Jouvet as Dr. Knock and Iza Reyner as the Lady in Black
in the first film version of Jules Romains's *Dr. Knock* (1933)

IV.

It is against this background of physician-patient interactions, which I have been considering as performance in a theatrical setting, that we can understand the emergence of medical simulations in the 1970s. Whereas the theatricality of medicine has been most thoroughly explored by the French, the simulated patient appears to be a distinctively American phenomenon, the co-creation of American medical schools, university departments of drama, and pharmaceutical companies. University drama students were occasionally recruited to play patients with the "right" symptoms and diseases, when no genuinely ill people with these specifications were on hand, in the training of medical students and in continuing education programs for practicing family physicians. A problem in medical education—the need for available and reliable participants in diagnostic demonstrations—proved the starting point for individual amateur performances by student actors.

In a more general and theoretical context, we can speculate that the simulated patient is also a consequence of postmodern medicine, which begins in the late 1940s as a result of the revolution in drug therapy, whose effects only became gradually felt a generation later in radically changed physician-patient relations. As Edward Shorter points out in *Bedside Manners: The Troubled History of Doctors and Patients*, the "new pharmacopoeia" led to "relentless persistence in diagnosis" and the categorization of symptoms, from which there could emerge a "chief complaint" treatable by drugs. As the postmodern doctor grew increasingly disease-oriented, prescription-prone, desirous of reducing the "avalanche of symptoms" to be classifiable material for drug therapy, the postmodern patient, overwhelmed by so many signs of sickness and a lowered threshold of illness, became hostile and suspicious, having lost faith in the authority of a distant and uninvolved physician. Alienated in the face of a biochemical approach to their well-being, the postmodern sick have a tendency to perceive doctors as enemies and organize movements in defense of their rights.[19]

As a stand-in for a possible uncooperative, inarticulate sufferer, the simulated patient can assist in the process of educating and re-educating physicians in the new high-technology drugs. If Dr. Knock is the ideal theatrical exponent of the modern physician's patriarchal authority, the actor-patient is the characteristic embodiment of postmodern pharmacological medicine. Further, the simulated patient is a paratheatrical counterpart of the impersonated sick and dying in the agonistic dramas of the 1970s and 80s. The phenomenon is an outgrowth of a media society and age of simulations, compatible with a medical sensibility nurtured on hospital novels, serials, and television commercials featuring actor-played doctors and patients.

V.

The medical theatrical company SIMULATIONS[20] had its origins in the period from 1975 to 1978 when its founder, Margaret McGovern, was a student in the Theatre Arts Department at Douglass College of Rutgers University, where she had been asked by the Rutgers Medical School to play the role of a patient suffering from anxiety and depression for demonstration classes. Mrs. McGovern recruited other student actors and actresses for similar purposes, and sensing that there might be a continuing demand from medical schools, medical conferences, and pharmaceutical conventions, she organized the Rutgers simulators into a professional company, which assumed its present features in 1979. Margaret McGovern is the president and artistic director, her husband Joseph the business manager; the project has prospered and now includes an affiliate devoted to sales and business simulations. The McGoverns create films and videos as well as live productions; they hope to develop scenarios to deal with environmental issues, such as toxic waste.

The medical company which Margaret McGovern casts, trains, and directs, consists of a group of Equity actors and actresses available to play the different roles in a repertory of over forty specialized ailments. Normally, the individual actor appears with the interviewing doctor on a podium in a lecture hall or hotel conference room before an audience varying from a few dozen to several hundred. Performances last roughly forty-five minutes, length being determined by the lecture/conference format. Like traditional drama, the "action" of the medical simulation is exciting and suspenseful. Ionesco has said, "There's always been a detective about. Every play's an investigation brought to a successful conclusion."[21] In this case, the doctor is the detective, the disease is the criminal, and the symptoms are the clues. The dramaturgical method is interrogative, consisting of questions and answers. The climax of the situation comes with the accurate diagnosis and recognition of the illness, and the resolution follows with the prescription of drug therapy. The perfect matching of patient and medicine (like marriage in comedy) results in the happy ending, or cure.

For the most part, SIMULATIONS is a "poor" theatre, using only a bare stage and two chairs. The performer's only resource is a disciplined body; there is no make-up, no costuming, no lighting (nor is the auditorium darkened). Although the simulated patient does not lie down or undress, the physical examination involving ailments such as arthritis requires great technical mastery on the part of the actor.

The most extended and fully staged dramatization ever presented by SIMULATIONS was the multi-media evocation, in a Dallas hotel auditorium, of a hospital emergency room to which are brought four different heart attack victims. Sponsored by a drug company introducing a new use for one of its products—recently approved for the treatment of patients undergoing a heart attack—the simulation covered the events of four days within a two-hour performance which mixed live action with elaborate video and audio effects. Parkland Medical Center-Dallas students and personnel first trained the cast in hospital procedures and the use of equipment and then played themselves in the dramatization.

At the beginning of the dramatic event, a siren wailed and an ambulance was shown on giant screens as it raced to bring the first victim to the hospital. Suddenly a real Dallas ambulance drove through the side doors of the auditorium and came up to the edge of the stage representing the emergency room. Next the cardiac care unit arrived to practice resuscitation, while the screens above the stage presented close-ups of the procedures being followed. Read-outs of the heart machines appeared on the screens, and the "blips" of the heartbeats were amplified over loudspeakers.

The drama itself was complex, involving three additional victims of heart attacks, all with different symptoms and case histories leading to varied diagnoses and treatments—options which raised questions as to when the new drug should be used. In subsequent cases, the four actor-patients could simultaneously be seen in four beds as a real doctor made his rounds with a group of his own medical students. This physician in attendance gave case histories and asked the students questions about suggested treatment, to which they spontaneously responded, while another doctor, serving as commentator, offered instructive interpretation and provided transition from scene to scene. Characterization and doctor-patient interplay were developed in the manner of the hospital-oriented soap opera, complete with comedy provided by an eager side-kick of one of the physicians. The denouement brought both good and bad fortune to the suffering heroes of the drama. The first victim, who had been rushed to the hospital by ambulance, died, but the one patient for whom the new drug had been the appropriate treatment, steadily improved and was finally discharged from the hospital, leaving hand in hand with his wife. Moved and enlightened, the audience of 500 sales representatives applauded enthusiastically. The simulation realized Horace's goal for poetry as *dulce et utile*, being both informative and entertaining.

Distinctive features of the medical simulation, not found in traditional theatre, are its use of real doctors as interlocutors, its improvised nature, and the interactive, participatory nature of the audience (consisting of doctors and pharmacists). As in commedia, the performance is spontaneous and non-scripted, based on the outlines of a scenario, derived from medical case histories and illness types, each actor specializing in certain diseases. Existing in an indeterminate realm between fact and fiction, the medical simulation infuses medicine with the transformative powers of theatre. The examining doctor plays himself, but the theatrical rendition enables him to be more himself, to realize fully his own essence as a physician-diagnostician. The actor, by contrast, impersonates someone else (a sick patient with an individualized case history), but cast according to physical type and wearing his own clothes, the simulator remains partly himself

A clinical demonstration of arthritic symptoms by SIMULATIONS with Dr. Stanley Alexander

The performance is punctuated by periodic comment by the examining physician, as well as by the doctor-moderator. The audience participates by asking the patients for additional information covering their histories and symptoms or by questioning the examining physicians about techniques, conclusions and therapy recommendations. Thus, the physician audience contributes to developing the proper denouement to the dramaturgical plot.

The appeal of the unpredictable is always present in these unrehearsed confrontations which draw upon the resourcefulness of all the performers. When, for example, at one demonstration, the simulated patient—playing a young woman stock broker addicted to cocaine—arrived for her consultation displaying obvious symptoms of being "high," the examining physician immediately refused to continue the interview, explaining that he never saw patients while they were under the influence of narcotics. The demonstration seemed to be about to break down, but the psychiatrist serving as moderator immediately suggested that the patient could return two days later free of the effects of her addiction, and the consultation resumed instantly. Due to the skillful intervention of the moderator, the temporary disruption became part of the performance, whereas the disturbance caused by an authentic patient would have stopped the show.

VI.

The above dramatic episode illustrates several of the ways in which the simulated patient is superior to the genuinely afflicted. The simulation is repeatable, interruptible, capable of being played back—with variations. Theatrically flexible time is subject to condensation, and may move backward or forward. In a single forty-five-minute class for medical students at New York University, Seret Scott, one of the group's seasoned performers and a well-known professional actress, was interviewed twice as a rape victim suffering from depression, first immediately after the attack, then two months later. As her principal character, Seret Scott plays a rheumatoid arthritic—able to be shown in all stages of the illness—whom she calls Alison Forrest, a name that retains anagrammatic relics of the actress's own.[22] Simulations make it possible to show the "disease state development" in different phases, follow its natural course, or alter its consequences with a variety of medications and other therapies. Past history can be relived and future effects studied, as in a film that can be stopped, rewound, or advanced at fast speed.

Most important, the simulation is a totally controlled learning device, offering risk-free realism. Eliminated are undesirable human variables. A genuinely sick person may have a good day and spoil the entire effect of the demonstration. With simulated patients, the physicians are "free from concerns that the patient will not cooperate, or perform up to the standards required to illustrate the disease state." No longer need physicians feel scruples about exploiting the truly afflicted; moreover, drug sales personnel, who are denied the opportunity to see real patients in their interactions with doctors because of medical ethics, can participate in the staged diagnoses leading to the prescription of their products.

The most celebrated and fascinating of all such shows featuring the mentally ill were those put on by Dr. Jean-Martin Charcot (himself a talented artist and showman with a highly developed histrionic talent who could both draw and impersonate his patients) at the Salpêtrière asylum in Paris at the end of the nineteenth century. "Like a film producer, Charcot possessed the ability to make breathtaking 'finds'" in his cultivation of talented patient performers. The music-hall artist Jane Avril, who went to the Salpêtrière as a troubled thirteen-year-old, was Dr. Charcot's most famous graduate. Writers, actors and actresses—including Sarah Bernhardt—as well as doctors and medical students flocked to the public demonstrations at which Charcot hypnotized his female patients and exhibited the various stages of their hysterical fits, causing them to win "fame in Paris and in the international world of medicine for their performances"[23] and became the main attractions at the hospital's annual post-Lenten *Bal des Folles*. Among his followers and admirers were Guy de Maupassant, August Strindberg, and Sigmund Freud. In his obituary tribute to his former teacher, Freud praised Charcot as a "seer" and "an artistically gifted temperament," and eight years earlier, in a letter of 1885, the founder of psychoanalysis had written that after Charcot's lecture-demonstrations, "My brain is sated as after an evening in the theatre . . . no other human being has ever affected me in the same way."[24] There is some evidence that the hysterical patients at the Salpêtrière were "coached and paid for their performances" by Dr. Charcot's assistants, and in any case, the play-acting element in hysteria was so strongly developed that it would have been difficult to distinguish true illness signs from those that were feigned.[25]   The histrionic appeal of hysteria is evident in the staged photographs of the stars of the Salpêtrière, given subtitles such as, "Amorous

A Clinical Lesson of Dr. Charcot at the Salpêtrière (1887), painting by André Brouillet

Supplication," "Ecstasy," and "Eroticism," and published by Charcot in three volumes from 1877 to 1880 as *Iconographie photographique de la Salpêtrière*.[26]

On a lower cultural level, displays of madness were the chief attraction in the Grand Guignol, a theatre of the sick, deformed, and demented, which had been inaugurated in Paris in 1898, five years after Charcot's death, and which reflected the same fascination with mental aberration and hypnosis. The favored setting for these early horror dramas was the insane asylum where sympathetically portrayed doctors attempted to diagnose and cure dangerous cases of psychic derangement. A direct link between the neurology and theatre of the time can be found in Dr. Alfred Binet (the psychologist best known for devising intelligence tests), a disciple of Charcot's, who collaborated with André de Lorde on several Grand Guignol medical plays. In fact, de Lorde's *A Lesson at the Salpêtrière*, dedicated to Binet, makes use of André Pierre Brouillet's celebrated painting *A Clinical Lesson of Dr. Charcot at the Salpêtrière* (showing a demonstration with the star performer, Blanche Wittmann, "Queen of the Hysterics") for its title, setting and atmosphere.[27] Dramatization of a picture (ekphrasis) was a frequent device of nineteenth-century melodrama. In de Lorde's play, Nicolo, a young intern (significantly, Argentinean, not French) performs an illegal operation on the hysterical Susanne, leaving her partially paralyzed; in revenge, she throws acid in his face during a demonstration.

A psychiatrist, marveling at the smoothness of a demonstration staged by SIMULATIONS, expressed his preference for actor-patients in these words: "There isn't the ambiguity, distrust, discomfort usually found in a first interview." Real patients are often neither willing nor able to share their pain and emotion with an audience; actors and actresses devote their careers to such sharing. The simulator is a producer of illness signs that are more consistent, compelling, and intelligible than the often vague and contradictory symptoms with which the truly sick must struggle. In other words, the actor as a disciplined performer can invariably give the response that the doctor—likewise a professional—expects to hear. In comparison, the genuinely sick are erratic amateurs (except in the case of hypochondriacs like Argan, where years of role-playing result in perfected techniques).

VII.

It should not be forgotten that real patients are also performers engaged in playing their role as the sick. This fact has been wittily noted by Dr. Jonathan Miller, a physician-director uniquely qualified to perceive the theatricality of medical practice (and the healing powers of the stage). "Most people who fall ill have chosen to cast themselves in the role of patient," Miller writes in *The Body in Question*. "Viewing their unfortunate situation, they see themselves as sick people and begin to act differently." The sufferer must then perform his symptoms for the physician. "Once someone has chosen to fall ill he has to apply for the role of patient: he auditions for the part by reciting his complaint as vividly and convincingly as he can."[28]

Psychiatric patients quite naturally strive to dramatize their illnesses in order to render them as striking as possible for the audience in attendance. Baudrillard points out that the Freudian patient will tell Oedipal stories and have analytic dreams to satisfy the psychoanalysts,[29] and Erving Goffman in *The Presentation of the Self in Everyday Life* observes that "sympathetic patients in mental wards will sometimes feign bizarre symptoms so that student nurses will not be subjected to disappointingly sane performances."[30]

The Surrealists were also inspired by Charcot's pioneering studies. In *La Révolution Surréaliste*, No. 11, March 28, Louis Aragon and André Breton celebrate "The Fiftieth Anniversary of Hysteria," marking the start of Charcot's work on youthful female patients at the Salpêtrière. The French authors call hysteria "the greatest poetic discovery of the late nineteenth century," considering it not "a pathological phenomenon" but "a supreme means of expression." And the proponents of *amour fou* are delighted that, after nightfall, Charcot's interns had love affairs with the hysterical patients, who, in turn, under the influence of passion enacted their supposedly pathological states of mind as demonstrations for the good of the medical cause.[31]

VIII.

SIMULATIONS offers authentic portraits of mental and physical illness, because of the thorough way in which the roles are created. In her capacity as producer and director, Margaret McGovern must do research on all the diseases in the large and ever-expanding repertory so that she can accurately select and then coach the performers. The simulator is to resemble the real patient as closely as possible, and therefore casting is done according to age, height, and body build, as well as particular acting abilities (use being made of the actor's demonstrated skills in standard theatrical roles). The actor or actress is given the case history of the patient to be simulated; next the performer selects a name for the patient, prepares a complete biography, and builds the character, sometimes meeting with the real patient who is being used as a model. In accord with methodology of the American Stanislavskian school, the actor-patient must be well versed in the preceding circumstances of his character's life and know precisely where he has been and what he has been doing prior to the consultation.

The physician/advisor who works with the performer in developing the case history and characterization to ensure clinical accuracy is not the same as the examining doctor who sees the simulated patient for the first time in the live demonstration. In these improvised dramatic confrontations, the performer has to play his role keeping in mind that his partner is not a fellow actor, but a doctor to whom he is simply to respond without intervening or leading. Although Margaret McGovern always announces that the presentation is a simulated office visit, the realism of the performance (in which the simulator never steps out of role or breaks the illusion) often convinces members of the physician audience that they are witnessing an interview with a real patient. Alarmed that the patient seemed deeply agitated and had begun to weep, a psychiatrist watching a dramatic demonstration actually wanted to stop the proceedings.

Working relations between doctors and actors are naturally collegial and creative. Both are professional performers who have high regard for craft and value the projection of an authoritative persona—hence their mutual admiration for one another's style (noticeably lacking in the genuinely afflicted). In general, physicians can be said to have a love of theatre and an appreciative understanding of the dramatic arts.

Medical simulations are more effective in a neutral theatre-like setting, such as a conference room with a bare platform stage, than in a hospital where the specific institutional environment and presence of so many truly suffering patients may inhibit the creation of a theatrical event dependent on feigned illness signs. In other words, the medical simulation—like more traditional forms of theatre—needs a semi-autonomous play-world protected from ordinary reality (the actual pain of the sick and dying).

The rewards of medical simulation for doctors are considerable. In the first place, as a training device in medical education, it is a dramatic way of enabling physicians to perfect their diagnostic techniques and strategies. Performance validates the diagnosis and therapy prescribed. What Jean-Francois Lyotard in *The Postmodern Condition* has called "the performance capability of the prescriber"[32] gives doctors participating in medical simulations a sense of power; their abilities are confirmed and even enhanced by playing roles that display professional dominance.

Behind these training and validating functions, the simulation is an occasion for emotional involvement, pleasurable in itself and gratifying evidence of the doctor's own humanity. Members of the physician audience can feel empathy for actor-patients in a way they scarcely could in the presence of the truly afflicted. Transformed for a few moments into spectators at a performance, they can indulge in compassion and be moved, sometimes to tears, by the pain and suffering they are witnessing, precisely because it is simulated, not real. In his study, *Role Playing and Identity: The Limits of Theatre as Metaphor*, Bruce Wilshire addresses the question of why performance is moving in a way that reality never is. "Inhibitions and defenses can come down and greater disclosures can be achieved than in comparable situations in the off-stage world," Wilshire maintains. "These are moments in which unprecedented extensions of our sympathy can occur, or in which regressions to archaic identifications and fusions with others can transpire."[33] Where the gulf between doctor and patient is naturally deep, the theatre of medical simulations may serve as a means for the physician to cultivate sympathy for those he is dedicated to healing. Identification comes only through the surrogate provided by the actor.

On the contrary, in enacting training scenarios, the police play both the cops and the criminals. The dramatic imagination readily accepts law-enforcers in the guise of lawbreakers (undercover agents are constantly cast in such roles). But for the doctor to play the sick would seem threatening to our belief in medicine and destructive of the healer's authority. The physician must cure the disease, not become it. That task falls to the actor, who has no other calling than to take on another's misfortune and ailments.

A third, and quite different, benefit of theatre for doctors is that medical simulations give physicians the opportunity to rehearse and refine the arts of "patient management" which will ensure their being in control of the sick. "The politics of medicine," Kathryn Staiano points out in her semiotic study of illness signs, dictates that "the imposition of one medical model . . . from among several . . . represents the struggle for control over information and resources." The result, Staiano asserts, is that "The ability to successfully impose a particular medical model usually indicates the relative social and political status of the several actors."[34] The interviewing of simulated patients, whose illness signs are generated according to doctor-established paradigms, serves to develop questioning techniques that can be used to lead the genuinely affected to respond according to the preferred medical models, which have been dictated by the postmodern technology of drug therapy.

Finally, medical simulation has an important commercial function in the fostering of product knowledge and acceptance. Here the theatrical complexity is heightened by the presence of the third actor in the medical drama, the pharmaceutical sales representative (already familiar to us as the old-fashioned apothecary in the plays of Molière and Jules Romains), whose promotional activities in drug development, introduction, and approval make possible the propagation of the "pharmaco-medical life."

IX.

Laboratories and pharmaceutical companies are among the chief patrons of SIMULATIONS, because their doctors who are pioneering and perfecting new drugs need to train sales personnel in the features and advantages of the product. To learn the relation of key symptoms to a given "treatment regime" the salesman must see the product being prescribed—which he is only able to do in an interview with a simulated patient.

A live demonstration presented by SIMULATIONS at a pharmaceutical company convention when a new drug for depression was being put on the market provides an example of the theatrical excitement of a product introduction—the equivalent of an "opening night" whose drama is heightened by the fact that huge sums of money are at stake in potential sales. The sales representatives who witness the diagnostic questions and answers—leading to recommended therapy—between examining psychiatrist and simulated patient suffering from extreme depression are then prepared to go out and present the product to leading psychiatrists, confident that they will appear "credible" in their own exchange of questions and answers with these knowledgeable specialists who must be convinced of the product's value. The simulation teaches the sales personnel about the product, about the illness, and about themselves, reminding them of their own vulnerability—an awareness which will make them all the more credible as salesmen. Having seen and experienced vicariously the actor-patient's pain and need, the sales personnel will make a stronger case for the new product. The psychiatrists who are to be convinced by the salesman's credibility will not even, in most cases, prescribe the antidepressant—that will be the role of the family physicians—but the psychiatrists have the authority to make the new product accepted on this lower echelon of the medical hierarchy.

The circularity of the simulation, with its chain of repeated questions and answers, is such that the truly afflicted appear only at the beginning and end of the process—as models and receivers.[35] The actor's rendering of illness signs is so compelling that the salesman acquires new insight into human vulnerability, lending authenticity to his performance in "showing" the product to psychiatrists who in turn lend their authority to its endorsement among the legions of prescribing physicians.

X.

I should diagnose the phenomenon of the simulated patient as a symptom of histrionic empathy (depth of feeling reserved for what can be performed) for the sick and suffering, comparable to that manifested by the patient-oriented dramas flourishing at the same time. The afflicted have found in actors' eloquent voices skilled mediums who can perform their pain and make drama out of their sickness.

In the distanced, critical reading of Zola's novel, *Germinal*, staged by the Théâtre National de Strasbourg in 1975, an invented character, Dr. Vanderhagen, is introduced as the spokesman for nineteenth-century science. Using photographs, charts, and case histories, Dr. Vanderhagen, who speaks in the manner of Zola and Claude Bernard, diagnoses the hereditary diseases ravaging the impoverished miners.[36] According to the playwright, Michel Deutsch, primary author of the collective creation, the medical theories sustaining Zola's Naturalism placed the entire working class in the ranks of the sick and took away their ability to express how they actually felt. "The sick person is forbidden to speak the language of his desire, he must speak the physician's language in order to formulate his request." Deutsch argues that the actor can restore the lost powers of articulation. "On the one hand, medical ideology reduces the body to silence, on the other, the theatre gives voice to the body."[37]

In *The Actor's Freedom*, Michael Goldman discusses how the actor gives voice to the body. "Acting is a way of learning to think with the body. It is a way of learning through the body to be free of all that limits or threatens the body, to give the body the freedom of the mind—to free the audience's mind through its response to the actor's freedom."[38]

Medical simulation is for the actor an opportunity to perfect one's technique and test one's powers of thinking with the body, before an elite audience of specialists, in pursuit of a "scientific" goal. The actor becomes the surrogate of an inarticulate patient whose pain he expresses. He is the double of the sick.

Simulations are risk-free for doctors, but what risks does the actor run? In Book 11, Chapter 25 of his *Essays*, "Not to counterfeit being sick," Montaigne provides "examples of people who became sick after pretending to be so."[39] In SIMULATIONS, Margaret McGovern never casts the sick to play the sick, but her performers know that they must draw upon something other than their normal, healthy selves. Seret Scott addressed the problems in these words:

> "Friends ask if I'm inviting evil," Mrs. Scott said. "On the contrary, I feel that portraying these people in whatever conditions they're in, in a safe environment like acting, frees me."

> "I have these parts of me that are arthritic, that have been raped, that are depressed and I can call them if you want them," she said. "I'm the sickest person I know, but my karmic debt is paid."[40]

In *Possessions et simulacres: aux sources de la théâtralité*, Jacques Bourgaux considers the possessed as the mythic model of the actor, finding certain stages of ritual possession to be counterparts to the hysterical states of Dr. Charcot's patients, their role-playing and simulations. To talk of theatre in relation to possession is to follow the path opened by Artaud. Thus in playing the psychically disordered, the actor is retracing his steps back to the roots of his art in the trance. Sickness is a privileged moment of contact

The Imaginary Invalid (1857) by Honoré Daumier

with the supernatural.[41] Like the sick and deranged, the actor was for many centuries an outcast from society; like a scapegoat, he took on the illnesses of others, which only then could be imaginatively experienced by the community.

In *Shamanism: Archaic Techniques of Ecstasy*, Mircea Eliade discusses the psychopathological origins of shamanism in nervous disorders, hysteria, and mental illness, and he examines the thesis that originally shamanism was a real sickness and that only later did the genuine trance come to be imitated dramatically.

> That such maladies nearly always appear in relation to the vocation of medicine men is not at all surprising. Like the sick man, the religious man is projected onto a vital plane that shows him the fundamental data of human existence, that is, solitude, danger, hostility of the surrounding world. But the primitive magician, the medicine man, or the shaman is not only a sick man: he is, above all, a sick man who has been cured, who has succeeded in curing himself.

Illness, Eliade argues, is a sign of election, and the "sickness-vocation" constitutes an initiation transforming the profane individual into a technician of the sacred. Through training and practice, the shaman can control the attacks and bring on the trance at will. Rather than being sickly, the medicine man has, during performance, a high degree of concentration, mastery of his body, unbounded energy in his gestures. By shamanizing, these technicians of the sacred have cured themselves and are able to cure others.[42] In playing the simulated patient, the actor rediscovers the power of his ancestor, the shaman, for, as Bourgaux suggests, acting is born from the demise of possession.

I shall end where I began, with Molière, the greatest of imaginary invalids. Whereas physicians and pharmaceutical companies now engage actors to play patients, the prosperous simulator, Argan, paid doctors and pharmacists to listen to his symptoms and confirm him in ill health. Choosing invalidism as a way of life, Molière's *Malade imaginaire* displayed a modern patient's sensitivities to his own body and its symptoms. Ahead of his time, Argan was already prepared to become a modern consumer of medical services and play a perpetual sick role in the advancing medicalizing of life.

The symptoms that Argan describes in the consultation scene in Act II are, in fact, accurate illness signs of hypertension.[43] In The *Birth of Neurosis*, Dr. George Drinka explains that in origin hypochondria was a medical category later subsumed by neurosis. "The hypochondrium is in the area below the rib cage—the stomach, the liver, and the pancreas, all body organs that partake in digestion—and the essential notion was that much hypochondria is caused by what one ate."[44] As the "site for the breeding" of symptoms, the hypochondrium makes Argan ever conscious of the gravity of his state. André Gide has best expressed what lies at the heart of the *malade imaginaire*'s obsessive apprehensions.

> And what solemnity, what a "*schaudern*" each scene receives from the secret contact with death. It is with death that everything sports; it is made a sport of, it is made to enter the dance; it is invited thrice . . . death is felt prowling about; it is seen reconnoitering; it is braved and flouted, even to the death of Molière himself, which comes at the end to round out atrociously this tragic farce. And all that, in the bourgeois key, achieves a grandeur that the theatre has never surpassed.[45]

In the words of Eliade, "the imminence of death felt by the sick man recalls the symbolic death represented in almost all initiation ceremonies." Argan's "sickness-vocation" confers on him the psychic isolation of "the elected" and brings on the initiation ceremony of suffering, death, and resurrection, leading to an ascent to the sky, various shamanic revelations and disclosure of secrets of the profession. The *malade imaginaire* is both a modern patient and an archaic medicine man.[46]

What, I wonder, would be the consequence for a performance of *The Imaginary Invalid* if the actor playing Argan was a skilled patient simulator specializing in gastrointestinal diseases? The *malade imaginaire* would then be able to hold an audience of doctors—on stage or off—spellbound by the virtuosity of his performance, causing perhaps even his skeptical family momentarily to believe in the authenticity of his illness signs.

The simulated patient is the apotheosis of the art of the actor in a world of manufactured illusions. As a performer, Molière at the end of the twentieth century would no longer be a pariah on the margins of society—quite the contrary. But as a truly afflicted patient, he could not simulate the *malade imaginaire*. Only the healthy can play the sick. And if we imagine that an actor expert in medical simulation falls sick one day and decides to consult one of the doctors with whom he has worked as a simulated patient, how would that diagnostic interview go?

NOTES

1. Friedrich Nietzsche, *The Birth of Tragedy* and *The Case of Wagner*, trans. Walter Kaufman (New York: Vintage, 1967), 179.
2. Friedrich Nietzsche, *Human, All Too Human*, trans. Marion Faber with Stephen Lehmann (Lincoln: University of Nebraska Press, 1984), 178.
3. "In Theatre of Pain, Jersey Acting Company Teaches Doctors," *New York Times*, February 16, 1986, 68.
4. Kathryn Vance Staiano, *Interpreting Signs of Illness: A Case Study in Medical Semiotics*, Approaches to Semiotics 72 (Berlin: Mouton de Gruyter, 1986), 1, xi. On the relation of medicine and semiology, see Tadeusz Kowzan. *Littérature et spectacle* (Warsaw: PWN Editions scientifiques de Pologne, 1975), 167.
5. Jean Baudrillard, *Simulations*, trans. Paul Foss, Paul Patton, and Philip Beitchman (New York: Semiotext(e), 1983), 5, 7.
6. W.H. Lewis, "The Medical World," *The Splendid Century* (New York: Morrow Quill, 1978), 177-94.
7. Robert Jouanny, "Notice" to *Le Malade imaginaire*, Molière. *Théâtre complet*, II (Paris: Garnier, 1960), 757. Jouanny suggests that Argan is a man whose sickness is knowing that he will die, played by the actor Molière who is almost dead.
8. Hamlet's simulated madness is another such problem.
9. Edward Shorter, "The Making of the Modern Patient," in *Bedside Manners: The Troubled History of Doctors and Patients* (New York: Simon & Schuster, 1985), 107-139.
10. Susan Sontag, *Illness as Metaphor* (New York: Farrar, Straus & Giroux, 1977), 18.
11. Zola, "The Experimental Novel," in *Documents of Modern Literary Realism*, ed. George J. Becker (Princeton: Princeton University Press, 1963), 162.
12. Maurice Gravier, "Introduction" to August Strindberg, *Théâtre cruel et théâtre mystique*, trans. Marguerite Diehl (Paris: Gallimard, 1964), 15-16.
13. Sidney Kingsley's *Men in White* (1933) is an early example of the genre, showing the life of a large metropolitan hospital and including an operating room scene (effectively staged by the Group Theatre). The American Medical Association praised the play and doctors rushed to see it.
14. From an interview in *New York Times*, June 25, 1978, cited in Bruce Wilshire, *Role Playing and Identity: The Limits of Theatre as Metaphor* (Bloomington: Indiana University Press, 1982), 88n36.
15. David Richard Jones, *Great Directors at Work* (Berkeley: University of California Press, 1986), 231.
16. Villiers de L'Isle-Adam, *Cruel Tales*. trans. Robert Baldick (London: Oxford University Press, 1963), 125, 120.
17. Jules Romains, *Knock*, trans. James Gidney (Great Neck, New York: Barron's, 1962), 12. According to Ludwik Flaszen, *Grotowski & Company*, ed. and trans. Paul Allain (Holstebro: Icarus, 2010), 227, in 1968 Jerzy Grotowski tended to fantasize about himself as "a doctor of some mysterious specialism, a medicine man. He would introduce himself thus: 'I'm Doctor Knock.'"
18. It is usual to interpret Dr. Knock as a parable of the totalitarian state, undoubtedly a valid reading of the play, but it is also a brilliant and prophetic dramatization of just what it says it is, *The Triumph of Medicine*, as cultural criticism of the profession makes clear. See Shorter, "Converting People into Patients," in *Bedside Manners*, 109-121 and the discussions of the expansionist medicalizing of society in *The Cultural Crisis of Modern Medicine*, ed. John Ehrenreich (New York: Monthly Review Press, 1978).
19. Shorter, *Bedside Manners*, 194-259.
20. Information about SIMULATIONS comes from my conversations with Mrs. McGovern as well as from the SIMULATIONS brochure, "Capabilities and Services," consisting of promotional materials, programs, letters, reviews, and articles. Quotations relating to SIMULATIONS come from these documents unless otherwise indicated.

21. Eugène Ionesco, *Victims of Duty* in *Three Plays*, trans. Donald Watson (New York: Grove Press, 1958), 119.

22. In a complex live demonstration at Caesar's Lake Tahoe, for the Nevada State Association of Family Physicians, "Alison" appeared first at home with her husband and then in the doctor's office for the consultation. The actual patient upon whom Alison is modeled has watched Seret Scott during a filming showing her advanced arthritis. These filmings sometimes take place in the real patient's home and bed.

23. George Frederick Drinka, *The Birth of Neurosis: Myth, Malady, and the Victorians* (New York: Simon and Schuster. 1984), 124, 89. Of Charcot's hysterics, Drinka explains "His presentation of them to an audience really encouraged their symptoms to grow more dramatic." (102). For more on Charcot, see Georges Didi-Huberman, *L'Invention de l'hysterie: Charcot et l'iconographie photographique de la Salpêtrière* (Paris: Macula, 1982).

24. Freud, quoted in Stanley Edgar Hyman, *The Tangled Bank: Darwin, Marx, Frazer and Freud as Imaginative Writers* (New York: Grosset & Dunlap, 1968), 302, 323.

25. Henry Miller, "Psychoanalysis: A Clinical Perspective" in *Freud: The Man, His World, His Influence*, ed. Jonathan Miller (New York: Little, Brown, 1972).

26. Elaine Showalter, *The Female Malady: Women, Madness and English Culture*, 1830-1980, New York: Penguin, 1987), 148-152.

27. In *Woman and the Demon: The Life of a Victorian Myth* (Cambridge. Harvard, 1982), 31-2. Nina Auerbach discusses Freud's attachment to this picture and gives her reading of its significance: "As a young man studying with Charcot he was so profoundly moved by a lithograph of the master in his clinic that he kept a copy all his life. The lithograph depicts a rigidly upright Charcot explicating the bosom of a seductively supine patient; the woman is supported by a bearded assistant, peering solicitously into her dress, who looks suspiciously like the young Freud. This prone, pliable woman psychically disrobed and recreated by the piercing eyes of men is the focus of a tableau closer in spirit to the popular image of Svengali and Trilby than du Maurier's actual illustrations are." In fact, the bearded assistant is Joseph Babinski. Dr. Charcot in this picture looks like Dr. Caligari, also a hypnotist and keeper of an insane asylum, who makes a display of his control over a patient. De Lorde's *Une Leçon à la Salpêtrière* was first performed at the Grand Guignol on March 3. 1906.

28. Jonathan Miller, *The Body in Question* (New York: Random House, 1978), 49, 53.

29. Baudrillard, 156.

30. Erving Goffman, *The Presentation of Self in Everyday Life* (Garden City, N.Y.: Anchor, 1959), 18.

31. Quotations from Dawn Ades, *Dada and Surrealism Reviewed* (Arts Council of Great Britain. 1978), 183. Michel Foucault, on the other hand, sees the Salpêtrière hysteric as a means by which Charcot could exalt "the doctor's marvelous powers." *A History of Insanity in the Age of Reason: Madness and Civilization*, trans. Richard Howard (New York: Vintage, 1965), 276.

32. Jean-Francois Lyotard, *The Post-modern Condition: A Report on Knowledge*, trans. Geoff Bennington and Brian Massurni (Minneapolis, University of Minnesota, 1984), 46.

33. Bruce Wilshire, *Role Playing and Identity: The Limits of Theatre as Metaphor* (Bloomington: University of Indiana, 1982), 25, 27. Freud developed the ability to empathize with the sick thanks to Dr. Charcot's lecture-demonstrations. "Freud had arrived at La Salpêtrière as a neurologist; he left it a 'hysteric'—having found that he was just hysterical enough to identify with Charcot's patients." Octave Mannoni, "Psychoanalysts and the Decolonization of Mankind," trans. Nicholas Fry, in *Freud: The Man, His Work, His Influence*, 93.

34. Staiano, xiii, xvi.

35. Baudrillard discusses the circularity of response in simulations where the interrogation produces the anticipated self-validating answer and so on ad infinitum, 130.

36. Bernard Dort, *Théâtre en jeu: Essais de critique*, 1970-1978 (Paris: Seuil, 1979), 180.

37. Daniel Lindenberg, Jean-Pierre Vincent, Michel Deutsch, Jacques Blanc, ed., *Germinal: Projet sur un roman* (Paris: Christian Bourgois, 1975), 115, 125.

38. Michael Goldman, *The Actor's Freedom: Toward a Theory of Drama* (New York: Viking, 1975), 89.

39. Montaigne, *The Complete Essays*, trans. Donald M. Frame (Stanford: Stanford University, 1976), 521.

40. *New York Times*, February 16, 1986, p. 68.

41. Jacques Bourgaux. *Possessions et simulacres: aux sources de la théâtralité* (Paris: EPI, 1973), 32, 42, 65, 80. Charcot recognized that the symptoms of hysteria correspond to those attributed in the Middle Ages to witchcraft and possession and he published studies, such as *Les démoniaques dans l'art*, featuring images of satanic convulsions from the early medieval period to the present and including his own drawings of his patients. See William J. McGrath. *Freud's Discovery of Psychoanalysis: The Politics of Hysteria* (Ithaca: Cornell, 1986), 156.

42. Mircea Eliade, *Shamanism: Archaic Techniques of Ecstasy*, trans. W.R. Trask (Princeton: Princeton University, 1974), 27, 28–34.

43. Pierre Valde, evidently from his book *La Malade imaginaire, essai d'interprétation* (Paris: Plon, 1946), quoted by Robert Jouanny, Molière, *Théâtre complet*, 2:755.

44. Drinka, 31.

45. André Gide, *Journals*, vol. 4, *1939-1949*, trans. and ed. Justin O'Brien (New York: Knopf), 71.

46. Eliade, *Shamanism*, 33.

PAUL MARGUERITTE AND *PIERROT ASSASSIN OF HIS WIFE*

Pantomime is thinking overheard. It begins and ends before words have
formed themselves, in a deeper consciousness than that of speech. [. . .]
And pantomime has that mystery which is one of the requirements of true
art. To watch it is like dreaming.
                    Arthur Symonds, "Pantomime and Poetic Drama,"
                    Studies in the Seven Arts, 1898

The pantomime, *Pierrot Assassin of His Wife*—one of the most extraordinary
solo performances of the late nineteenth century—was first created in 1881 by a stage-
struck twenty-one-year-old Parisian student, Paul Margueritte, who spent his summer
vacations outside the city putting on amateur theatre in an old barn loft. For the rest of
the decade, Margueritte, although embarked upon a successful literary career, continued
to present his pantomime whenever and wherever he could—for friends and relatives,
before peasants in rented rural ballrooms, in fashionable Parisian salons for elite private
audiences of artists and writers, and at special showings in professional theatres.

A radically new interpretation of the traditional comic figure derived from
commedia dell'arte, Margueritte's macabre Pierrot contributed directly to the revival of
pantomime that characterized the 1880s. Margueritte quickly became celebrated, and
his work was written up in popular magazines; Stéphane Mallarmé, Edmond de Goncourt,
Alphonse Daudet, and André Antoine were among the admirers of *Pierrot Assassin of His
Wife*. The history of this solo performance touches upon many aspects of artistic and
intellectual life in the early *belle époque*. Paul Margueritte identified passionately with
his role and became a harbinger of the Pierrotmania that soon swept through Paris
and later conquered the rest of Europe—as witness the youthful works of Picasso and
Meyerhold at the beginning of the twentieth century.[1]

The Theatre at Valvins: Prompter and Stage-Manager Stéphane Mallarmé

The story of *Pierrot Assassin of His Wife* begins in a picturesque country
village lost in the woods on the banks of the Seine somewhere between Fontainebleau
and Samois, about fifty miles southeast of Paris. It was there, in the little hamlet of
Valvins, that Madame Margueritte—widow of a French general killed at Sedan during the
Franco-Prussian war—rented a painter's atelier for her son Paul and his younger brother
Victor during the summers of 1881 and 1882. One climbed up a flight of wooden stairs,
used by hens as a roost, to a huge room above an enormous barn stuffed with hay and
oats. This studio served as a theatre where the two boys could put on Sunday evening
performances, including short plays, recitation, and mime.

The stage was a plank put across two trestles by the local carpenter. The curtain
was made of two white sheets. The footlights consisted of rows of candles. The costumes
had been purchased at the old clothes market in Paris. And the scenery was nothing but
several large folding screens covered with green foliage. For their repertory Paul and
Victor chose medieval farces, commedia, Musset, Banville, and verse by Daudet and
Hugo. For the Margueritte brothers, the theatre at Valvins—with its magical setting by
the forest and the river—was pure poetry.

—The Drama Review: TDR 23, no. 1 (March 1979): 103–112.

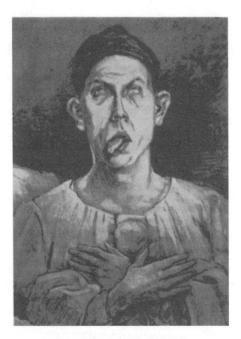

Paul Margueritte as Pierrot

Their next-door neighbors and relatives, Stéphane Mallarmé and his daughter Geneviève, contributed to the unusual atmosphere. The great Symbolist poet (the boys' uncle on Madame Margueritte's side) not only wrote a sonnet of inauguration for the theatre and a prologue for *The Farce of Master Pierre Pathelin*, but he also worked intimately on all aspects of the productions themselves.[2] Their charming cousin, Geneviève—with whom Paul was in love—played the female roles and recited poetry. Years later Paul Margueritte recalled the unique circumstances that made his first experience with theatre at Valvins so crucial for his development.

> As prompter and stage-manager, we had—rare honor—Stéphane Mallarmé himself, as audience, our family, and the peasants from the surrounding villages, who, bringing with them chairs or benches, came crowding together into the long, overly narrow room. A young neighbor, who created an entire orchestra with his violin, completed the company, as needed. My brother and I divided up the big roles. [. . .]

> This communion with naïve spectators, ever ready for laughter and enthusiasm, with an instinctive crowd, gave us a prodigious feeling of intoxication and a boundless sense of confidence.[3]

For Mallarmé, too, the theatre at Valvins proved to be an important influence. The poet's active participation in the productions helped him develop his ideas about a small coterie theatre—"an intimate gala for oneself"—as well as about a drama of popular entertainment.[4]

After rehearsals, Mallarmé would become involved in discussions on the destiny of the theatre and suggest that the poet should take the stage before a spellbound public, revealing beauty to the unlettered masses. For the author of "The Afternoon of a Faun," there were only two kinds of intelligent and lively spectators: poets and common people. In fact, both Mallarmé and the peasants at Valvins loved *Pierrot Assassin of His Wife*, the pantomime that Paul Margueritte created for the first season of their theatre. The audience watched in religious silence the sadistic cruelty of Pierrot, but howled with laughter at Hugo's *Hernani*, which they considered a farce. "A shudder ran along the rows of seats as soon as Pierrot glided along the boards, all white in his ample smock, with nothing black except the headband and the curve of the eyebrows," the author-actor later remembered.[5]

It was the use of silence that Mallarmé most admired in *Pierrot Assassin of His Wife*. In Margueritte's performance, "You could see the sonorous waves—alternatingly light or solemn, caressing or funereal—tremble as in a mirror on Pierrot's features."[6] Mallarmé's aesthetics of pantomime, formulated a few years later in his theoretical study, *Sketched at the Theatre*, is based entirely upon this single work. Unfortunately for Paul Margueritte, it was the young man's love for pantomime (according to J. H. Rosny) that made the Symbolist poet refuse to give him his daughter Geneviève in marriage. However much he esteemed his nephew's artistry, Mallarmé did not wish to have a professional mime as a son-in-law. "That boy will go into the Folies-Bergères!" the poet would say, shaking his head.[7] Such were the prejudices of even the most sympathetic writers with respect to performers in the popular arts. As a result of this setback, Paul Margueritte entered hastily into a disastrous marriage, followed by unhappy love affairs and a tragic personal life.

Becoming Pierrot

Pierrot exerted a fatal attraction for Paul Margueritte. His build, features, and temperament suited him to the role, as he had reconceived it in bold and original terms. The young mime was exceptionally tall, delicate, and frail. "He had," wrote Rosny, "an interesting, melancholy face. His eyes, which were gray with a yellowish tint, displayed a myopic softness. From time to time a sarcastic smile played upon his mouth, which an accident had slightly deformed. He did not speak much and his hearing was not acute."[8] To express his own nature and the spirit of the times, Margueritte created a modern, neurotic Pierrot, full of fear and malaise, obsessed by hallucinations, and capable of registering both tragic and burlesque emotions. "This incarnation of the man in white," as he himself put it, produced for Paul Margueritte during many years "a doubling of the personality and an irresistible vocation: the lunar phantom of Pierrot."[9] The new conception had been suggested to the young artist by a novella of Henri Rivière's, in which Pierrot appears as a jealous husband who, with a gigantic razor, cuts off the head of his rival, Harlequin, as well as by a couplet from Théophile Gautier's poem, *Posthumous Pierrot*:

> The story of a husband who, tickling his wife,
> Had in that fashion, laughing, made her lose her life.

For Margueritte, the traditionally comic and love-sick figure became "a Pierrot elegant in his cynicism, a jester in cruelty, at one and the same time sadistic and fantastic, swaggering and cowardly, deliberately perverse, taking pleasure in evil for its own esthetic beauty, an artist and Neronian in the invention and perpetuation of his crimes."[10] Gradually the self-taught amateur mime grew obsessed by his own creation. He wished to penetrate more deeply into the mysteries of the art of pantomime. He became fascinated by its techniques:

> These peripeteia without a voice, this rhythm of emotions translated into an eternal silence. the expressive anguish of a being who is unable to speak, who, while making himself understood, cannot express everything, and who is pursued by a relentless fatality for that very reason. Hence, the pathos of this mask where the power of a convulsed soul takes refuge. Hence, the eloquence of those movements, which, even in farce, lends to the drama something indefinably startling, as if we saw somnambulists in a state of crisis grow agitated, incoherent, and vehement, or the dead brought back to life.[11]

Despite the fact that he now had a clerk's job in the ministry concerned with administration of the Beaux-Arts and was starting to write successful novels, Paul Margueritte was determined to go on the stage as a professional mime. He shaved his forehead and temples in order to make his forehead larger. Finding the doors of all theatres closed to him, he began to call on famous artists to ask for their help and advice. At Mallarmé's suggestion, Margueritte first consulted the last of the great mimes, the living king of Pierrots, Paul Legrand, then almost forgotten, and asked him to teach him the mysterious language of the mime. Old and embittered, Legrand declared that there was no more use for such lessons and no future at all for pantomime, which was scarcely surviving in music halls between juggling acts and chorus girls. Then Legrand talked of his former rival, Deburau *fils*, and of his father, the great Deburau, who had popularized Pierrot in the first half of the nineteenth century and made him the favorite of a whole generation of artists.

After the young enthusiast presented a scene from his *Pierrot Assassin of His Wife*, the old master admitted that it was not bad for an amateur and then proceeded to correct some of Margueritte's movements and to show him various signs consecrated by the unwritten dictionary of mime that were capable of giving a comic aspect to the most tragic situations.[12] In writing about his early years, Paul Margueritte recalled some of these signs.

> Thus the idea of death was translated by the explosion of a being with a kick in the rear, or by the brusque gesture with which one deposits a suitcase on the sidewalk. The macabre and the terrible were tolerated by Paul Legrand only as something incidental, quickly transported by fantasy and dream. And my satanic Pierrot astounded him. He was for the white street urchin, the sympathetic type of which he had illustrated for so many years.
>
> The costume, too, had its tradition: the number of buttons, the fold of the cloak, the white skull cap topped by a black skull cap, in velvet, and the point of which made a "parson's nose," the shoes of buckskin with steel buckles; the make-up, lastly, an art of plastering oneself with grease or white fat to which white zinc in powdered form will stick, when applied by blows of a tampon made of lamp wicks.[13]

Still haunted by his *idée fixe*, Margueritte went to see the famous Comédie-Française actor, Coquelin, who showed no interest whatsoever, and he presented his Pierrot for André Antoine in his sixth-floor apartment in 1882 when the future founder of the Théâtre Libre was still with the Paris Gas Company and not yet in any position to offer the young artist a stage. Next he approached established poets and playwrights. He

Paul Margueritte as Pierrot in *Pierrot Assassin of his Wife,* first performed at the Théâtre de Valvins (Seine-et-Marne) and published in Paris (1882)

Images by H. Lanos in *L'Illustration*, March 26, 1887

went to see Jean Richepin, whose *Pierrot Assassin* was playing at the Palais du Trocadéro in 1883 with Sarah Bernhardt as Pierrot, and begged to be allowed to understudy Bernhardt. He visited Théodore Banville, who was known for his love of Deburau and the traditional pantomime of that time. The idea of a tragic Pierrot shocked Banville as a failure of taste in search of an absolute and eternal type. "If Pierrot is tragic," the poet asked Margueritte, "what advantage does he have over Thyestes?"[14] A projected performance at Banville's home did not take place because Madame Banville was afraid that her carpets would be damaged by the zinc powder used for whitening Pierrot's face.

Mallarmé's fear that his prospective son-in-law might decide upon a career in the variety theatre was not without foundation. Unable to gain acceptance as a performer in the world of officially sanctioned art, Paul Margueritte, whose fascination with the stage continued unabated, often thought of joining the lowest sort of popular artists.

> How many times have I wandered about dangerous-looking flea-bags and fetid music halls, with the irresistible desire of going in and offering myself up! Passionately fond of fairs, at once attracted and repelled by their raucous cacophony of sounds, their sizzling fried foods, their mountebanks in tights, how many times have I dreamed of appearing upon the crudely put-together stage of planks, in a fair booth made of canvas; how greatly have I envied the showman's roving wagon, the Thespian caravan of the humble![15]

> For Pierrot possessed me more than ever.[16]

Chez Daudet and at the Théâtre Libre

All the while Margueritte expanded his role as an amateur society entertainer, presenting *Pierrot Assassin of His Wife* before more and more distinguished and elite audiences. After the two summer seasons at Valvins, the young mime gave performances in the larger towns of Samois, Vétheuil, and Marlotte. Written up as a novelty by newspapers and magazines, Margueritte's Pierrot became fashionable in Paris, and there began a series of charity matinées, cafe productions, and private stagings in the homes of artists and writers, such as Paul Eudel, Roger Ballu, and Gilbert Stenger.

The most important of these salon performances took place in February 1887 at the home of the celebrated novelist and poet, Alphonse Daudet. The exclusive audience at Daudet's saw the first definitive version of *Pierrot Assassin of His Wife*, which Margueritte had been perfecting and refining for the past six years. With decor by the painter Montégut and music by the young composer Paul Vidal, the pantomime was now an integrated spectacle. Vidal, former conductor of the Opéra and musical director of the Opéra-Comique, rehearsed with Margueritte and worked closely on the production, as well as playing the score on the piano. The music, combining the themes of "Au clair de la lune" and "Dies Irae" of Le Corbeiller, accompanied and commented upon the play of facial expression, the attitudes, and the gestures, capturing Pierrot's changing moods with great precision. For Margueritte, such sculptural music was indispensable to pantomime and to the creation of its mysterious atmosphere.

In his *Journal* for February 6 and 10, 1887, Edmond de Goncourt describes the powerful impression that the performance produced.

> Daudet brought me home with him to attend the rehearsal of *Pierrot Assassin of His Wife*, presented by the author, Paul Margueritte. Truly amazing, the mobility of the author's mask, and the succession of anguished forms of expression that he makes appear beneath his neurotic flesh, and the admirable and panting designs that he gives to a terrorized mouth.

And for this macabre *pierrotade* in the style of an English clown show, the young musician Vidal has composed a little piece of music entirely suited to the neurotic quality of the play.[17]

Upon seeing the performance itself three days later, Goncourt—like Mallarmé before him—reveals a prejudice against performers that tells much about the cultural climate of the period. While praising Margueritte's "thoroughly macabre talent," the famous critic, novelist, and art historian cannot help but exclaim, "But really, what a strange ambition for an intellectual who has written a novel, *All Four*, to revive Deburau's pantomime!"[18] The Parisian literary world, although it patronized Margueritte and applauded private showings of his Pierrot, could not accept the fact that one of their own caste could aspire to be a mime.

Margueritte's greatest public triumph came on March 23, 1888, when he gave a performance of *Pierrot Assassin of His Wife* at the Théâtre Libre before a packed house. Antoine, long an admirer of Margueritte's "original and personal talent," had witnessed the salon production at Daudet's, affirming that the young artist mimed Pierrot's anguish "with a power that was truly the envy of professionals."[19] Now, a year later, due to a curious set of circumstances, Antoine at last had an opportunity to see Margueritte's *Pierrot* staged in his own theatre.

As a novelist of the Naturalist school centered around Emile Zola, Margueritte belonged to the group of young writers who, on August 18, 1887, after the publication of Zola's *The Earth*, issued in *Le Figaro* the "Manifesto of the Five," denouncing the master for crude excesses and breaking with the tenets of Naturalism. Zola good-humoredly encouraged Antoine to devote a whole program to the works of his opponents, thereby allowing the young dissidents to show what they could do. *Pierrot Assassin of His Wife* was the only pantomime on the program, the other dramas being one-act plays in a realistic idiom.

Paul Margueritte persuaded Antoine to try his hand at a new art. The director of the Théâtre Libre appeared for the first—and last—time in a pantomime, playing the role of the Undertaker's Man on March 23, 1888 at the Théâtre Montparnasse. "Paul Margueritte's pantomime was quite original," Antoine later wrote. "He has made a specialty of Pierrot, and consented to a public appearance on the condition that I support him as the mute."[20] Together Margueritte and Antoine produced an unforgettable effect. "I remember," Margueritte commented, "the stir in the auditorium when—as we both reeled drunkenly and he tried to support me—we surged in, the door banged open with a blow of the fist, beneath pallid rays of moonlight."[21]

Vidal accompanied the action on piano. The set was by H. E. Langlois. To the left hung Columbine's portrait, and to the right, pinned on the wall, was the announcement of her funeral. An iron bed with curtains stood to the rear, and by it, slightly to the right, a night table with two candles. Antoine's technical effects were brilliant: the portrait became lighted by magnesium and, during the fire at the end of the performance, long flames shot out of the doors and windows. When the curtain came down, Champfleury, who had directed the Théâtre des Funambules from 1847 to 1850, paid Marguerrite the supreme compliment by shouting, "Bravo Deburau!" In this way, the young amateur was likened to Jean Gaspard Deburau, who had created the long, pale, lovesick Pierrot in the 1830s and 1840s.

Precursor of the Pierrot Revival

For the past thirty years, pantomime had been a moribund art that no one thought possible to bring back to life. Then, suddenly, in the 1880s and 1890s, Pierrot and pantomime became all the rage. Although it was never performed, Huysmans and Hennique wrote their *Sceptical Pierrot* in 1881 for the English acrobatic troupe, the Hanlon-Lees. Bernhardt and Réjane appeared in Richepin's *Pierrot Assassin* in 1883. In 1885 Jean Lorrain published in *La Chat Noir* his one-act play for Chinese shadows, *The Damnation of Pierrot* (in which the hero's decapitated head appears on a platter), in the hopes that Bernhardt would star in it. The artist and illustrator, Adolphe Willette, produced books and albums filled with lunar Pierrots and started a small review, *Le Pierrot*; he also gave Pierrot parties, such as the "Bohemian night of gaiety" described by Antoine, which concluded with "the extraordinary sight produced by the dawn coming through the windowed roof-pale and exhausted people, all in Pierrot Costumes, the most glorious symphony in white imaginable."[22]

Substantial commercial successes for pantomime soon followed. Félicia Mallet starred in the popular *Prodigal Child* by Michel Carré II at the Bouffe Parisian in 1890, and in 1896 Catulle Mendès's adaptation of Deburau's *Old-Clothes Seller* was a hit with Sévérin in the title role. Paul Margueritte, with his *Pierrot Assassin of His Wife* in the loft at Valvins, had forecast this trend and helped to open the way for the revival.

After the performance at the Théâtre Libre, critical recognition came to Margueritte for his contribution to the resurrection of pantomime. Although some reviewers complained of the sadism and horror in *Pierrot Assassin of His Wife*, Francisque Sarcey, the conservative critic of *Le Temps*, praised the performance. In several different articles, Jules Lemaître, the influential drama critic of the *Journal des Débats* and the *Revue des Deux Mondes*, gave the most complete appraisal of Margueritte's accomplishments. Calling the young artist a major innovator, Lemaître wrote, "He was the first to create a tragic and neurotic Pierrot, totally similar to the sensual and deranged heroes of the novels of the young school."[23] According to Lemaître, Margueritte's new use of pantomime is prophetic of future directions in modern art.

> The Pierrot of M. Paul Margueritte is an impressionist and hallucinated Pierrot, quite akin to that of the great draughtsman, Willette.[24]

> You will recognize in this work one of the marks of the most recent literature—aesthetic delectation of the horrible, the mysterious, and the fatal. In fact, the mania of many young writers being the exclusive exploration of violent or subtle sensation, the whole essence of their books could be superbly expressed by pantomime alone. Pantomime would thus render superfluous much poetry and many novels. Circus and pantomime are perhaps the inevitable end product of the literatures of old.[25]

Extolling "the superiority of silence," Lemaître suggests that "pantomime is, of all the dramatic genres, the one with which the spectator collaborates the most."[26] Because it reduces everything to primitive emotion and presents what is unchangeable, essential, and eternal in human nature, pantomime also resembles the most ancient European drama and still retains its mythic power. Here the critic of the *Journal des Debats* draws an unexpected and illuminating comparison between the contemporary mime, Paul Margueritte, and the Greek tragic hero and concludes that, in order to experience the true effect of ancient Greek theatre, we should see the *Oresteia* mimed by a troupe of tragic Pierrots in the style devised by Margueritte.[27]

According to Lemaître, Pierrot became "a sort of theatrical effigy of generalized humanity," as were the characters in Greek drama.[28] Margueritte's eyebrows, eyes, and lips were like a tragic mask, and his white costume magnified him as did the Greek tragic robes and cothurnes.

> This head, simplified, artificial, without hair, without modeling, this oblong moon where one sees against the flat whiteness of the background only the holes of the eyes and the nostrils and the line of the eyebrows and the mouth, this head is truly tragic.[29]

> His mouth, when he turns down the corners, resembled the copper embouchure of the mask of Orestes or of Agamemnon, and the large folds of his smock and of his sleeves gave to his gestures a dignity, a grandiloquence, an extraordinary power of expression.[30]

No spectator ever laughed or even smiled. Margueritte's Pierrot was the embodiment of universal fear and terror. When, however, the artist abandoned his customary silence and at the Théâtre Beaumarchais attempted to reach a larger public by adding spoken dialogue to mimed action, the result was a fiasco.

Paul Margueritte composed a number of other pantomimes. From the youthful days at Valvins comes *Requiem*, in which Pierrot, who has murdered a butterfly in the flame of a candle, is pursued by an army of vengeful butterflies, but—violin in hand—succeeds in appeasing them by playing an expiatory requiem in honor of the departed. In 1910 the "Bibliophiles Fantasistes" published *Nos Tréteaux*, a collection of charades by Victor Margueritte and pantomimes by Paul, including *Pierrot, Dead and Alive, Pierrot Mormon,* and *Columbine Pardoned.*[31]

Margueritte has been remembered in France as a literary man, the author of a number of novels no one reads any more. Shouldn't he rather be known as the artist who reconceived Pierrot as a "tragic nightmare in the manner of Edgar Allan Poe"?

NOTES

1. On the cult of Pierrot at the turn of the century, see J. Douglas Clayton, *Pierrot in Petrograd: The Commedia dell'Arte/Balagan in Twentieth-Century Russian Theatre and Drama* (Montréal: McGill-Queen's, 1993); Martin Burgess Greene and John C. Swan, *The Triumph of Pierrot: The Commedia dell'Arte and the Modern Imagination* (New York: Macmillan, 1986); Jean de Palacio, *Pierrot fin-de-siècle, ou, Les Métamorphoses d'un masque* (Paris: Séguier, 1990); and Robert F. Storey, *Pierrot: A Critical History of a Masque* (Princeton: Princeton University Press, 1978) and *Pierrots on the Stage of Desire: Nineteenth-Century Literary Artists and the Comic Pantomime* (Princeton: Princeton University Press, 1985).

2. Henri Mondor, *Vie de Mallarmé* (Paris, Gallimard, 1941), 419.

3. Paul Margueritte, "Le printemps tourmenté: souvenirs littéraires 1881–1896," *Revue des deux mondes* 51 (1919), 244, 252. See also Francis Pruner, *Les luttes d'Antoine: Au Théâtre Libre* (Paris: Minard, 1964), 1:171–173.

4. Haskell Block, *Mallarmé and the Symbolist Drama* (Detroit: Wayne State University Press, 1963), 73.

5. Margueritte, "Le printemps tourmenté," 252.

6. Ibid., 246.

7. J.H. Rosny (Ainé), *Memoires de la vie littéraire* (Paris: G. Cres, 1927), 35–36.

8. Ibid., 31.

9. Margueritte, "Le printemps tourmenté," 245.

10. Ibid., 259.

11. Ibid., 246.

12. Ibid., 248-249.

13. Ibid., 245.

14. Ibid., 251.

15. Ibid., 73.

16. Ibid., 96.

17. Edmond and Jules Goncourt, *Journal: Mémoires de la vie littéraire—1887–1896* (Paris: Robert Laffont, 1989), 12.

18. Ibid., 13.

19. André Antoine, *Le théâtre par Antoine* 1 (Paris: Les Éditions de France, 1932).

20. Ibid., 223.

21. Margueritte, *Le printemps tourmenté* (Paris: Flammarion, 1925), 179.

22. Jean Chothia, *André Antoine* (Cambridge: Cambridge University Press, 1991), 90–91, 94.

23. Jules Lemaître, *Impressions de théâtre*, 2me serie (Paris: Lecène, Oudin et Cie, 1892), 347.

24. Ibid., 357.

25. Ibid., 358-359.

26. Ibid., 350.

27. Ibid., 356, 351, 352.

28. Ibid., 351.

29. Ibid.

30. Ibid., 352.

31. Paul Margueritte, *Nos tréteaux: charades de Victor Margueritte. Pantomimes de Paul Margueritte* (Paris: Les Bibliophiles Fantaisistes, 1910).

EULOGY FOR PIERROT
by
Paul Margueritte

Poor Pierrot! Enough ink has been spilled on your white smock to dye it black. You were smothered with funeral orations. Ironic, isn't it, at the very moment when you are coming back to life? A rather indelicate proceeding, they would like to bury you alive, in the sack with the old pantomime, under the crumbling ruins of the Funambules. Hypocritically they declare that you have died, hoping that you will be naïve enough to believe it, and that there is nothing more to be done but to carve upon your tombstone the words: Here lies Pierrot, interred by the arts of persuasion.

Fortunately, you are a hardy breed. Come now! Because the mimes Deburau, Kalpestri, Rouff, and others have lived, and because the inimitable Paul Legrand has grown old, shouldn't it be obligatory for you to disappear as well, along with the artists who incarnated you—you who are so dear to the poets that they compose masterpieces for you: Banville his charming *Kiss*, Richepin beautiful pantomimes, and Willette delightful albums of pictures; you in whose honor the devotees have opened a little funambulesque chapel; you who are the spotless and immutable symbol of the human soul, the perfect personification of its instincts and its vices, eternal and imperishable archetype—in the words of a discerning literary man, Gustave Geffroy—by the same right as Hamlet and Guignol!

I know exactly what is eating the critics.

They would pardon you for still living, if you confined yourself, at rare intervals, to stealing a bottle or a pâté. But since you have taken to assassinating women with refinements that even the late Pranzini was unaware of, they could no longer tolerate you. Think it over carefully, Pierrot, and as quickly as possible become once again what they always believed you to be: a comic character.

For, it seems, you amuse people. You make them laugh. They find you unusually funny. Did you have any inkling of it, Pierrot?

No, I am sure you did not, you never considered yourself as comic. Not even in the classic farces, the popular songs, and the chromo-lithographs. You are not what a frivolous people imagine. There has always been anxiety, malaise, and all but anguish in the nervous shudder which you produce in us. And I call to witness Gautier and Gérard de Nerval! To men of letters, to artists, to the refined and sensitive, haven't you almost always appeared, according to your different incarnations, as diabolic and mystifying in Deburau, as ever so slightly macabre in Kalpestri, as passionate and sentimental in Paul Legrand, but never, most assuredly, irremissibly comic as a buffoon?

After all, it's enough to look at you!

Your lunar pallor, your ample draperies flowing in shroud-like folds, your gait supple and fleeting as a shadow, your eye mysteriously shut, and the smile encrusted on your mask of plaster, all of this, your whimsical wit, your unexpected logic, and your disconcerting folly, doesn't it make of you a miraculous being, promenading, through the masks of the eternal comedy—foppish Leandres, grumbling Cassandres, flirtatious Harlequins, and such delightfully faithless Columbines—the living mystery, and the cold solemnity, of Galatea in marble or of the Commander's ghost?

– Translated by Daniel Gerould, New York, 1979.

Pierrot Assassin of His Wife, pantomime by Paul Margueritte,
print by Willette, *La Revue Illustrée*, 1888

Incontestably melancholy, consigned from the cradle to the influence of the moon, lover of the soundless night, which imparts to you its disturbing or criminal suggestions, why—if that amuses you—would you not disclose the sort of sacred horror which roves from the muscles of your pale face to the tragic folds of your clothes?

For if the thoughtless laughter of men—and how tired you must be of it!—confines you in a ring of tinkling bells, women and children have understood you better.

Their divining hearts have had presentiments of your own. And by simply appearing, with your unruffled smile, you chill them with a vague and tremulous terror.

*

If you could come back to us, Pierrot, otherwise than on a journey, and elsewhere than in the fantasies of artists and writers, I'll tell you where I should like to see you: at the Impossible Theatre.

On the elastic boards of a playhouse with scenery painted by the most delicate colorists, to the sounds of music that "enervates and cajoles," due to the suavest musicians, it would charm me to see presented—for the amusement of a few simple, or very complicated souls—the stupendous and tragicomic farces of life, love, and death, written exclusively by authors who are definitely not members of the Society of Men of Letters. Their imagination would romp in the dream, in the past, and in the strictest modernity. It would unite the fairy realm of gold, crude reality, and scathing satire. There, among the indispensable figurants, you would come forth, bitter clown; whether a black suit at once close-fitting and loose would accommodate you as an engaging skeleton, as an elegant parody of our anemia and our neurosis; or whether you would prefer, draped in huge white folds, to freeze in statuesque poses.

Columbine, at your side, more supple than a snake, lascivious in streams of gauze, or austere in stiff brocades, would express admirably—by a flash of her eyes, by a palpitation of her breasts, by a bird-like soaring, by a thousand gestures, intense or furtive, and nuanced ad infinitum—the passionate mobility of her soul, capricious as the ocean!

But what am I going to dream of next?—The Impossible Theatre?—Ah, most assuredly! . . .

Have you ever seen chimeras? Look, Pierrot, here's one. It is flying up, and up, and up into the blue, hesitating to alight on some roof, its wings frightened by the outcry of a people who rapturously acclaim, in the street as in the theatre, the triumphal advent of Mediocrity, and become hopelessly mired in the Great Marl-Pit, where doubtless they will remain.

But what does that matter to you, oh, prince of indifference, who know the vanity of things, the deceitfulness of appearances, and to whom it is all one, including even the familiarity with which I speak to you.

Forgive me for it, in any case. I know that I have less right to such familiarity than any one, and that it would be best to keep quiet. I plead as my excuse that you are one of the only beings who interest me, in this ugly democratic era, and that I love you, don't you see, for your cold skepticism, which mocks others and yourself.

Published in *Lecture*, February 25, 1891, 427–29.

Engraving by Henry W. McVikar

Portrait of Fyodor Sologub (1921) by Yuri Annenkov

SOLOGUB AND THE THEATRE

Fyodor Sologub is best known as a poet and novelist, famous for his elegant, musical verse and for his grotesque fictional masterpiece, *The Petty Demon*. But in the early years of the twentieth century he was also one of the most innovative, talked about, and widely performed playwrights in Russia.

Born in 1863 in St. Petersburg, Sologub was a man of humble origins whose real name was Teternikov. He grew up in poverty as the child of a tailor and an illiterate domestic servant, both former serfs. After his father's death when he was four, he lived with his sister and mother in the house of the well-to-do family for whom she worked. The boy was treated by turns as an inferior menial and as a favored godson, who was lucky enough to have a chance to develop his interests in literature, theatre, and the fine arts. As a result of these demeaning experiences, he grew up with a hatred of tyrannical authority and determined to be self-sufficient and independent-minded.

Sologub attended a community college and teachers' training institute in St. Petersburg and became a teacher of mathematics, and later a school inspector, in the provincial backwaters of Russia, where he observed close-up the crude pecking-order of a benighted society that ground down everything bright and fresh. Although his professional life as an educator would last for some twenty-five years, during which time he published many lengthy articles on pedagogy, he had begun writing poetry when he was twelve and soon embarked on a literary career. In 1892 he was able to move back to St. Petersburg, where he quickly became a prolific author of poems and stories and a leading member of the first generation of Russian Symbolists. In 1893 at the bidding of his publisher he adopted the pseudonym Sologub (pronounced Sulagoup, with the stress on the last syllable), which he was told would be more suitable for an aspiring writer than the uncouth-sounding Teternikov.

A gentle, melancholy, introspective, private individual, Sologub led a quiet, steady outer life, devoted first to his mother and sickly sister, then to his wife, Anastasia Chebotarevskaya, a fellow poet and translator with whom he frequently collaborated. Yet his writings were denounced as decadent, unwholesome, and even pornographic. In all his work he contrasted an ideal world of beauty and goodness as represented by the creative imagination, childhood, naked youthful bodies, and a longing for death to the real world of ugliness and evil represented by the rules and rigidities of adults and aging. A proponent of youth, Sologub himself, prematurely bald, had always looked old, even in his twenties.[1] Only in a world of dreams, the poet maintained, can one escape the evil of nature and the rampant stupidity of humankind.

Sologub was almost forty-five when he wrote his first play and had already been active in the literary world for over twenty years. Yet at this point the shy, secretive, and withdrawn poet embarked upon a new career in the theatre and became a major Symbolist dramatist and theoretician of a new stagecraft.

In 1906 Sologub met Meyerhold who was then just beginning his work as a director at the Vera Komissarzhevskaya Dramatic Theatre in St. Petersburg. The two men shared a number of the same ideas and soon became friends and associates, determined to carry out many joint projects. As a result of this meeting, Sologub, while continuing to write both poetry and fiction, came to devote much of his creative energies during the next fifteen years to the theatre, composing more than a dozen original plays as well as preparing adaptations and translations and writing many essays about the stage.

—*The Drama Review: TDR* 21, no. 4 (December 1977): 79–84.

Sologub was, above all, not simply a literary man who wrote plays, but a poet in the theatre, intimately concerned with the actual staging of his works and eager to challenge existing notions of theatrical performance, which he felt were inimical to the true nature of drama. Like Gordon Craig in his essay, "The Actor and the Über-Marionette," Sologub wished to subordinate the actor to the total spectacle; and like his fellow Russian Symbolists, Ivanov, Briusov, and Bely, he hoped to return theatre to its ritual origins and transform spectacle into mystery.

In late 1906, Vera Komissarzhevskaya organized a series of Saturday evenings at which poets would present their works for the stage to the company; Alexander Blok read his *The Puppet Show* prior to its production, and Sologub read his five-act tragedy, *The Gift of the Wise Bees (Dar mudrykh pchel)*, a ritual drama based on the Greek myth of Laodamia and Protesilaus. Meyerhold was impressed with Sologub's play and wanted to present it in the round, with the audience on all sides of the playing area, but Vera's brother, Fyodor Komissarzhevsky, opposed the idea on the grounds that the government, hostile to all innovation, would forbid the production. Despite Komissarzhevskaya's support, Meyerhold was forced to abandon the plan, but in 1912 he returned to his idea of staging *The Gift of the Wise Bees*. As is revealed in Meyerhold's correspondence,[2] the director discussed with Ida Rubinstein and Leon Bakst, both then in Paris, the possibility of staging Sologub's play as part of the Russian Seasons presented by Diaghilev in the French capital. Again the project was not realized, and *The Gift of the Wise Bees* remained unproduced.

The first of Sologub's plays to reach the stage was *The Triumph of Death (Pobeda smerti)*—a legendary drama on the theme of *Berthe aux grands pieds* (a medieval French romance)—that opened on November 6, 1907, at the Komissarzhevskaya Theatre under Meyerhold's direction and which was later played in Vitebsk by Meyerhold's own company. Sologub wrote a special prologue for the production in which modern characters in contemporary dress commented upon the drama; Meyerhold himself played the role of the poet. Sologub was crowned with a laurel wreath after the première. Meyerhold's highly stylized staging of *The Triumph of Death* brought to a head differences between the director and Komissarzhevskaya and led to Meyerhold's dismissal a few days after the opening. When Meyerhold unsuccessfully contested Komissarzhevskaya's action in a court of arbitration, Sologub acted as a witness on the director's behalf.[3]

During this period Sologub was closely associated with the Komissarzhevskaya troupe, participating in their activities and inviting members of the company to his house for his Sundays at home. Valentina Verigina, the actress who played Bertha in *The Triumph of Death*, recounts in her memoirs how Sologub went with her and the other members of the company to see Isadora Duncan perform in St. Petersburg in 1907 and how they all met with the American dancer backstage afterward—an extremely important experience for the evolution of Sologub's theory and practice of the drama.[4] The Russian poet was deeply influenced by the American dancer's use of bare feet and nearly nude body, since nakedness was central to his own mythopoesis. Here is how Sologub describes his encounter with Isadora.

> The spectator is enraptured and exults. He sees her half-naked body and does not lust. And if he were to see her completely nude, he would burn with a pure and ardent rapture. She dances. She is wearied. Her face grows red, and she is covered with drops of sweat, her bare hands turn red, her feet have reddened. She sweeps close, so close that the rustle of her light, lightly-fluttering clothing can be heard, and the smell of her body and of her sweat can be felt, and sweeter than spilt perfume is the smell of this sweat, poured

Scene from a production (circa 1910) based on Sologub's "Zarya Zaryanitsa"

forth in painful and joyous toil—for both painful and joyous is the toil of transformation, the herolc feat of transflguration.⁵

Also at this same time the poet worked with Meyerhold on his staging of Wedekind's *Spring Awakening*, editing the translation by Grigorii Feder that was used for the production at the Komissarzhevskaya Theatre in 1907.⁶ Sologub was drawn to Wedekind's play because of its lyrical and grotesque portrayal of adolescent sexuality warped by the cruel repressions of narrow-minded adults.

After Meyerhold's dismissal, Nikolai Evreinov shortly thereafter put on a new play by Sologub, at the Komissarzhevskaya Theatre. Opening on January 8,1909, *Vanka the Butler and the Page Jean (Van'ka kliuchnik i pazh Zhan)* was an ironic comedy presenting in a series of parallel scenes contrasting pictures of Russian and French amorous intrigues between masters and servants in olden times. The play proved unusually popular up to and even after the revolution. Alexander Kugel, who with Evreinov had founded the satirical cabaret-theatre, the Crooked Mirror, suggested to Sologub that he revise *Vanka the Butler and the Page Jean* for his theatre, since the original version was under a three-year contract to Fyodor Komissarzhevsky. In order to give the play a topical dimension, Kugel proposed that a third amorous intrigue involving a contemporary Russian bureaucrat be added for the production at the Crooked Mirror; Sologub agreed and rewrote the play as *Amorous Intrigues Forever (Vsegdashni shashni)*, which opened, under Evreinov's direction, on November 25, 1912 and made the author the most talked of playwright in Russia. The staging was a complete innovation; the three stories were played side by side, one after the other, in alternating scenes.

> Because the Crooked Mirror did not have a revolving stage, it was necessary to build a facsimile, in a handcrafted manner, which gave the possibility of presenting nonstop twenty-four scenes on three separate stages (each with its own curtain), lined up right in front of the footlights in such a way that there was visible to the audience: one stage with a raised curtain, and two others with lowered curtains.⁷

Other of his works were adapted for the small, after-hours theatres that flourished in St.Petersburg, and Sologub even considered opening a literary cabaret himself. The success of *Vanka the Butler* led to several other productions of Sologub's works in the period before World War I. During these years, Sologub was—along with Gorky, Kuprin, and Andreyev—one of the most celebrated Russian authors.

In the summer of 1909, Evreinov, assisted by Fyodor Komissarzhevsky, opened a new experimental stage, The Gay Theatre for Grown-Up Children, where he directed his own harlequinade, *A Gay Death (Veselaya smert')*, and Sologub's dramatic fairytale, *Night Dances (Nochnye plyaski)*, based on "The Secret Ball," which appears in Alexander Afanasyev's collection of *Russian Fairy Tales*,[8] and inspired by Isadora Duncan and her theatrical use of nudity.[9] Sologub saw Duncan's dancing as essentially democratic, liberating to the individual, and anti-authoritarian.[10]

Evreinov's production of *Night Dances* was one of the most extraordinary theatrical events of the time. It made use of almost total female nudity on stage; the dancers' only costumes were gossamer tutus and stockings. The cast consisted of famous writers and artists, including Alexei Remizov, Count Alexei Tolstoi, and Leon Bakst. Michel Fokine choreographed the dances in the style of Isadora Duncan, who is directly referred to in the play.

> KING: Did you follow my daughters?
>
> YOUNG POET: I gave my word—and I have done it. King, I followed the beautiful Princesses.
>
> KING: And where do they go?
>
> YOUNG POET: The beautiful Princesses go to an underground kingdom to see its enchanted king; there they dance all night long, doing dances in the style of the celebrated Isadora Duncan to the music of great composers of different times and nationalities.
> (*Night Dances*. Act III.)[11]

Rehearsals often took place in Sologub's home, and the poet insisted that the actresses playing the King's twelve daughters appear barefoot, a revolutionary and shocking procedure for the time. The production was also given at the Liteiny Theatre in St. Petersburg the same year (1909), and in 1915 *Night Dances* was revived at the Komissarzhevskaya Memorial Theatre in Moscow, under the direction of Fyodor Komissarzhevsky and Arkadii Zonov.

Sologub made an adaptation of his novel *The Petty Demon (Melkii bes)*, which was premièred at Solovtsov's Theatre in Kiev in 1909 and then directed by Konstantin Mardzhanov at the Nezlobin Theatre in Moscow in 1910. In 1912 two new Sologub plays appeared in St. Petersburg: *The Conqueror Dream (Mechta-pobeditel'nitsa)* at the Theatre of Comedy and Drama, and *The Hostages of Life (Zalozhniki Zhizn'i)* at the Alexandrinsky, directed by Meyerhold, who had not lost any of his interest in the works of the Symbolist poet. It was also played in Kiev in 1912 and in Penza in 1914. In 1912 also Sologub and his wife had published their adaptation of *War and Peace (Voina i mir)* in fourteen scenes.

In 1914 Sologub published *Love Over the Abyss (Lyubov' nad bezdnami)*, a drama in four acts (a semi-allegorical drama performed at the Burgtheater in Vienna in 1920); *The Farewell (Provody)*, a dramatic study in one act; and a translation of Kleist's *Penthesilea*. In 1915 his play, *A Stone Thrown in the Water (Kamen broshenny v vodu)*, dramatic scenes in four acts, co-written with Chebotarevskaya and directed by Nikolai Sinel'nikov, was given at the Kharkov Dramatic Theatre.

In his poems, stories, and plays Sologub holds to a Gnostic view of the world, seeing the god of the phenomenal world as a malicious creature punishing humans by consigning them to a miserable existence on earth. Above the phenomenal world is a world of quiet and beauty accessible to those spiritually attuned who seek escape from the prison of the real world through death.[12] A Manichean duality runs through all Sologub's works, expressed best by the pair from *Don Quixote*: Dulcinea and Aldonsa. Beauty is hidden by ugly reality. Beauty is created by human aspiration to other worlds in defiance of ugly, vulgar reality. In Sologub's private myth, art has transformative power, and the creative imagination can transform ugly reality into something higher.

In 1913–14 Sologub went on a lecturing tour for many months throughout Russia, and to Berlin and Paris, giving readings of his major essay, "The Art of Our Time (Iskusstvo nashych dnei)," in which Don Quixote appears as a foundational character in his aesthetic theory, and the poet expounds the Dulcinea/Aldonsa duality and its relation to Isadora Duncan.[13]

In the period 1910–16 Sologub wrote many essays on aesthetics and theatrical theory for *Theatre and Art (Teatr i Iskusstvo)*, in which he advances his views of a dualistic universe and the magical power of theatre to transcend the phenomenal world.

> Theatrical magic begins only when you see and do not see, hear and do not hear—when the voices of the actors blend with the voices of your own dream—when the light wings of the golden haired genius of dreams soar above the auditorium—when, during the intermission, you ask a theatre critic about his wife's health and smile upon hearing that she has the flu, smile at the voices of the dream which still are ringing in your soul.[14]

As an author who mixed spiritual quest, fantasy, political reality, and the perversely erotic, Sologub could not fail to be of interest to the growing Russian film industry. His novel *Sweeter than Poison (Slashche yada)* was filmed by Boris Svetlov, and his story *The Face of the Beast (Lik zverya)* was adapted as a film by Alexander Arkotov. In 1917 for the Moscow film company run by two Germans, Paul Thieman and F. Reinhardt, Meyerhold started shooting a film based on Sologub's trilogy of fantastic novels, *Phantom Spells (Nav'i chary)*—later renamed *The Created Legend (Tvorimaia legenda)*, a work said to anticipate magic realism by two generations,[15] but the project came to nothing.

During World War I Sologub was involved in various patriotic activities. As one of the founders of the Russian Society for the Study of Jewish Life, he co-edited with Gorky and Andreyev, *The Shield (Shchit)* in 1915, designed to combat anti-Semitism.

In the period of revolutionary upheaval, Sologub was active in a number of literary organizations designed to protect writers' freedom in opposition to the Bolsheviks' strongarm techniques. At the same time he worked on several adaptations. He dramatized Chateaubriand's novelette, *Les aventures du dernier Abéncerage* as a verse drama, *Love and Fidelity (Liubov i vernost')*, that was published in 1917 and performed at the Yalta Municipal Theatre in 1918, under the direction of Samuil Vermel from the Kamerny Theatre.[16] With his wife, Sologub translated from the French *The Wolves (Les Leonides)*, a drama by Romain Rolland about the French Revolution during the Terror in 1793, first published in 1906 under the pseudonym, C.-Godard d'Aucourt de Saint-Just. The translation was rejected in 1918 by the Petrograd Theatrical Commission, which was responsible for recommending plays to be staged. Sologub was regarded as a retrograde opponent of the new regime and its progressive values.

Sologub's *Triumph of Death* directed by Meyerhold at the Komissarzhevskaya Theatre, 1907
Set by Sergei Popov (following Meyerhold's design), sketch by Alexander Lyubimov

Sologub's fantastic stories, fables, and fairy tales, which draw on folklore, legend, and the occult are, like his poetry and plays, weird and eerie, and reveal the author's fondness for the grotesque and macabre. The mixing of perverse sado-masochistic sex and revolutionary politics in *The Created Legend* so offended Maxim Gorky that he referred to "that rotten, bald-headed bastard by the name of Sologub." Gorky continued, "You can say the filthiest things possible about Sologub and it would still not be enough for his vile, slimy, froglike soul!"[17]

The last of Sologub's works to be presented in the Russian theatre was *Arabesque of Roses (Uzor iz roz)*, the author's own adaption of his novel, *Lady Liza (Baryshnya Liza)*, that the Second Studio of the Moscow Art Theatre produced in 1920 under the direction of well-known actor Vassily Luzhsky. Praised by Lunacharsky and by Nemirovich-Danchenko, *Lady Liza*, which had been written in 1916, was also shown in the 1921–22 season in Tiflis and Petrograd, but in 1923 it was taken off as "too bourgeois," by order of a special commission on the theatrical repertory. From this point on, Sologub's plays—along with those of the other Symbolists, including Maeterlinck—were rejected as decadent and alien to the spirit of the revolution. Sologub was personally condemned by the Marxist-Leninist critics as a morbid and unhealthy writer whose dwelling on death and perverse sexuality (violating two principal Soviet taboos) went counter to the new revolutionary ethos.

During the difficult civil war years of 1920–21, Sologub made hand-written books of poems which he sold through bookstores and fellow writers. In 1921 Sologub had written to Lenin requesting a passport and permission to leave Russia; in the same year his wife committed suicide by drowning in the Neva. The poet spent his last years living quietly in Leningrad doing translations from a variety of different languages: French, German, English, Bulgarian, Greek, and Hungarian. He was honored on the anniversary of his forty years of literary activity, and he served as chairman of the Writers' Union. He died in 1927 and was buried in Smolensk cemetery.

In the Soviet era, *The Petty Demon* was reprinted, and a carefully annotated edition of Sologub's poetry appeared in 1975,[18] but his plays and theory of the theatre remained stigmatized as reactionary, psychopathic, and perverted. Only the Soviet director Sergei Radlov, writing two years after Sologub's death, praised Sologub for making a strong and decisive statement about the rights of the individual creator in the theatre.[19] Radlov ultimately rejected the notion that the author—a nonprofessional in the theatre—has sole possession of the spectacle, but he felt the charm of Sologub's "singing words." Since the fall of communism, there was been a revival of interest in Sologub and republication of his works; *The Petty Demon* has been performed on stage and was made into a film in 1995.

Sologub's chief theoretical work, "The Theatre of One Will (Teatr odnoi voli)," (published in 1908 in a famous collection of essays, *On the New Theatre*, including Meyerhold, Bely, Briusov, and Benois) should be read as a Symbolist text, a poetic fable—arcane and incantatory—containing the keys to the poet's mystical view of the universe. This world of deceptive appearances—our everyday life—is presided over by the evil Dragon, the sun, and by Aisa, the Greek Fate of chance and contingency; opposed to it is the higher world, supremely calm and unchanging, of Ananke and of Death. The theatrical spectacle—likened to the workings of the universe and to the workings of human consciousness—must cease simply to reflect the reality of the lower world and become transformed into a mystery that will make transparent the eternal truth that lurks behind all masks. "I take a scrap of life and make a legend out of it" was Sologub's motto.[20] Seemingly autocratic and elitist, subjectively individualistic and solipsistic in his critical theory, Sologub actually creates a legend in "The Theatre of One Will" whereby the spectator becomes a celebrant; barriers between stage and auditorium are broken down, the audience surges upon the stage, removes its clothes, and dances—a goal to some extent realized in Evreinov's production of *Night Dances*. It should be noted that the word used by Sologub for dance (in Russian *plyaska*)—as opposed to ballroom dancing and ballet—connotes a totally free form of self-expression, frenzied, strenuous, and transcendent. It is such a dance that the theatre must become according to Sologub's "Theatre of One Will."

Zamyatin said: "Cruel time will blot out many names, but Sologub's name will remain in Russian literature."[21]

NOTES

1. Murl G. Barker, Introduction to Fyodor Sologub, *The Kiss of the Unborn and Other Stories*, ed. and trans. Murl G. Barker (Knoxville: University of Tennessee Press, 1977), xvii.
2. *V.E. Meyerhold Perepiska,* ed. V.P. Korshunova and M.M. Sitkovetskaya (Moscow: Iskusstvo, 1976).
3. Catherine A. Schuler, *Women in Russian Theatre: The Actress in the Silver Age* (London: Routledge, 1996), 180. Iulia Petrovna Rybakova, *V.F. Komissarzhevskaya: Letopis' Zhizn'i i tvorchestva* (St. Petersburg: Rossiiskii Institut Istorii Iskusstv, 1994), 376–78.
4. Valentina Petrovna Verigina, *Vospominaniya* (Leningrad: Iskusstvo, 1974), 132.
5. Fyodor Sologub, *Sobranie sochinenii,* (St. Petersburg: Shipovnik, 1913), 10:163.
6. Iulia Petrovna Rybakova, *V.F. Komissarzhevskaya: Letopis' Zhizn'i i tvorchestva,* 365.
7. Nikolai Evreinov, "*Vsegdasni shashni [Amorous Intrigues Forever],*" *Russkaya Mysl'*, April 8, 1958, 4–5.
8. Alexander Afanasyev, "The Secret Ball," *Russian Fairy Tales* (New York: Pantheon, 1973), 224–26.
9. Evreinov was also intensely interested in nudity on stage and edited and contributed essays to an illustrated collection on the subject: *Nagota na stsene* (St. Petersburg: Tip. morskogo ministerstva, 1911).
10. Fyodor Sologub, "Ocharovanie vzorov (Aisedora Dunkan)" *Teatr i Iskusstvo,* no. 4 (January 27, 1913), 90. Quoted in Laura Engelstein, *Keys to Happiness: Sex and the Search for Modernity in Fin de Siècle Russia.* (Ithaca: Cornell University Press, 1992).
11. *Nochnye Plyaski,* in Fyodor Sologub, *Sobranie P'es* (St. Petersburg: Nav'i Chary, 2001), 1:184-85.
12. For an extensive discussion of gnostic drama, see Jane Goodall, "Introduction: The Gnostic Drama," *Artaud and the Gnostic Drama* (Oxford: Oxford University Press, 1994), 1-19.
13. "Iskusstvo nashykh dnei," in *Biblioteka Russkoi Kritiki: Kritika Ruskogo Simvolisma* (Moscow: Olimp, 2002), 1:352-9.
14. "Estetika mechty," *Teatr i Iskusstvo,* no. 5 (February 1, 1915), 84.
15. Robert Hadji, "Sologub," in *Penguin Encyclopedia of Horror and the Supernatural,* ed. Jack Sullivan, introduction by Jacques Barzun (New York: Viking, 1986), 394.
16. Alexander Borisovich Viner, "V Krymu," in *Vstrechi s Meyerholdom* (Moscow: Vserossiiskoe teatral'noe Obshchestvo, 1967), 173.
17. Quoted by Samuel D. Cioran, Introduction to Fyodor Sologub, *Drops of Blood, The Created Legend, Part One,* trans. Samuel D. Cioran (Ann Arbor, MI: Ardis, 1979), 18.
18. Fyodor Sologub, *Stikhotvoreniya,* ed. M.I. Dikman, *Biblioteka Poeta* (Leningrad: Leningradskoe Otdelenie, 1975).
19. Sergei Radlov, "O odnoi vole v teatre," in *Desiat let v teatre* (Leningrad: Priboy, 1929), 74-86.
20. Quoted by Pavel Markov in *O Teatre* (Moscow: Iskusstvo, 1974), 1:333.
21. Yevgeny Zamyatin, "Fedor Sologub" (1924) in *A Soviet Heretic: Essays by Yevgeny Zamyatin,* ed. and trans. Mirra Ginsburg (Chicago: University of Chicago Press, 1970).

Mayakovsky the Futurist (circa 1914)

RUSSIAN DRAMA AND THE POLISH THEATRE IN THE COMMUNIST ERA:
THE CASE OF MAYAKOVSKY

A history of the reception of one nation's dramatic literature in the theatre of another nation will always reveal much of interest about the social, political, and cultural relations of those two countries and of their distinctive traditions in matters of style and taste. When the two countries are Russia and Poland—nations with such close, yet troubled ties and with such radically dissimilar artistic and cultural traditions, in both of which theatre is central—then the story becomes particularly exciting and explosive. An account of the presentation and reception of Soviet drama on the Polish stage from 1944 to 1989 can open a window on key moments in the evolution of post-war twentieth-century Polish theatre.

The story is one of a brief, but painful enforced marriage and then a separation. The crucial dates are 1949, and then 1954 to 1956. And one Soviet playwright, Mayakovsky—and particularly his *Bathhouse*—played a decisive role in liberating Polish theatre, paradoxically enough, from the yoke of Soviet drama. But before turning to the story proper, first a word about the historical antecedents of the theatrical interchange between these two nations. From the 1830s until the First World War, in the Russian-occupied section of partitioned Poland, Tsarist administration and censorship controlled all theatres. Even at Warsaw's Rozmaitości Theatre, where plays were permitted to be performed in Polish, all Polish sentiments and national ideas were forbidden; in retaliation, the Rozmaitości Theatre presented no Russian plays.

When in 1906 the Moscow Art Theatre visited Warsaw, Polish actors felt obliged to stay away despite their great interest, or, if they did go, they sat in the least conspicuous seats out of public view—but published open letters to Stanislavsky explaining their feelings. After Poland had regained independence in 1918, the theatre became officially anti-Soviet throughout the period between the world wars because of the openly hostile relations of the two countries following the Russo-Polish War of 1920; the few Soviet plays presented were usually given a deliberately anti-Soviet slant, even though Leon Schiller and several other directors were sympathetic to Soviet theatre.

During the interwar years, Mayakovsky visited Poland twice, for a day in April 1927 on his way to Prague, and a month later on his way back in June 1927 for ten days. During the interwar years none of his plays was professionally staged in Poland, although there was a reading of the "Prologue" to *Mystery-Bouffe* at Witold Wandurski's Workers Theatre in 1924 in Łódź, and Leon Schiller had hoped, in vain, to stage *The Bedbug* at the Warsaw theatre school where he taught. Such was the not too promising background for the reception of Soviet drama in modern Poland.

From 1944 to 1949—the first period of postwar Polish theatre under the new communist regime—reconstruction of theatres, companies, and theatrical life was the prime task. There was little or no centralized control, and the future direction of Polish theatre remained undefined and uncertain. The repertory consisted of Polish classics, Shakespeare, new Polish plays and new foreign works by dramatists such as Jean Giraudoux, Armand Salacrou, and Arthur Miller. There were guest tours by the Moscow Art Theatre and the Leningrad Gorky Theatre, but Polish productions of Soviet plays

—*Contemporary Russian and Polish Drama, Theatre Perspectives*, no. 2 (1982): 28–32.

were rare. Konstantin Simonov's *The Russian Question* and *The Russians* were given, but *The Russians* closed in Cracow for lack of an audience. Only in Łódź and Katowice were Soviet plays successfully staged; the best of these was the Katowice production of Maxim Gorky's *Yegor Bulychov and the Others* in 1947, which was shown throughout Poland. Evgenii Petrov's *Island of Peace*, Sergei Esenin's *Pugachov*, and a dramatization of Vladimir Mayakovsky's poem *Khorosho* in 1948 virtually exhaust the list.[1]

Then in 1949 with the institution of Stalinism in Poland (later referred to euphemistically as the "period of errors and misdeeds"), everything suddenly changed, and for the next five years there came an influx of Soviet plays whose impact was immense. In January 1949, at the Congress of the Polish Writers' Union in Szczecin, socialist realism was proclaimed as the obligatory style for all the arts. Formalism, meaning any departure from the prescribed norms, was condemned, and a call for a change in the repertory was issued. A centralized administration for all Polish theatres under a Central Board of Theatres was established; as a result, individual directors lost all independence. If we ask why it took until 1949 for this tightening of controls to take place, the answer is that until then civil war and social instability in Poland were such that it was not yet possible for the regime to crack down in the cultural field. But by 1949 power had been sufficiently consolidated for the Soviet dogma of socialist realism to be enforced.

Consequently the Polish national classics of the Romantic repertory—the poetic, metaphoric, and political plays of Adam Mickiewicz, Zygmunt Krasiński, and Juliusz Słowacki as well as those of the Symbolist Stanisław Wyspiański—became outlawed during the five years of stagnation (only Słowacki's melodramatic *Mazeppa* was given during this entire period). Soviet theatre appeared on tour in Poland for the first time when, in 1949, the Moscow Dramatic Theatre (under the direction of Nikolai Okhlopkov) presented a number of plays, including Alexander Fadeyev's *Young Guard* and *Great Days* by Nikolai Virta, a leading proponent of the "No conflict" theory of drama (since there can be no conflict in socialist society).

The culmination of the newly announced policy was a huge Festival of Russian and Soviet Plays (proposed by the Congress of Polish-Soviet Friendship Society), in which all theatres took part: forty-seven theatres presented a total of sixty plays. One of the principal aims of the festival was to teach Polish playwrights how to deal correctly with modern problems and portray the new socialist man. We shall see shortly the results of this instruction. The most interesting productions included Mikhail Bulgakov's *Last Days*, Konstantin Trenyov's *Lyubov Yarovaya*, and Gorky's *Egor Bulychov and the Others*.

Much Gorky was given in 1949 and 1950, but the attempt to make his works fit the tenets of socialist realism and illustrate Russian social history rendered the productions dead and schematic. The style of the Moscow Art Theatre, its ensemble acting, and the concept of a realistic theatre dating back almost fifty years became the only acceptable model for Polish theatres. In 1952 Nikolai Pogodin's *Man With a Gun* was produced, giving rise to the first Lenin on the Polish stage. Vsevolod Ivanov's *Armored Train* was another major Soviet drama of the same year.

We should remember that in the early 1950s in Poland many young writers and artists who would slightly later become leaders of the post-thaw modern Polish theatre at this point enthusiastically embraced socialist realism, among others the director Kazimierz Dejmek, the critic Jan Kott, and the playwright Adam Tarn. Members of this younger generation, whether true believers or ambitious opportunists, were yet to grow disillusioned and cynical.

In 1949 at the Nowy Teatr in Łódź, which soon became famous for its

The Bathhouse, directed by Kazimierz Dejmek, Nowy Teatr, Łódź (1954)

scrupulously veristic realism, Dejmek did an outstanding staging of a productivity play, *Grinder Karhan's Team* (by the Czech Vašek Káňa, which had been staged in Prague by E.F.Burian), in which a whole factory was faithfully reproduced in the theatre.[2] In 1951 Dejmek won a state prize for his production of the Soviet educator Anton Makarenko's *Pedagogic Poem*.

At the Festival of Contemporary Polish Plays, held in 1951 to point the way for the new drama, it was in fact just such slavish imitations—Soviet productivity plays set in construction plants—that dominated the offerings and rendered the event a ludicrous failure. Besides productivity plays, Polish playwrights, attempting to follow the acceptable Soviet models, also showed at the Festival dramas on international cold war issues, attacking Western imperialism and the evils of capitalism (Adam Tarn won a prize for his *An Ordinary Affair* about miscarriage of justice in the USA) and Soviet World War plays, which had to be from a triumphal Soviet point of view. These propaganda pieces, and especially the productivity plays, were so foreign to the Polish tradition of an allusive, poetic drama that comic parodies soon began to appear, and it was even said that in their productions some directors deliberately pushed to absurdity the inherent folly of the factory play.

Visits from Soviet theatres continued, with the Pushkin Theatre of Leningrad in 1951, the Mossovet in 1952, and the Vakhtangov in 1953, but far more significant were two visiting groups from the West, Bertolt Brecht's Berliner Ensemble in 1952 with *Mother Courage* (officially disapproved of, but showing Polish artists that one could be socialist

The Bathhouse, directed by Kazimierz Dejmek, Nowy Teatr, Łódź (1954)

without being realist) and in 1954 Jean Vilar's Théâtre National Populaire with *Le Cid*, *Ruy Blas*, and *Don Juan*, demonstrating that a people's theatre need not be boring and colorless. Until this point the Polish theatre had been hopelessly isolated, cut off from all other countries except for the Soviet Union and its satellites.[3]

But by late 1954 (almost two years after Stalin's death) the situation had started to change, and the whole structure of rigid controls and enforced socialist realism was about to topple. The turning point can be seen to have come in December 1954 when Kazimierz Dejmek at the Nowy Teatr in Łódź (previously famous for its scrupulous realism) staged Mayakovsky's *The Bathhouse* (one year after its revival in the USSR at the Moscow Satire Theatre in 1953). This was the first—but by no means last—instance of the Polish theatre's use of avant-garde Soviet drama as a weapon against socialist realism and Soviet domination.

For the Polish theatre until the fall of communism Mayakovsky was the single most important Soviet playwright,[4] and the only one to be produced by almost all the major Polish directors: in addition to Dejmek, Grotowski, Szajna, Korzeniewski, Jarocki, and Swinarski all staged either *The Bathhouse* or *Bedbug*, sometimes both. The reason: not only did Mayakovsky serve to free the Polish stage from socialist realism, but he is perhaps the only Soviet playwright who is at one and the same time political, poetic, metaphoric, and fantastic, always capable of being contemporary—those very qualities that appeal to the Polish theatrical vision, as it is manifested in the Polish Romantic tradition. Dejmek's *Bathhouse*, with its platforms and moving scenery recalling

Meyerhold's staging, was an attack on bureaucracy, exposing the rotten structure of Stalinism in Poland; it proved to be a sensational success. Young people came from all over the country to see the production,[5] which served as a major inspiration to the student theatre movement that would soon help to transform Polish cultural life. Of this production, a Polish critic, Maria Czarnerle, has written that it was "the firework that threw light upon the hypocrisy and grayness of our cultural life, and the dynamite that blew up the fossilized social agreements, the theatrical conventions." Dejmek's *Bathhouse* introduced a new kind of political theatre, grotesque in technique, satirical in spirit

It was followed in December 1955 by *The Bedbug* at the Żeromski Theatre in Kielce, directed by Irena Byrska in such a way as to bring to the surface the play's ambiguous undercurrent and thereby make it a contemporary satire about the mechanization and soullessness of the present, rather than a critique of NEP men in Moscow in the 1920s. In this Polish *Bedbug*, in which the present was portrayed as in Huxley's *Brave New World* and Chaplin's *Modern Times*, Prisypkin came out as the most likeable and human character.[6]

I shall return a bit later to other important Polish interpretations of Mayakovsky on the Polish stage in the 1960s, but first we must return to 1955 and the social and political changes that were taking place then. The Polish theatre was decentralized, leading to greater regional control and flexibility in choosing repertory. Now the theatre was municipally financed and supervised, under the overall control of the Ministry of Culture and Art. After Khrushchev's speech disclosing Stalin's crimes in February of 1956, followed in Poland by the Poznań workers' riots in June and the bloodless October Revolution, Stalinism crumbled in Poland, and suddenly the shackles of socialist realism were irrevocably removed from the arts.

From 1956 to 1962 an extreme reaction set in, an opening to the West and away from the Soviet Union. And in no art was this more striking than in the theatre. In 1957 there were only three productions of Soviet plays, and none of these took place in a major center, such as Warsaw, Cracow, Wrocław, or Łódź. Instead a vast importation of Western drama, chiefly the new French avant-garde, took place. The Polish theatre became immediately responsive to Western influences and attuned to modern sensibility; the box set and veristic realism were discarded, and with them all the Soviet drama associated with socialist realism. Starting with the Polish production of *Waiting for Godot* in 1957, all of Beckett and also of Ionesco was translated into Polish and performed in Polish theatres, along with Ghelderode, Adamov, Genet, Dürrenmatt, Pinter, Osborne, Kafka's *Trial*, and Brecht. The entire Western avant-garde was immediately understood, accepted, and assimilated by Polish actors, writers, and audiences—much more rapidly than in the West, as a matter of fact.

In 1956 Adam Tarn (who a few years before had written a prize-winning socialist realist play) founded the influential drama magazine, *Dialog*, which introduced in translation the most significant foreign plays (including a number of inaccessible and officially shunned nonconformist Soviet plays from the 1920s and 30s) and made them available to both readers and theatres. And if the Polish theatre now avoided the official Soviet drama of the Stalin years, directors drew on the forgotten and often forbidden masterpieces of non-realistic Soviet playwriting from the interwar years. Evgenii Zamyatin's *The Flea* was given in Gdańsk in 1962, Evgenii Shvarts's *Dragon* in Nowa Huta in 1961, and many versions of Isaac Babel's plays and stories appeared on the Polish stage.

Mystery-Bouffe, directed by Jerzy Grotowski, Theatre of the Thirteen Rows, Opole (1960)

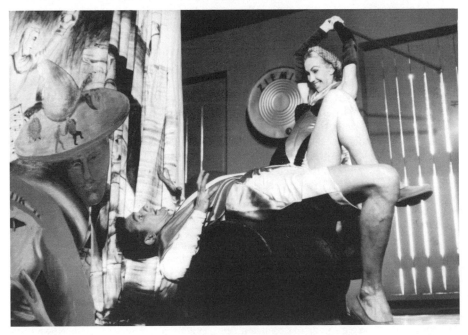

Mystery-Bouffe, directed by Jerzy Grotowski, Theatre of the Thirteen Rows, Opole (1960)

The Polish student theatres, which played a pioneering role in liberating the Polish theatre from official constraints in the period from 1954 to the early 1960s, did not present a single standard Soviet play, but instead offered dramatization of Babel's stories, Okudzhava's ballads, Esenin's *Pugachov* and *Confessions of a Hoodlum*, the first and only communist-era production of Daniil Kharms's *Elizabeth Bam* in 1967 (shown on tour in Yugoslavia), Zamyatin's *The Flea*, and poetic shows and recitations based on works by Akhmatova, Pasternak, Mandelshtam, and Mayakovsky.

Mayakovsky's plays continued to be important in the professional theatre as well. In 1960, following Mayakovsky's advice to future directors to make the play topical, Grotowski presented *Mystery-Bouffe* at his Theatre of the Thirteen Rows in Opole in a radically updated version. The scenario prepared by Grotowski cut half the original text and added interpolated sections of *The Bathhouse* as well as a prologue and epilogue made up of authentic fragments of Polish medieval mystery plays, accompanied by recorded Gregorian chant. The production, presented in a highly stylized manner that drew on puppet theatre and fairground conventions, stressed political and philosophical themes and attacked the bourgeois taste of the opponents of the Theatre of the Thirteen Rows.

Caricature, satire, and the grotesque set the tone. According to the program, the stage design was by "Hieronymous Bosch in collaboration with Wincenty Maszkowski." Six actors played all the roles, and the props consisted of a few painted shields bearing captions, a tin bucket that could be a desk, the ark, or part of the time machine (from *The Bathhouse*), and a bench painted black. All the characters wore similar costumes: shiny short pants, tight jackets, and suspenders. Optimistenko, a composite character combing Pobedonosikov and Ivan Ivanovich, stood on his head and spouted idiotic decrees and philistine pronouncements on art. In the epilogue all characters recited the late medieval *Dialogue of Master Polikarp with Death*.

Jerzy Jarocki's production of *The Bathhouse* in 1963 won a prize at the First Festival of Russian and Soviet Plays in Katowice (held every two years in October, alternating with the Festival of Drama of Socialist Countries). The entire action took place in front of Pobedonosikov's office, which was constantly present with its labyrinthine staircases, corridors, cubbyholes, revealing the sinister madness of the bureaucracy made manifest in the columns of waiting petitioners and uniformed officials. Jarocki staged *The Bedbug* in Wrocław in 1967 in a production that eliminated Act I, putting some fragments of its dialogue into Act III.

Józef Szajna staged *Mystery-Bouffe* at Nowa Huta in 1965 (the production was also shown at the International Festival in Florence the same year) and *The Bathhouse* in Cracow in 1967 in an original production that emphasized the changes that had taken place in the world, not only since Mayakovsky's time, but also since the earlier Polish productions. In Szajna's vision Pobedonosikov is no longer all-powerful, but rather undergoing an apocalypse. The single set consisted of ladders leading up to windows of the run-down apartment building where Pobedonosikov, who is shabby and tired, and speaks in a dead, colorless voice, reigns over a confused mass of paper. Chudakov and his associates are dressed in red overalls, constantly climb up and down the ladders, and invade Pobedonosikov's disintegrating regime.

Just before his death in a plane crash in 1975, Konrad Swinarski, who had first staged *The Bedbug* in German at the Schiller Theater in West Berlin in 1964, was nearing his final rehearsals of Mayakovsky's "fantastic comedy with fireworks" for the Narodowy

The Bedbug, directed by Konrad Swinarski, Teatr Narodowy, Warsaw (1975)

The Bathhouse, directed by Józef Szajna, Stary Teatr, Cracow (1967)

Theatre in Warsaw. The posthumous staging revealed Swinarski's intention to create out of all the ugliness and horror, which in his production reached Its apex in the wedding party, a morality drama about human destlny. In the sterile, alien world of a happy future portrayed in the second half of the play, the revolting, crude, and dangerous Prisypkin, brilliantly played by Tadeusz Łomnicki, seemed a desperate, lost, almost tragic figure.[7]

The final moment in the communist-era phase of the Russian writer's reception in Poland came in 1978 with Józef Szajna's homage drama, *Mayakovsky*, the last of his theatrical tributes to artist-heroes, following *Witkacy*, *Dante*, and *Cervantes*. In this overwhelmingly visual spectacle, the building of the "palace of communism" and its dismantling is represented by the stacking and collapse of a mountain of red chairs.

Although there were other productions of Mayakovsky in Poland in the 1970s,[8] with the rise of Solidarity and the open political challenge to the regime, Mayakovsky's plays had already performed their function as subversive counter-attacks on Soviet-imposed ideological art. They no longer seemed necessary.

But this was not the end of the story. After the fall of communism, at the time when Dejmek was named Minister of Culture from 1993 to 1996, the playwright Tadeusz Słobodzianek (the son of Polish political exiles born in Russia) started to write his *Bedbug's Dream* about Prisypkin's return to post-communist Russia thirty years after he was last seen in his cage at the Moscow zoo.

On September 15, 2001, Kazimierz Dejmek returned to Teatr Nowy in Łódź, where he had started his career, to direct the première of Słobodzianek's play (using the twin Janicki brothers from Kantor's Cricoteque). Filled with quotes from Mayakovsky, Dostoevsky, Blok, and Mandelshtam, and rich in allusions to Russian history, *The Bedbug's Dream* depicts a world of totalitarian capitalism where former communists have become wealthy spiritual gurus. Once again Mayakovsky's satirical vision transcended its own circumstances.

NOTES

1. Three Soviet plays were presented in 1945, none in 1946, three in 1947, and eight in 1948.
2. In 2008 the Nowy Teatr revived *Grinder Karhan's Team* in a prize-winning recreation of Dejmek's original production directed by Remigiusz Brzyk.
3. A curious side-effect of enforced socialist realism from 1949 to 1955 was the attempted popularization of the theatre to be achieved by means of free distribution of tickets, group outings to theatres from factories, schools, and military units, and other collective means of involving the masses in the cultural life of the country.
4. After 1989, Bulgakov became the most widely performed and highly esteemed twentieth-century Russian writer in Poland because he had never compromised with the Stalinist regime. After his failed attempt to get Stalin's permission for him to emigrate in 1929, Bulgakov went into a semi-state of internal exile and wrote his best work, *The Master and Margarita* "for the drawer." As a "non-Soviet" Soviet writer, he is an ideal writer for the postcommunist theatre, whereas Mayakovsky dropped from sight.
5. It was eventually taken to Moscow.
6. In Koszalin in 1961 *The Bathhouse* was made into a local satire.
7. August Grodzicki, *Polish Theatre Directors* (Warsaw: Interpress, 1979), 144–45.
8. Other Polish productions of Mayakovsky from the 1970s include *The Bathhouse* at the Teatr Polski in Wrocław in 1976, *The Bathhouse* at the Teatr im. Solskiego in Tarnów in 1978, and *The Bedbug* at the Teatr im. Mickiewicza in Częstochowa in 1979.

ENTER FORTINBRAS:
SHAKESPEARE'S STRONGMAN IN MODERN EASTERN EUROPEAN THEATRE

I first discovered that Shakespeare's Fortinbras is a well-known personage in Eastern Europe at a Warsaw performance of *Tango* in the fall of 1965. After some troubles with the censorship, Mrożek's play had only recently re-opened at the Teatr Współczesny to great critical acclaim, and was regarded as a major cultural event with far-reaching social and political implications. During an intermission, Adam Tarn, then editor of the Polish drama magazine *Dialog*, remarked that I, as a foreigner, would have difficulty in understanding all the allusions and hidden meanings obvious to Poles, and then went on to explain that *Tango* was based on, among other literary analogues, the opposition between Hamlet and Fortinbras.

Without the hint, it would scarcely have occurred to any Western theatregoer to look for that Elizabethan pairing at the heart of Mrożek's contemporary comedy of the grotesque. I grew intrigued by the paradox that in Poland Fortinbras is a figure of such notoriety that his presence is widely felt outside the Shakespearean tragedy in which he appears. In many surprising guises and incarnations, he has wandered into works by twentieth-century Polish poets, essayists, and playwrights.

As a result of that experience in the theatre, my awareness of Fortinbras became heightened, and since then, in my reading of Eastern European drama and literature, I have kept finding various traces—shadows, echoes, footsteps—of the warlike Norwegian Prince, who arrives unexpectedly at the very last moment to eulogize Hamlet and claim the throne of Denmark. In the West, on the contrary, Fortinbras is simply a very minor character in *The Tragedy of Hamlet, Prince of Denmark*. Whereas Hamlet himself and many of Shakespeare's other characters have independent existences, assuring them of a prominent position in the art and thought of the Western world, Fortinbras has no such life beyond the confines of the play—and not much life even within it.

In fact, it was customary in most nineteenth-century stagings of Shakespeare to omit the Norwegian Prince altogether. In 1894, after nearly two decades of frequenting London theatres, Bernard Shaw complained, "For all my Hamlet going, were I to perish this day, I should go to my account without having seen Fortinbras, save in my mind's eye."[1] An early and prophetic Fortinbras-watcher, Shaw recognized the value of the Norwegian Prince in combatting the romantic and sentimental interpretations of *Hamlet* that were dominant at the time. As long as the play was considered exclusively a psychological portrait of the hero, a personal tragedy of an exceptional individual, and a great acting role, Fortinbras was both unnecessary and unwanted. Goethe, for example, argued that it detracted from Hamlet's death to have Fortinbras suddenly appear and occupy center stage in the closing minutes of the drama, and he recommended cutting the role.

In the interests of reducing the number of characters and scenes, twentieth-century actors and directors have often continued the practice of eliminating what may seem an extraneous part in an overcrowded tragedy. The excision is easy to perform; Shakespeare gives us only the most fleeting glimpses of the character. Mentioned twice in Act I and once in Act II, Fortinbras appears on stage for the first time in Act IV, scene iv, and for the second and last time in Act V after Hamlet's death. The Norwegian Prince speaks twenty-seven lines in a total of six short speeches. Even Bernardo and Marcellus (who are present only in the sentry scene of Act I) are each allotted more lines and

—*Assaph: Studies in the Theatre* 1, section c, no. 1 (1984): 5–27.

Final scene from Edward Gordon Craig's *Hamlet*, Moscow Art Theatre (1912)
Fortinbras on platform at left

speeches than the Norwegian Prince.

What do we know of this most shadowy and enigmatic of Shakespearean characters? And how has it been possible for him to acquire in Eastern Europe a significance out of all proportion to the meager role assigned him in the text? Fortinbras is apparently Shakespeare's invention; he is not found in the known sources of the play (in *Belleforest*, only his uncle, Old Norway, appears). His name, from the French *fort en bras* (spelled Fortenbrasse in the first quarto of 1603) tells us almost all there is to know: he is strong of arm. Horatio provides an etymological gloss when he explains that Fortinbras hopes "to recover of us by strong hand" the lands lost by his father. The sole character in the drama to achieve his ends, the Norwegian strongman not only acquires the territory he maintained was rightfully his, but also all of Denmark.

Besides strength and success (in a tragedy of misspent energies and purposes gone astray), there is little that we can attribute to Fortinbras in the way of distinguishing traits. Can we remember the name of any actor who has played the role or recall seeing a single drawing or photograph of *Hamlet* that shows the Norwegian Prince (who never shares a scene with the hero until the latter is a corpse)?[2] Who is this faceless man of action, absent to the point of near invisibility?

Superstars of the English-speaking theatre, from Henry Irving to Laurence Olivier in his film version of *Hamlet*, have found Fortinbras to be dispensable. The Norwegian Prince lost out to the Danish Prince, in a reversal of what actually happened in the play. Not so in Russia and Eastern Europe. There Fortinbras has been the force to be reckoned with. It is he, not Hamlet, who wins the kingdom and holds the reins of power as the tragedy ends. In the new regime of the strongman, the philosopher prince is the one who can be dispensed with. In Moscow and Warsaw, Leningrad and Cracow,

Fortinbras holds the key to Shakespeare's tragedy—and to many later dramas as well. His lack of words, his non-appearance except at two crucial moments—at the head of an army, to the sounds of martial music—his very invisibility and anonymity all serve to make Fortinbras loom large in the Slavic imagination nurtured on cycles of oppression, revolt, coup, repression. In countries where the vicissitudes of history and power politics have borne down hard on intellectuals, the ironic juxtaposition of Hamlet and Fortinbras offers an instructive paradigm, and the strongman's surprising domination of the stage and the state in the ultimate minutes of Shakespeare's tragedy suggests possibilities for striking coups de théâtre that will also be coups d'état.

The first intrusion of Fortinbras into a modern Eastern European work that I have been able to find comes in the USSR in the late 1920s, as Stalin was consolidating power and forging the monolithic communist state. Conditions were right for the entry on stage of the Norwegian Prince. The devastations of the First World War and the upheavals of the Russian Revolution produced a generation of European writers obsessed with the workings of history. The violent changes brought about by these events convinced many artists that life would never again be the same and raised questions about the future of civilization. Apocalyptic thinking and anti-utopian fantasy became widespread in the literature and drama of the interwar years. Particularly in Russia and those adjacent Eastern European countries where the tremors of revolution could be strongly felt, the sense of rupture was acute, and all traditional values seemed in danger of being destroyed.

The slate would be wiped clean. In the Soviet Union the imminent arrival of the New Man was announced: he would be rational, socially-committed, selfless. The obsolete individualist would be forever replaced, and the bourgeois past liquidated. The march of history occasioned varying response; it could be joyfully accepted, viewed ambivalently with irony, or feared and castigated as a menacing catastrophe.

The second of these courses was followed by the Soviet novelist Yurii Olesha (1899-1960), who identified the march of history with the arrival of Fortinbras and his troops. In 1929 Olesha adapted his brilliant short novel, *Envy* (written the previous year), for the stage at the request of the Vakhtangov Theatre where it opened on March 13. The dramatic version, called *The Conspiracy of Feelings*, was a great success at both the Vakhtangov Theatre in Moscow and the Bolshoi Theatre in Leningrad, but it was officially condemned shortly thereafter for presenting a false picture of the new man as well as for various formalist heresies. The play disappeared from the stage and was never published in the author's lifetime.

Full of allusions to Shakespeare and analogues to a number of his plays, *The Conspiracy of Feelings* dramatizes the clash between old and new in the Soviet era by means of the Hamlet-Fortinbras opposition. In Olesha's comedy, two brothers—Ivan and Andrei Babichev—vie, like rival foster fathers, for control of the hero, Nikolai Kavalerov, a Hamlet-like dreamer (descendant of the nineteen-century Russian "superfluous man") and misfit in the victorious communist society, whose only possessions are his razor and volume of Shakespeare's plays. Spokesman for the old emotions of love, hate, jealousy, pride, and pity that are being eliminated from the antiseptic new world, Ivan attempts to organize a conspiracy, or sexual counter-revolution, by stirring up stifled feelings in the remnants of the petty bourgeoisie. Persuaded by Ivan—here functioning like the Ghost of Hamlet's father—that he should avenge the nineteenth century and its glorious feelings, Kavalerov resolves to kill the new Soviet man, Andrei, an efficient sausage maker obsessed with producing cheap salami and creating mass production kitchens.

As the play nears its climax at a football match where Kavalerov is to carry out his epoch-avenging deed, Ivan, the clownish champion of the victims of history, makes explicit the Hamlet-Fortinbras contrast upon which Olesha has built the play.

> You've read Shakespeare, haven't you, Kavalerov? Remember? Remember how Hamlet ends? Corpses, dire passions, misery, and suddenly enter Fortinbras. Enter the conqueror. And all passions come to an end. Enough is enough. Enter Fortinbras—who doesn't give a damn for passions or anguish. All soliloquies are over. Now begin the cheers and fanfares . . . (*A pause.*) There . . . look, Kavalerov. (*He points to the grandstand with a sweeping gesture.*) Now Fortinbras is going to enter, now the football players are going to enter, and they don't give a damn for your anguish or passions.[3]

At the last moment Kavalerov's plans for vengeance go awry, when the pragmatic, self-possessed Andrei takes the razor with which the vacillating hero is about to kill him and begins to slice his new salami with it. Bewildered and enraged, the introspective and tormented Kavalerov turns on his mentor Ivan and murders his own past, as a whistle blows and the football players, in uniform and in unison, march down the ramp. Andrei has the last word: "That's the end of the old passions . . . The new world is beginning." In Olesha's creative transformation of the Norwegian Prince into a team, Fortinbras's entry on stage signals the end of an era, the liquidation of the past, and the ushering in of a regimented world without doubts or hesitations, peopled by healthy, athletic, extroverted mass-men.

A comparable assessment of Fortinbras as the man of the future is central to the 1932 production of *Hamlet* at the Vakhtangov Theatre, which was directed by Nikolai Akimov, who had been the designer for *The Conspiracy of Feelings* at the same theatre three years earlier. With music by Dmitri Shostakovich and sets and costumes by Akimov himself, this was perhaps the most radical and inventive Russian re-interpretation of Shakespeare's tragedy ever staged; certainly nothing like it had ever been seen before.[4] To make the drama accessible to a popular audience of average Soviet theatregoers, Akimov transformed the tragedy into an entertaining adventure story by cutting the soliloquies and gloomy philosophizing and adding many vaudeville acts and farcical stunts. Hamlet was played by a short, stocky comic actor, Anatoly Goriunov. In the prologue, the audience is told:

> We are showing you today a Hamlet full of the will to fight for the throne, and his passionate struggle with Claudius; we are showing comic liveliness instead of a tragic carcass; we are showing the triumphant activity of Fortinbras.

In this action drama, the Ghost becomes simply a trick of Hamlet's to enlist support; the voice was simulated by speaking into an earthenware jar (an idea taken from Erasmus's fourth *Colloquy*, "Exorcism"). "To be or not to be" ceases to be an existential meditation and turns into a political option as the ambitious Danish Prince, in a philosophical discussion with Horatio in a tavern, points to a stage crown (left behind by the players) that he has jestingly placed on his head. Laertes delivers his warnings to Ophelia while mixing cocktails, and Ophelia herself, portrayed as a buxom slut and heavy drinker, falls into the brook while intoxicated.

As viewed by Akimov, Fortinbras is the efficient and admirable leader who wins victories for his country and finally triumphs because he is without inherited scruples, whereas Hamlet loses the struggle for the throne due to his still being too much the feudal lord. In the final scene, the Norwegian Prince and his mercenaries come crashing

Arrival of Fortinbras in Nikolai Akimov's *Hamlet*, Vakhtangov Theatre (1932)

through the gates; wearing a plumed helmet and seated on a white horse, Fortinbras rides to the forefront of the stage, the very image of the providential savior.

At about the same time, the poet, critic, and translator, Ivan Aksyonov—a long-time associate of Meyerhold and expert on Elizabethan drama—wrote a long essay on *Hamlet*, in which the question of Fortinbras occupies a central position.[5] Like Akimov, Aksyonov discovers an evolutionary pattern in Shakespeare's tragedy, as we witness the emergence of a new world of positive values through the breakdown of obsolete feudal imperatives to carry out ancestral blood vengeance. Laertes is the most backward, Fortinbras the most progressive; Hamlet tries to give up feudal morality, but is eventually trapped by it. "Fortinbras, alone of the three attains not only what he was striving for, but also what he did not even dream of. What did he do to deserve such kindness from tragedy?" Aksyonov asks. By renouncing vengeance and directing his energies against the Poles, the Norwegian Prince wins complete victory in Denmark. "There's Fortinbras, the author tells us: imitate him," is the conclusion that the Soviet critic draws from his analysis of *Hamlet*.

With the establishment of socialist realism as the sole mode of artistic expression by the mid-1930s, it was no longer possible in the USSR to write fantastic comedies, full of allusion and parody, such as *The Conspiracy of Feelings*, or to stage unorthodox and experimental readings of classics, like Akimov's *Hamlet*. With the terror unleashed by Stalin's purge trials, mass arrests, and deportations, it was now unwise to speculate too openly on what sort of a regime Fortinbras would inaugurate. It would appear that the strongman had already arrived. Not until some thirty years later, in the relatively free early 1960s, did Soviet writers take a somewhat more sober look at the Fortinbras world—and then only within the safe confines of Shakespearean production and scholarship.

The scene now shifts to Poland, where the experiences of the Second World War, the "liberation" of the country by the Red Army, the imposition of communist rule, the Stalinist years, and the thaw of 1956, followed by alternate loosening and tightening of the screws, all served to shape a national consciousness peculiarly attuned to the ironies of history. The Poles now became the foremost Fortinbrasologists in the world, and I shall devote almost all the rest of this study to Polish variations on the theme. Fascination with the Norwegian strongman on the part of Polish poets and playwrights is a natural consequence of their country's geopolitical situation. After all, in Shakespeare's tragedy Fortinbras leads his forces against Poland and returns a conqueror, and in the mid-twentieth century the totalitarian strongman repeatedly threatens to reappear on Polish soil enacting over and over again a collective national trauma and historical nightmare.

The opening statement of the Polish position was made by Roman Brandstaetter in his essay, "About Hamlet and Fortinbras," published in *Dialog* in 1956 (the first year of the magazine's existence).[6] Although written several years earlier, it could not appear until de-Stalinization set in and a new autonomous Polish cultural policy permitted a revival of the arts, which had been muzzled during the past six years. A Catholic poet and playwright dedicated to humanist values and historical perspectives, Brandstaetter traveled extensively in the Middle East, spent most of the war years in Jerusalem, served as a Polish cultural attaché in Rome, and returned permanently to his homeland only in 1949. It was then—at the beginning of the grim period of repression—that Brandstaetter started to keep a diary in which he jotted down his impressions from many readings of *Hamlet* as he worked on a translation of Shakespeare's tragedy. At that time thoughts on Shakespeare could be dangerous and subversive.

For the Polish poet, the play became a mirror of his own time and place. In the prison that was Denmark—Brandstaetter notes—all values have been shaken. Confronting the highly sensitive Hamlet was a world in which morality has become a relative concept, whereas the idea of authority has remained absolute and inexorable. The struggle against the tyrant is waged on both sides by any and all means, filling Hamlet with contempt for himself and others and desperate skepticism about all human endeavors. His double—and inverse image—is the Norwegian strongman.

> His opposite is Prince Fortinbras, who does not give in to any doubt, who does not reflect on the enigma of existence or the consequences of his plans. Aware of his own power, he acts in accord with his impetuous and uncompromising instincts.

A product of the *condottiere* mentality, it matters not at all to Fortinbras on what side or against whom he fights. If the Norwegian Prince cannot set out against Denmark, he attacks Poland. He wages war for war's sake, he wields power for power's sake. "Woe to Denmark when Fortinbras comes to reign on its royal throne," Brandstaetter declares, questioning whether this predatory young man, who says and does nothing out of the ordinary, could be Shakespeare's ideal. Rather, he is a historical necessity.

> Fortinbras must arrive. There must appear on stage the elegant prince with the rapacious instincts, the impetuous optimist, able in a simple fashion to cut without scruples all Gordian knots. And here we have an image of two victories. The easy victory of the handsome Norwegian, who conquers all with ease, and the difficult victory of Hamlet, which is at the same time his defeat.

In Hamlet's final words of support for his successor ("But I do prophesy the election lights / On Fortinbras; he has my dying voice") Brandstaetter sees subtle irony and an aftertaste of bitter musings on the vicissitudes of this world; to the empty and soulless enthusiasm of the people who tomorrow will unanimously vote for Fortinbras, Hamlet adds his "dying voice" in a gesture of contempt for society and its laws. Always ready to capitulate to the most powerful, humans are fickle and craven.

> Hamlet and Fortinbras are contrasting characters. The action involving Fortinbras, although secondary, develops parallel to the action involving Hamlet. These actions draw near each other, then again draw apart, but not even once in the entire drama do they intersect. When, in the glory of victory, Fortinbras enters on stage, Hamlet is already dead. They failed to meet. In this failure to meet lies the profound meaning of the drama and of the conflict. For what could Hamlet say to Fortinbras? The philosopher-poet to the brutal soldier? How might a scene in which poor Hamlet met powerful Fortinbras have ended? We know from history several such meetings that ended either tragically or sadly for the intellectuals. Archimedes perished by the blow of a brutal soldier's sword. Michelangelo bent his proud head to Baccio Valori, commissar of the occupying army in defeated Florence. It turned out for the best that Shakespeare's heroes failed to meet.

In Fortinbras's expressions of horror at the bloody sights that greet him, Brandstaetter finds further evidence of Shakespeare's irony. Having caused the death of several thousand of his soldiers in a senseless expedition, the Norwegian Prince, suddenly arrived in Elsinore, cannot stand the sight of a few royal corpses.

> Therefore, at the moment of Fortinbras's appearance at the finale of the tragedy, the entire stage should be drowned in gloom. Fortinbras assumes power over Elsinore. The last lights go out. Over the remains of the sole honest man in a cursed Sodom, the grandiloquent words of the Norwegian Prince inaugurate the rule of the long night. The powers of evil have triumphed.

Drawing parallels with Thomas Mann's *Tonio Kröger*, whose hero is a bourgeois Hamlet suffering from a Fortinbras complex and provided with two bourgeois Fortinbrases, Brandstaetter concludes his reflections with some psychological observations about the secret affinities between these two opposed types. According to this view, every weak Hamlet—in other words, every artist or intellectual—has his own powerful Fortinbras.

> We usually fail to meet our Fortinbrases, although we are constantly in their vicinity. We feel a special attraction for them, since they are our opposite; we often feel toward them genuine emotion and admiration, and most frequently jealousy. We envy them their joy of life, their impetuosity.

In 1961 one of the new generation of Polish writers whose careers began only after the thaw, Zbigniew Herbert, imagined what Fortinbras, man of practical action, might have said to the ineffectual idealist and dreamer in their sole confrontation after Hamlet's death. Playwright, poet, and essayist, Herbert created in his "Elegy of Fortinbras" a classic statement of the tension between real and ideal, political necessity and individual aspiration, that has been the keynote of post-war Polish literature. As "a poet of historical irony," in the phrase of Czesław Miłosz (to whom the poem is dedicated), Herbert adopts a more objective and balanced view of the two princes than Brandstaetter's, entering sympathetically into the strongman's psyche and weighing the pressures and constraints impelling him to action. Here is "Elegy for Fortinbras" in the English translation by Czesław Miłosz:

Now that we're alone we can talk prince man to man
though you lie on the stairs and see no more than a dead ant
nothing but black sun with broken rays
I could never think of your hands without smiling
and now that they lie on the stone like fallen nests
they are as defenseless as before The end is exactly this
The hands lie apart The sword lies apart The head apart
and the knight's feet in soft slippers.

You will have a soldier's funeral without having been a soldier
the only ritual I am acquainted with a little
There will be no candles no singing only cannon-fuses and bursts
crepe dragged on the pavement helmets boots artillery horses
        drums drums I know nothing exquisite
those will be my manoeuvres before I start to rule
one has to take the city by the neck and shake it a bit

Anyhow you had to perish Hamlet you were not for life.
you believed in crystal notions not in human clay
always twitching as if asleep you hunted chimeras
wolfishly you crunched the air only to vomit
you knew no human thing you did not know even how to breathe

Now you have peace Hamlet you accomplished what you had to
and you have peace. The rest is not silence but belongs to me
you chose the easier part an elegant thrust
but what is heroic death compared with eternal watching
with a cold apple in one's hand on a narrow chair
with a view of the ant-hill and clock's dial

Adieu prince I have tasks a sewer project
and a decree on prostitutes and beggars
I must also elaborate a better system of prisons
since as you justly said Denmark is a prison
I go to my affairs This night is born
a star named Hamlet We shall never meet
what I shall leave will not be worth a tragedy

It is not for us to greet each other or bid farewell we live on archipelagoes
and that water these words what can they do what can they do prince[7]

The critic Kazimierz Wyka sees the theme of Herbert's "Elegy" as a debate over conflicting values.[8] Which will triumph: the dissolution and disorder brought upon mankind by death, or the order and meaning which man imposes on his existence through the organization of history and culture? According to Wyka, it is this sort of order that Herbert's Fortinbras brings, thereby subduing the chaos of death that he encounters in the royal court of Denmark, and the critic speculates that Herbert may here be following the lead of two earlier Polish poet-playwrights who explored the same issue. The first of these is Zygmunt Krasiński in his Romantic tragedy *The Un-Divine Comedy* (published 1835). In this prophetic drama the revolutionary hero Pankracy realizes that if the revolution is to be successful it must solidify its victory by implementing changes in all aspects of everyday life and death must be redeemed by the works of life. After the bloody battle between radicals and reactionaries has left the field littered with corpses,

Pankracy—much like Herbert's Fortinbras—speaks with enthusiasm about his projects for the future.

> It is not yet time for me to sleep, my child, for only half the work is done . . . Behold those vast expanses, those immensities that lie crosswise between me and my thought. This wasteland must be peopled—these rocks must be leveled—these lakes united—the land dealt out to each so that twice as much life should be born on these plains as the death that lies on them now.[9]

The second antecedent that Wyka finds for Herbert's interpretation of Fortinbras comes in *The Hamlet Study* written by Stanisław Wyspiański (in 1904) in the form of notes on how to produce Shakespeare's tragedy. In his *Study* Wyspiański advances a fundamental principle of radically modern re-readings of Shakespeare: "The riddle of Hamlet can be answered by thinking about the current situation in Poland."[10] For Wyspiański, Fortinbras is the key to *Hamlet;* his accession to the throne without bloodshed closes the feudal cycle that began with the death of old Fortinbras. Fortinbras is the first sovereign who is neither executioner nor victim. It is worth noting that in 1964, at the Theatre of the Thirteen Rows in Opole, Jerzy Grotowski staged *The Hamlet Study*, with text by Shakespeare and Wyspiański, as an open rehearsal given before audiences.[11]

In the same year Shakespeare's Fortinbras appears in a contemporary Polish play, *The King the Fourth* by the poet Stanisław Grochowiak, who, in an introductory note, calls his grotesque drama "a fantasy (?) or parable (?)" and explains that it is pastiche of quotations from Shakespeare and the history of the Second World War.[12] Conceived in the spirit of political cabaret, *The King the Fourth* is a drama about the ineptitude of all political activity and the general impossibility of everything since all the actions undertaken by the puppet-like characters end in fiasco. The mechanism of power is shown to operate in a vacuum, and even the new order that comes to the fore after the overthrow of the old regime is incapable of introducing anything fresh or vital—it simply grinds on as part of the same broken-down machinery.

In a dreary, dilapidated kingdom somewhere in central Europe, inefficient conspirators plot the assassination of an equally ineffectual King the Fourth. Amateurishly stabbed, the shabby monarch takes a long, long time to bleed to death, all the while repeating over and over again Claudius's line from the last act of *Hamlet*, "O yet defend me, friends; I am but hurt." In the third act, entitled "The Ambitions of Fortinbras," the scene unexpectedly moves to the Norwegian Prince's palace.[13]

Even Shakespeare's strongman, "the king from the outside," has succumbed to the entropy from which the machine of power politics is suffering. We now see the Norwegian Prince in a very faded Elizabethan costume, nearly senile, dozing in a comfortable armchair, listening to lively Viennese waltzes on the radio, as well as to reports of how the strongman Fortinbras is coming to restore order throughout the world. The hope that is placed in his arrival remains only a hope, announced by the tapping of his cane on the floor. "I have always arrived too late on purpose," Grochowiak's Fortinbras declares, "To see what would happen." As evidence that the menace posed by the Norwegian Prince is only part of the illusory system of maintaining power, the General at the end of *The King the Fourth* informs the people that Fortinbras has reached the frontier and urges them to go resist his imminent attack; after they have left, the General explains that Fortinbras really does not exist.

Commenting obliquely on the deadly ossification of power in the Soviet Union and its satellites half a century after the revolution, Grochowiak, through the figure of

Fortinbras (holding helmet) leading his army to Elsinore in Grigorii Kozintsev's film of *Hamlet* (1964)

an octogenarian Fortinbras in *The King the Fourth*, reveals how the march of history has slowed down to an arthritic palsy. Hollow and creaking, the system of governance grinds on mindlessly in the void regardless of who is ostensibly in command. No matter who seizes power, the cycle is repetitive and closed.

In *Tango, or the Need for Order and Harmony* (published in late 1964 and first performed in April, 1965 in Belgrade), Mrożek is concerned with tracing a more dynamic, evolutionary sequence of events by means of the Hamlet-Fortinbras paradigm.[14] How does the vacuum—out of which brute force emerges as the sole mode of maintaining order—come into existence in the first place, Mrożek asks. He seeks out the origins of totalitarianism—be it fascist or communist—in the failures and frustrations of the intellectual bourgeoisie. In other words, Hamlet first creates the need for Fortinbras and then gives the strongman his opportunity. Re-interpreted along class and cultural lines, Mrożek's Fortinbras is an outsider who takes over in the sense that he is a "barbarian" or thug from below, a representative of the disgruntled underclass flattered, glorified, and promoted by educated apologists for brute strength.

In the guise of a ludicrous family drama, *Tango* offers an elliptical and parabolic history of civilization tracing the decline and fall of liberal Europe from the end of the nineteenth century through the rise of totalitarian dictatorships. The intelligentsia's responsibility for the celebration of force as the ultimate value is the central issue in Mrożek's ironic analysis—within the microcosm of a family composed of three different generations of the historical debacle that ended with Hitler and Stalin. Like Hamlet an idealistic student confronted with chaos at home, the young hero Arthur feels obligated to create order, despite the impossibility of re-instating the absolutes of tragedy in an absurd world of contingency and accommodation. The ethical and political promiscuity of a disoriented society is indicated by the fact that both Arthur's mother and new bride are sleeping with Eddie, the fat semi-literate butler and hanger-on lurking in the background whom all the members of the family find indispensable. The sexual is a metaphor for the political.

Abandoning his futile efforts to bring about a spiritual rebirth in his parents, Arthur realizes that only death-dealing can exist as a potent force in a world of chaos and nullity, but he is too much the intellectual to put his own brilliant insight into practice. Instead, it is the primitive and slow-witted Eddie who pre-empts the idea and suddenly kills its inventor with two sharp blows on the back of the neck with the butt of Arthur's own revolver. Thereupon, Mrożek's crude lumpen proletarian Fortinbras assumes power in the crumbling, decadent family.

Declaring that at last there will be order in the household, Eddie puts on Arthur's coat, which is too small for his stocky frame, and plays a recording of a tango (the dance that for Arthur's parents symbolized liberation and rebellious abandon) on an old wind-up gramophone with a large horn. Then the brutish strongman compels Great-Uncle Eugene—pitiful relic of old Europe—to dance *La Cumparsita* with him. The compelling music of the tango does not stop even after the curtain falls. Eddie, exponent of the new order, is dancing cheek to cheek with the doddering humane tradition that always capitulates to force and dances to its tune.

At the same time in the USSR, after more than forty years of the new order ushered in by Fortinbras, Soviet directors and scholars adopted a sober and disabused view of Shakespeare's opposition of the Danish and Norwegian Princes in *Hamlet* that is not dissimilar from the ironical position advanced by the Polish authors. In the second edition of *Our Contemporary: William Shakespeare* (translated in English as *Shakespeare: Time and Conscience*), Grigorii Kozintsev, in discussing his work on the Soviet film of *Hamlet* (1964), sees Fortinbras as the ineluctable march of history that sweeps away all before it like a whirlwind.[15] The very facelessness of the Norwegian Prince is deliberate on Shakespeare's part, according to the Soviet director. It is an ominous lack of features.[16]

> Shakespeare has roles that are contours. Only the most general sketching, and a total absence of detail. This is Fortinbras.
>
> Is it accidental?
>
> You have but to compare Osric and the Norwegian Prince, and it becomes clear that Fortinbras is vastly more important. Nevertheless, his outline is not filled in at all. Doesn't the answer to this lie in that the story itself fills in outlines like this? There isn't much of the human in that.
>
> The particularly difficult Fortinbras scenes begin. With a heavy tread, covered with dust, long unshaven, wearing dirt-stained boots and heavy armor, the men of fire and iron march. They go to act. The man of heart and thought is dead.

An even more explicit statement about Fortinbras as ruthless historical necessity—a bitter reflection on the Stalin years—occurs in the short monograph, *Shakespeare's Hamlet*, by the Soviet Shakespeare scholar Israil Vertsman, published in 1964. Vertsman stresses the surprise and irony of the Norwegian Prince's arrival in the last scene, pointing out that this second and quite unexpected denouement does not in any way follow from the previous development of the play. There is nothing to indicate that Hamlet would have seen Fortinbras as the ideal statesman or wanted him as King of

Denmark. Thus, according to Vertsman, the audience in the theatre, shocked by Hamlet's irreplaceable loss, hears in amazement the sounds of a rousing march, to the strains of which there appears on stage the well-built figure of the indefatigable Fortinbras in brightly shining armor at the head of an army with flying flags.

The Norwegian Prince offers the Danes a solid political order, which constitutes—in Vertsman's words—"the truth of historical action, national progress, which inevitably is accompanied not only by reasonable deeds but also by violence and the sacrifice, sometimes quite senseless, of the completely innocent." But the ethical and political principles in Shakespeare are forever irreconcilable. Fortinbras could not possibly understand Hamlet, since his measure of excellence is only the throne and the crown. He orders the cannons fired and says that Hamlet would have proved a successful monarch, when it is obvious that the Danish Prince and the role of king are incompatible.

> It is by no means accidental that the moral prince personified in Hamlet and . . . the political prince personified in Fortinbras never meet face to face throughout the entire play.

Hamlet cannot survive in a world where Claudiuses are replaced by Fortinbrases.[17] Both the Soviet director and the Soviet critic, in the guise of scientific scholarship, project back onto Shakespeare's Denmark, and its reflection of Renaissance historical reality, the collective experience of twentieth-century Russians attempting to endure the violence and senseless sacrifice engendered by the split between moral and political truth in the USSR. Polish writers and artists, on the other hand, working within a long tradition of metaphoric theatre saturated with multiple allusion and quotation, bring forward into the present and future the royal court at Elsinore and its familiar cast of characters considered as living exemplars of our times. In other words, the Polish dramaturgical method is to update borrowed images of heterogeneous cultural and literary provenance and superimpose one upon the other in a kaleidoscopically shifting series of fragments. In *Tango*, Mrożek's Hamlet, Arthur, realizes that to re-establish order and harmony he must have a formal wedding ceremony, following precedents set in plays by Wyspiański *(The Wedding)* and Gombrowicz *(The Marriage)*.

Polish dramatists often interweave the Polish Romantic classics of the nineteenth century (themselves richly allusive and the source of the national tradition of metaphoric theatre) with Shakespeare. A good example of this procedure is *Hamlet 70* by the journalist, editor, and poet, Bohdan Drozdowski, in which the prologue between Director and Playwright explores themes from Mickiewicz's *Forefathers' Eve* and Słowacki's *Kordian*, and the body of the play, set in an unspecified Latin American country, reconstitutes Shakespeare's tragedy in the form of a long philosophical discussion between a kidnapped Ambassador and an anti-government Guerilla set to guard him. Battling against a cruel dictatorship, the insurgents have seized the ambassador from a European country in order to win the release of political prisoners who have been condemned to death. When the government refuses to make the exchange and instead executes the prisoners, the Guerilla—known by the pseudonym of Hamlet—must shoot the Ambassador. It is at this point that the mob appears and revolution breaks out.

When asked earlier by the Ambassador who it was that had seized him, the Guerilla Hamlet replied, "It was Fortinbras," and he identifies the collective force that has been let loose as the Norwegian Prince.

Andrzej May as Fortinbras in *Hamlet* at the Słowacki Theatre in Koszalin, Poland (1960),
directed by Iadeusz Aleksandrowicz, set design by Zofia Wierchowicz

> The avalanche has started to come down [. . .]
> The mob storms the bastion of my pain.
> Fortinbras! Go forward! Charge, blasphemer!
> You're coming here? To us? A crazy chieftain!
> And when you start to shoot, the scherzo's over!
> It is your Forte on their raging Brass! [. . .]
> (*The din of doors being forced open, a mob headed by the Guerilla [Fortinbras] appears;*
> *it is the same mob that at the beginning of the play brought both the Guerilla [Hamlet]*
> *and the Ambassador.*)
> Take us, Fortinbras. I have carried out the sentence.
> I pulled out one stone—the avalanche comes down . . .
> (*The men carry out the Ambassador's body.*)
> A folktale ballad grows into a tragedy,
> Return me to the epic, take me away from Shakespeares . . .
> I pulled out one stone. I put it on my heart.
> (*An iron curtain comes down.*)[18]

Ambivalent about his own role and actions, the Guerilla-Hamlet considers the onset of
revolution as the arrival of Fortinbras—and the conclusion of his own drama.

An unusual and inventive reading of the Norwegian Prince was to have been a
central feature of a major Polish production of *Hamlet* that never took place because the
director, Konrad Swinarski, died in a plane crash on August 8, 1975 over Damascus while
traveling to the Shiraz Festival in Iran. One of Poland's leading theatre artists, Swinarski,
who had first directed *Hamlet* at Tel Aviv's Cameri Theatre in 1966, began rehearsals
for a new staging of Shakespeare's tragedy (to be given at the Teatr Stary in Cracow) in

November 1974 and continued them until May 1975. On the basis of stenographic notes taken during discussions with the actors, it is possible to derive a general notion of the director's conception of the play and of his plans for bringing it to life in the theatre.[19] Swinarski found within the tragedy existing simultaneously three different historical epochs and ideologies: the feudal age of England's wars and conquests, Shakespeare's own period of English monarchy maintaining itself through diplomacy, and the potential unfolding of a new era of individual freedom and humanistic values. The first of these is represented by Old Hamlet, the second by Claudius, the third by Hamlet. Swinarski decided to have the same actor play both the Ghost of Hamlet's father and Fortinbras because the two characters are akin in that both are conquerors, and the Norwegian Prince's last-minute arrival marks a return to the first epoch. But, Swinarski argues, it is not simply a blind cyclical return, since Fortinbras has borne witness to the mutual destruction wrought by Claudius and Hamlet on one another and understands quite clearly what has happened. Profiting from their errors, the Norwegian strongman deliberately mythologizes Hamlet's heroism in order to mold public opinion in favor of his rights to the Danish realm. Thus Fortinbras is a sophisticated conqueror who has experienced the defeat and death of both Claudius and Hamlet and resolved to enjoy a different fate. For the strongman's arrival, Swinarski planned to have Fortinbras's forces converge on Plac (Square) Szczepański outside the theatre in Cracow.

In 1979 Henryk Tomaszewski presented a *Hamlet* without words at the Wrocław Pantomime Theatre.[20] Called *Hamlet, Irony, Mourning*, Tomaszewski's ballet-pantomime adaptation of Shakespeare's tragedy opens and closes with a juxtaposition of art and power, comedians and barbarians, represented by the troupe of strolling players on the right side of the stage and by Fortinbras and his military troops on the left side of the stage. While the Norwegian Prince lays siege to the castle, the company of actors practices the art of pretending and rehearses scenes of "dying." Here it is clear that Tomaszewski is drawing not only upon the Polish Fortinbras tradition, but also upon Tom Stoppard's *Rosencrantz and Guildenstern Are Dead* with its theatricalist scenes of the Tragedians acting out episodes of violent death from *Hamlet*. Stoppard's play, published in *Dialog* in 1969 and performed successfully on the stage in Poland, exerted considerable influence on subsequent variations played on Shakespeare's tragedy by Polish authors. After Stoppard the actors (previously absent in Polish treatments of Fortinbras) assume an importance equal to Hamlet's.

In Tomaszewski's version, the strolling players at the royal court, which is surrounded by barbarian forces, present a psychodrama for Hamlet in which they "play" the chief events of the story. In the course of their "acting," the first player becomes transformed into the alter ego of the Prince and becomes the hero of a drama drawn from Hamlet's subconscious. Seemingly powerless when compared to the scheming courtiers and brutal soldiers, the actors take on a central role in the tragedy and actively participate in the search for truth and dignity initiated by Hamlet.

In the final scene, the first player refuses to swear the oath of loyalty to Fortinbras that the entire court has subscribed to with servile eagerness. Enraged at this defiance, the barbarian prince seizes the actor's stiletto and stabs him with it, unaware that this stage prop has a collapsible blade. Here Tomaszewski follows closely the episode in Stoppard's play in which Guildenstern apparently kills the Player with a dagger that proves to be a theatrical trick knife, but the Polish director uses the artist's enactment of death for a quite different purpose, in keeping with the political and philosophical theme of his Shakespearean adaptation. The old actor in *Hamlet, Irony, Mourning* plays dying to

Final scene of Konrad Swinarski's *Hamlet* at the Cameri Theatre, Tel Aviv (1966)
Horatio (Yossi Graber), Hamlet (Shimon Bar), and Fortinbras (Yossef Karmon)

perfection, but his protest against tyranny is none the less heroic since he could not have known the consequences of his act and willingly risked his life. The victorious barbarians cannot triumph over the comedians. Fascinated by the artifice and charmed by art, the Norwegian despot enters into a new stage of culture as a result of his contact with the players. Only artists can survive uncorrupted in a world of decadent courtiers and crude barbarians because they exist in realm of fiction that stands above reality.

In Tomaszewski's mime version of Shakespeare's tragedy, Fortinbras represents brute military force employed to maintain tyranny; his stifling grip can, however, be evaded through the dissembling of art, whose fictions serve truth and human dignity. The players are able to deceive—and delight—their totalitarian masters, a lesson that Polish artists have learned well and, in fact, the reason why they are drawn to the Hamlet-Fortinbras paradigm as an oblique comment on their own situation. By choosing actors as both the chorus and hidden protagonist of *Hamlet, Irony, Mourning* (in feigning death, they transcend it), Tomaszewski makes his version of the Shakespearean drama a self-reflexive study of the performer in an oppressive society that denies his freedom.

The rise of the Solidarity free trade union movement, starting in August 1980, and the attendant fears of a Soviet invasion or other repressive moves to crush the spreading liberalization made the presence of an invisible Fortinbras waiting at the border deeply felt in Poland and caused the imminent arrival of the strongman to seem a constant threat. It was only natural that the new generation of Polish writers making their debuts in the 1970s would turn, as had their predecessors, to *Hamlet* and the Fortinbras theme as a mirror for troubled times.

In *After Hamlet* (published in *Dialog* in April 1981, and performed shortly thereafter), the young playwright Jerzy Żurek traces the career of the Norwegian Prince from before his campaign against Poland until his arrival in Denmark immediately after Hamlet's death, showing us what Fortinbras is doing while the action of Shakespeare's tragedy is supposed to be unrolling offstage.[21] A playful set of variations on existing variations, full of multiple allusions and witty paradoxes, *After Hamlet* is a highly self-conscious literary and dramatic work of mixed extraction, indebted as much to Stoppard's *Rosencrantz and Guildenstern Are Dead* as to earlier Polish Fortinbrases.

In his ironic revision of *Hamlet* Stoppard promotes two minor characters to the center of the dramatic action, presents the court of Elsinore as seen from the periphery, and shifts perspective so that the major events in Shakespeare's plot occur behind the scenes until at the final moment the two lines join in the bloody denouement. So likewise in *After Hamlet* Żurek follows the happenings at the royal court in Denmark from the point of view of Norway and creates episodes that run parallel to those in Shakespeare's tragedy. Only when Fortinbras reaches Elsinore after the Danish Prince's death do we see Hamlet on stage for the first time as we step through the frame separating the modern Polish play from its Renaissance English prototype and witness the familiar Shakespearean ending, now attached to a completely new and different play.

The Polish playwright's aim in using these techniques derived from Stoppard is to explore the steps by which Fortinbras becomes the strongman who appears at the last moments of *Hamlet*. In order to reveal the inexorable workings of the mechanism of power, Żurek bases his drama on a surprising and paradoxical premise: his Fortinbras is by nature a sensitive and unwilling participant in the world of force and double-dealing, a true double of Hamlet, suffering from kindred scruples, who only gradually is drawn into the web of deceit practiced in the name of *Realpolitik*. *After Hamlet* thus becomes a study of the idealist who sells his ideals as the price of realizing them.

To provide his political thriller with a master intriguer whose manipulations predetermine the fate of both Hamlet and Fortinbras, Żurek invents a henchman for the King of Norway named Lizon who plots for his master to gain possession of Denmark. But in fact, Governor-General Lizon wants not only Denmark, but also England and Norway for himself and his son and heir, Vic. The atmosphere in Norway is even more permeated with scheming and treachery than is the royal court at Elsinore. "They spy on me, read my letters and slowly the noose gets tighter around my neck," Fortinbras complains, "Lizon watches over me as if I were a prisoner." Secret agents are everywhere. Lizon has even dispatched a theatrical troupe to Denmark to stage the Ghost of Hamlet's father as a conspiratorial show with the purpose of stirring up trouble between Hamlet and Claudius.

Exploited by Lizon, who eventually plans to eliminate Fortinbras in favor of his own son, the Norwegian Prince wishes to "withdraw from politics," explaining that "all these ambitions are alien to me." Żurek's Fortinbras hopes to flee to England to escape the responsibility of ruling and, in one of the play's many ironic twists, even thinks of retiring to a monastery (the allusion to Hamlet's "Get thee to a nunnery" is unmistakable in Polish since *klasztor*—English, cloister—means either monastery or nunnery). In another sardonic reversal of what we expect, it turns out that Fortinbras is ordered to attack Poland, to which command the reluctant warrior replies, "Well, friends, to Poland. By the way, where is it?" "Probably nowhere," he is told, directly recalling Alfred Jarry's quip about the setting of *Ubu* in Poland, that is, nowhere.

Pointing out that "Politics is for tough men only," Lizon explains how he will justify intervention in Denmark's internal affairs, much in the same way that a Soviet invasion of Poland might be defended and excused. "We want to help the Danes improve their lot. . . . We've heard that they are tired of anarchy in their country. . . . They want Fortinbras for their king. . . . If they ask for help we cannot refuse." And, the Governor General asserts, a pretext for military action can always be found. "Some riots will take place. . . . And we will have to punish them severely and quickly."

Despite his good intentions and desire to rule well, Fortinbras chooses expediency—so that he can achieve his goal of creating a just society. When his loyal friend, Grothe (even Fortinbras has his Horatio), warns him of the dangerous game he is playing, the Norwegian Prince responds, "For the time being—power and treachery are indispensable," and soon sets spies on Grothe, who is later killed. Finally trapped by his own compromises with the Machiavellian world he hoped to overcome, Fortinbras admits, "Power is the greatest whore in the world." Now this whorish power brings him to Denmark and puts him on the throne, while Hamlet lies dead.

Herbert's Fortinbras is a cool, efficient administrator, a modern technocrat. For Mrożek Shakespeare's strongman is a thug, a junta leader, raised to power by a coup. Żurek creates a Norwegian Prince who betrays his principles by trying to implement them; he is a decent man who discovers too late that you cannot improve the repressive system by serving it.

Another Polish playwright of the Solidarity years who saw analogies between the dangerous political situation and *Hamlet* was Janusz Głowacki. His macabre tragi-farce about power politics, *Fortinbras Gets Drunk*, although conceived several years earlier, was written in 1982 shortly after the establishment of martial law in Poland and the take-over by the new strongman, General Jaruzelski. Under a ban in communist Poland, the play was first performed and published in English.[22]

Fortinbras Gets Drunk, which takes place at the royal court in Norway during a long gloomy Scandinavian night, is the kind of masked political allegory that Polish playwrights had brought to perfection since the 1950s. Norway was the Soviet Union under Brezhnev, and Hamlet's Denmark Poland. The ghost of Hamlet I is interrogated, and Fortinbras's brother, Mortinbras, is secretly murdered. Polonius arrives from Denmark to get further orders from Sternberg, who is the power behind the throne, on how to deal with Hamlet and Claudius. Maurizio, a Finnish expert on Norwegian political intrigue (by allusion, a Kremlinologist), accuses Sternberg of having killed thirty thousand people in Finland. Since no one sees Fortinbras as a threat (because of his ploy of getting drunk). He is able, through his intricate schemes, to become ruler himself. Then Fortinbras gradually becomes yet another ruler who relies on coercion and brute force, because he is unable to cope with the complex political reality, which paradoxically he himself has created.

By the time *Fortinbras Gets Drunk* could be published and performed in Poland in 1990 after the fall of communism,[23] this sort of political parable about the mechanisms of power, making extensive use of allusion and Aesopian language, quickly went of fashion and lost appeal for audiences. Once independence as a nation brought freedom from censorship, there suddenly seemed no reason to write in such an oblique manner. For Polish spectators in the first decade of freedom, Głowacki's play seemed obsolete as a political genre, although the author created genuine theatrical excitement through farcical black humor and clever technological use of television projections of interlocking on and offstage action.

The era of Fortinbras in Eastern Europe may be said to be over, at least for the time being. In the new democratic world strongmen are no longer lurking at the gates, about to make a striking appearance at the final moment. Or are they?

To conclude with an ironic postscript. Just as the Eastern European Fortinbrases were making their final stage appearances before retiring, in the Western theatre playwrights and directors appear to have learned about the power of Fortinbras from their Russian and Polish colleagues. In the *Hamlet* that Ingmar Bergman directed in 1988, Fortinbras's new order is presented as much more violent and bloodthirsty than Claudius's. Fortinbras's soldiers, dressed in black leather, burst in, machine guns blazing, and mow down everyone to loud Danish rock music. Fortinbras gives orders to have Horatio shot and holds a press conference.

Lee Blessing, an American playwright who had explored American-Soviet relations in his *Through the Woods*, wrote a *Fortinbras* that received its première at the La Jolla Playhouse in June, 1991, directed by Des McAnuff. Blessing's play is an "after *Hamlet*," starting at the moment of Fortinbras's arrival in the final scene of Act V. The premise of the play is that Fortinbras does not believe Horatio's story of what has happened to produce such a bloody denouement and fabricates his own version to further his own political ends of consolidating all power. A modern, pragmatic, skeptical Fortinbras questions the intricacies of plot that have led to so many corpses on stage and comes up with a simpler political explanation that puts the blame on a Polish spy. To control reality one must manipulate it. There is no one truth, only versions of it increasingly conditioned by media. Fortinbras eventually loses his grip on the situation when the ghosts of all the dead appear offering alternative versions of the events at Elsinor. The strongman has all his certainties taken away and is finally left only with Hamlet's book that contains words from the soliloquies. For the American playwright Fortinbras's story is a legend about the relativity of the truth of all historical narratives and a warning about the deceptive use of words to manipulate political realities.

NOTES

1. Bernard Shaw, "The Religion of the Pianoforte," *The Fortnightly Review*, February 1894, quoted in *Shaw on Shakespeare*, ed. Edwin Wilson (New York: Dutton, 1961), 256. It was not until two years later, in 1896, at the Forbes-Robertson *Hamlet* at the Lyceum that Shaw saw his first Fortinbras on stage. For the author *of Arms and the Man*, the Norwegian Prince was a pre-Shavian version of the conventional military hero, whose "bellicose instincts and imperial ambitions are comfortably vulgar." Bernard Shaw, *The Saturday Review*, January 18, 1896, in *Our Theatres in the Nineties*, vol. 2 (London: Constable & Co., Ltd., 1931), 18. Another celebrated writer who, at about the same time, paid some attention to Shakespeare's strongman, was the French Symbolist Stéphane Mallarmé, whose essay, "Hamlet et Fortinbras," appeared in 1896. Later, during the "dark and bloody period" of Hitler's rise to power and the Second World War, Bertolt Brecht showed an interest in Fortinbras. See Ruby Cohn, *Modern Shakespeare Offshoots* (Princeton: Princeton University Press, 1976), 205—11. Twentieth-century British and American interpreters of Shakespeare (such as Harley Granville-Barker, Francis Fergusson, Robert Speaight) have, of course, recognized the importance of the Norwegian Prince in the structure of the tragedy, but for all that Fortinbras still has not become part of the cultural heritage in the West as he has in the East.
2. The illustrations that I have included are all of Eastern European Fortinbrases—the only pictorial representations that I was able to find.
3. Yurii Olesha, *The Conspiracy of Feelings*, and Konstanty Ildefons Gałczyński, *The Little Theatre of the Green Goose*, ed. and trans. Daniel Gerould (London: Routledge, 2002), 52. This passage occurs only in the dramatic version, not in the novel *Envy*; Olesha developed the Fortinbras theme as he worked on the play.
4. Akimov's production is described by Joseph Macleod, *The New Soviet Theatre* (London: G. Allen & Unwin, 1943), 158–63 and by Alma H. Law, *"Hamlet at the Vakhtangov,"* *The Drama Review* 21, no. 4 (T76) (December 1977): 100–110. Akimov was, in part, reacting against the mystical and symbolic Craig-Stanislavsky *Hamlet* presented at the Moscow Art Theatre in 1912. See the illustration for a celestial Norwegian Prince resembling an angel bearing divine tidings. "The archangel aspect of Fortinbras derived from his costume, which bore a golden cross on a white tabard and a nimbus-like shield he wore behind him," according to Laurence Senelick, "The Craig-Stanislavsky *Hamlet* at the Moscow Art Theatre," *Theatre Quarterly* 6, no. 22 (Summer 1976): 118.
5. Ivan Aksyonov, "Gamlet, prints datskii," *Gamlet i drugiye opyty v sodestviye otechestvennoi Shekspirologii* (Moscow: Federatsiya, 1930), 75–139.
6. Roman Brandstaetter, "O Hamlecie i Fortynbrasie," *Dialog* 8 (1956), 128–35.
7. "Elegy of Fortinbras" appears in Czesław Miłosz, *The History of Polish Literature* (Toronto: Macmillan, 1969), 473–74. It is also found in *Miłosz's Postwar Polish Poetry, An Anthology* (New York: Doubleday, 1965) and in Zbigniew Herbert, *Selected Poems* (Baltimore: Penguin, 1968). The translation was first published in *Encounter*, August 1961. It is discussed by Miłosz in *The History of Polish Literature* and by Alfred Alvarez in *Under Pressure; the Writer in Society: Eastern Europe and the U.S.A.* (Baltimore: Penguin, 1965), 31.
8. Kazimierz Wyka, "Tren Fortynbrasa," *Rzecz wyobraźni* (Warsaw: Państwowy Instytut Wydawniczy, 1977), 573–78.
9. *The Un-Divine Comedy*, trans. Harold B. Segel, in *Polish Romantic Drama*, ed. Harold B. Segel (London: Routledge, 1997), 245.
10. Stanisław Wyspiański, *Hamlet*, ed. Maria Prussak (Wrocław: Ossolineum, 1976), 97.
11. Zbigniew Osiński, *Grotowski i jego Laboratorium* (Warsaw: Państwowy Instytut Wydawniczy, 1980), 119–22.
12. Stanisław Grochowiak, *Krol IV, Dialog* 1 (1963): 19–43.

13. The Polish Romantic playwrights as well as the Symbolist Wyspiański had sometimes introduced a character from a work by a predecessor or contemporary into their own dramas, thereby producing a characteristic Polish tradition of theatre carrying on a debate with itself and its own creations. Closer in time and spirit to Grochowiak, Stanisław Ignacy Witkiewicz (1885–1939) continued this practice in a more grotesque vein, introducing Shakespeare's Richard III accompanied by two murderers into a domestic drama with a modern setting, *The New Deliverance* (1920), itself a response to Wyspiański's *Deliverance* (1903).

14. Sławomir Mrożek, *Tango, Dialog* 2 (1964): 5–44.

15. Grigori Kozintsev, *Shakespeare: Time and Conscience*, trans. Joyce Vining (New York: Hill and Wang, 1966). Because Jan Kott's *Szkice o Szekspirze* (*Sketches about Shakespeare*), published in Polish in 1964, was translated as *Shakespeare Our Contemporary*, Kozintsev's book, which had in its Russian edition of 1962 first used the title *Our Contemporary: William Shakespeare*, appeared in translation under a different title. In his discussion of *Hamlet* as a political drama, Kott follows the lead of Brandstaetter and other Polish Fortinbrasologists and comes to conclusions about the Norwegian Prince not unlike those of Kozintsev.

16. Kozintsev, it is interesting to note, had totally omitted Fortinbras from the stage version of *Hamlet* that he had directed in the 1950s. Pavel Gromov, "Dva *Gamleta*," *Geroi i Vremya* (Leningrad: Sovetskii Pisatel', 1961), 306.

17. Israil Vertsman, *Gamlet Shekspira* (Moscow: Khudozhestvennaya Literatura, 1964), 112.

18. Bohdan Drozdowski, *Hamlet 70, Dialog* 6 (1971), 33–34.

19. "Konrad Swinarski na próbie *Hamleta*," ed. Danuta Kużnicka, *Pamiętnik Teatralny* 1 (109) (1979): 3–52. See also Józef Opalski, *Rozmowy o Konradzie Swinarskim i Hamlecie* (Cracow: Wydawnictwo Literackie, 1988), 181.

20. Małgorzata Dzieduszycka, "*Hamlet* directed by Henryk Tomaszewski, with stage design by Kazimierz Wiśniak, at the Wrocław Theatre of Pantomime," *The Theatre in Poland* 2 (February 1980): 14–17; and August Grodzicki, "What's New in the Polish Theatre," *The Theatre in Poland* 3 and 4 (March/April 1980): 21.

21. Jerzy Żurek, *Po Hamlecie, Dialog* 4 (1981): 5–32. The English translation is by Michał Kobiałka.

22. *Fortinbras Gets Drunk*, translated by Konrad Brodzinski and Jadwiga Kosicka, was given its first English performance in a staged reading with Derek Jacobi as Fortinbras at the Playwright's Horizons in New York City on November 12, 1984. It was published in Janusz Głowacki, *Hunting Cockroaches and Other Plays* (Evanston, IL: Northwestern University Press, 1990). The first full-scale production took place in 1993 at the Fountainhead Theatre Group in Los Angeles.

23. *Fortynbras się upił* was published in *Dialog* 1 (1990): 24–55, and directed by Jerzy Stuhr at the Stary Teatr in Cracow in late 1990.

Fregoli in the "danse serpentine" of Loïe Fuller (1907)

FREGOLI, WITKIEWICZ, AND QUICK CHANGE

At the beginning of *The Pragmatists*, the entrepreneur and director of the Department of Poisons at the Ministry of Trade, Graf Franz von Telek, tells his corpse-like friend, the suicidal Plasfodor Mimecker, "Stop pretending, you quick-change artist!" (*"Nie udawaj, transformisto!"*).[1] It is evidently Plasfodor's skills at mimicry and rapid transformations that make von Telek wish to engage his friend as a performer in the cabaret theatre that he is planning to open.

Taking the word *transformista* as my point of departure, I propose to examine Witkacy's theory and practice of transformation on two levels: first, as a theatrical technique by which a performer effects quick changes in physical appearance, costume, voice, and bearing; and second, as a psychic manifestation by which an individual strives to overcome any single, fixed identity through the constant creation of new selves and lives. My argument will be that the startling and incongruous superimposition of physical "quick changes" on psychic aspirations to endless self-renewal, produces the specifically Witkacian brand of metamorphosis. Finally, inherent in Witkacy's theory and practice of transformation is his ambivalent attitude towards *spectaculum* in general, and toward acting, theatricalization and impersonation in particular. From all of these considerations it follows that although transformation is the central dynamic in Witkacian dramaturgy, it is always presented as a questionable stunt or theatrical trick, to be regarded with admiration for its virtuosity of form but not for its authenticity of substance.

Let us return now to the beginning of this exploration and the word *transformista*, which is defined as "an actor who quickly changes characteristics, appearing in several roles during a single show" (*"aktor szybko zmieniający charakteryzacje, występujący w kilku rolach podczas jednego spektaklu"*).[2] The word is a neologism in Polish, derived from the French *transformiste* and Italian *trasformista*, which are special theatrical terms which came into use at the end of the nineteenth century with the popularity of the quick-change artist in the variety theatre. The normal meaning of "transformist" is a believer in the biological theory of transformism, which is the theory of biological evolution developed by Lamarck and Darwin. In Russian the term is *transformator*, usually associated with clowns and the circus. In English, the transformist is called a "quick-change artist" or "protean artist"; in the nineteenth century the words "metamorphosist" or "transfigurator" were sometimes used. A distinction was often made between quick-change acts, in which different costumes succeeded one another, and protean acts, in which a single performer played all the characters in a sketch with a plot.[3]

Although the theatrical art of quick change goes back several centuries and was part of the circus and fairground tradition, it became a highly fashionable and popular form of entertainment at the turn of the century due to the music hall appearances of Leopoldo Fregoli, the most celebrated transformist of all time.

Fregoli (1867–1936), was a mime, singer, musician, dancer, ventriloquist, and magician, who could change voices, faces, figure, shape, even sex, in a matter of seconds. In the course of a single performance at a music hall (such as the Parisian Olympia,

–*Theatre Three* 3 (Fall 1987): 47–60.

Witkacy as Napoleon (circa 1930)

located on the Boulevard des Capucines), this protean artist—known as a Master of Faces, a living museum of Masks—would undertake 80 to 100 transformations, aided by a staff of dressers and making use of a scientifically organized wardrobe in the wings that contained 800 costumes and 1200 wigs. But above all, it was Fregoli's personality—mercurial, unstable, changeable—that gave him a "multiple unity" and made him known as "multiform man." He did imitations of music-hall artists, dancers, and actors and actresses such as Loïe Fuller and Eleanora Duse, as well as of writers, musicians, and conductors, including Ibsen, D'Annunzio and Verdi. And he would present parodies of operas in which he sang all the roles (including an hour-and-a-half version of *Faust*) and his own short plays in which he played all the characters. Or he would stage a trial in which he would appear as the accused, the victim, the prosecuting attorney, the defense counsel, the judge, and the jury.[4]

Above all, Fregoli favored tricks and surprises, leaving the stage, for example, to the left, and re-entering a moment later from the right as a totally different character. His theatrical museum was full of oddities. Rapidity of effect, rhythm, dynamism, improvisation, and a flowing series of tableaux—these were the characteristics of Leopoldo Fregoli's "art of transformation" that made him a popular celebrity and won him the admiration of artists like Duse, D'Annunzio and—most interesting for our purposes—Filippo Marinetti, who, when he was on tour with a group of Futurists, saw the master of the quick change at the Teatro Belini in Naples. In his Manifesto, "The Variety Theatre" of 1913, Marinetti praises Fregoli, whose protean art incarnated for the Futurists an aesthetic of surprise, speed, and astonishment. The Futurist author Cangiulli even put Fregoli into one of his plays.[5] "Fregolism" became a word signifying the ability to change costumes, attitudes, and feelings repeatedly and rapidly. He inspired many imitators who claimed to be the American or French Fregoli.

It should be stressed that in all cases the audience derived its enjoyment not from a perfect illusion created by the actor losing himself in the role, but from the awareness that it was Fregoli the quick-change artist playing all the parts. The transformist called attention to his artistry and to his own multiple identity, saying, in effect, "Look, now you are seeing Fregoli as Loïe Fuller, doing the famous serpentine dance." And often, in the vocabulary of the Russian formalists, Fregoli "bared the device," showing how the trick was done, and like a magician revealing his secret, thereby heightened the wonder at his technique. For example, in one number called "The Theatre Wrong Side Around," he sang and danced facing the back of the stage, which represented an imaginary auditorium filled with spectators, and then he came back to the forestage where he made his quick changes under the audience's very eyes. In another he used a transparent set so that the spectators could see how he made the quick changes offstage. In yet another self-referential number featuring the device of the theatre-in-the-theatre, called "The Fregoliad," the action takes place on a music-hall stage, and Fregoli first plays an unsuccessful transformist imitating Fregoli and then various other inept variety-theatre artists, all of whom are roundly hissed. Finally, the master plays Fregoli, who arrives and saves the situation by replacing the lackluster transformist and enacting the roles of all the variety artists himself.

From 1900 to 1910 Fregoli made twenty-six films, functioning both as actor and director, and creating his own projector—the Fregoligraph—with a special screen surrounded by light bulbs. At the end of his stage shows, Fregoli showed several of his films, providing sound by standing behind the screen and speaking, in synchronization, the dialogue for all the roles. L'Homme Protée (The Lightning Change Artist), directed and produced by Méliès in 1899, presented Fregoli making twenty changes of character in two minutes; others revealed his secrets, showing the protean artist in the wings performing the transformations. As with his stage presentations, Fregoli's films stressed technical virtuosity and exploitation of the medium itself (rather than realism and verisimilitude).[6]

In fact, there was a strong affinity between the aesthetic of the transformist's art and that of early cinema, making Fregoli's move from one medium to the other quite natural. The period from 1895 to 1905 was the heyday of the short trick film, in which the newly evolving genre explored the magical possibilities of its own resources, thereby fostering presentation of the fantastic, grotesque, impossible, and absurd. Incredibly fast metamorphoses—as well as ghosts and apparitions, ghoulish games, gallows humor, and uninhibited mayhem—delighted spectators through the repudiation of all physical restrictions on human life. The transformist's art, like the early trick films, was a form that called attention to itself, deliberately stressed its nature as a clever stunt, and held up for admiration the performer's skill at the same time that it freed the human body from the restraints of real-life limitations.

Fregoli in two transformations

Witkiewicz and two transformations

A precursor of Fregoli was the French actor Pierre Thomas Levassor (1808–1870), who played as many as ten different roles in comedy-vaudevilles at the Palais Royal during the 1840s. This master of protean changes was admired by Théophile Gautier and Alexander Sukhovo-Kobylin.[7] In his notes to *The Death of Tarelkin*, Sukhovo-Kobylin cites Levassor as the model to be followed for the two-fold transformation of Tarelkin-into-Kopylov that he wishes to take place on the stage and in full view of the audience. The Russian author declares:

> This transformation should be executed quickly, suddenly, and accompanied by a change of the expression of the face and its features. This is a matter of mimicry and a task for an artist. Here one could point, for example, to the French comic Levassor, who developed this into a high art and acquired a very great reputation because of it. He carried the play of his facial muscles to such a degree of mobility, that he could even change the shape of his nose at will and with the aid of a toupée, beard and moustache almost instantaneously assume the external appearances of the most varied types.[8]

Now it is time to return to Witkacy and to consider the nature of his attachment to the art of the transformist. Whether the author of *The Pragmatists* ever saw or heard of Fregoli is not the issue, although the then-world-famous Italian artist appeared in Moscow and St. Petersburg in 1898 and 1899 and may well have performed in Warsaw in transit, and, in any case, his films and reputation must have been known in Poland. What is certain, however, is that Witkacy himself was by nature a *transformista* and that many of the characters in his plays are also quick-change artists. In all his writing for the theatre, Witkacy asks for a display of the techniques of transformation and an exploration of the resources of the actor's art in such a way as to call attention, self-consciously and self-referentially, to the medium itself and to the nature of theatre as impersonation. This predisposition to quick change is hardly surprising. Given Witkacy's ambivalent attraction to the popular arts of cabaret and cinema, and his reaching artistic maturity under the impress of fin de siècle ideologies, it is perfectly consistent with these points of departure that he should have embraced the aesthetics of surprise, speed, and astonishment characteristic of the protean performer and the early trick film.

From all we know of the playwright's life—from his letters, from accounts provided by his friends, and above all from the hundreds of "mugging" photographs—it is clear that the author of *The New Deliverance* was a talented metamorphosist who could change his voice, facial expression, and physical appearance at will, and who enjoyed staging scenes in which he played different roles and wore different costumes. Moreover, Witkacy had a "multiple" personality in which a plurality of selves did battle with any attempts to impose unity. Although he earned his living as a painter, he might well have enjoyed a career as a performer. In a letter to Malinowski, written in 1927, Witkacy, lamenting his impoverished financial state, declares: "Maybe I'll become a movie actor (Quite seriously—I have several offers)."[9]

In his plays, from *Maciej Korbowa and Bellatrix* in 1918 to *The Shoemakers* completed in 1933, Witkacy incorporates aspects of quick change or the art of protean transformations. Let us look briefly at three kinds of metamorphoses.

1. Transformation of gender. In Witkacy's very first work for the theatre (after the childhood plays), we find a dual transsexual protean act put on by the twin protagonists, Bellatrix and Korbowa. As her voice changes back and forth from feminine to masculine, Bellatrix claims, "Now I'll be a boy—now a girl—now a girl—now a boy,"[10] making gestures appropriate to the transformation. While Bellatrix turns into a man, she often addresses Korbowa as though he were a woman—and in fact, at these moments, his body grows soft and his voice high pitched. It is worth noting, in passing, that the Italian clowns Antonet and Beby (Umberto Guillaume and Aristodemo Frediani) performed a circus act known as "He and She" in which Beby changed sex back and forth, saying "He" and "She" at each transformation, while Antonet commented on the efforts of his partner at playing the role of a would-be Fregoli.[11]

2. Transformation of costume. In almost every play of Witkacy, there are sudden changes of dress, by which a character attempts to put on or off a second self and in this fashion become "other" than he has hitherto been. Edgar in *The Water Hen*, striving to lead a new life, changes in and out of his eighteenth-century costume (tri-cornered hat, wide-topped boots, old-fashioned jacket and trousers, based on an illustrated edition of Defoe's *Robinson Crusoe*). The would-be dictator Hyrcan IV in *The Cuttlefish* removes his impressive purple robe and helmet with a red plume and reveals himself to be an ordinary twentieth-century man in a well-tailored business suit. The deranged poet Walpurg, in *The Madman and the Nun* pulls off a complex stunt (comparable to the trick effects in early films) whereby he appears to hang himself with his strait jacket and then quickly appears on stage in a completely different costume and makeup, clean shaven and elegantly dressed, a yellow flower in his buttonhole.

3. Transformation of character type. At the end of *Mr. Price, or Tropical Madness*, the hero casts off his former mask as business tycoon and goes out into the storm in his pajamas, reborn as an artist. Conversely, in *The Cuttlefish* the painter Rockoffer abandons his persona as artist and assumes the identity of the political strongman, declaring himself to be Hyrcan V. In *Gyubal Wahazar*, the monstrous director alternately blows up in dreadful dimensions and shrivels to almost nothing. Gyubal's size actually seems to change throughout the play; as we watch, the actor playing the role must appear to grow now bigger, now smaller. The most spectacular of all Witkacy's physical transformations occurs in *The Beelzebub Sonata*, when the Brazilian planter Joachim de Campos de Baleastadar turns into the Prince of Darkness before our very eyes. Like all Witkacian "transformational exercises" (the term comes from *Janulka, Daughter of Fizdejko*),[12] the process is a physiological permutation, in this case requiring the performer to arch and swell, writhe and go into convulsions, undergoing all the birth pangs of creating a new self—much in the style that Eugène Ionesco was to propose in *Rhinoceros* more than a generation later.

Baleastadar's growing a tail and horn, like Bellatrix's sexual oscillations and Father Unguenty's transformation into Wahazar II in *Gyubal Wahazar*, is something natural and biological in its intended effect, but artificial and synthetic in the means employed to bring it about. In the emergence of Beelzebub from within the Brazilian planter, emphasis is focused on how the trick is done. A tail and horns do indeed grow out of Baleastadar, but we are constantly reminded that they are false. The horns are made of rubber, inflated through a tube by means of a bulb in the actor's pocket. In these Witkacian metamorphoses, the second self grows over and encrusts the original form which is never lost sight of. Although he may strive to become the devil, Baleastadar will never cease to be himself. He is both a planter of vineyards and the Prince of Darkness, while at the same time always remaining the skilled performer impersonating the interchanges between the two.

To conclude the first section of my analysis, I would suggest the following proposition. From the art of the transformist and the trick film, Witkacy adopted for his own special purposes a technique of physical quick change that emphasizes precision of movement, exact timing, and externals of costume and appearance. Surprise and astonishment are the principal effects sought, and the artistry of the transformation is flaunted, not hidden. From this point of view I believe that we gain a new understanding of the role of the actor in Witkacy's theory of pure form in the theatre. The actor becomes a pure instrument, a performer executing a series of numbers, and the principal mechanism in the total composition.

All this may be true, but it is only the physical dimension. The second component of Witkacian transformation is philosophical, based upon the Nietzschean concept of man as his own creator seeking constant renewal of the self by means of endless transformation in both his life and work, Witkacy's central obsession is with problems of identity. "Who am I really"[13] is the question that each of his heroes never ceases to ask. The pursuit of identity through metamorphosis becomes the arduous task of an entire lifetime.

As a boy, young Staś had been the object of his father's endless exhortations to rise above himself and create his own individuality, and the confused young man, overburdened with selves, responded with a resolve to give form to himself. But as his friend Brummel tells Witkacy's alter-ego Bungo in his early autobiographical novel: "You're always beginning a new life, but I don't ever see the slightest change in you."[14]

The Nietzschean burden of self-sufficiency imposed on young Witkacy by his father was immense. The boy was given total freedom to be his own creator, required always to transcend himself and seek ever higher achievement. In Nietzsche's call to creativity, the entire responsibility is laid upon the individual, who must give laws to himself and follow the highest commandments. The as-yet-uncharted path the individual must follow is dangerous and lonely; the authentic creator is not sustained by any outside structure or order of society, but must look within for all sources of strength. Since man has no objectively identifiable nature, the Nietzschean watchword, "Become what you are," condemns the creative personality to ambiguous indeterminacy, in which he remains free to choose among open possibilities.[15]

The heroes of Witkacy's plays and novels feel themselves to be under similar compulsion to be someone, to create themselves from nothing at each moment, although they do not know who they are, who they should be, or who they will be tomorrow. The Nietzschean imperative leading to transvaluation in art, in thought, and in individuality, is expressed as a relentless battle of self against the void:

> The world is nothingness; the midnight bell wakes us from that nothingness to struggle with nothingness, and in that struggle we forge and continuously re-forge our destinies.[16]

The pressing need to be someone at every moment and to have the inner strength to realize one's potential through an endless play of possibilities reduces Witkacy's young heroes to despair. "I must live all the things that I have in me," Bungo muses; "But a man creates himself solely out of the struggle with himself."[17] And Athanazy Bazakbal, the young hero of *Farewell to Autumn*, overcome by the challenge of identity, muses: "The whole charm of life lay in staying undefined," and finally concludes: "Endure life not knowing what one is—perhaps that amounts to a certain kind of greatness."[18] Bewildered by a multiplicity of selves, Gyubal Wahazar finds at the moment of death release from the oppression of identity, by submitting to the ecstasy of protean existence:

I live in indeterminacy, I feel I'm everything. . . . Oh! What happiness! What bliss! Not to know who one is—to be everything!![19]

In *The Crazy Locomotive*, the two heroes, Prince Tréfaldi and his associate Travaillac, have been masquerading under the borrowed identities of a railroad engineer and his fireman, until the moment when they suddenly disclose—in a psychic quick-change act—their new individualities as master criminals. "I hardly even resemble myself," Tréfaldi exclaims, to which Travaillac answers, "Of course, we all have to keep changing, constantly."[20] In *Janulka*, none of the characters has an identity, except the one that is being fabricated at each moment by the construction of artificial selves. Under the supervision of the Grand Master and his Director of Séances, Der Zipfel, the group of "corpses on vacation" engages in a series of transformational exercises, starting from nothing and returning to it, and then beginning all over again.

The Witkacian dramatis personae are constantly inventing new forms of existence, changing costumes and styles of performance, forging cards of identity, undergoing metamorphosis through death, real or feigned, and suddenly being reborn as someone else. By joining the histrionic techniques of physical quick change to the spiritual goals of psychic self-transcendence, by combining Leopoldo Fregoli with Friedrich Nietzsche, Witkacy produces transformations that disconcert and delight as protean theatrical tricks both serving and subverting lofty philosophical pretensions. The speed and precision of the theatrical mechanics—the changes in facial expression, voice, costume, wig, beard, girth, height—harnessed to grandiose notions of psychic renewal and creation out of the void, give rise to an unexpected amalgam of the abstract and concrete capable of provoking the laughter of astonishment.

The consequences of these observations for a Witkacian acting style are as follows. First of all, it should have the external sharpness of outline, the speed and the accuracy of the seasoned music-hall and variety-theatre performer trying to grapple with Nietzschean injunctions to create oneself. In other words, Zarathustra as a quick-change artist. Whether or not the director and actors choose to follow literally Witkacy's intricate and explicit stage directions about costume, makeup, and physical appearance is hardly important. It is however essential that the precision, tempo, physicality, and surprise characteristic of the transformist's art be maintained, whatever the style or period of costuming.

Second, a Witkacian acting style, based on quick change, is necessarily eclectic, devoid of any single set of conventions or fixed method. The protean artist's style is an absence of style, since he imitates the style of the character which he adopts at one moment, only to drop it several moments later. In their unstable, ever-shifting role-playing and ceaseless quest for identity, Witkacy's characters discard old forms and put on new ones, abandoning theatrical masks and conventions with bewildering speed and nonchalance. A Witkacian hero like Edgar in *The Water Hen*, who suffers from self-multiplication and contains many characters, is in search of a style; all that he can do is, one after the other, try out and quote different acting styles.

The person who cannot find himself is doomed to change constantly. Thus the Witkacian dramatis personae, to conceal their inner emptiness and the surrounding void, must play, be actors, adopt roles, put on theatre, stage themselves. Performance becomes a way of survival. But in Witkacy's world the theatricalization of life is a risky business, threatening the integrity of the personality and leading to the fake and the pseudo. Endowed with a protean nature and drawn to all forms of playing, the young

Witkacy underwent a prolonged crisis of identity in which he came to regard himself as an actor on the stage, and to consider acting as synonymous with lying.[21] Dramatizing the instability of his alter-ego Bungo, who plays at both art and life, Witkacy uses the actor as the very image of alienation from self:

> "I must have a mask," he muttered through clenched teeth.
> "Don't you know that a mask is a dangerous thing?" Tymbeusz asked.
> "To trade away life for a mask, to be only an actor at the beck and call of another person lurking within oneself, an alien being, Mr. Bungo. You won't be able to bring that off artistically, you'll lose yourself, but not in a creative fashion. [. . .]
> You can't be an actor in life. [. . .] You won't succeed, because you won't be able to turn yourself *entirely* into a lie."[22]

Athanazy, in *Farewell to Autumn*, expresses the common longing of Witkacian heroes when he exclaims "To be oneself, only what one really is. Not to create those lying doubles in spheres of the spirit alien to one's nature."[23] For the author of *They*, the theatricalization of life is a sure sign of the inauthenticity that has infected modern life, and the stage and play-acting are indices of degeneration. The more theatrical Witkacy's characters become, the less they can be true to themselves. As the mystery dies out, the theatricalization of life blossoms as a substitute, as the ultimate in the ersatz. Failure to locate the mystery of existence leads to the theatrical poses and stagey gestures designed to recapture what has been lost forever.

Like von Telek, who planned to turn his friend's spectral changeability into a show, the bizarre group of degenerates at the end of *The 622 Downfalls of Bungo* announces, "We'll set up a cabaret." Once Bungo decides to create an artificial self, and ceases trying to be himself, he declares, "Now it's theatre," and "I have the feeling that I'm employed by some theatre." And finding that he is an even better performer at falsifying himself than the actress Acne, with whom he has been having a love affair, he tells her, "Even though I'm not a professional ham, I act better than you do."[24]

Witkacy's reservations about the art of acting sometime seem as far-reaching as those expressed by Jean-Jacques Rousseau in the *Lettre D'Alembert sur les spectacles*:

> It is the art of dissimulation, of assuming a foreign character, and of appearing different to what he really is [. . .] of saying what he does not think as naturally as if he really did, in a word, of forgetting himself to personate others. What is the profession of a comedian? A trade in which a man publicly exhibits himself with a mercenary design [. . .] would you support the shame of being meanly metamorphosed into kings and obliged to play a part so different from your own, exposing your majestical personages to the rude shouts of the populace.[25]

In *Insatiability* the demonic Persy tells the young hero Zipcio, "But soon you will start thinking deceitful thoughts, and you will tell them to me, and I will make them my life and through them create my own deceitful act. You see, I need it for the theatre."[26]

The result of the collective theatricalization of life, by which acting and lying, playing roles and developing masked selves become widespread, is that society itself and its institutions become subject to endless transformation. All forms grow blurred and identities unstable; regimes and ideologies succeed one another in the body politic, as selves do in the individual psyche. The only law is ceaseless change.[27]

The most highly theatricalized societies are those on the eve of social upheaval, and the classes who feel themselves on the margin of events, watching from outside as spectators or actors without parts experience most concretely the quality of the coming changes.[28] The transformation of all of life into revolution, into a vast show, is commented upon ironically by the Bolshevik poet Sajetan Tempe, in *Farewell to Autumn*:

> You'd like to watch the revolution from the best seat in the orchestra as though it were a play—better still, to have it staged by those new, self-proclaimed social artists who try to make a pseudo-artistic performance out of everything—a mass meeting, rally, street shooting, even work.[29]

In *Homo Ludens*, Huizinga points out that the growth of play elements, used to deaden a growing sense of menace and emptiness, precedes the collapse of civilization and leads to a dangerous world of impostures. The theatricalization of revolution, by transforming it into entertainment to provide thrills for the bored, renders the process fraudulent and incapable of producing anything new.[30] In both the personal and the social spheres, transformation in Witkacy is unable to effect real change, but can only repeat the old life in deformed shapes by trying to twist to fresh purposes the established forms of art and society. The failure is due to the distorting weight of pseudomorphosis. In *Farewell to Autumn*, Witkacy explains that he has taken the term from Oswald Spengler's *Decline of the West* and applied it to the characters in his novel. Spengler himself, Witkacy points out, adapted the word from mineralogy where it refers to the process by which new molten masses from volcanic outbursts, not free to find their own special forms, are forced to fill hollow molds in rock strata whose crystals have been washed out.[31] "They must fill up the spaces they find available," Spengler writes. "Thus there arise distorted forms, crystals whose inner structure contradicts their external shapes, stones of one kind presenting the appearance of stones of another kind."

Applied to the growth of civilizations, historical pseudomorphosis occurs when a new culture cannot develop its own forms. "All that wells up from the depths of the young soul is cast in old moulds, young feelings stiffen in senile works, and instead of rearing itself up in its own creative power, it can only hate the distant power with a hate that grows to be monstrous."[32]

As used by Witkacy, pseudomorphosis serves to characterize the new trapped in old forms, and the futility of endless transformations that change nothing. The eternal shell remains, while a radically different inner content surreptitiously attempts to grow within. Witkacian transformation remains stunted and incomplete, the products only deformed pseudo-types.

Fregolian quick change and Nietzschean creative renewal are held in perpetual check by Spenglerian pseudomorphosis. Witkacy's living museum of masks fails to achieve self-transcendence and remains forever arrested in the deformed grimaces of old forms struggling with a Sisyphean task of endless transformation.[33]

NOTES

1. Stanisław Ignacy Witkiewicz, *Dramaty*, vol. 1 (Warsaw: Państwowy Instytut Wydawniczy, 1996), 182. In English, *Witkiewicz: Seven Plays*, trans. and ed. Daniel Gerould (New York: Martin E. Segal Theatre Center Publications, 2005), 15.
2. Jan Tokarski, ed., *Słownik wyrazów obcych* (Warsaw: Państwowe Wydawnictwo Naukowe, 1971), 770.
3. Joe Laurie, Jr., *Vaudeville—From the Honky-Tonks to the Palace* (New York: Holt, 1953), 96.
4. Jean Nohain and François Caradec, *Fregoli 1867–1936: Sa Vie et Ses Secrets* (Paris: La jeune Parque, 1968). Little new information is to be found in Patrick Rambaud, *Les mirobolantes aventures de Fregoli, racontées d'après ses mémoires et des témoins* (Paris: Éditions François Bourin, 1991).
5. Giovanni Lista, "Esthétique du music-hall et mythologie urbaine chez Marinetti," in *Du Cirque au théâtre*, ed. Claudine Amiard Chevrel (Lausanne: L'Age d'Homme, 1983), 55–56. Fregoli also appears in Nikolai Evreinov's play, *The Chief Thing* (1919), as a fictional character called Doctor Fregoli. The contemporary quick-change artist Arturo Brachetti starred in the long-running 1994/5 Italian musical *Fregoli*, by Ugo Chiti and Bruno Moretti, directed by Saverio Marconi.
6. Erik Barnouw, *The Magician and the Cinema* (Oxford: Oxford University Press, 1991), 85–105. See also Paul Hammond, *Marvelous Méliès* (New York: St. Martin's Press, 1975), 42.
7. Théophile Gautier repeatedly refers to Levassor in *L'Histoire de l'art dramatique en France depuis vingt-cinq ans* (1858–59) (Geneva: Slatkine Reprints, 1968).
8. *The Trilogy of Alexander Sukhovo-Kobylin*, trans. Harold B. Segel (The Netherlands: Harwood Academic Publishers, 1995), 210.
9. "Listy Witkacego do Bronisława Malinowskiego," ed. Jan Witkiewicz, *Puls* 21 (Spring 1984), 104–5.
10. *Dramaty*, vol. 1, 151. *Maciej Korbowa and Bellatrix*, trans. and intro by Daniel Gerould (Ashby-de-la-Louch, UK: InkerMen Press, 2009), 84.
11. Tristan Rémy, *Les Clowns* (Paris: Bernard Grasset, 1945), Chapter 9; *Klouny*, trans. Ya. Z. Lesyuk (Moscow: Iskusstvo, 1965), 135.
12. *Dramaty*, vol. 3 (2004), 135. *The Witkiewicz Reader*, ed. Daniel Gerould (Evanston, IL: Northwestern University Press, 1993), 183.
13. *Dramaty*, vol. 3, 144. *The Witkiewicz Reader*, 190. Fizdejko himself poses the question.
14. Stanisław Ignacy Witkiewicz, *622 upadki Bunga, czyli Demoniczna kobieta*, ed. Anna Micińska (Warsaw: Państwowy Instytut Wydawniczy, 1992), 304.
15. Karl Jaspers, "Man as his own creator," in *Nietzsche—A Collection of Critical Essays*, ed. Robert C. Solomon (Garden City, NY: Anchor Press/Doubleday, 1973), 144–54.
16. Morse Peckham, *Beyond the Tragic Vision: The Quest for Identity in the Nineteenth Century* (New York: George Braziller, 1962), 368.
17. *622 upadki Bunga*, 43, 256.
18. Stanisław Ignacy Witkiewicz, *Pożegnanie jesieni*, ed. Anna Micińska (Warsaw: Państwowy Instytut Wydawniczy, 1992), 55, 115.
19. *Dramaty*, vol. 2 (1998), 276. *Witkiewicz: Seven Plays*, 160.
20. *Dramaty*, vol. 3, 574. *The Madman and the Nun and The Crazy Locomotive, with The Water Hen*, ed. and trans. Daniel Gerould and C.S. Durer (New York: Applause Books, 1988), 98.
21. Witkacy shared the general modernist denigration of the actor. On this subject, see John Stokes, "The Legend of Duse," in *Decadence and the 1890's*, ed. Ian Fletcher (New York: Holmes & Meier, 1980), 150–71. Witkacy could also have found support for his views in Nietzsche, who in *The Case of Wagner* talks about the actor's "talent to lie." See John Burt Foster, Jr., *Heirs to Dionysus: A Nietzschean Current in Literary Modernism* (Princeton, NJ: Princeton University Press, 1981), 107.
22. *622 upadki Bunga*, 31, 237.
23. *Pożegnanie jesieni*, 747.

24. *622 upadki Bunga*, 409, 420, 426.

25. Jean-Jacques Rousseau, *Lettre d D'Alembert sur son Article Genève* (Paris: Garnier-Flammarion, 1967), 163; in English, "An Epistle from J.J. Rousseau, Citizen of Geneva to Mr. D'Alembert (1758)," anonymous translator, in *Theatre/Theory/Theatre*, ed. Daniel Gerould (New York: Applause Books, 2000), 214.

26. Stanisław Ignacy Witkiewicz, *Nienasycenie*, part 2 (Warsaw: Państwowy Instytut Wydawniczy, 1992), 427. Citation in English from *Insatiability*, trans. and ed. Louis Iribarne (Urbana: University of Illinois Press, 1977), 291.

27. Witkacy himself underwent constant political transformations. "I have undergone strange transformations, shifting from aristocratic aestheticism to the ideology of the Social Revolutionaries, and then of the Bolsheviks, and now recently through a temporary flirtation with fascism to a certain version of communism." In *Bez kompromisu*, ed. Janusz Degler (Warsaw: Państwowy Instytut Wydawniczy, 1976), 385. In English, *The Witkiewicz Reader*, 283.

28. Elizabeth Burns, *Theatricality* (London: Longman, 1972), 11.

29. *Pożegnanie jesieni*, 151.

30. Johan Huizinga, *Homo Ludens* (Boston: Beacon, 1967), 204–6.

31. *Pożegnanie jesieni*, 152.

32. Oswald Spengler, *Perspectives of World History*, vol. 2, *The Decline of the West*, trans. Charles Francis Atkinson (New York: Knopf, 1961), 189.

33. Another important form of Witkacian transformation that results in deformation is linguistic.

Caricature of Ibsen by Olaf Gulbransson, Norwegian artist (1873–1959)

GEORGE BERNARD SHAW'S CRITICISM OF IBSEN

Edmund Gosse introduced Ibsen to England, William Archer translated his works, but it was George Bernard Shaw who became the self-appointed exponent of Ibsen's message to the British public. Yet, from Ibsen's time until the present day, the critical estimate of Shaw's writings on Ibsen has been almost uniformly unfavorable. On July 18, 1890 Shaw made his first public pronouncement on Ibsen in a speech before the Fabian Society, in which he called Ibsen a socialist. In *The Daily Chronicle* of August 28, 1890 an indignant critic, answering Shaw, discredited his interpretation; he answered with some authority, for the writer was Henrik Ibsen himself. "I never belonged, and probably never shall belong, to any party whatever. I may add here that it has become an absolute necessity to me to work quite independently and to shape my own course."[1] This protest is typical of the reception of Shaw's advocacy of Ibsen as a man with a social message. Innumerable writers and critics have sprung to defend Ibsen from "Mr. Bernard Shaw's victimization of him."[2]

As early as 1889 Archer, who knew Shaw well and probably had him in mind, warned against just such a misrepresentation. "A grave injustice has been done Ibsen of late by those of his English admirers who have set him up as a social prophet, and sometimes omitted to mention that he was a bit of a poet as well."[3] *The Quintessence of Ibsenism*, Shaw's revision in book form of his original Fabian exposition of Ibsen, has become the classic example of misguided Ibsen criticism, which all writers on either Ibsen or Shaw feel obliged to denounce or ridicule. In *Iconoclasts: A Book of Dramatists* (1905), James Huneker entitled his chapter on Shaw "The Quintessence of Shaw." The American critic did not believe that Shaw's book had much to do with Ibsen.

> This pamphlet, among the first of its kind in English, now seems a trifle old-fashioned in its interpretation of the Norwegian dramatist—possibly because he is something so different from what Mr. Shaw pictured him. We are never shown Ibsen the artist, but always the social reformer with an awful frown.[4]

This view was repeated, with slight modifications, by Miriam A. Franc in *Ibsen in England*, which appeared in 1919. The author regarded some of Shaw's writings on Ibsen as of historical importance, but had grave reservations about Shaw's interpretation: "Himself a preacher lacking all poetry, Shaw always regarded Ibsen as a moralist rather than a poet. He invariably stressed the didactic elements . . . constantly overemphasized the propagandist in the poet."[5]

Mid-twentieth century English and American criticism of Ibsen carried still further the discounting of the social prophet in Ibsen in order to reinstate the poet. In *The Poet in the Theatre*, a book whose title alone indicates a new critical orientation, Ronald Peacock sees Ibsen not only as a poet but as a poet with affinities in the past, "possibly in fact the great belated dramatist of the whole Romantic movement."[6] What once seemed most important in Ibsen is actually least important. "The detached spectator of today can more easily see how the social problem plays of Ibsen do not compare for artistic unity with his earlier or later work."[7] It is not surprising that Shaw's Ibsen criticism became unfashionable in this critical atmosphere. Raymond Williams, in his critical study, *Drama from Ibsen to Eliot*, cites T. S. Eliot's dictum, "Shaw *was* a poet—until he was born, and

Caricature of Shaw and Ibsen by William Cotton, American artist and playwright (1880–1958)

the poet in Shaw was stillborn."[8] From this premise it follows that Shaw the non-poet is incapable of understanding Ibsen the poet. According to Williams, *The Quintessence of Ibsenism* "has to do with Ibsen only in the sense that it seriously misrepresents him."[9]

If we turn to critics generally sympathetic to Shaw and to social import, we find almost the same reaction to Shaw's criticism of Ibsen. Both Edmund Wilson and Eric Bentley are convinced that Shaw seriously misrepresented Ibsen; Wilson, however, feels that Shaw misrepresented himself at the same time, while Bentley thinks that Shaw was really talking about himself rather than about Ibsen. Bentley suggests that, "for 'Ibsen,' throughout *The Quintessence of Ibsenism*, we should read 'Shaw.'"[10]

The Swedish critic Martin Lamm is virtually alone in praising Shaw's interpretation of Ibsen, and it is noteworthy that Lamm holds that both Shaw and Ibsen wrote problem plays in which they expounded their ideas. "Before Shaw had published any play, he had already written *The Quintessence of Ibsenism* (1891), in which he shows how well he understood, and how greatly he admired, all Ibsen's work to date."[11] Lamm's judgment lends authority to the belief that there may be more in Shaw's criticism of Ibsen than the English critics choose to find. The school of criticism of the theatre inspired by T. S. Eliot represents a reaction against the whole social drama of the late nineteenth and early twentieth century, and these critics, like Shaw before them, turn to Ibsen to find substantiation for their own preconceptions and ideals.[12]

In order to determine whether Shaw misunderstood and misrepresented an author for whom he professed the greatest admiration and respect, it is necessary to examine all his Ibsen criticism and to distinguish the different kinds. When did he write it? For what audience? With what purpose? Shaw was a novelist, socialist, journalist, critic, and dramatist; in which of these several capacities did he write about Ibsen? It is misleading to divorce a book like *The Quintessence of Ibsenism* from Shaw's particular purpose in writing it or from the rest of his criticism.

Shaw's criticism of Ibsen falls into three principal phases, represented by: *The Quintessence of Ibsenism* (1891, enlarged 1913); *Our Theatres in the Nineties* (criticisms contributed week by week to *The Saturday Review* from January 1895 to May 1898); and *The Prefaces* (1893 to 1933). In *The Quintessence of Ibsenism*, Shaw was writing as a novelist, socialist, and playwright-to-be; in *Our Theatres in the Nineties*, as a professional play reviewer and dramatist on the threshold of success; and, in *The Prefaces*, as a famous playwright and essayist of world renown. As we might expect, these several stages in Shaw's life experience are reflected in his criticism; the socialist, the drama critic, and the great master consider Ibsen from three different points of view.

The first edition of *The Quintessence of Ibsenism* consists of two principal parts: (1) a long introductory section concerning the false ideals of the nineteenth century, and (2) analyses of Ibsen's plays that are little more than summaries. In the first section, Shaw advances the thesis that Ibsen in his works is attacking false ideals, but he devotes most of the three introductory chapters to a discussion of false ideals in other nineteenth-century writers or in social and intellectual contexts that have but slight relation to Ibsen. In the second section, he illustrates his thesis by giving a summary of each Ibsen play.

Shaw states that his purpose is "to distill the quintessence of Ibsen's message to his age,"[13] and he insists that the value of the plays lies in their message. He discusses the plays as if they were novels, without attention to their dramatic form. He refers to characters who don't appear in the plays as if they did: "Whilst the general reads the paper in the afternoon, Løvborg and Hedda have long conversations."[14] The summaries concentrate on unravelling the exposition rather than on explaining the dramatic values.

There is no mention of any of the symbolic values in the plays, not even of the wild duck or of the white horses of *Rosmersholm.*

Certainly these are grave and absurd misinterpretations if that is all there is to *The Quintessence of Ibsenism.* Yet Shaw had read Ibsen carefully; he must have known that General Gabler never comes on the stage and that the wild duck is a complex symbol essential to the meaning of the play. Why does Shaw insist on the message of the plays, and ignore completely the most basic sort of dramatic concerns that would be obvious to any amateur lover of the theatre?

In the Preface to the first edition, Shaw discusses the genesis of the work; it was one of a series of lectures on socialism in contemporary literature before the Fabian Society. He explains, apologetically, that it was a makeshift series and that the topic was not "the result of a spontaneous internal impulse on my part." He "purposely couched it in the most provocative terms" and, after the lecture, "laid it aside as a *pièce d'occasion* which had served its turn." However, the "frantic newspaper controversy" launched by *Ghosts* in 1891 caused him to publish his lecture, which, he says, had at least the value of a consistent approach.[15]

> At any rate, the controversialists, whether in the abusive stage, or apologetic stage, or the hero-worshipping stage, by no means made clear what they were abusing, or apologizing for, or going into ecstasies about; and I came to the conclusion that my explanation might as well be placed in the field until a better could be found.[16]

Shaw concludes his Preface with "a reminder that [the book] is not a critical essay on the poetic beauties of Ibsen, but simply an exposition of Ibsenism."[17] Shaw's purpose was clearly polemic. Writing at the outset of the virulent Ibsen controversy which raged in England for five years, he was primarily concerned with creating public interest in Ibsen by inciting people to read and to discuss his works.

He places special emphasis on reading, rather than seeing, Ibsen's plays. In the early 1890s the reading of plays, a habit uncommon among the British since the eighteenth century, once again became prevalent—creating a new audience for the drama, an audience receptive to new ideas and new methods.[18] The average Victorian theatregoer who attended farces and melodramas had little literary or intellectual interest in the drama; the new play readers came from the public of late Victorian fiction, accustomed to serious reading in which they could expect to find a discussion of ideas, a philosophy of life, an examination of moral and social questions of contemporary significance, and sometimes a direct message. As play reading became popular, the traditions of the novel of the period, with stress on moral and intellectual seriousness, came to the aid of the drama and gradually modified the superficial theatrical conventions that had persisted for almost a century. It was this new public which made possible Ibsen's great success with British readers, even though he never was completely victorious on the English stage.

In *The Quintessence of Ibsenism* Shaw addressed this new public. When he first conceived the book, it seemed unlikely that there would be much opportunity for this public to see many of the plays performed; when they were performed, it was usually under adverse circumstances for very short runs. There were also problems of censorship, as well as difficulties with actors and producers. Furthermore, Shaw knew that the English considered literature and the theatre as irreconcilably opposed; the only place where the British public could have full access to Ibsen and where they could take him seriously was in the library.

Shaw was trying to make Ibsen interesting to novel readers; his summaries in novelistic form were designed to unravel the complexities of the exposition so that a reader uninitiated in Ibsen's technique could make sense of the plays. Illustrative comparisons and analogies are drawn, not from dramatic literature, but from the whole tradition of European thought, especially nineteenth-century thought as expressed by novelists and philosophers. Shaw places Ibsen—in a context of content rather than of form—with Shelley, Dickens, Samuel Butler, and Darwin. In introducing Ibsen to the British reading public, he could have found no better method, since there was at the time no valid dramatic tradition. In *The Quintessence of Ibsenism* we see the meaning Ibsen had *vis-à-vis* a particular audience at a particular time. Shaw is primarily concerned with the way the public reacts to Ibsen. His analysis of *Ghosts* consists of a sampling of newspaper reviews, which enables us to gauge the mental, moral, and artistic perceptions of the British press with respect to Ibsen.

However, Shaw enunciates three of the cardinal principles of all serious Ibsen criticism: one must know all Ibsen's work to understand any of it; one must study the plays chronologically in order to grasp all the relationships between them; one must recognize a continuous theme running through all the plays. On these points Shaw is not at variance with the modern critics; it is only his success in carrying out these principles that is open to question.

He begins his study of Ibsen's work with *Brand* and discusses all the other plays in chronological order, except *Emperor and Galilean*, which he considers before *The League of Youth*. Despite the omission of the early plays, he demonstrates a thorough knowledge of them in many references and comparisons. He also traces relationships back and forth between various plays, using *Brand* and *Peer Gynt* as fixed points of reference. He calls the theme which runs through Ibsen's plays an attack on idealism; Ibsen is attempting to expose the false ideals of society. Nonetheless, Shaw's final words reveal skepticism about any attempt to make Ibsen a social reformer with a positive message for the world.

> What Ibsen insists on is that there is no golden rule; that conduct must justify itself by its effect upon life and not by its conformity to any rule or ideal. . . Here I must leave the matter, merely reminding those who may think I have forgotten to reduce Ibsenism to a formula for them, that its quintessence is that there is no formula.[19]

The second edition of *The Quintessence of Ibsenism* appeared in 1913, more than twenty years after the original publication of the essay. The additions, designed to complete the work and bring it up to date, indicate a shift in critical emphasis which reveals a new approach to Ibsen. By 1913 Ibsen was an accepted classic, no longer controversial, and Shaw was a famous and original playwright, having written the majority of the plays for which he is best known; and audiences were being exposed to new dramatists such as Galsworthy, Strindberg, and Chekhov. In all his dramatic criticism Shaw writes a history of audience reactions; by 1913 the change in generations had brought about an audience re-evaluation of Ibsen.

In the first place, the audience for Ibsen was no longer primarily composed of readers, for the modern drama had triumphed modestly and won a place on the stage. Small repertory theatres like the Independent Theatre and Court Theatre were successfully presenting the new drama to a growing public. Shaw recognized this development; in his discussion of Ibsen's last four plays he distinguished clearly between the dramatic form of the plays and the novelistic summaries which he still provided, with the avowed purpose of making it easier to follow the play in performance.[20]

Second, the audience was much more sophisticated and had already outgrown Ibsen in some respects. Shaw's aim was no longer polemic, for the battle had been won. Now he was able to look back dispassionately and assign Ibsen his place in the evolution of ideas and form in the modern drama. He makes use of two comparisons which serve to locate Ibsen in the proper perspective—one with Dickens, the other with Strindberg. Ibsen has outdistanced Dickens and has been himself outdistanced by Strindberg. Shaw believed in progress in the arts and took the side of the Moderns versus the Ancients.

In this retrospective evaluation of Ibsen's place in the drama, Shaw realized that he himself, along with Ibsen's other followers, may have been responsible for creating a false picture of Ibsen in the vehemence of the polemics.

> When an author's works produce violent controversy, and are new, people are apt to read them with that sort of seriousness which is very appropriately called deadly. . . . I remember a performance of The Wild Duck, at which the late Clement Scott pointed out triumphantly that the play was so absurd that even the champions of Ibsen could not help laughing at it. It had not occurred to him that Ibsen could laugh like other men.[21]

In the chapter, "The Technical Novelty in Ibsen's Plays," Shaw discusses the impact of Ibsen on younger dramatists, and issues a general manifesto for the new drama, in particular for his own kind of play. In many ways this program goes beyond or runs counter to Ibsen's own work; it is this fact that has caused critics like Bentley to say that *The Quintessence of Ibsenism* is about Shaw, not Ibsen. Shaw is, however, careful to keep separate what he attributes to Ibsen and what he claims for the newer writers, though he maintains that Ibsen prepared the way for later developments in which he had no part. He makes two important observations on the new technique: it adds a new element of discussion, and it deals with people like ourselves.

> Formerly you had in what was called a well made play an exposition in the first act, a situation in the second, an unravelling in the third. Now you have exposition, situation, and discussion; and the discussion is the test of the playwright . . . The discussion conquered Europe in Ibsen's Doll's House; and now the serious playwright recognizes in the discussion not only the main test of his highest powers, but also the real centre of his play's interest.[22]

Because of Ibsen, audiences now demand "a moralist and a debater as well as a dramatist."[23] It is now possible for a dramatist like Shaw to write plays that begin with discussion rather than end with it—or that are all discussion.

Shaw says that the new drama deals with "people exactly like ourselves"— broaching the classic question of nature and the natural in dramatic literature. "Now the natural is mainly the everyday. Crimes, fights, big legacies, fires, shipwrecks, battles, and thunderbolts are mistakes in a play."[24] Since such events occur in Ibsen's work, the reader tends to rebel against Shaw's conception of the subject of the new drama, insofar as it is supposed to refer to Ibsen. But, if we read a little further, we discover that Shaw is not talking about Ibsen's work itself, but only about what came after Ibsen as a result of his pioneering. In certain respects he is now critical of Ibsen; he judges Ibsen from the vantage point of the new post-Ibsen theatre which has continued the task which the master began, the development of a new drama.

> Perhaps the most plausible reproach levelled at Ibsen by modern critics of his own school is just that survival of the old school in him which makes the death rate so high in his last acts . . . The post-Ibsen playwrights apparently think that Ibsen's homicides and suicides were forced.[25]

If we are to understand *The Quintessence of Ibsenism*, we must recognize that Shaw is telling us how Ibsen conditioned audiences for developments that go beyond his own accomplishments and how Ibsen influenced the whole new school of dramatists, himself included. If *The Quintessence of Ibsenism* does not tell us a great deal about the plays as plays, it is full of information about Ibsen in relation to British public opinion and to the new drama in England.

It is not true that Shaw emphasized the social plays at the expense of the earlier and later work. The plays to which he devotes the most space are: *Emperor and Galilean, When We Dead Awaken, Little Eyolf, Peer Gynt, Ghosts, Rosmersholm,* and *Hedda Gabler.* Surprisingly, *When We Dead Awaken* excited Shaw's greatest admiration, as it did James Joyce's at about the same time. Shaw analyzes the changes in technique which he regards as improvements rather than senile falterings. "It shews no decay of Ibsen's highest qualities: his magic is nowhere more potent . . . There is no falling-off here in Ibsen."[26]

The Quintessence of Ibsenism is not the grotesque misinterpretation that it has been called by the critics. It has value as a general introduction to Ibsen for the uninitiated and as a study in the relations between Ibsen and the English theatre. Nevertheless, as a critical examination of Ibsen's plays for one who already knows them, the book is hardly satisfying or even stimulating. His treatment of the characters is inadequate; Shaw gives no indication of the dramatic form in which the plays are cast, of the exposition, dialogue, and symbols. Since it is by his creation of character and his power of construction that Ibsen lives, these are serious faults. Did Shaw fail to see where Ibsen's power lay?

We find the answer in his next writing that touches frequently on Ibsen, his dramatic criticism in the *Saturday Review* from 1895 to 1898. These reviews supply the qualities that were lacking in *The Quintessence of Ibsenism.* Since Shaw is now writing practical dramatic criticism, he must perforce deal with plays as plays—and consider the form of the plays and the meaning this form has for spectator, producer, director, stage manager, and actor. On these topics he writes with the authority of a playwright, lover of the theatre, and dramatic critic—and shows a solid knowledge of the English stage and its conditions, of Ibsen's plays, and of the adaptation of the one to the other.

The Quintessence of Ibsenism gave an abstract and lifeless picture of the plays; *Our Theatres in the Nineties* creates a vivid and detailed impression of the characters, dialogue, and atmosphere. The Ibsen controversy, but recently won, is still fresh enough in Shaw's memory to add warmth to his advocacy of Ibsen; yet tempers have cooled and reason once again prevails, so that he feels free to correct the exaggerations of his earlier fanaticism and to moderate his praise. The causes and abstractions of his Fabian days occupy a less prominent role in his criticism; as a playwright himself, he is now especially sensitive to the technical side of the dramatic and scenic arts.

Shaw now points out what for him is the distinctive feature of all of Ibsen's later plays—they begin with the catastrophe. By his use of exposition, Ibsen avoids wasting an act or two on tiresome explanations and preparations, and can begin at an advanced state of action when the curtain rises.[27] This technique, Shaw believes, follows from the new subject matter Ibsen is exploring—marriage. His dramas thus open where the normal romantic play ends. "The Ibsen drama is preeminently the drama of marriage . . . That is

"Ibsen" (1942) by Sergei Eisenstein from *Theatrical Drawings*

just where an ordinary play leaves off, and just where an Ibsen play begins."[28] Although these observations are true and perceptive as far as they go, Shaw fails to emphasize sufficiently the role of the past in Ibsen and its influence as a nemesis on the present.

In *The Quintessence of Ibsenism* Shaw talked little about Ibsen's characters as rounded creations of living human beings and gave the misleading impression that the plays lived by their ideas and themes alone. In his dramatic criticism, he takes the opposite position—stressing the pre-eminence of character in Ibsen and recognizing the many brilliant roles offered to actors. He repeatedly calls attention to the numerous excellent acting parts for women and tries to convince famous actresses that they should play Ibsen, if only for their own glory. He now places a sense of character above social doctrine.

> Imagination, humor, and a sense of character . . . These qualities will carry a good deal of psychology and social doctrine about the unhappiness of marriage, the emancipation of woman, and so forth, if the loading be judiciously done. But the psychology and the doctrine can be done without, whereas the imagination, the humor, the sympathetic sense of character, whether blunt and vulgar or acute and subtle, are indispensable.[29]

In his reviews Shaw devotes a great deal of attention to analysis of the actors' interpretations and to comparison of these interpretations with Ibsen's conception of the characters. He is concerned with fidelity to the text, and sees the danger of making the characters mere abstractions, not real characters.

> Mr. Martin Harvey, as Erhart, was clever enough to seize the main idea of the part the impulse towards happiness—but not experienced enough to know that the actor's business is not to supply an idea with a sounding board, but with a credible, simple, and natural human being to utter it when its time comes and not before.[30]

Related to Shaw's preoccupation with character in Ibsen is his concern lest the plays be taken as pompous, humorless masterpieces. Since he was in part responsible for the picture of Ibsen as a bearded prophet with a ponderous moral message, he is now anxious to stress Ibsen's humor and to show that all the plays are full of vitality and human life.

> I beg the conventional stage manager to treat Ibsen as comedy. That will not get the business right; but it will be better than the tragedy plan . . . But the Ibsenite actor marks the speeches which are beyond him by a sudden access of pathetic sentimentality and an intense consciousness of Ibsen's greatness. No doubt this devotional plan lets the earnestness of the representation down less than the sceptical one; yet its effect is as false as false can be; and I am sorry to say that it is gradually establishing a funereally unreal tradition which is likely to end in making Ibsen the most portentous of stage bores.[31]

He blames this "Mesopotamian solemnity" with which Ibsen is treated on the British public, who love moralizing but cannot understand the comic spirit.[32]

Shaw finds that the only thoroughly satisfying productions of Ibsen's plays are those which create a pervasive poetic atmosphere, such as the productions of M. Lugné-Poë. For Shaw, the reform designed to bring the stage into closer connection with contemporary life was only a first step toward an ultimate goal, "an indispensable preliminary to any movement towards beauty, individuality, and imaginative setting."[33] After Ibsen, however, the photographically realistic treatment is no longer desirable.

Besides, there has come along the terrible Ibsen . . . the atmosphere of poetry, imagination, tragedy, irony, pity, terror, and all the rest of it, suddenly rising from the theatre from which they had been swept . . . The drawing-room comedy of furniture and manners, with a tastefully conducted intrigue as a pretext, is as dead as Donizetti and deader.[34]

A long review of the Paris production of *Peer Gynt* in 1896 presents striking evidence that Shaw was sensitive to the poetry and myth in Ibsen and that he could write a close analysis of the sort of play that he supposedly could not even understand.

Peer Gynt will finally smash anti-Ibsenism in Europe, because Peer is everybody's hero. He has the same effect on the imagination that Hamlet, Faust, and Mozart's Don Juan have had. Thousands of people who will never read another line of Ibsen will read Peer Gynt again and again; and millions will be conscious of him as part of the poetic currency of the world without reading him at all . . . Nobody who is susceptible to legendary poetry can escape the spell if he once opens the book.[35]

The summary of *Peer Gynt* in *The Quintessence of Ibsenism* is abstract; the later review is full of concrete detail and vivid realization of character and situation, and shows an unusual understanding and appreciation of the symbolism.

In *Our Theatres in the Nineties*, the critical orientation centers around the play itself—the organization of its elements, its mood, and its artistic effect. At the same time Shaw continues his development of the principal idea in *The Quintessence of Ibsenism*— the effect of Ibsen on the audience. This was Shaw's special province as a critic; he had an intuitive sense of what was important at the time that it was happening. He knew the British theatre and its audience so thoroughly that he was able to prophesy with great accuracy the effect Ibsen would have on future trends and developments. Shaw was the historian of the stage for his own age, a task which demands a critic with a highly sensitive response to audience reaction and with a long view of development within an art form. He perceived that the immediate success or failure of Ibsen was relatively unimportant; what mattered was his ultimate influence on public taste.

When Mr. Charrington produced Ibsen's Doll's House at the Royalty in 1889, he smashed up the British drama of the eighties. Not that the public liked Ibsen: he was infinitely too good for that. But the practical business point is not how people liked Ibsen, but how they liked Byron, Sardou, and Tom Taylor after Ibsen . . . Never mind whether these experiments were pecuniary successes or not: the question is how far they altered the fashion in pecuniarily successful pieces . . . The change is evident at once. In short, a modern manager need not produce The Wild Duck; but he must be very careful not to produce a play which will seem insipid and old-fashioned to playgoers who have seen The Wild Duck, even though they may have hissed it.[36]

Shaw's Ibsen criticism in *Our Theatres in the Nineties* makes up for most of the deficiencies of *The Quintessence of Ibsenism*. The style is also improved; instead of a colorless and monotonous rhetoric, we now find sentences that are terse, logical, yet sinewy and rhythmic, packed with specific details and concrete illustration.

The final stage of Shaw's Ibsen criticism is found in the *Prefaces*, which include prefaces to Shaw's own plays, novels, and essays and prefaces to works by other authors, such as plays by Brieux. The comments on Ibsen which we find here are less systematic than those in the reviews, since his method is now discursive and his range of subject matter unbounded. More often than not, he mentions Ibsen's name only in passing or uses him to illustrate a point at issue. There are, nevertheless, enough references scattered throughout the *Prefaces* to bear witness to his continuing interest in Ibsen and to warrant a formulation of his final estimate of a writer whom he had studied and admired for many years. The *Prefaces* date from 1893 to 1933, but most of them were written in the twentieth century, and the Ibsen criticism they contain is in large part later than any of Shaw's other writings on Ibsen, except the additions to the second edition of *The Quintessence of Ibsenism* in 1913.

There is now an entirely new relationship between the critic and the author criticized; Shaw the world-famous modern dramatist looks back into the nineteenth century at the old Norwegian master whom he revered in his younger days and whom he still admires—with reservations. These reservations become the substance of his final estimate of Ibsen. Shaw is no longer the young socialist championing a revolutionary new writer in the battle of the Ancients and the Moderns, for the Moderns have become Ancient already. Shaw, who was then the eager disciple, is now himself the master; he is not as interested in Ibsen as he is in his own theories of the drama; and, where these theories come into conflict with Ibsen's practice, he is openly critical.

In the *Prefaces*, Ibsen is seen as a necessary stage in the evolution of the drama and of Shaw's own evolution as a dramatist. But the Ibsen period is now past history, and Shaw can now recognize more clearly Ibsen's limitations and shortcomings and measure his debt to the past and his relation to what came before him as well as to what came after him. Although Shaw still feels the genius of Ibsen, he has a sense of superiority in the light of the progress made since those bygone days.

In *The Quintessence of Ibsenism*, Shaw stressed the novelty of Ibsen's ideas and techniques and suggested what they would mean for the future; the twentieth century has seen these new developments quickly incorporated into European dramatic culture and then soon outdistanced by still newer modes of thought and expression. In the *Prefaces*, Shaw places Ibsen back in the perspective of the nineteenth century and in relation to his antecedents; he is less anxious to dwell on Ibsen's descendents, among whom he feels he has been classed too long, even after he has come of age.

It is easy to understand why Shaw, establishing his own reputation as a playwright, would be concerned to dissociate himself from an older and more famous author under whose influence he had begun writing plays and whose cause he had argued with enthusiasm. When the critics accused him of being nothing more than an imitator of Ibsen, a belief which Shaw himself had fostered, it is only natural that he would deny such an influence and gradually attempt to set himself up in a position of equality with and even superiority to the master. The reviewers of his first play, *Widowers' Houses*, labeled him "the London Ibsen" and "the high priest of Ibsenism." As early as 1893 he was trying to emancipate himself.

> Now the first two acts of Widowers' Houses were written in 1885 when I knew nothing about Ibsen . . . There is not one idea in the play that cannot be more easily referred to half a dozen English writers than to Ibsen; whilst his peculiar retrospective method, by which his plays are made to turn about events supposed to have happened before the rise of the curtain, there is not a trace in my work.[37]

Shaw's chief method of repudiating Ibsen's influence is to show that he found or could have found the same inspiration in English writers: the ideas on heredity in Spencer, Darwin, and Huxley; the ideas on the emancipation of women in Mary Wollstonecraft and Mill; and the complex characters in George Eliot and Meredith. He tries to re-establish himself in the English tradition and is at pains to deny any corruption by foreign ideas. It is interesting to note that, in his return to the British tradition, he aligns himself with the novelists. He tells us that a minor Irish writer, Charles Lever, gave him many of the ideas that critics attribute to Ibsen's influence, and praises Samuel Butler as his real inspiration.

> It drives one almost to despair of English literature when one sees so extraordinary a study of English life as Butler's posthumous Way of All Flesh making so little impression that when, some years later, I produce plays in which Butler's extraordinarily fresh, free, and future-piercing suggestions have an obvious share, I am met with nothing but vague cacklings about Ibsen and Nietzsche.[38]

We also find a debunking of the influence that Ibsen's social dramas were reputed to have on Shaw.

> The revolt of the Life Force against ready-made morality in the nineteenth century was not the work of a Norwegian microbe, but would have worked itself into expression in English literature had Norway never existed. In fact, when Miss Lord's translation of A Doll's House appeared . . . its novelty as a morally original study of marriage did not stagger me as it staggered Europe . . . Indeed I concerned myself very little about Ibsen until, later on, William Archer translated Peter Gynt to me *viva voce*, when the magic of the great poet opened my eyes in a flash to the importance of the social philosopher.[39]

In the Preface to *Three Plays by Brieux*, Shaw explained how he first came under the influence of and then rejected the naturalistic movement with which Ibsen was sometimes associated because of *Ghosts*. Shaw regarded this movement as a necessary reaction against taboo, especially sexual taboo; he felt these social restrictions could best be destroyed by shock treatment—by mentioning forbidden subjects. Yet, at the same time, he recognized that such scientific natural history was in spirit anti-artistic. Instead of works of literary art, the movement produced things that really happen, the accidental rather than the probable, the sordid rather than the normal, the extreme rather than the mean. In the *Brieux* Preface, he condemned this movement for its deviation from everyday reality.

In his moderate approach, in his first tentative compromise with Naturalism and then his final rejection of it, Shaw follows the time-honored practice of many English writers. Although he calls Ibsen and Zola the best representatives of this school, even they have serious limitations and cannot be considered as models.

> Their imitators assumed that unmentionability was an end in itself—that to be decent was to be out of the movement. Zola and Ibsen could not, of course, be confined to mere reaction against taboo. Ibsen was to the last fascinating and full of strange moving beauty; and Zola often broke into sentimental romance. But neither Ibsen nor Zola, after they once took in hand the work of unmasking the idols of the bourgeoisie, ever again wrote a happy or pleasant play or novel.[40]

Shaw finds himself in reaction against the reaction. He calls Ibsen bitter and hopeless and regards his works as morbid and negative. Thus he reaffirms the English belief that literature should, on the whole, be pleasant and contain positive values, such as Shaw's own faith in the Life Force and Creative Evolution.

In *The Quintessence of Ibsenism* Shaw had proclaimed the originality of Ibsen's technique; in the *Prefaces* he points out the residue of mechanical tricks and devices that still remains at the core of Ibsen's work—"melodramatic forgeries, spinal diseases, and suicides."[41] He postulates the everyday, the average, and the usual as the correct view of human nature and the natural. Since it is one of his cardinal principles that changes in technique follow changes in subject matter, the technique of the drama should be modified in accordance with this new concept of real life. Once the sordid and violent subjects of Naturalism are excluded as unnatural and negligible accidents, the melodramatic technique used to dramatize these subjects will disappear and a new dramatic method will evolve. Since the everyday theory of nature rules out not only suicide but any violent form of death, Shaw finds Ibsen especially unacceptable in his handling of the dénouement.

> The tragedy of Hedda in real life is not that she commits suicide but that she continues to live . . . The tragedy of modern life is that nothing happens, and that the resultant dullness does not kill . . . In Ibsen's works we find the old traditions and the new conditions struggling in the same play . . . Not only is the tradition of the catastrophe unsuitable to modern studies of life: the tradition of an ending, happy or the reverse, is equally unworkable. The moment the dramatist gives up accidents and catastrophes, and takes "slices of life" as his material, he finds himself committed to plays that have no endings.[42]

Shaw had once extolled the rejuvenating effect which Ibsen had on the English drama of the 1890s. With the passage of time, he recognized another less beneficent effect; he perceived that certain British playwrights, such as Pinero and Jones, adopted superficial aspects of Ibsen's work without the real Ibsen spirit, and turned out spurious problem plays which seemed daring and modern to contemporary audiences, but were in reality a very old commodity dressed up in fancy new clothes.

> I did not find that matters were improved by the lady pretending to be "a woman with a past," violently oversexed, or the play being called a problem play . . . In fact these so-called problem plays invariably depended for their dramatic interest on foregone conclusions of the most heartwearying conventionality concerning sexual morality. The authors had no problematic views: all they wanted was to capture some of the fascination of Ibsen. It seemed to them that most of Ibsen's heroines were naughty ladies. And they tried to produce Ibsen plays by making their heroines naughty. But they took great care to make them pretty and expensively dressed. Thus the pseudo-Ibsen play was nothing but the ordinary sensuous ritual of the stage become as frankly pornographic as good manners allowed.[43]

Shaw was thinking in particular of Pinero and his heroines with a past—Mrs. Tanqueray, Mrs. Ebbsmith, and the rest. He did not hold Ibsen guilty of sensationalism, but he realized that Ibsen's treatment of women, marriage, and love had a negative as well as a positive influence on the English drama.[44]

Shaw had for Ibsen a lifelong admiration; but his attitude was never fixed and dogmatic, but always dynamic and changing. He did not see in Ibsen only the didactic social reformer with an awful frown; with most modern critics, he would call *Peer Gynt* Ibsen's supreme work. As a study of Ibsen's impact and influence on the English drama, Shaw's criticism is an invaluable document of literary history.

NOTES

1. Henrik Ibsen, quoted in Miriam A. Franc, *Ibsen in England* (Boston: The Four Seas Co., 1919), 34.
2. Miriam A. Franc, *Ibsen in England* (New York: Scribner's, 1908), 243.
3. Ibid., 35.
4. James Huneker, *Iconoclasts: A Book of Dramatists* (New York: Scribner's, 1908), quoted in Louis Kronenberger, ed., *George Bernard Show: A Critical Survey* (Cleveland and New York: World Publishing Co., 1953), 12.
5. Franc, 29.
6. Ronald Peacock, *The Poet in the Theatre* (New York: Harcourt, Brace, and Company, 1946), 79.
7. Ibid., 82.
8. T. S. Eliot, *Selected Essays 1917-1932* (New York: Harcourt, Brace, and Company, 1932), 38.
9. Raymond Williams, *Drama from Ibsen to Eliot* (London: Oxford University Press, 1952), 138.
10. Eric Bentley, *Bernard Shaw* (Norfolk, Conn.: New Directions Books, 1947), 116–17.
11. Martin Lamm, *Modern Drama*, trans. Karin Elliott (Oxford: Blackwell, 1952), 252–53.
12. Since my article appeared in 1963, later scholarship and critical writing have moved in the same direction and continued the rehabilitation of Shaw as a critic of Ibsen. See J.L. Wisenthal, "Shaw and Ibsen," in *Shaw and Ibsen: Bernard Shaw's* The Quintessence of Ibsenism *and Related Writings*, ed. J.L. Wisenthal (Toronto: University of Toronto Press, 1979), 3–73; Keith M. May, *Ibsen and Shaw* (N.Y.: St. Martin's Press, 1985); Michael Holroyd, *Bernard Shaw: Volume I, 1856-1898.* (London: Chatto & Windus, 1988), 198–203; Katherine E. Kelly, "Imprinting the Stage: Shaw and the Publishing Trade, 1883–1903," 32–34, and Charles A. Berst, "New Theatres for Old," 55–61, both in *Cambridge Companion to George Bernard Shaw*, ed. Christopher Innes (Cambridge: Cambridge University Press, 1998).
13. George Bernard Shaw, *Selected Prose* (New York: Dodd, Mead, 1952), 576.
14. Ibid., 622.
15. Ibid., 543
16. Ibid., 544.
17. Ibid.
18. The lack of copyright protection had contributed to the decline in the publication of plays; the introduction of adequate legal safeguards toward the end of the century was responsible for renewed interest in the publication and reading of plays. Clayton Hamilton, Introduction to Henry Arthur Jones, *Representative Plays* (Boston: Little, Brown, 1925), 1:xxiii.
19. Shaw, *Selected Prose*, 663–64.
20. Ibid., 679.
21. Ibid., 671–72.
22. Ibid., 675.
23. Ibid., 677.
24. Ibid., 680.
25. Ibid., 683.
26. Ibid., 646–47.
27. Shaw, *Our Theatres in the Nineties* (London: Constable and Company, 1931), 2:84.
28. Ibid., 2:258.
29. Ibid., 1:195.
30. Shaw, "*John Gabriel Borkman*, May 8, 1897," in *Our Theatres in the Nineties*, 3:134.
31. Ibid., 3:131.
32. *Our Theatre in the Nineties*, 3:32–33.
33. Ibid., 1:278.
34. Shaw, "*Mr. John Hare*, December 21, 1895," in *Our Theatres in the Nineties*, 1:293–94.
35. Shaw, "*Peer Gynt* in Paris, November 21, 1896," in *Our Theatres in the Nineties*, 2:60–61.
36. Shaw, "*Mr. Daly Fossilizes*, June 29, 1895," in *Our Theatres in the Nineties*, 1:173–74.

37. Shaw, Preface to *Widowers' Houses* (1893), in *Prefaces* (London: Constable and Company, 1934), 672.
38. Shaw, Preface to *Major Barbara* (1905), in *Prefaces*, 123.
39. Shaw, Preface to *The Irrational Knot* (1905), in *Prefaces*, 657.
40. Shaw, Preface to *Three Plays by Brieux* (1911), in *Prefaces*, 199.
41. Preface to *The Irrational Knot*, 657.
42. Preface to *Three Plays by Brieux*, 199–200.
43. Shaw, Preface to *Three Plays for Puritans* (1900) in *Prefaces*, 707.
44. There is an interesting parallel between Shaw's criticism of Ibsen and his own early collections of plays, *Plays: Pleasant and Unpleasant* and *Three Plays far Puritans*. The unpleasant plays represent Shaw's experiments with Naturalism, the pleasant plays his turning away from negative to positive values, and the plays for Puritans his answer to the pseudo-Ibsen sex play. The closest parallels with Ibsen's work occur in the unpleasant plays, written in 1892 and 1893 during the height of the Ibsen controversy. *Mrs. Warren's Profession*, in particular, offers many points of comparison with *Ghosts*, and comes as close as Shaw ever did to the formula of Naturalism.

Back Cover of *Pchela (The Bee)*, from *Blood and Laughter: Caricatures from the 1905 Revolution*

THE APOCALYPTIC MODE AND THE TERROR OF HISTORY:
TURN-OF-THE-CENTURY RUSSIAN AND
POLISH MILLENARIAN DRAMA

History has meaning only because it ends.
Nikolai Berdyaev, *The Russian Idea*

1. THE APOCALYPTIC SENSIBILITY

On December 26, 1908, the poet and playwright Alexander Blok made the following entry in his notebook: "Feeling of catastrophe, disease, anxiety, rupture (humankind like people next to a bomb). The bomb was planted by history and split everything."[1]

This bomb of history gave rise to a sense of impending apocalypse that marked Russian society from the 1890s to 1917 and produced a vast outpouring of eschatological poems, novels, plays, painting, music, and essays.[2] The immediate context was the Russo-Japanese War (1904–5) and the Revolution of 1905, although the Slavic culture of last things had roots going back several centuries. Russians had habitually turned to apocalyptic prophecies about the Antichrist in times of social upheaval.[3] During the partitions of their country, captive Poles, particularly those living under the czarist yoke, also cultivated the apocalyptic sensibility and impatiently awaited the catastrophic end of the Russian Empire, which would bring them liberty.

Unlike Western European writers at the turn of the century for whom tales of the Antichrist and the coming end were, for the most part, merely poetic fictions in an apparently stable bourgeois society that put its faith in progress, the Polish and Russian apocalypticists believed in the imminent destruction of the present world. Living through the violent death throes of a tottering *ancien régime*, they knew what Mircea Eliade calls the "terror of history" that always gives rise to millenarian movements and apocalyptic visions. "Paradise will be regained," Eliade points out. "All millenarian and eschatological movements show signs of optimism. They react against the terror of history with a force which only utter despair can call forth."[4]

The idea of gradualism and continuity has held sway in the West, at least since the French Revolution, but Russian thinking embraced the concept of the new as a radical break with the past, a total eschatological change, producing the either/or mentality of apocalypticism.[5] The antecedents for Russian messianic sensibility go back to the fall of Constantinople in 1453, which, in the view of the sacred historiographers, served as a basis for belief in Moscow's divinely chosen position as the Third Rome. What followed for the faithful was an unending battle against the new, the secular, and the Western. As a result of the Great Schism in the seventeenth century, the Old Believers, who refused to accept the modernized Orthodox Church promoted by the czar, were persecuted by the state. Their former Third Rome messianism transformed into an apocalyptic denunciation of Moscow as "the Whore of Babylon."

Peter the Great's enforced Westernizing led to nostalgic visions of Holy Rus, an atemporal, transcendental land of salvation opposed to the materialistic czarist

–*Theater* 29, no. 3 (Winter 1999): 47–70.

empire mired in the sin and corruption of historical time. Because present events were interpreted as echoing the sacral past, the seventeenth-century peasant revolt of Stenka Razin and all subsequent popular anti-czarist uprisings came to be seen as struggles against the Antichrist. Convinced of the coming *ekpyrosis* (great fire)—perceived as a counterpart to the *kataklysmos* (great flood)—Old Believers burned themselves alive, hoping to make contact with eternity through a fiery death.

In *The Diary of a Writer*, Dostoyevsky predicted that "the Antichrist is coming to us! He is coming! And the end is near—nearer than they think," and in *The Devils*, he warned that "the end of the century will be marked by a calamity, the likes of which has never yet occurred."[6] Some years later the Russian apocalyptic mood was given definitive expression by the philosopher and poet Vladimir Solovyov (1853-1900). In his poem of 1894, "Panmongolism" he described the invasion of Russia by Mongolian hordes—a high-art version of the theme that soon began appearing in popular fiction as the "yellow peril." Decadent European civilization will be destroyed by the barbarians from the East when divine retribution for her sins is visited on Moscow, the Third Rome, which will fall as surely as did Byzantium, the Second Rome. In his posthumous testament, *The Tale about the Antichrist* (1900), Solovyov predicts war and world catastrophe, chaos and revolution, and the eventual coming of the Antichrist—perhaps disguised as materialistic Western civilization and bourgeois capitalism. In the inevitable clash between good and evil, cleansing fires will burn away the old world and give rise to a new one.[7]

In Russia at the turn of the century, both Christian mystics and Marxist utopians were millenarians expecting a radical break with the past. Both eagerly anticipated the end of the world, but each located the agency of the final reckoning in a different place. The apocalyptic Christians viewed history as determined, from the outside, by God, while the utopian Marxists made human beings the source of their own transformations through violent change within history.

The religious philosopher Nikolai Berdyaev (1874-1948), a follower of Dostoyevsky and former Marxist who initially welcomed the Revolution, maintained that "Russians are apocalypticists or nihilists. Russia is an apocalyptic revolt against antiquity (Spengler). This means that the Russian people, in accordance with their metaphysical nature and vocation in the world, are a people of the end."[8] Overcome by a sense of impending catastrophe, preachers of the end rose up in all classes of Russian society.

2. 1905

As the czarist empire started to crumble, apocalypse suddenly seemed immanent in contemporary history, and Revelation became the basic text of the times. The historical events of the Revolution of 1905 were viewed as fulfilling biblical prophecies and interpreted in the light of eschatological symbolism; the imagery, dramatic properties, and stage effects of the New Testament apocalypse were read into them.[9]

After the catastrophic defeats of the czarist forces in the Russo-Japanese War, revolution flared up throughout the empire during the entire year of 1905. For a while it seemed that autocracy might fall, but in the end the rebellion was brutally put down, and the repression that followed was savage. For writers and artists in Russia and Poland, 1905 was a time first of hope, then of despair, of ecstatic longing for a purifying apocalypse and horror at the ruthless crushing of the masses' struggle for freedom.

Revolution, the central event in modern Slavic messianic thought, fascinated the fin de siècle poets, giving rise to the millennial expectations expressed in the works of Andrei Bely, Alexander Blok, and Tadeusz Miciński, all of whom frequented Vyacheslav Ivanov's "tower" (his St. Petersburg seventh-floor penthouse), then the center of Russian apocalypticism. But with the crushing of the Revolution of 1905, the hopes of these poets seemed betrayed, leading to terrifying visions of the future instead of joyous anticipations of a New Jerusalem.

The nightmare imagery of bloodshed, madness, and death connected with the events of 1905 is powerfully evoked in the work of the Russian artists and illustrators contributing to the revolutionary satirical journals that sprang up at that time, often to be quickly suppressed by the censor and forced to go underground. With such titles as *Vampire, Bugbear, Machine Gun, Arrows, Octopus, Hell-Post, Bombs, Flame*, and *Storm Wood*, these journals questioned the authority of the czar, his ministers, and the government, and revealed the savagery with which the people's demands were met. The stark, strident illustrations, whose imagery often comes from Revelation, convey the mood of the times from the perspective of those in revolt, the downtrodden and oppressed screaming in pain.[10] By positing the rapidly approaching end of human history and the reuniting of the temporal with the eternal, the eschatological sensibility imparted an urgent expectancy to the human drama. Anticipations of such a spectacular denouement to the *theatrum mundi* could not fail to have repercussions on works for the stage.

As the satirical posters powerfully demonstrate, the visual arts were able to represent directly the most sweeping apocalyptic events; so could poetry and fiction. Theatre, on the other hand, was more suited to a portrayal of waiting for the apocalypse or the Antichrist than to actually showing "last things." Waiting itself—most often for someone or something that never appears—becomes a major thematic and structural motif. The feared, yet longed for, final event draws near, but does not come.

3. BELY'S WAITING FOR THE ANTICHRIST

Andrei Bely, chief representative of the Russian eschatological mode, proclaimed "the approaching End of Universal History" and called for the spiritual transformation of the world. He saw himself sometimes as a Christ figure, sometimes as the "white horseman"—offspring of the "Woman Clothed with the Sun" of Revelation, who had come to reign victorious over the new era. And he created the drama of waiting for the Antichrist.

Before writing his two apocalyptic novels, *The Silver Dove* (1910) and *Petersburg* (1913), Bely experimented with the idea of a modern *mysterium*. He first conceived this work in 1898, anticipating by two years Solovyov's "A Tale about the Antichrist." The only two completed fragments of Bely's projected mystery play—*Jaws of Night* (1898) and *He Who Has Come* (1903)—have as their theme "the coming of the Antichrist under the mask of Christ."[11]

At the age of seventeen on the Tuesday of Passion Week in 1898, Bely had a vision in church that provided the inspiration for his play: "It was as if one wall of the church opened into the void. I saw the End (I don't know of what—my life or the world's), but it was as if the road of history rested upon two domes—upon a Temple; and crowds of people thronged toward it. To myself, I called the Temple I saw the Temple of Glory and it seemed to me that Antichrist was threatening this Temple. I ran out of the church like a madman. [. . .] In the evening in my little room, I drafted the plan for a mystery drama."[12]

Although Bely's *mysterium* is set in the early Christian period, its portrayal of spiritual confusion, hearkening unto false prophets, and feverish expectation of the end are direct reflections of the temper of the poet's own times. "The gulf over which we are hanging," Bely declared, "is deeper and darker than we think."[13] In the two fragments, the early Christians awaiting the coming of the Messiah are overcome by the "sensation of the abyss." Dread, doubt, and satanic laughter subvert what should be their joyous anticipation of the Second Coming. Before the glow of a new dawn comes the glacial darkness ushered in by the reign of the Antichrist, the appearance of false messiahs, and the return to primordial chaos.

Jaws of Night and *He Who Has Come* are dramas of eschatological premonition, played out in murky interstellar space and indeterminate time. Except for interminable waiting for the redeemer—who may be no redeemer, who may never come, or who may already have come unnoticed—they have no action. Members of the commune awaiting the end fall into dissension over whether "He Who Has Come" is Christ or Antichrist, and although the prophet Ilya declares that the millennium has already begun, life goes on as before, and the waiting continues. Since the sun has been extinguished and all entities subjected to the power of negation, night and day are no longer distinguishable. Darkness prevails in this battle between spiritual enlightenment and the forces of evil. The action is concentrated in the light given off by different objects and personalities. But all signs are ambivalent.

The bold theatrical concept and unorthodox Gnostic theology of Bely's Antichrist fragments made them seem more literary than theatrical and prevented even the most daring directors from attempting to perform them. No Symbolist plays had yet been staged in Russia. The first such production took place in 1904 when the Moscow Art Theatre—at Chekhov's urging—presented Maurice Maeterlinck's three one-act plays: *The Blind*, *Interior*, and *The Intruder*. The Polish theatre was somewhat more advanced in its readiness to put on dramas in the new mode; the plays of Stanisław Wyspiański began to be staged as early as 1898, but often in truncated form. Particularly in Cracow (in the liberal Austro-Hungarian sector of partitioned Poland), the Polish theatre enjoyed a relative freedom that permitted some experimentation and allowed the first staging of Adam Mickiewicz's great national drama, *Forefathers' Eve*. The national Romantic tradition, dominant in Catholic Poland, was receptive to the apocalyptic mode.

4. MILLENNIAL PLAYHOUSES

Because of strict political and religious censorship in czarist Russia and the inherent incompatibility of "last things" with the restrictive conventions of an illusionistic stage, few apocalyptic dramas were written (in comparison to the torrents of poetry and prose), and none of these could be performed until after the 1917 Revolution. But although the prevailing mode in Russian theatre at the turn of the century was realistic, Symbolism was the innovative new movement with international connections and prestige. Through their theoretical writing and activity, Blok, Bely, and Briusov had an impact on the theatre that far transcended the marginal status of their plays.

In addition to problems with censorship, theatrical resources and imagination lagged behind the playwrights' vision. In their quest for a theatre-temple, the apocalypticists rejected not only the nineteenth-century theatre of entertainment but also Naturalism as both worldview and dramatic technique, objecting to its attempted confinement of the eternal spirit to a narrow box. Instead they made grandiose plans to establish sacral playing areas on mountain summits and in holy places. Wyspiański proposed a stage on "sacred national soil" next to Wawel Royal Castle and dreamed of creating an enormous theatre under the open skies in the Tatra Mountains, with their lofty peaks serving as the wings and the deep blue waters of a crater lake evoking the auditorium. In the same Polish mountain range, associated by poetic analogy with the Himalayas and the origins of ancient Indian religions, Miciński called for the creation of a universal temple of beauty, where Sanskrit dramas such as *Shakuntala* could be performed, and "where in an amphitheatre of the dead and the living, carved in the mountains, under the azure sky and among the deep forests, there will be revealed the mysteries of life on earth."[14]

A few years later the Russian composer and mystic Alexander Scriabin first conceived the idea for a vast *mysterium*, which would represent a synthesis of the arts of music, song, dance, and theatre, and began composing a cosmic symphony of sounds, lights, colors, scents, and tastes. Designed to usher in the end of the world in a triumphal conflagration, Scriabin's *mysterium* was to be given on the banks of the Ganges or at the foot of the Himalayas (the London theosophists recommended Darjeeling). Sunrise and sunset would serve as elements of the stage setting, bells would be suspended from clouds over the mountains, and thousands of spectators would sit in a huge semicircular auditorium with spiral steps facing a semicircle of reflecting water.

The composer had been deeply impressed by the rhythmic rendering of a chorus from *Antigone* presented at Vsevolod Meyerhold's studio in 1913 and hoped to use the same technique.[15] As part of his work on the *mysterium*, Scriabin studied Sanskrit, became a disciple of Yogi Ram Charak, and planned a trip to India in the winter of 1914, buying a white suit and pith helmet and spending hours in the sun to prepare himself for the tropical climate. Although he continued to work on the project until his death in 1915, Scriabin completed only a fragmentary sketch of the Prefatory Action, which was to last seven days: at the end of the twelfth hour of the seventh day, a new humanity, combining male and female traits, would be born. The *mysterium* itself was never realized.[16]

The failure of these visionary artists to create—except in their imaginations—a feasible new playing area outside the theatre of commerce might at first suggest that their dream was futile and unproductive. But if the theatre could not be moved to the mountains and holy places, at least the mountains and holy places could be brought into the theatre. In emulation of Greek, medieval, and Indian models, Polish dramatists Wyspiański and Miciński forged a paradigm of the theatre-temple that transformed the secular stage into a sacred arena for ritual performance. They were heirs of the Romantic era, when Poles developed a messianic vision of their country's destiny, according to which Poland, the Christ of nations, had been chosen by God to fulfill a higher purpose. Martyred Poland would now redeem Europe, as she had already once saved Christianity from the Turkish threat in 1683 by lifting the siege of Vienna. In Eastern Europe Symbolism was almost always tied to nationalism, native folk traditions, and the mother tongue, as opposed to the aim of the occupying forces to impose an alien culture. The theatre was a primary place in which resistance could be openly manifested. Thus, for Poles the apocalyptic was invariably linked to the idea of gaining freedom for their country from the Russians, from the Prussians, and from the Austrians.

5. WYSPIAŃSKI'S APOCALYPSE: *ACROPOLIS* (1903)

At the turn of the century Wyspiański transformed this mythic reading of Polish history into an apocalyptic plot. Seeing the world and its history as a whole, rather than scientifically compartmentalized, Wyspiański made daring leaps between past and present times. Positivism, which had gained dominance in the second half of the nineteenth century, was the standard against which he and other Symbolists reacted. The apocalyptic represented a return to medieval thinking, bypassing the rationalism of logical cause and effect. In his drama of death and rebirth, *Acropolis* (written in 1903, but not performed in its original form until 1926), Wyspiański fashioned a syncretism of Judaic, Greek, and Christian religious mythology through a series of correspondences—a central device of apocalyptic poetics—whereby the Old Testament, Homer, and Polish history were fused in an eternal moment.[17]

By setting *Acropolis* in Wawel Royal Castel and Cathedral, overlooking the city of Cracow and the river Vistula, Wyspiański, who had a double vocation as painter and playwright, was able to make the entire action of the drama grow out of the visual images associated with the sacral place. Instead of human characters (none ever appears in the work), sculptured figures in wood and marble and heroes woven on tapestries depicting scenes from the Bible and Homer come to life and reenact their eternal stories at the magical hour of midnight preceding Easter Sunday.

Utilizing the syncretic theory advanced by Edouard Schuré that all known religions contain one and the same esoteric doctrine, Wyspiański links Easter to pagan rites of seasonal renewal and the primordial rhythms of nature. By occult analogy, Poland is the living Troy, Wawel becomes the Acropolis on the holy hill of Athens, and the sacred rivers Jordan and Scamander flow again in the waters of the Vistula. The present reenacts the past. Resurrection, awaited as a spiritual, biological, and national event, follows an apocalyptic ending, when, amidst thunder and the extinction of the old world, a luminous Christ-Apollo appears at dawn in the chariot of the sun drawn by four white horses to the pealing of the cathedral bells.[18]

6. SCIENCE FICTION AND THE APOCALYPSE: BRIUSOV'S *THE EARTH* (1904) AND STANISLAVSKY'S *THE COMET* (1908)

The Russian avant-garde produced a form of apocalyptic drama, futurological and cautionary in nature, that deals with the extinction of life on earth due to a great catastrophe brought about by misguided faith or by innovations in science and technology. This drama took the form of science fiction, which, as David Ketterer writes, is the "purest outlet" for the apocalyptic imagination.[19] Valerii Briusov, leader of the Russian Symbolists, anti-Naturalist theatrical theorist, and Meyerhold's dramaturg, took a cool, ironic stance on the approaching end of the world. He wrote a number of science fiction stories and plays, including *The World of Seven Generations* (1923), named after a comet destined to collide with earth and destroy human civilization.[20]

In his essay about Alexander Blok, Briusov interpreted the apparent failure of the apocalypse as the cause of the sardonic mood of the time: "Those same feelings which the whole of Europe had experienced around the year 1000 A.D., when it expected the end of the world and the Last Judgment, were relived in the circle of young Moscow mystics. But the fearful time came and went and their prophecies had not come true.

A period of disillusion and disbelief followed, which led them at times to mock what they had once held sacred."[21] Sharing the French decadents' feeling of crisis and consciousness of standing at a turning point in history, the Russian poet welcomed the demise of an over-refined civilization at the end of its life span.

As a member of a degenerate, exhausted culture, Briusov identified his society with the later years of the Roman Empire, when the barbarians were at the gates, and he longed for the destruction that the modern Goths would bring, even if that meant his own annihilation, which perhaps he longed for most of all. For the Russian intelligentsia, the Russo-Japanese War and the Revolution of 1905 made the coming of barbarians a reality. Briusov equated their arrival with the triumph of socialism, which he welcomed, and in 1904–5 he wrote essays, stories, and poems in which revolution is celebrated as the unleashing of a destructive, rebarbarizing force that will cause humanity's regression to a primitive state of nature.

The death of culture and the end of history are the themes of Briusov's major work for the stage, *The Earth*, a proto-science-fiction drama subtitled *A Tragedy of Future Times*. First conceived in 1890 and completed in 1904, *The Earth* depicts the self-destruction of an advanced technological civilization after humankind has cut itself off from the natural world by creating a huge enclosed city with a special roof that blocks out the sky and air. One of the strange sects to spring up in this artificial atmosphere is the Order of Deliverers, who worship death and darkness, hoping to free humanity from the scourge of life and all its earthly passions. A rival group, led by a sage, urges a return to the sun and stars that must inevitably shine above the black dome that shuts them in. Aspiring to restore humanity to its rightful place in the universe, the sage actually brings about the apocalypse when he orders the dome to be slid back. The last words of the final stage direction read: "The entire hall, now silenced, turns into a cemetery of motionless wizened bodies upon which there shines through the open dome the deep sky and, like an angel blowing a golden trumpet, the blazing sun."[22]

In his search for new forms, Konstantin Stanislavsky evidently looked to Briusov for direction and, under the influence of *The Earth*, began work on an apocalyptic drama, *The Comet, a Fantasy in Four Acts* (1908), portraying the final day of life on earth. Stanislavsky's play, of which only some fragments of act two exist, begins at the point where Briusov's ends, with the final catastrophe. This act, depicting the cataclysm that has struck humanity, opens with the following stage direction:

> The comet falls to earth and destroys everything, it kills all the people except two: A Man (a miner) and An Old Woman. The action takes place at a cross-roads, amidst debris, scorched ruins, and scattered bodies. In the background there is the office of a joint-stock company of mines. From the half-open door there protrude the legs of a corpse outstretched in the doorway. An on-duty policeman lies in the middle of the street. The windows are broken. A coach for hire—the coachman has fallen from the coach box and lies on the sidewalk. The fare lies tipped backwards in the coach. Total silence. The wind raises some papers—money and sometimes the flaps on the policeman's uniform.[23]

Act one evidently showed the corrupt way of life on earth—drunken slaves worshipping their oppressors—for which divine retribution has been taken. "The planets have descended to the earth. They have burned away and wiped out the old life."[24] The last remaining Man curses the old world of injustice and calls for freedom from the oppressive system that kept the slaves working underground for their masters and searches for another living soul with whom he can start a new life. There is a cry from a window, where a young woman appears. At sunset, as the tail of the comet recedes, the Last Man calls out, "You who are living respond!"[25]

7. PROMETHEUS IN A GARBAGE CAN: MICIŃSKI'S *THE REVOLT OF THE POTEMKIN* (1905)

By its very nature the turn of the century points in two different directions. Bely described the sense of eschatological tension felt by members of his generation in the following terms: "The failure of the old ways is experienced as the End of the World; the tidings of the new era—as the Second Coming. We sensed the apocalyptic rhythm of the time. Towards the Beginning we strive through the End."[26] The apocalypse awaited by the Russian and Polish Symbolists was expected to bring not only the end of an old world, but also the beginning of a new age—in Mircea Eliade's words, "the end of one humanity, followed by the apparition of a new humanity."[27]

It is only natural that apocalyptic dramatists caught between two epochs should make extensive use of dualistic and antithetical pairs—such as Christ and Antichrist, birth and death, light and dark, heights and depths (found throughout Revelation)—and strive for unity of polar opposites. What the fifteenth-century mystic, churchman, philosopher, mathematician, and political theorist, Nicholas of Cusa, called *coincidentia oppositorum* (or union of contraries in God) became an essential technique whereby the mystery of totality finds affirmation and "ultimate reality is defined by pairs of opposites."[28]

Nowhere is this reliance on duality more apparent than in Tadeusz Miciński's vast five-act epic, *The Revolt of the Potemkin*. Begun at the time of the mutiny, completed within a few months, and published in 1906 at the author's expense, Miciński's *Potemkin* is the first and strangest of twentieth-century apocalyptic dramas dealing with war and revolution—a subgenre that includes Leonid Andreyev's *King Hunger* (1908), Carl Hauptmann's *War: A Te Deum* (1914), and Karl Kraus's *Last Days of Mankind* (1919).

Weird, misshapen, and seemingly unstageable, Miciński's play includes a cast of hundreds of sailors, Cossacks, and beggars, a pornographic Easter egg, the port of Odessa on fire, a putrescent man in the garbage can (half a century before Beckett's *Endgame*), the ghost of the infant Dalai Lama, and a version of the Whore of Babylon, the Syphilitic Madonna. The Polish poet's visionary drama proved too radical, in both form and content, to gain any hearing in the author's lifetime, but its startling mixture of revolutionary politics and Eastern mysticism, piety and eroticism, documentary history and occult science, now strikes us as surprisingly contemporary in spirit. What once seemed a bizarre and unplayable poetic text has become an early example of total theatre—a multimedia spectacle calling upon all the resources of the modern stage.[29]

Approximately one-fourth of *The Revolt of the Potemkin* is a verbatim transcript (with only slight editorial emendations) of original Russian documents about this revolt; the author refers to his drama in the afterword as "little more than a quotation from the great document of Truth."[30] Events now known to a wide audience thanks to Eisenstein's film, such as the doctor's examining the rotten meat crawling with maggots, the covering of the protesters with a tarpaulin in preparation for their execution, the solemn procession for the funeral of Vakulinchuk—the first martyred sailor—the revolutionary council of the rebels, and the bearing of gifts to the battleship from the city in an armada of small boats, are here presented for the first time in all their historical particularity, utilizing the actual reported words of the participants.

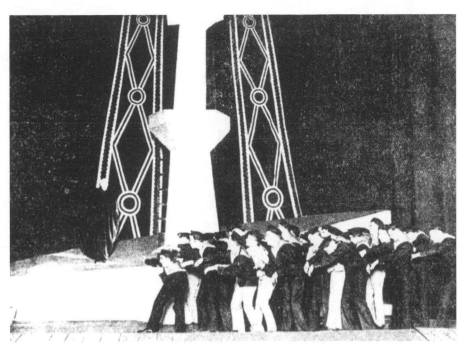

Tadeusz Miciński's *The Revolt of the Potemkin*, Boguslawski Theatre, Warsaw (1925), directed by Leon Schiller

Miciński focuses not only on the mutiny itself, but also on the social, political, and cultural contexts that produced it. Compressing historical material of epic dimensions into the first four acts of the play, he creates a vast panorama that stretches the framework of dramatic form to the breaking point. He paints a horrifying picture of inhumanity and injustice, capitalist rapacity and imperialist exploitation, and age-old superstition and barbarity. We witness the cruel military discipline in the armed forces and the atrocities of the Russo-Japanese War, the Jewish pogroms by the government-backed Black Hundreds, the punitive detachments of Cossacks terrorizing villages, and the repressive police forces breaking up factory strikes and fomenting riots.

The Revolt of the Potemkin is a cry of protest against ignorance, hatred, and war. In this respect Miciński's portrait of the times resembles the savage and grotesque caricatures of a world in flames and an empire reduced to corpses and skeletons that appeared in the revolutionary satirical journals. But he is not simply content to show the death and destruction sown by the oppressors or to urge violent retribution. Miciński's view of apocalypse is redemptive. Since the blind and unthinking mutiny that took place aboard the real battleship *Potemkin* ended in senseless defeat, Miciński argues that the entire action aboard his imaginary battleship must simultaneously be perceived from the viewpoint of a higher truth if the mutiny is to have any meaning. Thus he offers a philosophical drama that runs parallel to the documentary drama, commenting upon it and investing the realistic details with mythic significance. This symbolic dimension gives *The Revolt of the Potemkin* its unique shape. Drawing upon a vast library of mystical literature, both Christian and Eastern, Miciński creates a mythic ship burgeoning with complex symbols.

Miciński's perspective has its roots in turn-of-the-century occultism and Gnosticism. "We've got the earth, the sky, and the seas!" Matiushenko, the leader of the revolt, exclaims.[31] The entire drama is played out among the four elements and their shifting symbolism. Fire is associated with the coming apocalypse, as it had been by the seventeenth-century Old Believers, who desired that all Russia and then the whole world be destroyed by flames in order to escape the Antichrist. The burning of Odessa by the bums from the lower depths is also a self-immolating conflagration, annihilating and purifying. The sea is a source of freedom and renewal, but also the *mare tenebrarum*, a graveyard of all things, upon which sails the phantom ship of death.

In Miciński's iconography the *Potemkin* becomes a redemptive ship bearing the human soul—the soul of both the tormented individual and the entire Russian nation—through hell and purgatory on a harrowing journey of purification and enlightenment. Rather than view the mutiny from the perspective of the later, "inevitable" triumph of the Revolution (as does Eisenstein), Miciński perceives it *sub specie aeternitatis*. Miciński's boldest modification of the historical record places Lieutenant Schmidt, the idealistic martyr-hero of the Sevastopol uprising in October, aboard the *Potemkin*. Such a confluence of two separate but similar events gives the playwright as his protagonist an apostle of Christian love, suffering, and passive resistance to evil who seeks at all costs to avoid bloodshed, but proves an ineffectual and impotent leader of the Revolution.

As Schmidt's dialectical antagonist, the Polish poet chooses Wilhelm Ton, an actual officer aboard the *Potemkin* killed in the mutiny. Ton becomes in Miciński's reinterpretation a nihilistic destroyer and prime mover of revolution guided solely by cold reason. The ideological superstructure of *The Revolt of the Potemkin* takes the form of a running debate between Schmidt and Ton, representing Christ and Lucifer. Following the Gnostic myth that God and the Devil are blood brothers, Miciński develops the *coincidentia oppositorum*, central to all his work, that Lucifer—"the elder brother of Christ in his pre-eternal existence"—must complete what God alone could not successfully accomplish.[32] In turn-of-the-century eschatology, as God ceased to be regarded as the judge and became the accused, going on trial for having created an unhappy and destructive race of men, Lucifer was rehabilitated as the champion of poor and downtrodden humanity.[33]

Russian apocalypticism, as practiced by Bely or Briusov, often drew upon fears of "Asiatics," barbarians, other races. Because the notion of unity among all peoples and nations is central to Miciński's *The Revolt of the Potemkin*, the plight of the Jews as the victims of brutal pogroms is a recurring motif. The officers on the battleship, the governor of Odessa, and the waterfront bums incited by the Black Hundreds all try to make the Jews the scapegoats responsible for the uprising and the other troubles plaguing Russia, and Miciński shows how in the Russian popular imagination the Jews have been linked to Antichrist. Police and government records of the time bear out the accuracy of these charges of anti-Semitism.

Toward the end of the third act there is a moment of terrifying silence when Lieutenant Schmidt and a group of sailors holding aloft a red flag carry in the corpses of the Jews and workers killed by the Cossacks. Prominently displayed are the small coffins of the slaughtered Jewish children. Deeply moved, the living kneel down, or sit or stand by the dead. In this entirely mute scene, Miciński's use of broken human bodies—some naked, some clothed, all distorted in pain—reveals the horror of the Cossacks' violence by purely theatrical means, creating an effect as powerful and moving as Eisenstein's Odessa steps sequence.

In the mystical fifth act, a sudden shift in perspective offers a sustained view of another world. The leaders of the mutiny and the crew of the battleship, some already dead, others still alive, are seen against a cosmic landscape beyond time and space—a device first introduced by Strindberg at the end of *The Dream Play* (1902). Mysteriously transported to a "reef in the midst of the sea which in the darkness glows phosphorescently throughout its blue depths,"[34] the epileptic, Christ-like Schmidt—clinging to a rock and surrounded by strange sea monsters—describes his vision of a Tibetan journey to the mountain temples and holy places in a series of shifting, phantasmagoric pictures: mirages of the giant Himalayas rise up from the sea, the sacred city of Lhasa with its golden palaces can be seen, and the ghost of the infant Dalai Lama appears.

Schmidt's revelation (*apokalypsis*) is that of a seer who stands outside history and mediates for members of humanity still trapped within chronology. He points to the threshold city or New Jerusalem at the end of history's road, providing glimpses of an otherworldly order in the midst of worldly chaos. The apocalypse of revolution achieved through violent political means must be transformed into an apocalypse of consciousness achieved through suffering and poetic imagination.[35] Against this backdrop of eternity, the bloody searchlights of the battleship struggle to cut through the darkness, but the *Potemkin* appears to be heading straight for the reef—until at the last moment, guided by the mystic light emanating from the Dalai Lama, the phantom ship glides safely past and continues on its eternal wanderings.

At the time of its publication, the playwright Alfred Nowaczyński caustically observed that "the anarchistic element of the Russian Revolution has found its counterpart in the absolute compositional anarchy of Miciński's drama."[36] Leon Schiller, who first brought *The Revolt of the Potemkin* to the stage in 1925, more sympathetically declared of this kind of anomalous drama that the "scenic shape was a mystery for the authors themselves."[37] Schiller's production at the Bogusławski Theatre, Warsaw, was as successful as it was controversial, running for a record-breaking forty-eight performances. The two most talented designers of the period, Andrzej and Zbigniew Pronaszko, did the sets and costumes, and the musical interlude preceding the fifth act was by Karol Szymanowski, the outstanding Polish composer of the interwar years. Special agents of the government were on watch in the auditorium, fearing that radical demonstrations might be occasioned by the play's revolutionary content, while most leftists criticized the drama as being too negative and pessimistic to be effective propaganda. The play was definitively less utopian than dystopian. In its treatment of character and theme as well as in its fluid use of stage space—involving vast multiple-action scenes and huge masses of people—Miciński's polyphonic drama anticipated many aspects of German Expressionism by almost a decade.

8. ANDREYEV'S *KING HUNGER* (1908) AND PROTO-EXPRESSIONISM

Another drama of social unrest called forth by the Revolution of 1905, Leonid Andreyev's *King Hunger*, exemplifies the same apocalyptic mode as *The Revolt of the Potemkin*. Written in 1907 and published in 1908, Andreyev's play was forbidden by czarist censorship and could not be performed until after the Revolution of 1917, when it was premièred at the City Theatre in Saratov. With its monstrous machines to which men are harnessed, glaring red furnaces, and lurid urban landscape, *King Hunger* creates an image of the nightmarish metropolis as terrifying as that of *The Revolt of the Potemkin*, and the uprising of the rabble, goaded by King Hunger, recalls the drunken orgy of Miciński's waterfront bums.

Andreyev's rhythmic use of percussive noises, choral chants, and screams brings *King Hunger* even closer to the techniques of German Expressionism than *The Revolt of the Potemkin*. Unspecified as to time and place, *King Hunger* exists only in the abstract, with, on the one hand, allegorical personifications, such as Death, Time, and Hunger, and, on the other, generic groups of workingmen, rabble, and upper-class visitors, all of whom behave like automatons and deliver an exclamatory text which, for the most part, is unassigned to any individual speakers. The schematic, poster-like scenes are reminiscent of the stark, brightly colored illustrations in the revolutionary satirical journals and were an influence on the young Mayakovsky when he wrote his *Vladimir Mayakovsky: A Tragedy*, a Futurist urban apocalypse.[38] There is, however, no theme of redemption or possibility of transcendence in *King Hunger*; the abortive revolt provoked by King Hunger pits a disreputable rabble bent on vengeance against a soulless power structure that inevitably triumphs. No vision of a New Jerusalem is possible.

9. POLISH CATASTROPHISM AND KANTOR'S ENDLESS APOCALYPSE

In the Soviet Union, the triumph of communism led to the attempted elimination of the apocalyptic or its transformation into the utopian. Blok and Bely, who believed in Russia's messianic destiny, initially welcomed the Revolution as a cataclysm of purifying power that would do away with the obsolete humanist civilization of Europe and usher in the "culture of eternity." But after 1917 the Soviets, who were intent on building their own New Jerusalem, engaged in a militant antireligious campaign that ridiculed traditional apocalypticism, although it has been argued that socialist realism with its obligatory triumph of the working class had a thinly disguised eschatological structure.

Such was not the case in neighboring Poland, newly independent in 1918 after a century and a half of oppression by occupying powers. An apocalyptic mood afflicted poets and artists. Poland's spectacular last-minute victory in its brief war with Soviet Russia (1920–21) could not dispel the ominous warnings emanating from an over-civilized, decaying social structure that revealed little talent for governing itself.

The playwright and novelist Stanisław Ignacy Witkiewicz (Witkacy) was one of Poland's leading catastrophists between the wars.[39] In Witkacy's works the apocalypse takes the form of a dystopian vision of totalitarian dictatorship. In *The Water Hen* (1921), the decadent Alice, duchess of Nevermore, delights in the annihilation of her former social class and joins forces with the criminal element that welcomes the cataclysm. In *The Anonymous Work* (1921), the unruly mob of "people in black pointed caps" led by the gravedigger Lopak creates the "anonymous work"—revolution from below which has as its goal the total destruction of existing civilization. In *The Cuttlefish* (1922), the would-be dictator and superman Hyrcan—self-fabricated ruler of an imaginary kingdom—is simply a modern barbarian interested in power for its own sake.

In his final surviving play, *The Shoemakers* (written from 1927 to 1933), the triumphant hordes who take over at the last minute are no longer terrifying barbarians, but chillingly ordinary technocrats in business suits, mouthing pragmatic, pseudocommunist platitudes. Witkacy's catastrophic novel *Insatiability* (1930) gives comically exaggerated treatment to the racist nightmare of the "yellow peril." Witkacy's parodic theatricalization of the stereotypes of cultural catastrophism is truly innovative

Apocalyptic Horse from Tadeusz Kantor's *Let the Artists Die*, La MaMa, New York (1985)

and modern in sensibility.

Tadeusz Kantor, who began his career under the German occupation, reinterpreted Witkacy's catastrophism as a national trauma experienced by the individual. In Kantor's manifestos, and theatrical works, the apocalypse becomes personal, autobiographical, and internalized. "The last things" are his lost childhood and past, which he attempts to recover through memory and artistic legerdemain. Kantor—the principal player in his dramas, whether as medium, witness, or participant— curses the present in which he is an alien. The world that the artist has experienced most intensely—the world of his parents—no longer exists. It came to an end long ago. The apocalypse that destroyed that world happened in the distant past—but it keeps being played over and over in the artist's memory.

Events of 1914, 1917, 1939, the occupation, the Holocaust come back again and again. The recurring nightmare of Polish history takes the shape of a vicious circle, endlessly reenacted by Kantor's traveling band of players in their frantic circular procession or round dance of death. What is most characteristic about the apocalypse for the creator of *The Dead Class* is its repetitiousness.

War is Kantor's perennial "end of the world." The somnambulistically marching soldiers who sweep through Kantor's dramas are repeatedly gunned down or slaughter

Stanisław Wyspiański's *Acropolis*, staged by Jerzy Grotowski and Józef Szajna, Opole (1962)

others *ad infinitum*. In *Wielopole, Wielopole*, the dead regiment cyclically bursts through the gates separating the stage from the world beyond. In *Let the Artists Die* the eight ashen-faced generals in faded silver uniforms who accompany the commander on his apocalyptic charger (a skeletal horse recalling Arnold Böcklin's painting *War*) move like automatons but fall over like tin soldiers whenever pushed. For Kantor the only apocalypse that could be final would be the death of art.[40]

Jerzy Grotowski, who died in January 1999, was the last major Polish theorist and practitioner of the fin de siècle apocalyptic sensibility in the theatre, a mode that seemed destined to die out by our own turn of the century. In their five versions of Wyspiański's *Acropolis* from 1962 to 1967, Grotowski and Józef Szajna moved the action from Wawel Royal Castle in Cracow to Auschwitz thirty miles to the southeast. It is now the inmates of the death camp who, after carrying out their meaningless and dehumanizing tasks, reenact the stories of the Biblical and Homeric heroes before descending into the ovens.

Rope suggesting barbed wire fences off the camp from the audience, who can never enter into the world of the Holocaust, where prisoners are given the job of building their own camp, or grave-cum-crematorium. As they construct the trash bins for bodies, simple hammers and nails become instruments of destruction and the dummies of victims are carted off in wooden wheelbarrows on their journey to death.

In this cemetery of human values and culture—Wyspiański's phrase, "the cemetery of the tribes" is repeated again and again[41]—the prisoners play out the marriage of Jacob and Rachel, Jacob's battle with the Angel, the love of Paris and Helen, and Cassandra's prophecies. Instead of an Easter apotheosis, there is the death of civilization and the end of humankind. No longer grandiose and cosmic, the apocalypse has become an anonymous everyday experience, full of ordinary objects and unrelieved terror. The sun chariot has become a wheelbarrow. Szajna, who designed and created the costumes and properties, was a prisoner in Auschwitz and Buchenwald from 1941 to 1945. Szajna explained, "I showed a day in the life of a man who had become only a number from his birth to his death, i.e. from dawn till night."[42]

Szajna re-created the directly experienced sense impressions of the Holocaust— its sights, noises, textures. He made by hand the black berets (concealing the hair, turning faces into emaciated masks, obliterating differences of gender, age, class) and the rag uniforms cut from partly burned sacks, mottled with wound scars revealing naked arms and legs, the heavy wooden clogs that rattle like chains, the wheelbarrows, old bathtubs, and the rusty scrap iron and stove-pipes.

Ludwik Flaszen, dramaturg of the production, described the ironic "end of the world" that occurs in the last moments of *Acropolis*:

> The group of human wrecks, led by the Singer, finds its Savior. The Savior is a headless, bluish, badly mauled corpse, horribly reminiscent of the miserable skeletons of the concentration camps. The Singer lifts the corpse in a lyrical gesture, like a priest lifting the chalice. The crowd stares religiously and follows the leader in a procession. . . . The procession evokes the religious crowds of the Middle Ages, the flagellants, the haunting beggars. . . . The Singer lets out a pious yell, opens a hole in the box, and crawls into it dragging after him the corpse of the Savior. The inmates follow him one by one, singing fanatically. They seem to throw themselves out of this world. . . . After a while a calm, matter-of-fact voice is heard. It says simply, "They are gone, and the smoke rises in spirals." The joyful delirium has found its fulfillment in the crematorium. The end.[43]

Grotowski retained the turn-of-the-century apocalyptic mood in his final work for the theatre, *Apocalypsis cum figuris* (1969), utilizing a collage of citations from the Bible, Dostoyevsky's *Brothers Karamazov* (the Grand Inquisitor), T. S. Eliot, and Simone Weil. This is a mystery play about the second coming of a redeemer, who may be only a pseudo-savior. Cast by the master of ceremonies, Simon Peter, and played out among a group of present-day drunken revelers, the drama at first seems a blasphemous twentieth-century profanation of the sacred, but as happened in *Acropolis*, once the debased modern characters are given mythic roles to enact, they start to call forth echoes of the gospel stories, which they gradually inhabit. When an outcast village idiot called Ciemny (meaning dark, shady, suspect, ignorant, as well as simpleton), who is imbued with strange powers, is assigned the Christ role, he is mocked and tormented. Destined to be sacrificed but surviving crucifixion, this ambiguous figure dressed in black disrupts the social order by acting out the Gospels and is told, "Go and come no more." Is this "simpleton" Christ or Antichrist? Turned psychically inward, Grotowski's apocalypse, by removing masks and stripping humanity bare, aims to reveal a new man, but leads instead to the expulsion of a scapegoat.[44]

Alexander Blok's "bomb planted by history" has exploded; the pieces are lodged within us. Apocalypse—an anxiety and foreboding in Bely, a directly experienced documentary reality in Miciński—is in Grotowski and Kantor an obsessive memory, fragmentary, hallucinatory, inescapable.[45]

NOTES

1. Alexander Blok, *Sobranie Sochinenii* (Moscow: Biblioteka "Ogonek," Izdatel'stvo "Pravda" 1971), 5:162.
2. David M. Bethea, *The Shape of the Apocalypse in Modern Russian Fiction* (Princeton, NJ: Princeton University Press, 1989), 109-25.
3. W. Bruce Lincoln, *Between Heaven and Hell* (New York: Viking, 1998), 223, 230; Bethea, *Shape of Apocalypse*, 117.
4. Mircea Eliade, *Aspects du mythe* (Paris: Gallimard, 1963), 88.
5. Y. M. Lotman and B. A. Uspenskii, "Binary Models in the Dynamics of Russian Culture (to the End of the Eighteenth Century)," in *The Semiotics of Russian Cultural History*, ed. Alexander D. Nakhimovsky and Alice Stone Nakhimovsky (Ithaca, N.Y.: Cornell University Press, 1985), 32.
6. Quoted in Lincoln, *Heaven and Hell*, 164. Konstantin Mochul'skii, *Dostoevsky: His Life and Work* (Princeton, N.J.: Princeton University Press, 1967), 652.
7. Czesław Miłosz, "Science Fiction and the Coming of the Antichrist;" in *Emperor of the Earth* (Berkeley: University of California Press, 1977), 15-30. S.L. Frank, introduction to *A Solovyov Anthology* (New York: Scribner's, 1950), 26; Lincoln, *Heaven and Hell*, 274.
8. Nikolai Berdyaev, *The Russian Idea* (Boston: Beacon, 1962), 193; translation revised.
9. Samuel D. Cioran, *The Apocalyptic Symbolism of Andrei Bely* (The Hague: Mouton, 1973), 13.
10. David King and Cathy Porter, *Blood and Laughter: Caricatures from the 1905 Revolution* (London: Jonathan Cape, 1983), 17-45.
11. Andrei Bely, *Na Rubezhe d'vukh stoletii* (1930; repr., Letchworth, U.K.: Bradda, 1966), 401-2. For an analysis of the uncertainty prevailing in turn-of-the-century Russia "as to whether disaster or deliverance was at hand," see James H. Billington, *The Icon and the Axe* (New York: Knopf, 1966), 59.
12. Quoted in Aleksandr Vasil'evich Lavrov, *Andrei Bely v 1900-e Gody: Zhizn'i literaturnaya deyatel'nost'* (Moscow: Novoye Literaturnoye Obozreniye, 1995), 31.
13. Andrei Bely, "Budushchee Iskusstvo," in *Simvolizm* (1910; repr., Munich: Wilhelm Fink, 1969), 453.
14. *Theatre-Temple*, "Teatr-Świątynia" in *Myśl teatralna Młodej Polski*, ed. Irena Sławińska and Stefan Kruk (Warsaw: Wydawnictwa Artystyczne i Filmowe, 1966), 197. See also Elżbieta Rzewuska, *O dramaturgii Tadeusza Micińskiego* (Wrocław: Ossolineum, 1977), 121-23.
15. Vera Verigina, "Po dorogam iskanii," in *Vstrechi s Meyerholdem* (Moscow: Vserossiskoye Teatral'noye Obshchestvo, 1967), 58.
16. Boris Schloezer, *Scriabin, Artist and Mystic*, trans. Nicolas Slonimsky (Berkeley: University of California Press, 1987), 157-306; and Faubion Bowers, *The New Scriabin* (New York: St. Martin's, 1973), 72-73, 92-100, 124-26. Schloezer's work was originally published in Russian in Berlin in 1923.
17. Tymon Terlecki, "Stanisław Wyspiański and the Poetics of Symbolist Drama," *Polish Review* 15 (1970): 60-61. See also Claude Backvis, *Le Dramaturge Stanislas Wyspiański* (Paris: Presses Universitaires de France, 1952), 253-54.
18. Antonina Maria Terlecka (Tola Korian), "Acropolis," in "Stanisław Wyspiański and Symbolism," *Antemurale* 27-28 (1985-1986): 86-103. See also Wojciech Natanson, *Stanisław Wyspiański: Próba nowego spojrzenia* (Poznań: Wydawnictwo Poznańskie, 1969), 215-23.
19. David Ketterer, *New Worlds for Old: The Apocalyptic Imagination, Science Fiction, and American Literature* (Garden City, N.Y.: Doubleday, 1974), 15, 91.
20. N. G. Andreasyan, "Dramaturgiya V. Ya. Briusova (1907-1917)," in *Russkii Teatr i Dramaturgiya, 1907-1917* (Leningrad: Leningradskii Gosurdarstvennii Institut Teatra, Muzyki i Kinomatografii im. M. K. Cherkasova, 1988), 22-25; Galina Yur'evna Brodskaya, "Briusov i Teatr." in *Valerii Briusov: Literaturnoye Nasledstvo* (Moscow: Nauka, 1976), 85:167-79.
21. Valery Bryusov, "Alexander Blok," in *Blok: An Anthology of Essays and Memoirs*, ed. and trans. Lucy Vogel (Ann Arbor, Mich.: Ardis, 1982), 108; Alexander Blok, *Sobranie Sochinenii* (Moscow: Khudozhestvennaya Literarura, 1975), 6:434. See also Avril Pyman, *A History of Russian Symbolism* (Cambridge: Cambridge University Press, 1994), 232-33.

22. Valerii Briusov, *Zemlya*, in *Zemnaya Os'* (Moscow: Skorpion, 1907), 165–66.

23. Konstantin Stanislavsky quoted in Marianna Stroeva, *Rezhisserskie Iskania Stanislavskogo, 1898–1917* (Moscow: Nauka, 1973), 221–22.

24. Ibid., 222.

25. Ibid.

26. Quoted in Cioran, *Apocalyptic Symbolism*, 22.

27. Eliade, *Aspects du mythe*, 72.

28. Mircea Eliade, *The Two and the One*, trans. J. M. Cohen (New York: Harper and Row, 1965), 95. Chapter 2, "Mephistopheles and the Androgyne or the Mystery of the Whole," is devoted to *coincidentia oppositorum*.

29. For an introduction to Miciński, see Daniel Gerould, "The Magus Tadeusz Miciński," *yale/theatre* 7 (1975): 58–64.

30. Tadeusz Miciński, *Utwory Dramatyczne*, ed. Teresa Wróblewska (Cracow: Wydawnictwo Literackie, 1996), 240. All quotations from *The Revolt of the Potemkin* are from an unpublished translation by Daniel Gerould and Jadwiga Kosicka. Page citations are keyed to the Polish text cited in this note.

31. Ibid., 150.

32. Tadeusz Miciński, *Xiądz Faust* (Cracow: Książka, 1913), 113.

33. Adam Ważyk, "U Modernistów," *Twórczość* 8 (1977): 83-84.

34. Miciński, *Utwory Dramatyczne*, 233.

35. Bethea, *Shape of Apocalypse*, 37–45. Miciński's epilogue fits the pattern of Bethea's formulation of the structures of Russian apocalyptic fiction. It also shows analogues to the Old Believers' fear of the coming flood and need to escape to the mountaintop. See Billington, *Icon and Axe*, 368.

36. Alfred Nowaczyński, "O Tadeuszu Micińskim," in *Wczasy Literackie* (Warsaw: Nakładem J. Fiszera, 1906), 286–99.

37. Leon Schiller, *Teatr Ogromny*, ed. Zbigniew Raszewski (Warsaw: Czytelnik, 1961), 143.

38. In his mock apocalypse, *Mystery-Bouffe*, Mayakovsky presented the world revolution in the guise of the biblical flood. Throughout his plays and poetry the Russian Futurist poet appropriated the language and imagery of the Christian apocalypse and applied them to his own self-legend. But later apocalyptic works, such as Boris Pasternak's *Doctor Zhivago* and Mikhail Bulgakov's *Master and Margarita*, were suppressed. See L. K. Shvetsova, "Tvorcheskiye printsipy i vzglyady, bliskiye k ekspressionizmu," in *Literaturno Esteticheskie Kontseptsi v Rossii kontsa XIX-nachala XX v.* (Moscow: Nauka, 1975), 275–83.

39. For the philosophical bases of Polish catastrophism, see Leszek Gawor, *Katastrofizm konsekwentny: O poglądach Mariana Zdziechowskiego i Stanisława Ignacego Witkiewicza* (Lublin: Uniwersytet Marii Curie-Skłodowskiej, 1998).

40. Elżbieta Morawiec, "Tadeusz Kantor—ostatni kapłan umarłego świata" in *Powidoki Teatru* (Cracow: Wydawnictwo Literackie, 1991), 270–75, 371. See also Krzysztof Pleśniarowicz, *Kantor:Artysta końca wieku* (Wrocław: Wydawnictwo Dolnośląskie, 1997), 235, 244; and Jan Kłossowicz, *Tadeusz Kantor: Teatr* (Warsaw: Państwowy Instytut Wydawniczy, 1991), 183.

41. Zbigniew Osiński, "In the Theatre," in Tadeusz Burzyński and Zbigniew Osiński, *Grotowski's Laboratory* (Warsaw: Interpress, 1979), 25–33. Osiński points out that the production took inspiration from the stories of Tadeusz Borowski, author of *This Way for the Gas, Ladies and Gentlemen*.

42. August Grodzicki, *Polish Theatre Directors* (Warsaw: Interpress, 1979), 155. For attempting to escape, Szajna was condemned to death and taken to the place of execution.

43. Ibid., 48–49.

44. Zbigniew Osiński, *Grotowski i jego Laboratorium* (Warsaw: Państwowy Instytut Wydawniczy, 1980), 106–10, 160–64.

45. That we live permanently in that apocalypse is a central premise of the poetry, stories, and plays of Tadeusz Różewicz, such as *Death in an Old Setting*, *The Old Lady Broods*, and *The Trap*.

Valerii Briusov, portrait by Mikhail Vrubel' (1906)

VALERII BRIUSOV—RUSSIAN SYMBOLIST

The most versatile and prolific of the Russian Symbolists, the poet Valerii Briusov (1873–1924) became the acknowledged leader of the new movement shortly after the turn of the century. From 1904 to 1909 he edited the major Symbolist review, *The Scales (Vesy)*, while at the same time demonstrating his mastery of almost every poetic form and literary genre. By 1906, with the acceptance of Symbolism as the dominant voice in Russian artistic circles, Briusov emerged as an important influence, not only on the development of Russian prosody, but also on the rapidly evolving poetics of the new Russian drama and theatre.

As chief theoretician of Russian Symbolism, Briusov—following his French models, Verlaine, Mallarmé, and Rimbaud—insisted that the author's task is to evoke moods through hints and suggestions rather than to present a total picture by means of precise statement. In his view, Symbolism reveals essences, not appearances, and the goal of art is to express the creative personality of the artist, which is inevitably unique, mysterious, and subjective. "The whole world within me" was one of Briusov's mottoes. Yet at the same time—and unlike the French Symbolists, who most often looked backwards nostalgically to a vague medieval past—Briusov believed that art should be contemporary in spirit and that the artist should stand in the vanguard. As an apostle of the new, Briusov urged his fellow writers to live in the future.[1]

"We live in the world of the telegraph, the telephone, the stock-exchanges, the theatre, the scientific congress, the world of ocean liners and express trains, but poets continue to use images, which are completely alien to us," he wrote in 1909, rejecting the obsolete poetic conventions of the past and welcoming the Futurists because of their commitment to modernity and the machine age.[2] Briusov himself was a pioneer in the field of Russian science fiction, writing of interplanetary travel and of the collapse of industrial civilization, stifled by its own technology,[3] and he also was the first Russian poet of the city, his urban cycle, "The Spirits of Fire," "The Glory of the Crowd," and "The White Horse" (1903–5), opening the way for Mayakovsky.

An omnivorous reader, immensely curious about all fields of knowledge, Briusov threw himself into the most diverse projects with characteristic energy. For example, when in 1915 he was asked to edit a selection of Armenian poetry in Russian translation, Briusov—a brilliant linguist who knew most of the European languages as well as Sanskrit—set out to study Armenian, mastered it within a year, and did most of the translations himself. In the light of this constant espousal of new interests and innovations, it is not surprising that the relatively apolitical Symbolist poet enthusiastically welcomed the Bolshevik Revolution of 1917 as opening up unexplored poetic possibilities, wrote admiringly about Lenin, and even promoted proletarian art as the appropriate reflection of contemporary Soviet society.

In his attitude towards theatre, Briusov was also a proponent of innovation. He became the theoretician behind the theatrical revolution against Naturalism that began around 1900, and he played a crucial role in shaping the new directions taken by the Russian stage in the early twentieth century. Stanislavsky, Meyerhold, and Komissarzhevskaya—the three most influential figures in the Russian theatre of that time—all looked to Briusov for support, guidance, and criticism.

–Performing Arts Journal 3, no. 3 (Winter 1979): 85–91.

A frequent spectator at the Moscow Art Theatre, Briusov felt that Stanislavsky's productions of Hauptmann's *Sunken Bell* and *Lonely Lives* (in 1898 and 1900) and Chekhov's *Uncle Vanya* (in 1899), despite their originality and perfection, were misguided in their excessive attention to external realism. The creativity of the actor became submerged at the Moscow Art Theatre, Briusov maintained, in detailed reconstructions of everyday life and painstaking stage effects. Imitation of reality was being substituted for artistic imagination, according to Briusov, who liked to cite Grillparzer's saying that art bears the same relationship to reality as wine to the vineyard.

Then, on January 1, 1900, while visiting friends outside Moscow, the poet saw a production of the traditional folk play, *Tsar Maximilian*, presented by the workers at a local factory (one of the many excellent amateur theatres flourishing at the time), using only a bare stage and the simplest scenery and symbolic properties. This seemingly primitive and naïve performance came as a revelation to Briusov and enabled him to grasp for the first time that theatre is an art with its own language, comprising a stylized system of expressive signs superior to any attempts at achieving a direct correspondence with reality.[4]

Now that his ideas on the futility of realism in the theatre had crystallized, Briusov published in 1902 an attack on the Moscow Art Theatre, entitled "Unnecessary Truth," which proved to be the opening shot in the Symbolists' battle against the sort of naturalistic staging for which Stanislavsky had become famous.[5] Instead of representing the theatre of the future, as its supporters claimed, the Moscow Art Theatre was, Briusov pointed out, merely a continuation and perfection of an old nineteenth-century tradition. With its elaborately simulated chirping crickets and windblown curtains, Stanislavsky's theatre, along with most of the other theatres in Europe, was pursuing a false ideal of verisimilitude to surface details of life. Such futile efforts to reproduce reality on stage constitute "unnecessary truth," in contrast to the higher truth of the theatre which is achieved through self-conscious stylization. Here Briusov formulates one of the cardinal principles of the twentieth-century stage: that theatre is a matter of agreed upon conventions, like those of sculpture with its white statues, like those of painting with its flat surface, like those of engraving with its black tonalities.

Once it is realized "what powerful means of its own the theatre possesses and how vainly it seeks support from scene painters and technicians,"[6] Briusov declares that the actor can be restored to his rightful place of pre-eminence on a stage consciously accepted as acting space, where everything external has been stripped away. Briusov develops a daring and radical position that theatrical performance should not have as its goal to serve and illuminate the playwright's text, but rather that "the sole purpose of the theatre is to assist the actor to reveal his soul before the spectators."

> Artistic, aesthetic enjoyment in the theatre we receive from the performers, and not from the play. The author is the servant of the actors. If it were otherwise, the theatre would lose its right to exist. It would become an aid to imagination, helping to present clearly what the author wrote. People with powerful imaginations would never need to go to the theatre: they could he satisfied with reading dramas. The theatre would turn into an almshouse for people with a weak sense of fantasy or as illustrations of the text. Whoever wants to know Shakespeare should read him; in the theatre he will come to know the actors.[7]

Briusov's call for a drastic change in theatrical values came at a decisive moment. During the first decade of the twentieth century, the Russian theatre was in

Alberto Martini's *In the Mirror* (1910), illustration for Briusov's story "The Mirror"

a state of crisis because of the dead weight of old traditions which stifled the talents and creativity of the actor. Stanislavsky himself, feeling that he had reached a dead end in his previous work, now embarked in the period from 1903 to 1907 upon a series of experiments with plays by Maeterlinck, Hamsun, and Andreyev, making the Moscow Art Theatre the first Russian theatre to stage Symbolist drama.[8] In a further application of the revolutionary ideas enunciated in "Unnecessary Truth," Stanislavsky organized a laboratory theatre specifically designed to search for new scenic forms and he appointed Meyerhold the director of this Theatre Studio, with Briusov as the head of its literary bureau.

In this capacity, the Symbolist poet became the theoretician of the short-lived Theatre Studio on Povarskaya Street, and his ideas on conscious stylization became the basis for Meyerhold's new stage language, revealed in the production of Maeterlinck's *The Death of Tintagiles*. Writing of the experiences at the Theatre Studio, Briusov criticized Meyerhold only for not going far enough and making a complete break with the naturalistic acting style created by Antoine and Stanislavsky.

> The theatre must renounce all its age-old traditions which have come into being during the period from Shakespeare to Ibsen . . . Not to complicate the stage, but to simplify it, not perfect counterfeiting, but give something genuine, albeit stylized, to recognize that symbolism is the sole principle of all art—this is the path to the "new theatre."[9]

Briusov continued his campaign for a theatre of conscious stylization giving a series of three public lectures on "The Theatre of the Future" in 1907 and contributing the essay, "Realistic and Stylized Theatre," to the important collection, *On Theatre* (1908), to which Meyerhold, Bely, and other leaders of the new movement contributed. During these years Briusov modified his initial position to some degree, endeavoring to find a balance between realism and stylization which would give greater freedom to the actor. In the course of his work with Vera Komissarzhevskaya on *Pelléas and Mélisande*, which he translated for the production directed by Meyerhold,[10] Briusov defended the actress against the director and argued that the performer should not be turned into a marionette or mechanism. Sounding sometimes almost like Brecht in claiming that theatre should be a learning experience and activity of cognition, Briusov now rejected his friend Vyacheslav Ivanov's notion of a Symbolist theatre-temple.

> Least of all should the theatrical performance be transformed, as some demand, into a blind vision. The auditorium should be filled, not with a crowd of dreaming somnambulists, but with an audience of strenuously attentive spectators. Unconscious art is as absurd as nonsensical science.[11]

Yet Briusov continued his advocacy of non-naturalistic acting styles. Commenting in 1912 on the Craig-Stanislavsky *Hamlet* at the Moscow Art Theatre, he defended Craig's position against Stanislavsky's.

> A stylized production demands stylized acting: in the production of Hamlet the Moscow Art Theatre did not understand this. Instead of a palace there was the suggestion of a palace; correspondingly, we should have heard the suggestion of a scream rather than a scream. The terrace was replaced by parallelepipeds stretching upwards: real life movements and real life gestures should have been replaced by stylized gestures similar to those that we see in old Byzantine icons. The houses without windows, doors, or ceilings, the naked, monochromatic walls, even the stony cemetery itself with its quadrangular posts would not have seemed strange or out of place if we had seen there the life of equally "stylized" beings, with stylized gestures, with stylized intonation of voice.[12]

As a playwright, Briusov was also an experimental and prophetic innovator, but because most of his dramas remained unpublished or unperformed, his impact on Russian theatre was far greater as a critic and theoretician. Fascinated by the stage throughout his career, Briusov became involved with theatre at an early point. He wrote his first plays in his late teens at the same time that he embarked on his career as a poet. In August 1893 he planned to put on as an amateur production his one-act light comedy, *Country Passions*, intending also to play the lead role of the young poet Vladimir Findesieclev, but the performance was stopped by the censor on grounds of immorality (because of a frivolous kiss). Several months later he wrote a short dramatic *stsenka* (scene) *Prose*, in which he appeared in the role of the poet hero when it was staged for several performances at the German club.[13]

By the time of his death in 1924, Briusov had produced over twenty dramas, as well as plans and sketches for many other theatrical works, in almost every genre and style: realistic comedy, history play, mythological drama, and verse monologue.

Briusov's most original creations were fantastic cosmic dramas, such as *The Earth, a Tragedy of Future Times* (published in 1905), which depicts the death throes of advanced technological civilization, in much the same manner as his science fiction

Alberto Martini's *The Destruction of the Earth* (1910),
an illustration for the final scene of Briusov's play *The Earth*

story, *The Republic of the Southern Cross*. The inhabitants of the mechanized city of the future, which is covered by a special roof shutting out the sky, breathe artificial air and exist by artificial light. Sensing the coming apocalypse, the Order of Deliverers worship death and darkness, while the Wise Man, Nevalt, urges a return to the stars and sun above the antiseptic lid. Hoping to save mankind, the Wise Man actually brings about the catastrophe; once the city-dwellers make a breakthrough to the world of nature, the blazing sun and fresh air kill them all.

Although Meyerhold had been interested in staging *The Earth* as early as 1905 and Alexander Pavlovich Lenskii had hoped to produce it at the Maly Theatre during the 1907–8 season, Briusov's play did not reach the stage until after the Revolution, when it was given twice in Leningrad, first at the Bolshoi Dramatic Theatre in 1922, and then at the State Experimental Theatre in 1923. Based in part on Plato's allegory of the cave and on Egyptian and Assyrian cosmological myths and rituals, *The Earth* has been regarded as Briusov's masterpiece and a great philosophical drama akin to Goethe's *Faust*.[14] Long obsessed with the Faust legend (both Dr. Faustus and Mephistopheles appear in *The Fiery Angel*, a historical romance set in the sixteenth century), Briusov projected an unrealized drama, *Faust in Moscow*.[15]

In 1920 Briusov published under a pseudonym *The Pythagoreans, a Dramatic Study*, which contains covert criticism of party discipline that results in the suppression of individual creativity. When a young member of the secret society of Pythagoreans gains possession of a scroll discovered in Egypt that contains symbols about the island Atlantis, the authorities take the papyrus away from him and give it to the elders to be studied, causing the acolyte's death.[16]

Briusov consulted with the Russian pioneer in rocketry, theory of cosmic travel, and science fiction, Konstantin Tsiolkovsky (1857–1935), whose work he much admired. Unpublished science fiction plays composed by Briusov include *Piroent*—or Pyroesis, the ancient name for the planet Mars—whose hero is a Russian engineer aboard an interplanetary space ship, and *The World of Seven Generations* (1923), which takes place on a comet of the same name.

The Dictator, written in 1921 but first published only in 1986, was Briusov's major post-revolutionary play and the first work in Soviet drama about the threat of dictatorship and the cult of personality. The tyrant Orm (who is ultimately assassinated) attempts to establish armed dominance over the cosmos by earthmen, threatening galactic warfare.

> The earth has ripened in order to wield power in the cosmos . . . Man must be emperor of the universe. Our commands will spread throughout space, and they must be heeded like the word of god. The earth is the new god, and I am called to be its prophet. Mankind is destined to conquer the entire world, and if it does not understand this, I shall compel it to.[17]

When the author gave a reading of the play to an overflow crowd at the Moscow House of the Press, the audience didn't accept or understand the play, objecting that in the evolving socialist state, there would be no grounds for a dictatorship to arise. Briusov answered that "the artist is obliged to notice the dark side of life and to point out the looming dangers." Briusov's persistent efforts to publish the tragedy were unsuccessful, but until the end of his life he kept listing it among his works so that its existence would not be ignored and the play forever lost.

The Wayfarer, Briusov's one-act psychodrama about insurmountable human loneliness, was written in 1910 and published in 1911. Although Briusov claimed in his *Autobiography*, written in 1912–13, that *The Wayfarer*, along with *The Earth* and *Protesilaus Dying* (1912), was not written for the stage,[18] it was successfully performed in St. Petersburg and toured in the provinces by Georges Pitoëff (before his emigration to Switzerland and eventually France).

The projection of a single consciousness and its inner workings, *The Wayfarer* is an example of monodrama, a genre favored by the Symbolists and given theoretical foundation by Nikolai Evreinov in his *Introduction to Monodrama* (1909) as well as in Sologub's *Theatre of One Will*. Briusov's revelation of Julia's secret self through her response to the mute wayfarer calls to mind Harold Pinter's similar technique in *A Slight Ache*, in which the silent Matchseller calls forth Flora's hidden dreams and longings. *The Wayfarer* perfectly illustrates Briusov's contention that

> There is no fixed boundary between the real world and the imaginary world, between "dreaming" and "waking," "life" and "fantasy." What we commonly consider imaginary may be the highest reality of the world, and the reality acknowledged by all maybe the most frightful delirium.[19]

Briusov succeeded in creating both a theory and practice of Symbolist drama based on a view of reality that penetrated deep into the underground. His work is never in danger of dissolving into ethereal vagueness. "The poet," Briusov declared, "always like Antaeus, gains strength only from contact with the earth."[20]

NOTES

1. D. Stremoukhoff, "Echos du Symbolisme français dans le Symbolisme russe," *Revue des Sciences Humaines*, No. 78, (April-June, 1955): 297–319.
2. Quoted by T. J. Binyon, "Valery Bryusov and the Nature of Art," *Oxford Slavonic Papers* (Oxford: Clarendon Press, 1974), 7:109.
3. Darko Suvin, "The Utopian Tradition of Russian Science Fiction.' *Modern Language Review* 66, no. 1 (January, 1971): 145.
4. Valerii Briusov, *Dnevniki 1891–1910* (Moscow: M. and S. Sabashnikov, 1927), 79.
5. "Nienuzhnaya Pravda (Unnecessary Truth)" first appeared in the influential art journal, *Mir Iskusstva*, No. 4, 1902, and is reprinted in Valerii Briusov, *Sobranie Sochinenii* (Moscow: Khudozhestvennaya Literatura, 1975), 6:62–73.
6. Ibid, 73.
7. Ibid, 67.
8. Tat'yana Rodina, A. *Blok i Russkii Teatr Nachala XX Veka* (Moscow: Nauka, 1972), 61–69.
9. Originally in *Vesy*, No. 1. 1906, 75; quoted by B. I. Rostotskii, "Modernizm v teatre," *Russkaya Khudozhestvennaya Kul'tura Kontsa XIX-Nachala XX Veka (1895–1907)* (Moscow: Nauka, 1968), 1: 197–98.
10. Briusov also translated D'Annunzio's *Francesca da Rimini* and Wilde's *Prince of Padua*, both which were staged at the Maly Theatre. Valerii Briusov, *Zarya Vremeni: Stikhovorenia, Poemy, P'esy, Stat'i*, ed. Sergei Gindin (Moscow: Panorama, 2000), 24.
11. From the lecture. "Teatr budushchego (The Theatre of the Future)," quoted by G. Yu. Brodskaya. "Briusov i Teatr," *Literaturnoye Nasledstvo,* vol. 85, Valerii Briusov (Moscow: Nauka, 1976), 177.
12. Quoted by Marianna Stroeva, *Rezhisserskie Iskaniya Stanislavskogo 1898–1917* (Moscow: Nauka, 1973), 288–89.
13. Valerii Briusov, *Zarya Vremeni*, 474–75.
14. Ellis (Lev Kobylinskii), *Russkiye Simvolisty* (Moscow: Musaget', 1910), 196–97. *The Earth* perhaps influenced Stanislavsky in the writing of his apocalyptic symbolist drama, *The Comet, a Fantasy in Four Acts* (1908), portraying the final day of life on Earth (Stroeva, 221–22), and the Order of the Deliverers may have been the inspiration for the death-seeking mystics in *The Puppet Show* (1906) by Alexander Blok, who greatly admired Briusov's play. See A. V. Fedorov. *Teatr A. Bloka i Dramaturgiya ego Vremeni* (Leningrad: Leningrad University, 1972), 45–47.
15. *Literaturnoye Nasledstvo,* vol. 85, Valerii Briusov , 68. Briusov translated Goethe's *Faust*.
16. Briusov, *Zarya vremeni*, 475.
17. Briusov, *Zarya vremeni*, 421. For a discussion of the play, see K. S. Gerasimov, "'Shturm neba' v poezii Valeriya Briusova," *Briusovskiye Chteniya* (Erevan: Aiastan, 1964), 134.
18. Briusov, *Zarya vremeni*, 24.
19. Valerii Briusov, *Zemnaya Os'* (Moscow: Skorpion, 1910), vii.
20. Valerii Briusov, *Dalekie i blizkie*, no 41, 1906, 177.

HISTORICAL SIMULATION AND POPULAR ENTERTAINMENT:
THE *POTEMKIN* MUTINY

FROM RECONSTRUCTED NEWSREEL TO BLACK SEA STUNT MEN

Modern man [. . .] is continually having a world-panorama unrolled before his eyes by his historical artists. He is turned into a restless, dilettante spectator, and arrives at a condition when even great wars and revolutions cannot affect him beyond the moment. The war is hardly at an end, and it is already converted into thousands of copies of printed matter.
    —Friedrich Nietzsche, *The Use and Abuse of History*[1]

Appearances have always played a much more important part than reality in history, where the unreal is always of greater moment than the real.
    Crowds being only capable of thinking in images are only to be impressed by images. It is only images that terrify or attract them and become motives of action.
    For this reason theatrical representations, in which the image is shown in its most clearly visible shape, always have an enormous influence on crowds. [. . .] The unreal has almost as much influence on them as the real. They have an evident tendency not to distinguish between the two.
    —Gustave Le Bon, *The Crowd*[2]

In striving to produce deceptively lifelike changes in their presentation of nature, the panoramas point ahead, beyond photography, to films and sound films. [. . .] The panoramas, which declare a revolution in the relation of art to technology, are at the same time an expression of a new feeling about life.
    —Walter Benjamin, *Reflections*[3]

Revolution, war, and natural disaster were converted into spectacle, and simulated news became a form of entertainment for mass audiences after 1789. Gigantic paintings and panoramas as well as their animated counterparts in theatrical representations were in vogue during the French Revolution and the Napoleonic era, but pictorial simulation of news events reached its largest public 100 years later at the turn of the next century when the mechanical means of production offered by cinema enabled the show to be inscribed on celluloid, copied, and endlessly replayed. Land engagements, naval battles, shipwrecks, fires at sea, explosions, volcanic eruptions, and earthquakes were popular spectacular reconstructions in the nineteenth-century entertainment industry that were quickly taken over by early film.

    The catastrophic defeats of the Tsarist forces in the Russo-Japanese War, the wave of assassinations and anarchist attacks, and then the revolution of 1905 provided exciting material for these reconstructed newsreels. The revolt aboard the battleship *Potemkin* that took place in late June 1905 in the Black Sea was given its first cinematographic incarnation as a French *actualité reconstituée*—or simulated news event—almost as it was happening and exactly twenty years before Eisenstein's film, *The Battleship Potemkin*, a mythologized version of the same episode from Russian history. Before looking more closely at this first documentary simulation about the *Potemkin*, I must briefly reconstruct the history of the historical reconstruction.

–*TDR* 33, no. 2 (Summer 1989): 161–184.

The Masses on the Stage of History: Supernumeraries as Protagonists

The French Revolution was the first great European political and social upheaval that its creators immediately perceived as a spectacle to be enacted and reenacted. The Fall of the Bastille, the Meetings of the Convention and Committees, the Sessions of the Revolutionary Tribunal, and the Terror and the Guillotine were all history theatricalized which could be constantly replayed. In the festivals and rites staged by revolutionary choreographers to celebrate and commemorate these events, audience and performers became one. "The most magnificent of spectacles is that of a great people assembled," Robespierre declared; "the spectacle of the spectators themselves" was the essence of the show.[4]

These mass spectacles and popular rituals expressing the unity of the people sometimes took the form of reenactments, such as *La Prise de la Bastille*, a musical *hiérodrama*, presented in the Cathedral of Notre Dame on the eve of the first anniversary.[5] More often they were pageants and processionals in authentic outdoor settings involving the participation of hundreds of thousands. Such was the *Festival of the Supreme Being*, devised and directed by the painter David in celebration of a deistic god, with Robespierre officiating.[6] Later, the revolutionary ceremonial might be repeated in simulated form in professional theatres, as was the case with the *Festival of the Unity and Indivisibility of the Republic*. Originally organized by David on the first anniversary of the overthrow of the monarch (August 10, 1793) and staged processionally with chariots and floats moving from the Place de la Bastille to the Champs de Mars, this *fête* was subsequently transformed into a dramatic *sans-cullotide*, or revolutionary show in five acts to be performed in playhouses by actors taking the parts of the real people who had played themselves in the earlier version.[7]

The spectacles reflected the new role of the masses in the making of history. A collective act of the people, the taking of the Bastille marked the advent of the French Revolution. On the London stage it was reenacted as early as 1789 with *The Triumph of Liberty, or the Destruction of the Bastille* at the Royal Circus, and *Paris in an Uproar, or The Destruction of the Bastille* at Astley's Amphitheatre.[8] But it was military history that brought the masses on stage and provided the greatest impetus for new forms of pictorial journalism in the popular arts. Never before had there been such huge mass-conscripted armies or battles on such a vast scale. French attempts to defend—and export their revolution—against the foreign intervention of a British, Austrian, and Prussian coalition, and then the ensuing Napoleonic Wars, engulfed all of Europe in conflict. Military campaigns in far-off places became of interest to the general public everywhere.[9]

Large numbers of people were curious to see with their own eyes the events of the day involving large numbers of people like themselves; simulated news became a form of entertainment. Large-scale history painting portraying current happenings flourished. At the same time there appeared a new pictorial genre of popular entertainment, the panorama, which placed the spectator in the center of an immense circular painting shown in a special rotunda. Invented and named by an Irishman, Robert Barker, the panorama came into being at the time of the French Revolution. Its vogue spread from London to Paris, Berlin, and St. Petersburg and its popularity lasted throughout the nineteenth, and even into the early twentieth century, when it was supplanted by cinema.[10]

The new mass public that followed the warfare in the newspapers was willing to pay admission to look at the latest military paintings on view in galleries and special

The *Potemkin* reaches Constanta, Romania on July 8, 1905,
and surrenders to Romanian authorities

exhibition sheds or to visit one of the panoramas—at first fixed, later moving through the use of canvas on rollers—that were "the newsreels of the Napoleonic era."[11] Battle artists on assignment accompanied the armies; panoramas were painted from drawings made at the scene of battle, while details were adjusted according to late dispatches.

London theatres competed with historical paintings and panoramas in representing current events, although the historicity of the staged versions of military and naval exploits was less exact than in the graphic arts. With its huge tank of water in which scale models of warships floated, the Sadler's Wells specialized in nautical drama— an imitation of the *naumachia* of the ancient Romans—such as *The Battle of Trafalgar* (1806) and *The Battle of the Nile* (1815).[12] With its stable of trained horses, sometimes numbering up to ninety, Astley's was a hippodrome in which action could move back and forth from ring to stage. It featured cavalry engagements, such as *The British Glory in Egypt* (1801) with "REAL CAVALRY and INFANTRY" and *The Battle of Waterloo*, the greatest favorite of all, which in a number of different versions was constantly revived. Cavalry charges, bugle calls, cannon fire, and military music lent authenticity.[13] The presence of a special spectator could also serve to authenticate the representation of a battle in which he had been a leading participant, as when the Duke of Wellington attended *The Battle of Waterloo* or Nelson praised Robert Barker for keeping alive the memory of the Battle of the Nile by the creation of his commemorative panorama of 1815.[14]

Simulated pictorial representation on canvas was often combined with real objects in three-dimensional space. Panoramas could be incorporated in theatrical pantomimes or used in pleasure-garden settings behind lakes and free-standing models in something approaching a motion picture set.[15] Such was the case when the Battle of Waterloo was reconstructed as a total event at the Vauxhall Gardens in 1827 with the participation of 1,000 soldiers.

In France during the reign of Napoleon, the imperial ceremonies were the outstanding historical spectacles, and would subsequently be simulated in the theatre. After Waterloo and the restoration of the Bourbon monarchy, the huge popular theatres on the boulevards, like the Cirque Olympique with its more than fifty horses and complex stage machinery permitting simultaneous action in the ring and on the stage, satisfied the popular longing for former military glories with mass spectacles. Despite censorship forbidding the presentation of Napoleon on stage, homage was paid to the Emperor by means of plays glorifying his generals and the French army, such as in *La Morte de Kleber, ou Les Français, Cadix et la France* (1819) and *La Prise de la Flotte, ou la Charge de Cavalerie* (1822) in which the French cavalry made a charge across the frozen North Sea to attack and capture the Dutch fleet.[16] Military spectacles like *Les Pyrénées, Cadix et la France* (1824) celebrating the French forces in Spain were given special performances for soldiers (including the disabled) newly returned from the Spanish campaign. A contemporary observer wrote in 1821, "A few years ago the people of Paris went to battles as to the theatre; now they go to the theatre as to a combat."[17] At the Cirque Olympique the smell of smoke and of horses made veterans imagine that they were back on the battlefield.

After the revolution of July 1830, with the installation of Louis Philippe as king and the lifting of censorship, the Napoleonic myth flourished in the popular theatres, achieving pictorial authentication as history through iconic evocation of the best-known images of Napoleon in historical paintings.[18] Different aspects of the heroic life and campaigns of the Emperor were shown in over 500 melodramas and military spectacles, whose acts were sometimes called "Epochs." In *L'Empereur*, staged at the Cirque Olympique in 1830, the entire career of Napoleon was presented, ending with the obligatory apotheosis in heaven. "It was no play, it was reality," wrote a spectator.[19] Every theatre now had its own Napoleon and contests were held to choose the actor who best simulated the Emperor; one performer finally came to believe that he actually was the great man whom he portrayed.

Claims of authenticity extended to the costumes and properties. The director of the Ambigu consulted with Napoleon's old valet for the design and measurement of the Emperor's small hat and gray cloak to reproduce the right texture and exact color.[20] In London, British dramas on the Emperor's life, although less chauvinistic than their French counterparts, were equally concerned with scrupulous historical reconstruction. For the "Grand Historical and Military Spectacle" entitled *Napoleon* at Covent Garden in 1831, the management claimed that the costumes, imported from France, had actually been worn by Napoleon and his staff.[21]

Panoramists were not to be outdone. As an attaché in St. Petersburg, Jean-Charles Langlois (1789–1870), an ex-colonel who had served with Napoleon at Waterloo, made on-the-scene studies near Borodino and Moscow for his panoramas, *The Battle of Moskva*, *The Battle of Borodino*, and *The Burning of Moscow*.[22] For his panorama *The Battle of Navarino*, shown in 1830 at the rotunda he established in Paris, Langlois bought the poop of the *Scipion*, a vessel of seventy-four cannons which had taken part in the naval engagement on the Ionian Sea, and made it the platform for the spectators, who entered by corridors replicating those of the battleship. When they reached the deck, the spectators found themselves in the midst of the battle, confronted by an approaching

Turkish fireship that the sailors of the French, English, and Russian coalition attempted to drive off.[23]

Chronometrically, topographically, and logistically exact, the panorama of *The Battle of Sedan*, first shown in Berlin on September 1, 1883, with the Kaiser in attendance, represented the moment on the afternoon of September 1870 between 1:30 and 2:00 that proved to be a turning point in the engagement leading to the Prussian triumph over the French. To achieve such an effect of reportorial accuracy, the artist—Anton von Werner (1855–1927)—used strategic maps, went on maneuvers, and studied the amount and extent of smoke emitted by different caliber guns, assisted in his research by a staff of weapons experts. Bismarck approvingly viewed himself meeting Napoleon III for the French capitulation, commenting on the lifelikeness of his horse, Rosa. The artist, however, was to complain of the impermanence and disposability of the panorama as an art form undervalued by the cultural establishment.

> All these works, spatially and artistically powerful, vanished after the sightseers had seen their fill—and the stockholders had no further prospects of high dividends. I wonder if some future book on art history will mention any of them as a characteristic phenomenon of the last third of the nineteenth century?[24]

It is precisely this constant unrolling of a world-panorama before the glazed eyes of the passive spectator that led Nietzsche to assail the hypertrophy of the "historical sense" and "historical culture" in the new democratic age.[25]

Projected on Smoke and Imprinted on Wax

Impermanence was characteristic of the popular arts. Two other genres of visual simulations of historical personalities, important in determining how the nineteenth century perceived itself and imagined its heroes and villains, were the phantasmagoria and the waxworks. For six years, starting in 1789, Etienne Gaspard Robertson, a Belgian inventor and balloonist, presented his *Fantasmagorie*, or optical illusions, in an abandoned chapel on the grounds of an Old Capuchin monastery in Paris. By means of a magic lantern he projected ghostly apparitions onto smoke or semitransparent screens.[26] In addition to luminous images of Gothic specters and skeletons—fashionable in an age enamored of sorcery, magic, and phantoms—the *Fantasmagorie* included famous figures from the French Revolution and its aftermath, such as Marat, Danton, Robespierre, and Napoleon—specters still haunting Europe.[27] A mobile lantern and adjustable lens allowed the images to be enlarged or contracted, creating the illusion of ominously advancing or retreating figures who seemed to approach the spectators and almost touch them, spreading terror among the audience.[28] These shows, presented in London and New York in the first decades of the nineteenth century, also featured re-creations of eruptions of Mt. Vesuvius and spectacular fires currently in the news. They placed the spectators directly at the center of the spectacle.

When Madame Tussaud established her waxworks in London in 1802 at the Lyceum, her museum was located next to Paul de Philipstal's Phantasmagoria.[29] Waxworks offered three-dimensional dramatic representations of current events and personalities in the news, and since Madame Tussaud insisted on keeping up with the headlines, the exhibits changed with the times. Rigorous authenticity was proclaimed. For her French Revolutionary figures, such as Charlotte Corday, Marie Antoinette, and

Robespierre, the effigies were modeled either from death masks or from casts made of the severed heads brought directly to the cemetery from the guillotine.[30]

Where possible, the figures were dressed in their actual clothes. "The Effigy and Personal Effects of Napoleon" was one of the special attractions, particularly admired by the Duke of Wellington, a frequent visitor at Madame Tussaud's. Seeing him contemplating his defeated enemy, the Tussaud brothers commissioned William Hayter to paint this scene, thereby obtaining a historical painting—which subsequently hung in the waxworks—that reflexively comments on simulation.[31] One great historical player, now aging, admiringly confronts a replica of his former rival, fixed by death at an earlier moment that has been captured forever by the art of the wax-worker. Two time frames co-exist and several layers of simulation intersect, producing a modern perspective (not unlike that present in the Mabou Mines' 1983 historical reconstruction, *Cold Harbor*, in which General Grant is brought out of his museum case) pleasing to those with an increasingly democratized interest in the makers and making of history.[32] Whereas, given present technologies, the Iron Duke would be interviewed on television and shown footage of his former adversary to be commented upon, in the silent Victorian simulation each viewer is required to read Wellington's reflections according to the expression on his face and his stance vis-á-vis the fallen foe.

War by Correspondence in the Crimea and in India: Imperialist Entertainment

An expanding mass-circulation press, financed by advertising and furthered by new telegraphic technology, set out to create and then satisfy curiosity about current events. In its reliance on the power of visual effects, the new pictorial journalism transformed politics and war into entertainment. The Crimean War (1853–56), the bloodiest in Europe between Waterloo and World War I, was the first to be covered by eyewitness reporters. The foreign correspondent of the *Times* of London wielded such power in mobilizing popular support for the war that it was said that the country was actually being governed by the *Times*.[33] War correspondents watching from hillsides sent telegraphic dispatches, but photographers actually present still posed and staged battle scenes which would not shock the public. Langlois created a striking photographic panorama of the devastated countryside around Sebastopol, but avoided battle scenes altogether. The gallantry of war, not the spectacle of death, was the subject of patriotic journalism that aimed at pictorial distraction (the American Civil War photographer Matthew Brady was ruined when he showed genuine horrors and atrocities).[34]

At Astley's hippodrome, *The Battle of Alma* was presented in October 1854, less than a month after the event. With 400 extras, brass bands, and vast processions of troops, it put on stage a *Times* correspondent as a character who assists in defeating the barbarian Russians, killing one and capturing several others himself.[35] For the first time a historical simulation placed within its frame the newsgatherer who was the source of its existence. It was not until Karl Kraus's vast drama of World War I, *The Last Days of Mankind* (1922), that war correspondents were portrayed not simply as reporters of what happened, but rather as major causes of the war. Kraus indicts journalists as instigators of hatreds responsible for the bloodshed.

Newspapers in the mid-nineteenth century offered enthusiastic support for imperial and colonial wars, and no one questioned the inspiration provided by chauvinistic journalism for popular entertainment. The playwright Dionysius Boucicault records in his memoirs (talking of himself in the third person) that while visiting New York in the 1850s he found in the accounts of historical events in the popular press new subjects for his dramas.

> Boucicault had used these three years in the study of the American people, their tastes, and the direction of their intellectual appetites. The poetic and romantic drama had no longer its old charm; the actual, the contemporary, the photographic had replaced the works of the imagination. It was in turning over the *Illustrated Journal* that the idea struck him that the stage might be employed in a similar manner to embody and illustrate the moving events of the period. The Russian war, the Indian mutiny, the adventures of Dr. Kane in polar regions, the slave question, were all live subjects of the period. But the most immediate and burning matter in the public mind was the Indian mutiny. The news of the massacre at Cawnpore had filled the world with horror, when we learned that a small garrison of Europeans were shut up in Lucknow, besieged by an overwhelming force of Indians. This article was seized on by Boucicault when he wrote "Jessie Brown, or the Relief of Lucknow," and this play was produced in New York while the siege was still in progress.[36]

All the major battles of the Crimean War—Inkerman, Balaclava, Sebastopol, as well as Alma—had military spectacles devoted to them. Indian and Afghan wars and mutinies were the subjects of panoramas and spectacles in London: *The Battle of Kabul in the Afghan War*, a panorama in 1842 commemorating a defeat; *The Afghanistan War; Or, The Revolt at Kabul and British Triumphs in India*, a huge spectacle of 1843, making use of elephants as well as horses; *The Storming and Capture of Delhi*, at Astley's in 1857, as well as panoramas on the Sepoy Mutiny and the Mutinies at Delhi and Lucknow; and *The Fall of Khartoum and the Death of General Gordon* at the rebuilt Astley's in 1885.[37]

At the Great Paris Exhibitions of 1890 and 1900, reconstructions of battles and naval engagements continued to be popular, as were panoramas showing scenes from the French Revolution, the battle of Austerlitz, and other episodes in French history.[38] But it was the many "little wars" of the early twentieth century that provided the best material for the entertainment industry. In 1901 the Cirque d'Hiver presented a military pantomime, *The Allies in China*, while the Nouveau Cirque in 1905 gave a pantomime of the Russo-Japanese War. At the Châtelet, where the Cirque Olympique had moved in 1862 when the theatres on the Boulevard du Temple had been razed, the sinking of a Russian battleship by the Japanese was staged as late as 1911. At the end of the old century and the beginning of the new, news as visual entertainment still took the form of picture postcards, figures at the wax museum, panoramas, and theatrical spectacles; film, the product of the latest technology, would enter into competition with these earlier forms of news simulation, and the power of its pictures was such that it eventually supplanted all others.

Reconstructed Newsreel

Almost immediately the new film studios which appeared in the mid-1890s went into the news business. Louis Lumière sent cameramen throughout the world to make newsreels and documentaries, but George Méliès, a magician by training, chose to follow the earlier traditions of spectacle and panorama and to reconstruct current events in his studios.[39] Actually, the mass-circulation papers, such as *Le Petit Journal* and *Le Monde Illustré*, were doing much the same thing at this time when they had graphic artists copy or re-create photographs; because of difficulties in photographic reproduction, engravings were preferred for use as illustrations.[40]

Méliès began his pioneering work in reconstructed newsreels with scenes from the Greco-Turkish War of 1897: *War Episodes, Massacre in Crete*, and *Sea Fighting in Greece*. In 1898 he reconstructed scenes of the American intervention in Cuba and the Philippines: *A View of the Wreck of the Maine* and *Divers at Work on the Wreck of the Maine*, in which a painted backdrop representing the sunken battleship was photographed through a large aquarium containing real water and fish.[41] Lumière had shot a brief simulated Dreyfus Affair in 1897. During the summer of 1899, Méliès made a thirteen-minute *Dreyfus Affair* with eleven sets that reconstructed the illustrations in the weekly papers.[42] Because of the passions these reconstructions aroused, the government prohibited the filming or showing of works about the Dreyfus case.[43] Using actors and painted sets based on a published photograph, Méliès prepared *The Coronation of Edward VII* in the studio at Montreuil in 1902 several days before the event itself took place so that the film could be shown on the evening of Coronation Day at the Alhambra music hall in Leicester Square.[44]

We should remember that Méliès was making his famous fantastic "trick" films—such as *A Trip to the Moon* (1902) and *The Impossible Voyage* (1904)—at the same time as his *actualités reconstituées*. The distinction between true and false, then as now, was hard to draw and for many nonexistent. In certain Third World countries today people believe that the film of the 1969 moon-landing is "simulated"—a kind of Méliès trick film.

The ten years from 1897 to 1906 were the high point in the reconstructed newsreel. In 1906 a cinema was opened which was devoted entirely to authentic *actualités*, or so it was advertised. Once techniques of photographing and developing had become sufficiently advanced, current events were increasingly filmed on location rather than in the studio. Starting in 1900, the *Pathé Journal* or newsreel appeared on a regular basis.

But for a number of years at the turn of the century audiences were most deeply moved and affected by simulations which effectively dramatized events that could not be captured or adequately filmed while in progress. Starting with their own six-part *Dreyfus Affair* in 1899, Charles and Emile Pathé began to create a series of *actualités reconstituées* under the general direction of Ferdinand Zecca, a young Corsican in charge of the studios at Vincennes on the outskirts of Paris. Although Zecca continued to produce comedies, trick films, and adventure and crime stories, special emphasis was placed on the increasingly popular simulated documentaries about disasters, such as *The Great Chicago Theatre Fire* and *The Catastrophe in Martinique* (1902; about the volcanic eruption that killed 40,000). The ancestor of this simulated disaster newsreel was a theatrical spectacle, *The Earthquake in Martinique*, by Lafout and Desnoyer, given at the Porte-St.-Martin and Gaîté theatres in 1840.

Using eyewitness accounts, photographs, and drawings from newspapers and magazines such as *L'Illustration* and the picture supplement of *Le Petit Journal*, the Pathé artists (already experienced in historical reconstructions such as *Quo Vadis* and various lives of Jesus) were able, in the course of only a few hours, to prepare painted backgrounds of cities and ports so precisely detailed that they could be taken for the real place. For *The Catastrophe in Martinique*, the painted backdrop represented the town and the volcanic mountain Pelée, in front of which a large trough of water served as the ocean. One studio assistant burned sulfur behind the mountain, another on a ladder out of view of the camera manipulated a large tray so as to bring smoke down upon the set in

Body of Vakulinchuk, the martyred hero, in Lucien Nonguet's film version of the *Potemkin* mutiny, *The Events of Odessa* (1905)

imitation of lava, while yet another, perched on a ladder, threw sawdust to create a rain of cinders. A fourth assistant shook the trough of water to simulate waves and at the end of the film hurled the entire contents at the backdrop to produce a gigantic tidal wave.[45]

The New York studio, Vitagraph, filmed a tabletop battle of Santiago Bay—with cigar smoke, explosives, and cardboard ships going down in inch-deep water—because actual footage of Theodore Roosevelt going up San Juan Hill was dull and disappointing. Such practices cause the documentary film historian Erik Barnouw to talk of fakery and deceit. He cites as further evidence of fraud the work of the British filmmaker James Williamson whose *Attack on a Chinese Mission* (1898) was shot in his backyard, and whose Boer War scenes were filmed on a golf course, while Biograph's *Battle of Re Yalu* and Edison's *Skirmish Between Russian and Japanese Advance Guards* were reconstructed on Long Island and New Jersey.[46]

Although the British painter John Constable had said of the panoramas and dioramas, "It is without the pale of art, because its object is deception,"[47] the very nature of the nineteenth-century media for news simulations kept the audience from being truly deceived. No matter how spectators standing at the center of the rotunda exclaimed that the panorama seemed reality itself, they did not really believe that they had been transported from London or Paris back in time to the battlefield at Waterloo. Likewise, for all its three-dimensionality, smoke, noise and smells, real water and real horses, and hundreds of authentically costumed soldiers at the Cirque Olympique or Sadler's Wells, the immediacy of the theatrical representation, the audience's knowledge that the performance was happening here and now limited the possibility of any complete illusion. That the film reconstructions—flat, silent, without color, often involving only several dozen performers, and lasting one or two minutes—seemed so real as to deceive audiences and raise charges of fakery is due to the reportorial nature of cinema. Film portrays something that purportedly happened somewhere else at an earlier time; its record of distant events can be played over and over again in other places and at other times. Its very essence is deception.

Lucien Nonguet, who was the *chef de figuration*—director in charge of supernumeraries and crowd movements—at the Châtelet, Ambigu, and Renaissance theatres in Paris, at first only provided his friend Zecca with extras and supervised their placement and grouping.[48] Soon, however, Nonguet undertook the *mise-en-scène* himself and became Zecca's principal co-worker at Pathé. In 1902–3 the two filmmakers collaborated on a lengthy *Life and Passion of Our Lord Jesus Christ* in eighteen tableaux, and Nonguet alone produced a number of spectacular fairy tales, such as *Puss-in-Boots* and *Sleeping Beauty*, as well as a version of Zola's *Germinal* (without acknowledging its source). But it was in the field of *actualités reconstituées* dealing with nihilists and assassinations, war and revolution, that Nonguet demonstrated his skill in handling crowds.[49]

Starting in 1903 with *The Assassination of the Royal Family of Serbia*—followed by *The Assassination of the Minister Plehve* and *The Assassination of the Grand Duke Serge*—Nonguet began to reconstruct, in a series of carefully researched films, the bloody events taking place in Eastern Europe and Russia. The Russo-Japanese War in 1904 offered spectacular opportunities to make front-page news come alive. *The Catastrophe of the Petropavlovsk in the Roads of Port Arthur* used small-scale models and a theatrical setting to present the sinking of the Russian flagship, whereas another of the *Scenes from the Russo-Japanese War* was filmed outdoors, making use of 150 extras costumed and armed as Russian and Japanese soldiers; alternate titles in six languages proclaiming either "Long Live Russia" or "Long Live Japan" were available, to be chosen according to the political sympathies of the audience, and attesting to the objectivity and neutrality of the representation.[50]

The revolution of 1905 provided Nonguet with his most important subject.[51] *The Disturbances in Saint Petersburg* dealt with Father Gapon and the workers' march to the Winter Palace to petition the Tsar on January 9, known as Bloody Sunday because of the massacre which took place when troops fired on the unarmed demonstrators. In July 1905, twenty years before Sergei Eisenstein commemorated the revolt, the first film about the *Potemkin* mutiny was shot at the Vincennes studio of the Pathé brothers one month after the revolution. This two-and-one-half-minute documentary, a part of the series "The Revolution in Russia," is called *The Events in Odessa*.[52] It tells the story of the mutiny aboard the largest and newest warship in the Russian navy, the *Potemkin*, and the impact of the rebellion on the port of Odessa.

Like all the Pathé reconstructed newsreels, Nonguet's *Potemkin* is based on journalistic reports and designed to compete with the illustrated newspapers by means of painted backdrops that are skillful copies of photographs; it strives to be factual and give the spectators the impression that they are witnessing actual historic events. Its fast-moving narrative represents the principal stages of the revolt and its effects in all their concrete particularity, quite unlike Eisenstein's attempt to universalize and create a symbolic ship of revolution. Rather than mythos, the French filmmaker offers montage—in its embryonic state to be sure, but nonetheless montage—and herein lies

Nonguet's montage device, the telescope iris, shows a view of the shore as Cossacks attack the citizens of Odessa. The mound of earth and the fence are real, not a painted set.

the innovation of *The Events in Odessa*.[53]

In this brief one-reel film, Nonguet creates a panoramic series of images that include many of the well-known episodes that now make up the *Potemkin* legend given definitive shape by Eisenstein. Reconstructed in short scenes lasting no more than a few seconds are the sailors' refusal to eat the soup made of spoiled meat, the murder of the sailor Vakulinchuk, the throwing of the officers overboard, the display of the martyr Vakulinchuk's dead body on the pier to the emotional crowd, the shelling of the city, and the cossacks' assault on the people. As the title indicates, the focus of Nonguet's reconstructed newsreel is not upon the battleship itself (we never learn what happens to the crew), but rather upon the impact of the mutiny on Odessa and the inciting of violence there.

Montage results as the camera alternates between ship and shore during the bombardment of the city. First we see the mutinous officer, who has assumed command of the ship, directing cannon fire against Odessa from the side of the deck; next we witness the consequences of the shelling on the people in the burning town, as perceived through the telescope of the now jubilant officer. The point of view of the mutinous commander is juxtaposed to that of his victims, as the camera moves rapidly from his enthusiastic gesticulating to the suffering of a family driven out of their flaming home.

Next the authorities order the massacre of the citizens of Odessa in reprisal for the uprising. Nonguet's documentary ends unresolved, at the moment when a band of

Cossacks, armed with whips, beat a group of women and children trapped against a wall; this scene of Tsarist repression is comparable—on its own small scale—to Eisenstein's famous Odessa steps sequence, arousing the same feelings of pity and indignation. A sense of lively reality is imparted to the scene when the women fight back furiously and a small dog bites at the heels of one of the Cossacks.

Nonguet's primitive montage device of the telescope iris enables the filmmaker to show repercussions in the community caused by the presence of the revolutionary ship in the harbor. The final nine-second sequence reveals much of the city engulfed in flames. Uncertainty remains as to who is responsible for the disorder: the officers, the mutineers, or the Cossacks—but the people are clearly the ones who suffer. The *Potemkin* mutiny was chosen as a reconstructed newsreel because it was topical and sensational, capable of arousing feelings of outrage in French audiences at the shocking events in Russia. The reconstructed newsreel had no room for interpretation; the events were all that mattered.

In 1907 Nonguet directed a remake of the Pathé *Dreyfus*,[54] but gradually the *actualités reconstituées* died out as a film genre, unable to survive the competition posed by the new illustrated newspapers and the authentic news films (*actualités véritables*) which were coming into vogue. During World War I newsreels of battles and atrocities were sometimes simulated in the service of propaganda, further discrediting simulation as deceptive manipulation.

Eisenstein's Battleship Potemkin *as Actualité Reconstitutée and Mass Spectacle*

Like Nonguet's works for Pathé, Eisenstein's film, *The Battleship Potemkin*, displayed the concern for pictorial authenticity characteristic of the reconstructed newsreel; the director and his assistants went to French and Italian illustrated newspapers of the time and reproduced as faithfully as possible the pictures and drawings of Vakulinchuk's body in the tent on the pier and the crowd on the steps looking out to sea at the ship. Eyewitness accounts by the French journalist Gustave Babin— "The Revolt of the *Potemkin* and the Rioting in Odessa" and "The True Adventure of the Battleship *Potemkin*"—appeared on July 15 and 22 in *L'Illustration*, and there were also newspaper articles and published memoirs by a number of the leaders of the revolt as well as a commemorative volume of historical documents for the twentieth anniversary of the mutiny, all of which Eisenstein consulted.[55]

Commissioned for the anniversary of the 1905 revolution, Eisenstein's *Battleship Potemkin* is part of the tradition of the mass spectacle that goes back to the festivals of the French Revolution. Soviet mass spectacles, inspired by the theories of Romain Rolland in his *Le Théâtre du peuple* (*The People's Theatre*, 1903), had flourished after the October Revolution; thousands of workers, soldiers, and citizens joined professional actors, circus clowns, and acrobats to reenact revolutionary scenes from Russian and world history in the great historic squares of Petrograd and Moscow.[56] These huge pageants were staged on major dates in the history of world revolution according to a new revolutionary calendar of holidays designed to replace old Christian celebrations. Where possible, as in the case of the 1920 *The Storming of the Winter Palace* (with 8,000 participants and 100,000 spectators), the mass spectacle was enacted in the original setting of the historical event with the participation of those who had shaped history. In *The Overthrow of Autocracy*, staged in Petrograd in 1919, the revolution of 1905 was presented as the first important step in the crumbling of the Tsarist monarchy; Bloody Sunday, which had taken place in the same city fourteen years earlier, was the episode chosen for dramatization. In June 1920, there was staged in Odessa, along Maritime Boulevard overlooking the port, a grandiose concert-meeting entitled "The Revolt of the Battleship *Potemkin*" in which actors played the roles of the heroes of the rebellion.

In the Petrograd mass spectacle, *Toward a World Commune*, staged in 1920 in front of the former Stock Exchange and played partly on the broad steps leading up to the building, the first section devoted to the Paris Commune showed a group of communards trapped on the stairs by the Versailles troops. Moving upwards from below in detachments, soldiers fired a volley into the crowd; the writhing bodies of the wounded and dying communards fell on the steps, while others leapt off the stairs in frenzied attempts to escape.

The aesthetics of the mass spectacle had enduring impact on later dramatic versions of the *Potemkin* mutiny, including Eisenstein's. The aim of these commemorative pageants was to celebrate and strengthen feelings of unanimity and indivisibility by means of ceremonies and processionals, religious in nature but seeking to replace Christian belief with socialist faith, while often retaining the old iconography. In *The Battleship Potemkin*, Eisenstein, long attracted to religious art and the pathos of spiritual ecstasy as found in the paintings of El Greco, stresses themes of martyrdom and brotherhood through repeated religious motifs and imagery.

Filmed almost entirely in Odessa, in the places where the actual events took place, Eisenstein's *Potemkin* made use of a huge cast of several thousand, composed of a few professional actors and masses of local Inhabitants, some of whom would actually have witnessed the happenings they were re-creating. The student agitator Konstantin Feldman—one of the key figures in the real drama—was played by Feldman himself in an early example of autoperformance; he also served as an advisor on historical detail and authenticity. Like the mass spectacles, *The Battleship Potemkin* is a reenactment of a famous episode in the revolutionary calendar, in which historical facts are subordinated to the central idea of glorifying revolution. Eisenstein inscribes history into eternal time and transmutes the events in Odessa into myth. As Adrian Piotrovsky (theoretician, classicist, translator, critic, scenarist, deviser of mass spectacles, and film studio head) observed, Eisenstein's *Potemkin* is a film without plot or psychology, devoid of stars or heroes, and glorifying only a collective protagonist, the sailors and the people of Odessa.[57] Rather than the division between ship and shore as in Nonguet's neutral, ironic *actualité reconstituée*, Eisenstein imposes a wholeness upon history, eliminating all signs of discord and violence among the people and the sailors, still slightly discernible in the scenario but absent from the film. In the scenario, the rabble-rouser from the reactionary Black Hundreds who cries, "Beat the Jews," is himself beaten by the angry crowd, but in the film he is only driven away—in reality, he was killed on the spot.

In 1925 there was already a sizable body of prose, poetry, and drama about the *Potemkin* and an evolving tradition of imagery and motifs upon which the filmmaker could draw. Eisenstein makes extensive use of the general store of poetic images that the now legendary battleship invariably called forth and gives us the breaking waves, the mist, spray, and fog, the soaring seagulls, and the inevitable revolutionary flag—tinted red by hand for the black-and-white film.

Eisenstein's own attitude toward reconstructed actuality was ambivalent. He both affirmed his film's historicity by his use of sources and consultants and then later denied that some of the famous episodes had any basis in fact. But the innovative spirit of

The student agitator, Konstantin Feldman, playing himself
in Eistenstein's *The Battleship Potemkin* (1925)

the film is best revealed by how the artist handles the now conventionalized and almost obligatory episodes and themes rather than in claims to original invention. Eisenstein himself is responsible for confusion as to how much of the *Potemkin* legend is the creation of his film. Thus even an event as strictly historical (found in all the eyewitness accounts) as the covering of the sailors with a tarpaulin before the order is given to have them shot was, according to the filmmaker, an artistic fabrication shocking to a naval officer present at the filming who declared that such a procedure was absolutely impossible.[58]

Likewise, it has been implied that the massacre on the Richelieu Steps never took place and was Eisenstein's invention. Despite some conflicting testimony, the evidence clearly indicates there was a terrible slaughter on the famous stairs leading from the town to the port. The Social Democrat and Menshevik, Kirill (one of Eisenstein's sources), reports that the sailors who went to army headquarters to arrange for Vakulinchuk's funeral saw bodies on the steps: "In the port and on the stairs leading to the sea-front, they had to pick their way through piles of workers killed during the night."[59] During the "red night" of June 28, extensive looting and burning by an unruly mob took place, and the cossacks and soldiers shot those trying to escape from the burning port by the only possible route, the stairs. Eisenstein's originality lies in his skill in dramatizing an authentic element of the historical reality through the transformation of its details. He staged the attack in the daytime with the innocent and unsuspecting people in a festive mood—descending the stairs, rather than trying to escape up them— and falling suddenly victim to the relentlessly advancing, machinelike cossacks. Here

Eisenstein has appropriated the basic situation of Bloody Sunday, in which Tsarist troops opened fire on a peacefully assembled crowd of men, women, and children. The Soviet filmmaker absorbed and synthesized the most diverse ideas, suggestions, and raw materials to create a "song" or hymn to revolution.

All that did not further the revolutionary pathos and heroic grandeur of the mutiny was judged irrelevant. The "eccentric" elements in the scenario—grotesque or satirical incidents of overt theatricality, related to the circus numbers in the mass spectacles and similar to the stunts that dominated Eisenstein's staging of Alexander Ostrovsky's *Wiseman* at the Proletkult Theatre and his first film, *Strike*—were rhythmically and tonally disruptive and were cut from the final version of the film. One of these eccentric numbers introduces two journalists, dressed in black and wearing derbies, who stand back to back on the pier and lean against each other as they jot down the words written on the placard on Vakulinchuk's chest as he lies in the tent: "On account of a spoonful of borscht." These bourgeois newsmen, with their music-hall costumes, do not make news, but prey upon those who do; ultimately they are irrelevant to the revolutionary event and were discarded in the cutting room.[60]

Eisenstein's most striking intervention in the historical record was his turning a humiliating defeat into a great revolutionary victory by ending his film with the triumphant meeting of the battleship *Potemkin* with the squadron sent to attack it. The *Potemkin* cuts directly through the fleet without a shot being fired—the rebellious battleship sails on.

In his essay "Constanta (Where Does the Battleship *Potemkin* Go?)"—written in 1926, but not published until 1969—Eisenstein explains why he decided not to show the desperate and futile wanderings of the *Potemkin* across the Black Sea, its flight to Romania and final surrender to the Romanian authorities in Constanta. Because the meeting with the squadron was the "high point representing the maximum of revolutionary spirit conceivable under the circumstances," the Soviet filmmaker chose to conclude his drama at that moment, fixing forever a triumphant image.[61] By treating a momentary success rather than an ultimate defeat, Eisenstein was able to show the *Potemkin* as moral victor over the Tsarist forces.

The Red Admiral and the Singer Sewing Machine Company

Revolutionary dramas are always in quest of heroes, but the *Potemkin* mutiny could produce no candidates, except for the dead martyr, Vakulinchuk. Afanasii Matiushenko, the haunting, enigmatic leader of the revolt, refused to fit neatly into the heroic mold or to play his expected part in the legendary pageant. In Nonguet's reconstructed newsreel, there is no such protagonist developed as leader of the revolt, and in Eisenstein's scenario he remains unnamed and scarcely visible. In the film, however, Matiushenko assumes a major role as a generalized and idealized representative of the entire crew, forcefully expressing their harmonious will—the perfect revolutionary sailor.

Such is the picture of Matiushenko that appears in a characteristic Soviet form of reconstruction: the retouched photograph of the revolutionary hero, with all blemishes removed. In Boris Pasternak's short poetic epic on the *Potemkin*, "Mutiny at Sea" (1926), which takes place on the first glorious day of freedom (before complications and contradictions set in), Matiushenko strides into view for a moment, "towering tall." In fact, he was small and exceptionally short, as unretouched photographs taken in Romania show.

After crisscrossing the Black Sea for a week—frantically searching for a friendly port—and failing to kindle the spark of revolution elsewhere, the demoralized crew of the *Potemkin* returned to Constanta (their first port of call) and capitulated on Saturday, July 8, 1905, at 3 A.M. sailing under the Tsarist Saint Andrew Flag. The red flag had been buried at sea the day before. Over 600 members of the crew elected to stay in Romania, where they were given asylum but kept under strict surveillance. The remaining 117 returned to the ship and swore allegiance to the Tsar once again. They were immediately arrested and imprisoned on the ship, soon to be returned to Russia where they were given summary trials and sentenced to labor camps. A Russian fleet under Rear Admiral Pisarevsky towed the *Potemkin*, which had been partially sunk, back to Sevastopol.

The French journalist Gustave Babin gave the following portrait of the leader of the revolt:

> All those who, at Constanta, have come near Matiushenko remain as it were haunted by this alarming brute of a man, with the prominent cheekbones of a Kalmuck, with hate-filled eyes, with a stupid, gloomy countenance teeming with cruel ideas. [. . .]

> He ruled by terror. He went back and forth along the passageways on the bridge and in the batteries, always frenzied and enraged, clutching his revolver, constantly threatening. Every one trembled on seeing him appear.[62]

In his dramatic poem, *The Battleship Potemkin* (written in 1922 and thus the first Soviet version, performed in 1927 by the TRAM theatre in Perm), the poet Georgii Shengeli gives an unorthodox portrait of Matiushenko as a bitter, disillusioned man confronting a passive, fearful, and disunified crew, threatening to shoot anyone who disagrees with him (an account supported by the memoirs of Feldman and Kirill). After throwing off the Tsarist yoke, there is immediate need to reintroduce even harsher authority; Matiushenko must use revolutionary terror if he is to maintain order. In the final moment of the dramatic poem Matiushenko contemplates suicide and reflects on the failure of the mutiny, while members of the crew have gone to find solace and distraction in the brothels of Constanta. This Matiushenko—with his revolver in hand, his need to assert authority, his hatred of prostitutes—is an unorthodox Soviet study of the revolutionary temperament.

Nicknamed the Red Admiral, the real Matiushenko was a wanderer, like the battleship itself. In his wanderings in Europe after the failure of the mutiny, he met Lenin in Geneva as well as Father Gapon, whose protégé he became, but the Red Admiral was not able to settle down and accept the role of revolutionary-in-exile that many of the leading Potemkinites found congenial. In Paris, the hero of the *Potemkin* hoped to start an armed uprising and associated with anarchists. A solitary man of action mistrustful of intellectuals, he could not understand or tolerate party politics and intrigues.

In June 1906, Matiushenko came to the United States where he remained until March 1907. The former machinist on the *Potemkin* worked for the Singer Sewing Machine Company in New York and lived on the Lower East Side, where he made contact with Russian radical circles. On October 11, 1906, Matiushenko met Maxim Gorky, who attempted to help the former sailor get his autobiography published (failed revolutionaries often become authors).

In June 1907, Matiushenko returned to Russia, using a false name and forged passport. There the Red Admiral was soon arrested, still carrying his revolver, probably betrayed by a seeming comrade. He was tried by a military tribunal, sentenced to death, and executed under conditions of high security with several companies of troops standing guard. Even the Red Admiral's lonely death agony was a public spectacle at which he conducted himself with exemplary courage and heroism.

Not long before his return to Russia, Matiushenko wrote from Paris to his friend Zamfir Arbore in Romania:

I'm completely fed up with the mugs around here, talking incessantly, screaming about freedom incessantly, while they are nothing but slaves themselves, the most despicable slaves of their own lusts. There are many socialists here, but very few real people. They all talk, scream, argue, abuse one another, and are ready to gouge out each other's eyes, without even knowing why. Well, to hell with them, let them argue to their heart's content—the people know what they need without any help. [. . .] I think a lot about the happiness of the people and I shall never cease to do so. But I am now afraid of one thing: will the Russian people, in return for the blood which is now being shed in Russia, achieve what they did in Western Europe and America? If so, I wash my hands of it in advance. I do not need freedom of that sort.[63]

The poet Dmitrii Petrovsky (a friend and disciple of the Futurist Velimir Khlebnikov) in his *Black Sea Notebook* (1925)—a collection of poems on the revolt of the *Potemkin*, other naval mutinies, and seascapes—created a documentary poem describing Matiushenko's execution taken directly from an eyewitness account.

I did not see the execution.
This is what they said:
While they read the sentence,
He paced up and down before the line of soldiers.
They finished and he said: *Farewell,*
Comrades
And he stood on the table.
Akimov started yelling.
He responded.—"Why are you screaming?"
And on the table he said:
—Do your hanging, cowards!
The professional hangman
Put the noose over his neck and gave a shove.
The table flew off.
They started beating on a drum.
He hung there for almost fifteen minutes;—Then they let him down.
They took his fetters off:
It seemed a waste to bury the iron
In the grave;
They twisted his feet
So as not to have to unlock the chains.
And threw him in his overcoat into his coffin.[64]

Such was the lonely death of Matiushenko.

The Potemkin's *Last Prodigious Adventure: Super-Châtelet and Black Sea Stunt Men*

On the seventieth anniversary of the mutiny, The *Potemkin* reached its final destination in Paris at the huge 80,000-seat Palais des Sports. The stage and film actor and director Robert Hossein presented a mass spectacle, *The Prodigious Adventure of the Battleship Potemkin*, recapitulating and synthesizing all the traditions of nineteenth- and twentieth-century historical simulation. Taking part in Hossein's *Prodigious Adventure* were more than 100 professional actors, crews of technicians, special effects people, lighting experts, and the recorded Chorus of the Red Army singing Jean Ferrat's popular *Potemkine* in Russian. The replica of the battleship *Potemkin* constructed in the middle of the vast arena of the Palais des Sports—twenty-six meters long, ten meters wide, and twelve meters high—was an authentic scale model, about one-fourth the length of the actual battleship. It provided a stage on which the crew of extras—more highly disciplined than the Russian sailors—did their daily chores, fell in for roll call, marched, and ran. Called by one critic "Hossein's Black Sea stunt men," the sailors made incredibly high leaps in the air and during the climactic meeting with the squadron jumped from one moving battleship to another.

The Prodigious Adventure dealt in epic fashion with the entire mutiny from joyous exaltation to bitter defeat. Hossein, whose image was projected on a huge screen fourteen meters high, served as a filmic chorus throughout, except at the beginning and ending of each performance when the actor himself appeared on stage.

For the leftist French creators of *The Prodigious Adventure*, the *Potemkin* mutiny is a mirror for studying their own failed revolution, the Paris student-worker uprising of 1968. The dominant ideological role is given to the student Feldman (minimized in Eisenstein's film) as the activist-intellectual who attempts to act as a bridge between the armed services and the working classes; the revolt fails in large part because his call for firm and decisive action is not heeded. *The Prodigious Adventure* achieves its impact by its striking visual effects, returning to the traditions of the nineteenth-century military and naval spectacles. The performance opens and closes with a vision of the wanderer-ship, its enchanted crew forever frozen on the deck in a tableau, eternally dreaming the dream of revolution. The title, *The Prodigious Adventure of the Battleship Potemkin*, comes from Gustave Babin's firsthand reporting in 1905 from Constanta for the popular Parisian weekly, *L'Illustration*. But whereas Babin called his account "The True Adventure of the Battleship *Potemkin*," the Palais des Sports version is prodigious rather than true.

Several French critics with long memories—half-admiringly, half-mockingly—called Hossein's *Potemkin* "super-Châtelet," referring to the 3,600-seat Théâtre du Châtelet which had perfected the traditions of the Cirque Olympique. Nonguet had come to Pathé from the Châtelet, and the filmmaker Robert Hossein is his direct descendent. For the audience in 1975, *The Prodigious Adventure* was a modern live version of the reconstructed newsreel, a grandiose silent film with accompanying musical score and Hossein's recorded spoken subtitles and intertitles superimposed on the action. For both Nonguet and Hossein, the goal is the same: to recreate the historical event so vividly that spectators would have the sense of witnessing what had actually happened. Apart from technological improvements and contemporary ideological viewpoints, the only significant change that has occurred in the seventy years separating the primitive Pathé *Potemkin* from its Palais des Sports grandchild is that the French spectators of *The Prodigious Adventure* knew in advance what they were going to see and realized that they were participating in the ritual celebration of an already sanctified legend.

The "Black Sea Stunt Men" of Robert Hossein's
The Prodigious Adventure of the Battleship Potemkin (1975) at the Palais des Sports in Paris

From Revolutionary Icon to Cardboard Cruiser

What remains for the Battleship *Potemkin*? Can it continue its wanderings and reach new shores? Or has it become a profitable restoration, a reconstruction of an old ship to be visited by tourists?

The repertory of revolutionary imagery and gesture is severely limited; to be effective its signs must be external, public, and instantly recognizable. Crowd emotions are by their very nature large and unsubtle, and therein lies their power. The *Potemkin* tradition would seem to have reached the stage of development where all it can do is repeat itself; newer versions quote earlier versions, sometimes unconsciously, more often deliberately. In several modern films, the famous battleship, canonized by Eisenstein, serves as the occasion for cinematographic homages, in-jokes, and allusions. In Jean-Luc Godard's *Les Carabiniers* (1963), a pretty female revolutionary about to be executed places a kerchief over her head and calls out "Brothers!" while in Dušan Makavejev's *Sweet Movie* (1974) one of the young protagonists wears a *Potemkin* sailor hat during much of the action. In Ettore Scola's *We All Loved Each Other So Much* (1974), late one night in a deserted plaza Nicola recreates the Odessa Steps sequence, while in Brian DePalma's *The Untouchables* (1987), in gangland Chicago the final train station shootout reprises the Odessa Steps massacre. Also from 1987, Zbigniew Rybczyński's *Steps* superimposes contemporary American tourists over Eisenstein's famous sequence of the Cossack's slaughter of the innocent victims trapped on the stairs. Oblivious to the horrors taking place around them, the sightseers take snapshots of one another and eat hamburgers.

The old ship of revolution is starting to mirror its own image, rather than present or future realities. Growing obsolete as a living symbol (sooner or later all symbols become nostalgically cherished and slightly ridiculous fossils), the *Potemkin* has turned into a theatrical prop, and the revolution that failed has proved successful as popular entertainment and icon. In 1987, a Polish youth movement, Orange Alternative, marked the seventieth anniversary of the Russian Revolution by staging a mock battle between cardboard cruisers named the *Potemkin* and *Aurora*.[65]

The journalist Babin—with a bourgeois Frenchman's sharp eye for the centrality of money and theatre in life—reported that from the very start the mutiny became the occasion for a show and a source of profiteering. In Romania, speculation in *Potemkin* buttons and caps began as soon as the sailors set foot on shore; by the next day, simply the bands from the caps were bringing fifteen francs each. Complete uniforms went for the highest prices, since they would be in demand for the *Potemkin* masked balls that would be all the fashion next season.

NOTES

1. Friedrich Nietzsche, *The Use and Abuse of History*, trans. Adrian Collins (Indianapolis: Bobbs-Merrill, 1957), 29.
2. Gustave Le Bon, *The Crowd: A Study of the Popular Mind* (New York: Viking, 1960), 68–69.
3. Walter Benjamin, *Reflections: Essays, Aphorisms, Autobiographical Writing*, trans. Edmund Jephcott (New York: Harcourt, Brace Jovanovich, 1978), 149–50.
4. Frederick Brown, *Theater and Revolution* (New York: Viking, 1980), 76–77.
5. Marvin Carlson, *The Theatre of the French Revolution* (Ithaca, NY: Cornell University Press, 1966), 44–45.
6. See Hassan El Nouty, *Théâtre et Pre-cinéma: Essai sur la problématique de spectacle au XIXe siècle* (Paris: A.-G. Nizet, 1978), 43–44; and James H. Billington, *Fire in the Minds of Men* (New York: Basic Books, 1980), 45–46.
7. Régis Michel, *David: L'Art et le politique* (Paris: Gallimard, 1988), 74–75.
8. Michael R. Booth, *English Melodrama* (London: Herbert Jenkins, 1965), 93; Allardyce Nicoll, *A History of English Drama, 1660–1900* (Cambridge: Cambridge University Press, 1962), 3:54.
9. Martin Meisel, *Realizations* (Princeton, NJ: Princeton University Press, 1983), 204.
10. "The panorama struck a responsive chord in the nineteenth century. It satisfied, or at least helped to satisfy, an increasing appetite for visual information. A revolution in travel made the world seem smaller. The newspaper industry meant that many people were aware of a greater number of happenings over a larger area of the globe. It is not surprising that people should desire visual images of a world of which they were becoming increasingly aware through the printed word." Scott B. Wilcox, "Unlimiting the Bounds of Painting," in *Panoramania!*, ed. Ralph Hyde (London: Trefoil Publications in Association with the Barbican Art Gallery, 1988), 37.
11. Richard D. Altick, *The Shows of London* (Cambridge, MA: Harvard University Press, 1978), 174–75, 136.
12. Frank Rayhill, *The World of Melodrama*. (University Park, PA: University of Pennsylvania Press, 1967), 133; Booth, 100.
13. Arthur Saxon, *Enter Foot and Horse: A History of Hippodrama in England and France* (New Haven, CT: Yale University Press, 1968), 46, 137; Booth, 93–94; Altick, 175.
14. See Altick, 136.
15. Ibid., 325.
16. Marian Hannah Winter, *The Theatre of Marvels* (New York: Benjamin Bloom, 1964), 176; El Nouty, 56.
17. Quoted in El Nouty, 46.
18. See Meisel, 215–17.
19. In Saxon, 123–24.
20. See Saxon, 121.
21. See Meisel, 219-21.
22. Dolf Sternberger, *Panoramas of the Nineteenth Century*, trans. Joachim Neugroschel (New York: Urizen, 1977), 187.
23. See El Nouty, 56.
24. von Werner, quoted in Sternberger, 15.
25. Nietzsche, 48, 49.
26. Erik Barnouw, *The Magician and the Cinema* (New York: Oxford University Press, 1981), 19–27.
27. Etienne Gaspard Robertson, *La Fantasmagorie* (Paris: Cafe livre. 1985), 13.
28. See El Nouty, 51; Altick, 219.
29. See Altick, 333.
30. Anita Leslie and Pauline Chapman, *Madame Tussaud* (London: Hutchinson, 1978), 70–75.
31. Altick, 223. What survives is an engraving, reproduced in *The Shows of London*, of Sir William Hayter's *The Duke of Wellington Visiting the Effigy and Personal Relics of Napoleon at Madame Tussaud's* (1852), now destroyed.

32. See Altick, 222–23; Meisel, 234–35. Daniel Gerould, *Guillotine, Its Legend and Lore* (New York: Blast Books, 1992), 79–81.
33. See Billington, 314–17, 337–38.
34. Gay Cogeval, *From Courbet to Cézanne: A New 19th Century* (Catalog. Paris: Editions de la Reunion des musées nationaux, 1986), 71–74.
35. J.S. Bratton, "Theatre of War: the Crimea on the London Stage 1854–5," in *Performance and Politics in Popular Drama*, edited by David Bradby, Louis James, and Bernard Schratt, 119–37. (Cambridge: Cambridge University Press, 1980), 129–33; Saxon, 144.
36. Dionysius Boucicault, "Leaves from a Dramatist's Diary," *The North American Review* 19 (August 1889): 230.
37. See Nicoll, 5:579, 675; Saxon, 144, 205, 221.
38. Charles Rearick, *Pleasures of the Belle Epoque* (New Haven, CT: Yale University Press, 1985), 208.
39. Paul Hammond, *Marvelous Méliès* (New York: St. Martin's, 1975), 34.
40. Jacques Deslandes, *Le Boulevard du cinema à l'époque de Georges Méliès* (Paris: Cerf., 1963), 62.
41. See Hammond, 36; Deslandes, 62–63.
42. See Hammond, 42.
43. Norman L. Kleeblatt, *The Dreyfus Affair* (Berkeley: University of California Press, 1984), 276–77.
44. See Hammond, 53–54.
45. René Jeanne, *Cinema 1900* (Paris: Flammarion, 1965), 127; Jean Mitry, *Histoire du cinema.* (Paris: Editions Universitaires, 1967), 5:219–20.
46. Erik Barnouw, *Documentary* (New York: Oxford University Press, 1974), 24–25.
47. Quoted in Harold Osborne, ed., *Oxford Companion to Art* (Oxford: Oxford University Press, 1986), 317.
48. See Mitry, 216.
49. See Jeanne, 131.
50. Georges Sadoul, *Histoire générale du cinéma*, vol. 2, 5. (Paris: Denoel, 1975), 302; Hughes Laurent, "Le décor de cinéma et les décorateurs," *Bulletin de l'Association française des ingénieurs et techniciens de cinéma* 16, 4.
51. Alain Lacasse, Sonia Lemelin, and Andre Michaud, "La Révolution en Russie. Fiche signalétique/Découpage technique," in *Les Premiers Ans du Cinéma Français*, ed. Pierre Guibbert (Perpignan: Collections des Cahiers Cinémathèque, Institut Jean Vigo, 1985), 259–66.
52. Restored in 2004 by the Finnish Film Archive to the correct speed, the film actually runs five minutes.
53. See Mitry, 222. See also Alain Lacasse, Sonia Lemelin, and André Michaud.
54. See Sadoul, 302.
55. Ignatii G. Rostovtsev, *Bronenosets Potemkin* (Moscow: Isskustvo, 1962), 78–81.
56. For descriptions and photographs see František Deák's 1975 article in *TDR* 19, no. 2 (T66).
57. Adrian Piotrovsky, *Teatr. Kino. Zhizn'* (Leningrad: Isskustvo, 1969), 218.
58. See Rostovtsev, 100–101.
59. Kirill [A.P. Berezovsky], *Drama v tenderovskoi Bulehtye* (Moscow: Molodaya Gvardiya, 1934), 90.
60. Naum Kleiman and K. Levina, eds., *Bronenosets Potemkin* (Moscow: Isskustvo, 1969), 85.
61. Sergei Eisenstein, "Konstantsa. (Kuda ukhodit 'Bronenosets Potemkin')," in Kleiman and Levina, 290–92.
62. Gustave Babin, "Le Véritable Aventure du Kniaz Potemkin," *L'Illustration*, July 22, 1905, 56–57.
63. Afanasii N. Matiushenko, "K prebyvaniu Potiomkintsev v emigratsii," in *Istoricheskii Arkhiv* 3 (1955), 147.
64. Dmitrii Vasilevich Petrovsky, *Izbrannoe*, with an introduction by Viktor Shklovsky (Moscow: Gosudarstvennoe Izdatel'stvo Khudozhestvennoi literatury, 1957), 1.
65. John Tagliabue, "The Very Young Decide to Form a Cutting Edge," *New York Times*, June 14, 1988, A4.

Andrzej Bursa

ANDRZEJ BURSA

Almost fifty years after his death in 1957 at the age of twenty-five, Andrzej Bursa remains a cult figure and marginal presence in the history of Polish literature, although the emotions that his work arouses have changed over the years. The hopes and fears of the post-Stalinist thaw in Poland half a century ago are now distant memories and no longer of vital interest to present-day Polish readers. Yet Bursa's poetry, fiction, and drama have not ceased to fascinate because all his creative works spring from the artist's angry protest against the fraudulent world in which he found himself. His disillusioned response was both lyrical and grotesque, denunciatory and cynical, marked by an acute awareness of the senselessness of everything including himself, a total rejection of the accepted social norms, and an obsession with impermanence and death.

The Stalinist period in Poland from 1949 to 1955 was one of political repression and censorship, fear and conformity, isolation from the rest of the world, cultural stagnation, provincialism, and boredom. Feeling hopelessly behind the times and out of touch with the new currents of European thought, Polish youth was intellectually curious and ready to shake off Soviet imposed socialist realism and rejoin the "avant-garde."

After the thaw of 1956 the Polish arts exploded and began to attract international attention in the fields of music, film, theatre, and literature. Like Bursa, Krzysztof Penderecki, Jerzy Grotowski, Sławomir Mrożek, Marek Hłasko, and Stanisław Grochowiak—all in their early twenties—came of age as artists at this time.

This was a period in which there sprang up literary cabarets, poetry readings, jazz clubs, and young people's art associations. A new style of writing took shape in which Polish heroics were ridiculed and ugliness, poverty, and suffering became objects of infatuation. Irony and the grotesque came into fashion. A reaction set in against the big institutional, state-run theatres in favor of the alternative student theatres like Bim-Bom, STS, and Kalambur (which in Poland existed within universities, but enjoyed a certain freedom and independence from adult control and had no connection to professional theatre training).

Bursa was a member of an immensely talented generation and a highly creative milieu; many of his contemporaries have become much better known, but he shared their concerns and sensibility, and if it had not been for his premature death, he might have achieved the same kind of fame. Seen in this context, his work is exemplary but kindred in spirit to that of his peers

Andrzej Bursa was born in Cracow in 1932 to well-to-do parents from the intelligentsia. Despite the war and occupation, he completed his secondary schooling and went on to the Jagellonian University where he was an indifferent student at languages and literature; he briefly switched to art school and then abandoned his formal education. He worked as a journalist for Cracow newspapers; he had married at twenty and had a wife and son to support. He was for a short period a member of the Communist Party, as were many of his contemporaries. He made his literary debut in 1954 with the short poem of some 100 lines, "A Voice in the Discussion about Our Youth," a sweeping condemnation of the hypocrisy and lies of the Stalinist era and an attack on the older generation for their deceit and moral cowardice. This was a daring and controversial opening statement on the part of an unknown twenty-two-year-old.

—PAJ: A Journal of Performance and Art 27, no. 2 (PAJ 80) (2005): 99–113.

Bursa's promise seemed great, but it would remain unfulfilled. In 1957 he died of inoperable heart disease. During his lifetime a few of his poems appeared in the press. A volume of his poetry was published posthumously in 1958, causing a sensation and giving rise to a growing legend, but it was only in 1969 that a comprehensive collection of his work in all genres, including his plays, finally came out.[1]

His brief creativity, condensed essentially into two years—1956 and 1957—was intense. He wrote three micronovels, eight short dramas, hundreds of essays, reviews and articles, short stories, and a great deal of poetry. Bursa was active in Cracow's burgeoning artistic life, whose epicenter was Tadeusz Kantor's theatre Cricot II, located in an artists' café. Kantor called it a street theatre since it continued the action of the street and aimed to be equally provocative, full of surprises and absurd associations.

From its inception in the autumn of 1955, Bursa appeared at Cricot II both as an artist and as a member of the audience. The plays started at 10 PM, and a jazz band played before the show. The audience was seated at the tables, eating and drinking throughout. During the intermission and after the show the audience took to the floor and danced. In May 1956 the first two plays staged were Witkacy's *The Cuttlefish* and the painter Kazimierz Mikulski's pantomime, *The Well*. Kantor also introduced a new element: an "intervention" (actually planned beforehand) by "poètes maudits" who would burst onto "the stage," recite their poems, and verbally abuse the audience. Andrzej Bursa was one of the poets, along with the seventeen-year-old Ireneusz Iredyński (also a future playwright).

In January 1957, Kantor presented Mikulski's *Circus* as "commedia dell'arte in abstracto." Then from April to June 1957, *Circus* was played on the same bill with Andrzej Pawłowski's *Kinoforms*—a form of "visual music" consisting of moving abstract images projected on a screen to the rhythm of music produced by a "special machine for kinoforms"—and *Carbuncle*, a theatre of horrors written by Bursa and his friend, Jan Guntner, an actor at Cricot and also at the Piwnica (wine-cellar), the new literary cabaret that would become a landmark in Cracow. The text of *Carbuncle*, which survives only in fragments, is a scenario full of magical transformations and stunts. In a shadow sequence, a gentleman in a tail coat strokes the silhouette of a naked girl. Then a spotlight reveals the same girl, live, with blood dripping from the spots that the man has touched. The actions resemble the happenings that Kantor would stage in 1966.

For Bursa, his "theatrical experience" at Cricot II and his subsequent connection with Piwnica, where his poetry and dramatic sketches often featured, were seminal. He loved theatre, wrote occasional reviews, and dreamed about "writing good dramatic pieces." All of his eight short dramas, which he called "dramatic experiments," were written in rapid succession during the last two years of his life. He also worked on stage adaptations of Saint-Exupéry's *The Little Prince* and Ilf and Petrov's *The Twelve Chairs*.

In order to understand the creative stimuli for *Count Cagliostro's Animals*, we should take into account that Bursa participated in Kantor's production of *The Cuttlefish* and would certainly have been acquainted with other of Witkacy's plays, including *The Shoemakers*, which had been published in 1948. For Polish theatre artists Witkacy was the link to the pre-war Polish avant-garde and its greatest representative. Intrigued by commedia, Bursa could well have seen Krystyna Skuszanka's productions of Gozzi's *Turandot* and Goldoni's *Servant of Two Masters* at Teatr Ludowy in nearby Nowa Huta. And his drama perhaps owes something to Jarry's *Ubu Roi* and its view of history as a monstrous farce. The super-showman Cagliostro had captured Jarry's imagination too; his one-act opera-bouffe, *Le Manoir enchanté* (1905), takes place in Cagliostro's "magic chateau" and sings the praises of the illustrious sorcerer, even though he never appears.

At the time of the thaw everything was in motion. The new theatre magazine, *Dialog*, which published its first issue in January 1956, began introducing the latest trends in Western theatre, with translations of the plays of Sartre, Camus, Ionesco, Beckett, and the theatre of the absurd in almost every issue. After 1956, Konstanty Ildefons Gałczyński's *Little Theatre of the Green Goose*, an on-going series of nonsense plays by a major poet, began to exert an influence on the student theatres. Gałczyński's irreverent debunking of Polish history and myth, his poetic fantasy, and his mastery of parody made him an elder the young could emulate.

In 1955 Bursa wrote a short poem "Cagliostro" in which he sets out his view of the famous swindler as a demagogue, hoodwinking the working classes.

> Cagliostro—bastard of a slut from Naples
> Sipping wine now plays baccarat with marquises
> Luck spins across the table like a golden ducat
> Wigs bow low before a rogue out of the gutter.
>
> When faint hearts quaked fearing for their necks
> And sentries at the Bastille were reinforced
> He showed the Queen inside a crystal sphere
> An ingenious machine for chopping heads off.
>
> The Queen went pale, for there beneath the guillotine
> She saw the shape of her own face in the glass
> And next day the Master floated over rooftops
> To the "ahs" and the "ohs" of cobblers and masons.
>
> So when the heads began to roll in earnest
> And the enraged masses swayed like a flag
> The cry went up: "Now Master—In some former church
> Celebrate a black mass for the pope's demise"
>
> But Cagliostro—tightly clutching his bag
> Of peddler's tricks, pursued by a half moon
> Urged his servant on to keep the horses flying
> Across a quaggy border into Flanders.

Written two years later, *Count Cagliostro's Animals* is Bursa's most mature play and his most political; it parodies different theatrical genres and modes, such as pantomime, commedia dell'arte, and circus, with rapid shifts of action and mood. The choice of subject reflects the poet's fascination with the histrionic personality, public performance of the self, and theatrical manipulation of the populace. Joseph Balsamo (1743–1795) from Palermo—alias Count Alessandro di Cagliostro—was a famous eighteenth-century charlatan posing as a magician, fortune-teller, medium, and healer, selling elixirs of youth and love potions, and conducting séances in Parisian high society. So many legends have swirled about Cagliostro that he has no fixed identity or shape and exists in a fictive world of rumor, slander, and gossip. He has been the subject of numerous novels, romances, operas, operettas, and ballets. To some he is a genius of the occult, to others a crass adventurer. Astutely, Bursa never brings Cagliostro on stage, making the impostor all the more elusive and spurious as the creation of his animals' fears and paranoia.

From its first appearance *Count Cagliostro's Animals* has been interpreted politically as a satire on totalitarianism and a reaction to Stalinist abuses of power, but it is a marked departure from the deadly serious variety of philosophical-political drama characteristic of Polish drama prior to Mrożek. In adopting an absurdist, non-didactic approach, Bursa anticipates the ironic, mocking tone of the new Polish drama of the 1960s.

The psychology of Cagliostro's animals is patterned after the fear and opportunism of the Stalinist era. The two protagonists, Albandine and Bartholomew, are, like members of Bursa's generation—deformed morally as well as physically. They condemn Cagliostro's brutality and support freedom only when he appears to be losing; they re-affirm their allegiance to Cagliostro when he reasserts his tyranny. Bartholomew, the revolutionary worker-demagogue, has had a classic childhood of deprivation and received indoctrination in class consciousness at the tannery where he was apprenticed. Albandine is the eager convert, and Catherine the victim, branded as a counter-revolutionary. Fear rules the lives of the workers who are ready to do anything that they are told to by those in power. Morally corrupted, they serve the debauched and depraved Cagliostro, a low-born impostor playing a bogus count.

People's Poland was ruled by countless Cagliostros. The ordinary people were duped and manipulated. Only Catherine, Cagliostro's medium and lover, is courageous enough to have her own opinion, but for her convictions she must pay with her life. Catherine uses her common sense and clear vision to strip away the myths of revolution. She has seen the Master remove his artificial eye and walking about with his nightshirt raised above his navel.

The revolt in the cellar by the animals imitates the revolt in the streets. When the street exclaims, "Liberté!" the cork pops out of Albandine's head. The phallus of the King of Nipuans, once an implement for begetting tyrants, briefly serves as the tree of liberty before becoming the weapon with which Catherine is killed.

The charlatan-trickster Cagliostro has his own "animal farm," or troop of actors to play out the scenes of revolution. We see the great revolutionary events only from the perspective of "down below," from the "lower depths." From the grotesque perspective of underneath, people become judged only by the condition of their shoes.

Cagliostro's cellar is a storehouse, or property room, of revolutionary "props," including all the banners, songs, and slogans of revolution. The trio of animals performs the allegory of revolution, an old show number that they have given many times before. Revolution and its language and gestures have become a tired variety act, performed by the lowly monsters who mouth its empty words and phrases. Revolution is nothing but theatre in the theatre, a parody and pastiche. The ending of the drama brings us back to the beginning and the shoes that are passing by. Has anything changed? Has any revolution actually taken place?

Count Cagliostro's Animals can also be interpreted as a drama about the artist. The actor is a key figure in Bursa's aesthetic theory. In his poem "The Defense of Beggary," Bursa puts the case for beggars as hard-working actors who are playing themselves and who deserve our admiration for their daring self-exposure of their own wounds.

The three figures that appear in Cagliostro's theatre of biological curiosities are artificially raised monsters who must enact their deformities by putting their bodies on display. Their bodies are also subject to torture by their director and the master of theatrical ceremonies, whom they hate. Cagliostro has made them into freaks. Actors are like beggars, who must perform their own deformities and misfortunes. Tadeusz Kantor's traveling band of players from the lowest level of society has much in common with Cagliostro's group of animal performers.

The first production of *Count Cagliostro's Animals* took place on May 2, 1958, at the Teatr Atelier in Poznań, where it was directed by Stanisław Hebanowski, managing and artistic director of the small experimental theatre, founded in November 1957. He had opened the theatre with the first Polish production of Beckett's *Endgame*. The Atelier did not have space of it own, but played in different places in Poznań. The actors received no pay. Hebanowski gained recognition for selecting and introducing new authors and interesting literary texts, among others, Beckett, Ingmar Bergman, Albee, Tadeusz Miciński, Evreinov. His productions appealed to the elite by their intellectual rigor; the church and the party objected to the obscenity and anti-proletarian sentiments of the performances.[2] A second production of *Count Cagliostro's Animals*, directed by Zofia Jaremowa, took place in Cracow at the Groteska Puppet Theatre in April 1972.

Since the 1980s there has been a revival of interest in Bursa, characterized by a strong element of nostalgia. The writer is seen to personify rebellious youth at a crucial turning point in modern Polish cultural history, and his tragic early death has made him the James Dean of Polish literature.

NOTES

1. Andrzej Bursa, *Utwory wierszem i prozą*, ed. with an introduction by Stanisław Stanuch (Cracow: Wydawnictwo Literackie, 1969). It contains *Zwierzęta hrabiego Cagliostro*,131–43. See also Stanisław Stanuch, *Życie moje . . . : o twórczości i życiu Andrzeja Bursy* (Toruń: C & T Editions, 1995); Ewa Dunaj-Kozakow, *Bursa* (Cracow: Wydawnictwo Literackie, 1996); and *Czytanie Bursy*, ed. Anna Czabanowska and Grzegorz Grochowski (Cracow: Księgarnia Akademicka, 2004).
2. Andrzej Żurowski, *Hebanowski* (Warsaw: Wydawnictwa Artystyczne i Filmowe, 1984), 63–81. See also *Teatry Stanisława Hebanowskiego: odkrycia, powtórki, rewizje* (Gdańsk: Tower Press, 2005).

Tadeusz Sabara as Albandine, Jerzy Kaczmarek as Bartholomew, and Irena Maślińska as Catherine in *Count Cagliostro's Animals*, Atelier Theatre, Poznań (1958), directed by Stanisław Hebanowski

COUNT CAGLIOSTRO'S ANIMALS
by
Andrzej Bursa

ALBANDINE—A fellow raised from childhood in a bottle, approximately three feet tall.
BARTHOLOMEW—A creature thin as a rail with extremely long legs, played by an actor on stilts.
CATHERINE—CAGLIOSTRO's medium.

COUNT CAGLIOSTRO's *property room in a Parisian cellar.*

BARTHOLOMEW *is standing with his face at the cellar window, which is too high for* ALBANDINE *and* CATHERINE *to look out.*

ALBANDINE: Any news?

(BARTHOLOMEW *shakes his head negatively.*)

ALBANDINE: I don't like it . . . But tell me, Bartholomew . . . has nothing really happened? . . . Well, I mean, it can't keep on like this forever . . . The uncertainty has me terrified (*tearfully*), it isn't our fault, is it . . . But tell me, Bartholomew, tell me, what kind of shoes did you see most often in the street today?

BARTHOLOMEW: I already told you, the number of shabby black shoes with low heels has been on the increase since yesterday. Oh, look there . . . too bad you can't see the sort of legs that just went by. They must belong to an apprentice. Lots of apprentices have been walking down the street for the last two days.

ALBANDINE: Lots of apprentices? That's odd. Might be worth pondering.

CATHERINE: Dumbbell.

ALBANDINE: What? . . . What's that supposed to mean, Catherine?

CATHERINE: Just what I said. You're a dumbbell—period. What of it if apprentices are walking down the street? That's some reason to get agitated.

– Translated by Daniel Gerould, New York, 2005.

BARTHOLOMEW: It may be more significant than you imagine.

ALBANDINE: I imagine . . .

CATHERINE: Who cares what you imagine? Cagliostro hasn't given us anything to eat for two days. And that idiot is hatching theories about . . . apprentices. If this goes on much longer, I'll go beserk. But maybe what you're saying about those apprentices is right after all. It's beyond me. I'm a simple down-to-earth girl. I feel sad and I'm hungry. (*She begins to cry*.)

ALBANDINE: Stop it, Catherine.You know how susceptible I am to women's tears. You know that when I was bottled up in the flask, my tear glands floated to the top of my head. So now I can't burst into tears because Cagliostro corked me before he went out. So I'm suffering terribly.

CATHERINE: I'll try to pull the cork out for you. You'll feel better.

ALBANDINE: Can't be done. The cork is kept firmly in place on the strength of a spell known only to Cagliostro. Besides, if I don't cry, it doesn't particularly bother me.

BARTHOLOMEW: The cork will pop out when the walls of Paris echo the spell.

ALBANDINE: What's that you're saying, Bartholomew, maybe you have some news from town? Bartholomew, why don't you answer? Bartholomew, you must know something . . .

BARTHOLOMEW: No use talking with you two as long as you belittle the lot of the apprentices.

ALBANDINE: But we're not belittling anything, Bartholomew, how can you say that . . . we assure you, Bartholomew, the lot of those you mentioned is close to our hearts. Isn't that right, Catherine, we didn't belittle the lot of the apprentices?

CATHERINE (*softly*): Go on, Bartholomew.

BARTHOLOMEW: When Cagliostro bought me as a young lad, he decided to make me long in the legs. You probably know that story, but unless you do, you'll never understand the problem of the apprentices. So he hung me by the legs in a tannery which had been leased by one of his freemason friends. My childhood and tender youth were passed in a gentle swinging amidst the aroma of raw ox hide. Every so often the master stretched my legs on a machine especially constructed for that purpose, whose patent Cagliostro sold a year ago to the Kingdom of Switzerland. You remember that abominable performance we gave for the Swiss in June last year . . .

CATHERINE: Oh, of course. That's when Cagliostro stuck a sharp wire into me in a spot not indicated at the rehearsals. That was a dirty trick on his part.

BARTHOLOMEW: But that's beside the point. I simply made a little digression back to my childhood days. So while I was hanging there among the ox hides, I got to know some of the apprentices. Those weren't always agreeable meetings. Sometimes an apprentice in a hurry mistook me for one of the hides and tried to tan me. But on the whole they were decent fellows. In the evenings they got together in groups and started whispering among themselves. Their eyes were full of fire.

ALBANDINE: Then what?

BARTHOLOMEW: Their eyes were full of fire. The fiery eyes of the apprentices. These days the apprentices are coming out into the streets. Doesn't that tell you anything?

ALBANDINE: Nnno . . . I can't figure it out.

BARTHOLOMEW: You're not up to the situation.

ALBANDINE: Obviously I'm not up to it. But you shouldn't get angry at me. It's not my fault I was enclosed in a bottle. I too was tempted by the smell of meadows in May and shepherdesses' smiles. I too had a mother.

CATHERINE: Who hasn't? But memories won't take the place of meals.

ALBANDINE: Catherine, Bartholomew's words have inspired me with high hopes. Great things await us. What do you see, Bartholomew?

BARTHOLOMEW: Shoes.

ALBANDINE: Are they . . . apprentices' shoes?

BARTHOLOMEW: Yes, for the most part . . .

ALBANDINE: Catherine, Bartholomew sees apprentices' shoes. The apprentices' eyes are full of fire. Isn't that so, Bartholomew?

BARTHOLOMEW: I don't know. I see only the shoes.

ALBANDINE: Can signs of high hopes be found in what you see? Tell us, Bartholomew?

CATHERINE: Be quiet. It's not enough for a person to be cooped up in this basement on an empty stomach, but that idiot has to crack bad jokes. High hopes. You're running on at the mouth about high hopes, while I'm here for the entire springtime of my girlish life rotting in this cellar with two monsters. Count Cagliostro's medium. The mysteries of Paris. I used to get the most exquisite letters from princes and marquises, but Cagliostro intercepted everything and slapped me around too. But even if he hadn't intercepted my letters, I still couldn't have read them, because I don't know how to read.

BARTHOLOMEW: Catherine, the time is drawing near when your illiteracy will be a title of ennoblement. The reign of reason is approaching.

ALBANDINE: Didn't I tell you, Catherine, Bartholomew knows something.

BARTHOLOMEW: Keep calm. Don't be startled by the explosions and all that racket. We'll soon be freed.

CATHERINE: Oh, dear God . . . if only I can somehow get out of this wretched dump.

BARTHOLOMEW: The apprentices' shoes are on the run. Any minute now the revolution will break out.

ALBANDINE: Oh, revolution, you beam of valor . . .

(*They all huddle together and freeze in a fixed pose. The sounds of revolution. The people beat out the syllables: "Li-ber-té!" The cork pops out of* ALBANDINE's *head.*)

ALBANDINE: Oh!

BARTHOLOMEW: Oh!

CATHERINE: Oh!

THE ALLEGORY

ALBANDINE: Oh, revolution, you beam of valor
                                In golden robes with flaming sword
                                You steel weak nerves and dispel pallor

CHORUS: Our hearts burn bright

BARTHOLOMEW: With reason's light

CATHERINE: Sword in one hand, palm branch into the other

CHORUS: You'll lead us where the banner gleams
                                And blood of foes pours out in streams

ALBANDINE: Oh, flying high on sky-born wing
                                Quick as lightning or the lion's spring

CHORUS: When masses jab with sticks and rakes
                                Then blood will flow in crimson lakes.

SONG FROM THE STREET: Blue blood spurts
                                Blue blood of the aroostercruits
                                True blood squirts
                                Blue blood of the aroostercruits.

ALBANDINE: Watch out, Mr. Cagliostro! The age of potentates is over.

BARTHOLOMEW: Brute force's days are numbered.

CATHERINE: A good riddance to bad rubbish. Now I'll fix that rat. For all the wrongs he's done me, for all the girlish tears I've shed. A medium, a medium was what he felt like having . . . But to roast somebody over flames and stick wires into that person's flesh—was that nice, Monsieur le Comte? That's what I'll say to him: was that nice, Monsieur le Comte? . . . The rat would press me with a hot iron and smirk at all those whores in the box seats, making believe I didn't feel a thing because I was under the influence of his fluids. I felt them all right, those fluids of his—in the marrow of my bones. And when I tried to run away with Anatol, a sweet boy who loved me, he caught us barely two miles from Paris. He beat me to a pulp, turned Anatol into a billy goat, had him slaughtered and made his guts into mandolin strings. Oh, Anatol, my poor Anatol. (*She takes the mandolin down from the wall and strums it tearfully. The mandolin bleats like a goat. The preceding monologue by* CATHERINE *is punctuated by exclamations from* ALBANDINE *and* BARTHOLOMEW: "What infamy! Death to the villain! Liberty! Fraternity! Etc.")

ALBANDINE: Cagliostro, you turned me into a bottle, but the wine of revolution fermented in the flask. Revolution has opened my eyes to new perspectives. I refuse to be a bottle any longer. My backbone will straighten and I shall grow taller.

BARTHOLOMEW: And I shall shrink . . .

ALBANDINE: I'll become a real man, handsome and strong, and I'll cultivate the vineyard like my father before me. On nights in May I'll entice young maidens and bed them on the fragrant riverbank. But death to the criminal. (*He bubbles over, a small jet of foam gushes out of the flask.*) I boiled over just a bit. But that's nothing. Getting back to normal will restore my equilibrium.

BARTHOLOMEW: Plant the tree of liberty.

ALBANDINE: Yes, in this gloomy place of torture, the tree of liberty . . . symbol of the dawning day. Catherine, look in the trunk and see if there isn't something that could serve as the tree of liberty.

(CATHERINE *rummages in the trunk, tossing miscellaneous junk about. Nothing fits the bill. Finally she pulls out an elongated object of ambiguous shape.*)

CATHERINE: Maybe this . . .

BARTHOLOMEW: The King of the Nipuans' phallus. The most valuable item in Cagliostro's collection.

CATHERINE: What a lark! He'd drop dead if he could see his precious treasure now.

ALBANDINE: A tool that once begat tyrants today sprinkles the earth with intoxicating blossoms of liberty.

(*They plant the tree of liberty, join hands, dance, and sing: "Blue blood spurts . . ."*)

ALBANDINE: We'll hang Cagliostro on that tree.

BARTHOLOMEW: Better throttle him.

CATHERINE: I'd settle for sticking a few pins into him. So he'd know what it feels like.

ALBANDINE: Oh, nooo. That's far too little. First we'll break him on the wheel, roast him over a slow flame, impale him on a stake, pull out his fingernails, and only then will we kill him . . .

CATHERINE: Oh, nooo. No need to kill him. He wasn't any worse than many others. We'll beat him up, make him behave, and call it quits.

ALBANDINE: Ah-ha, Catherine, I see you're defending Count Cagliostro. Could it perhaps be that those nights you spent in his secret boudoir near the Templars' monastery made you so cozy? Once revolution has rooted out tyrants, it extends its just arm to strike their concubines.

CATHERINE: You're a swine. I'm not defending him just because I slept with him. Anyway it wasn't so bad. Better than those performances when I acted as his medium. But now that we're enjoying liberty, why kill him? I'm not that vengeful.

BARTHOLOMEW: Vengeance is not the motive force of he revolution. Cagliostro ought to be eradicated because it's dictated by the infallible laws of reason.

ALBANDINE: Yes, he ought to be eradicated; do you hear, Catherine, he ought to be eradicated.

BARTHOLOMEW: Tortured to death.

ALBANDINE: At the stake, on the wheel, on the spit, on the grill . . .

BARTHOLOMEW: Yes, and not to slake our thirst for vengeance, but as a consequence of the laws governing humanity.

ALBANDINE: Yes, that's right.

(*They dance circling in the other direction and singing the song.*)

CATHERINE (*cries out*): Stop it, boys, this is madness, come to your senses.

ALBANDINE: Here, in this cellar, his moans and groans will resound. He'll crawl and whine: "Forgive me." And we'll say: "We don't have anything against you, but this is mandated by the eternal laws of reason" and then I'll burn his eyes out with a red-hot poker.

CATHERINE: Cagliostro has one glass eye.

ALBANDINE: Oh, what rotten luck. One less option. So I'll burn out his only remaining eye with a red-hot poker. And then armed with a sharp knife I'll sidle up to him and cut off his . . .

BARTHOLOMEW: Quiet . . . The multitudes are returning from the field of battle.

(*The footsteps of the mob can be heard, cries, songs.*)

ALBANDINE: My heart is overflowing with honey and joie de vivre . . .

CATHERINE: I think I hear Cagliostro's name . . .

ALBANDINE: I hope they won't hang him without us . . .

BARTHOLOMEW: Be quiet . . .

(*They strain their ears to listen. The mob beats out*:
"Ca-gli-ost-ro, Ca-gli-ost-ro.")

BARTHOLOMEW: Cagliostro has been elected to the convention . . .

CATHERINE: That rat will never be eradicated . . .

ALBANDINE: Bartholomew . . . What is that supposed to mean . . . Where's my cork, Bartholomew?

BARTHOLOMEW: Look, didn't I always tell you that the revolution is guided by reason. Towering above the median, I've always seen farther and had a broader outlook. And why shouldn't Cagliostro become a member of the Convention? After all, he's a man of intellect, learned, astute, coming from a working-class background. And we all know that his title as count is bogus.

ALBANDINE: But you said he ought to be eradicated.

BARTHOLOMEW: I never said anything of the sort. I just gave you an example of the inexorable workings of the law of reason. If Cagliostro had opposed the people, he would have had to be done away with. Done away with while suffering the worst agonies, I won't back down on that. But I didn't say the circumstances warranted it. You, however, wished to settle accounts with a member of the Convention by means of various kitchen utensils. For that the revolution exacts a head as punishment.

ALBANDINE(*tearfully*): But you wanted to strangle him . . .

BARTHOLOMEW: Let's stop trying to outshine each other. You have no reason to be afraid, Albandine.

CATHERINE: Ha . . . ha . . . ha . . .

ALBANDINE: Hi . . . hi . . . hi . . .

(*General laughter.*)

ALBANDINE: We've got to arrange a little surprise for him.

CATHERINE: For whom?

ALBANDINE: For Cagliostro, of course. He'll be pleased that we've remembered him.

BARTHOLOMEW: We can put on our allegory. It's lost none of its topical relevance.

ALBANDINE: And we'll say we were worried the whole time wondering if something bad hadn't happened to him.

BARTHOLOMEW: It would be nice to have Catherine present him with a bouquet of flowers.

CATHERINE: I'll present him with a punch in the nose.

ALBANDINE and BARTHOLOMEW: What?

CATHERINE: I said I'll sock him in the jaw. I'll tell him right to his face so he won't forget in a hurry. The rat.

BARTHOLOMEW: Catherine, you'll be branded as a counter-revolutionary.

ALBANDINE: Catherine, how can you!

CATHERINE: Oh, I can very easily! You were just Count Cagliostro's animals. But I slept with him. I've seen him with his night shirt hoisted above his belly button and watched him take out his artificial eye. From my viewpoint Cagliostro is no Prince Charming!

ALBANDINE: Hush her up, Bartholomew; for God's sake, hush her up.

BARTHOLOMEW: Don't get excited, Catherine. After all, the minor set-backs we met with in our work cannot be the cause of such rancor. We're artists, we're the elite. A glorious future awaits us. In the present state of the rule of reason, endless possibilities are open to me because of the length of my lower limbs.

ALBANDINE: And to me because of my shape. To be a bottle—a perfect bottle—is also a proof of the iron-clad nature of the laws of reason. The triumph of human thought over the forms of nature.

BARTHOLOMEW: You're right, Albandine, I see you've grasped a thing or two.

CATHERINE: I'm no bottle or any other kind of freak. I'm a simple down-to-earth girl. I'd like to get out of here and get married, and I'll tell that stinker right to his face. Don't you worry . . .

ALBANDINE: Catherine, don't you dare!

CATHERINE: I'll tell him, I'll tell him . . . "Oh, you cad, you crook, you cheat! With your tail coat you wiped the floors in antechambers of the rich. You slurped your soup from golden bowls. Now you want to be back in the limelight. Fat chance of that. The people of Paris you can take in, but you won't dupe your Katie. Oh, you booze-hound, you whore-monger, you swindler! (*Panting, she grabs the poker.*) I'll grab this poker, I'll hide here in the corner and when he comes in, I'll . . .

ALBANDINE: Catherine, stop, I implore you!

CATHERINE: Shut your trap, monster!

BARTHOLOMEW: Catherine, you better get back in line!

CATHERINE: And when he comes in, I'll smash him with the poker . . .

ALBANDINE: Hold it, Catherine, that's enough. (*He hits her.*)

CATHERINE: What's going on? You're pummeling me! I'll tell him everything, you'll see . . .

(ALBANDINE *and* BARTHOLOMEW *beat up* CATHERINE.)

CATHERINE: You've gone mad! Don't beat me! Think I won't defend myself . . . (*She aims at them with the poker. At this point* BARTHOLOMEW *hits her in the head with the King of the Nipuans' phallus.*)

CATHERINE (*collapses*): I'm dying . . . May angels escort my soul . . .

(ALBANDINE *and* BARTHOLOMEW *huddle together in a corner. After a moment.*)

BARTHOLOMEW: Cagliostro loved that little brat.

ALBANDINE: He won't forgive us for this. (*After a moment.*) Bartholomew, you don't know, do you, what's happening in town, do you? . . . It's grown strangely quiet . . .

(BARTHOLOMEW *goes over to the window.*)

ALBANDINE: What do you see?

BARTHOLOMEW: Shoes . . .

THE END

The Laocoön Group, Vatican collection

LAOCOÖN AT THE FRONTIER, OR
THE LIMIT OF LIMITS

FATHER: I had a bit of bad luck. I get there, I go over to the blindingly white Laocoön Group, of course there's a crowd, a mob, a lot of tourists. I elbow my way through. And there's a sign on the base of the statue: "Laocoön te—Calco in Gesso. Dello Originalle in Restauro." What could I do?

SON: But, Daddy, what makes the Laocoön Group so beautiful?

FATHER (*pacing up and down the room*): My boy, it contains all the inner harmony of the ancient Greek. Ancient man developed his body, mind, and soul harmoniously, and that is why he created an art that is unique in its form. Truth and beauty were one. In the marvelous harmony of the human forms that are entwined by the serpents, the Laocoön Group expresses even suffering in a form that is harmonious and full of moderation. . . . I'm a bit tired. . . .

SON: Is that true of the snakes too?

FATHER: The snakes?

SON: Did the snakes too live in that marvelous harmony that's expressed by their coils?

FATHER: Of course they did.

SON (*enthusiastically*): Ave, Imperator, morituri te salutant.

FATHER: You've got the periods mixed up.

SON (*shrugging his shoulders*): I only just . . . (*The Son raises his thumb up in "Caesar's gesture," then turns it down.*) ingula!

FATHER: What's that supposed to mean?

SON: Oh, nothing. . . .

Tadeusz Różewicz, The Laocoön Group (1961)[1]

Almost all the classical myths—the House of Atreus, Return of Odysseus, Medea, Oedipus—providing impetus for modern versions and offshoots have been transmitted in literary form as dramatic or epic poetry. An interesting exception is the Laocoön, which exists spatially as something seen—a sculptural myth less remembered for its narrative content than for the immediacy of a single visual anecdote.

Although recounted at length in Book II of *The Aeneid*, the myth of Laocoön finds its enduring shape in the Hellenistic Greek statue mentioned by Pliny as standing in the palace of the Emperor Titus, lost for many centuries, and then rediscovered in the Italian Renaissance. Laocoön is thus exceptional on two counts: it has made its mark on Western consciousness as an image rather than a story, and this process began in modern times. Not surprisingly, the sculpture gave rise to other works of art—by El Greco and Blake, most notably—rather than to drama.[2]

The Laocoön Group has always had something of a public, rhetorical character, lending itself to doctrines and declarations. The sensational unearthing of the statue on Esquiline Hill on January 14, 1506, was a major cultural event. Within an hour Michelangelo was on the scene to view what was immediately acclaimed to be one of the greatest masterpieces of ancient art. On June 1, under the sponsorship of Pope Julius II, who had purchased the sculpture and placed it in the Vatican Museum, Romans held a festival to honor the finding of the Laocoön.[3] The statue became the object of such admiration that the pious and moral Pope Adrian VI referred to it as *idola antiquorum* and tried having the entrance to the museum closed off.[4]

—Modern Drama 29, no. 1 (March 1986): 23–40.

William Blake's 1822 engraving of the Laocoön Group,
titled "Jehovah and his two Sons Satan and Adam"

Soon after its discovery the statue became a much discussed and highly coveted object. A contest, judged by Raphael, was held among artists to make a wax copy of the sculpture. International rivalry sprang up for its possession. After the French victory of Marignano in 1515, Francis I through his ambassadors at the Vatican made clear that he expected the Laocoön as a spoil of war, but Pope Leo prepared a plaster copy to put him off with a fake.

Some two hundred years later the French succeeded in acquiring the Laocoön as a trophy of war. In 1796, after Napoleon's victories in Italy, the Pope ceded to France one hundred works of art. Four convoys of wagons left Rome in 1797 and brought the Laocoön and other trophies over the Alps to France. The journey was commemorated in art works depicting the journey, and on July 27, 1798, a huge celebration began in Paris when the captured treasures arrived. The prize statue was paraded before large crowds to the Champs-de-Mars, accompanied by poetry recitations and musical performances. A painting was made of Napoleon viewing the Laocoön Group at night in the Louvre, and a Sèvres vase was issued depicting the arrival of the Laocoön at the Louvre. It was not until 1816 that the statue was returned to Rome. During its decade at the Louvre, the Laocoön was seen by far larger numbers of viewers than had ever seen it before. It had become a tourist attraction.[5]

So there arose in the Renaissance a second myth—not of Laocoön, priest of Apollo, but of the sculpture itself. The world's reactions, not what gave rise to them, became the center of attention. The Laocoön Group as an artifact to be confronted became high drama, starting with a discovery and containing many reversals of assessment and interpretation. Without a context, detached from its original setting and housed in the Vatican as a museum piece, the Group was above all an object provoking speculations on aesthetics, each age finding in it verification of its own principles and predilections. A cultural monument, the Laocoön saw other, figurative monuments erected in its name. Ever since Pliny declared it to be unequaled among ancient sculpture, the Group has been taken as an exemplar to be defined and categorized.

If the late Renaissance found in the Hellenistic sculpture the pathos of the baroque, Germany in the second half of the eighteenth century discovered support for a new classicizing impulse. Winckelmann, Lessing, Herder, Goethe, and Schiller saw the Group as a monument to the noble simplicity, serenity, and greatness of soul which they took to be the classical heritage. So labeled and stereotyped, Laocoön became a rallying cry and watchword, signaling "the tyranny of Greece over Germany"—in the colorful phrase of Eliza Butler.[6] Laocoön was synonymous with an ideal of posed classical beauty to be extolled and imitated.

Lessing's treatise *Laocoön, or The Limits of Painting and Poetry* (1766)— growing out of a description of the sculpture in Winckelmann's pamphlet *Thoughts on the Imitation of Greek Works in Painting and Sculpture* (1755)—is the most celebrated response to emerge from the long preoccupation with the work, rivaling the Group itself in influence and becoming the focal point for subsequent theorizing about art and literature. Due to Lessing, a continuing dialogue on aesthetics in the name of Laocoön has become a part of cultural history.

Often called "theatrical" (usually in the pejorative sense of something mannered and calculatingly effective), the Laocoön nonetheless remained only a topic for aesthetic discourse in non-dramatic forms until very recently. Then, in the 1960s and 1970s, for reasons I shall attempt to explain, two Eastern European playwrights, quite independently, disclosed for the first time theatrical uses for the Group by placing it in plays about mass culture, copies, and bureaucratization.

It is true that in *The Tyranny of Greece over Germany*, Eliza Butler did forecast the possibility of making theatre out of theorizing about art occasioned by the Laocoön in her witty and ingenious analysis of Lessing's essay as a five-act nineteenth-century drama (about the liberation of poetry from the bondage of art) in the Ibsenite mold, with the author himself as *raisonneur* bringing about the gradual revelation of the truth, but her perception remains only a playful literary analogy attached to the obsolescent form of "drama of ideas."[7] For aesthetic discourse on the theme of Laocoön to come to life on the modern stage, there first had to take place the revolution in the concept of theatrical form of the late 1940s and 1950s, and the resulting rejection of two ideas central to Lessing's argument: the separation of genres and the idea of drama as action. The banality of earnest disquisition must be rendered as such, and not disguised by plot and character or elevated to the rank of "serious" ideas.

In 1961, the Polish poet and playwright Tadeusz Różewicz turned to the Laocoön for both the title and principal topic of his second play, which exemplifies a modern, non-narrative use of myth as cultural icon. Różewicz refuses to mythologize. His *The Laocoön Group* is not a retelling, modernization, transposition, or adaptation of Greek myth on stage. It is not a copy, but it is about copies and copying. Nor is it an imitation of an action, but rather a series of conversations that are imitations of what has already been written and said.[8]

Everyone in the play is engaged in artistic discourse, and the most diverse cultural experiences and products are offered for sampling. Two housewives read Spinoza and await impatiently a new edition of his letters, quote Ortega y Gasset, debate the merits of experimental stagings of naturalistic plays and reworkings of Shakespeare, and evaluate new movements in painting. Customs officials know the works of Kierkegaard and talk of the "disintegration, alienation, frustration" resulting from the cultural crisis as something quite routine. Even a tired bureaucrat quotes Kokoschka in German, talks of Burckhardt's views of the Renaissance, and analyzes theories of cubism.

In the midst of this world of proliferating cultural images (now available to all on a mass scale) and ready-made phrases and stereotypes designed to make art manageable as a commodity for consumption, Różewicz introduces the Laocoön as an instance of a great work that will elicit awed responses. Making no attempt to reanimate the myth or reinterpret it, he provides a theatrical context in which the sculpture will be viewed as a dead fact of cultural history about which nothing new can be said, but much old repeated. To this purpose, the playwright creates a pseudo-intellectual family consisting of three generations of two interlocking pairs of fathers and sons (fitting respondents to the entwined fathers and sons of the Laocoön). Theirs are no longer the elite reflections of a Lessing or Winckelmann, but the average man's parrotings of received opinions. Różewicz's family is a primary consuming group with insatiable aesthetic demands who desire instant and constant artistic experiences which the culture industry will supply by its skills at imitation, duplication, reproduction.

A professional himself in the cultural establishment (art historian, curator, professor—we never know exactly what his position is), the Father returns home from Rome "completely saturated with beauty," having seen among other masterpieces the Laocoön Group, which, unfortunately, was on display only in a plaster copy, while the original was being restored. Aided and echoed by Grandfather and Mother (everyone repeats what has already been said, whether by himself or others), the Father tries to inspire the Son, interested in cars and machines, with the higher values of art embodied in the Laocoön by mouthing platitudes out of Lessing. The Son, hesitating between careers as a musicologist or as a dentist, goes off to a friend's house to watch a TV show on how to look at a work of art. But all the fine sentiments and lofty views about art are nothing but plaster copies.[9]

The diffusion of culture in a mass society results not in philistine rejection of art, but rather in the total embrace of it. In the West, under capitalism, where everything is to be bought and sold, the product is culture as a commodity, or the commercialization of art. In Eastern Europe, under communism, where all art is state promoted, financed, and controlled, a leveling pseudoculture is created by the bureaucratization of aesthetic experience.[10] Despite differences in the degree of government involvement, the institutionalizing of culture has led to the same proliferation and vulgarization in both East and West (where grants, subsidies, arts councils, and foundations take the place of direct state support), although the claustrophobic self-containment of communist societies makes the cliché-ridden formulas more rigid. It is precisely because the official fostering of culture has been so complete in Eastern Europe that writers in those countries have been among the first to register and analyze the linguistic consequences.

Różewicz chose the Laocoön as the unifying motif for a play about mass culture and copies—consisting of four disconnected scenes, without beginning, middle, or end, and devoid of action—even though the statue is the subject of aesthetic discourse only in Scenes 2 and 4, whereas Scene 1 takes place in a train compartment at the frontier, and Scene 3 presents the committee meeting of an arts jury deciding on the selection of a monument to honor a great poet. In this respect the Polish playwright has followed the example of Lessing, who in the Preface to his treatise explains: "Since I started, as it were, with the Laocoön and return to it a number of times, I wished to give it a share in the title too."[11]

In the opening scene of *The Laocoön Group*, the First Gentleman (who subsequently becomes the Father) in his exchanges with the Customs Officials talks of beauty as though it were a consumer good acquired abroad that must be declared at the border. The traveler in quest of aesthetic experience returns from the land of classical culture with a "great treasure" which he does not try to conceal from Customs. This enlargement of cultural possessions is part of the tradition of "The Italian Journey" that each voyager shares with all his predecessors.[12]

Shortly after Różewicz's first trip to Italy in the summer of 1960, he wrote both *The Laocoön Group* and the anti-pastoral poem *Et in Arcadia Ego*, which opens with an epigraph from Goethe and closes with the line: "I have tried to return to paradise."[13] Like the German poets, Różewicz—"an inhabitant of a small town in the North" from the area near Wrocław (which once was Breslau)—is drawn to the ideal of classical beauty to be found in Rome. His *Italienische Reise* takes him to view the cultural monuments:

> In the Vatican Museum . . .
> the guides hurriedly copulate
> with the beauty in the tourists' eyes
> ....
> an original in original marble
> but of course[14]

Yet following his experiences of war (Różewicz fought in a guerrilla unit), the paradise of a naïve faith in art has been lost. Deprived of innocence, the poet is now a believer who has ceased to believe:

> It was no accident that I chose to study the history of art. . . .
> I was full of reverential wonder at works of art (the aesthetic
> experience replaced religious experience) but simultaneously I felt . . .
> that something had come to an end for me and for humanity.[15]

Great cultural monuments like the Laocoön, invested with so much meaning over the centuries, are no longer to be revered—or even taken seriously. Those who speak of art in the solemn tones appropriate to religious experience are using the wrong language. Plaster replicas and proliferating images destroy the exceptional status of the work of art. A plurality of copies causes "the decay of aura" and "the liquidation of the traditional value of the cultural heritage," according to Walter Benjamin in "The Work of Art in the Age of Mechanical Reproduction."[16] The realm of art has moved from sacred ritual to politics, as mass society strives to overcome uniqueness and distance gives way to familiarity. A culture of the ersatz and the inauthentic comes into being.

For Różewicz, the plaster of copies is a negation of vitality, suggesting the death mask and the corpse. At the end of Part II of *Et in Arcadia Ego*, the author cites—from one of his early postwar poems, "Mask" (1946)—the following lines describing a Venetian carnival:

> huge effigies with monstrous heads
> laugh noiselessly from ear to ear
> and a maid too beautiful for me
> an inhabitant of a small town in the North
> rides astride an ichthyosaurus
> Objects excavated in my country have small black
> heads sealed with plaster and horrible grins[17]

The "Objects excavated" make reference to the Nazi practice during the occupation of sealing with plaster the mouths of Poles about to be shot in public executions so that they could not shout insults or "Long live Poland!"[18]

The Laocoön is likewise an excavated object, an artifact of human culture, available for study by the historian of civilization. According to the Father, the classical ideal of *kalokagathia*—that beauty and goodness are united, and the body and soul are in perfect harmony—is most fully expressed in the Laocoön Group, where even suffering takes on a beautiful form.[19]

But is this a valid principle for the present? The "small black / heads sealed with plaster" indicate that the old forms are anachronistic and that the time of beauty is long since past. Can physical pain, torture, agony ever be expressed harmoniously and with moderation?[20] The Son—with the clear vision of a child—looks in fascination at the snakes, wonders if their lives have the same marvelous inner harmony expressed in the statue by their coils, and denies that he himself is a manifestation of beauty. And as for plaster casts, he reports matter-of-factly that he sees copies everywhere and thinks nothing of it.

An alternate picture of violent death in antiquity, more consonant with the experience of Różewicz's generation, confronted the poet years before in the Polish capital, itself a recent scene of slaughter. Coming to Warsaw for the first time since the end of the war, in October 1945, when the city was still in ruins, the twenty-four-year-old Różewicz found on a path overgrown with grass a few pages torn from *The Iliad*, including the lines:[21]

> A cloud of dust rose where Hektor was dragged, his dark hair falling
> about him, and all that head that was once so handsome was tumbled in the dust
> . . .
>   So all his head was dragged in the dust; and now his mother
> tore out her hair, and flew the shining veil far from her
> and raised a great wail as she looked upon her son. . . . [22]

Whether or not the Laocoön Group is the perfect expression of the classical ideal of harmony and moderation ("noble simplicity and serene greatness") is not the issue.[23] Różewicz joins in the discourse initiated by Lessing not by stating his own views (he has none and remains objective) or making the statue a symbol or metaphor, but by having the characters repeat the famous quotations, hackneyed phrases, and banalities to which the Laocoön has given rise. No interpretation of the sculpture is offered other than the clichés advanced, thereby rendering the discourse theatrical, not ideological or instructional.

The playwright simply shows how such excavated cultural objects and monuments "impinge on a modern consciousness."[24] The heritage left by the Laocoön is an accumulation of received opinions, piled layer upon layer; the response is no longer to the work of art, but to responses to previous responses. Not only is the Laocoön Group subject to reproduction, but so are all the ideas about it. The clichés of cultural discourse about the arts are the results of a process of endless duplication.

In *Human, All Too Human* Nietzsche writes of "Copies": "Not infrequently, one encounters copies of important people; and, as with paintings, most people prefer the copy to the original."[25] Although they pay lip service to the concept of the original, the characters of *The Laocoön Group* live contentedly in the realm of copies. Everything in their world is a replica, including the Mother's paper flowers. Human beings likewise have become counterfeits, their thoughts and words imitations. The need for copies is, Benjamin argues, an expression of the desire felt by the masses to bring the formerly inaccessible work of art closer—that is to say, to put it on their level, at their disposition."[26]

The reproduction of art leads to its bureaucratization. Prizes and competitions, as for the statue to honor the great poet in Scene 3, are functions of the cultural apparatus. The jury must decide on the Słowacki monument project. Should it be in the shape of a grandfather clock with a cuckoo-Słowacki who awakens the nation every hour? Or should the poet be represented as an ordinary civil servant with Wawel castle in the background, creating the impression that his poetry resembles a soap bubble, but can thunder when necessary? Or should it be a folk-art creation, with Słowacki in a bottle in the shape of a ceramic jar? The jury become involved in a discussion of poetry and "aesthetic revisionism," and as the scene ends they declaim Słowacki's verse.[27]

Behind the words of *The Laocoön Group*—produced automatically, proliferating mechanically, reverberating hollowly—there is nothing, except paper, on which the various citations quoted by the characters have been transmitted. These are all paper feelings and paper problems, as real as the paper rose which for the Mother is so "alive" that she changes its water daily. Paper is the ultimate reality for bureaucracy, subject to constant reproduction and proliferation, and the management of the arts is accomplished through the power of paper and its multiple copies.

Różewicz's theme of mass culture—state-supported, bureaucratized, rendered an ersatz commodity—is a peculiarly modern one. Yet replication is a time-honored practice in the arts, and a reliance on copies cannot be used as a test to distinguish the debased present from an earlier elite age. And here lies another dimension in the choice of the Laocoön Group as the cultural icon to be viewed and discussed in Różewicz's play. The plight of the Father, who laments missing the original on his visit to the Vatican Museum, becomes more ambiguous when we learn that Winckelmann had never been to Rome and had seen only a plaster cast of the Laocoön when he wrote his famous description of the statue that inspired Lessing, who quotes it at length on the first page of his treatise.[28] Quite insensitive to the visual arts, Lessing at the time of his writing Laocoön knew only a series of engravings and had not even looked at a plaster cast.[29] When years later in 1775 he finally made his Italian journey, he included no mention of the sculpture in his diary but is said to have decided, after hours of contemplating the original, that he preferred the plaster cast. Winckelmann himself, in his *History of Art among the Ancients* (1764), in which he repeats his earlier description of the Laocoön, has something positive to say about copies: "We study the copies of the originals more attentively than we should have studied the originals themselves."[30]

All the later German enthusiasts of the Laocoön followed suit. Herder cited Winckelmann, and Schiller copied verbatim the archaeologist's now canonical description. Goethe, who called the Group "the most complete masterpiece of sculptured art," worshiped at the feet of a plaster reproduction in Mannheim in 1771.[31] And all of these copies (apparently of poor quality) were of an incorrectly restored original; the right arm of the father and the right arm of the son are raised high in the air when they should be bent back.

Out of these layers of copied opinions about a copy of a falsely restored original which recedes farther and farther in the distance, there grew up the myth of the Laocoön—in the modern, negative, political sense of a misleading and potentially harmful belief that has gained currency through constant repetition. For in actual fact, the idea, first put into circulation by Winckelmann, that the Laocoön Group exemplifies "noble simplicity and serene greatness" seems in no way whatsoever to correspond to the intricate, realistic original, which gives a heightened and harrowing depiction of physical pain.

In this tangle of copies, it is natural that Różewicz's Father, as he recounts for the benefit of Son and Mother his impressions of the plaster cast he saw in Rome, quotes word for word Winckelmann's description as cited by Lessing, in which there is, in turn, repeated the commentary of the Italian Latinist and poet Sadolet (who in Różewicz's system of deformation becomes Gadolet, from the Polish *gad*, meaning reptile). Thus, the myth of the Laocoön—a mistaken interpretation based on a faulty copy and then endlessly recopied—is passed down from Father to Son, who is—or soon will be—a copy of his father. The repetition of clichés and slogans is a political device—as is the constant citing of authorities—used to promote uniformity and suppress deviation.

Transferring these techniques from the political to the aesthetic realm and creating out of them a dramatic style, Różewicz reveals the totalitarian power of words. But even in a world of carbon copies, the characters of *The Laocoön Group*, as they "hunger for beauty," experience a longing for authenticity. Constant immersion in culture leads to a creative urge. Grandfather asks Father: "Couldn't you put it in your own words?" "Tired of the polytechnicalization and catastrophic situation in the arts," the Mother paints in her spare time and may soon have an exhibition. Both Mother and Son voice the desires to "be themselves"—that is to say, an unrepeatable original—and lead an "authentic" life. But these are further clichés which they have copied from the popular jargon of the day. All talk of the cultural crisis and the need for authenticity is another banality as spurious as the rest. It is impossible to escape from the ready-made phrases recurring in tightening loops and entwining the family, much as the serpentine coils twist about Laocoön and his sons.

Culture plagiarism is at work. With its name-dropping (Arp and Giacometti, Moore and Calder) and use of fashionable words ("alienation," "crisis," "inner values"), Polish intellectual life is mimicking the West. Each generation adopts a different imitative pose. For the Son, there is the mythology of popular youth culture with its heroes to be aped (paralleling those for the intelligentsia of his parents' age). When the Son enters the room to assert his individuality, he copies slavishly James Dean's movements.[32]

Since culture consists of ever growing piles of copies and reproductions, Różewicz proposes a correlative poetics of accumulation and proliferation that mixes genres and styles, based on the view that the chaos of reality overflows all formal bounds, and affirming the triumph of trash and apotheosis of cultural refuse. In this respect, the Polish poet is anti-Lessing, whose Laocoön was written to set limits between the arts of painting and poetry.

In *The New Laokoon* (1910), Irving Babbitt, an American *epigonos* of the classical ideal striving to defend the frontiers against barbarians who would blur genres, says approvingly of Lessing that he "is a lover of boundaries and distinctions, and of the clearly defined type."[33] Różewicz, on the other hand, as a writer who intermingles lyric, epic, and dramatic, is an opponent of limits interested in overstepping bounds, breaking forms, crossing frontiers. *The Laocoön Group* opens at the frontier; the word, *granica*, is the same as for limit in the title of Lessing's treatise. In Eastern Europe boundaries are most often confining, and frontiers threatening. Różewicz's challenge to limits consists of breaking down fixed forms and striving for maximum impurity through the creation of junk art out of scraps of quotations, clippings, lists, and documents.

In the theatre this challenge results in what he calls open dramaturgy. The openness lies in the denial of a perfect, finished, unchangeable work, in favor of what is fragmentary, lacking in internal cohesion: a collage of citations, different styles, found objects (newspapers, overheard conversations).[34] The play can be realized—if at all—only in the theatre through active collaboration with the director and actors. Not the form, but the struggle with it (breaking it open), is what attracts the author of *The Laocoön Group*. "What I like best in the theatre," Różewicz writes, "are the rehearsals. When the director is fighting with everything and everyone. The drama involved in shaping the 'performance.'"[35]

Once again the Polish poet sets himself against the classical ideal as interpreted by its humanist guardians. "For Lessing," Babbitt argues, "the highest thing in art is the plot or design and the subordinating of everything else to its orderly development."[36] The concept of limits dictates that poetry, and thus drama, is temporal, action-oriented, whereas painting and the visual arts are spatial. For Różewicz, standing at the frontier, amidst the different genres, this is simply not the case. "The themes of my plays do not develop through time," he writes, "so the action does not 'develop' either."[37] Without beginnings or endings, his dramas unfold spatially (or geographically) in a circular structure. Poland and the West, the journey to Italy and the return, discourse always coming back to its point of departure—these are spatial perceptions in a work about the contemplation of a piece of sculpture.

A sense of history as well as of geography permeates *The Laocoön Group*, allowing us to see the layers of cultural residue on display in cross section. Greek, Roman, Renaissance, Enlightenment, and Modern are the periods of history so amassed, each having its relationship to the statue. So too the three ages react according to generational perspectives: Grandfather, the old-fashioned humanist, holding that beauty makes life harmonious; Father, the overworked bureaucrat, lecturing about his travels; and Son, latest product of popular culture, interested in the snakes.

By his Latin citation, "*Ave, Imperator, morituri te salutant,*" the Son locates the Laocoön in a Roman rather than a Greek context, attracted to the mass culture of Rome, its public shows and games. Instead of ascribing the sculpture to high culture, as do Father and Grandfather, he places the Laocoön in the category of "bread and circuses" as an example of the man-versus-beast gladiatorial combats popular in the reign of Claudius. The Father immediately squelches the boy's enthusiasm, telling him he has the wrong historical period, but if we accept the current dating of the work as circa 55 B.C., the Son is actually less off the mark than either Winckelmann or Lessing.[38] In any case, the date of composition remains uncertain, and the Laocoön has proved adaptable to many different settings.

The Son's placing the Group in the Vatican Circus rather than in the Vatican Museum may reflect his own interests in the more brutal aspects of mass culture, but it has its justification. According to Suetonius, Claudius's public shows in the Vatican Circus alternated chariot races with gladiatorial combats; wild-beast shows, panther hunts, and other novelties involving men and animals. Finding in the Laocoön a gruesome and sensational depiction of pain and suffering—and not the noble simplicity and serenity of soul perceived by his elders—the Son quite naturally associates the statue with the Roman Circuses.[39]

The Son's reading of the Laocoön is not out of keeping with the judgments of art historians in the nineteenth and twentieth centuries who have found the subject repulsive and the work weird, distressing, melodramatic, pathological, horrifying. "The snakes have no truth to nature," one Victorian scholar objects, "but are zoological monstrosities . . . one of them is biting like a dog."[40] Snakes may be venomous or constrictors, but they do not bite and crush their victims. There is something abnormal and astounding about the anecdote contained in the sculpture. In other words, the Laocoön Group can be perceived as a *fait divers*—the ultimate expression of popular culture for the masses. The *fait divers* is a short, fragmentary news item about crimes, horrors, calamities, monsters, and curiosities of nature, lending itself to a brief text and striking headline.[41] The Laocoön considered as a bizarre accident involving monstrous creatures becomes myth as *fait divers*: "Priest of Apollo and two sons killed on beach by sea serpents," or "Priest killed trying to save sons from water snakes," or "Huge snakes crush and bite priest and two sons."

The arousal of curiosity, the taking inavowable pleasure in disaster, the anomalous nature of the event allowing the viewer to project his own fantasy are all characteristics of the *fait divers*, explaining its mass appeal (shown in the Son's obsession with the snakes). The Laocoön Group is "a monstrous item" that illustrates "the structure of the *fait divers*" as analyzed by Roland Barthes.[42] It is autonomous, a closed structure without context, requiring no outside reference or explanation, and consisting of two terms related by a causality that is aberrant or a coincidence so improbable as to suggest a hidden design. In the case of the Laocoön Group, the disproportion between cause and effect—the break with the norm introducing the paradoxical and irrational—lies in the fact that a priest in the act of protecting his sons is struck down, that three members of the same family have been attacked at the same time, and that the snakes bite and crush simultaneously. The illogicality of the world is affirmed by the *fait divers* as it casts doubts on the everyday workings of causality and gives a glimpse of the unfathomable mystery of the universe. Another theorist, Cl. Sales, places the *fait divers* at the "Frontiers of the Known World":

> It invalidates our way of thinking the world and begins at exactly that point where our intelligence is revealed as unable to understand the universe and get a grip on it. Its discourse is located on an ambiguous frontier where the world ceases being classified, repertoried, subjected to discernible laws and where there is disclosed an unintelligible universe in which all our certitudes vanish.[43]

The cheap journalistic form of *fait divers* offers amore penetrating reading of the Laocoön Group than the high-art criticism of serious journalism which succeeds only in repeating cultural clichés. In his poetry, fiction, and drama, Różewicz has shown a preference for the *fait divers*, for the simple enumeration, in disjointed fashion, of brute fact, or what Barthes calls "the unorganized discard of news."[44] Wartime experiences taught him to mistrust all ideologies, abstractions, and intellectual speculations, and rely only on the concrete. Sensing the impossibility of making reality submit to artistic conventions, he makes assemblages of disparate pieces of trash and bits of old newspaper. Posed on "an ambiguous frontier where the world ceases being classified," Różewicz confronts, on one side, the non-art of the *fait divers*, and, on another, the pseudo-art of kitsch.

If the Son reads the Laocoön Group as *fait divers*, his parents turn it into kitsch. According to Matei Calinescu in *Faces of Modernity*, kitsch is grounded on the idea that "artistic culture can be turned into something fit for immediate 'consumption,' like a commodity," and arises with the "proliferation of cheap . . . imitations" and "spurious replicas or reproductions of objects whose original aesthetic meaning consisted . . . in being unique and therefore inimitable." Even masterpieces can have their aesthetic significance destroyed by being "consumed" as kitsch by philistine sensibilities:

> A kitsch-man . . . is one who tends to experience as kitsch even nonkitsch works or situations, one who involuntarily makes a parody of aesthetic response. In the tourist's role . . . the kitsch-man will "kitschify" . . . cultural monuments.[45]

This description fits Różewicz's Father perfectly. In his *Italienische Reise* to see the plaster copy in the Vatican Museum, he "makes a parody of aesthetic response," but the words he uses are directly quoted from others. When did the process of "kitschifying" the statue begin? Even at the time of its discovery—trumpeted in advance as the summit of ancient art—the Laocoön was already on its way to becoming a cultural cliché. Francesco, son of the architect Giuliano da San Gallo, recounts how he, his father, and Michelangelo went down to the ruins of the Palace of Titus:

> We set off, all three together; I on my father's shoulders. When we descended into the place where the statue lay, my father exclaimed at once, 'That is the Laocoön , of which Pliny speaks.' The opening was enlarged, so that it could be taken out; and after we had sufficiently admired it, we went home to breakfast.[46]

Not unlike the Son in Różewicz's play, the boy Francesco was introduced to classical beauty by his father by means of the Laocoön. But contact with the sublimity of art soon arouses an appetite for something earthly—just as in *The Laocoön Group*, Grandfather, having lost his belief in the supremacy of beauty, asks for Gorgonzola, a cheese brought from Italy providing physical rather than aesthetic sustenance. After buying the sculpture for 500 crowns, Pope Julius II placed the Laocoön in the Vatican Museum, where it could be "sufficiently admired" by crowds of fathers and sons who would then go for breakfast, lunch, or dinner, and repeat the obligatory phrases, revealing their natures as dutiful receivers of culture.

Is it the crowds of gaping tourists who have turned the Laocoön into kitsch, or is Lessing himself to blame for having given currency to the stereotype of "noble simplicity and serene greatness" which he took from Winckelmann? Perhaps in the last analysis the unknown team of artists who created the Laocoön Group should be held responsible. In *Authenticity and Kitsch*, Paweł Beylin points out that we hesitate to call ancient works kitsch simply because history triumphs over aesthetics.[47]

Yet Andrzej Banach in his study, *On Kitsch*, has no reluctance to place the Laocoön in the chapter on "Museum Kitsch," including, appropriately, a very poor photographic reproduction of what appears to be a bad copy of the Group, perhaps taken from a Polish illustrated journal of the second half of the nineteenth century intended for mass consumption. According to Banach, the stereotype of canonical beauty in classical works leads to kitsch. The danger, he argues, lies in exaggerated perfection, aiming for power of expression, especially when it is imitated or reproduced, as it is in his own book.[48]

Różewicz's turning loose his family of pseudoaesthetes on the Laocoön can be seen as a defacement comparable to Marcel Duchamp's drawing mustaches and a goatee on a reproduction of the *Mona Lisa*.[49] But can we tell if the abuse is of the masterpiece or of the inferior copy? Are the two distinguishable anymore? Has Różewicz brought out the kitsch in the Laocoön Group or in the regimented, bureaucratized society of mass culture and consumer art?

In a similar spirit, the Russian novelist and playwright Vasily Aksyonov invokes the Laocoön as a cultural icon in his comedy *The Heron*.[50] Here the sculpture provides a visual equivalent for the entrapment by slogans and clichés and the constrictions of the bureaucratic mentality. Like Różewicz, Aksyonov is an author who refuses to be confined by boundaries and distinctions. Combining short prose poems and lengthy stage directions with dialogue and songs, he writes a play, at "an ambiguous frontier where the world ceases to be classified," which transcends the limits of dramatic form. The genre breaking of *The Heron*, Aksyonov tells us, grew out of the impossibility of having the work staged:

> I wrote this play in the winter of 1979, sitting in my own dacha, in Peredelkino, a writers' village near Moscow, having already been ousted from the Writers' Union and all official Soviet literature. . . . I didn't expect it to be staged at all, so I wrote a lot of very prolonged remarks there, and some verses too. I adapted it for reading, because I didn't expect any changes in the attitude toward me. I couldn't imagine that this play would be suitable for the Soviet theatre at all.[51]

Aksyonov's play takes place at a frontier in a second and more literal sense; the action occurs in a Baltic Health Resort for Garment Workers seven kilometers from the Polish border, and the Heron—a strange bird girl, a mysterious swamp creature—flies over from Poland every night, arousing yearnings for a different life in the Soviet characters who are mired in a banal reality. The comedy is, according to Aksyonov, a modern version of *The Seagull*, and a paraphrase (or copy) of the whole genre of Russian dacha plays as developed by Chekhov, Gorky, and Andreyev. The drama unfolds as a pastiche of Chekhovian motifs and devices, including a rhythmic interweaving of arrivals, eating and drinking, talking and love affairs; three sisters dream of going not to Moscow but to Poland, which represents for the Soviets a glamorous and decadent Western country, source of consumer goods, pop culture, and romance.

Caught up in the stereotypes of mass culture, parroting clichés and slogans from newspapers and TV, copying the most banal aspects of consumer society, Western and Soviet, the characters in *The Heron* have lost their souls and identities, and their meetings with the Heron make them aware of their fall from grace. Shot at the end of the play because of the "law of drama" requiring that a gun hanging on the wall be used, the Heron undergoes a last-minute resurrection, appearing with an enormous snow-white egg upon which she sits. To exemplify the mongrel lineage of contemporary mass culture (shown at a lower and less pretentious level than in Różewicz's play), Aksyonov creates a rich stylistic mishmash of foreign phrases, pidgin Russian, slang, Soviet jargon, pop songs, folklore, and literary and classical imagery.

The image of the Laocoön Group dominates the first half of Act II, as we see the old revolutionary turned *apparatchik*, Kampeneyets, who runs the Health Resort as his own family enclave, making deals about buying and selling household goods (Iranian detergent, Dutch shampoo) over the telephone, and at the same time slowly entangling himself and all the other characters in the long cord until they finally become immobilized in a group sculpture called in a stage direction "our Laocoön."[52]

A glancing allusion, a mythic quotation, the Laocoön does not inform Aksyonov's play as fully as it does Różewicz's, nor does it engage as many layers of cultural history (Chekhov and the Russian dacha tradition assume that role). Here the famous sculpture suggests not the tyranny of Greece over Germany, but the triumph of bureaucracy over Russia. As in Różewicz's play, the Laocoön Group in Aksyonov's *The Heron* signals the politicizing of culture, the babbling of empty phrases, the copying of copies. The telephone cord sending words along prescribed lines becomes the linguistic chain that fetters all the characters and takes away their ability to move beyond a fixed set of responses. "Our Laocoön" binds us to rigid categories of thought, inflexible systems of belief, and prevents seeing and feeling the world afresh.

Making copies has always been the traditional way of studying and transmitting art. Shortly after its discovery, the Laocoön Group gave rise to Renaissance engravings, marble copies, bronze models, etchings, and plaster casts. From a cast of Laocoön, Titian copied the Christ for his *Altarpiece of the Resurrection*. But copying need not always be official and reverential. Titian also made a comic version of the Group in which Laocoön and his sons are depicted as apes.[53] Reacting to the idolatry of his fellow Germans, Heine wrote the following poem:

> Now come and embrace me sweetly,
> You beautiful bundle of charms;
> Entwine me supply, featly,
> With body and feet and arms!
>
> She has coiled and twisted round me
> Her beautiful sinuous shape—
> Me, the most blest of Laocoöns,
> She, the most wonderful snake.[54]

Różewicz claimed that it was only a regrettable compromise with the "laws of drama" that made him abandon his initial plan to create a marmalade Laocoön:

> The group was to have been a sculpture made of marmalade. Not of marble, not of plaster, but of ordinary marmalade. It was to have been the undoing of aesthetes and pseudoinnovators sculptured in marmalade. It was to have been the "*cloaca maxima*" of putrid aesthetics. But in the process of "work on the play" the hand of the playwright started to glue together an "action." The theatre (the "authentic" one) insisted on its rights and there arose a nearly authentic comedy with settings and an intermission. Out of the marmalade there flowed a group of characters. If only they had "dissipated."[55]

I failed to mention earlier that Sophocles wrote a tragedy on the subject. If only Sophocles' *Laocoön* existed, the entire situation would be different.[56] A dramatic version of the myth from classical times would surely have resulted in later narrative and dramatic treatments. But the original was lost, and no copies had been made.

NOTES

1. Tadeusz Różewicz, *Teatr niekonsekwencji* (Wrocław: Zakład Narodowy im. Ossolińskich, 1979), 62–64. Translation my own.

2. El Greco's painting shows Laocoön lying passively on the ground holding the serpent at his head and the sons scattered beneath a stormy landscape. Blake's engraving, based on a visit to the cast room of the Royal Academy Schools, entitles the Group "Jehovah and his two Sons Satan and Adam" and the serpents "Good and Evil." The work is covered with aphorisms on the nature of art.

3. Margarete Bieber, *Laocoön: The Influence of the Group since Its Rediscovery* (New York, 1942), 1, 2, 19. In "Laocoon," one of his *Historical Miniatures* published in 1906 (the four-hundredth anniversary of the statue's discovery), Strindberg places a young German monk in Rome in 1506. He witnesses the excavation of the Laocoön and observes the excitement and joy that its discovery produces among the Romans. As the statue, decorated with flowers, is carried through the streets in a triumphal procession by ecstatic crowds and church bells are rung, the monk at first thinks that it must be the statue of a church martyr. The monk is Martin Luther and the Laocoön celebration that he observes is the first of many pagan manifestations that arouse his ire and denunciation as betrayals of true Christianity. Although the episode is Strindberg's invention, Luther was in fact in Rome at about this time and could have witnessed the theatrical hoopla occasioned by the statue's discovery. See August Strindberg, "Laocoon," in *Historical Miniatures*, trans. Claud Field (Freeport, N.Y.: Books for Libraries Press, 1972), 238–61.

4. Jacob Burckhardt, *The Civilization of the Renaissance in Italy* (New York: Harper, 1958), 1:169.

5. Francis Haskell and Nicholas Penny, *Taste and the Antiques: The Lure of Classical Sculpture 1500–1900* (New Haven: Yale University Press, 1981), 243–47. See also Jean-Pierre Cuzin, Jean René Gaborit, and Alain Pasquier, *D'après l'antique* (Paris: Reunion des Musées nationaux, 2000), 228–73.

6. Eliza Marian Butler, *The Tyranny of Greece over Germany* (London: Cambridge University Press, 1935; Boston: Beacon Press, 1958). Citations are to the Beacon edition.

7. Ibid., 57–58.

8. Stanisław Gębala, *Teatr Różewicza* (Wrocław: Zakład Narodowy im. Ossolińskich, 1978), 100–108. In the sub-chapter "Kopia i oryginał," Gębala treats at length the theme of the copy (100–119).

9. Józef Kelera, *Kpiarze i Moraliści* (Cracow: Wydawnictwo Literackie, 1966), 121–25. (On Różewicz's first play, see Halina Filipowicz, "The Card Index: A New Beginning for Polish Drama," *Modern Drama* 27 (March 1984): 395–408).

10. Gębala, 108–111.

11. Gotthold Ephraim Lessing, *Laocoön*, trans. Edward Allen McCormick (Indianapolis: Bobbs-Merrill, 1962), 5–6.

12. Henryk Vogler, *Tadeusz Różewicz* (Warsaw: Państwowy Instytut Wydawniczy, 1972), 40.

13. Kazimierz Wyka, *Różewicz parokrotnie* (Cracow: Wydawnictwo Literackie, 1977), 47–55. Translation my own.

14. Tadeusz Różewicz, *Conversations with the Prince and Other Poems*, trans. and intro. Adam Czerniawski (London: Anvil Press, 1982), 110.

15. Ibid., 11.

16. Walter Benjamin, *Illuminations*, trans. Harry Zohn (New York: Harcourt, Brace and World, 1968), 223–24.

17. Różewicz, *Conversations with the Prince*, 117.

18. Lesław M. Bartelski, *Genealogia Ocalonych* (Cracow: Wydawnictwo Literackie, 1969), 198.

19. Werner Jaeger, *Paideia: The Ideals of Greek Culture*, trans. Gilbert Highet (New York: Oxford University Press, 1963), 2:194.

20. Kelera, 123.

21. Tadeusz Różewicz, "Tarcza z pajęczyny," *Próba rekonstrukcji* (Wrocław: Zakład Narodowy im. Ossolińskich, 1979), 482–83.
22. Homer, *The Iliad*, trans. Richmond Lattimore (Chicago: University of Chicago Press, 1962), 446.
23. Winckelmann's phrase is *edle Einfalt and stille Grosse*.
24. Adam Czerniawski, "Introduction," Różewicz, *Conversations with the Prince*, 17.
25. Friedrich Nietzsche, *Human, All Too Human*, trans. Marion Faber (Lincoln: University of Nebraska Press, 1984), 176.
26. Benjamin, 225.
27. Juliusz Słowacki (1809-1849), one of the greatest Polish Romantic poets, regarded as a national bard.
28. Butler, 47.
29. Edward Allen McCormick, "Translator's Introduction," Lessing, *Laocoön*, xxviii.
30. Butler, 56, 77.
31. Ibid., 81.
32. Gębala, 115–19.
33. Irving Babbitt, *The New Laokoon: An Essay on the Confusion of the Arts* (Boston: Houghton Mifflin, 1910), 39. Clement Greenberg wrote an essay on abstract art, "Toward a Newer Laocoon," *Partisan Review* 7, no. 4 (July/August 1940). In 2007 the Henry Moore Institute presented an exhibition entitled, Toward a New Laocoon, which explored the legacy of the sculpture.
34. "I tend to find any old newspaper more absorbing than the finest edition of poems," Różewicz told Czerniawski, cited in *Conversations with the Prince*, 16.
35. Różewlcz, "Sobowtór," *Proba rekonstrukcji*, 499. Translation my own.
36. Babbitt, 97.
37. Tadeusz Różewicz, *Birth Rate: The Biography of a Play for the Theatre* in *Twentieth-Century Polish Avant-Garde Drama*, ed. and trans. Daniel Gerould (Ithaca, NY: Cornell University Press, 1977), 276.
38. McCormick, xi, and Bieber, 12.
39. Suetonius, *The Twelve Caesars*, trans. Robert Graves (Baltimore: Penguin Books, 1957), 193–95.
40. Ernest Arthur Gardner, *Handbook of Greek Sculpture, 1896–1897*, cited by Bieber, 18. In a late twentieth-century study of Lessing's treatise, there is unexpected affirmation of the "noble simplicity and serene greatness" of the sculpture. "Winckelmann's empirical observations of the Laocoön statue . . . are entirely sound" (David E. Wellbery, *Lessing's Laocoon: Semiotics and Aesthetics in the Age of Reason* (Cambridge: Cambridge University Press, 1984), 101).
41. Georges Auclair, *Le Mana Quotidien: Structures et fonctions de la chronique des faits divers* (Paris: Anthropos, 1970), 9–23.
42. Roland Barthes, "Structure of the Faits-Divers," *Critical Essays*, trans. Richard Howard (Evanston, IL: Northwestern University Press, 1972), 165–95.
43. In Musée national des arts et traditions populaires, *Le Fait Divers, 19 November 1982–18 Avril 1983* (Paris: Réunion des musées nationaux, 1982), 58.
44. Barthes, 185.
45. Matei Calinescu, *Faces of Modernity: Avant-Garde, Decadence, Kitsch* (Bloomington: University of Indiana Press, 1977), 226, 259.
46. John Addington Symonds, *The Life of Michelangelo Buonarroti* (New York: Charles Scribner's Sons, 1911), 1:154.
47. Paweł Beylin, *Autentyczność i kicze* (Warsaw: Państwowy Instytut Wydawniczy, 1975), 189–90. Beylin, like other theorists of kitsch, maintains that it differs from authentic art in being repeatable and reproducible.
48. Andrzej Banach, *O kiczu* (Cracow: Wydawnictwo Literackie, 1968), 292.
49. Calinescu, 254–55.

50. In Vasily Aksyonov, *Aristofaniana s lyagushkami* (Ann Arbor, MI: Ardis, 1981). *The Heron* is dedicated to friends and co-workers on the almanac *Metropol*, an uncensored anthology of Soviet writing which was suppressed at the time Aksyonov was writing his play (January–April 1979). It has been performed in Paris, in alternation with *The Seagull*, in February 1984, at the Théâtre de Chaillot, directed by Antoine Vitez. A reading of *The Heron*, translated by Edythe Haber, was given by the Open World Theatre Company in New York in March 1985. The translation by Haber is published in Vasily Aksyonov, *Quest for an Island* (New York: PAJ Publications, 1987).

51. *Eastern European Drama and the American Stage: A Symposium, sponsored by the Academy for the Humanities and Sciences of the City University of New York, April 30, 1984* (New York: Center for the Advanced Study of Theatre Arts, 1984), 24–25.

52. Aksyonov, *Aristofaniana*, 355.

53. Bieber, 5–7.

54. Cited in Butler, 251.

55. Tadeusz Różewicz, *Sztuki teatralne* (Wrocław: Zakład Narodowy im. Ossolińskich, 1972), 312–13. Translation my own.

56. The English translation of Różewicz's *The Laocoön Group* by Adam Czerniawski is also lost. Unfortunately, the translator tells me he has no copy.

Tadeusz Kantor. Photo by Jacek Barcz

TADEUSZ KANTOR (1915–1990)
A VISUAL ARTIST WORKS MAGIC ON THE POLISH STAGE

One of the major creators in Polish and world theatre, Tadeusz Kantor was a constant and uncompromising artistic innovator for over forty years. His work embraces and combines painting, graphic arts, stage design and costumes, and directing. Striving for an integral theatre in which all arts will have equal rights, Kantor realized Gordon Craig's ideal of the total theatre artist. In each endeavor he was rigorously avant-garde, always seeking a radically new artistic position and refusing to remain enclosed in any currently fashionable formulas, including his own. As a stage designer and as a pioneer in the development of Happenings, Kantor exerted a profound influence on the new generation of theatre artists in Poland. His work is known throughout the world because of his exhibits, many appearances at theatre festivals, and close contacts with the international artistic community. Starting with *The Dead Class* in 1976, all his major productions are seen throughout the world. The following chronology is an attempt, in survey form, to indicate the extent, variety, and depth of Kantor's work as both practitioner and theorist.

1915
Born April 6 in Wielopole, a small town near Cracow. Shows an early interest in theatre, but decides to become a painter. Draws and paints under the influence of Stanisław Wyspiański and Jacek Malczewski, Symbolists from Cracow.

1934–1939
Attends the Academy of Fine Arts in Cracow, where he studies stage design with Karol Frycz (1877–1963), painter, designer, director, and theatre manager, a follower of Craig and Wyspiański and one of the creators of modern Polish stage design. Since the turn of the century, Cracow has been the center of stage design and the avant-garde tradition in the visual arts in Poland, and its artists frequently become directors and theatre managers.

1938
Stages his first play, Maeterlinck's *Death of Tintagiles*, at his own Little Marionette Theatre.

1942
With a group of young painters, organizes the underground, experimental Independent Theatre in Cracow during the German occupation, when the public theatre is either trivial or collaborationist. Clandestine performances are held in private homes.

–*Performing Arts Journal* 4, no. 3 (1980): 27–38.

1943

Directs and designs Juliusz Słowacki's Romantic tragedy *Balladyna* (1834) at the Independent Theatre. Presented in a room in an apartment without stage or setting, with the actors playing amidst the spectators. Kantor makes an asset of this limitation to create a total performance out of costumes, properties, and movement. Instead of the character Balladyna, there is an abstract figure with masks in the middle of the room.

1944

Directs and designs Jean Cocteau's *Orpheus* and Stanisław Wyspiański's *Return of Odysseus* (1907) at the Independent Theatre. Wyspiański's dark and sinister drama is interpreted as the contemporary story of a soldier returning from the war. The setting includes something resembling the barrel of an old rifle on a slightly raised platform with a mast-like object above it. Wearing a German general's uniform, the painter Tadeusz Brzozowski plays Odysseus.

Kantor on the Independent Theatre:

> The theatre is not a place for the reproduction of literature. The theatre is an autonomous art. Each element of theatre must become autonomous and acquire its own expressiveness so that it can exist independently in its own right. Theatrical elements such as actor, shape, light, color, sound, and movement, once they are stripped of their real-life logic and naturalistic existence, become liberated and acquire enormous energy and expressiveness. They become *forms*.

> The text is not a form, but the text is that "something" that binds all the elements of theatre together into one entity.

> The duality: stage/auditorium kills theatre.

> The theatre has to avoid creating the illusion of the reality contained in the drama; the reality of the drama must *become reality* on the stage.

> *The most essential* is to create the impression that the audience is on the stage.

> Skepticism with regard to the illusory and make-believe appearance of the external world, abstraction treated as an objective system which carries in itself intellectual truth, and desire to create a work of art independent of nature, whose perfection could be seriously doubted.

1945

The Return of Odysseus is repeated as a student production at the Stary Theatre in Cracow. Begins an active career as a scene designer, doing sets and costumes for fifty productions throughout Poland. Designs *The Death of a Faun* by painter and poet Tytus Czyżewski (first presented in 1934 at Cricot 1) at the Dom Plastyków in Cracow.

1946

Directs and designs Corneille's *Le Cid* in Czechowice and designs Wanda Karczewska's *Our Eyes are Open Now* and Jerzy Szaniawski's *The Two Theatres* in Cracow. Member of the group "Young Graphic Artists."

Set design for *The Return of Odysseus*

1947
Studies in France.

1948
Organizes the first post-war exhibition of modern Polish art in Cracow. Appointed professor at the Cracow Academy of Fine Arts.

1949
Professorship revoked. Beginning of the Stalinist period in Poland and the imposition of socialist realism in the arts.

1950
Works privately with Maria Jarema (1908–1958), an important sculptor and painter, who did scene design for Cricot 1 and created almost abstract forms out of hands, faces, and heads.

1951
Designs Calderón's *The Mayor of Zalamea.*

1952

Designs Henri Becque's *Les Corbeaux.*

1953

Designs Lesage's *Turcaret* and Musset's *On ne badine pas avec l'amour.*

1954

Designs Shakespeare's *Measure for Measure* at Opole. Interpreting the play as a conflict of old and new, Renaissance humanism and medieval obscurantism, Kantor puts colorful individuals against a set suggestive of the Middle Ages.

1955

Designs *Legend about Love* by Nazim Hikmet, the Turkish socialist poet who had lived in the Soviet Union and become a Polish citizen, and *Summer in Nohant* (1936) by Jarosław Iwaszkiewicz, about Chopin and George Sand, which the following year goes to Paris (Festival of Nations) and Vienna. Designs Konstantin Trenyov's *Lyubov Yarovaya* (1925), a Soviet melodrama about the civil war following the revolution.

1956

Stalinism crumbles after Khrushchev's revelations, and after the bloodless October Revolution, Poland achieves greater autonomy, at least in cultural matters. The modern Polish theatre flourishes. Kantor's activities grow more intense and varied. Designs and directs three Prosper Mérimée one-act plays (*The Occasion, African Love,* and *Heaven and Hell*) and Garcia Lorca's *The Shoemaker's Prodigious Wife* in Katowice (moving to Cracow the following year), Shaw's *Saint Joan* in Cracow, Shakespeare's *Hamlet* and a second *Measure for Measure* at Nowa Huta, the newly created industrial city near Cracow. The stage in *Saint Joan* is dominated by three huge mannequins of Pope, King, and Knight, showing the three powers ruling in the Middle Ages; in between the mannequins are functional objects defining the place of action: palace window, conference table, ramparts, cannons. In *Measure for Measure* the stage space is enclosed by a long, high wall running the entire width of the playing area; above it, there is a watch-tower that seems made of bones. The action takes place in this police state and concentration camp run by the usurper-dictator. At the Dom Plastyków opens his own theatre, Cricot 2 (named after Cricot, an important avant-garde artists theatre in Cracow between the wars). Eventually housed in the basement Gallery Krzysztofory in Cracow, which will be Kantor's headquarters when in Poland, Cricot 2 is a theatre of actors, painters, and poets in search of new possibilities in the arts. The first creation is *The Cuttlefish* (1922) by Stanisław Ignacy Witkiewicz (Witkacy), who will provide Kantor with the texts for many of his subsequent productions (Kantor: "We don't play Witkiewicz, we play with Witkiewicz."). Previously performed at Cricot 1 in 1933, *The Cuttlefish*, a play about art and totalitarianism, is the first post-war performance of any of Witkacy's work, until then banned from the stage, and an important step in liberating the Polish theatre from the constraints of Stalinism. Maria Jarema designs the sets and costumes and plays one of the roles. On the same program is a surrealistic pantomime. The *Well, or Depth of*

Thought by Kazimierz Mikulski, a well-know painter and stage designer for the puppet theatre Groteska, who becomes a regular actor with Kantor's theatre. Cricot 2 always uses both professional and amateur actors and never receives any subsidy or support from the state.

Kantor on Cricot 2:

> The theatre must be treated as creativity which cannot be standardized, regularized, and made dependent on red tape. Cricot 2 insisted that a performance grow as a work of art: autonomously, not for an "opening night," and its exploitation, but as an act of creation of a new situation in the evolution of art, in what is called "the totality of art." That distinguishes Cricot 2 from professional theatres.
>
> One cannot be entirely enclosed in professionalism and claim purity of theatrical activity. One has to surpass the theatre as well; that does not mean the creation of some kind of anti-theatre, but it does mean the necessity of dealing with all that lies within art's domain. Placing theatre within the totality of art guarantees that the theatre will evolve. The man of the theatre must be an artist too, that is, he must be involved in art, accept the risks it brings and search for the unknown and the impossible. We work a very long time on each new production; our aim is something more than opening night. Our aim is a slow transformation, achievement of a new "consciousness," a search for new means of expression, the process of building a new stage development, a new situation in art; that is why premières and opening nights are not important for Cricot 2. What is important are the stages of Cricot 2: The Informel Theatre, The Theatre of Death, etc . . .

1957

Designs Jerzy Zawieyski's *Masks of Maria Dominika* in Warsaw and Jean Anouilh's *Antigone* in Cracow (directed by Jerzy Kaliszewski, with Jerzy Grotowski as assistant

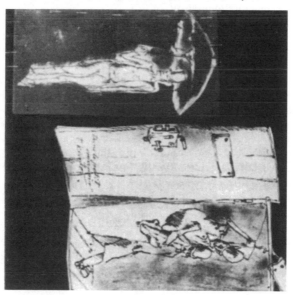

Witkacy's *Country House*, drawing by Kantor

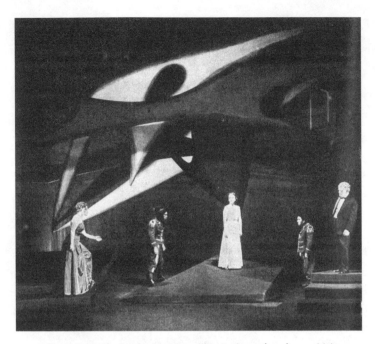

Kantor's set design for Jean Anouilh's *Antigone* (1957), on which
Kantor and Grotowski (Assistant Director to Jerzy Kaliszewski) work together

director—the only collaboration between Kantor and Grotowski). The decor in *Antigone* represents a startling employment of images, heightening dramatic tension by the changing use of sinister shapes, in a manner that is metaphoric, abstract, and kinetic, similar in spirit to Gordon Craig's *Hamlet*. As each new catastrophe threatens the tragic heroine, sharp, angular forms, suggesting lances, spears, and axes, come down from above over the characters, cutting off the perspective on open space and creating an atmosphere bristling with danger. At Cricot 2 presents *Circus* by Kazimierz Mikulski, revealing a fascination with umbrellas and displaying the first elements of *emballage* (French, "packing") and Happenings—two currents soon to be central to Kantor's art. The actors, completely de-individualized, are placed inside a huge black sack filling the stage and isolating the performers from the audience; the actors become transformed into a homogeneous pulsating structure of matter, only their heads and hands are visible, squeezed out through narrow holes.

1958
Travels to Switzerland, Sweden and France. One-man show in Sweden. Does illustrations for a new edition of Witold Gombrowicz's play, *Ivona, Princess of Burgundia.*

1959
Exhibits in Düsseldorf. (Throughout his career, exhibits regularly either in one-man or group shows: Paris, New York, Stockholm, London, Venice, Lausanne, Sao Paulo, etc.)

1960

Publishes the "Manifesto of the Informel Theatre" (from the French, *informe*, meaning formless or misshapen). The informal method uses scenic techniques appropriate to the concept of "shapeless matter," in all its possible senses: "accidental, spontaneous, impetuous, incandescent, fluid, elemental, hallucinatory, spasmatic, obsessive, ecstatic, insane, profligate, exaggerated, unexpected, informal." The process and stages of creation—the resistance of matter and the artist's struggle with it—are more important than the finished work of art.

1961

Designs Ionesco's *Rhinoceros* in Warsaw; the characters and setting are abstract with the result that the transformation into rhinoceros does not seem in any way extraordinary. At Cricot 2 inaugurates the Informel Theatre with Witkacy's *Country House* (1921). The creation of roles is shown as the actors at first follow the text. Destroying all form, the theatrical material bursts forth and rejects the rigidity of the text. The performance turns into an orgy. Actors jammed into a wardrobe hang inertly like old clothes and are reduced to a mass of objects of the lowest rank.

Kantor on wardrobes and sacks:

> The WARDROBE has for a long time (since 1957) played an important role in my theatre. As in the circus, or a surrealist game, the wardrobe was a catalyst for many human things, human fate, its mysteries. The ridiculous paucity of space inside a wardrobe easily deprived the actor of dignity, personal prestige, will, transformed him into a common mass of matter, almost of clothing.
>
> SACKS are similar objects. In the hierarchy of objects, sacks belong to the lowest and as such are or can become almost purposeless matter.

The Wardrobe (1966)

Travels to Italy, France, Sweden, and Germany. Professor at the Akademie der Künste in Hamburg. Publishes "Ist Orpheus Rückkehr möglich?" ("Is Orpheus's Comeback Possible?")

1962

Designs Massenet's opera, *Don Quichotte*, in Cracow, using a large number of whirling windmills. Wins a Polish state prize. Writes "Emballages Manifesto": "The tying and wrapping of packages, multiplied and tangled, becomes an exciting and almost disinterested process." Sacks, bags, envelopes, and umbrellas hoard, protect, and isolate; they offer a descent to the lowest, neglected region of the despised, scorned, and ridiculous. The object, having lost the significance and symbolism imposed upon it from outside, is shown as leading an autonomous, empty existence, without any function whatsoever.

1963

Designs Bartók's *Bluebeard's Castle* for the Warsaw opera house. The space is created by only two walls painted with spots of color and covered with fragments and nets of tulle curtain. The costumes of Bluebeard's wives are made of jute, satin, brass and silver plate, and beads, which create richly dressed figures who are macabre and repellant. Publishes the "Emballages Manifesto" in Switzerland and the "Theatre Zero Manifesto" in Cracow. At Cricot 2 presents Witkacy's *Madman and the Nun* as Theatre Zero, in which there is radical destruction of the dramatic text and the stage creates its own reality. The play itself is not performed, but the text is quoted, commented upon, and repeated. Actors and objects are equalized; an enormous pile of folding chairs almost fills the entire playing area, forcing the actors to struggle to stay on stage and to fight against

Happening, "Grand Emballage" (1966)

Concert "Panoramic Sea Happening," at Osieki on the Baltic (1967)

the chairs. "The annexation of objects is central to all art." Fascination with the refuse of life: bums and bag-ladies, "wandering people" roaming about outside society, always wrapped up in multiple layers of clothing, bags, blankets, strings, and straps. A Popular Exhibition or "Anti-Exhibit" at the Gallery Krzysztofory.

1964
Creates first compositions with umbrellas attached to canvas. Travels to Sweden and West Germany.

1965
Travels to the United States. Organizes the first "Happening-Cricotage" at the Hall of the Society of the Friends of the Fine Arts in Warsaw; the participants are artists associated with the society (1 hour). A "Cricotage" is a small theatrical event drawing upon the experiences of Cricot 2.

1966
Happening "Line of Division" at the Association of Art Historians in Cracow; the participants are painters and art historians (45 minutes). *Country House*, now called *The Wardrobe*, presented in Baden-Baden. Saarbrücken TV makes a film, *The Journey*, about Kantor's art, which abounds in images of travel and "Eternal Wanderers."

Kantor on the theme of the Journey:

> The idea of the journey is connected by its subject matter with all my creative work. It is the idea of art as a mental journey and an exploration of new territories. Since 1963 props connected to travel have appeared in my pictures: packs, bags, suitcases, knapsacks, figures of "Eternal Wanderers."

Emballage, "Traveler" (1967)

Happening "Grand Emballage" at the Gallery Handschin in Basel.

1967

Happening "The Letter" at the Foksal Gallery, Warsaw (30 minutes). Panoramic "Sea-Happening" at Osieki on the Baltic coast, making use of the beach and sea. Sixteen artists participate as well as an audience of 1600 (2 hours). Géricault's painting, "The Raft of the Medusa," serves as an analogue.

Kantor on Happenings:

> A Happening for me is a kind of subjugation of an object, an attempt to catch it *in flagranti*. The artist must show great precision in tracking down the object's qualities, errors, crimes, peripeties, hidden and masked details.

Shows a series of compositions with umbrellas at the Biannual in Sao Paulo. Begins work on Witkacy's *Water Hen*, based on the idea of a journey and in part conceived as a Happening.

1968

Travels to Italy, France, and West Germany. *Premio Marzotto* awarded in Rome for umbrella compositions. Happening "The Anatomy Lesson according to Rembrandt" at the Kunsthalle, Nuremberg. With students of the Institut für moderne Kunst as the participants watching, Kantor recreates the painting and cuts through the layers of clothes on the body into the pockets, the organs of the human instinct for preservation, and displays the contents. A film, *Kantor ist da*, is occasioned by the Happening. Happening "Eine Konferenz mit dem Rhinozeros" in Nuremberg. Happening "Hommage to Maria Jarema" at the Krzysztofory in Cracow takes place at the opening of a posthumous exhibit of Jarema's painting and sculpture. Issues "Manifesto Theatre Happening." Appointed Professor at the Academy of Fine Arts in Cracow for the second time. *The Water Hen* given at Cricot 2. Real waiters serve coffee and eggs to the audience; real cleaning women pour water into the tub and wring out wet towels. The character, "The Water Hen," sits throughout the entire performance in the tub full of water. The performance takes place amongst the audience, with full lights and the actors making contact with the spectators. The wanderers and their luggage become part of the Human Reserve of Cricot 2, some of them reappearing in later works.

1969

Professorship at the Academy of Fine Arts in Cracow revoked a second time. Creates the Impossible Theatre and in Bled, Yugoslavia, assembles a group of actors of different nationalities to realize the new program. Rejecting conventional notions of theatrical place and time, the Impossible Theatre transforms the actors into a "wandering corpse" that presents each scene in a different place: on a glacier in the Julian Alps, on the shore of the Adriatic, in a Casino in Bled, in a station, in a chateau, and with a two month interval. *Country House* made as a TV film by German Television (Saarbrücken). The spoken text is from Witkacy; the action of the Happening follows an independent course. Happening "The Anatomy Lesson II" given at the Foksal Gallery, Warsaw. German TV film, *Schrank, Säcke, und Regenschirm. The Water Hen* shown at the Premio di Roma Festival (plays in Rome, Modena, Bologna).

The Water Hen (1968)

Dainty Shapes and Hairy Apes, drawing (1973)

1970
Publishes "Manifesto 1970" at the Foksal Gallery, Warsaw. Creates "Exhibition Multipart" and issues "Multipart Manifesto." Creates a Chair in Concrete Symposium in Wrocław.

1971
The Water Hen presented at the International Theatre Festival in Nancy, France, and at the Theatre 71 de Malakoff, Paris. Creates *The Great Chair* and the Happening, "The Anatomy Lesson," at the Sonia Henie-Onstad Art Center, in Oslo. "The Anatomy Lesson, III" presented at the Atelier International de Théâtre in Dourdan, France. While vacationing on the Baltic in 1972, chances upon an empty one-room schoolhouse. Flattening his nose against the dirty pane of a window, peered into past. The "negatives of memory" activated, the Theatre of Death was born in this illusory return to the lost homeland of childhood. Looking through window frame at a non-existent world of the past, saw himself as a six-year-old sitting on the bench. For his next production, *The Dead Class*, he places on stage wooden benches, which he makes himself, at which sit thirteen old men and women, who carry their childhood with them, in the form of mannequins attached to their sides and backs.

1972
Takes *The Water Hen* on tour in England, presenting the production at the Edinburgh Festival. Presents Witkacy's *The Shoemakers* at the Theatre 71 de Malakoff in Paris, using French actors speaking the text in French.

1973

Creates Witkacy's *Dainty Shapes and Hairy Apes, or the Green Pill* (also known as *Lovelies and Dowdies)* at Cricot 2 in Cracow as a Theatre Impossible performance. Publication of the "Theatre Impossible Manifesto." "The theatre should make use of the sustained radicalism of painting." *Dainty Shapes and Hairy Apes* presented at the Edinburgh Festival. Actors and objects are fused, as seen in the man with the board in his back and the man with bicycle wheels grown into his legs. The Forty Mandelbaums, who are found in Witkacy's text, are costumed as Hasidic Jews with beards, black hats, and gowns, and are played by members of the audience, coached by the head Mandelbaum (a Cricot actor). Voices for the Mandelbaums heard over a loudspeaker are based on the cries of Jews approaching the gas chambers. Kantor disregards Witkacy's detailed stage directions and indications for costuming since he regards the playwright's characters as actors impersonating others and playing roles—hence the seemingly conventional and realistic surface of the plays.

Kantor on Witkacy:

> While reading Witkiewicz's plays, I always have the impression that they are everlasting continuations of those famous Witkacian "séances" (all night parties with friends), in which philosophical palaver, intellectual orgies of gargantuan proportions, perverse creativity, and eroticism are all mixed up and intertwined. Therefore, my performances of Witkacy's plays are presented as an attempt to penetrate to the inner essence of the play, not to follow its plot or philosophical substance.

1974

Shows *Dainty Shapes and Hairy Apes* in Nancy, Paris (the Théâtre National at the Palais de Chaillot), Rome, Essen, Germany, and at the Shiraz Festival in Iran.

The Dead Class, drawing (1975)

1975

Creates *The Dead Class*, "A Dramatic Séance," as a Theatre of Death performance at Cricot 2, Cracow. Based in part on Witkacy's *Tumor Brainiowicz* (1920), Witold Gombrowicz's *Ferdydurke* (1938), and Bruno Schulz's *Street of Crocodiles* (1934, especially "The Treatise on Mannequins") and his drawings of life in the Jewish town of Drohobycz. Follows Schulz's concept of degraded reality and inferiority of material. In *The Dead Class* the pupils are senile old people at the edge of the grave, sent back to school bearing with them little dummy-children, who are the dreams lost in the pragmatic process of living and growing up. They endlessly repeat the same suspended gestures, which they will never finish, because they are forever imprisoned within them. All psychological and biological processes are reified, through the use of machines that are infantilely primitive and without any practical utility, such as the Family Machine, which makes the victims legs keep opening and closing. Death the Sweeper, the ultimate confrontation with the great Void, brings on the Mechanical Cradle, which looks like a small coffin. Reversion to the infantile, the childish pranks and degraded experiences of schooldays, seems immature from the adult point of view, but is in fact the original matter of life. "Their fortuitous quality, their lack of social efficacy, relate them to the realms of art." Throughout, the woman behind the women is always watching. Publishes the "Theatre of Death Manifesto," Foksal Gallery, Warsaw. "Life can be expressed in art only by the absence of life, by reference to death." In *The Dead Class*, Kantor himself is the factotum who directs the inner dynamism between text and theatrical material, braking the independent force of the latter so that it does not go out of control and thereby preserving the unity of stage action and dramatic text. For Kantor, the text serves to animate the theatrical material—the actor and visual matter—which then acquires an autonomous life that must be held back and kept in check. To the music of the waltz "François" (a popular melody of the between-the-wars period), Kantor conducts and orchestrates the

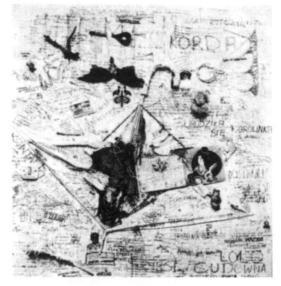

"Multipart"

The Dead Class (1975)

performance. After *The Dead Class*, Kantor abandoned Witkacy's texts and moved on to the two great Polish religious myths of crucifixion and redemption, aiming to become both a universal artist and a national bard in the style of Mickiewicz.

1976
Presents *The Dead Class* at the Edinburgh Festival, in London, and in Amsterdam. It is filmed by both Andrzej Wajda and Denis Bablet.

1977
Presents *The Dead Class* at the International Festival in Nancy and at the Autumn Festival in Paris, as well as in Holland, Germany, Belgium, and Iran. *Théâtre de la Mort*, a collection of manifestoes and documents, is published in France.

1978
Presents *The Dead Class* in Florence, Milan, Zurich, Geneva, Caracas, and Australia.

Wielopole, Wielopole (1980)

1979

Presents *The Dead Class* in Mexico and the United States (La MaMa). The Cricotage, *Where are the Snows of Yesteryear?* (after François Villon's poetry), is created in Rome. The Regional Theatre of Tuscany and the City of Florence provide Cricot with a home and funding.

1980

Wielopole, Wielopole is created and first presented in the Church of Santa Maria in Florence. It is financed by the City of Florence and uses Italian actors in minor roles. No longer based on pre-existing texts, *Wielopole* explores the artist's memories to trace the social and cultural history of his family. Establishment of archival centers called Cricoteques in Florence and Cracow.

For Kantor, the stage is a "poor room of the imagination," a place of community between the living and the dead—out of time and out of space—where a profane sacrum is celebrated every evening.

> I maintain that the theatre is a fording place on a river, a place across which dead characters from the other shore, from the other world, cross into our world, now, into our life. And what happens then? I can give you the answer; the Dybbuk, the spirit of the dead, who enters into the body of another person and speaks through him.

Once called forth, the dead passionately burst through the doors from the other side and repeat the unending cycle of living and dying. Repetition of the senseless words and events of daily life is sole key to the mystery of past existence.

1981
Wielopole is presented in Italy, Switzerland, Venezuela, Germany, Spain, and Poland.

1982
The Dead Class and *Wielopole* are presented in Japan, England, Mexico, the United States, and France.

1985
Let the Artists Die is first presented in Nuremberg with financing by a wealthy German patron. The production is inspired by Wit Stwosz, the late medieval wood and stone carver from Nuremberg who spent twelve years in Cracow creating the great altar for Saint Mary's Church. *Let the Artists Die* also draws upon Zbigniew Uniłowski's novel, *The Shared Room* (1932) and its artist-hero, Lucjan.

It is the dead who are sharply differentiated and delineated; the living are all alike. Life after death is stronger than life here and now. Once dead, the characters truly begin to exist—nothing limits them. The returning dead (suggested by Witkacy's risen corpses) are comically posturing and gesticulating automatons ; the other world is like this one for all eternity.

1986
The Cricotage, *The Marriage*, is presented at the Piccolo Theatre of Milan. Delivers a series of lectures at the School of Dramatic Art in Milan, which are published as *The Milano Lessons*.

1987
The Cricotage, *The Machine of Love and Death*, is given in Kassel, Germany, at Documenta 8. It is a fiftieth anniversary recreation of Kantor's *Death of Tintagiles*.

1988
I Shall Never Return is created in Milan. A retrospective of the artist's life in the theatre, *I Shall Never Return* recalls characters and scenes from earlier productions, going back to *The Return of Odysseus*. For the first time, Kantor himself appears as a character in the drama, whereas previously he has functioned only as a director of séances, conducting the proceedings from the sidelines.

A modern Charon on the river Styx, Kantor by his constant presence on stage violates a central convention of theatrical illusion and thereby vouches for the authenticity of the séance.

As revenants, Kantor's actors did not play the dead; rather it was the dead who played the role of the actors. And as Kantor drew closer to death, he more and more played the principal role of himself in his productions. The process of posthumous reduplication started early, while the artist was still alive. A master at self-replication and hand-crafting of secondary symbolic bodies, Kantor made doubles of himself already dead in the form of mannequins, photographs, and portraits.

His last theatrical productions were rehearsals for the staging of his death. Appears with his own coffin—the same coffin that was used for his actual funeral.

1989

The Cricotage, *Oh, Sweet Night*, is presented at the Festival d'Avignon.

1990

Kantor dies of a heart attack in Cracow on the night of December 7–8 after one of the final rehearsals for his new creation, *Tomorrow is My Birthday*.

Kantor's Catholic funeral in Cracow was a huge affair attended by tens of thousands.

Kantor made the first model of his gravestone in 1984, ostensibly for his mother's grave. An avant-gardist who once scorned museums and said art hates commemorations, Kantor created a museum for himself, the Cricoteka, as a repository of memory and designed his own monument. Buried next to his mother, he lies under the stone with the sculpture of the boy sitting on the school bench at his desk—the self he had seen through the dirty window pane. Now frozen, immobilized in stone, eternalized forever.

1991

Tomorrow is My Birthday is given in Toulouse on January 10 and in Paris on January 21.

Bibliography

Borowski, Wiesław. "Happeningi Tadeusza Kantora." *Dialog* 9 (1972): 103–7.

———. "Założenia Kantora." *Dialog* 8 (1973): 130–33.

Czartoryska, Urszula. "'Teatr Śmierci' Tadeusza Kantora." *Dialog* 5 (1976): 154–57.

Kantor, Tadeusz. "Happeningi." *Dialog* 9 (1972): 84–102.

———. "'Kurka Wodna'—Scenariusz." *Dialog* 8 (1973): 118–30.

———. *Tadeusz Kantor, Emballages 1960–1976*. Nuremberg: Galerie Johanna Ricard, 1976.

———. "The Theatre of Death." *Canadian Theatre Review* (Fall 1977): 34–73.

———. *Le Théâtre de la Mort*. Edited by Denis Bablet. Lausanne: *L'Age d'Homme*, 1977.

———. "Na Konferencji Prasowej." *Dialog* 7 (1978): 111–16.

———. *A Journey Through Other Spaces: Essays & Manifestos, 1944–1990*. Edited and translated by Michal Kobialka. Berkeley: University of California Press, 1993.

———. *My Creation, My Journey*. Edited by Oka Shigemi and Suzuki Takashi. Translated by Tokimasa Sekiguchi. Tokyo: Sezon Museum of Art, 1994.

———. *Od Małego dworku do Umarłej klasy/From The Country House to the Dead Class*. Cracow/ Wrocław:Muzeum Narodowe we Wrocławiu/Cricoteka, 2010.

———. *Scenografia dla teatrów oflcjalnych*. Cracow: Cricoteka, 2006.

Kobiałka, Michał. *Further On, Nothing: Tadeusz Kantor's Theatre*. Minneapolis: University of Minnesota, 2009.

Miklaszewska, Agata. "Kantora 'Teatr Informel.'" *Dialog* (1978): 124–31.

Miklaszewski, Krzysztof. *Encounters with Tadeusz Kantor*. Edited by George Hyde. London: Routledge, 2002.

Pieniążek, Marek. *Akt twórczy jako mimesis: "Dziś są moje urodziny"—ostatni spektakl Tadeusza Kantora*. Cracow Modernizm w Polsce. Cracow: Universitas, 2005.

Pleśniarowicz, Krzysztof. *Kantor: Artysta końca wieku*. Wrocław: Wydawnictwo Dolnośląskie, 1997.

Skiba-Lickel, Aldona. *L'Acteur dans le theatre de Tadeusz Kantor*. Bouffonneries (1991) No. 26–27.

Sogliuzzo, A. Richard. "Tadeusz Kantor and the Theatre Cricot 2 of Cracow, Poland." *Theatre Annual* (1973): 54–76.

Szpakowska, Małgorzata. "Tekst Witkiewicza a scenariusz Kantora." *Dialog* 8 (1973): 133–37.

Jerzy Grotowski, 1971

JERZY GROTOWSKI'S THEATRICAL AND PARATHEATRICAL ACTIVITIES AS COSMIC DRAMA: ROOTS AND CONTINUITIES IN THE POLISH ROMANTIC TRADITION

Jerzy Grotowski's work falls into five phases: The Theatre of Productions (1959–69), The Theatre of Participation (1969–75), the Theatre of Sources (1976–82), Objective Drama (1983–86), and Art as Vehicle (1983–99).

Jerzy Grotowski's paratheatrical activities (Theatre of Participation), which starting in 1969 took the Polish director farther and farther away from traditional theatre performed in a playhouse for an audience, can be seen as a natural, even inevitable extension of his earlier work, begun at the Theatre of the Thirteen Rows in Opole in 1959 and continued by his Laboratory Theatre in Wrocław, starting in 1965. Both the theatrical and the paratheatrical explorations conducted by Grotowski were dedicated to the revelation of a secular mystery (the only kind possible in an age of disbelief), a ceremonial capable of uniting actor and spectator, a communal and collective creation that will transform its participants and reorder their lives. In the words of Ludwik Flaszen, Grotowski's longtime associate and literary advisor, "Grotowski's performances wish to revive the utopia of those elementary experiences, supplied by the collective ritual, in whose ecstatic elation a community, as it were, dreamed a dream about its own essence, its place in total reality, not particularized into separate spheres, where Beauty was not different from Truth, emotions from intellect, spirit from body, joy from suffering; where man felt an affinity with the Totality of Being."[1]

In the first phase of his career, within the framework of traditional stage performance at Opole and Wrocław, Grotowski eliminated from theatre everything but the essential relationship of actor to spectator and developed training techniques stressing gymnastics, acrobatics, yoga, and pantomime. At the Theatre of the Thirteen Rows in Opole, from 1959 to 1964 Grotowski staged poetic works played against the texts as arguments with past cultural monuments and designed to transform traditional actor-audience relationships: Byron's *Cain*, Goethe's *Faust*, Mayakovsky's *Mystery-Bouffe* and Kālidāsa's *Shakuntala* in 1960; Mickiewicz's *Forefathers' Eve* in 1961; Słowacki's *Kordian* and Wyspiański's *Acropolis* (co-created with Józef Szajna) in two versions in 1962; Marlowe's *Faustus* in 1963; a third variant of *Acropolis* in 1963. In 1965 Grotowski moved the group to Wrocław, adopting the name Laboratory Theatre. There he created a fourth and fifth variant of *Acropolis*, three versions of Calderón's *The Constant Prince* (in Słowacki's translation), and three variants of *Apocalypsis cum figuris*, his final production.

In the second phase of his creative quest, the Theatre of Participation, Grotowski, moving from the playhouse into the world of nature and society, organized paratheatrical events that broke down barriers between actors and spectators, as they both engaged in structured and spontaneous activities in natural surroundings. These developments come as no surprise if we examine the Polish tradition of mystical, cosmic drama, and place Grotowski in its context.

The three great Polish poets of the nineteenth century, Adam Mickiewicz (1798–1855), Juliusz Słowacki (1809–49), and Zygmunt Krasiński (1812–59), who had left their partitioned homeland and lived abroad in political exile, created a unique form of Romantic drama, written for a theatre that existed only in the imagination of its authors

–*World Literature Today* 54, no. 3 (Summer 1980): 381–383.

and designed to transcend the bounds of reality and the prosaic stage that imitated it. These national heroes were not simply playwrights, but bards or seers (in Polish, the word is *wieszcz*) who envisaged an art of the drama that would overcome the separation of stage and auditorium, draw the spectator into the performance and directly influence his life. The aim of Polish Romantic drama was nothing less than to transform the viewers from passive onlookers to active participants. Although seemingly alone and defeated, the heroes of these Romantic dramas embody a supra-personal ideal and identify themselves with the entire nation, for which they become willing martyrs. The spectators are incited to join in the process.

These visionary dramas, created without regard for the material conditions necessary for performance and existing in a cosmic dimension beyond ordinary categories of time and space, are the very basis of the Polish theatrical tradition. As the Polish critic Jan Błoński has remarked, the plays of Mickiewicz, Słowacki, and Krasiński present a religious mystery in which the public joins together as celebrants in a common sacrifice and collective gesture that will lift the veil of illusion and convention.[2]

Take, for example, Mickiewicz's *Forefathers' Eve* (*Dziady*, 1823–32), which has become Poland's national sacred drama. A modern passion play celebrating the martyrdom of Poland, Mickiewicz's cosmic mystery depicts the entire universe of heaven, hell, and earth, with man at the center, surrounded by supernatural powers and struggling for salvation. In one prolonged scene a group of peasants, chanting incantations, gather on All Souls' Day to enact the primeval pagan rites of calling on the dead and offering them food. Mickiewicz revives drama by returning to the ancient roots of sacred theatre. During a night of visions, the protagonist of *Forefathers' Eve*, Gustaw, is transformed from an individual preoccupied with personal problems to a hero dedicated to the cause of his nation and of humanity.

Showing the cruel oppression of his fellow countrymen under the tyranny of the Czar, Mickiewicz poses the problem of human suffering, portraying Poland as the Christ of nations and its agony as comparable to Christ's crucifixion. Now renamed Konrad as a sign of his spiritual metamorphosis, the hero of *Forefathers' Eve* challenges God and accuses him of injustice for allowing a people to suffer such a destiny. Despite this blasphemy, Konrad is ultimately saved by his good angels, and the drama contains messianic prophecies telling of a great man who will lead Poland and all humanity to a bright future.

In the sixteenth lecture of his course on Slavic literatures given in French at the Collège de France in 1843, Mickiewicz declared that the actual theatres of his day could not stage plays such as *Forefathers' Eve*, and he predicted that the Slavic theatre of the future would be the true heir to Greek tragedy and the medieval religious theatre, revitalizing the mystery play and dramatizing the interplay of natural and supernatural worlds.[3]

At the turn of the century in Poland, the Symbolist poet, painter, and playwright Stanisław Wyspiański went back to the tradition of cosmic drama started by the Romantics. In fact, it was Wyspiański who for the first time staged *Forefathers' Eve* in Cracow in 1901. Continuing the Romantics' search for the mythic origins of drama, Wyspiański envisaged a holy stage erected on sacred national soil by Wawel Royal Castle in Cracow overlooking the river Vistula, which he associated with the Greek Scamander, and he dreamed of a gigantic theatre under the open sky in the Tatras Mountains, with the lofty peaks serving as the wings and the deep blue waters of a small lake suggesting the auditorium.

Such are the principal Polish antecedents for the ideas of Jerzy Grotowski, who, like the Romantics, identifies theatre with religion and yearns for a spiritual drama of involvement dealing with the tragic forces controlling man's fate on earth. It is no accident that Grotowski built his repertory at Opole and Wrocław on the Polish Romantic and post-Romantic classics. These productions include Mickiewicz's *Forefathers' Eve*, Słowacki's *Kordian* (1834) and *The Constant Prince* (after Calderón), and Wyspiański's version of *Hamlet* as well as his *Acropolis* (1904), set in Wawel Royal Castle at midnight before Easter. For Grotowski, Polish Romantic drama was a metaphysical art that strove "to go beyond everyday situations in order to reveal a wide existential perspective of human existence; one could call it a search for destiny." "It contained," Grotowski asserted, "a trait for which Dostoevsky's work came to be known—the penetration of human nature from the aspect of its unclear motives, through prophetic madness."[4]

Not the performance, but the theatrical process itself was always the goal of all Grotowski's work. Rejecting what he calls the falsehood of traditional theatre, in which the actor plays a make-believe role in front of a passive audience of paying spectators, Grotowski wanted neither pure play or an imitation of life in the theatre; rather, he aspired to absolute truth and reality and speaks of the need for a spontaneous, organic, authentic life in art. In order to be more than a kind of prostitute exhibiting himself for money to please an audience, the actor must annihilate his own body and free it from all psychic restraints. By such a sacrifice, the artist repeats the act of redemption and comes close to sanctity.

It was from primeval rites that theatre first arose, according to Grotowski, and it was his wish to return drama to the form of a ritual or ceremonial that takes place between actors and viewers. Thus Grotowski's theatre is poor in that it is reduced to this single relationship without any other accessories. Once the idea of a show performed by one group and watched by another has been abolished, all are free to become participants in a quest for truth, wisdom, and holiness. The actor then becomes the celebrant for the community of spectators, inciting them to take part in the ritual.

Such for Grotowski was the ideal. But since true religious ritual was no longer possible in a world of crumbling values, Grotowski could only hope to approach sacred theatre through myth and archetype in a profane rite: a modern and ironic confrontation with the experiences of past generations. For contemporary man, living without any fixed set of beliefs, each myth must be tested through blasphemy and sacrilege, which are alone capable of rekindling some spark of feeling for the divine.

In Grotowski's version of *Forefathers' Eve*, Konrad's great monologue was transformed into a grotesque rendering of the Stations of the Cross; the hero bears a broom as his cross, subjecting the Christian ritual to ironic scrutiny. In his staging of Słowacki's *Kordian*, the second great Polish Romantic drama, Grotowski restructured the myth of the hero's spiritual transformations by using as the frame for the entire play the scene in which the hero is confined in an insane asylum; now all his dreams of self-sacrifice for his country may be viewed as the dreams of a madman. Grotowski's final work for the theatre, *Apocalypsis cum figuris*, was a collectively created scenario or score for stage action, made up of quotations from the Bible, liturgical chants, Dostoevsky, T. S. Eliot, and Simone Weil. In it the Christian myth of the death of Christ and salvation through his sacrifice—Grotowski's constant obsession—is put to the test of blasphemy and profanation. The hero of the piece—a Simpleton who may be Christ, Satan, or simply the village idiot— undergoes in metaphoric fashion the Passion of Christ in a series of scenes that blend mysticism and the erotic.[5]

Grotowski created no new work for performance after 1968, when *Apocalypsis cum figuris* was first shown. Instead, he moved outside the theatre to new forms of spiritual endeavor. As a seer and master of enlightenment, Jerzy Grotowski always opposed the playing of roles and every form of social custom, habit, and pattern of behavior in the name of total integrity. "Theatre," Grotowski maintained, "means something only when it gives us the opportunity to transcend our standard imaginings, conventional emotions and opinions . . . and after discarding all our everyday pretenses . . . shows us in a state of absolute helplessness, disclosing, giving and finding ourselves. Through shock . . . we will be able to give ourselves to that something that we cannot describe, but in which Eros and Caritas live."[6]

The literary text, which for Grotowski had never been anything more than a point of departure reduced to its essentials, can at this point be dispensed with entirely. Performance likewise was never more than a means, not an end in itself. In Grotowski's paratheatrical activities, actor and viewer merged into participant or celebrant in a process whereby inner inhibitions and acquired habits are thrown off in an effort to reach the spiritual essence common to all. The evolution of Grotowski's visionary goals was toward ever greater purification: first the playwright was abolished, then the stage, finally the actor. All that remained were the celebrants and the master.

In his paratheatrical seminars and exercises—"Holiday," "The University of Explorations of the Theatre of Nations," "Opening," "Special Projects," "Venture Mountain," and "The Tree of People"—Grotowski brought together people of various nationalities and professions, ages and races, meeting in different countries and settings, as part of his unending quest to break down barriers that prevent man from reaching what lies hidden in his soul. Both Grotowski's poor theatre and his paratheatrical activities had in common the desire to strip away false layers of convention, to penetrate the myths that link past, present, and future, and to uncover the symbols that are common to all. In this way, Grotowski declared, we can re-create the feeling of unity and purification known in ancient tragedy but lost to us in modern society. Suggesting that each of us can participate in the cosmic drama that constantly surrounds us, Grotowski advised that we should forget ourselves, make less noise and learn to coexist with the wind, trees and stars.[7] The true theatre is everywhere around us.[8]

The Theatre of Participation was the last predominantly Polish phase of Grotowski's work, conducted primarily in Poland and inspired by Polish writers, artists, places, and ideas. In the third phase, the Theatre of Sources, Grotowski and members of his circle sought the roots of theatrical experience beyond the Polish tradition and takes them across national borders and cultural boundaries. Travel to diverse cultures and invitations to native practitioners from abroad became the prime means for Grotowski to further study of ritual performance techniques. The fourth and fifth phases of Grotowski's work, first Objective Drama in California and Art as Vehicle (Ritual Arts) in Italy, marked a return to the ancient mysteries in which there is no spectator, actor, or theatrical performance, but only the performer. But these later phases are other stories to be told elsewhere, subjects for separate investigation. Suffice it to say here that in 1997 Jerzy Grotowski was appointed to the Collège de France and gave his inaugural lecture, continuing the work and tradition of his predecessor Adam Mickiewicz. [9]

NOTES

1. Ludwik Flaszen, quoted in Tadeusz Burzyński and Zbigniew Osiński, *Grotowski's Laboratory*, trans. Bolesław Taborski (Warsaw: Interpress, 1979), 59.
2. Jan Błoński, "Grotowski and His Laboratory Theatre," *Dialog*, Special Issue (1970): 144.
3. See Adam Mickiewicz, "Lectures on Slavic Literature: Lesson 16 (4 April 1843)," trans. Daniel Gerould, *TDR* (T111), (Fall 1986): 91–97. Reprinted in *Theatre/Theory/Theatre*, ed. Daniel Gerould (New York: Applause, 2000), 330–35.
4. Jerzy Grotowski, quoted in Burzyński and Osiński, *Grotowski's Laboratory*, 61.
5. Konstanty Puzyna, "A Myth Vivisected: Grotowski's Apocalypse," *Polish Perspectives* 2 (1970): 18–30.
6. Jerzy Grotowski, quoted in Maria Krzysztof Byrski, "Grotowski a tradycja indyjska," *Dialog* 8 (1969), 69.
7. Jerzy Grotowski, "Działanie jest dosłowne," *Dialog* 9 (1979): 97—99, and "Świat powinien być miejscem prawdy," *Dialog* 10 (1979): 140–41.
8. For more on the paratheatrical phase, see *The Grotowski SourceBook*, ed. Richard Schechner and Lisa Wolford (London: Routledge, 1997), Pt. II: Paratheatre (1969–78) 207–47, and the following works by Zbigniew Osiński: "Grotowski and the Reduta Tradition," in *Grotowski's Empty Room*, ed. Paul Allain (London: Seagull Books, 2009), 19–54; *Jerzy Grotowski. Źródła, inspiracje, konteksty* (Gdańsk: słowo/obraz/terytoria, 1998); *Pamięć Reduty. Osterwa, Limanowski, Grotowski* (Gdańsk: słowo/obraz/terytoria, 2003); "Tradycja Reduty u Grotowskiego"; and "Utopia praktykowana. Na przykładzie wypowiedzi Grotowskiego: Święto I Przedsięwzięcie Góra: the Mountain of Flame," *Grotowski wytycza trasy: Studia I szkice* (Warsaw: Wydawnictwo Pusty Obłok, 1993), 185–278.
9. Allen Kuharski, "Grotowski's First Lecture at the College de France," *Slavic and East European Performance* 17, no. 3 (Summer 1997): 16–20.

Engraving of Maxim Gorky (ca. 1900)

GORKY, MELODRAMA, AND THE DEVELOPMENT OF EARLY SOVIET THEATRE

Maxim Gorky began his career in the theatre with *Smug Citizens* and *The Lower Depths* in 1902 at the age of thirty-four; for the next decade the novelist and story-writer devoted much of his creative energies to the stage. When, in 1915 shortly after his return to Russia from exile abroad, Gorky put the finishing touches on *The Old Man*, it was his thirteenth play in as many years, but immediately thereafter, in a period of revolution and civil war, Gorky the established dramatist fell silent. For the next fifteen years, the author of *The Lower Depths* did not complete a single play and returned to major playwriting only in the early 1930s.

However, Gorky had not lost all interest in the theatre, but like the other revolutionary artists and intellectuals of the period was seeking for new directions in keeping with the radical temper of the times. In the years of violent upheaval in Russia from 1916 to 1919, Gorky worked on an unfinished play and made sketches for a verse drama about the ancient Normans, as well as writing film scenarios, circus pieces, and texts for improvisation.[1] These ventures are evidence that, under the impress of revolution and civil war, Gorky's ideas about the theatre changed significantly, particularly his attitude to his own previous plays and the realistic tradition which they represented.

In the early days of the new Soviet era, avant-garde theatres and directors regarded Gorky's plays as pedestrian and old-fashioned and in some cases refused to stage them. The playwright himself now shared these views, as the following anecdote will show. On March 27, 1919, Gorky went to talk with the actors at the Alexandrinsky Theatre where his first play, *Smug Citizens*, was being revived as part of the official Soviet celebration in honor of the great writer's fiftieth birthday. When one of the actresses asked Gorky which of his plays was his own personal favorite, he would give no answer. Of *Smug Citizens*, he merely commented, "Is it really a play?" And the revered author finally declared, "I don't like Gorky."[2]

At the same time that he paid his visit to the Alexandrinsky Theatre and expressed aversion to his own playwriting, Gorky was engaged—along with his good friend Anatoly Lunacharsky—in an unusual project which enabled him to promote his conception of a new popular drama for the revolutionary era. This project was a melodrama contest for playwrights sponsored by the Petrograd branch of the Theatre Section of the Commissariat of Education, of which Gorky was an active member and Lunacharsky the head. The following announcement appeared in *The Life of Art* (*Zhizn' iskusstva*) on February 28, 1919;[3] a similar notice was published in other prominent artistic and theatrical journals during the same week.[4]

MELODRAMA CONTEST SPONSORED BY THE THEATRE SECTION OF THE COMMISSARIAT OF EDUCATION OF THE UNION OF COMMUNES IN THE NORTHERN PROVINCE

Information about the Rules of the Contest:

The Theatre Section announces a melodrama contest. The rules of the contest are as follows: four acts; choice of historical epoch and national setting is left to the discretion of the authors.

—yale/theatre 7, no. 2 (Winter 1976): 33–44.

Since melodrama is based on psychological primitivism and on simplification of the feelings and the interrelationships of the characters, it is advisable that the authors stress clearly and explicitly their sympathies and antipathies towards the protagonists and antagonists, it is also advisable that they include in the text fine songs, rhymed couplets, duets, etc.

Deadline for the submission of manuscripts—April 15. The manuscripts are to be submitted without the authors' signatures, each with a motto; the motto, name, and address of the author is to be given separately, in a sealed envelope.

The manuscripts are to be sent to: A.M. Peshkov, 23 Kronverskii Prospect, Petrograd.

> First Prize—10,000 rubles.
> Second Prize—7,000 rubles
> Third Prize—5,000 rubles.
> Fourth Prize—3,000 rubles.

Jury for the contest: A. V. Lunacharsky, N.F. Monakhov, F.I. Chaliapin, Yu. M. Yuriev, secretary of the jury, A.M. Peshkov.

People's Commissar A. Lunacharsky, Theatre Commissar M. Andreyeva

Of course, the secretary of the jury, A.M. Peshkov, is Maxim Gorky, who not only devised and organized the contest, but also wrote the announcement himself[5] and then, as we shall see, gave evaluations of thirty of the forty-one plays submitted. Besides Lunacharsky, the other members of the jury were close friends and associates of Gorky's from the theatre world who were working with the Soviet government in bringing culture to the new mass audiences. The great operatic bass Fyodor Chaliapin was then director of the Mariinsky Theatre, and Nikolai Monakhov and Yurii Yuriev were outstanding actors at the Bolshoi Dramatic Theatre which they had recently helped to organize along with Lunacharsky, Gorky, the poet Alexander Blok, and the actress Maria Andreyeva, Gorky's life-long companion and common-law wife, who was also the Theatre Commissar.

Why, we well may ask, were so many talented artists and intellectuals actively interested in melodrama, and what were their reasons for thinking that a new version of this old form would constitute the revolutionary drama of the future? To answer these questions, it is worth taking a closer look at the melodrama contest and Gorky's role in it. Much more than an interesting curiosity in Soviet theatre history, the contest not only reflects many of Gorky's principal concerns and activities in the period 1917–1921,[6] before he left Russia for Western Europe, but it is also expressive of a major current in the theatrical life of the new country during the civil war.[7]

A few words need to be said about the general situation in Petrograd in the winter of 1919 at the time of the contest, if we are to appreciate the unusual importance given to melodrama at a moment when the struggle for survival might have seemed so overwhelming as to preclude any concern with dramatic genres. Famine, typhus, cholera, freezing temperatures, counter-revolution, foreign intervention, and conspiracies on all sides had turned Petrograd into a beleaguered city in a state of total siege. Surrounded by countless enemies, the city was battling for existence against the elements. The allied blockade had cut off all trade with the outside world. Ordinary daily life came to an end as food supplies and fuel ran out, and the inhabitants of Petrograd were reduced to eating horses and burning their own books and furniture. Even so, many starved or froze to death. All of life became exaggerated, extreme, and fantastic; everywhere there was devastation and suffering as chaos and breakdown seemed imminent. Resistance to cold, hunger, and disease paralleled the unremitting fight against an inexhaustible number of antagonists: the Whites, Greens, Blacks, British, Americans, Germans, Czechs, Japanese, and their legions of agents, spies, and traitors.[8]

Called the heroic age of the revolution, the period of the civil war was in itself inherently melodramatic with the orphaned and outcast Soviet Union righteously combatting rich and powerful villains under a myriad of disguises.[9] Gorky, who had, at first opposed Lenin and the Bolsheviks, but then come to see the Soviet regime as the only salvation for Russia from bloody anarchy,[10] now argued for the heroic art of Romantic melodrama as befitting the new revolutionary ethos. The old realistic drama, with its detailed depiction of the dying bourgeois world and its intricate psychological techniques, was, in Gorky's opinion, worn out and no longer valid; melodrama was better suited to presenting the grand ideas and ideals of the new era and to encompassing the magnitude of its feelings and deeds. Starting from these premises, Gorky set about to rehabilitate melodrama and to encourage new playwrights to write works in the genre.[11] The following essay, which Gorky evidently worked on at the same time that he composed the rules for the contest, but never finished or published[12] clarifies his ideas on psychological primitivism and simplification of feelings in melodrama and elaborates the didactic and pedagogic effects which he expected of the genre.

ON THE HEROIC THEATRE

The people no longer are passive figures living their lives according to the dictates of the classes which formerly controlled their will, the people have ceased to be spectators of events, they wish to be the actors and create new forms of social life.

But the psychological habits of the great mass of people still persist.

Therefore we observe in the revolutionary way of life a process of pouring "new wine in old bottles," a process of inculcating new ideas in old forms of relationships—the old coarseness and cruelty in the interrelations among people do not disappear, the feeling of solidarity grows feebly, the word "comrade" still is not imbued with a feeling of sincere friendship and respect of equal for equal—everything continues more or less "in the old way," and man does not become more humane.

Beginning with this incontestable phenomenon, we must recognize as urgently necessary the education of the great masses of people with respect to feeling and will. Let us remember that the tangled web of economic conditions which has created a jumble of impressions, opinions, and attitudes in both the people and the intelligentsia has its parallel in the tangled web of psychological relationships which should now wither away and die out along with the dying economic system.

Everyone, and especially the great mass of people, must return to clarity of feeling, even to primitivism of feeling, if we understand by primitivism the fundamental sensations natural to every man, those "great" feelings upon which the supreme experts on the human spirit have based their dramas—the Greek tragic authors, Shakespeare, Schiller, Goethe, and the like. This primitivism of heroic drama is in truth its strength, not only not simplifying the complexity of the human soul, but concentrating the spirit according to its fundamental aspirations. Whereas realistic and psychological drama is, for the most, part, an apolitical drama eroding and destroying a clear, integral relation to man, heroic drama, tragedy, and melodrama are more or less successful attempts at a synthesis of feeling, consolidations of the spirit, an organizing force.

Beyond these general considerations in favor of tragedy and melodrama, the conditions of the time imperatively dictate to us the necessity of giving the masses a new and different kind of drama, rather than plays which depict a dying way of life full of hypocrisy, lies, cruelty, and the like, with which the spectator all by himself, without our theatre, is quite sufficiently acquainted.

If the old is dying, it should be buried, and in any case it is not the plays of Ostrovsky, Chekhov, Gorky, and so on—the usual repertory of our theatre—which will inspire people with new ideas, feelings, and thoughts, and it is not in such works that rest can be found for man living in such tragic days as ours, in such infernal work of destruction and creation as the work of our days.

The masses must be given beautiful theatrical performances in which their eyes can find rest and which will call forth in them the desire to put beauty into their own everyday lives.

A beautiful theatrical performance must contain a significant subject capable of exciting the fundamental principles of the human spirit. From the stage words must be spoken about courage, selflessness, about love for one's fellow man and respect for him, about the feeling of friendship, about man as a citizen, but the drama of man as a philistine, about man as a passive spectator of the tragedy of life—this drama should die out. The theatre should be a temple where man, resting from everyday life, without doing violence to himself, without even noticing it, learns to be a citizen and learns to be more a man than he is now.

For Gorky, as for the other artists and intellectuals, writers and actors who, like him, joined forces with the Bolsheviks, the most important task in 1919 was the creation of a new revolutionary culture and, at the same time, the preservation of the highest humanistic values of the past. All were in agreement that the education of the masses for the new society was the first priority and that the theatre must be the chief forum.[13] Thus, in the days of starvation and epidemics, theatrical performances—often given in unheated buildings—stirred great excitement; among the theorists of the new regime, fierce debates raged about dramatic genres in an attempt to find the right mode for the new revolutionary theatre.

Very much in tune with the times, Gorky attacked realism and traditionalism in Russian theatre and favored the experimentation prevalent in those years. In the struggle to build a new drama, Gorky, like most of his associates, proposed Romantic melodrama as the genre most consonant with the titanic nature of the October Revolution and civil war. The melodrama contest which he proposed and organized as a call for heroic art was designed to stimulate creativity in this new direction.

In 1919 the crucial problem for the Soviet theatre was to find a new repertory since the same old pre-revolutionary plays and playwrights continued to dominate the stage even after the revolution.[14] Well-made plays, bourgeois problem dramas, comedies by Labiche and Halévy, as well as decadent works by the ever-popular Andreyev continued to be played because there was no revolutionary repertory. The playwriting competitions were designed to remedy this lack, and in the period of the civil war, from 1918 to 1922, dozens of these contests, similar to Gorky's for melodrama, were held in Petrograd and Moscow and also in the smaller provincial cities.[15] On the juries were well-known writers and directors, such as Alexander Blok, Kornei Chukovsky, Mikhail Kuzmin, and Sergei Radlov; prizes consisted of relatively large sums of money (which had to be constantly increased because of inflation) and, often, the opportunity for performance.

Among the most important and characteristic activities of the early Soviet theatre, these contests were instrumental in creating a new repertory and new playwrights as well as in bringing about the involvement of vast numbers of people and organizations in producing revolutionary drama. Peasants, workers, and Red Army soldiers not only started attending the theatre for the first time, they actually began writing plays.

The contests, sponsored by the various new Soviet agencies and organizations, called for many different kinds of plays, although most specified a revolutionary content. The Proletcult quite naturally held a contest for proletarian drama. Recalling the medieval guilds which had presented mystery plays related to their trades—the plasterers staging the creation of the world, the water carriers the flood—the Soviet labor associations organized competitions for works about their own professions. For example, the All-Russian Miners Union ran a contest for plays about the life of miners, and the Union of Water Transport Workers for a drama about the struggles of Water Transport Workers. One of these announcements opened with the words: "Workers and Peasants! Create your own works of art!"[16]

There were competitions for children's theatre and children's opera, designed to serve specific pedagogic functions. Numerous contests were held for works of a ceremonial and ritual nature, to celebrate key events in the life struggle of the working classes and peasant masses, such as the October Revolution, or to commemorate proletarian holidays, like May 1 and the 50th anniversary of the Paris Commune. These mass spectacles—made famous by grandiose shows such as *The Pantomime of the Great Revolution*, *The Taking of the Winter Palace*, *The Mystery of Freed Labor*, and *The Blockade of Russia*[17]—were monumental and popular in style, totally rejecting psychological realism, and their kinship with Gorky's notion of heroic melodrama and its primitivism is evident,[18] as the following Red Army contest shows.

Starting with the premise that "the repertory should be elevated and heroic, a theatre of great emotions,"[19] the Political Department of the Petrograd Military Command sponsored a competition for revolutionary drama. The first prize of 5,000 rubles was awarded for the trilogy *The Red Year* written collectively by the soldiers in the Red Army Theatre Workshop, and the play itself—we are informed in the announcement of results of the contest—was a communal mass spectacle making "no distinction between actor and audience. The events of the February and October Revolutions unfold amidst the spectators."[20]

Gorky, who of course hoped to promote a revival of the literary genre of melodrama and to encourage young playwrights to produce a new Soviet version of an old dramatic form, was not as successful with his contest. At this period there were simply not any young writers equipped to handle melodramatic form as Gorky understood it.[21] Because of the inferior quality of the plays submitted, the competition deadline was extended one month, from April 15 to May 15.[22] Then the following announcement appeared in *The Life of Art* (*Zhizn' iskusstva*) on July 2, 1919.[23]

INFORMATION FROM THE JURY OF THE MELODRAMA CONTEST ABOUT THE RESULTS OF THE CONTEST

Forty-one plays were sent to the contest, the majority of the plays turned out to be purely realistic depictions of everyday life and failed to meet the formal requirements of melodrama, the rest were devoid of literary merit. The jury found it possible to award the second prize to the play *At Daybreak* by Nikolai Isidorovitch Misheyev.

Yu. Yuriev, N. Monakhov, F. Chaliapin, Secretary A. Peshkov

Gorky's handwritten comments, preserved for thirty of the plays, are all negative.[24] They reveal that the famous author, who was always anxious to help young writers and willing to read everything which was sent him[25] could be caustic and ironic in his judgments and that he would not tolerate mediocrity. At this point in his career, Gorky was especially impatient with realism and also did not like narrowly conformist propaganda plays. Typical of his opinions on the entries devoid of literary merit are the following:

> (9) The Queen. Motto: "The path for the living is with the living."
>> A feeble little thing. No queen, no strength, no character, no sonorous words. No talent either.

> (10) Motto: "Life for life's sake."
>> A realistic play. Serfdom, the landowner is a despot, a petty tyrant, he is involved in brigandage, he oppresses his daughter, his stepson, the peasants, and—especially the reader.
>> The daughter is a fool, the step-son is a fool, and so is the landowner.
>> There is no action, no thought, no talent either, only oppressions.[26]

Gorky's harshest comments are reserved for an anti-religious play which extols as its hero a member of the secret police. At precisely this time, in 1919, Gorky was frequently intervening to save those arrested by the Cheka (the acronym for the first Soviet secret police: the Extraordinary Commission for Repression against Counter-Revolution, Speculation, and Desertion); in *Memoirs of a Revolutionary*, Victor Serge observes, "Often at the Cheka I would meet the man whom I came to dub mentally as the 'great interceder,' Maxim Gorky . . . He never refused to intervene."[27] It is not surprising that the "great interceder" judged the propaganda play about the Cheka in the following hostile terms:

> (6) Motto: "Let there be light."
>> The play is singularly communistic, but as literature it is almost illiterate and exceptionally boring. The hero is president of the Cheka, the son-in-law of an Orthodox priest and a former political prisoner; he exposes the relics of a holy [indecipherable]. The priest, smearing his cassock with phosphorus, incites the people to insurrection against the power of the Soviets. A commissar—a former zemgusar, swindler, and traitor—gets a bullet in the back of the head from the revolver of a certain Cheka man. The priest's daughter—a former political prisoner—misses her father somewhat, but loves her husband and the revolution extraordinarily [N.B. the play on words with Cheka, "Extraordinary Commission"], understanding by revolution the exposing of religious relics. A heavy dose of red-journalistic verbiage. But no action.[28]

Only two of the plays submitted to the contest—Vyacheslav Yakelovich Shishkov's *The Old World* and Alexander Alexandrovich Vermishev's *The Red Truth*—enjoyed subsequent success on the stage. In both cases, Gorky recognized that the authors had talent and that, with only minor changes, their plays could be staged, but neither Shishkov nor Vermishev received a prize since, in Gorky's opinion, their entries were not melodramas at all, but realistic plays of a political nature on contemporary themes.

From Gorky's strictures on the works submitted to the contest, we can infer what qualities he felt a true melodrama should possess: strong dynamics, sharp contrasts and conflicts, characters drawn in high relief, and clearly defined feelings and attitudes. "Drama," Gorky wrote in a reader's report for the Bolshoi Theatre, "demands movement, activity on the part of the heroes, strong feelings, rapidity of experiences, brevity and clarity of expression. If this is lacking, there is no drama."[29] For these reasons, the author of *The Lower Depths* turned his back on his own previous playwriting and favored melodrama as the true school for future dramatists and the best way to infuse new blood into the Russian theatre.

These ideas of Gorky's, sharpened by the revolution and civil war, were, however, not simply occasioned by the political situation which arose when the Bolsheviks gained power, but are rather the results of a decade of slow and thoughtful maturation. Gorky's interest in melodrama antedates by at least ten years the playwriting contest, and as early as 1908 the celebrated author of realistic fiction and drama had intuitively and prophetically grasped the importance of melodrama as a future direction in the evolution of Russian theatre.

Writing in 1908, Lunacharsky reported, "In a private conversation our famous writer told me that he was getting ready to write a play in the style of the old melodramas. I warmly greeted the idea. Unfortunately M. Gorky still has not carried it out."[30] Two years later, in 1910, Gorky wrote to Leopold Sulerzhitsky, Stanislavsky's disciple and director of the First Studio of the Moscow Art Theatre, "I am thinking about a melodrama, but a melodrama of a special type. I consider melodrama the most genuine need of the time and a necessity for Russia."[31] In his reply, Sulerzhitsky reported that Stanislavsky himself was very interested in Gorky's ideas about Russian melodrama; and the director and playwright talked about melodrama when Stanislavsky visited Gorky in Capri in 1911. In a letter to Stanislavsky in 1912, Gorky again mentions "melodrama of a new kind."[32]

Upon his return to Russia in 1914, Gorky gave an interview to journalists in which he discussed the future of contemporary theatre and the role of melodrama in creating a repertory accessible to all: "Melodrama should be a part of the basic repertory of such a theatre, but it must be artistic melodrama, full of spirited words, challenging us to live and participate actively."[33] In a second interview, Gorky declared that the old form of drama had outlived its time, and that the new form had yet to be born, but he predicted that "The dramatic work of the immediate future will be melodrama, melodrama permeated with an atmosphere of Romanticism."[34]

In June, 1918, in his column "Untimely Thoughts" in his journal *Novaya Zhizn'* (just a month before it was closed by Lenin and the Bolsheviks), Gorky argued that art should be superior to life and serve as a purifying and elevating contrast to crass reality which degrades man's spirit. Fearing that culture would be destroyed by the excesses of revolution on the part of uncivilized peasant masses, Gorky felt that drama and theatre were powerful forces capable of "raising the receptive spectator above the chaos of the everyday and the ordinary."[35] Accordingly, melodrama would have a humanizing, elevating effect which realism could never hope to achieve.

> I will pose an apparently paradoxical question: which is more useful for the social and aesthetic education of the masses—Chekhov's *Uncle Vanya* or Rostand's *Cyrano de Bergerac*, Dickens's *Cricket on the Hearth*, or any play of Ostrovsky? I am for Rostand, Dickens, Shakespeare.[36]

In stating his preference for the heroic and melodramatic, Gorky is referring to plays actually in the repertory at that very time. *Uncle Vanya* and Ostrovsky's *Enough Simplicity in Every Wiseman* were playing at the Moscow Art Theatre in 1918, and *The Cricket on the Hearth*, created by Boris Sushkevich in 1914 as a theatricalist melodrama based on Dickens's tale, was still being staged at the First Studio with Sulerzhitsky, Vakhtangov, and Mikhail Chekhov in the principal roles; shortly before that, in the 1915–1916 season, Tairov had presented *Cyrano* at the Kamerny Theatre.

In his desire to move Russian theatre away from the tired traditions of realism, represented by Chekhov and Ostrovsky, towards the bright, colorful, expansive world of heroic melodrama, Gorky joined forces with the major innovators of the time, stimulated fruitful debate on dramatic genres, and pointed the way to a new conception of theatrical art which was soon to flourish on the Russian stage. The first and greatest period of Soviet drama, from 1918 to 1928, was a decade of melodrama. Especially characteristic of these years was the growing interest on the part of the artistic intelligentsia in the revival of Romantic and heroic melodrama which seemed both the most theatrical form of drama and the most genuinely popular species of art, well suited to the needs and interests of the masses.[37]

Melodrama soon became a dominant genre in the early Soviet repertory and the center of intense critical discussion. The Bolshoi Dramatic Theatre, organized by Gorky, Lunacharsky, Blok, and associates in 1918 to present the classics of world drama, had as its slogan: "Heroic Theatre for Heroic People." At first the plays of Schiller and Shakespeare, heavily "Schillerized," served the goal, proposed by Gorky, of "idealizing the individual" and showing "man as a hero, chivalrously selfless and passionate in his devotion to the cause in which he believes."[38] The style of the acting in plays like *The Robbers* and *Don Carlos* (with Monakhov as the King and Yuriev as the Marquis de Posa) was grandiose and Romantic, with broad, expressive gestures speaking directly to the masses about tyranny and oppression.

In charge of repertory, Alexander Blok explained the program of the new theatre as one of Romantic celebration. "I think that most of the spectators come to our theatre to brighten their daily lives and participate in a kind of festivity. We do our part to sustain this feeling of holiday by presenting lofty drama which is Romantic in the broadest sense of the word."[39] In a speech to the actors in March 1919, the great Symbolist poet explained why they were planning to present the French melodrama *God's Mercy, or the New Fanchon* by D'Ennery and Lemoine in Nekrasov's nineteenth-century adaptation called *A Mother's Blessing, or Poverty and Honor*:

> Having done Shakespeare, Schiller, and Hugo we now wish to finish the season with melodrama which grew out of romantic drama. In choosing one of the classic melodramas, we are planning to organize a kind of theatrical festivity; we need no film studios here for that purpose although in recent times that is where melodramas have been staged; what is required in a lavish production, authentic old music, unusual ease of movement from tears to laughter—all those things so becoming to the theatre.[40]

Although *The Mother's Blessing* was not actually presented at the Bolshoi Dramatic Theatre, Blok's instructions as to how it should be played reveal the similarity of his views of melodrama with Gorky's primitivism, simplification, and clarity of feelings. According to Blok, the melodrama "should be played so that the public would weep fine, purifying tears, tears such as civilized people have long since forgotten how to weep."[41]

In fact, the primitivism of melodrama at this early stage of Soviet theatre had wide appeal both for Symbolist poets and intellectuals and also for avant-garde directors. The radical wing of the experimental theatre, interested primarily in theatricalization and circus effects, admired melodrama for its fast-paced action, vivid characters, and strong

Alexander Anders and Maria Titova in Adolphe D'Ennery's *The Two Orphans*,
called *The Sisters Gerard* in a version by Vladimir Mass, at the Moscow Art Theatre (1927)

situations and emotions, much as Gorky did, but less on didactic grounds than for the
excellent opportunities offered for sheer "play." Combining clowning, the American
silent film, and the adventure and detective story, directors like Sergei Radlov and Nikolai
Foregger turned melodrama into exciting shows. At his Theatre of Popular Comedy in
January 1921, Radlov presented his "urban melodrama" *Love and Gold*, based on motifs
from the popular French novelist and playwright Pierre Decourcelle, using cinema
cutting to move about the streets of Paris and penetrate into its underworld haunts and
underground sewers.[42] At about the same time Foregger presented D'Ennery's *The Child
Snatcher* at his theatre Mastfor (Foregger's Workshop), utilizing a frantic tempo and
projectors with flashing shutters so that the production resembled a silent film.[43]

By the early 1920s, a major revival of D'Ennery, Dumas *père*, and nineteenth-
century French melodrama appeared to be in progress in revolutionary Russia.[44] This
realization of Gorky's program was given theoretical sanction by Lunacharsky in 1922
when a new theatre was organized with his support and blessing specially to be devoted
to French Romantic melodrama. The creation of Valerii Bebutov, who had co-directed
Verhaeren's *Les Aubes* with Meyerhold, the Romanesque Theatre, as it was called,
presented two plays by Dumas *père* in its only season in existence, *The Tower of Nesle*
and *The Count of Monte Cristo*. Writing of the Romanesque Theatre in an essay entitled

"The Right Path," Lunacharsky, who claims to have attended virtually all the rehearsals of *The Tower of Nesle*, states: "The fact is that for almost twenty years now, both verbally and in my writing I have stressed the great significance of melodrama and the Romantic drama of France in the 30s, 40s, and 50s as the basis and starting point for the creation of a genuinely popular theatre."[45]

Acknowledging his debt to Romain Rolland, who in *Le Théâtre du peuple* (1903) argues that melodrama is the truly popular theatre of the future,[46] Lunacharsky explains his own position that the new Soviet drama, if it is to be genuinely democratic and revolutionary, must appeal to the masses and grip their emotions. Melodrama, in Lunacharsky's opinion, "a theatre of effects, contrasts, broad poses, sonorous words, intense beauty and caricatural deformity, a theatre relying at one extreme on titanic emotions, and at the other, on reckless buffoonery," is the basis for any popular theatre and, what is more, "the highest form of theatre as such."[47] The Commissar of Education concludes his discussion with the following injunction: "in the realm of the theatre we must go back to Dumas *père*."[48] It is interesting to note that Lunacharsky's advice to Soviet dramatists to learn the art of entertainment and enthrallment from the author of *The Count of Monte Cristo* comes a year before his better known slogan, "back to Ostrovsky."

Like his friend Gorky, Lunacharsky stressed both the artistic strength and the didactic purpose of the popular genre which he ranked with film in importance. For Lunacharsky, melodrama should have these traits: "A fine, gripping subject; next richness of action; character traits defined with colossal relief; clarity and sharp expressiveness of all the situations and the capacity to call forth undivided and total emotional reactions; compassion and indignation; the action connected to simple and therefore sublime esthetic premises, and to simple and clear ideological positions."[49] For these reasons, the Commissar of Education believed that melodrama would have the same powerful impact on the masses as Gorky did.

Lunacharsky promoted melodrama not only in his theoretical works, but also in his own playwriting, producing at least three works clearly in that genre: *The Incendiaries* (1923), *The Bear's Wedding* (1924, based on a Mérimée tale), and *Poison* (1926). Other well-known Soviet melodramas of the mid-1920s include Golichnikov's *Comrade Semivzvodnii* (1923), Slavianskii's *The Red Eagle* (1925), Romashov's *The End of Krivorylsk* (1926), and Lavrenyov's *The Break* (1927), which are all plays of the civil war pitting embattled communists against capitalist villains.[50]

Perhaps the best-known Soviet writer of melodrama in this period was Alexei Faiko whose early plays like *Lake Lyul'*, "A Melodrama in Five Acts" (1923) were produced by Meyerhold. However, by 1928, when Faiko's *The Man with the Briefcase* was staged by Akimov at the Theatre of the Revolution, a change had already taken place in the Soviet Union which brought to an end not only the era of melodrama, but also the period of freedom to debate which style of theatre would be appropriate for the new society. When the critics attacked *The Man with the Briefcase* savagely, the vogue of melodrama subsided. [51] By the early 1930s, all experimentation was over, the revolutionary intellectuals silenced or repentant, and primitivism seen as formalistic heresy.[52] With the reinstatement of psychological realism and the deification of socialist realism, melodrama could only be judged an aberration and obstacle to the perfection of Soviet drama.

When Gorky returned to the Soviet Union and began the final phase of his career as a playwright, the atmosphere had totally changed. Concerned with presenting Gorky as the founder of socialist realism, the critics overlooked his earlier advocacy of melodrama and stressed Gorky's opposition to avant-garde experimentation rather than his criticism of psychological realism. Gorky himself had apparently forgotten the melodrama episode; he went back to the dramatic mode in which he had written most of his plays and achieved his greatest success, and he now produced his masterpiece in that genre, *Egor Bulichov and the Others* (1932). Soviet criticism tended to regard Gorky's struggle for heroic melodrama as a case of abstract idealism lacking historical concreteness and a direct consequence of the writer's political errors in opposing Lenin and the Bolsheviks.[53]

The striking fact still remains that, at the time of the revolution when he was fifty years old, the future father of socialist realism lost interest in the old psychological tradition, participated actively in the new Soviet theatre of the time, and, along with all the best talents of the age, promoted the innovative forms of circus, cinema, and melodrama.

NOTES

1. Boris A. Bialik, *Maxim Gor'kii, Dramaturg* (Moscow: Sovetskii Pisatel', 1962), 368.
2. David I. Zolotnitskii, "M. Gor'kii," in *Russkie Dramaturgi: XVIII–XIX VV., Vtoraya Polovina XIX Veka*, ed. B.I. Bursov (Leningrad-Moscow: Iskusstvo, 1962), 3:433.
3. Reprinted in "Dramaturgicheskie Konkursy," ed. N.S. Plyatskovskaya, in *Russkii Sovetskii Teatr 1917–1921: Dokumenty i Materialy*, ed. A.Z. Yufit (Leningrad: Iskusstvo, 1968), 359.
4. The contest was first announced on February 27, in *Severnaya Kommuna*, No. 46, according to *Letopis' zhizni i tvorchestva A.M. Gor'kogo* (Moscow: Akademiya Nauk, 1960), 3:113. The same notice also appeared in *Iskusstvo Kommuny*, No. 13, March 12, and in *Vestnik Teatra*, No. 43.
5. Yuriev told I. Berezark that Gorky himself wrote the announcement. See I. Berezark, "V bor'be za pravdy dramaticheskogo obraza," in *Gorkii i voprosy sovetskoi literatury* (Leningrad: Sovetskii Pisatel', 1956), 315. A comparison of the announcement with the essay "On the Heroic Theatre," which Gorky wrote at the same time, confirms his authorship of the rules of the melodrama contest.
6. Zolotnitskii, "M. Gor'kii," 436.
7. S.S. Danilov, "Rannyaya Sovetskaya Dramaturgiya (1917–1920)," in *Ocherki Istorii Russkoi Sovetskoi Dramaturgii 1917–1934*, ed. S.V. Vladimirov and D.I. Zolotnitskii (Leningrad-Moscow: Iskusstvo, 1963), 10.
8. For a vivid personal picture of the situation in Petrograd in 1919, see Victor Serge, *Memoirs of a Revolutionary 1901–1941*, trans. Peter Sedgwick (London: Oxford University Press, 1963), 70–114. Serge gives a more objective account in his *Year One of the Russian Revolution*, trans. Peter Sedgwick (New York: Holt, Rinehart and Winston, 1972), 350–64. Gorky himself described the desperate circumstances and horrors of starvation in 1918 in his articles "Untimely Thoughts" in his journal *Novaya Zhizn'* for May 23 and June 1, 8, and 9. The articles for May 23 and June 1 are included in Maxim Gorky, *Untimely Thoughts*, trans. Herman Ermolaev (New York: Paul S. Eriksson, 1968), 203–6, 216–19.
9. Boris Thomson, *The Premature Revolution: Russian Literature and Society 1917–1946* (London: Weidenfeld and Nicolson, 1972), 39–40.
10. A detailed study of Gorky's relations with Lenin and the Bolsheviks is given in Bertram D. Wolfe, *The Bridge and the Abyss: The Troubled Friendship of Maxim Gorky and V.I. Lenin* (New York: Praeger, 1957).
11. D.I. Zolotnitskii, "Gor'kii," in *Ocherki Istorii Russkoi Sovetskoi Dramaturgii 1917–1934*, 78. See also Bialik, 372 and Danilov, 10–11.
12. Published for the first time in *Arkhiv A.M. Gor'kogo* (Moscow: Goslitizdat, 1951), 3:220–22.
13. Nikolai A. Gorchakov, *The Theater in Soviet Russia*, trans. Edgar Lehrman (New York: Columbia University Press, 1957), 116.
14. "Teatry Moskvy," ed. G.A. Khaichenko, in *Russkii Sovetskii Teatr 1917–1921: Dokumenty i Materialy*. See also Danilov, 9.
15. "Dramaturgicheskie Konkursy," in *Russkii Sovetskii Teatr 1917–1921: Dokumenty i Materialy*, 358–69.
16. Ibid., 362.
17. "Massovye prazdnestva," ed. E.D. Volodarskaya, in *Russkii Sovetskii Teatr 1917–1921: Dokumenty i Materialy*, 262–76.
18. L. Tamashin, *Sovetskaya Dramaturgiya v Gody-Grazhdanskoi Voiny* (Moscow: Iskusstvo, 1961), 139.
19. Ibid.
20. "Dramaturgicheskie Konkursy," 362.
21. Berezark, 315.
22. Tamashin, 271.
23. Reprinted in "Dramaturgicheskie Konkursy," 360.
24. *M. Gor'kii: Materialy i Issledovaniia*, ed. V.A. Desnitskii (Moscow: Akademiya Nauk, 1934), 1:102–7.
25. Irwin Weil, *Gorky: His Literary Development and Influence on Soviet Intellectual Life* (New York: Random House, 1966), 113.

26. *M. Gor'kii: Materialy i Issledovaniia*, 104.

27. Serge, *Memoirs of a Revolutionary*, 82. Additional testimony as to Gorky's intercessions is given in Alexander Kaun, *Maxim Gorky and His Russia* (New York: Benjamin Blom, 1968), 507.

28. *M. Gor'kii: Materialy i Issledovaniia*, 103.

29. Ibid, 113. Gorky's comments on a play called *The Madman* (author unknown) date from the same period, 1919–1920. Followers of Chekhov, such as Chirikov and Surguchev, had produced pallid mood pieces, called "small dramas of little people" by Marc Slonim in *Russian Theater From Empire to the Soviets* (New York: Collier, 1962), 242. It is as an antidote to this dead end that Gorky promotes melodrama.

30. Bialik, 287.

31. Ibid.

32. A.O. Boguslavskii and V.A. Diev, *Russkaya Sovetskaya Dramaturgia 1917–1935* (Moscow: Akademiya Nauk, 1963), 1:31.

33. Bialik, 287.

34. Ibid.

35. Ibid., 371.

36. Ibid. These passages can also be found in the English translation of *Untimely Thoughts*, 224–28.

37. Boguslavskii and Diev, 30–31. Not long after Gorky gave his interviews about the revival of the genre upon his return to Russia in 1914, Meyerhold, in collaboration with Vladimir Solovyov and Yurii Bondi, wrote a patriotic war melodrama *Fire*, designed to awaken heroic feelings in the audience. See Gorchakov, 73.

38. S. Mokul'skii, "V Bor'be za Klassiky," *Bol'shoi Dramaticheskii Teatr* (Leningrad: Bol'shoi Dramaticheskii Teatr, 1935), 46. Gorky's statement about the aims of the Bolshoi Theatre first appeared in "Dela i dni Bol'shogo Dramaticheskogo Teatra," No. 1, 1919, 7–8.

39. Mokul'skii, 49.

40. Ibid., 49–50.

41. Ibid., 51.

42. Mel Gordon, "Radlov's Theatre of Popular Comedy," *The Drama Review*, 19, no. 4, (December 1975): 113–16. See also Gorchakov, 131.

43. S.I. Yutkevitch, quoted in *Istoriya Sovetskogo Dramaticheskogo Teatra*, ed. K.L. Rudnitskii (Moscow: Nauka, 1966), 2:134–35.

44. Stanislavsky, who had already expressed his interest in melodrama to Gorky, became part of this movement somewhat later when, in 1927, the Moscow Art Theatre presented D'Ennery and Cormon's *The Two Orphans*, adapted as *The Sisters Gerard* by V.C. Mass, under Gorchakov's direction. Stanislavsky's comments on the acting of melodrama are found in Nikolai A. Gorchakov, *Stanislavsky Directs*, trans. Miriam Goldina (New York: Funk & Wagnalls, 1954), 277–349. It is also worth noting that Hugo's *Marion de Lorme* was billed as a "melodrama" at the Vakhtangov Theatre in 1926. French melodrama, not English or American, was the inspiration for the Soviet theory and practice of the genre, although Edward Sheldon's *Romance* and adaptations of *Trilby* were popular on the Soviet stage in the early 1920s. In film, of course, the American influence was the greatest.

45. A.V. Lunacharsky, *Sobranie Sochinenii* (Moscow: Khudozhestvennaya Literatura, 1964), 3:112. The essay was originally published in 1922.

46. Rolland's book, published in Russian in 1908, undoubtedly was known to Gorky as well.

47. Lunacharsky, 114.

48. Ibid. The striking fact is that in urging Soviet drama to go forward, its theorists have almost always proposed that it go back to something earlier. Innovation has taken the form of a return to tradition.

49. Quoted in Boguslavskii and Diev, 35, from the essay "Kakaya nam nuzhna melodrama?" ("What kind of melodrama do we need?"), originally published in 1919.

50. Boguslavskii and Diev, 36–37.

51. Vladimir Frolov, *Zhanry Sovetskoi Dramaturgii* (Moscow: Sovetskoi Pisatel', 1957), 67. Arbuzov attempted to revive the genre once again in 1961 with his melodrama *The Lost Son*.

52. A.A. Gvozdev and Adrian Piotrovskii, "TEO NARKOMPROSA i Teatral'naya Teoriya," in *Istoriya Sovetskogo Teatra* (Leningrad: Gosudarstvennaya Akademiya, 1933), 136–37.

53. Bialik, 371.

Caricature of Sławomir Mrożek by Andrzej Stopka (circa 1960)

CONTEXTS FOR *VATZLAV:*

MROŻEK AND THE EIGHTEENTH CENTURY

During Sławomir Mrożek's long career writing for the theatre, two distinguishing marks of his work have been a preference for parable forms and an obsession with dialectical polarities of nature and culture, instinct and reason, primitivism and civilization, experience and theory. Now these are characteristics typical of many French writers in the Age of Enlightenment, but Mrożek's affinity for eighteenth-century thought and literature might pass unnoticed if it were not for *Vatzlav*, a play that is the dramatic equivalent of a *conte philosophique*, such as *Candide*, and that was given an eighteenth-century staging in its first and most influential Polish production.

At pains to show the playwright's avant-garde credentials, critics have tended to focus their attention on Mrożek's relationship to the theatre of the absurd, the impact of Beckett and Ionesco, and the influence of his Polish predecessors Witkiewicz and Gombrowicz.[1] Yet *Vatzlav* reveals another side of Mrożek's art that has antecedents in the eighteenth century. As a modern philosopher, satirist, and moralist in the tradition of Voltaire and Diderot, the Polish playwright shares their concerns with what Lester Crocker calls the problems of "our existence, the nature of man, the organization of society and the integration of the individual within it."[2] Even Mrożek's nihilistic black humor may be closer to "the philosophy of the absurd that was one child of the Enlightenment"[3] than it is to that of Beckett and Ionesco, and his critique of extreme rationalism has its roots in the eighteenth century.

Mrożek is a masterful assimilator and parodist who has been able to adapt for his own purposes a wide variety of literary styles and genres,[4] but in the case of his eighteenth-century personation, I believe that the author of *Vatzlav* goes beyond mockery, mimicry, and pastiche. Mrożek, a disabused rationalist, finds congenial the oblique techniques and social themes of the philosophical tale in the Age of Enlightenment; for the playwright to treat ironically a form that is itself deeply ironic is simply to continue its traditions.

As is often the case with Polish drama, which is fatally entangled in national history, everything about *Vatzlav* is complicated and unclear. The play exists in a critical limbo, its nature and position anomalous and undefined. And yet this enigmatic work is in some crucial way an important transitional work, about a hero in transit, by an author in transit. I propose to explore *Vatzlav*'s place in Mrożek's playwriting and Mrożek's place in *Vatzlav* by discovering contexts for the play—above all, in the eighteenth century.

Written in the summer of 1968—and probably not finished until after the Soviet invasion of Czechoslovakia in late August—*Vatzlav* was the first of Mrożek's plays not to be published in Poland, and for this and other reasons that I shall look at shortly, it was almost completely ignored in criticism of Mrożek in Polish for over a decade.[5] *Vatzlav* received its world première in Zürich at the Theater am Neumarkt on February 11, 1970, and was first published in German translation that same year. Ralph Manheim's translation, presumably made from the German, also appeared in 1970, and the English-language première took place in August at the Stratford Festival in Stratford, Ontario.

It was not until nine years later that the Polish première could be given, on April 21, 1979, at the Teatr Nowy in Łódź, directed by Kazimierz Dejmek, one of Poland's

—*Modern Drama* 26, no. 1 (March 1984): 21–40.

greatest theatre artists.[6] Unlike Mrożek's previous plays, which had been widely performed at many different theatres throughout the country, *Vatzlav* initially received only this one production, which, although invariably referred to as brilliant, was not reviewed in Poland.[7] The play was in effect partially banned by being confined to this one staging. After he became manager of the Teatr Polski in Warsaw, Dejmek revived the production in April 1982, with a different cast but the same stage design.[8] In 1989 he made a TV adaptation shown on January 1, 1990.

Vatzlav was published in Polish for the first time in 1982, along with Mrożek's 1981 play *The Ambassador*, in a single volume issued by the Parisian émigré press, Kultura.[9] The published Polish text, representing the cut and slightly rewritten version used by Dejmek for his production, differs considerably from Mrożek's manuscript, which is the basis of the German and English translations. All scenes involving Mrs. Bat and her oedipal relationship with her son after her first two appearances have been omitted, as have the episodes in which Oedipus serves as a spy and informer for Bat. Occasionally small but important additions and changes have been made in the dialogue.[10] Also, Mrożek has added to the printed play an opening description of the characters and a two-page interpretative commentary on their natures and significance, which was evidently included in the program of 1979; previously, the playwright had never provided any such information about his dramatis personae.

1968—the year of composition for *Vatzlav*—was a turning point for Mrożek. Although he had been living abroad (in Italy) since 1963, the playwright now definitively made a break with his homeland and settled in Paris, the traditional place of exile for Polish émigré artists and intellectuals; eventually he became a French citizen. Mrożek's attraction to the *conte philosophique* and the literary traditions of his adopted country of residence at this point in his career is not surprising.

Political events had recently produced a climate of repression in Poland, bringing to a standstill the more than a decade of creative ferment in the arts that had followed the liberalization of 1956. In March 1968, student unrest at Warsaw University led to political infighting, exploitation of anti-Semitism, and the expulsion of a large number of Jews in high positions in the government, the army, and the arts, many of them Communist Party members, including Adam Tarn, Mrożek's friend and the editor of the drama magazine *Dialog*, in which until then all of his plays had appeared.

In the fall, after Mrożek published in Yugoslavia a letter protesting the Soviet invasion of Czechoslovakia, his works came under a ban. The last opening of a Mrożek play took place in June 1968, and productions already in the repertory soon disappeared; his last book, a volume of cartoons entitled *Seen through Sławomir Mrożek's Glasses*, was printed in July. No new work by Mrożek was published or performed for the next five years,[11] and his absence from the Polish theatre created a great void.

Not until the spring of 1973 did Mrożek's plays return to the Polish stage and to the pages of *Dialog*. He soon resumed his position of preeminence in contemporary Polish drama, enjoying the second great success of his career with *Émigrés* in 1975 (*Tango* in 1965 had been the first). His plays were now performed everywhere in Poland, and the government indicated that he would be welcomed back if he chose to return. Mrożek did come back, but only for short visits. Yet *Vatzlav* still remained under the cloud that had darkened the horizon at the time of its creation: it was neither printed, performed, nor discussed.

Vatzlav, in fact, opens under a lowering sky, with thunder and lightning, as the shipwrecked hero is tossed by the sea on an alien shore. Permitting his double—former self, fellow man, brother, past history—to drown, so that there will be no witness to what he once was, the former slave, now a free man in a free world, sets out on a series of adventures in which he attempts to improve his lot and achieve wealth, fame, and honor. After failing to realize these self-seeking goals—the true springs of action in a society that pays only lip service to the ideal of equality—Vatzlav finds himself at the end of the play back at his starting point: on the shore retreating into the sea and hoping to reach the other, far-distant shore. The free world has shown him much the same injustice and abuse of power and authority that existed in the slave world which he has left forever, but the taste of freedom, however empty it proved in practice, has made the ex-slave able to think and choose for himself.

Anomalies in *Vatzlav* begin with the title of the play and the name of its hero. Rarely do characters in Mrożek's plays have specifically Polish names. They have, instead, generic names (Policeman, Prisoner, Husband, Wife, Newcomer), international names (Arthur, Amelia), borrowed names (Paganini, Othello), or invented names (Onucy, Onek, Onka).[12] Here for the first time the hero has a Polish name, Wacław, but contrary to what we would expect, the name is spelled—in the Polish text as well as in the German and English translations—Vatzlav, in a westernized phonetic transcription. The character appears to have adopted a foreign way of writing his name to make it easier to spell and pronounce. Starting a new life abroad, Vatzlav sheds an earlier self (much as he let his double drown) and hopes to assume an identity that will replace that of shipwrecked slave. The changed orthography of his name indicates assimilation and accommodation to the surrounding culture.[13]

"V" is not a letter in the Polish alphabet, as the military government in Poland was at great pains to point out in attempting to discredit the victory sign used by Solidarity supporters. Vaclav is the Czech form of the same Slavic name, which is in fact Czech in origin—it does not exist as a native Russian name.[14] It means wreath or garland of glory. Given the year 1968, Vatzlav could suggest a Czech émigré who has left his country after the Soviet invasion and is creating a new life for himself in the West.

There are storms and shipwrecked slaves in Plautine comedy, but the basic frame of Mrożek's drama—arrival and departure of the castaway on the alien shore—has its true prototype in *Robinson Crusoe* and the many eighteenth-century adaptations and imitations that it inspired. In one of these *Robinson Crusoe* offshoots, the travels of an earlier Polish hero, shipwrecked during a storm and flung by the sea onto an unknown island, offer an interesting analogue to Vatzlav's story. The first Polish novel, *The Adventures of Nicolaus Doświadczyński*, written by Ignacy Krasicki—the bishop of Warmia—in 1776, is a philosophical tale of education, modeled on Defoe's narrative and influenced by Rousseau's ideas.[15] Unlike Mrożek's hero, who soon discovers all the discontents of civilization on his alien shore, the dissipated and already corrupted Nicolaus finds utopia on the island of Nipu. The inhabitants live in perfect equality and freedom, without any government, army, police, written laws, or money.

When Nicolaus, who considers the natives savages, wishes to enlighten them as to the advantages of European civilization, the wise old sage Xaoo explains the shortcomings of the supposedly rational system of Western education. Reason is a faulty guide and leads to futile metaphysical speculation. Nature and experience are worth more than abstract thought, and it is preferable to live simply and happily as a savage. Accordingly, there is no place for dissent in such a paradise, and anyone traveling to foreign lands and bringing back the vices of civilization is accused of treason, tried, and stoned.

Too deeply depraved by reason to tolerate the natural simplicity of the good life, Nicolaus escapes from the island—to his later regret—and is captured and made a slave by Spanish pirates. At the conclusion of this picaresque drama of ideas, the wandering hero finally reaches home. Vatzlav, on the other hand, comes to an anti-utopia where reason is perverted and prostituted to justify all the vices of society; where equality is proclaimed, but injustice rules; and where the ultimate argument is always that of coercion and violence. Condemned to death for his attempts to come to terms with this hostile world, the former slave flees, departing for an uncertain destination and an unknown future. Having severed his ties to the past, he no longer has a homeland to which he can return.

Although Krasicki presents a utopian vision and Mrożek an anti-utopian nightmare, their attitudes toward civilization, their concerns with reason and experience, and their premises about human nature are not dissimilar. The worldly-wise bishop of Warmia was also the author of *Fables and Parables* (1779), animal tales in epigrammatic verse, whose moral lesson is often cruel and ironic: the strong survive, the weak and foolish perish. In the fable "The Lamb and the Wolves," for example, when the lamb, attacked by two wolves, asks by what right, the predators reply, "You are tasty, weak, and in the wood." Because of their dramatic power, Krasicki's fables and parables became the basis for theatrical works by other authors.

Man and beast comparisons, essential to eighteenth-century ethical thought,[16] run throughout Mrożek's plays, where hunters, dogs, the chase, and the prey are recurring images of man's life in society. In a tetralogy of animal fables—*Serenade*, *Philosopher Fox*, *Fox Hunt*, and *Aspiring Fox* (1976–1978)—the characters, both human and animal, act out and attempt to rationalize their predatory existence in a cannibalistic social order. The Bear sequences in *Vatzlav*, in which the hero must become game in the woods, make use of the conventions of the animal fable and serve to illustrate the mechanisms governing communal victimization. "What good is freedom when you're not the hunter but the hunted?" asks Vatzlav as the Bear.[17] Similar aphoristic lessons are drawn by the eighteenth-century French *conteurs* in their explorations of the man-animal nexus and their reflections on cannibalism as the basis of human society. Consider the following maxims:

> In Nature all species devour each other; all classes devour each other in society.
>> Diderot, *Rameau's Nephew*

> Let us try, my dear Leader, to keep in the ranks of the eaters; the role of the eaten is only for the weak and the fools.
>> Retif de la Bretonne, *Le paysan perverti*

> The weak must be the food of the strong.
>> Marquis de Sade, *Juliette*

As a literary genre, the *conte philosophique* has much to recommend it to a writer like Mrożek. The eighteenth-century philosophical tale is an ironic form of narrative, an extended parable dealing with a general theme, usually some aspect of the human condition, man's moral life, or the history of humanity. The plot, consisting of wild and implausible adventures, is treated in a cavalier fashion and serves only to illustrate a thesis; the characters are overtly manipulated puppets who stand for ideas and function as parts of the argument. The highly schematized story exists on two levels: that of the

Vatzlav, directed by Kazimierz Dejmek at Teatr Nowy in Łódź (1979)

events described, and that of the camouflaged inner situation to be interpreted on the basis of a secret understanding or complicity between the author and his audience.[18]

The product of an oppressive political climate, the *conte philosophique* is a dangerous game which must deceive or at least circumvent the censor and cover its polemical attack by allusion, inversion, fable, false names, anagrams, plays on words, and other ruses. In the entry on "Fable" in his *Philosophical Dictionary*, Voltaire writes: "One can scarcely speak to a tyrant except by parable, and yet even this subterfuge is dangerous."[19]

Didactic in intent, the philosophical tale is antagonistic to metaphysical systems and concerned rather with the practical moral issues of man's life in society. It often takes the form of an educational journey, both ethical and ethnographic, showing the bewildering variety of manners and morals operative in the world and the relativity of all systems of belief. The innocent and naïve hero, wandering from country to country, grows progressively disabused by experience which exposes the falsity of all *a priori* notions of what life should be. Abstract dogma is punctured by the pragmatic testing of an individual whose empirical questioning discloses the limits of rationality. Theory must constantly be adjusted to the realities of a world dominated by self-interest and ruled by arbitrary power.

The lesson taught by the philosophical tale is one of doubt, skepticism, resigned wisdom, and tolerance. Human reason is unable to penetrate to the ultimate nature of God or the universe. Perpetual, unanswerable questioning often takes the place of a resolution, as the hero of the *conte* searches for order and moral sense in a physical world that is the result of chance and where endless change is the only law.

Yvon Belaval calls the *conte philosophique* an ideogrammatic form of discourse, an intellectual experiment to determine how pure qualities react in different settings and circumstances. The innocent hero—or natural man—is the principal ideogram used pedagogically by the *conteur* in his exploration of the paired terms: nature and culture. In the Enlightenment philosophical tale, the reality of experience confronts and confounds the unreality of systems that are the product of false rationality or reason's unreason. Despite serious content, the tone of the philosophical tale is light and humorous: the author maintains a distanced attitude toward his characters and their adventures. Erotic episodes and sexual innuendoes are frequently the means employed to reveal the lower half of man's nature and unmask his pretended aspirations. Ideas are expressed in images, and fast-paced action renders the tale amusing.

Mrożek, who studied the fine arts and has published several volumes of cartoons and illustrated his own stories, could not help but find the diagrammatic visual method of the *conte philosophique* to his liking. Parable works in sharply outlined extremes and contrasts. Broad, bold strokes and bright primary colors are more suited to illustrate ideas than realistic, psychological portraiture.

The technique of the philosophical tale is episodic, fluid, and open. Time and space are free, and transformations kaleidoscopic and unceasing. Commenting on the structural resemblance between Sade's novels and the *conte philosophique*, Lester Crocker observes: "We have a series of situations rather than a plot; each is composed, as it were, like a tableau, and held as long as interesting; then rapidly liquidated by a sudden event, often involving change of place."[20]

Vatzlav has the verve and rapidity of movement of the *conte philosophique*. Both the first version in seventy-seven scenes and the second in sixty scenes appear cinematographic in the fast deployment of brief tableaux. In the mid 1970s, Mrożek wrote film scenarios—*The Island of Roses* (1975) in ninety-four scenes and *Amor* (1976) in seventy-six scenes—which were made into television films in West Germany, and there is reason to believe that the author at one point thought of *Vatzlav* as a work that could be adapted for cinema. When it was eventually staged and then published in Polish, the reduction by seventeen in the number of scenes and the increased focus on the central character appear designed to give the play a more concentrated structure without changing its basic narrative pattern as a series of loosely connected adventures befalling a picaresque wanderer.

The use of episodic open form represents a departure for Mrożek from his previous practice of creating closed circular structures. The playwright's usual technique is to present model situations—reflecting social, historical, and cultural processes—in small-scale reductions.[21] By diminishing large political and national issues to domestic situations and trivial, everyday activities (eating, sleeping, dressing, and undressing), the model not only reveals the underlying mechanisms behind the solemn masks of public life, but also renders them ridiculous.

In other words, Mrożek functions as a social structuralist, comparing different systems of ordering existence by the creation of hypothetical constructs. Concerned with the operation of power in a monolithic regime, in works prior to *Vatzlav* he locates his microcosmic world, or scale model, within a single confined setting from which there is no escape. Structural change is impossible within closed systems; only self-perpetuation can occur as one oppressive set of power wielders replaces another. In *Tango*, for example, the scale model is a family consisting of three generations—by extension of membership it can become a community, a political entity, a nation. Within this self-contained world, everyone is related and shares the same preoccupations. One is never alone or able to leave, but stays trapped in fixed positions and predetermined roles. Boredom holds sway in the closed world, and one plays ironic games to counter it. *Tango* opens with a card game in which the cards are called by rhyming jingles, and it closes with travestied dance. There are only shifts in which players occupy the seats of power; the same repetitious game goes on—the same steps, with different partners. The structure of *Vatzlav*, in keeping with the open form of the *conte philosophique*, is not built on a single model situation. Although it demonstrates the operation of a number of power mechanisms, as in Mrożek's earlier plays, the world of *Vatzlav* is chaotic and not fully delimited. The hero is only passing through, and it is possible for him to escape.

Vatzlav stands apart from the world in which he finds himself and from the characters who surround him. Given unusual relief and centrality as an individual hero, the shipwrecked ex-slave is frequently alone, communing with himself—and the audience—in lengthy speeches. No longer confined in a "no-exit" situation, he suffers from a new kind of restriction and alienation: isolation. Monologues by the hero alternate with scenes of meeting and confrontation.

The play opens and closes at the edge of the water, at the border of land and sea, where Vatzlav arrives and departs. He is by himself—a circumstance which means here that he is accompanied by his alter ego. Paradoxically, like all concepts and states of being in Mrożek, solitariness is paired with and defined by its opposite, or negation. Vatzlav's first double—his fellow countryman—he allows to drown, killing his past and former identity so that he may live for himself and start a new life. His second double— Justine's son—he saves so that he can live again in another being whose future may be brighter.[22] At the front of the stage, facing the sea—that is, the audience—Vatzlav speaks to the child:

> Do you see the other shore? Neither do I. But if we could get there, you might grow up to be something worthwhile. Because here at best you'll be brought up by the executioner.[23]

The conclusion of *Vatzlav* is symmetrical, even circular in the sense that the play ends where it began: the hero's journey is starting again. The sea is a source of both death and birth. Vatzlav kills his double and gives it life; he dies and is reborn. Although his future is problematic, by choosing to take the child (whom Justine would drown), the ex-slave leaves the shore a different and wiser person than when he arrived. The closed circle is broken.

Of what then is *Vatzlav* a parable? What is its second level of meaning about which author and audience have complicity? Interpreting Mrożek's parables, deciphering the camouflage, is a tricky business. Polish critics, such as Józef Kelera and Andrzej Wirth, suggest that Mrożek's plays present autonomous structures, reflecting abstract and general processes, without exact parallels or analogues outside themselves.[24] Wirth argues that such dramatizations of concepts are prognostic, not descriptive of particular circumstances, and therefore hard to verify beyond the criterion of internal consistency. Denial of concrete referents for his parables accords with the author's own cautionary poetics. In the "Author's note on the production of *The Police*" (his first play, written in 1958), Mrożek categorically rules out extrinsic readings of his text, calling for a strict theatrical presentation:

> This play does not contain anything except what it actually contains. This means that it is not an allusion to anything, it is not a metaphor, and it should not be read as such. The most important thing is to present the naked text, as exactly as possible, with a firmly underlined sense of logic in the opinions and scenes.[25]

The rest of the "Author's note" consists of a series of negations, disallowing the play to be committed to any genre or style, and concluding with the following theoretical principle:

> While I know what this little play is not, I do not know what it is, and it is not my duty to explain what it is. This must be discovered by the theatre.[26]

Mrożek's characteristic method of definition is by opposition, exclusion, and rejection.[27] For example, the playwright's brief letter of protest published five days after the imposition of martial law in Poland on December 13, 1981, is entitled "What It Was Not."[28] In this ironic sketch, Mrożek contravenes the regime's contention that what happened was exceptional by pointing out that, since the Soviet imposition by force of a Communist system in 1945, everything in Poland has been anomalous—the point being a clear echo of Arthur's dictum in *Tango* that "Abnormality is the new norm." The playwright concludes that the Polish army is not a third force between the Party and Solidarity, and that only if General Jaruzelski arrested himself would this proposition become credible—a conceit that is the basic principle of reasoning in *The Police*.[29] The fact that Mrożek feels free to apply the model situations in his own plays to subsequent political events indicates that, no matter how purely conceptual these theatrical mechanisms may have been originally, history constantly supplies analogues and transforms them into ever shifting metaphors and allusions.

As a public forum, *Vatzlav* is an ironic reflection in theatrical images on the nature of freedom and equality, a series of dramatized paradoxes about morality and civilization, power and the rebellion against authority. But the play has a more personal and private theme with application to the author and to all who share his experience.[30] Louis MacNeice comments that parable writing is analogous to dreaming, giving voice through the inner situation to the unconscious and repressed.[31] In *Vatzlav*, an individual dimension of reference exists within the satirical and polemical debate.

Vatzlav is a modern everyman, cut off from his roots, wandering homeless, adapting to circumstance, ready to compromise and to be what the world asks of him in order to survive. The ex-slave has left the security—and paradoxically the equality—of serfdom ("Where do you find more equality than in prison?") and now faces the cruel, competitive world of freedom. The broader theme of Mrożek's parable is the frightening experience of being set free and starting a new life, unburdened of the past and all the chains that bind. Freedom means anxiety, because of the constant need to make a place in a hostile or indifferent world.

Deprived of parents and family—the restrictive group in *Tango*—Vatzlav is a displaced person, forced to contend in an arbitrary, alien society synthetically composed of fragments, dead myths, and living inequities. A political exile and émigré, Mrożek's hero becomes, figuratively, a representative of all who feel uprooted and outcast, even in their own homelands, of all who live in isolation and flee in fear.

Émigrés (1975) depicts a later stage in the journeys of the displaced. Two halves of a single national self, an intellectual and a peasant who have settled abroad in lonely emigration, suffer extreme alienation from the surrounding foreign world and create between themselves a surrogate family to satisfy their longings for the abandoned nation. The circle is closed again. In the vacuum of freedom, the ex-prisoners of an oppressive state can only strive to reconstruct the ties that once bound them.

Yvon Belaval points out that the *conte philosophique* moves effortlessly from realism to abstract allegory, from daily life to the enigma of symbols, in its dramatization

Vatzlav, directed by Kazimierz Dejmek at Teatr Nowy in Łódź (1979)

of philosophy; characters are illustrations of ideas, and images convey the play of thought.[32] *Vatzlav* is a collage of characters from different provenances. The dramatis personae—a colorful mixture of types with generic names, animal names, label names, real names, and names taken from literature—are the ideograms by which the playwright conducts his discourse. In his introductory comments, "Traits and Significance of the Characters," Mrożek actually uses the term "ideogram" in discussing the bloodsucking capitalist Bat, a semi-allegorical figure with interesting iconographic ancestry who illustrates the playwright's technique of making a metaphor literal:

> In externals he recalls a capitalist in the propaganda posters from the early period of the Russian revolution, except that he is thin. The "bloodsucking" motif is a theatrical ideogram, taken from the repertory of the stereotypical poetics of propaganda.

The Genius is the standard-bearer of abstract thought in his plans to reform society through reason alone. He typifies the optimistic eighteenth-century philosopher who believed that nature could be the basis for a civilized and ethical social order; but his daughter Justine, sprung from his head, is his ultimate misconception and becomes the refutation of his ideals in the harsh world of experience. Justine—"the just one"—calls to mind the heroine of Marquis de Sade's novel *Justine, or The Misfortunes of Virtue*, in which goodness is invariably punished and vice rewarded, and the state of nature is revealed to be perpetual warfare of the strong against the weak. Mrożek's Justine, like Sade's, is brutally violated, offering a paradigm of the fate of justice in the real world.

Vatzlav's display of Justine's naked body in an ideological striptease for paying customers degrades the virtue of justice in the manner of a Sadean voyeuristic spectacle. The play-within-the-play has additional eighteenth-century connections. In his prefatory remarks, Mrożek calls Justine "the biological counterpart of abstraction," revealing his device of paired extremes. The theatrical elaboration of the device takes the following form: Vatzlav quotes verbatim from "The Declaration of the Rights of Man and the Citizen" (passed by the French National Assembly on August 27, 1789) as Justine strips.[33] The exhibition of a scantily clad young woman as the personification of justice (another metaphor made literal) also recalls the revolutionary festivals and pageants celebrating virtue: for instance, the Festival of Reason held in 1794 in Notre Dame Cathedral, which had been converted into the Temple of Reason, where "The Declaration of the Rights of Man" was read, and a beautiful young lady, dressed in white drapery, her flowing hair covered with the cap of liberty, represented the goddess of Reason—to cries of "Reason forever!" from the mob.[34] Such popular imagery from the poetics of propaganda could not fail to appeal to Mrożek as material for theatrical ideograms.

In "Traits and Significance of the Characters," Mrożek stresses that there is nothing satanic about General Barbaro (Barbar in the Polish text). He is simply the embodiment of brute force, a vital figure of crude good nature doing what is right from his point of view: that is, instinctively subduing everything around him. Vaguely sensing the need for ideological justification, Barbaro makes use of the mummified Genius as a magic talisman to sanction his indiscriminate depredations. Although Mrożek is careful to specify in his introductory gloss that the costumes of Barbaro's troops should be universalized soldiers' uniforms without particulars of time or place, the General and his boys—simple souls who subjugate their neighbors under the banner of an embalmed foreign ideology—inevitably suggest to any Pole the barbarians from the East and their fossilized Marxism.

Barbaro orders the castration of camels, without ever defining just who is a camel. Everyone is suspect as a potential enemy of the state and subject to liquidation; any political, racial, or social group or class can be identified as "camels" and hunted down.[35] The barbarian general also tells his boys to "screw" Oedipus, the incarnation of law, and a moral and psychological exemplar in myth, drama, and Freudian psychoanalysis.[36] The blind king and riddle solver—fountainhead of the Western tradition of tragic guilt and responsibility, whose hidden transgressions inspired awe and whose fate became spiritually redemptive—is cheerfully gang-raped by an entire army in a sadistic orgy of buggery, where violence and sacrilege are casual, impersonal, and without scruple. Culture is desecrated by nature in its most brutish form.

The two sly peasants, Quail and Maciej, are natural in quite a different sense.[37] In his prefatory comments, Mrożek cautions against presenting them as clownish caricatures, stating that he regards them with much sympathy and even a certain degree of seriousness. Such characters are not by nature grotesque, because they are neither, déracinés nor dépaysés. They are the only figures perfectly at home in their world, and therefore cannot be ridicule, ridiculous, although they may be amusant, funny.[38] In other words, the two peasants truly belong—the other characters come from outside, trying to take something from or impose something on a traditional order of life, rooted in place and validated by time. Barbaro and his roving band of boys are not connected to this organic way of existence and therefore not restrained from committing whatever atrocities the mood of the moment may dictate.

Vatzlav, too, no longer has any such ties, having left the inflexible world of slavery, where everyone's place is defined, for the unstable, unpredictable world of freedom. In "Traits and Significance of the Characters," Mrożek describes his hero in these terms:

> His name suggests that he is Slavic. Yet Vatzlav is the representative of the lower half of humanity in general, of humanity making its way up toward material prosperity, full of longings and complexes. Humanity in an undefined, transitional phase. Subject to corruption, leading a marginal existence, a potential opportunist of great vitality. His outspokenness is childlike rather than cynical. His craftiness is more a consequence of an instinct for self-preservation than of ill will. At the end of the play he permits himself disinterested reflection, which indicates the ability to grow. A complex character.

Vatzlav is a natural man in two senses: he is driven by self-interest and the desire to survive, and he is an innocent open to experience and capable—perhaps—of learning. He is a common man, midway between the thug Eddie and the reformer Arthur in *Tango*, and as close to the lout XX (near the end of the alphabet) as to the intellectual AA in *Émigrés*. According to Mrożek's cast listing, he is "a healthy extrovert, rather stocky"—a mark of his plebeian origins.

A man on the move, trying to climb up, Vatzlav is a nobody aspiring to be somebody, and his aspirations are viewed sympathetically, if ironically, by the playwright. He is caught between classes and forces in his attempts to rise in the world, beaten from above and below, by the Bats and the Peasants. In his eagerness to be part of the system, he identifies first with the hunted, then with the hunters, switching slogans without the slightest hesitation. When the pack of yelping dogs—a recurring image in Mrożek for the myrmidons of authority—chase after Vatzlav, the former slave flatters the hounds and proclaims his belief in them: "I'd rather be bitten now and then than go without their protection."[39]

Becoming petty bourgeois in his desire for possessions and showing an emigrant's fascination with material things, Vatzlav defends dogs because they protect private property, such as his litter—otherwise wild forest animals would take over. A have-not hoping to become a have, the ex-slave sides with civilization and its laws rather than with the forces of anarchy represented by the Bear and the forest. Starting from a privileged position, Józio—the twenty-year-old son of the capitalist Bats—follows the opposite path in his generational rebellion against his own class and parents, and becomes a Bear.[40] But it is the former slave Vatzlav who has true mobility, breaks out of psychic confines, and goes beyond self-interest. At the end of the play, the opportunist who has looked out only for himself takes Justine's baby in the wild hope of giving the child a better chance.

Where is the alien shore to which chance has brought Vatzlav? What is its location on the map of political geography? It appears to be both the new free world and the old slave world, not only because in fact these two worlds do share many characteristics, but also because parable can represent two different, even contradictory, systems at the same time. The referents may be double, or multiple. For example, Evgenii Shvarts's parable drama *The Dragon*, written during the Second World War and at the height of Stalinism, shows the workings of tyranny both under Fascism in Nazi Germany (the ostensible referent) and under Communism in Soviet Russia (the hidden referent).[41]

In *Vatzlav*, the new world resembles the old: it is as arbitrary a mechanism, but not as enclosed or restrictive. To a degree, the free system and the slave system mirror each other; equality is the great illusion and hypocrisy of both.[42] The individual is as lost in democracy as in totalitarianism, but in a different manner. In slavery there is belonging; freedom is empty. It is within this absence that Vatzlav, no longer a part of the system, starts to exist solely for himself—until he finally discovers a small tie with another human creature.

Vatzlav, directed by Kazimierz Dejmek at Teatr Nowy in Łódź (1979)

The other shore that he cannot see and may never reach will not be radically different from the land that he is leaving. All shores will be more or less the same. Vatzlav does not believe in great revolutions, catastrophes, or crashes; and small coups d'état change only the wielders of power, not the power structure. Abstract ideology and grandiose ideals are incapable of having a beneficial influence on the course of man's daily life. Even the apocalypse is subjected to sarcastic questioning. "How can you tell when it's the end of the world?" Vatzlav asks. "First it gets very dark," Sassafras replies.[43] Like revolution, doomsday has become a banal, oft repeated experience. Life goes on in its normal routine; the world is not ruled by justice or reason, nor is it affected by cultural clichés. Rendering the apocalypse commonplace and reducing it to the dimensions of an everyday event constitute part of Mrożek's demystification of national myths.

In several scenes of *Vatzlav*, Mrożek parodies the language and sentiments of the great Polish Romantic dramas of the early nineteenth century, written by émigré poets about the fate of Poland and the national cause.[44] Here as elsewhere in his work, the playwright adopts an ironic attitude toward the inflated sentiments and heroics of the Romantic exiles, preferring instead the laconic cynicism of the Age of Enlightenment. The style, distance, and coolness that characterize the approach of the eighteenth-century *conteurs* to the most serious subjects are the antithesis of the passionate idealism of Romanticism.

For Eastern European writers and artists, whose countries have undergone revolutionary upheavals followed by oppressive tyrannies, similarities between their own age and the late eighteenth century have been striking. Both historical moments constitute a turning point in civilization, the end of an *ancien regime*, the destruction of a social and political structure that had lasted for many years. When established order breaks down, the stability of the world suddenly seems menaced.

Accordingly, a catalog of the anxieties and uncertainties prevalent in the Age of Enlightenment can also serve to explain the tortured sensibility of Vatzlav ("My father begot me in fear, my mother bore me in dread").[45] The sudden metamorphosis of all previously held values and fear of an apocalyptic cataclysm follow when objective ethical universals are subverted by a new materialism.[46] Rationalistic attempts to reconstruct society by revolution may end in terror, in the style of either Robespierre or Stalin. The failure of social institutions and culture to transcend human nature, and the dangers of reason pushed beyond the limits of reason in the name of ideological schemes for social perfection, are known to those living in the orbit of Soviet Russia as well as to philosophers in the Age of Enlightenment.[47]

An eloquent statement of Eastern Europe's fascination with the French eighteenth century has been given by the Czech novelist and playwright Milan Kundera in the preface to his dramatized version of Diderot's *Jacques le fataliste*.[48] When the Russians invaded Czechoslovakia in 1968, Kundera experienced a need to go back to Diderot's *conte philosophique*. Because his own works soon came under a ban, it was proposed that Kundera adapt Dostoevsky for the stage: the play would appear under the director's name, but Kundera would receive the royalties. Despite the practical benefits of the offer, Kundera felt too repelled by Dostoevsky's over-emotionality and by the novel's surcharged atmosphere of portentous exaggeration to accept. The Czech satirist could not tolerate the Russian sentimentality and irrationalism which he saw expressed in the genuine affection that the Soviet occupiers constantly voiced for the occupied whom they were oppressing.

In reaction, Kundera was drawn to the French eighteenth century for its reason and doubt, its sense of play, and its understanding of the relativity of all things human. "When heavy Russian irrationality fell on my country, I experienced an instinctive need to inhale deeply of that spirit." *Jacques le fataliste* was for the Czech novelist and playwright the highest expression of Enlightenment intelligence, humor, fantasy, and liberty— qualities of mind that he desperately clung to as darkness descended on Prague. The Soviet invasion brought down the curtain on Western culture, which is based on the individual and reason, tolerance and pluralism of thought. It was the end of the West, the apocalypse, Kundera explains, that made him write his *hommage á Denis Diderot*.

Vatzlav can be considered Mrożek's homage to the *conte philosophique*, and its first Polish production in 1979, a salute to eighteenth-century theatre. When Kazimierz Dejmek was finally able to stage the play, he chose the rococo style of performance, with spectacular visual effects, painted scenery that moved before the eyes of the spectators, and elegant period costumes, as though *Vatzlav* was being given at a court theatre in the Age of Enlightenment.

Polish enchantment with eighteenth-century French theatre goes back to the *siècle des lumieres*, when cultural ties between the two countries were unusually close and the repertory of the Polish theatre was largely composed of French works. In 1979— the year of the Polish première of *Vatzlav*—the following eighteenth-century French plays were newly staged: Beaumarchais's *Le Mariage de Figaro*, Marivaux's *Le Jeu de l'amour et du hasard*, *Le Triomphe de l'amour*, and *La Dispute*; and there were adaptations of Diderot's *La Religieuse* and Laclos's *Les Liaisons dangereuses*. A Polish version of *Jacques le fataliste* had been in the repertory since 1976.[49]

When the production of *Vatzlav* was permitted to reach Warsaw in January 1981, Mrożek's parable had acquired new meanings as a consequence of the rapidly changing political situation. In a discussion between Dejmek (himself an exile from 1969 to 1973, after he lost his post as artistic director of the National Theatre in March 1968)[50] and Anna Schiller published in a Solidarity weekly in the spring of 1981,[51] the director explains that his *Vatzlav* embarrassed the critics and they deliberately ignored it; Schiller comments that theatre administrators have prevented the production from appearing at theatre festivals. In fact, *Vatzlav* was excluded from the Wrocław Festival of Contemporary Polish Plays in the summers of 1979 and 1980, and from the Warsaw Theatre Encounters in the winter of 1980.[52]

After the accords signed by the Polish government with Solidarity in August 1980, leading to a new spirit of freedom and the relaxing of censorship, *Vatzlav* was at last shown as part of the Warsaw Theatre Encounters in January 1981, where it was enthusiastically received. The whole drama now seemed to build to the final exhortation, in which the hero speaks directly to the audience about their collective drama:

> I've heard that it's possible to walk on the water. I've also heard that the sea parted and a people passed through to the other side. . . . Then you can follow me.

The references to the biblical miracles—Jesus walking on the water (Matthew 14) and Moses leading the children of Israel through the Red Sea to the promised land (Exodus 14)—had special meaning for a people who in 1981 expected miracles and wanted hope that they could pass to the other shore. Vatzlav's injunction that they should follow him and do the impossible corresponded to the mood of the audience who wished to believe in the power of dreams.[53] The model situation in Mrożek's parable is no longer a vicious circle or *reductio ad absurdum*, but an open perspective on a realm where free choice is possible. Yet it would require a miracle to reach that realm, as the playwright reminds us ironically.

According to Yvon Belaval, for the *conte philosophique* to thrive in the eighteenth century three conditions were necessary: a special limited public, censorship, and the art of conversation (by which he means finely honed wiliness and subterfuge in polemical battles). When these conditions ceased to exist, the philosophical tale disappeared. Yet in the postwar Polish theatre, the situation for playwrights has been comparable to what prevailed in eighteenth-century France with regard to the triad of audience, censor, and polemics. In these circumstances, Mrożek has been able to develop a dramatic art of the parable that has great impact and resonance in Eastern Europe. But in the West, where these conditions do not hold, Mrożek's plays, although highly esteemed, do not have the same importance or generate as much excitement in the theatre.[54]

Even after leaving Poland and living in exile, Mrożek has continued to write for the Polish stage and the elite Polish theatre audience who understand their complicity with the author in circumventing the censor. Even the censor knows his role in applying pressure. Parable thinking—saying more than you seem to be saying—has become second nature for the playwright, and not simply an externally imposed necessity: East European writers learn to derive strength from the restrictions with which they must live. Mrożek's "art of conversation" permits him to speak a polysemic, equivocal, multileveled language, rich in allusion, covert meaning, hidden resonance; and yet whatever is obscure and recondite becomes theatrically clear through the use of evocative stage images that speak directly to the imagination—just as Vatzlav speaks directly to the audience at his departure for the other shore.

NOTES

1. Regina Grol-Prokopczyk, "Sławomir Mrożek's Theatre of the Absurd," *The Polish Review* 24 (1979): 45–56. The author makes a convincing case for Mrożek's fundamental difference from the Western absurdists, citing Ionesco's comment that "practical, moral absurdity" based on the "gap between ideology and reality" is distinct from "metaphysical absurdity."
2. Lester G. Crocker, *An Age in Crisis: Man and World in Eighteenth-Century French Thought* (Baltimore: Johns Hopkins, 1959), 473.
3. Ibid.
4. Jan Kłossowicz, *Mrożek*, trans. Christina Cenkalska (Warsaw: Czytelnik, 1980), 18. The author, who regards Mrożek as a rationalist rather than an absurdist, is one of the few Polish critics to deal with *Vatzlav*, although only briefly, since his entire monograph is less than fifty pages. See also Jan Kłossowicz, "Mrożek czyli Kasandra," *Mgliste Sezony* (Warsaw: Wydawnictwa Artystyczne i Filmowe, 1981), 170–75.
5. There is no mention of *Vatzlav* in the following: Krzysztof Wolicki, "W poszukiwaniu miary: Twórczość dramatopisarska Sławomira Mrożka," *Pamiętnik Teatralny* 1 (1975): 3–37; Lesław Eustachiewicz, *Dramaturgia polska w latach 1945–77* (Warsaw: Wydawnictwa Szkolne i Pedagogiczne, 1979); Szczepan Gąssowski, *Współcześni dramatopisarze polscy1945–1975* (Warsaw: Wydawnictwo Artystyczne i Filmowe, 1979). See Halina Stephan, "Vatzlav," *Mrożek* (Cracow: Wydawnictwo Literackie, 1996), 157–64, and Małgorzata Sugiera, *Dramaturgia Sławomira Mrożka* (Cracow: Universitas, 1996), 228–33.
6. It is discussed in the foreign-language *The Theatre in Poland* (in French and English): Elżbieta Morawiec, "New Productions: *Vatzlav*," *The Theatre In Poland* 10 (October 1979): 13–16.
7. In an attempt to win support, the military government permitted all of Mrożek (except *The Ambassador*) to be played.
8. There was a second production of *Vatzlav*, directed and designed by Marcel Kochańczyk at Teatr Wybrzeże in Gdańsk in June 1982; Kochańczyk repeated his production in Wrocław in 1986.
9. Sławomir Mrożek, *Vatzlav—Ambassador* (Paris: Instytut Literacki, 1982). It is only after the fall of communism that there is extensive discussion of *Vatzlav*.
10. The following scenes from the version used for the English translation have been omitted: 25–30, 33, 38–42, 44, 49, 52, 53, 56, and 73. The English translation itself is often at odds with the Polish original in matters of style and tone. Whereas the Polish text is a mosaic of different styles, the English translation is contemporary, vulgar, and full of slang throughout.
11. On International Theatre Day, in the spring of 1969, an extended section of *Tango* was shown on Polish National Television—a typical instance of Polish inconsistency and an indication that the workings of censorship in Eastern Europe are far from logical.
12. Mrożek's onomastics would make an interesting study: Onucy, in *The Tailor*, comes from onuca, cloth wrapped around feet in bast shoes; Onek and Onka, in *The Hunchback*, derive from on and ona, he and she.
13. Mrożek's early novella, *Moniza Clavier* (1963), deals with a Pole living in Venice, trying to adapt to foreign ways; and there are similar problems of name and identity.
14. Rising from peasant background, the Přemysl dynasty in the Middle Ages produced a series of kings of Bohemia named Vaclav. The first of these, known to us in the Latinized form, was "Good King Wenceslaus" of the English Christmas carol.
15. "Doświadczyć" means to learn by experience. See Ignacy Krasicki, *Mikołaja Doświadczyńskiego Przypadki* in *Wokół "Doświadczyńskiego": Antologia romansu i powieści*, ed. Jerzy Jackl (Warsaw: Państwowy Instytut Wydawniczy, 1969), 393–525. For discussions of the novel in English, see Julian Krzyżanowski, *A History of Polish Literature* (Warsaw: PWN—Polish Scientific Publishers, 1978), 193–94, and Czesław Miłosz, *The History of Polish Literature* (New York: Macmillan, 1969), 176–80.
16. Crocker, 83–106.
17. *Vatzlav*, trans. Ralph Manheim (New York: Grove Press, 1970), 20.

18. Angus Martin, *Anthologie du Conte en France 1750–1799: Philosophes et coeurs sensibles* (Paris: Union générale d'éditions, 1981), 25–35, 55–59.

19. Yvon Belaval, "Le conte philosophique," in *The Age of Enlightenment: Studies Presented to Theodore Besterman*, ed. W.H. Barber et al. (London: Oliver and Boyd, 1967), 308–17.

20. Crocker, 10, n. 15.

21. Mrożek's use of model situations is discussed by Kłossowicz, 20–26, and also by Józef Kelera, "Dramaturgia Polska 1945–1978," *Dialog* 4 (1979): 93–94, and Andrzej Wirth, "Dramaturgy of Models," in *Theatre Byways: Essays in Honor of Claude L. Shaver*, ed. CJ Stevens and Joseph Aurbach (New Orleans: Polyanthos, 1978), 102–4.

22. It is important that Justine's child is male, not female as in the English translation, only in that the baby is a second Vatzlav.

23. The Polish text of *Vatzlav*, 58. The final sentence in the English translation of this passage is abbreviated to "Not here."

24. Kelera, 94, and Wirth, 102–4.

25. Mrożek, *The Police* in *Six Plays by Sławomir Mrożek*, trans. Nicholas Bethell (New York: Grove Press, 1967), 7.

26. Ibid, 8.

27. Wirth points out that East European writers have a negative concept of truth: "they know only what is not true." Wirth, 101.

28. The letter appeared in *Le Monde* and in the *International Herald Tribune*, December 18, 1981. It is reprinted in the *Performing Arts Journal* 17 (1982): 76.

29. To justify its own existence, the police force—in a utopian state of obedient citizens—must arrest one of its own officers posing as a revolutionary.

30. Morawiec discusses the autobiographical aspects of the play.

31. Louis MacNeice, *Varieties of Parable* (Cambridge: Cambridge University Press, 1965), 77–78.

32. Belaval, 313.

33. Paragraphs 1, 2, 4–6, 9–11 are cited directly.

34. Described in vol. 3 of *The History of the French Revolution* by Louis Adolphe Thiers, trans. Frederick Shoberl. Perhaps at this point Mrożek was reading in French political and cultural history as he prepared to become a French citizen and enjoy the rights of man.

35. Here Mrożek returns to the theme of his one-act play *Charlie*, written in 1961, in which all "Charlies" are to be shot. English translation by Nicholas Bethell in *The Mrożek Reader*, ed. Daniel Gerould (New York: Grove Press, 2004), 109–34.

36. The discordant insertion of a character from classic or Romantic drama into a modern play is a device used by Wyspiański, Witkiewicz, and several contemporary Polish writers.

37. Maciej is a common Polish first name, in literature often given to peasant characters. Mrożek also uses the name for one of the peasants in *The Turkey* (1960). In Manheim's translation, the character is named Sassafras.

38. In French and English in Mrożek's text.

39. *Vatzlav*, trans. Manheim, 71.

40. In the English translation, Józio becomes Bobbie and is erroneously listed as being in his forties. The Józio episodes reflect the French student revolution of May 1968.

41. Parables are malleable. *The Dragon* has even had as its referent American capitalism, in the production by the Théâtre des Amandiers directed by Pierre Debauche at the Festival of Nanterre in 1967. See Claudine Amiard-Cherrel, "*Le Dragon* d'Evgeni Schwartz," in *Les Voies de la création théâtrale III* (Paris: Éditions du Centre National de la Recherche Scientifique, 1972).

42. See Sławomir Mrożek, "How to be Better," trans. Edward Rothert, *Polish Perspectives* 25 (1982): 37–41; rpt. from *Dialog* 2 (1982): 151–52.

43. *Vatzlav*, trans. Manheim, 62.

44. *Vatzlav* contains allusions to and citations from Słowacki's *Balladyna* and *Kordian*, and especially Part II of Mickiewicz's *Forefathers' Eve* (with its cruel landlord who oppressed his peasants). Through the use of internal rhymes, rhythm, and alliteration, Mrożek creates a pastiche of Romanticism. The play can also be seen as a response to Gombrowicz's *Trans-Atlantic* (1953), a novel about a Pole starting a new life abroad, caught between different cultures. But these are other contexts for *Vatzlav*, requiring separate studies. See Janina Katz Hewetson, "*Vatzlav*," *Kultura* 6/429 (1983): 147–51. I am also indebted to David Brodsky's unpublished essay "Gombrowicz and Mrożek."
45. *Vatzlav*, trans. Manheim, 22.
46. Martin, 55–56.
47. Crocker, 447.
48. Milan Kundera, *Jacques et son maitre: Hommage à Denis Diderot en trois actes* (Paris: Gallimard, 1981). "Introduction à une variation" is dated Paris, July 1981, but the play was written in Czech in the early 1970s in Prague and smuggled out in manuscript in 1972 by the French director Georges Werler. It was translated into French by the author around 1980.
49. Excellent translations by Tadeusz Boy-Żeleński (1874–1941) have contributed to the popularization of eighteenth-century French literature in Poland.
50. Dejmek's production of Mickiewicz's *Forefathers' Eve* was alleged to have provoked the student riots; tumultuous applause greeted the anti-Russian sentiments in the play.
51. *Solidarność*, May 1, 1981, 5. Most of the interview appears in *Theatre in Poland* 8 (August 1980): 5–6.
52. Bożena Frankowska, "XVI Warszawskie Spotkania Teatralne," *Teatr* 6, March 15, 1981, 4.
53. Teresa Krzemień, "XVI Warszawskie Spotkania Teatralne: Polowanie na treści," *Kultura* (Warsaw), February 15, 1981, 11. The sentence about walking on the water does not appear in the English-language version of the play.
54. Martin Esslin observed that the première of *Tango* in Warsaw gave one an idea of what seeing *The Marriage of Figaro* in Paris on the eve of the Revolution would have been like.

Witkiewicz double portrait by Bronisław Linke (1958)

WITKACY'S DOUBLES

One of the Polish artists of the younger generation whom Witkacy knew and admired in the 1930s was the painter Bronisław Linke (1906–1962), twenty years his junior. With characteristic generosity and prophetic insight in matters of undiscovered talent (Bruno Schulz was another of his enthusiasms), Witkacy recognized Linke's originality and wrote in praise of his genius.[1]

In 1958, ten years after Witkacy's suicide, Linke paid homage to his friend and early champion by painting his portrait—or rather I should say, his double portrait, for in Linke's drawing, against a hostile background, with a towering sky, five leafless trees, and a stony soil, there appear two Witkacies. As Irena Jakimowicz has suggested in an inventive interpretation of the picture, one of these Witkacies has the face of a thinker, the other that of a sufferer, consumed by passion and inner conflict.[2] The two twin figures in Linke's double portrait do not seem to be totally at ease with each other or even in a state of communication; they do not confront each other directly but stand side by side on slightly different planes—one behind the other. One Witkacy is the intellectual, theoretician of Pure Form, opponent of irrationalism; the other is the explorer of the mystery of existence, experimenter with drugs, defender of the unique experience of the individual. Man is divided against himself.

However we choose to interpret these two figures—and there is a good deal of deliberate ambiguity involved there is no doubt that Linke has captured an essential trait of his subject and projected an image central to the older artist's work. Duality runs through Witkacy's life, art, and philosophy. Splits and fragmentation scar the psyche in the Witkacian universe; the personality no longer holds together but is in a state of perpetual decomposition.

Gifted with a peculiar artistic vision, Witkacy saw double. In a long series of self-contemplating portraits, whether the medium is oils, pastels, or photography, the playwright-novelist-artist-philosopher is both the observer and the observed. Witkacy's literary works, dramatic and fictional, are no less peopled with doubles—alter-egos of the creator and of his creations. And since these doubles themselves often submit to doubling, we enter a deceptive world of reflections and refractions seen in ingeniously positioned mirrors where myriads of selves seem to pass back and forth.

The double can then serve as a key to our understanding the multiplicity of a protean artist who is so intensely himself that he must constantly play at being others and watch himself so doing. And I should like to weave a few variations on the theme of Witkacy and the double—with special emphasis on the fact that the double— *Doppelgänger, dvoinik, sobowtór*—is a time-honored artistic and literary device self-consciously used and abused by the artist playwright who respects its sanctity no more than he does any of the other serious conventions that he appropriates and desecrates. In other words, I am concerned with the artifice of Witkacy's doubles, not their sincerity or psychoanalytic truthfulness.

The first and most enduring double that Stanisław Ignacy Witkiewicz created was Witkacy—an amalgam of his last and middle name—originally devised to distinguish the young painter from his more famous father. When the thirty-three-year-old artist returned to Poland in 1918 after four years in Russia, he began signing his paintings "Witkacy" and throughout the rest of his career the son used the signature Witkiewicz

—*Colloque de Bruxelles: Cahier Witkiewicz*, no. 4 (Lausanne: L'Age d'Homme, 1982), 129–145.

Witkiewicz, Double Self-Portrait: Witkacy as *Dr. Jekyll* (1938)

The two self-portraits painted in pastels overnight on 26/27 April 1938 are among the last of Wit-kacy's double self-portraits and reflect his mature insights on the duality of existence. They both belong to "Type E" according to *The Rules of the S.I. Witkiewicz Portrait Painting Firm:* "Spontane-ous psychological interpretation." Witcacy indicates on his drawings the date, type of painintg, and coded indication of his use of stimulants.

Witkiewicz, Double Self-Portrait: Witkacy as *Mr. Hyde* (1938)

Dr. Jekyll (left) was painted under the influence of beer and cocaine; *Mr. Hyde (above)* after an additional dose of cocaine and alcohol. There is a split running through the length of the paper in the middle of the face of Mr. Hyde, which appears to be an act of self-destruction willed by the artist.

Source: Irena Jakimowicz, "Metaphor and Realism: Witkacy's Late Works ...," see page vi.

or Ignacy Witkiewicz for his conventional realistic portraits done for money, but saved Witkacy for those works to which he attached special importance. The name and identity—Witkacy—served as a mask, alternatingly tragic and humorous, sinister and playful, handsome and grotesque, and was artfully designed both to conceal and reveal the artist's personality.[3]

The innumerable auto-Witkacies on canvas painted over a period of more than thirty years—the intense photographic self-studies of the prolonged psychological crisis suffered by the artist in the half-decade before the First World War, and the dozens of mugging poses, or "faces," from the 1930s showing Witkacy as priest, opium smoker, cowboy, colonial capitalist, Mayakovskyesque proletarian, and melodramatic villain—all these visual projections of the self offer us a remarkable and unprecedented record of narcissistic contemplation on the part of the artist. In projecting his double, Witkacy could not keep a straight face. The self-studies are all carefully staged, and we are allowed to witness the long-running production of the double with the model himself as actor, stage designer, regisseur, and audience. For this reason, Witkacy's *Doppelgängers* are less confessional than theatrical; the artist plays a double game—with himself and with us.

Before turning to my major concern—the double in its literary manifestations— let me mention several of the painter-playwright's visual projections of other selves. In a self-portrait of 1922, the face of the artist's alter-ego—the right side lost in shadows— looks out, lips tightly pursed, eyes askance, from an oval mirror, the favored lurking-place of the anguished Romantic *Doppelgänger*. A photographic study of twelve years earlier shows the young artist's other self looking out through a broken pane of glass—or is it reflected in a shattered mirror? It is only the presence of the cracks on the left side that reveals the glass—the face itself is engulfed in darkness; the eyes shine dimly; and the chin, corners of the lips, nose, and brows gleam amidst small clusters of nebulae in a dark cosmic night.

In a remarkable quintuple photographic portrait done in St. Petersburg while Witkacy was serving in the Imperial Army during the First World War,[4] the artist's alter ego in the uniform of a Tsarist officer sits at a pentagonal table, his back to us; at the four sides of the table sit two pairs of identically dressed doubles, the two end figures in profile, the paired central projections full face at a slight angle. The upturned eyes, full of mistrust, stare straight ahead, rather than at those of the other partners. Partners in what, we may ask: a conspiracy? a secret brotherhood? an ordeal? In this black box illuminated from above, an interrogation may be in progress, the parts of the self undergoing a trial conducted by the ruling member of the junta. The expression of the four visible faces is one of unbearably tense self-control, a struggle to suppress any tell-tale emotion that might betray or endanger; yet fear and guilt lurk in the eyes, and the hands are placed on the table as though to keep from trembling and to have something to hold on to. Or perhaps it is nothing more dangerous than a game played among the fragments of the self seated around the gaming table, and the figure with his back towards us is, in this case, the double dealer.

Yet another variety of double portrait that Witkacy specialized in was of two distinct, and yet somehow closely related individuals. An example in which Witkacy himself is one of such a pair is the photograph of father and son seated at a table, taken in 1911 in Lovranno where Stanisław Witkiewicz senior, who was dying slowly of tuberculosis, had gone for reasons of health. Certainly the two Witkiewiczes were an antagonistic and at the same time complementary duo, opposing selves making up a composite whole. In this picture the facial expression, eyes, and even the taut pose of

Quintuple portrait of Witkacy, St. Petersburg (circa 1915)

the body of the younger artist suggest those of the five Tsarist doubles.[5]

But Witkacy's practice of doubling in portraiture was not limited to exercises in introspection and self-projection. In the pastel studies of his intimate circle of friends as opposed to the purely commercial works by which he earned his living), the artist developed a characteristically Witkacian double portrait, which might be either of two separate but kindred individuals, who were joined together like Siamese twins, or of a single individual grown apart in two divergent strands. In this category belong the double portraits of couples—often, but not necessarily, male and female—such as the picture of Helena and Teodor Birula-Białynicki, in which the two heads appear joined at the eyes. In the second category there are two-headed creatures, as in the double portrait of Dr. Stefan Glass, where the two contrasting faces appear to grow organically out of a number of round stones or seed-shaped objects on a plate and the selves are attached at the ears as well as at the neck.[6] I should add parenthetically that the identification of the figures sometimes varies from one exhibition catalogue to another and is open to question.

By the time that Witkacy began his experiments in doubling in the early twentieth century, the double had a long and rich tradition in Western literature, as well as in primitive religion, folklore, and superstition. But doubles and doubleness were—at least in European drama—purely comic themes until the end of the eighteenth century; we have only to think of Plautus's *Menaechmi* and *Amphitryo* and such later adaptations as Rotrou's *Les Sosies*, Molière's *Amphitryon*, and Shakespeare's *Comedy of Errors*.

Two illustrations of "William Wilson" from collections of Poe's works,
Alberto Martini (circa 1905), left, and Harry Clarke (1923), right

Around 1800 a major shift took place in literary sensibility about the double, as witness Kleist's tragic *Amphitryon* in which the once laughable confusions of identity now undermine the characters' belief in themselves and in a stable, meaningful universe. It was the German Romantics who first made duality and doubleness a serious theme in modern literature. The double became an obsessive nineteenth-century motif under the threefold influence of Fichtean philosophy, the new psychology of the unconscious soul, and Mesmer's theory of the magnetic union of souls whereby two separate beings were viewed as complementary halves of a single entity.[7]

It was Jean Paul who invented the term *Doppelgänger* and first created heroes fragmented into a self that participates in life and a self that merely observes. Fascinated by the duality of the human personality, he also presented pairs of similar or contrasting characters who sometimes exchanged identities. In *The Titan*, the librarian Schoppe is terrified by the fourfold reproduction of himself that he sees reflected in mirrors hung facing each other in a deserted room, and he tries to smash the deceptive surfaces. In *Hesperus*, the hero Victor while still a child discovered that after having been put to bed he had the ability to leave his body and be aware of the distance separating him from his "outer bark of alien flesh."[8]

The Romantic double was closely connected with magic and the supernatural and served as a means for exploring the newly discovered realm of the unconscious where dark and suppressed aspects of the human personality lay hidden.[9] E.T.A. Hoffmann was the great master of Romantic *Doppelgängerei*, creating in his tales the figure of the diabolical alter-ego and calling forth the hallucinations, madness, and feelings of ontological insecurity that accompany its appearance. "I can no longer find myself," the hero of his novel *Die Elixire des Teufels* exclaims, "I cannot solve the problem of myself: my 'self' is split in two." Due to the great popularity and literary impact of Hoffman's tales, doubles spread rapidly throughout the world, finding an especially receptive welcome in hinterlands such as America and Russia.

Edgar Allan Poe carried on the Hoffmann tradition in *Tales of the Grotesque and Arabesque*. In "William Wilson," the unprincipled hero is pursued by an identical character, also named William Wilson, who always appears when the first Wilson is engaged in some shameful act. But since no one else ever sees this alter ego, it becomes clear that he exists solely in William Wilson's imagination. Finally, the divided hero forces his *Doppelgänger*, who functions as his judging half or conscience, into a duel and plunges his sword through his alter-ego's heart. At this moment the first William Wilson sees himself in a mirror, "all pale and dabbled in blood," and realizes that he has murdered himself.[10]

Although it was Antony Pogorelsky with his novel *The Double* who first introduced the Russian term, *dvoinik*,[11] unquestionably Dostoevsky is the most important Slavic follower of Hoffmann, and his early novella, *The Double*, is the classic mid-nineteenth-century version of the theme. Golyadkin Senior, a pitiful failure in life, is followed everywhere by his identical twin, Golyadkin Junior, a man of action and accomplishment—the inverse mirror image of the hero and embodiment of all that he both fears and desires. Having seen his double and been unable to rid himself of this constant nightmare, Golyadkin falls victim to feelings of dread and menace, loses his reason, and ends in a lunatic asylum.

As Dmitri Chizhevsky has pointed out, the double is a major problem in Dostoevsky and all of nineteenth-century Russian literature because it raises ethical and ontological questions about the fixity, stability, and reality of individual experience. If the main trait of individual existence in all its concreteness is that it cannot be repeated or duplicated, then the appearance of the double is a direct challenge to the reality of the human personality. Once Golyadkin Junior has appeared, there is no place for Golyadkin Senior. The anthill society and its rationalistic ideal of identical happy lives for all, so abhorred by Dostoevsky, constituted the real threat posed by the double.[12]

By the fin de siècle in decadent, Symbolist, and occult literature the double had undergone internalization. Psychic explorations in the world of dreams and visions led writers to probe what lay on the other side of the mirror and behind its images. Such was the case with Valerii Briusov in his fantastic tale, "In the Mirror," where the heroine, obsessed with her reflection in the looking glass, pursues her double through the surface of the glass and then looks out at reality from within the mirror image. It is no longer possible to distinguish the heroine herself from her reflected alter ego.

At a time when Freud and Jung were already starting to make their discoveries known, but before their impact was felt in the world of art, poets, novelists, and playwrights were quite independently putting the Hoffmannesque double to work in the fields of abnormal psychology and pathology in order to study cases of mental derangement, alienation, and disintegration. In *To Damascus*, August Strindberg's alter ego, The Stranger, meets himself everywhere in other characters who are he himself at different stages or periods in his life, representing what he was and what he will be. The "I" of the present confronts the "I" of the past or future. This asynchronistic double appears elsewhere in modernist literature.[13] The French Symbolist poet Saint-Pol-Roux built his one-act monodrama, *Les Personnages de l'individu*, on a meeting on a bridge over a stream between two characters who are both the same hero at different points in his life. Luigi Antonelli's *L'uomo che incontro se stresso* is a drama about a forty-five-year-old man who encounters himself as a youth. More recently, Jorge Luis Borges in "L'otro" tells of sitting on a bench which existed in two times and talking with his youthful other self.

Stanisław Przybyszewski dramatized the hysterical paranoia of the persecuting double. In the dramatic epilogue in one act, *Guests*, Adam is tormented by his shadow or phantom double that has become detached from his body, only to reappear when the moment of his death draws near. Returning to the source of its being, the shadow now exacts revenge on the creature who once had projected it and drives Adam to his death. Leonid Andreyev, deeply versed in Hoffmann and Poe, made use of the double in his plays and stories to expose the dichotomy in his heroes' neurotic personalities. In *Black Masks* the Duke Lorenzo, who has lived as a recluse in the castle that is his soul, gives a ball to which all are invited, but the revelers who come wear grotesque and hideous masks; they are, the Duke is told, the projections of his own heart, thoughts, and lies. And among these black maskers there appears a second false Lorenzo whom the Duke must engage in mortal combat and eventually kill.

In *The Strange Case of Dr. Jekyll and Mr. Hyde*, Robert Louis Stevenson presented, in vivid and easily intelligible terms, the divided self as the embodiment of the aggression and savagery slumbering within the respectable citizen, but, after many lurid thrills, closed the tale with the suicide of the evil-doing alter ego who has gained control of his better half. Because of the popularity of Stevenson and the dominance of English literature, the double reached a modern mass audience for the first time with *Dr. Jekyll and Mr. Hyde*, which was printed in cheap editions that sold widely, quickly became a classic for young readers, and served as the basis for many early films, including one with John Barrymore.[14] Oscar Wilde's *Picture of Dorian Gray*, in which the portrait double is a variation on mirror double and the hero, like Poe's William Wilson, dies as he stabs his own image, further contributed to the vogue of the *Doppelgänger*, which had now entered the popular consciousness. Joseph Conrad lent his prestige to this process with his novella, *The Secret Sharer*, which tells of the confrontation of the narrator, a young captain on his first command, with the fugitive Leggatt, who is his double and embodiment of a more instinctive, primordial self; from this crisis of identity and plunge into the abyss of his own unconscious, the captain emerges as a stronger and more fully integrated personality.

The final modernistic manifestation of *Doppelgängerei* occurred in Germany in the period just before and after the First World War. Drawing upon both the Romantic double and Strindberg's psychic alter-egos, the German expressionists created a highly subjective form of drama in which the characters are the projections of the author's consciousness and no more than emanations of a single soul who perceives reality as an ever-shifting dream. In Ernst Toller's *Die Wandlung* and *Masse Mensch* fragments of the heroes' personality are dispersed among other figures, and minor characters—extreme instances of alienation—are simply reduplicated types, robot-like abstractions representing aspects of society or the state. In Franz Werfel's *Spiegelmensch*, the hero Thalmal in an attempt to annihilate his sinful alter-ego liberates him instead; the mirror man leaps out of the looking glass and leads the protagonist through a series of ordeals in the real world. Only when Thalmal commits suicide does the mirror image return to its proper place.

The expressionist double had soon filtered down to the level of popular

Franz Werfel's *Spiegelmensch* (Mirror-Man), A. Baranowsky, Altes Theater, Leipzig (1921)

Double exposure photograph of Richard Mansfield as Dr. Jekyll and Mr. Hyde
in his stage adaptation of Stevenson's tale (1887)

Yuri Brusovani's illustration for Dostoevsky's *The Double,* Leningrad, 1981
Black Pencil on Paper, The Dostoevsky Museum

Vitalii Kovalenko and Dmitri Lysenkov in a stage adaptation of Dostoevsky's *The Double*,
directed by Valerii Fokin, Alexandrinsky Theatre, St. Petersburg (2005)

literature and to that new form of mass entertainment, the silent film. Hanns Heinz Ewers, a successful author of sadistic and bloody horror stories (and later an admirer of Hitler), twice adapted for the cinema—first in 1913 and again in 1926—his own fantastic tale, *The Student of Prague* (*Der Student von Prag*). In this now classic treatment of the diabolic other self, the poor student Baldwin signs a compact with the satanic sorcerer Scapinelli on condition that the wizard be given the student's mirror reflection. Lured out of the looking glass, the mirror image acquires an independent existence and sets out to persecute and destroy Baldwin and the better self that he has betrayed. In desperation, the student shoots his reflection in the mirror, but kills only himself. An obvious pastiche of incidents and motifs from Hoffmann, Chamisso, Poe, and others, *Der Student von Prag* was itself a double of other literary works that it exploits and plagiarized.

But as the filmmaker Paul Wegener, who played the role of the student in the first version pointed out, cinema was ideally suite to render the fantastic world of Hoffmann and the theme of the *Doppelgänger*. And Kracauer, in *From Caligari to Hitler*, has shown that the obsession of German cinema with the double was symptomatic of collective uneasiness and deep and fearful concern with the foundations of the self. In the ambiguous and uncertain world of the expressionist film, the characters are unsure of their identity and can lose it at any moment.[15]

From the cinema and popular literature it was but a short step for the double to pass into the realm of trash art—such as comic book versions and imitations of *Dr. Jekyll and Mr. Hyde*—and third-rate horror films. The schematic device of the *Doppelgänger* rapidly fell victim to commercial exploitation, seemingly beyond redemption. For this reason, in his study, *Doubles in Literary Psychology*, Ralph Tymms alluded to the debased status of the motif and its pitfalls for serious artistic work when he wrote: "Superficially, doubles are among the facile, and less reputable devices in fiction."[16]

My brief excursion through *Doppelgängerei* in nineteenth and early twentieth-century literature, drama, and film has shown how thoroughly worked over and overworked the motif of the double was by the time that Witkacy took it up in his major plays and novels. The very proliferation of doubles seemed to indicate that the device itself—like one of its own heroes—had seen its image reflected too often in too many mirrors, that it had lost its individuality and unique identity, and that it was in danger of stabbing itself as an artistic cliché and thus committing suicide.

Now we know that Witkacy, an omnivorous and eclectic reader, had absorbed the basic literature of the double; Poe, Stevenson, Wilde, Conrad, and Strindberg were among his favorite authors, and he was acquainted with Dostoevsky, the major German Romantics, and some of the expressionist dramas and films, as well as with such a popular exponent of *Doppelgängerei* as Ewers. Rather than avoid worn-out themes and devices that had slipped down from the level of serious art to that of popular culture, Witkacy displayed a marked preference for shabby material, obsolescent character types, and outdated stereotypes.[17] Along with the vampires, demonic women, Nietzschean supermen, and decadent artists that people his works, doubles are likewise leftovers from the past, dusty bric-a-brac from the fin de siècle. The *Doppelgänger* is an old stage prop that can be used to comment on its own history or made to serve unexpected new purposes.

Witkacy's technique with the threadbare is to pull apart the fabric, display the threads, expose the weave. Making no attempt to conceal borrowings, the artist is a show-off, gives a virtuoso performance, flaunting his sources at the same time that he self-consciously parodies them and himself. Taking the now secondhand motif of the double out of its former context and tradition, Witkacy pushes the device into alien territory, updating its resonances, stretching its contours, transposing its tonalities. By calling attention to its staleness, he makes the device fresh again. Although he expects his audience to recognize the conventions with which he plays so capriciously, the playwright-philosopher follows no set of coherent or consistent rules. The double is for him a piece of a puzzle, a point of departure for a free play of associations.

Before I take a look at the open form doubles in several of Witkacy's plays, it may be helpful to locate his technique of disorientation in relation not to those who precede him, but to those who have come after. In spirit and sensibility Witkacy is closer to the present age than to his immediate fin de siècle roots.

The conscious art of self-reflexive fictionality has been called by John Barth, one of its leading practitioners, "the literature of exhaustion." It starts with the hypothesis that literature has used up all its possibilities and that it is impossible to write anything original any more. All that remains is to explore that exhausted state of literature and create self-contemplating artifice, virtuoso displays of technique, and Chinese box effects. Jorge Luis Borges, another specialist in the genre, calls it "the Baroque" which, he explains, is "that style which deliberately exhausts (or tries to exhaust) its possibilities and borders on its own caricature."[18] In the hands of Vladimir Nabokov, the literature of exhaustion becomes a complex game of allusion. Not surprisingly, all three writers—Barth, Borges, and Nabokov—elaborate and complicate the technique of the double to the point of ambiguity and self-parody.[19]

Readers of Witkacy's *Insatiability* will recall that the narrator of that self-exhausting novel complains that all a writer can do is repeat with certain variations things formulated a long time ago. And as if to stress the inability of literature to say anything new, Witkacy deliberately directs attention, by means of allusion and quotation, to his principal models and precursors. During the climax of the novel at the most intense moments, Witkacy ironically points out parallels to *Macbeth* and *Le Rouge et le noir*, from both of which he has repeated famous episodes. Thus Witkacy's characters have literary doubles in Shakespeare and Stendhal.

In Nabokov's *Despair*, Hermann learns with pleasure that he can "split off" in such a way as to observe his body as it copulates with his wife and he manages to "have the bed reflected in the oblique speculum or spiegel" on the wardrobe. Nabokov's bizarrely absurd voyeuristic double, grotesquely parodying the Romantic-mirror image, calls to mind the young Genezip in *Insatiability* as he watches through the distorting lens of the stained-glass window his slightly older cousin and double Toldzio making love to the demonic princess in a replay of his own recent initiation.

By the early 1920s Witkacy was already playing intricate games with burlesque and self-exhausting doubles. In *The Water Hen*, the uncertain, guilt-ridden hero Edgar Valpor, who is in search of something irreversible and unique—experience that cannot be repeated or duplicated—so that he can discover his essential identity, finds himself beset by doubles. In an ersatz world of inauthenticity, where artificial selves are constantly being manufactured, Edgar has no place and is in fact replaceable at every point. His new wife Alice is instantly accompanied by a lover, the scoundrel Korbowski, who looks like Edgar and is his inverse double, representing all those male traits of decision and aggression that the hero lacks and desires.

But the doubling soon grows more confusing. Alice's first husband was also an Edgar—Edgar Nevermore (who was devoured by a tiger in the Jahjapara Jungle while reading Russell and Whitehead's *Principia Mathematica*) and a close friend of Edgar

Valpor. And now in the play of doubling names, the game extends beyond the boundaries of the stage and the internal life of the drama and spills over into the realm of antecedents and ancestors. Alice, Duchess of Nevermore, derives her title given in English by Witkacy from the refrain of a poem by another Edgar—Poe's "The Raven," a famous American literary bird paired off against the Polish *Water Hen*, itself a double for Ibsen's *Wild Duck*, Chekhov's *Seagull*, and Maeterlinck's *Blue Bird*, as well as a hidden anagram for the word for "whore."[20] Finally, Edgar and Alice are the names of the artillery captain and his wife in Strindberg's *Dance of Death*. When, at the end of Act 2 of *The Water Hen*, Witkacy's hero and heroine announce that, like condemned prisoners, they will drag on and on together until death, they echo the exact language and hideous plight of their namesakes in Strindberg's drama about the torments of married life. It is no longer possible to talk of true and false selves in a world in which all that Edgar can do is to re-enact dramas that have already been played and repeat the lines of other Edgars in other plays. Surrounded by doubles, the hero's identity has dwindled to the vanishing point.

Elsewhere Witkacy pumps new life into the figure of the double by bringing it abruptly into the non-Euclidean world of totalitarian politics and modern science. Instead of the old forms of magic—the enchanted mirrors and haunted portraits—that ushered in the Romantic doubles, Witkacy shows how psychiatry, medicine, mathematics, social engineering, and technology can work towards the production of identical doubles *ad infinitum*. Witkacy's fantastic scientist-magicians—Professor Green, Dr. Grün, and Dr. Rypmann—are prepared to reduplicate the human personality, reduce individuality to uniformity of mind and feeling, fabricate selves indistinguishable from one another.

Whereas in Edgar's case in *The Water Hen* the doubling was by division resulting in the decomposition of the self, in the "six-dimensional continuum" that is the realm of the monstrous dictator in *Gyubal Wahazar*, we encounter the ancient, archaic, and tribal multiplication of doubles. Images of the tyrant proliferate, in the form of life-size Gyubal Wahazar dolls, recalling those of necromancy and sorcery, and in the person of his many imitators who have spring up in Albania. But these *Doppelgängerei*, rather than attesting to the dictator's unique individuality, mark his vulnerability and show that he can be replaced. On the basis of his experiments with gland transplants and the fission of psychic atoms the sinister Dr. Rypmann concludes that he will soon be able to turn anyone, or anything—even a hyena, jackal, or bedbug—into a Wahazar.

In the hands of the mediumistic child Piggykins, Wahazar falls into a hypnotic trance in which he has an autoscopic vision of himself as he was as a young man. This dissociation in time, brought about by splitting in two and looking back at the person he once was, offers the weary dictator at least a moment's rest from the heavy burden of being Wahazar. Finally there takes place the ritual killing, dismemberment and eating of the divine victim, as the doddering Father Unguenty, reinvigorated with the former dictator's glands, served piping hot by Dr. Rypmann, is proclaimed Wahazar II. Magic and science joined hands to make of the great tyrant a gesticulating mechanical puppet, whose movements could be copied by synthetic doubles.

Another type of double occurring throughout Witkacy's work is the duo of opposing, but complementary selves, found in two distinct individuals who together make up a composite psychological whole. Such a pair need not be look-alikes or even have any external traits in common. Freud has argued convincingly for viewing Macbeth and Lady Macbeth as constituting two halves of a single personality; they interchange responses of defiance and remorse after the murder of Duncan. "Together they exhaust the possibilities of reaction to the crime," Freud writes, "like two disunited parts of the mind of a single individuality, and perhaps they are the divided images of a single prototype."[21]

In Witkacy such pairs of opposing but complementary selves are represented by von Telek and Plasfodor in *The Pragmatists*, Professor Alfred Green and Tumor in *Tumor Brainiowicz*, Seraskier Banga Tefuan and Balandash in *They*, Dr. Grün and Walpurg in *The Madman and the Nun*, and Baleastadar and Istvan in *The Beelzebub Sonata* among others. Although the duo takes widely different forms in each play, the two fragments of one mind are, in the most general sense, authority and instinct in the realm of creativity. Closely bound together in a symbiotic relationship, the opposing but complementary selves are in Conrad's phrase, "secret sharers," deeply attracted to each other. They reveal the complex life of the mind and enable us to penetrate into the recesses of the brain.

The supervisor, regulator, and executor oppresses and exploits, spies upon and imprisons the intuitive creator. In *The Pragmatists* the authoritarian, entrepreneurial von Telek desires to be the director of "events in life" and to set up a cabaret displaying his friend and alter ego, Plasfodor, who is a passive receptacle and dark abyss of unshaped creative forces. In *The Beelzebub Sonata* Baleastadar extracts the work of genius that he seeks from his artistic well-spring, Istvan, and having squeezed him dry, discards the useless shell. The controlling mind of *They*, Seraskier Banga Tefuan—advocate of the total suppression of art—is pitted against the apostle of aesthetic indulgence and pleasure, Balandash. But these two ideological opponents secretly share many of the same impulses. Both are frustrated artists, united by their love for the same woman, and Balandash's zeal in amassing art is matched by Tefuan's in destroying it. The manipulative British mathematician, Professor Alfred Green of the M.C.G.O., attempts to shackle and subdue to the purposes of civilization the volcanic creative forces of Tumor Brainiowicz in the play that bears his name.

Perhaps the most interesting of all these complementary doubles can be found in *The Madman and the Nun*, in the case of the Freudian psychiatrist Grün and his prize patient, the mad poet Walpurg, of whom the doctor is so proud. Grün (German for green, and thus related to Professor Green in *Tumor*) is both an observing self, watching voyeuristically the uninhibited, instinctual behavior of his alter ego, Walpurg, and at the same time a controlling self, attempting to curb the lawless conduct of his double and suppress his explosive creative energies. Almost in love with his primordial opposing self, Dr. Grün alternatingly provides Walpurg with paper and pencil—the tools of creation—and binds his arms in a strait jacket. Blinded by his faith in a theory that would enforce consistency on a chaotic self determined to be free of all restriction, Dr. Grün turns his supposedly new psychoanalytic method into a mechanistic and reductive system for fabricating mechanical puppets, mass-produced doubles uniform in thought and feeling and ready for the anthill society—thereby achieving the same results as Dr. Rypmann had with his medicine.

Here we reach the final instance of doubling in Witkacy's work that I shall mention here: the puppet or mannequin. And of all the virtuoso devices and coups de théâtre practiced by the playwright none is more spectacular, theatrical, or characteristically Witkacian than that of the "dead double" and the risen corpse. The ultimate theatricalization of the division of the self occurs in *The Madman and the Nun* and in *The Mother* when at one and the same time we see before us on stage the same character living and dead.

After the psychiatrically imprisoned madman Walpurg hangs himself and his

Doubles by Witkacy. Charcoal drawing (1910–14)

corpse lies on the floor of the insane asylum, the poet and dandy Walpurg—very much alive, elegantly dressed, and freshly shaved—enters the cell to bid his former keepers farewell forever. In primitive belief, the spirit-double, or wraith, is thought to be visible just before or just after death. Dying, Walpurg has "split off," to use Nabokov's flippant term, and left behind the "outer bark of alien flesh," in the Romantic vocabulary of Jean Paul. This remarkable feat of dissociation is accomplished without explanation, rationalization, or psychologizing. As Witkacy himself stressed, his invention of the rising of the dead depends for its effect on the resurrected figures appearing not as ghosts but live people. The immense theatricality derives from the concreteness and matter-of-factness, as well as the suddenness of the return to life of the mad poet who has just killed himself.

In the context of the history of the double, the presence of the two Walpurgs living and dead in the last act of *The Madman and the Nun* works a number of variations and inversions on the traditional patterns of *Doppelgängerei*. In the first place, it is a non-meeting of the two selves. The younger, handsome, risen Walpurg does not once look at his dead double on the floor. The poet "splits off" to leave behind his earthly remains, which he discards as a worn-out skin or shell that could only encase him in a second-rate, debased version of himself. Instead Walpurg becomes what he once was or might have been. For the poet, the double is a triumph of mind over matter, but for mad-house keepers it turns out to be a nightmare.

As we have noted, in nineteenth-century tales of the double, such as Dostoevsky's, characters like Golyadkin who see the *Doppelgänger* go mad. In *The Madman and the Nun* it is not Walpurg who confronts his double, but rather Grün and his associates who see simultaneously both the dead and the living victim of their system of psychiatry oppression—and as a result they go mad and are locked into the lunatic asylum cell. It is appropriate that the mad-house keepers who treated Walpurg like a thing to be manipulated and turned him into a puppet of their theories should see the mannequin double that they have created and grow terrified of their own work of fragmentation and mechanization.

That this corpse double is not something human, but only a wooden dummy, a theatrical prop, a piece of stage trickery, remains implicit in *The Madman and the Nun*, where only in the stage directions is the artifice disclosed and the illusion uncovered. But in *The Mother*, where the double mothers meet at different period in their lives—the one old, used up, dead of an over-dose of cocaine, the other at twenty-three, attractive, vital, bearing the hero Leon in her womb—there is a revelation of the fraudulent nature of the corpse. The younger self exposes the deceit and tears apart the false double, which life and time have rendered rigid and inhuman, and death has made a parody of a woman. Repudiating what she would become, the young mother-to-be speaks across gulf of years to her full-grown son: "Look here, Leon. All of this is just one big phony." And she rips the wooden head off the body and scatters the straw and rags across the stage. "This isn't a corpse, it's just a manikin."[22]

Here in the third act of *The Mother*, which serves as an epilogue, Witkacy not only bares the device, to use the Russian formalist terminology, and undermines the bogus stage illusion of realism, under attack throughout the play, but he also exposes the sham—the straw and rags—of the roles imposed on individuals by family, society, and the very nature of existence. Witkacy's virtuoso displays with the double—playful and parodistic, inter-textual, social, ontological, and above all theatrical—reached an apogee in *The Mother* when the young mother destroys her *Doppelgänger* and throws the pieces about the stage.

NOTES

1. Stanisław Ignacy Witkiewicz, "Hut ab, meine Herren—ein Genie!" (Rzecz o twórczości malarskiej Bronisława Linkego) in Bez kompromisu. Pisma krytyczne i publicystyczne, ed. Janusz Degler (Warsaw: Państwowy Instytut Wydawniczy, 1976), 109–13.
2. Irena Jakimowicz, Witkacy, Chwistek, Strzemiński: Myśli i Obrazy (Warsaw: Arkady, 1978), 8.
3. This is particularly evident in his letters to his friends, which Witkacy signs with various versions of this pseudonym: Witkaś, Witkrejus, Saint Witkacy à la Fourchette, de St. Vitecasse, Witkatze, Witkacjusz, Vitcatius, Vitcacius, Witkos, Mahatma Witkac, etc . . .
4. Marcel Duchamp had a similar quintuple photographic portrait taken in New York in 1917.
5. This photograph is reproduced in Stanisław Witkiewicz, Listy do syna, ed. Bożena Danek-Wojnowska and Anna Micińska (Warsaw: Państwowy Instytut Wydawniczy, 1969), 336.
6. Both portraits are reproduced in Stanisław Ignacy Witkiewicz: Twórczość plastyczna. Katalog Wystawy (Cracow: Muzeum Nardowe w Krakowie, 1966).
7. Theodore Ziolkowski, Disenchanted Images (Princeton: Princeton University Press, 1977).
8. Lotte Eisner, "The World of Shadows and Mirrors," in The Haunted Screen (Berkeley: University of California Press, 1973), 129–50.
9. See Maria Janion, Gorączka Romantyczna (Warsaw: PIW, 1975), 178–79. See also Albert J. Guerard, "Concepts of the Double" in Stories of the Double, ed. Albert J. Guerard, (Philadelphia: J.B. Lippincott, 1967), 1–14; Otto Rank, The Double. A Psychoanalytical Study (N.Y.: New American Library, 1979); and Robert Rodgers, A Psychoanalytical Study of the Double in Literature (Detroit: Wayne State University Press, 1970).
10. Edgar Allan Poe, "William Wilson" in Complete Poems and Stories of Edgar Allan Poe, ed. Arthur Hobson Quinn (New York: Knopf, 1967), 1:292.
11. Dmitrii E. Maksimov, "Ob odnom stikhotvorenii (Dvoinik)." Poeziya i proza Al. Bloka (Leningrad: Sovetskii Pisatel', 1975), 144–74.
12. Dmitri Chizhevsky, "The Theme of the Double in Dostoevsky," in Dostoevsky, ed. Rene Wellek (Englewood Cliffs, NJ: Prentice-Hall, 1962), 112–29.
13. Maurice Gravier, Strindberg et le Théâtre Moderne, vol. 1, L'Allemagne (Lyon-Paris: IAC, 1949).
14. See Karl Miller, Doubles: Studies in Literary History (Oxford: Oxford University Press, 1987), 209. "During the Eighties and Nineties of the last century duality underwent a revival which carried the subject, together with its predicated psychic state, into the century that followed [. . .] Anglo-America and well beyond rang to the cry of Robert Louis Stevenson's Dr. Jekyll: 'This too was myself.'"
15. Siegfried Kracauer, From Caligari to Hitler (New York: Noonday Press, 1959). See also Eisner, The Haunted Screen, and Jean-Michel Palmer, L'Expressionisme comme revolte (Paris: Payot, 1978).
16. Ralph Tymms, Doubles in Literary Psychology (Cambridge: Bowes & Bowes, 1949), 15.
17. Lech Sokół, Groteska w teatrze Stanisława Ignacego Witkiewicza (Wrocław: Ossolineum, 1973).
18. John Barth, "Literature of Exhaustion," Atlantic, August 1967, 29–34.
19. John Stark, The Literature of Exhaustion (Durham: Duke University Press, 1974).
20. See Daniel Gerould, Witkiewicz as an Imaginative Writer (Seattle: University of Washington Press, 1981), 174–76.
21. Sigmund Freud, "Some Character Types Met with in Psychoanalytic Work," in Collected Papers, translated under the supervision of Joan Riviere, ed. Ernst Jones (London: Hogarth Press, 1953), 4:331–33.
22. Stanisław Ignacy Witkiewicz, The Mother in Stanisław Ignacy Witkiewicz, The Mother and Other Unsavory Plays, trans. Daniel Gerould and C.S. Durer (New York: Applause, 1993), 199.

Sketch of Anatoly Lunacharsky by Leonid Pasternak (1920)

LUNACHARSKY ON MELODRAMA

The Russian theatrical theorists of the early twentieth century were the first to attempt a serious rehabilitation of melodrama and other popular arts such as music hall and circus. With the publication of "What Kind of Melodrama Do We Need?" in *The Life of Art* (*Zhizn' iskusstva*) on January 14, 1919,[1] the New Soviet Commissar of Education, Anatoly Lunacharsky, began his campaign for the acceptance of a nineteenth-century bourgeois dramatic genre as the form best suited to advance the new Bolshevik morality and Communist ideology. A month and a half later, on February 28, 1919, the same journal ran an announcement of a melodrama contest sponsored by the Petrograd Theatre Section of the Commissariat of Education and designed to encourage young playwrights to create new works in the old genre. The notice (written by Maxim Gorky) contained the following specifications that correspond closely to Lunacharsky's concept of the genre:

> Since melodrama is based on psychological primitivism and on simplification of the feelings and the Interrelationships of the characters, it is advisable that the authors stress clearly and explicitly their sympathies and antipathies toward the protagonists and antagonists; it is also advisable that they include in the text songs, rhymed couplets, duets, etc.[2]

The jury consisted of Lunacharsky, Gorky, the operatic bass, Fyodor Chaliapin, and two actors: Nikolai Monakhov and Yurii Yuriev.

Lunacharsky had long been a proponent of melodrama. As early as 1908 in the collection, *Theatre: A Book About the New Theatre* (to which Meyerhold and the Symbolists also contributed), Lunacharsky had argued for melodrama as the best vehicle for socialist drama. The theatre of the future, he argued, would be a barbarian theatre:

> The socialist artist-intellectual should create in the sphere of the fantastic vividly, lushly, graphically, hyperbolically, actively, in the spirit of the old melodrama.
>
> It will be a powerful, energetic, courageous theatre of a generation under the red banner, by the light of dawn, with the cold and bracing breath of a pre-dusk wind; it will be a theatre of rapid action, great passions, sharp contrasts, whole characters, powerful sufferings, and lofty ecstasies. Yes, it will be an ideological theatre.
>
> The new theatre, if it is destined to arise, will be a barbarian theatre. Yes, yes. It will rid itself of nuances, details, and all the flavors needed by the refined and hysterical palates of our "cultured" public. It will thunder, glitter, be noisy, rapid-firing, and crude both for the nervous young ladies and the soured "cream" of society. Its satire will strike one's cheek loudly; its woe will make one sob uncontrollably. Its joy will make one forget oneself and dance; its villainy will be terrifying.
>
> Lovers of half tones, those half alive people can rest satisfied with their half theatres. We need a real theatre, even if it is barbarian. The salvation of civilization is in its barbarians. They are the bearers of real culture; they open the bright, long paths, while the so-called cultured society rots.[3]

—*Slavic and East European Performance* 14, no. 3 (Fall 1994): 57–64

Lunacharsky here voices the then widespread admiration of Russian intellectuals for barbarism as a radical cure for the ills of a decadent, dying society. After the Revolution, melodrama for Lunacharsky becomes humanist, not barbarian. In 1919, the problem for Soviet authorities in the field of culture was to provide politically instructive yet entertaining art for the new mass audience. Lunacharsky, who had spent three years in Paris, knew the tremendous appeal that melodrama and other popular forms like music-hall had for working-class audiences. The Bolsheviks had to wrest the genre away from the capitalists, rid it of cheap, commercial values, and appropriate it for the proletariat. The essay reflects Lunacharsky's concern in the early Soviet years with the democratization of art and the bringing of culture to the masses by the use of popular forms—such as melodrama, music hall, and circus—purified of the dross of vulgar trash.

The concluding sections of the essay are cast in the form of a narrative melodrama. Himself a playwright, Lunacharsky turns his theory into a drama of a stolen child. Popular art is the young beauty kidnapped by the capitalist pimp-entrepreneur who decks her out in tawdry finery and garish make-up until she is hardly recognizable amongst all the thin and refined false beauties of the "higher sphere." But the hero, the people, recognizes true beauty beneath all the wretched attire and restores popular art to her former simplicity and purity.

As Commissar of Education, Lunacharsky encouraged variety and experimentation in the arts, but at the same time he was for conserving the best of past European drama. He was an innovative traditionalist. Soviet melodrama was to be new content in old bottles. Lunacharsky saw its accessibility, ethical instruction, and theatrical simplicity and strength as the great virtues of melodrama; he also stressed the genre's inherent partisanship and polarization, which made it serviceable for propaganda and vilification of enemies.

Lunacharsky's active promotion of melodrama led to some interesting experiments in the Soviet theatre of the 1920s, but the genre was eventually condemned as bourgeois and socialist realism became the only acceptable dramatic formula.[4]

NOTES

1. Anatoly Lunacharsky, "What Kind of Melodrama Do We Need?," *The Life of Art* (*Zhizn' iskusstva*), no. 58, January 14, 1919, 2–3.
2. *The Life of Art* (*Zhizn' iskusstva*), February 28, 1919. My discussion of Lunacharsky's theories of melodrama draws upon the earlier essay in this book, 223–33: "Gorky, Melodrama, and the Development of Early Soviet Theatre."
3. Anatoly Lunacharsky, "Sotsializm i iskusstvo," in *Teatr—kniga o novom teatre* (St. Petersburg: Shipovnik, 1908), 34–35, 39.
4. Renewed interest in Lunacharsky as a theatre theorist is indicated by the translation of his assessment of Ibsen: "The Last Great Bourgeois: on the Plays of Henrik Ibsen" (1907), translated and introduced by Edward Braun in *New Theatre Quarterly* 10, no. 39 (August 1994): 223–41.

WHAT KIND OF MELODRAMA DO WE NEED?
by
ANATOLY LUNACHARSKY

In his celebrated book on theatre for the people, Roman Rolland, after having rejected with unmatched and excessive severity almost all the values of the old theatre and, of course, having quite correctly passed judgment on the maudlin spinelessness and inner emptiness of most melodramas, nonetheless—for the reader, perhaps, suddenly—dwelt on this form with tremendous partiality and frankly declared that, in his opinion, the future of people's theatre was tied to a new development of melodrama. The only people who could be surprised, by Rolland's unexpected conclusion are those unacquainted with the laws of social psychology on the one hand and with the fundamental characteristics of melodrama on the other, above all its socio-psychological aspect. We know only too well what a despicable kind of person chases after success. Much ink has been wasted exposing, with an admixture of haughty sneering and fiery indignation, all the vulgarity of so-called success with the crowd. And conversely, unusual sympathy goes out to the supposedly misunderstood genius who creates in an exceptional and subtle fashion and is accessible only to the chosen few and so on and so forth.

As democrats, we ought to reassess this hierarchy of values. Yes, success with a bourgeois public, with an idle and profligate public, very often amounts to a connivance with the worst passions that cannot have anything in common with the great concepts of democracy. And it is also true that the broad masses are ignorant, their tastes are utterly unrefined, and it is not difficult to sweep them off their feet with trumpery and purely external effects. And it is an incontestable fact that private entrepreneurs of various kinds, seeking to flatter the taste of the very democratic street, achieve their goal by not disdaining to use any means and in most cases corrupt the taste of the public, because instead of the true soul of the people they imagine some yawning and heehawing hydra, which in fact does not exist. All these circumstances have also prevented many from grasping the inner meaning of what is called success with the broad masses, although all the signs have always indicated that the people highly esteem the plays of the classic repertory and respond with astonishing seriousness to what is serious when it is shown to them. They are deeply moved or joyously delighted by the sorrowful or the comic if it is well presented on stage. But such deference to the tastes of the peasantry or the working class is shown only when these tastes have seemed to coincide with the established tastes of what passes for the better part of the intelligentsia. Where these tastes diverged, opinions also immediately became divided and even went in the opposite direction. What scornful aristocratic remarks won't you hear about the taste of the boor who jumps so readily at the bait of film, café-chantant, and melodrama "of the very lowest kind."

Instead of turning up their noses and averting their gaze, serious-minded people should ask themselves what it actually is that draws the crowd to such shows, and they should conduct the following experiment: after having eliminated the intolerable crudity from all these forms of art "for the people," they should try to retain what has nothing in common with crudeness, but which may offend supposedly refined taste. Then they will have to admit that film and melodrama have a fine, gripping subject; next richness

— Translated by Daniel Gerould, New York, 1994.

of action; character traits defined with colossal relief; clarity and sharp expressiveness of all the situations and the capacity to call forth undivided and total emotional reactions of compassion and indignation; action connected to simple and therefore grand ethical positions, to simple and clear ideological positions.

I dare say that if someone would try to construct a film, or melodrama according to these specifications, he would to his surprise become convinced that through their correct use (if he were talented) there would result, in essence, a true tragedy that was monumental, simple, typical in its cast of characters and in its basic lines. Herein are defined our demands concerning a new melodrama.

We are sometimes told: the writer should write as his innermost god inspires him to, with total disregard for whom he is writing.

That may well be the right course for purely lyrical geniuses. So be it, let them write for themselves, if they wish, without giving a thought to success. But there are talents of a different sort, talents in which the sermonizing bent is strong, social talents, which confront directly and openly a certain problem: I wish to tell the truth in an accessible and even strikingly emotional guise to my era and to my people. In this situation one has to know for whom one is writing. Therefore we have no objections whatsoever if the writer, who has set out to create a melodrama, pictures to himself with absolute clarity his mass audience, and if he writes for the people. If that means he must be insincere, he would do better not to write at all. If he has something to say to the people, then let him write in a form that is acceptable to the people. And be certain that this will not be a simplified, vulgarized, debased form, as the aesthetes think but will be a transformation of our arbitrary, refined, hypercultural pursuits, of our satiety, of all that is dictated by too much nervous agitation, into something healthy, monumental, simple, clear, and strong. Have these concepts really become alien to us? Are we really stuck in the rut of that decadent art to which simplicity, clarity, and strength seem a bugbear and something demeaning?

So, from the point of view of form we have nothing to fear from melodrama. Melodrama simply as theatre is superior to other dramatic genres. It is superior to realistic drama because it is free of the laborious and quasi-photographic portrayal of everyday life, and of probing into psychological minutiae, which quite simply is not suited to the stage and invariably requires a more or less pronounced transition from a theatre of the masses to an intimate theatre, and this in and of itself marks the decline of the theatre. It is superior to symbolic drama because the latter toys with the reader and sets him riddles. It is superior to tragedy because tragedy—unless it is melodrama—is marked by a certain bombast and purely literary poetic quality, pursues the goal of being noble and impressive, sticks to the heights aspired to by the aesthetic avant-garde and therefore quite frequently sins by being bookish. Musical accompaniment of the more spectacular and pictorial actions enters into the concept of melodrama. This is by no means a shortcoming. There is no reason to think that musical drama, which was the basis of Greek theatre, cannot be reborn in a truly magnificent form. I think that even tragedy (ancient, Romantic, Shakespearian, Schillerian, Pushkinian, and so on) should be accompanied by suitable music.

A few words concerning the inner content of the desired melodrama. As has been graphically observed, today's playwrights are toothless and do not excite people, or rarely excite them, because according to their ethical doctrine no one knows the nature of good and evil. The playwright is almost always a skeptic. And since he cannot preach from the stage with full clarity on the nature of good and evil, real emotionality is absent from his work, because tragedy, in any case, is only great when it contains a golden nugget of instruction ethically uplifting for the spirit.

Undoubtedly there is much truth in this, if only we take into consideration that it is, of course, a question not of copy-book good and evil, but of these concepts in the broad sense. Schiller understood that the strength of will and iron energy of the villain is the essence of good and that we can make a tragic hero out of such a villain; he will be highly sympathetic to the public, and the public will mourn his death precisely because he appears as the desired type of hero, a man of will and strength. Having posed such a question, we can say: the playwright who dares to undertake melodrama, in our view the sole possible form of broadly-based tragedy for the new age, should clearly take sides for and against. For the melodramatist, the world should be polarized. At least while he writes, he should cast off all skepticism and all doubt. On the melodramatic stage there should be no place for doubts. As in frescoes, the colors must be vivid and pure, the lines simple.

What must be done to put this into practice is, of course, in no way the subject of the present essay, but the business of the writer himself. In the final analysis it is worth remembering Maeterlinck's great yet simple formula, which he was not the first or the last to express everything that furthers the growth of life is good, and everything that opposes it is evil. Therefore choose any great force whatever that furthers the growth of life in its struggle with anything that is detrimental to life, and present this struggle as a matter of burning actuality, not stinting on the episodes, revealing the conflict in the light of striking situations that arouse anger and compassion in a simple soul capable of becoming boundlessly angry and tearfully compassionate, and you will have the soul for our dramatic work.

Here is not the place to talk about the other very important aspect of art for the people—café-chantant, or music hall—which also seems to us not only not to be some kind of trash bin but, on the contrary, a shining pinnacle of art, at the present time occupied by disgusting mountebanks. Here too it is necessary to understand what constitutes the secret of success. You will see, as was the case with melodrama, that if the crowd, the broad-based crowd, took a fancy to a particular kind of work of art, it was not just because it was decked out in the wretched splendor of finery, hung with trinkets and gaudily painted, but because its forms were healthy and beautiful, its gait full of strength and purpose, its voice resonant and entrancing. Take off the filthy make-up which the hand of the pimp-entrepreneur put on her, and then, laid bare, compare her, this beauty of the people, with the sickly and refined beauties of your "higher spheres," and you will then understand that the people were right, that they simply discerned the forms of genuine art beneath all the frightful exterior of that art of the third and fourth sort, which had been fed them.

Fear not, the people will also understand your art of the first class, if you create for them something in the slightest degree equal to that first class art of yours. But before you teach the people anything, learn something from them yourselves.

Young Witkacy, Warsaw (circa. 1889)

PICTORIAL CITATION:
WITKACY AND SELOUS'S SHAKESPEARE

In Witkacy's dramas, the literary text is part of a rich theatrical setting—composed of scene, costume, and gesture—that renders pictorially precise and concrete even the most abstruse philosophical argumentation or psychic disquisition. Visual imagery sustains verbal statement; the written word becomes three-dimensional spoken dialogue. As a painter-playwright, practicing two arts at the same time, Witkacy had extraordinary ability to hear with his eyes; he assigns exact colors, shapes, and sculptural relief to all forms of discourse.

Witkacy's dramatic imagination was from earliest childhood nurtured on images and evolved as much in pictorial as in literary terms. Evidence to support this claim can be found in what would at first glance appear to be a purely literary phenomenon: Witkacy's extensive use of quotation and allusion.

For the youthful Witkacy, reading was in large part a visual experience. As a prime instance of this pictorial tendency, let us examine the case of Shakespeare, an author to whom Staś was introduced as a child in his most formative years.[1] *Romeo and Juliet*, *Richard III*, and *Hamlet* became an inspiration to the boy in his first attempts at playwriting, which often took the form of parody, and also served him as a major source of citation throughout his subsequent career as a writer. In his "Reminiscences about Staś," Witkacy's childhood friend, Władysław Matlakowski, describes how the future author of *The Water Hen* discovered Shakespeare and his own vocation simultaneously.

> Very early he began to read Shakespeare's works which were lent to him by my father who was then working on *Hamlet*. Under the influence of this reading he tried writing works for the stage.[2]

It is clear that Shakespeare's plays had a seminal influence on the development of Witkacy's dramatic imagination, but what is less evident is that for the young creative-artist-to-be Shakespeare's words were always accompanied by pictures. Witkacy's Shakespeare was an illustrated Shakespeare, and his frequent quotations from and allusions to the tragedies and histories are pictorial citations, in which the words serve as captions for the illustrations. Writing of his first meeting with Witkacy in 1921, the musicologist Roman Jasiński recalls the playwright's unusual visual-verbal powers which enabled him to remember dozens of such captions.

> Then we talked of Shakespeare. Witkacy loved him and made random citations. He remembered perfectly the captions placed under Selous's illustrations that adorned the three-volume complete Polish edition of his plays. I for my part cited him several analogous captions, because (as luck would have it!) I had had that edition at my finger tips since childhood and somehow the quotations had got fixed in my memory. That impressed him a lot and he was amazed that someone else could have had such a number of quotations engraved in his memory. The upshot was that we established something of the order of a duel with those quotations.[3]

The three-volume illustrated Shakespeare, from which Witkacy drew his pictorial citations, was the best known and most widely disseminated edition of the British poet in Polish translation at the end of the nineteenth century. Published in

—Pamiętnik Teatralny (1980): 529–540.

Warsaw in 1875–77, the three large volumes that stimulated young Staś's imagination contained 545 woodcuts by Henry Courtney Selous (1811–1890), a London painter of portraits, landscapes, and historical and literary subjects. Son of the painter George Slous (he altered the spelling of his name in 1837), Selous achieved his greatest fame as an illustrator and lithographer. His popular works include Biblical subjects, such as *Scenes from the Life of Moses, Jerusalem in her Grandeur*, and *The Parable of the Prodigal Son*, and illustrations for Bunyan's *Pilgrim's Progress* and for Shakespeare's plays. The Shakespeare woodcuts originally appeared in Cassell's *Illustrated Shakespeare*, edited and annotated by Charles and Mary Cowden Clarke, first published in 1864 and many times reprinted. Selous's illustrations have appeared not only in the Polish edition of Shakespeare but also in a Hungarian edition of 1889 and probably accompany other Eastern European translations. Selous was himself an author of children's books, such as *Granny's Story Book* (1858), *Sunny Days* (1871), and *The Young Governess: A Tale for Girls* (1872).[4]

In his reading of Shakespeare it was Selous's highly dramatic and often nightmarish illustrations to the tragedies and histories (the comedies interested him less) that most fascinated the eight-year-old Staś. Each of the Shakespearean quotations and allusions that Witkacy utilizes in his own early plays is based on one of Selous woodcuts. Practicing pictorial citation, the young author selects striking images, which are accompanied by two or three lines of dialogue providing short captions to the illustrations. He then quotes this dialogue. In some case, Witkacy cites the picture alone as a visualization of the action and entirely omits the captioned dialogue.

The survey that follows of some of Selous's illustrations to *Romeo and Juliet, II Henry VI, Hamlet*, and *Macbeth* reveals Witkacy's device of pictorial citation, as practiced throughout his career in both drama and fiction.

Plate 1 from *Romeo and Juliet*, Act V, scene iii, shows Juliet stabbing herself and falling upon Romeo's body.

> JULIET: O happy dagger!
> This is thy sheath; (*Stabs herself.*) There rust, and let me die.

The illustrated passage is cited by Staś in *The Princess Magdalena*, one of his childhood plays. The young author in a footnote indicates his Shakespearean source.[5] The double suicide—by knife and by poison—that captures the child's imagination will be replicated in his own case fifty years later.

Plate 2 from *II Henry VI*, Act III, scene i, portrays the Duke of York speaking in soliloquy at the moment when he decides to seize power by means of a coup d'état and resolves to make use of Jack Cade and his levelers for this purpose.

> YORK: Now, York, or never, steel thy fearful thoughts,
> And change misdoubt to resolution:
> Be that thou hop'st to be . . .

This speech is cited by the artist-hero in Witkacy's first autobiographical novel, *The 622 Downfalls of Bungo, or The Demonic Woman*.[6] Here Witkacy mistakenly attributes the words to Richard III, confusing the Duke of York with his son, the Duke of Gloucester; in fact, the image of the scheming and ruthless nobleman determined to become monarch by whatever means he can applies equally well to the one as to the other. It is likely that Staś did not always read the entire play, but in some instances simply looked at the pictures.

The idea of self-fashioning through an exercise of will, here expressed by York, is a call to action for the irresolute Bungo and corresponds to Witkiewicz senior's program of character formation designed to give his son a greater sense of purpose.

Plate 3 from *II Henry VI*, Act IV, scene ii, shows the rebel Jack Cade with his army of workmen-levelers.

> CADE: But then are we in order, when we are most out of order. Come, march forward.

The picture of Cade and his levelers stayed with Witkacy throughout his career, merging with the Bolshevik revolutionaries he saw at close hand in Russia. In *They*, Seraskier Banga Tefuan, ideologue for a levelers' revolution, quotes this passage at a crucial moment in his own attempted rise to power. Further, Cade's workmen-levelers who murder and maim indiscriminately serve as models for the worker-thugs at the end of *The New Deliverance*, for the Grizzlovik workers in *The Anonymous Work*, and for the six automated workers who appear from the pipe at the end of *The Mother*.

Plate 4 from *Richard III*, Act V, scene iii, presents the ghosts who appear to Richard on the eve of the battle of Bosworth Field; we see the apparitions accusing the guilt-ridden tyrant of his many crimes and tormenting his sleep. This plate, which appears as the frontispiece to the play, impressed itself deeply on Witkacy's imagination, and many echoes of it are found throughout his works. In *The Anonymous Work* the Princess says of Giers, "The ghosts of those he condemned to death are tormenting him, the way they did Richard III."[7] In *A Normal Person* (a 1924 drama that has survived in an incomplete text), Joseph says of himself, "Like Richard III I am tormented by spirits."[8] Most significantly, the trapped and tormented figure of Richard III in *The New Deliverance* is derived from this image, as well as from another woodcut depicting the Two Murderers with Clarence. In Witkacy's transposed version, the Murderers turn their daggers against Richard himself.

Plate 5 from *Hamlet*, Act IV, scene v, shows Ophelia "larded with sweet flowers," an image which Witkacy takes up several times. First in *Bungo* we read, "I see Ophelia, but with a bouquet, in a first class car."[9] Then, ten years later in *The Crazy Locomotive*, this figure reappears as Janina, the demented wife of the Railway Guard, dressed like Ophelia with flowers.

Plate 6 from *Hamlet*, Act V, scene i, portrays the Gravediggers, an image which dominates Act I of *The Anonymous Work*. Throughout this act, Girtak and the Second Gravedigger continue to dig a grave for Giers. In fact, Girtak as a leader of the levelers will be the undertaker for a whole rotten society.

Plate 7 from *Macbeth*, Act III, scene iv, presents the Ghost of Banquo appearing in Macbeth's seat. This image is explicitly invoked at the end of *Insatiability*, when Slobowicz upon seeing the apparition of an officer he condemned to death remembers the fear inspired in him as a child by Selous's woodcut of the Ghost of Banquo.[10]

Plate 8 from Macbeth, Act IV, scene i, depicts Macbeth's visit to the Witches in a dark cave.

> MACBETH: How now, you secret, black, and midnight hags, What is't you do?
>
> ALL: A deed without a name.

The Witches' line is rendered in the Polish translation by Józef Paszkowski (1817–1861) as "Bezimienne dzieło," or "anonymous work," suggesting to Witkacy the title of one of his major plays dealing with the seemingly spontaneous creation of a revolution from below. The woodcut, teeming with winged beasts, strange monsters, and hideous little creatures, undoubtedly left a profound mark on Staś's creative imagination and served as a model for the grotesque figures which would later people then artist's paintings and drawings.

The subjects and themes, found in those of Selous's illustrations to Shakespeare which Witkacy chose for pictorial citation, reveal a kinship with the playwright's own obsessive concerns. The images from Selous's Shakespeare that most fascinated Witkacy are: from *Romeo and Juliet*, a double suicide piling one corpse upon another; from *II Henry VI*, an aspiring strongman and a leveler's revolt; from *Richard III*, ghosts of the dead appearing to torment the living; from *Hamlet*, an insane woman and a pair of gravediggers; and from *Macbeth*, a terrifying hallucination and swarming monsters and demons.

Shakespeare, rendered pictorial by Selous's illustrations, touched the wellsprings of Staś's imagination at the time when his creative energies were first awakening. Images from Selous's Shakespeare—never long buried—come to the surface in a number of Witkacy's mature works. The madmen and suicides, tyrants and levelers, ghosts and monsters that people the Witkacian universe were first conjured up in the young playwright's burgeoning imagination by the combination of Shakespeare's words and Selous's woodcuts.

Romeo and Juliet
JULIET: O happy dagger!
            This is thy sheath; (*Stabs herself.*) There rust, and let me die.
                                                    Act V, scene III

York. Teraz lub nicdy przyszedł dzień, Yorku,
W stal odziać twarzą twoje trwożne myśli,
I koniec wszystkim położyć wahaniem.

Akt III, Scena I.

II Henry VI

YORK: Now, York, or never, steel thy fearful thoughts,
          And change misdoubt to resolution:
          Be that thou hop'st to be . . .

                                        Act III, scene I

II Henry VI
CADE: But then are we in order, when we are most out of order. Come,
march forward.

Act IV, scene ii

KRÓL RYSZARD III.

Richard III

Act V, scene iii

Hamlet
OPHELIA: (*Song*) Larded all with sweet flowers
Which bewept to the grave did not go
With truelove showers.

Act IV, scene v

Hamlet
SECOND GRAVEDIGGER: Who builds stronger than a mason, a shipwright, or
a carpenter?
FIRST GRAVEDIGGER: Ay, tell me that, and unyoke.

Act V, scene i

Macbeth
MACBETH: Which of you have done this?
LORDS: What, my good Lord?
MACBETH: Thou canst not say I did it.

Act III, scene iv

Macbeth
MACBETH: How now, you secret, black, and midnight hags,
What is't you do?

ALL: A deed without a name.

Act IV, scene i

NOTES

1. Władysław Matlakowski, "Wspomnienie o Stasiu (*Wiadomości*, no. 22, 1957)," quoted by Anna Micińska, "Stanisław Ignacy Witkiewicz, Iuvenilia," *Dialog* 8 (1965): 17.
2. Ibid.
3. Roman Jasiński, "Witkacy," in *Stanisław Ignacy Witkiewicz. Człowiek i twórca. Księga pamiątkowa*, ed. Tadeusz Kotarbiński and Jerzy Eugeniusz Płomieński (Warsaw: Państwowy Instytut Wydawniczy, 1957), 308.
4. For a discussion of Selous as an illustrator of Shakespeare, see Stuart Sillars, *The Illustrated Shakespeare, 1709–1875* (Cambridge: University of Cambridge Press, 2008), 291–305.
5. Daniel Gerould and Jadwiga Kosicka, "The Playwright as a Child: The Witkiewicz Childhood Plays. *The Princess Magdalena*," *yale/theater* 5, no. 3 (1974): 58.
6. The passage appears in a fragment not included in Witkacy's final version of the novel. Stanisław Ignacy Witkiewicz, *622 Upadki Bunga czyli Demoniczna Kobieta*, ed. Anna Micińska (Warsaw: Państwowy Instytut Wydawniczy, 1992), 547.
7. *The Anonymous Work*, Act I, in *Seven Plays by Witkiewicz* (New York: Segal Center Publications, 2005), 188.
8. Stanisław Ignacy Witkiewicz, *Dramaty*, vol. 3 (Warsaw: Państwowy Instytut Wydawniczy, 2004), 448
9. *622 Upadki Bunga*, 16.
10. "The general recalled how terrified he had been by the dark, opaque spirit of Banquo and how afterwards he had lain awake for hours unable to get rid of the horrible vision which had haunted him." *Insatiability*, translated by Louis Iribarne (Urbana: University of Illinois Press, 1977), 406.

Oscar Méténier (circa 1890-1900), Photo by Pierre Petit, Collection of Felix Pottin

OSCAR MÉTÉNIER AND *COMÉDIE ROSSE*:
FROM THE THÉÂTRE LIBRE TO THE GRAND GUIGNOL

In the spring of 1887, André Antoine was an employee of the Gas Company and an amateur actor dissatisfied with the existing state of French theatre. He founded the Théâtre Libre and began the revolution in theatrical art that would bear fruit throughout Europe with the creation of the Freie Bühne in Berlin, the Moscow Art Theatre, and J. T. Grein's Independent Theatre in London. The Théâtre Libre was a small private enterprise that gave only two or three performances of each of its programs in rented halls for a limited number of subscribers and invited guests (thereby escaping the constraints of censorship). Its role in establishing Naturalism as a dominant theatrical mode was out of all proportion to the limited number of spectators that it reached directly. Antoine presented the first French performances and often the world premières of pioneering foreign works such as Tolstoy's *Power of Darkness* (1888), Ibsen's *Ghosts* (1890), Strindberg's *Miss Julie* (1893), and Hauptmann's *Weavers* (1893). Premiers of French works included adaptations of novels and short stories by Zola, the Goncourt brothers and others.

In their desire to show life as it is, the Naturalists in the theatre insisted on direct observation, research and documentation, precise notation of fact, and objectivity of technique. They applied to drama the discoveries and methods of nineteenth-century science, particularly those of experimental medicine, to produce authentic case histories and clinical studies. Pursuing these principles, Zola and his followers opened new areas of theatrical subject matter by exploring the seamy underside of the belle époque.

In slum tenements and neighborhood bistros the struggle for existence could be studied among poor day-laborers, rag-pickers, and street walkers. The Naturalists defended their preference for the most brutal aspects of life by arguing that the essential relationships between man and society could be more vividly revealed in primitive characters and sordid situations than when disguised by wealth, complex psychology and hypocritical pretense.[1] Unconcerned with matters of form, the playwrights working with Antoine rejected the old theatrical formulas and devices such as clever plots, carefully prepared climaxes and tidy, and definitive endings in favor of simplicity of action, a "slice of life" (a term coined by Jean Jullien, dramatist, journalist, and critic).

The Théâtre Libre helped bring about the end of the declamatory rhetoric that had been part of the French theatrical tradition for centuries. To create a new mode of dialogue appropriate to their documentary approach, the Naturalist playwrights turned to dialect and slang, reproducing the crude and often obscene colloquial speech of specific low-life milieux. For the first time the language of uneducated working-class characters was heard on stage. The dramas and comedies presented by Antoine shattered long-standing taboos with their uncensored dialogue and frank treatment of sexual matters.

It is little wonder that the Théâtre Libre became celebrated for the scandals that it created. It tore away the veils of piety, discretion and decency that had always shielded audiences from contact with certain shocking facts of life. Antoine's theatre gained a reputation for a kind of bitter cynicism known as *rosserie*, a word derived from *rosse*— literally, a worn-out old horse and, figuratively, someone maliciously ironic and nasty.

—*The Drama Review: TDR* 28, no. 1 (T101) (Spring 1984): 15–28.

Oscar MÉTÉNIER

LES

VOYOUS

au Théâtre

(Histoire de deux Pièces)

BRUXELLES
chez HENRY KISTEMAECKERS, *éditeur*
73, RUE DUPONT, 73

1891

Book Cover of Oscar Méténier, *Hooligans in the Theatre*, Brussels, 1891

Comédie rosse takes sardonic pleasure in undermining the high ideals of traditional religious morality by showing how harsh economic facts and biological drives render those ideals hollow and inoperative. Without comment or condemnation—and only the trace of an ironic sneer—the playwright allows the bare truth to expose the falsity of society's hypocritical pretensions. The Polish actress and playwright Gabriela Zapolska, who appeared at Antoine's theatre from 1892 to 1895, defined *comédie rosse* in these terms:

> *Être rosse* in French means to be cruel in speaking the truth, to be not only malicious, but to make that malice so biting it draws blood. The French writer who created that school was Henri Becque, author of *The Crows* [1882] and The *Parisian Woman* [1885]. [. . .] The dramatic literature fostered by Antoine has one great and incontestable virtue: it makes its authors look directly at life. Initially these writers tore aside the veil with rather playful a hand. Then suddenly something surprising confronted them. Life revealed itself to them in all its nakedness, with all the vices of the social organism. The most daring of them abandoned the playful manner and began to look directly at those vices and the human misery arising from them. And that gave rise to social drama, which is undoubtedly the genre of *rosse* comedies.[2]

One of the first and best practitioners of *comédie rosse* was the novelist and playwright Oscar Méténier (1859–1913), a co-founder of the Théâtre Libre and an author very much at the center of Naturalist controversy toward the end of the nineteenth century. At Antoine's second program on May 30, 1887, the work that attracted the most attention was Méténier's one-act play *At Home* (*En Famille*). Méténier adapted the play from his own short story of the same title about a drunken family gathering of shady characters: the father, a receiver of stolen goods; the daughter, a prostitute; and the son, a pimp who recounts in lurid detail the execution by guillotine of a criminal friend.[3] Public performances were forbidden by the government as an offense to morals.

Two years later, in May 1889 at the Théâtre Libre, Méténier's one-act *Stool-Pigeon* (*La Casserole*), a violent story of betrayal and murder among prostitutes and pimps at a cheap dance hall, created an even greater sensation. In the bloody conclusion, a pimp stabs the whore who informed on his male lover. In the program, Antoine warned the spectators that those of delicate sensibilities should leave before the beginning of *Stool-Pigeon*, scheduled last on the program, which would start at 12:30 a.m. Because of the advance publicity, Méténier's thirty-minute drama played to a packed house and enjoyed great popular success. It was attacked by critics as repulsive and revolting. For verisimilitude, a real strongman, Leo Will, played the strongman's role and lifted real weights, and the extras (*figurants*) representing the criminals populating the dance hall were authentic underworld figures with long police records.[4]

Oscar Méténier was particularly suited by training and temperament to his position as militant Naturalist chronicler of the lower depths of Parisian society. At the beginning of his career, to earn a living and gather material for his literary work, the young writer served as secretary to the police commissioner. For a period of five years, Méténier worked in thirty-four different metropolitan districts, including several of the toughest working-class areas, where he could closely observe the life of the common people and the street types of Paris.[5]

Méténier considered himself a historian of manners and morals, and his job as police clerk proved a rich source of documentation and an inexhaustible mine of observations. Early in his career, Méténier decided to leave to other writers the bourgeois world and complex psychology of the fashionable upper crust and instead to specialize in the common people, recognizing quickly that no class in society was so interesting or so little known.[6]

Gaining the confidence of the inhabitants of the notorious La Roquette district, Méténier became their friend, learned their secrets, and mastered their slang. The young author discovered that these low-life figures, who were ignorant of good and evil and simply followed their instincts, had a stronger sense of courage, honor, friendship and gratitude than the supposedly civilized bourgeois citizens. Because it was frank and spontaneous, the criminal world was more decent and honorable than the hypocritical upper classes.[7]

"I developed the opinion," Méténier declared in a lecture he gave in Brussels in 1891 prior to a performance of *La Casserole*, that "there is no absolute honesty. . . . I would go even further: In the strict sense of the word, virtue is a myth, and that is why our books appear bitter . . . because they are true. After all, morality is only a convention that is relative and modifiable according to the climate, epoch and latitude. In our case, in Paris, each class of society has its own particular morality."[8]

Having interrogated 2,000 working-class girls who became prostitutes, Méténier pointed out that "they come to consider their calling as a perfectly normal profession," which the circumstances of their lives had dictated.[9] Most were initiated into sex at an early age, often by a member of their own family. "Incest," Méténier observed, "far from seeming a monstrosity to them, is so ordinary that half the prostitutes born in Paris had a brother or sometimes their father as a first lover."[10] Méténier perceived that it was the injustice of the world that condemned the poor to go hungry and forced them into a life of crime.

"I pity them," Méténier affirmed. "Since I have seen them, since I have lived among them, I excuse them and I feel for them nothing except immense pity. I love them even!"[11] Bourgeois virtues and values were quite extraneous to lower class life. "The worker who has a regular job prefers concubinage to marriage," Méténier observed, "since marriage is only a source of difficulty . . . and at the same time a cause of expense."[12] The only honesty recognized by the common people, the writer asserted, was a natural honesty that consisted in not taking someone else's property.

After he gave up his job with the police commissioner to become a full-time writer, Méténier continued his explorations of the other Paris's bizarre haunts and dives. He based his books and plays on what he saw and heard there. Even when he served as an adaptor of Russian drama, he drew upon his experiences living among the dregs of society. Méténier collaborated with the Russian Isaac Pavlovsky on the translation of *The Power of Darkness* for Antoine's famous production in 1888. Although some critics questioned the French playwright's wisdom in having the Russian peasants speak Parisian underworld slang, Tolstoy himself read and approved Méténier's adaptation.[13]

By the 1890s Naturalism had lost its novelty as an avant-garde movement. The Théâtre Libre, after a number of highly creative and innovative seasons, began to repeat itself. The Naturalist impetus in drama had set out to destroy all formulas, yet eventually became a formula itself. The Symbolist reaction, with its affirmation of spiritual values, had its moment of triumph in small independent theatres that staged the mystical and otherworldly plays of Maurice Maeterlinck. In June 1894, Antoine, feeling that he had accomplished his mission in bringing Naturalism to the stage, closed the Théâtre Libre.

At the moment when Naturalism ceased to be a new force in the avant-garde, many of its motifs and techniques started to filter down into the popular arts and general consciousness. By the early 1890s, themes of low-life achieved wide popularity in the graphic arts of poster and lithograph as well as in the fusion of music and poetry in song. The French popular song became transformed into the *chanson réaliste* with street slang lyrics that celebrated the urban poetry of the prostitute and the apache to whom she gave her heart and money. The picturesque aspects and character types of proletarian life—bums, unemployed workingmen, poor girls forced to solicit on the street—became the subjects of popular entertainment for the working classes at the *café-concert* and for more fashionable audiences at the *cabaret artistique*, such as the Chat Noir and Mirliton.

The most famous creator of these songs of low-life and social protest was the poet-singer Aristide Bruant (1851–1925), who, coming to Paris from the country, studied life in the poor districts on the outer boulevards. Frequenting little bars, cheap restaurants, and shabby cafes where he noted down the colorful street slang, Bruant wrote his own lyrics and sang them before predominantly working-class audiences. Bruant explored the dangerous world of thieves and thugs, prostitutes and pimps with the former police clerk Oscar Méténier as his guide and mentor.

In 1893 Méténier wrote a short monograph about his friend, *Le Chansonnier populaire, Aristide Bruant*, to which the poet-singer appended a note emphasizing their close artistic kinship: "Of all writers at the present time the one with whom I have the greatest affinity is unquestionably Oscar Méténier. The same spirit of observation applied to the same subjects, the same profound knowledge of the common people and their way of life, the same pity for the downtrodden, the déclassé, and the disinherited. Engaged in the same battle, we were fated to meet."[14] The Swiss-French artist Théophile Steinlen (1859–1923), who held the same radical views as the playwright and the singer, illustrated the book.

In April 1897, Oscar Méténier made his most important contribution to popular culture when he founded his own theatre, the Grand Guignol, in painter Georges Rochegrosse's studio (originally a Jansenist convent) on the rue Chaptal in the ninth arrondissement. Although the Grand Guignol would soon become world-famous as a horror theatre, during the two years of Méténier's management it was a direct offshoot of the Théâtre Libre and attracted many of Antoine's authors. Alternating farces with serious drama, Méténier specialized in staging short, often sensationalistic plays in which scrupulous attention was paid to realistic details.

The inaugural program on April 13, 1897, consisted of a prologue and seven plays, including three by Méténier himself: his adaptation of Guy de Maupassant's story about life in a brothel during the Franco-Prussian war, *Mademoiselle Fifi* (that had first been given at the Théâtre Libre and would eventually be played 2,000 times); his dramatizations of two of his short stories, *Meat-Ticket* (*La Brême*), slang for the prostitute's police card; and *Little Bugger* (*Le Loupiot*), slang for child. Also on the first program was a one-act comedy, *Gun Shot* (*Coup de Fusil*), by the well-known humorist Georges Courteline.[15]

Méténier's expertise in Parisian crime and the underworld oriented the Grand Guignol toward the violent and macabre *fait divers* or news item. A special formula gradually evolved for the ultra-realistic staging of bloodcurdling situations with sudden, unexpected endings that would arouse intense emotions of horror in the spectators. Méténier's *Him!* (*Lui!*), performed November 11, 1897, about a prostitute who brings home a customer only to discover that he has recently committed a particularly grisly murder, points clearly to the style that would be the trademark of the Grand Guignol. It illustrates how Naturalism, originally a serious, pseudo-scientific dramatic form, could be exploited for sheer thrills and entertainment.

Meat-Ticket and *Little Bugger*, however, are not horror plays, but pure examples of *comédie rosse* as developed at the Théâtre Libre. Sociologically acute in their depiction of working-class life and aesthetically innovative in their simple presentation of everyday reality, Méténier's miniature dramas expose the fraud of bourgeois morality when foisted on the poor. The common people in Méténier's plays parody the values of their supposed betters by adapting the precepts taught by the church and state to their own lowly circumstances. They demonstrate that the best way for a poor girl to take care of her parents is through prostitution. The self-styled anarchist in *Little Bugger* exposes the institution of marriage as a swindle and shows how to beat the system by outwitting the landlord. Méténier's character Leonidas Grelu is an ironic comment on the French obsession of 1897 with bomb-throwing anarchists, who were seen as dangerous terrorists threatening civilization.

Short single-scene one-act plays, like *Meat-Ticket* and *Little Bugger*, were known at the Théâtre Libre as *quarts d'heure*, or quarter-of-an-hour dramas. During his association with the Naturalist movement, August Strindberg declared that such brevity was "the type of play for contemporary theatregoers."[16] He wrote several of these short ironic works—*Pariah*, *The Stronger*, and *Simoon*—for the Scandinavian Experimental Theatre Company in Copenhagen (1887–1889). In a letter to the Danish actor, Carl Price, in December 1888, Strindberg mentions his copy of Méténier's *En Famille*, which he has lent someone and wants to get back.[17]

In *comédie rosse*, as represented by *Meat-Ticket* and *Little Bugger*, Oscar Méténier was able to focus briefly and deftly on an aspect of contemporary reality, with humor and irony and without the cumbersome superstructure of traditional dramaturgy.

NOTES

1. In a diary entry for December 3, 1871, Edmond de Goncourt wrote, "But why, you will ask me, choose these [repulsive] milieux? Because, as a civilization is in the process of disappearing, it is at the bottom that the character of things, of persons, of the language, of everything, is preserved." Edmond and Jules de Goncourt, *Journal: Memoires de la Vie Littéraire*, ed. Robert Ricatte (Paris: Robert Laffont, 1989) 2:479.
2. *Słowo Polskie*, 1900, no. 569. On *rosserie*, see also Jean Chothia, *André Antoine* (Cambridge: Cambridge University Press, 1991), 92–96.
3. Samuel Montefiore Waxman, *Antoine and the Théâtre-Libre* (Cambridge, MA: Harvard University Press, 1926), 71–72. See also Chothia, 10–11.
4. Waxman, 109. See also Chothia, 88–89.
5. Oscar Méténier, *Les Voyous au Théâtre* (Brussels: Henry Kistemaekers, 1981), 68.
6. Ibid., 63–64.
7. Ibid., 74–75.
8. Ibid., 71.
9. Ibid., 80.
10. Ibid., 79.
11. Ibid., 82.
12. Ibid., 80.
13. Tolstoy's daughter Tatiana wrote to Méténier to convey her father's approval of the translation and to indicate the few small corrections that he required. Méténier published the letter in *La Vie moderne* (February 11, 1888), and it also appeared in *Le Monde Illustré* (November 13, 1888). See Francis Pruner, *Le Théâtre Libre d'Antoine: Le Répertoire Étranger* (Paris: Lettres Modernes, 1958), 26–28 n. 16, and Chothia, 40–41, 202.
14. In Oscar Méténier, *Le Chansonnier Populaire Aristide Bruant* (Paris: Au Mirliton, 1893), 45–46. See Jerrold Seigel, *Bohemian Paris: Culture, Politics, and the Boundaries of Bourgeois Life, 1830–1930* (New York: Viking Penguin, 1987), 237–38.
15. For a discussion of Méténier's career and establishment of the Grand Guignol, see Agnes Pierrot, "Preface," *Le Grand Guignol: Le Théâtre des Peurs de la Belle Époque* (Paris: Robert Laffont, 1995), iii–vi. The collection includes Méténier's *Lui!*
16. August Strindberg, "On Modern Drama and Modern Theatre," in *Selected Essays*, ed. and trans. Michael Robinson (Cambridge: Cambridge University Press, 1996), 85.
17. *Strindberg's Letters*, comp., ed., and trans. Michael Robinson (Chicago: University of Chicago Press, 1995), 1:309.

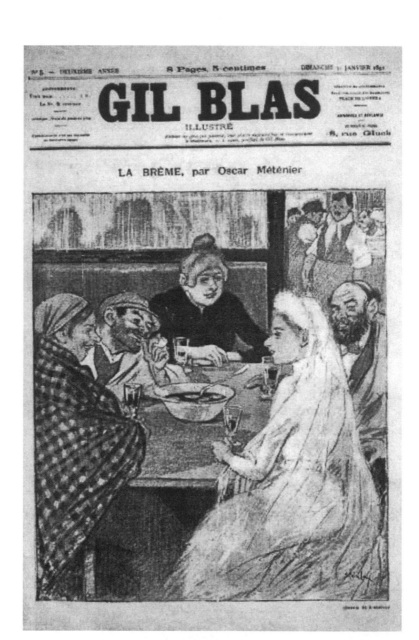

Cover for *La Brême* (*Meat-Ticket*), Paris: Paul Ollendorff, 1897,
reprinted in *Gil Blas*

MEAT-TICKET

A PICTURE OF THE LIFE OF THE PEOPLE IN TWO SCENES

by Oscar Méténier

Presented at the Theatre of the Grand Guignol on April 13, 1897.

FATHER PICHARD
FATHER PINSON
A WAITER
MOTHER PICHARD
NINI
LOUISA

The backroom of a wine shop, rue Sainte-Marguerite.

Scene 1

FATHER PICHARD, FATHER PINSON, *and afterwards* MOTHER PICHARD *and* NINI, *and later on a* WAITER.

(FATHER PICHARD *is seated at a table with* FATHER PINSON, *with a bowl of hot wine in front of them, when* MOTHER PINCHARD *enters with her daughter* NINI *dressed for her first communion.*)

FATHER PICHARD: Well, how about it? Is all that hocus-pocus of yours finally over and done with? You know, I invited Father Pinson to join me . . . I got bored sitting here all by myself waiting for you to come . . . but at least we got something to wet the old whistle . . .

(MOTHER PICHARD *and* NINI *sitting down.*)

MOTHER PICHARD: And where's Louisa? Ain't nobody seen her come yet?

FATHER PICHARD: What you talking about? The great Louisa came already . . . She's in there . . . She'll be back in a minute . . . She just went to say hello to the folks in the next room . . . Hey! Everybody asleep? (*To the WAITER who puts in an appearance*) Bring a glass for mother and the kids here! (*He pours hot wine into the glass.*)

– Translated by Daniel Gerould, New York, 1984

MOTHER PICHARD: You know what, Pichard, the parish priest was real fair and square . . . Just now when the whole thing was over, he had me bring the little one with me into the sacristy, and he slipped me . . . guess what he slipped me . . . a five-franc piece! (*She takes a five-franc piece out of her pocket.*)

FATHER PICHARD: What of it? That's no great shakes . . . We earned it all right . . . He puts us through enough trouble . . . (*He pockets the coin.*)

MOTHER PICHARD: Oh! You're dead wrong about that, Pichard! I'm telling you, Father Pinson, first off Pichard wouldn't hear nothing . . . about letting the kid make her communion . . . He got his dandruff up . . .

FATHER PICHARD: First off, sending the little one every day to their confounded catychyzum messed up our work . . .

MOTHER PICHARD: But I stuck to my guns no matter what . . . Now you take somebody like me, Father Pinson, you see, I always been for religion, I mean after all, where we going to find another guy halfways as decent as the parish priest of Saint Margot's? . . . and it would have been a dirty shame to let him down and not do what he wants . . . And anyhow you never know what's coming later on, I mean, do you?

FATHER PINSON: Pichard, you know, you're wife is right! Here's to you! (*He drinks to her health.*)

MOTHER PICHARD: And then, there's another thing I'm going to tell, Father Pinson, those ladies in the parish have been real good to us . . . They got Nini her outfit . . . Nini and me just about bust out crying when we opened the box and saw the dress . . . You'd of thought it was made special for her! Get up, Nini! Just look at that material, Father Pinson! Pure muslin! Oh! You can't beat that! I'll tell you! There's nothing like religion to give you them feelings . . . But that's not all . . . You know what the parish priest's got in his head now? . . . He wants us to get married . . .

FATHER PICHARD: Oh, no! Not on your life! Those confounded holy water sprinklers are all the same! I already made enough confessions letting him have the little one . . .

FATHER PINSON: Since he showed his appreciation of what you done for him! No reason to regret it!

MOTHER PICHARD: I'm telling you, he's taking care of everything! He sent for our papers! . . . And we don't have to do nothing, he says!

FATHER PICHARD: That's a lot of rot! We lived together fine for twenty years without ever getting married . . . And we can go on like that for as long as we got yet to live . . . Marriage! Marriage is for the rich!

MOTHER PICHARD: If that's all that's bothering you! It won't cost us nothing . . . we might even get something out of it!

FATHER PICHARD: Hogwash! Look here, Pinson, you're an intelligent man . . . tell me, would you get married?

FATHER PINSON: Oh! With the parish priest presiding, I don't know about that . . . but I'm pretty sure if I had to do it over again I'd set up housekeeping with some woman or another . . . When you're young, it's okay to live by yourself . . . But when you're old, it really gets rough . . . Sometimes when I come back home after making the morning rounds in winter and I take the basket off my back and put it in the corner I say to myself: "Look! There's Pichard next door, he's got a wife who fixes all the meals . . . And then, when there are two of you . . . it's a lot easier to keep warm . . . in the sack . . . He's got children . . . two swell girls . . . real dolls who won't never let their father starve to death on the sidewalk . . . and look at me . . ." Of course . . . you don't get to be married for that! Oh! Kids . . . Say! Just looking at Nini! . . . does something to me . . . I wish she was my kid!

FATHER PICHARD: Oh! Sure, children are a consolation alright, but they're a headache too . . . You're always worrying they'll turn out bad!

MOTHER PICHARD: That's just what the parish priest was saying, too . . . He asked if we ain't got no plans to apprentice her so as to make her into a good worker. The ladies in the parish who dressed her up think she's real sweet . . . They want to help us out all they can . . . They're ready to look after her . . .

FATHER PICHARD: There you go again with your parish priest! I don't want any part of that! There's only one sure way to hold onto your children, and that's never to go against the job they choose themselves . . .

FATHER PINSON: But then they got to know what it is they want to do.

FATHER PICHARD: Look here, Nini! Now that you've taken your first communion, you're almost a full-grown woman . . . You don't want to be an old clothes dealer like me, do you?

NINI: Oh, no! Not me!

FATHER PICHARD: Then want to be a seamstress . . . a laundress . . . a nursemaid? It's up to you!

NINI: I know just what I want to be! Been thinking about it for a long, long time now! . . . Because I'm a serious girl, I am!

FATHER PICHARD: On that score, got to hand it to her! Nini never gave us nothing but real satisfaction! . . . I got nothing to reproach her with . . . Not a bit like Louisa! Oh! That little silly monkey gave us a miserable time up until she was eighteen years old! It's been not much more than a year since she started to behave herself! And it wasn't for lack of getting some good lickings! Would you believe it, Pinson, at Nini's age, she'd already run away from home two or four times . . . with good-for-nothings, total trash . . . I had to go get her at least a dozen times at the Police Station . . . Mademoiselle got nabbed all over the place . . . A regular little devil!

MOTHER PICHARD: And how! She didn't have her little sister's quiet disposition!

NINI: Oh! That's for sure! She got off to a real terrible start, Louisa did! . . . You won't catch me getting into stupid scrapes like that!

MOTHER PICHARD: No chance of that! She set you some example, that girl did! . . . Sure, but I'm telling you, too, that Louisa settled down real nice since . . . One day when she had enough, she asked Pichard's permission to go get her card at the Police Station, you know, what she calls her meat-ticket! . . . Naturally, Pichard agreed . . . She got someone—I don't remember who anymore—to recommend her to Madame Trollon, the proprietor of Number 116 boulevard de la Vilette! It's a well-run house, I don't got to tell you more, do I? . . . and since then I only heard nice things about her . . . Oh! I'm telling you! It's a decent job . . . keeps her busy . . . She makes a lot of money, and those ladies there like her a lot . . . Well, speak of the devil and there she is! Say, Louisa, I was just talking about you!

Scene 2

(*The same characters and* LOUISA.)

LOUISA (*kissing* NINI): Well, I never! Look at how big you are, kid! And ain't she pretty in her white dress! Oh! Say, seeing you like that does something to me . . . makes me remember my first communion! . . . (*She kisses her again.*)

FATHER PICHARD: Ain't you going to sit down?

LOUISA (*sitting down*): Sure I will! So you was just talking about me . . . But you didn't even leave me a glass of hot wine, you bunch of selfish characters! Waiter, another bowl, and I'm treating everybody!

MOTHER PICHARD: So you're in the chips?

LOUISA: Listen! When I go out! . . . I take a little money with me! (*She clicks the coins in her apron pocket.*) Got to have a little fun some of the time! And who we got more precious than our parents, right?

FATHER PICHARD (*touched*): What was I telling you, Pinson? May be a little headstrong sometimes, but the heart's in the right place!

MOTHER PICHARD: Oh, it runs in the family!

LOUISA: And now the little one here is a grown woman, and what do you want her to become?

FATHER PICHARD: I said I'll let her choose her own kind of life . . . I won't go back on my word! I know she's sensible! And anyhow that's just what we was about to ask her when you came in . . . All right, kid, tell us about it . . . the whole story!

NINI: I'll always remember what the parish priest told us . . . how you mustn't never abandon your parents, even if they do you wrong . . . So then I'm going to wait till I come of age . . . and then right away I'll go to the Police Station and ask for a meat-ticket . . . like my sister . . . so as to have peace and quiet . . . Then I'll work with Louisa in the house run by Mother Trollon . . . and then I'll earn lots of money so as to help papa and mama when they get old! My mind's made up!

MOTHER PICHARD (*kissing* NINI): That's a dear girl! See, Pichard, parish priests *do* have a good influence!

FATHER PICHARD (*full of enthusiasm*): Didn't I tell you, Pinson, that the kid's a real angel!

FATHER PINSON (*his glass in his hand*): I see it all now, I made a real mistake not getting married! (*He clinks glasses with* NINI *and lets out a big sigh.*) Here's to a successful career, my girl!

MOTHER PICHARD (*toasting*): Here's to a happy future, my child!

THE END

Cover for *Le Loupiot* (*Little Bugger*), Paris: Paul Ollendorff, 1897

LITTLE BUGGER

A PICTURE OF THE LIFE OF THE PEOPLE IN TWO SCENES

by Oscar Méténier

Presented at the Theatre of the Grand Guignol on April 13, 1897.

GAUTRON
EUGENIA
THE WAITER
GRELU

The backroom of a wine shop.

Scene 1

JEAN GAUTRON, EUGENIA, *and afterwards a* WAITER.

(JEAN GAUTRON *and* EUGENIA *are seated at a table with a bottle of wine.*)

EUGENIA (*very upset and almost in tears*): No! I mean it, Jean, let's get out of here! I don't want to stay no more.

GAUTRON: All right, let's have it! Will you just tell me what's eating you . . . You been whining for the past hour, and you can't sit still for one minute . . . it's no fun . . .

EUGENIA (*the same business*): But . . . no . . . nothing's wrong with me . . . I swear it . . .

GUATRON: I'm telling you something is wrong! With that long face of yours, you're spoiling my whole Sunday . . . it's the only day we got to go out together . . . I been looking forward to it all week . . . Don't try to bullshit me! . . . Ever since this morning, it's been the same old wailing and moaning . . . Come on, Genie baby, did I do something to hurt you?

EUGENIA: Oh! Good lord, no! My poor, poor man! You're much too good to me!

GAUTRON: Well, what is it then?

EUGENIA (*very disturbed*): I told you, nothing's wrong . . . That's what! Let's just go, please, for my sake!

GAUTRON: What for? It's real nice here . . . Where else is there to go?

– Translated by Daniel Gerould, New York, 1984.

EUGENIA: Let's go home.

GAUTRON (*looking all around suspiciously*): Oh! There's something fishy going on here! And I don't like that secret stuff . . . You better tell me what it is that's bugging you. (EUGENIA *leans her head on* GAUTRON*'s shoulder and bursts out crying.*) Great! Now you're squawking all over the place! Hey, will you stop that blubbering, crybaby! (*Tenderly, comforting her.*) Come on, Genie girl, tell me what's eating you . . .

EUGENIA (*sobbing*): All right! The trouble is . . . I didn't want to tell you right off . . . but since you want to know so bad . . . here's what it is . . . (*She looks down.*) For the past two months I thought I might be . . . Now I'm sure . . . That's what it is . . .

GAUTRON: Boy, am I relieved! I thought it might be something much worse! Say, does the idea of having a little bugger really make you all that unhappy? You know, it kind of tickles me! I'm not such a bad guy, right? Just because we didn't get no scrap of paper at the mayor's office don't mean you and I don't love each other any less, right? That little guy is mine; I mean, I'm the one who made him! I'll own up that he's my kid, and we'll put his name in the big book at the Town Hall! Take a look at those paws . . . You can always knock out a lot of work if you're built like an ox the way I am . . . A few extra swings with the sledge hammer at old man Ansteque's iron works, that's all it takes! Cut it out! Come on, give me a smile, you spoiled little brat!

EUGENIA: You'll own up that he's your kid . . . that's a good one!

GAUTRON: I suppose you don't believe me?

EUGENIA: Sure! I believe you all right! But you won't be able to own up that he's yours, my poor man, because . . .

GAUTRON: Because? . . .

EUGENIA: Because . . . forgive me, I never told you this before . . . because . . . I'm married!

GAUTRON: Married? Did you hear that! She's really gone too far! (*He gets up and paces back and forth without saying a word while* EUGENIA *cries, then comes back to her.*) So, in that case, I'm going to have a kid, but he'll have somebody else's name! You're some broad, you know, you never said a word to me about that bird! Mind telling me what his name is?

EUGENIA: Oh! Forgive me! I was so afraid you'd leave me! I didn't dare! His name was Grelu, he was a cabinet maker . . . We got married real young . . . In the early days, he worked hard, we was happy . . . Then he got in with the wrong crowd . . . He started drinking . . . absinthe . . . and going to meetings till he finally got mixed up in politics . . . It went to his head, he started beating me . . . I had a baby that died . . . of malnutrition, they said . . . and then we broke up . . . When you got me, it had been all over with him for more than a year . . . I didn't dare tell you nothing . . . That was wrong of me . . . now I'm paying for it!

GAUTRON: How about that! That's real nice! Eh! Grelu! Mrs. Grelu!

EUGENIA (*getting excited*): Shut up! For my sake, please shut up! Don't ever say that name again . . . and now let's get out of here!

GAUTRON (*suspicious*): How come? What are you so scared of?

EUGENIA: Listen, since I started to tell you everything, I might as well tell you everything . . . Since me and my husband broke up, I never seen him again, I swear it . . . But just now . . . when we come in here . . . I noticed him . . . sitting there drinking . . . in the side room . . . He's here . . . That's why I'd like us to get out of here . . .

GAUTRON (*exploding*): He's here! All right then! We're going to have some fun, if he's here! I'm going to tell that guy a thing or two!

EUGENIA (*pleading*): Jean! Jean! Please, for my sake! Look, he don't even know you! He never did nothing to you! Please, for my sake, Jean, don't do nothing wild! Sit down, will you!

GAUTRON (*grimly*): You're right, you know: He don't know me. But see, the idea that our kid, that we made together, could be called Grelu . . . that really pissed me off . . .

EUGENIA: Please, for my sake, Jean, don't make no trouble!

GAUTRON: OK, I promise you I won't, Genie baby! . . . But I got an idea . . . Do you really love me, I mean . . . do you really love me?

EUGENIA: How can you ask me that!

GAUTRON: Would you be ready . . . even to go to jail . . . to stay with me?

EUGENIA: Go to jail? What are you talking like that for?

GAUTRON: Because . . . here's what it is . . . that Grelu of yours won't eat me . . . I mean, he's not ten feet tall, right? All right then! Since he's here, I'm going to go get him and no nonsense about it . . . I'll tell him, I'm with your wife now and she's going to have my kid . . . I'm living with her on such-and-such street, at such-and-such a number . . . If you're not some kind of goof-off, you'll report us and have them come get us! . . . That'll do it! So what? They'll lock us up for a while, but you'll be able to get a divorce from him . . . And then our kid will have the same last name as me!

EUGENIA: Oh! But if you're sent to jail!

GAUTRON: What do I care? Just as long as it's not for stealing . . . Are you willing? Come on! We got to take the chance while we got it!

EUGENIA: OK, but I want to stay here with you . . .

GAUTRON: No! This is one of those things that we got to settle just between men. You're going to take off like a good girl, go home and wait for me, while I go talk with him . . .

EUGENIA: Then promise me you'll take it easy . . . and not make any trouble . . . You know, he's not a bad guy . . .

GAUTRON: Don't be scared! OK, I promise I won't make any trouble! Now off you go, Genie baby!

EUGENIA: Just one more thing! Swear to me that whatever happens you won't ever abandon me . . . Swear that you'll always love me . . .

GAUTRON: Are you dumb! Didn't you just hear me? I'm even ready to go to jail for you!

EUGENIA: Oh! You got a big heart, my dear, dear Jean! (*She gives him a prolonged kiss.*) See you!

GAUTRON: See you! (EUGENIA *leaves.*) Waiter!

WAITER (*coming in*): What can I do for you?

GAUTRON: Say, isn't that Mr. Grelu in there in the side room?

WAITER: That's right!

GAUTRON: Would you mind telling him that there's somebody here who's got to speak to him right away. (*The* WAITER *goes out.* GAUTRON *sits down muttering to himself.*) Oh! Now we're going to see . . . I'll take care of you, Mr. Grelu.

Scene 2

GAUTRON, GRELU, *and the* WAITER.

GAUTRON (*seeing* GRELU *appear in the doorway and coming forward hesitatingly, his forehead wrinkled and his eyes betraying suspicion*): Mr. Leon Grelu, if you please!

GRELU (*curtly*): Never heard of him.

GAUTRON: But they told me . . .

GRELU: The only Grelu I know is Leonidas Grelu . . . and that's me!

GAUTRON: Well, then, you're the one I want to see anyhow . . . If you'd be willing to have a drink with me . . . I've got to have a talk with you . . .

GRELU (*curt as ever*): Go ahead, I'm listening.

GAUTRON: It's with regard to your Missus, Eugenia!

GRELU (*bursting out enthusiastically*): Oh! Eugenia! It's okay if you come from Eugenia! Should have said so right off! Oh! No, that's a riot! You won't believe it, but at first I took you for a police fink! Oh! So you're here from Eugenia! Then that means you're one of her brothers! You wanted me to have a drink with you just now! Now I'm going to buy you a drink so we can drink to Eugenia's health! It just so happens that I've got some dough . . . It don't happen every day, but my skinflint of a landlord just paid me my month's rent today! You're really flabbergasted by that, eh? Nothing easier once you know how! You tell Eugenia how it's done! All you got is a bed, a table, and a chair, just like me, right? So they can't lay their hands on your belongings . . . You don't have any! They give you your notice . . . You don't get out . . . They've got to throw you out. Then you go find old money bags, and you tell him, "It'll cost you eighty francs to kick me out in the street . . . Give me forty, and I get out of my own accord!" He always gives it to you, and you start again somewhere else three months later . . . It's a regular sort of income!

GAUTRON: That's not what I came here for . . . I wanted to tell you . . .

GRELU (*sitting down*): Stop . . . not until we've clinked glasses . . . Waiter, two absinthes!

GAUTRON: Not for me, I don't drink . . .

GRELU (*pointing to the bottle of wine*): Just that cheap swill, ugh! Better swear off it! The thing to do is drink absinthe! Absinthe is good for your health . . . Like vinegar for pickling cucumbers! Hey! Pal, you was flabbergasted when you found out my name was Leonidas . . . You see, I'm a member of a Club, the E-gal-i-tar-i-ans, I'm an anarchist . . . I couldn't be caught with a name like Leon, it's a name for a priest, it's a name for a papist! (*While the* WAITER *serves the absinthe, he tosses two twenty-franc coins on the table.*) How about that, eh? Pretty wild, to spend the proprietor's coin, eh? (*To the* WAITER.) Take it out of that! (*He drinks.*) To your health! But here I am yakking away . . . Come on, it's something else altogether . . . tell me what's up? How's Eugenia doing?

GAUTRON: Eugenia's doing fine! Listen, you strike me as a decent guy, I'm not going to beat around the bush! After she left you, she moved in with me . . . Now it works out she's going to have a kid . . . I'm here to ask you to bring charges against me so she can get a divorce.

GRELU: Hey now! My sincere congratulations, comrade . . . What's your name?

GAUTRON: Gautron!

GRELU: Comrade Gautron! Well then! What do you expect me to do about it? I lived with Eugenia in a free union, because as for that little sideshow in front of the mayor, a trinket vendor who stuck a pretty colored ribbon across his belly button especially for the occasion, well, you got to realize the marriage ceremony just didn't count for me! It was just a big joke! So I lived with her in a free union. When she had enough, she just left . . . Then she took up with you! That's her business! I can't do nothing about it! I wash my hands of the whole thing!

GAUTRON: But what about the law! . . .

GRELU: The law? Don't know any such thing! The only thing I know is freedom, comrade! Eugenia is free, and so am I! Equality, that's the only true law! I gave a speech on the subject at the last meeting of my social studies Club, the E-gal-i-tar-i-ans, and I can tell you . . .

GAUTRON (*growing irritated*): Listen, buddy, those stories of yours are beginning to get on my nerves. You lost interest in your wife, but she suits me just fine! And, you know what, I don't want the kid that's on the way to be called Grelu . . . My wife will get a divorce, take Gautron's word for it, and you'll agree to it, or else . . . (*He is on his feet, his hand raised;* GRELU *pulls back to the other end of the table clutching his glass, which he quickly drains.*) Well now! Did you get that?

GRELU: Look here, pal, it strikes me as pretty funny for you to come tell me all about your family troubles as if that I give a damn, Eugenia got herself a bulge in the belly, that's her problem! In nine month's time, they'll be work for Mrs. Pop-'em-Out, alias Watch-by-the-Crack, but not for me! Since you're getting up on your high horse, I'll take off, I don't like scenes! And then, anyhow, say your kid was called Grelu, you know, Grelu's as good a name as Gautron! Now I don't hold no grudge against you! Once I've found a new place, if you feel like it and want to be friendly, no reason why any of this should stop you from dropping by to see me . . . We'll have a bite to eat and drink a glass of grape to the little bugger's health . . . Meantime, so long, comrade! (*He leaves.*)

GAUTRON: (*thinking hard; after a moment's silence, picking up his hat*): You know! He's right! The law! Must be a piss-poor kind of law if it don't allow kids to have the same last name as their fathers!

THE END

NOTE

The first performance of these translations of *Meat-Ticket* and *Little Bugger* took place on April 11, 1983, at the Brooklyn Museum, NY. The plays were directed by Carol Ilson and performed by Jon Kent, C. Peter Goslett, John Birkin, Loretta Ehrhardt, Jill Caryn, and Frank Vitale.

Anatoly Lunacharsky (1928)

LUNACHARSKY ON REVOLUTIONARY LAUGHTER

Anatoly Lunacharsky first set out his ideas on revolutionary comedy in his essay, "We Are Going to Laugh," published in early 1920,[1] at the height of the civil war, just as the tide was beginning to turn in favor of the Bolsheviks. For the Commissar of Education laughter is the expression of the triumph of progressive values over reactionary enemies.

Thus laughter—Lunacharsky argues—is a major weapon of class warfare in the battle of the Soviets for control of Russia, and in his view it has always played a key role in the struggle for the liberation of humanity from the shackles of the past. When the new world conquers a dying old order, the laughter of victory rings out as an expression of strength.

The sources for Lunacharsky's ideas in "We Are Going To Laugh" are many and complex. The Commissar of Education had read widely in the theory and practice of comedy, and he drew upon the classics, medieval and Renaissance masters, enlightenment philosophers, and nineteenth-century Russian social thinkers. While arguing for a distinctly new Soviet form of comedy, Lunacharsky stresses continuity with earlier humanist concepts, going back to the notion of release from constraint found in Roman Saturnalia and in medieval and Renaissance festive holidays. Carnival is at the heart of his theories. He offers a vigorous defense of the Russian popular culture of festivity.

Lunacharsky argues that markedly social and satirical nature of Russian popular culture is a legacy of the traditional Russian buffoons (*skomorokhi*), known for their allusive jests and pointed witticisms. The Commissar of Education is firmly committed to the world of merriment represented by the clown, who was always scorned by the Orthodox church and Tsarist state, but will be acclaimed—Lunacharsky hopes—by the new Soviet republic. His concept of victorious laughter has its roots in traditional notions of the contest between summer and winter in the seasonal cycles of the year, the generational battle between impetuous young lovers and repressive aging parents, and the clash between freedom and ritual bondage. Lunacharsky also finds inspiration in Marxist theory, particularly in the commentary on history and comedy by the twenty-six-year-old Karl Marx based on his reading of the Greeks:

> History is thorough and goes through many phases as it conducts an old form to the grave. The final phase of a world-historical form is comedy. The Greek gods, already tragically and mortally wounded in Aeschylus' *Prometheus Bound*, had to die again comically in Lucian's dialogues. Why this course of history? So that mankind may part from its past happily.[2]

Throughout the 1920s Lunacharsky in his position as Commissar of Education spoke out in favor of Soviet satire, including the plays of Mayakovsky. He encouraged festive holiday celebrations (sports, games, shows, and pageants) and mass spectacles on revolutionary anniversaries re-enacting historic events, and he actively promoted popular culture in its many forms: circus, clowning, musical hall, cabaret, ballroom and modern dancing, song, and film,

–*Slavic and East European Performance* 26, no. 1 (Winter 2006): 58–66.

Stanislavsky, Lunacharsky, and Shaw in Moscow (1931)

In 1929 during an acrimonious debate over the supposed demise of humor and satire, the opponents of laughter—doctrinaire party hacks supporting Stalin and the monolithic state—called for the eradication of satire as something useless and even harmful in the new Soviet society where there never were—and never could be—any vices or foibles. Although no longer Commissar of Education, Lunacharsky came to the defense of satire, and, at the end of 1930 under the auspices of the Academy of Sciences, he established a Commission for the Study of the Satiric Genres, which was to prepare monographs on individual authors and topics as well as a general bibliography.

In January 1931 Lunacharsky read to the Commission at the Academy of Sciences his lecture on "Laughter," in which he discussed the comic culture of the new society and analyzed the special place of satire. Lunacharsky's projected but never written book on the social role of laughter was to include the following topics: the philosophy and psychology of laughter; the concept of the risible; the comic, its aesthetics and philosophy; the theory of satire and humor; the history of the satirical genres in their historical development; the problem of wit; and the problem of irony.[3]

In his lecture on "Laughter," Lunacharsky includes a short section on carnival and its importance in the history of satire as "open mockery." Mikhail Bakhtin was thinking along similar lines at the same time and may have been encouraged by Lunacharsky's essay to make his own in-depth study of carnival in *The World of Rabelais*. The former Commissar would later defend Bakhtin's book on Dostoevsky. For Lunacharsky carnival is a time of abundance and equality for all, in which the lower classes are temporally liberated.

Carnival is a custom that goes back to the distant times of the history of Babylon and comes up to our own days. Carnival plays a huge role in Roman and pre-Roman culture. In carnival there can be found both magical disguise and also the replacement of a more ancient custom—human sacrifice—which represents a cultural phenomenon of immense importance, It is not only a question of replacing a precious sacrifice by a less valuable one, but it also a question of replacing a sacrifice which formerly the aristocratic class made by a sacrifice which the plebeians make. Moreover, carnival served the ruling classes as a kind of safe-valve, since during carnival a certain public freedom was given to the oppressed classes. In ordinary times the lower classes could laugh at the upper classes only on the sly, during carnival open mockery became possible. The organizers of carnival felt that, on the one hand, this was an outlet for feelings of mounting class dissatisfaction, and, on the other, that this outlet was not serious.[4]

Lunacharsky sees revolutionary laughter as a healthy and joyous reaction to a lowering of tension when obstacles are overcome. It is a physiological response of the human mechanism to dissipating pressure. Channeled in an ideologically progressive direction, laughter purges the nightmares of the past.

NOTES

1. Anatoly Lunacharsky, "We Are Going to Laugh" ("Budem Smeyat'sya"), *Vestnik Teatra*, no. 58, March 23–28, 1920. Reprinted in A. V. Lunacharsky, *Sobranie Sochinenii*, vol. 3 (Moscow: Khudozhestvennaya Literatura, 1964), 76–79.
2. "Toward the Critique of Hegel's Philosophy of Law: Introduction," in *Writings of the Young Marx on Philosophy and Society*, trans. and ed. by Lloyd D. Easton and Kurt H. Guddat (Garden City, NY: Doubleday and Company, 1967), 254.
3. "Laughter has always been an extraordinarily important part of social progress. The role of laughter is also great in our struggle, the final struggle for humanity. Therefore we will be happy and proud, if we succeed in tracing and in analyzing in concrete examples the historical development and thus sharpen the weapons of our humorists and satirists." From "O Smekhe," a lecture first given in 1931 and published in 1935. Reprinted in A. V. Lunacharsky, *Sobranie Sochinenii*, vol. 8 (Moscow: Khudozhestvennaya Literatura, 1967), 538.
4. Ibid., 535.

Anatoly Lunacharsky reading the Soviet satirical journal *Chudak* (*The Eccentric*), Vol. 5, 1929

WE ARE GOING TO LAUGH

by

ANATOLY LUNACHARSKY

I often hear laughter. We live in a cold and hungry land, which recently was being torn to pieces. But I often hear laughter, I see laughing faces in the streets, I hear throngs of workers and Red Army men laughing at entertaining shows or at an amusing film. I have heard booming peals of laughter even at the front not far from where blood is being spilt.

That shows that we have a vast reserve of strength, for laughter is a sign of strength. Laughter is not only a sign of strength, it is strength itself. And since we have it, we need to direct it into the right channel.

Until now, despite several attempts, we have not succeeded in creating a satirical literary magazine. Individual caricatures in the ROSTA window series or in the form of placards have been successful, but even here we have not found our own style or a scale worthy of the revolution. Perhaps Demian Bedny is our best laughter-crafter, but he is somewhat of an isolated case in this respect and only gradually and in very small measure is beginning to leave the half-dead columns of the newspaper for the living stage.

All this is nothing compared to the great task of directing the elemental force of popular laughter into a worthy channel.

Laughter is a sign of victory. A subtle thinker says: "There is nothing more festive, sacred, and joyful than the first smile of a child; It means that its psyche is beginning to dominate its organism and surroundings, it indicates the triumph of the first ray of consciousness."

Spencer, Sully, Bergson and others have maintained with absolute certainty that laughter signifies the discharge of inner tension as the result of a feeling of one's own superiority, as the result of a simple solution to some sort of problem in real life.

As long as man is weak in the face of his enemy, he does not laugh at him, he hates him; if at times a sarcastic smile full of hate appears on his lips, it is laughter poisoned by bile, laughter that rings uneasily. But once what was bowed down grows up straight, laughter rings out louder and stronger. That is indignant laughter, that is irony, biting satire. In this laughter can be heard the crack of the whip and at times the peal of the approaching thunder of the struggle. That is how Gogol began laughing, before he started drying the tears in his eyes, and that is how Saltykov laughed, trembling with indignation.

And what comes after that?

After that laughter becomes more and more contemptuous as the new feels its strengths. This contemptuous laughter—defiant, cheerful, already sensing its victory, already signifying relaxation—is indispensable as a very real weapon. It is the stake that is driven into the freshly killed dark wizard ready to return from the grave, it is the hammering of strong nails into the black coffin of the past.

When you have defeated a vile but powerful enemy, don't think that it is final, especially if what's involved is an entire class and an entire civilization. The enemy

– Translated by Daniel Gerould, New York, 2006.

entangles you from all sides with a thousand toxic threads, and has flung some of those tentacles into your very brain, into your very heart, and, like other hydras, can come back to life. Such threads need to be torn out, need to be extirpated. It cannot be done mechanically, it cannot be done by force, it cannot be done by an operation, which would mean tearing the entire body of a living being to shreds and even then nothing would be accomplished. But it can be done chemically. There is such a substance, such a disinfectant that causes the evaporation of all that noxiousness—it is laughter, the great sanitizer. To do something by means of the comic means to inflict a wound in the vital nerve itself. Laughter is audacious, laughter is blasphemous, laughter kills with the venom of poisoned arrows.

And in our time, when we have overthrown the gigantic enemy only in Russia, when we are indeed entangled by the threads of the former civilization, still poisoning all our air, when on all sides that same enemy exults and awaits the moment to land a new blow—at such a time, without letting go of the sword in one hand, we can take in the other hand a subtle weapon—laughter.

Will we find among us actors for the great social comedies, will we find among us satirists who could anew shake off all the detritus of the past? Will it be enough to revive the old laughter from Fonvizin to Chekhov?

We shall not immediately set our sights on doing something great and at the same time we shall not content ourselves only with foreign works, only with our former literature—we are alive and should create; if we are not immediately up to creating on a grandiose scale (remember: we are creating the grandiose in another theatre—the theatre of military operations and international relations, we are creating the grandiose in the field of national economy), then we shall start on a small scale.

If we already have among us interesting, successful attempts at parodies, vaudeville couplets, satirical jabs, caustic diatribes, why wouldn't satirical theatre simply be an extension of that?

Long live the jesters of his majesty the proletariat! If even their fools sometimes, with a grimace, told the truth to czars, they remained slaves all the same. The jesters of the proletariat will be the workers' brothers, their beloved, joyful, smartly dressed, lively, talented, vigilant, eloquent advisers.

What's to keep that from actually happening? At fairs, in the squares of cities, at our political rallies, why shouldn't there appear, as a beloved figure, the figure of some kind of Russian Petrushka, some sort of popular town crier, who could make use of the inexhaustible treasures of Russian facetious sayings, of the Russian and Ukrainian languages with their truly titanic strength in the realm of humor? Why shouldn't there ring out such a catchy, danceable tune, such a rousing Russian humorous song, and why shouldn't all of that run through the revolution, shaking everything with acerbic laughter?

A satire studio, a satire theatre is what we need. This will enable us to begin to bring together the best of the young professionals with the people and to begin a selection of the best popular amateur forces in this guild of artists from the people, which we must organize.

Comrades, organize a brotherhood of rollicking red buffoons, a guild of truly popular jesters, and let help be provided to you by even our party publicists, in whose essays there sometimes sparkles such splendid laughter, and our party poets, writers and proletarian poets, as well as those of the old generation, whose hearts have already begun to beat in unison with the thunderous heartbeats of the revolution.

Let visual artists help, by devising special costumes, special kinds of compact, movable scenery, platforms, wagons for strolling buffoons. Let musicians help, by creating in Russian cadences, in the Russian manner new humorous, satirical, dance-inflected, easily memorized couplets.

The Russian church paved the way for the autocracy and hated gudok-players and rollicking buffoons. They represented ancient, republican, pagan Rus, free of asceticism, and now it should truly go back to that, only in a totally new form, having passed through the crucible of much, much civilization, possessing factories and railroads, but equally free, communal and pagan.

The French kings and Cardinal Richelieu once trembled upon hearing beneath the windows of their palaces the vaudevilles of olden times, the biting tales of bards from the common people. The Italian revolution gave birth to carnival masks like the Turinese marionette Gianduia.

Russian revolutionary laughter will have excellent precursors.

Embark boldly on this course, young artists of the stage, of the word, of the brush. The shades of Swift and Henrich Heine bless you; somewhere in the grass beneath the hedge, forgotten, lies the heroic whistle of Dobroliubov.[1] Find it, and may it emit ringing trills above the heads of the awakened people and of their enemies who, just barely overthrown, still nourish evil hopes.

NOTE

1. Nikolai Dobroliubov (1836–1861), progressive literary critic who founded the satirical journal *Svistok* (*Whistle*) in 1859.

Tadeusz Kantor, *Dead Class* (circa 1975)

ICONOGRAPHIC IMAGES IN THE THEATRE OF TADEUSZ KANTOR

Pictorial inspiration in the theatrical works of Tadeusz Kantor is rich and diverse. Kantor's theatre was overwhelmingly, obsessively visual, and he himself was by training and profession a painter and graphic artist. It is therefore hardly surprising that we can locate many antecedents and affinities from the fine arts for his stage creations. In fact, Kantor—lucid analyst and brilliant theorist of his own work—pointed out these sources himself. From whatever provenance, Kantor's "borrowings" were always transformed into something uniquely his own.

Magisterially self-reflexive, Kantor incorporated motifs from his own art work into his theatrical compositions; he cited himself and played new variations on images that he created earlier in different contexts. We can consider three of Kantor's major works—*The Dead Class* (1975), *Wielopole, Wielopole* (1980), and *Let the Artists Die* (1985)—as a trilogy illustrating the quintessence of his iconography. Each had a long period of incubation, and collectively they represent the summation of the Polish artist's lifelong immersion in pictorial imagery.

The first of Kantor's iconographic sources is personal and self-perpetuating, as the artist repeats and modifies from event to event—exhibit, *emballage*, happening, theatre—certain objects and activities: chair, umbrella, suitcase, mannequin, packing, washing, journeying, which he has accumulated in his storehouse of images. A second type of inspiration we may call international. Kantor stressed his appropriation of whatever he could use at any given moment from the various twentieth-century avant-gardes: Craig, Appia, Futurism, Dada, Constructivism, Bauhaus, Oskar Schlemmer, Surrealism. Having studied these historical "Isms" and absorbed their lessons, Kantor went beyond them, rejecting the institution of what he called the "Omnipresent Avant-Garde," finding its routines as conformist as the orthodox theatre.

A third earlier pictorial tradition—that of Symbolism—was one to which Kantor remained loyal; he was a living part of this tradition and its present-day representative. In this respect he was the heir of a specifically Polish tradition in the fine arts associated with the city of Cracow. For all its international dimensions, Kantor's entire career and work were centered around Cracow; Wielopole, the town where he was born and that served as his nexus of memory, is not far distant. Kantor attended the Cracow Academy of Fine Arts from 1934 to 1939, later becoming a professor there for two brief periods. It was in Cracow that in 1938 he put on his first play, Maeterlinck's *Death of Tintagiles*, and it was there that he established the clandestine Independent Theatre during the Nazi Occupation. Then after the liberalization of 1956 and the break with Stalinist control of the arts in Poland, Kantor opened his theatre, Cricot 2 in the Cracow art gallery Krzysztofory. And in 1980, in recognition of his worldwide fame, Cracow gave him a new larger theatre and a special museum, called Cricoteque, devoted to his work. No matter how much he may have traveled, Kantor was a Cracow artist who stayed close to his roots in the ancient Polish city renowned for its tradition in the visual arts and for its painterly theatre.

It is Kantor as a Cracow artist drawing upon the city's unusual heritage that I wish make the center of this study of his iconography. Cracow, which had declined from its former glory as Poland's capital in the Middle Ages and Renaissance into a sleepy provincial seat under the Hapsburgs and Austrian rule (during the partitions of Poland) came to life in the late 1890s and became the artistic breeding ground for innovation in the fine arts, particularly for the new modernist-Symbolist movement. And it was the

—*Sacred Theatre*, ed. Daniel Gerould, Bettina Knapp, and Jane House (New York: 1989).

headquarters for a number of multi-talented artists, such as the painter-playwright, Stanisław Wyspiański, whose play *The Wedding in* 1901 ushered in modernism in the Polish theatre, and the painter-poet, Jacek Malczewski, who first studied and then taught at the School of Fine Arts. Stirring up controversy at the helm of the new movement was the playwright and novelist Stanisław Przybyszewski, back from Germany and Scandinavia to edit the new journal *Life*. He also functioned as a pioneering art critic, introducing the work of his Norwegian friends, Edvard Munch and Gustav Vigeland, and helping to bring about the European discovery of El Greco and Goya, then little known outside of Spain.

Born in 1915 when this modernist current was still very much alive in Poland, Tadeusz Kantor grew up painting and drawing under the influence of Wyspiański and Malczewski, and he studied stage design at the Cracow Academy of Fine Arts (from which he graduated in 1939) with Karol Frycz, a painter, designer, director, and theatre manager, as well as a disciple of Craig and Wyspiański. Kantor's second production at the underground theatre during the occupation was Wyspiański's *Return of Odysseus* in 1943,

As painter, artist, man of the theatre in the Cracow modernist tradition—in which poetry, drama, and literature are cultivated in symbiosis with the visual arts—Kantor can be seen as a custodian of the past, which he preserved by the radical transposition and deformation necessary to give it new life. Kantor's theatre was a theatre of retrieval—both of the artist's past and of the artistic past—in the form of iconographic images from the Cracow tradition. External resemblance is not the issue; Kantor did not aim to reproduce faithfully on stage celebrated paintings from the past, but rather to refashion them for his own aesthetic premises and purposes.

For Kantor, as for the turn-of-the-century Cracow modernists, art was a religion, theatre a spiritual voyage—a journey into the past undertaken by making contact with the dead. Instead of a *theatrum mundi*, Kantor like his Cracow predecessors, created a *theatrum mortis*. As it had been for the Symbolists, his central theme was the interpenetration of death and life. The stage for Kantor was a special place, a point of transition between the other world and this world, a passage through which the dead can enter our life, not as ghosts or unreal figures, but as tangible beings. Shifting fragments of the past, floating images of a life that no longer exists are called up by what Kantor referred to as "the negatives of memory." The Polish artist himself, whose presence on stage violated a central convention of theatrical illusion, was the master of ceremonies at a dramatic séance at which the dead are called forth.

In its earlier sacred phase, Polish Symbolism dealt with the artist's mission and the charismatic chosen individual. In its later manifestations there was a change of emphasis toward the profane, toward banal, ordinary characters and experience, including the grotesque and the aesthetics of ugliness (and its power to provoke laughter). Both currents are present in Kantor's work, which combined the sacred and the profane. "But isn't profanation the best and perhaps the only way of making a ritual live?" the Polish artist asked. He had a preference for "degraded objects" and "reality of the lowest order," trash so useless and inadequate that it makes a "hole" for the imagination. The grotesque helps the artist penetrate through the outer layer to reach the sacred essence.

Wielopole, Wielopole, which was created and first presented in the church of Santa Maria in Florence, makes explicit use of religious iconography; crucifixion, resurrection, redemption are constantly recalled, although blocked from ever being completed as a cycle. Death and rebirth, taken from both Greek and Christian mythologies, are likewise central to Wyspiański's dramas, such as *November Night* and *Acropolis*, where the playwright cross-cuts characters from Homer and the Bible with heroes of Polish history. In *Wielopole, Wielopole*, Kantor invokes Leonardo da Vinci's *Last Supper* (during some of the rehearsals he had a reproduction in hand), but the Biblical scene is subject to profanation. The guests accuse one another of stealing the soup, and soldiers encircle the table, interrupting the ceremony and preventing any hope of change through mythic re-enactment.

In Kantor's dark vision, repetition plays a decisive role. The vicious circle of repeated brutality and boredom cannot be broken; the same sequences of trite words and gestures come back again and again, and the whole "show" assumes the form of a round dance, or circular procession. The living dead appear tied to the endlessly repetitious rituals of Polish history and culture, to the fixed images of old myths out of which they would like to break, but are unable. Determined by Poland's political history and the treasury of national memories, the dramatis personae cannot get off the treadmill of horrors. Here the weight of myth is oppressive, comprising patterns of national behavior and experience that have been perceived as an inescapable destiny. Archetypes spring from a national collective unconscious that enchains all Poles. In Kantor's theatre, history as fate is a notion to be demystified through irony, sarcasm, and humor.

The living dead and the circular dance are two interrelated motifs highly prominent in the iconography of the Polish turn-of-the-century modernists and Symbolists that Kantor made a central part of his theatre. In a revival of medieval imagery, so favored at that time, the round dance became a modern version of the *danse macabre*. This vicious circle, hopeless in its circularity, is emblematic of the closed cycle of birth, life, and death in which beginning and ending are joined, making impossible any action that could bring a resolution to the inevitable turning of the wheel. The results are the monotonous rituals of regressive behavior that recall children's games. In *The Dead Class* the old men and women have tried to murder the memory of their childhood, and now each must carry about attached to his or her body the mannequin of the child that was killed, as they all return to the school benches and repeat endlessly the lessons they could never learn.

A sense of history weighs heavily upon the characters of *Wielopole, Wielopole*, recalled to life from the last days of the Hapsburg Empire. The past suffocates the present, creating a claustrophobic sense of helplessness in the face of what has been and what will be again. Daily life repeats sacred history in ironic and debased forms. The Biblical myths of Golgotha and Calvary, the story of the Passion are enacted over and over again, as crucifixion is inflicted on many different characters—without anything being changed, or anything being learned. As controller of the séance, Kantor supervised these rites of repetition whereby a reality gone forever is constantly restaged. *Let the Artists Die* deals specifically with the problem of the creative personality in his relations to society and with the creative process itself as seen in the workings of memory. In fact, all Kantor's work was about the artist, about Kantor himself and his reclaiming of the past and its dead through the creative life. "But my theatre is not my autobiography," the Polish artist insisted. Despite the many references to Kantor's family and the events of his life, his family as it appears in his plays is "suspect, mean, reduced to the lowest rank of reality."

Now it is time to look more closely at the painters whose imagery appears reborn in Kantor's theatre. In the work of Jacek Malczewski, men, women, and children are portrayed as subject to an ominous and mysterious universe in which impenetrable forces control man's destiny. Yet in all his paintings the human figures are also rooted in concrete social and political times and places: nation, town or village, plot of land. In other words, Malczewski's view is both abstract and existential on the one hand and precise and contextual on the other.

The artist himself often appears in his own pictures, a wanderer attempting to return home to the lost paradise of his childhood and the house of memories where time past can be recaptured. Kantor will make a similar appearance. It is interesting to note that whereas the physical presence of the artist in his own work has long been accepted in the visual arts, it was always thought to be impossible in the supposedly objective form of drama—until the time of Symbolism (for example, Mayakovsky's autoperformance in *Vladimir Mayakovsky, A Tragedy*). For Malczewski and the Polish Symbolists, significance is to be found in the autobiographical connection of the artist to a particular spot on this earth and to its local traditions and folklore. The process of recollection is nurtured by deep attachment to that past and those customs. Kantor continues this tradition, in *Wielopole, Wielopole* returning to his native town and the hidden forces that direct the creative life. For the first time in the dramatis personae of *Let the Artists Die* there appears the following character at the head of the list: "I, a real person, the Prime Mover," played by Tadeusz Kantor, who calls forth and watches three other selves. These are "I-Dying," "The Author of the Stage Persona," and "I-When I Was Six." Such interplay among different phases and parts of a single personality recalls the monodramas developed by Saint-Pol-Roux in France and Nikolai Evreinov in Russia at the turn of the century.

In Malczewski's country of memories, the artist-dreamer surrounded by phantoms and lost in recollections, is no less obsessed by the nation's struggle for independence—and tormented by his inability to act in the face of Poland's tragic history and continuing enslavement. Consider Malczewski's large canvas, *Melancholy* (1890–94), cited by Kantor as a work he admires. Its vortex of swirling human bodies provides an image of the ages of man's life (a favorite Symbolist motif), from childhood through maturity to old age, but it also offers images of the suffering of Poland. For example, the elderly men wear the gray overcoats of those exiled to Siberia following the crushing of the January Uprising of 1863. In *Wielopole, Wielopole* the figure of the deportee (cranking an old wooden musical instrument), who has returned from Siberia, is similarly dressed and alludes to the same historical experience.

The contemplative painter seated at the easel in the background is Malczewski, the artist who is creating the scene, while the enthralled figure in the foreground is his double, who unknown to his creator is taking part in the whirling procession, the ever-renewed yet ultimately ineffectual struggle for freedom and independence. Beyond the open window—a frame for transitions from earthly life to another dimension of being—is the woman in black, both Polonia in mourning and also the figure of death looking in and waiting for the moment to strike. The woman behind the window is a recurring iconographic figure in Kantor, appearing in *The Dead Class* as well as in *Wielopole, Wielopole*. Claustrophobic in its anxieties, *Melancholy* shows mankind isolated in dreams and the artist imprisoned in his art. Each figure, each group is forever separated from those nearest. Rings of separation radiate outward concentrically, cutting off communication, as circles within circles enclose all within fixed boundaries of memory and tradition. The rings of history endlessly repeat themselves; art is such a ring, cutting off the artist from reality. In another large canvas, *The Vicious Circle* (1895–97), Malczewski again presents the dance of life that is a dance of death, while in a series of

Melancholy by Jacek Malczewski (1890–94)

The Vicious Circle by Jacek Malczewski (1895–97)

paintings entitled *Thanatos*, he explores the Symbolist penchant for uniting Eros and Thanatos by portraying the winged angel of death as an attractive semi-nude androgyne, who often appears at a gate that serves as the threshold between this transitory life and eternity.

In *Wielopole, Wielopole* as well as in *Let the Artists Die*, Kantor has built a gate or door (that will be placed prominently at the rear of the stage) through which the characters out of the past seek admission, through which recollection flows, through which the dead can enter the "poor room of memory" and repeat the words they used in life. In *Let the Artists Die*, the androgynous angel, Thanatos, has been metamorphosized and degraded to a cabaret whore, on whose shoulders black wings are attached during the play, and who then rides a skeletal horse, waving the black flag of death—or perhaps of anarchy. In this image the whore becomes one of the horsemen of the Apocalypse, evoking the painting *War* by the Swiss proto-Symbolist, Arnold Böcklin (and the various woodcuts of Dürer which were his inspiration.)

Constant transformation is a cardinal principal of Symbolist art; nothing stays itself for long or can be unequivocally defined. Likewise people and objects in Kantor's theatre undergo perpetual metamorphosis, change shape and size, become their own opposites, remain forever variable and ambiguous. The standing camera on a tripod in *Wielopole, Wielopole* used for taking portraits (of the recruits, of the bride and groom, of the family) becomes a machine gun. By taking photos, it kills; by fixing reality forever, it renders that reality dead. Art is death unless it does more than reproduce. In a reversal of this murderous shot from the camera-machine-gun, the faded old photograph of the group of recruits repeatedly grows animated.

One of Kantor's most striking transformations occurs in *Let the Artists Die*, in which the late medieval wood and stone carver from Nuremberg, Viet Stoss (in Polish, Wit Stwosz), who spent twelve years in Cracow doing a great altar for Saint Mary's Church, has turned into a fin de siècle bohemian artist wearing what Kantor called a Toulouse-Lautrec or Picasso cape. As the artist and the prostitute dance the tango, they recall the black-clad couple in *We and the War* (1917–23) by the Polish Art Nouveau painter, Edward Okuń. The idea of making Wit Stwosz a dramatic character came to Kantor when his friend, Dr. Karl Gerhard Schmidt, a banker and gallery owner, suggested his native Nuremberg as the site for the Polish artist's new production. The 450th anniversary of Wit Stwosz's death occurred in 1983, but Kantor, declaring that "Art hates celebrations and anniversaries," wanted to establish an anti-commemorative and non-reverential tone. To avoid the expected, Kantor uses his technique of "associative montage"—a form of cultural syncretism whereby different personal, historical, and mythical layers are juxtaposed and combined. The title was provided by a remark ("Qu'ils crèvent les artistes!") made by an angry *fille de joie* to a gallery owner in Paris. Other elements come from Zbigniew Uniłowski's novel, *A Shared Room* (1932), that Kantor chanced upon. About the literary bohemia of Warsaw, the book gave Kantor the artist-hero, Lucjan; the author himself, who died in 1937 at the age of twenty-eight, is another *poète maudit*, whose biography, alongside that of the medieval craftsman, is examined in *Let the Artists Die*.

Wit Stwosz is for Kantor a "found character," analogous to a found object (*objet trouvé*); he "came all by himself" halfway through the show. A visitor from the other world, out of his own age, but not yet of ours, the Nuremberg Master occupies a privileged position in the drama. The historical Wit Stwosz was a multitalented innovator, combining in his famous altar triptych both sculpture and painting and capturing the life

We and the War by Edward Okuń (1917–23)

of the Middle Ages in his animated figures whose gestures were like those of actors in the theatre. For Kantor, he was "one of the most interesting artists of the period" and "a perfect illustration of the artist's conflict with society." When he returned to Nuremberg after achieving fame and fortune in Cracow, Wit Stwosz was imprisoned for serious financial irregularities, tortured and branded by the executioner by having his cheek pierced with a nail, deprived of his rights, and allowed to die in misery. In a series of surprising reversals, Kantor's decadent bohemian becomes a torturer and creates art by torturing; the literal imprisonment of the Nuremberg craftsman becomes the figurative imprisonment of the modern artist. The construction of the altar—the work of art as a prison—brings the actors to the pillory, revealing their situation in the theatre.

    Let the Artists Die is called a "revue" by its creator; Kantor explained that while he was rehearsing in Italy, the last revue theatre in Milan closed and he wished to continue the tradition. The performance takes the shape of a circus or fairground show (Kantor cites Alexander Blok's *Puppet Show* as another source), in which dying artists are intermixed with members of a traveling theatrical troupe.

    The greatest of Cracow Symbolist artists whose line Kantor continues was Stanisław Wyspiański (1869–1907), a painter, book illustrator, and total man of the theatre. Like Kantor, Wyspiański looked to national folklore and to the village remembered from childhood for his imagery, and as an artisan he made by hand his costumes and objects (which are not props, but the real thing).

Mulches by Stanisław Wyspiański (1898–99)

Wyspiański likewise created a *theatrum mortis* in which death signifies, rather than simple biological annihilation, the torpor and immobility of being mired in the past. The linking of the dance and the wedding, prominent in *Wielopole, Wielopole*, has its origins in Wyspiański's *The Wedding*, where at dawn the drunken guests, weary of waiting for the great revelation that never comes, put down the scythes with which they have armed themselves to fight for national liberation and begin a slow somnambulistic dance that becomes a powerful image of stagnation and hopelessness, death-in-life, the vicious circle from which Poland cannot escape. Presiding over these nocturnal revels is the fantastic figure of the strawman or mulch (the straw cover put over rosebushes in winter) who plays a halting dance melody on a broken stick and conducts a kind of séance. In his painting, *Mulches* (1898–99), Wyspiański had already created a haunting picture of these straw figures in the Cracow city park growing animate and joining the dance of death; they are images of the sleep of the captive nation during the long night of winter and of the dormant seed waiting to be reborn, according to the Eleusinian mysteries of which the painter was an adept.

In *The Wedding*, Wyspiański draws upon folk motifs and village customs, and popular ceremonies, particularly the Polish *szopka* or Christmas puppet show featuring Herod, Death, and the Devil. The characters at the all-night celebration move like puppets and are in fact marionettes in the hands of larger forces, both historical and cosmic, that hover above them and pull their strings. Like Wyspiański, Kantor creates a total, overpowering effect by building the rhythm of his plays out of repeated and broken strains of music to which his figures move like mannequins. Analogous to the images, the music creates an associative montage, contrasting the sacred and the profane, the religious and the popular. In *Wielopole, Wielopole*, Psalm 110 (in a special version prepared by mountaineers from a village church) is juxtaposed to the *Gray Infantry March* and a fragment of Chopin's *Scherzo in B Minor*.

In *Let the Artists Die* a striking effect is produced by the eight ashen-faced generals in faded silver uniforms and the skeletal horse on which the Commander rides to the accompaniment of a well-known match of the Piłsudski legions. (Piłsudski was Poland's nationalist strongman in the 1920s and 30s.) According to Kantor, the generals were patterned after his tin soldiers and childhood nightmares; they move like mechanical automatons, swarm over the room like cockroaches, and fall when pushed by the little soldier in the self-propelled wagon who is the artist at the age of six. The wagon, which his grandfather had bought him in Vienna, he remembered from his childhood. The Apocalyptic charger he had seen at Piłsudski's funeral in 1935, when the hearse was followed by the General's horse. Behind these dreams and reminiscences there is one of Wyspiański's pastels, a preparatory sketch for stained-glass windows in the Cathedral at Wawel Castle in Cracow (never executed), showing Poland's fourteenth-century king, Kazimierz Wielki, in his coffin. The decaying corpse in royal robes, with crown and scepter, is a nightmare image of past glory forever gone and an emblem of *Vanitas vanitatum*.

These parallels between the theatrical images of Tadeusz Kantor and those of his Cracow predecessors at the turn of the century attest to the creative presence of Symbolist iconography and aesthetics in the work of a living practitioner. It would be possible to find many other kinds of visual sources in Kantor's work: for example, in *Wielopole, Wielopole*, after the rape of the bride, when the soldiers throw the doll in the air, Goya's *Blindman's Buff* is cited; and in *Let the Artists Die*, as the crucified artists on the barricade attack the public, Delacroix's *Liberty Guiding the People* is recalled. But above all it is to Polish Symbolist roots that Kantor's theatre remained loyal. In its absolute freedom and originality it pays glorious tribute to the artistic ancestors that it invokes.

BIBLIOGRAPHY

Bablet, Denis, ed. *Les Voies de la création théâtrale XI. T. Kantor: La Classe Morte; Wielopole, Wielopole*. Paris: Éditions du Centre National de la Recherche Scientifique, 1983.

Dobrowolski, Piotr. "Tadeusz Kantor i iluzja powtórzenia." *Przestrzenie Teorii* 8, Poznań, 2008, 105–22.

Fik, Marta. "Umarła Klasa." In *Przeciw, czyli za,* 64–71. Warsaw: Czytelnik, 1983.

Jenkins, Ron. "Ring Master in a Circus of Dreams." *American Theatre* 2, no. 11 (March 1986): 4–11.

Juszczak, Wiesław. *Malarstwo polskie: Modernizm*. Warsaw: Auriga, 1977.

Kantor, Tadeusz, "Tadeusz Kantor." *The Drama Review* 30, no. 3 (T111) (Fall, 1986): 98–198. (Special section of an issue devoted to Polish theatre, including "Tadeusz Kantor's Journey" by Jan Kłossowicz, "The Writings of Tadeusz Kantor: 1956–1985" translated by Michał Kobiałka, "Let the Artists Die? An Interview with Tadeusz Kantor" by Michał Kobiałka, and "Bibliography: Writings by and about Tadeusz Kantor" by Michał Kobiałka.)

———. *Le Théâtre de la mort*, ed. Denis Bablet. Lausanne: L'Age d'Homme, 1977.

———. "The Theatre of Death." *Canadian Theatre Review* (Fall 1977): 33–73.

———. *Wielopole, Wielopole*. Cracow: Wydawnictwo Literackie, 1984.

Kłossowicz, Jan. *Tadeusz Kantor: Teatr*. Warsaw: Państwowy Instytut Wydawniczy, 1991.

———. "Scenariusz przedstawienia, postzapis." *Dialog* 2 (1977): 121–34.

———. "*Umarła klasa*—odtworzenie scenariusza." In *Mgliste sezony*. Warsaw: Wydawnictwa Artystyczne i Filmowe, 1981.

Marandel, J. Patrice, ed. *Symbolism in Poland: Collected Essays*. Detroit: Detroit Institute of the Arts, 1984.

Miklaszewski, Krzysztof. "*Let the Artists Die*. Tadeusz Kantor Speaks about the Production." *Le Théâtre en Pologne/The Theatre in Poland* 1–3 (1986): 11–16.

———. *Encounters with Tadeusz Kantor*. Ed. George Hyde. London: Routledge, 2002.

Morawiec, Elżbieta. "Wyspiański a Teatr Śmierci Kantora." *Dialog* 2 (1979): 141–48.

Morawińska, Agnieszka. "Polish Symbolism." In *Symbolism in Polish Painting, 1890–1914*, 13–34. Detroit: Detroit Institute of the Arts, 1984.

Pleśniarowicz, Krzysztof. "Kogo posadzono w tej klasie?" *Zeszyty Naukowe Uniwersytetu Jagiellońskiego* 738, no. 58 (1985): 221–30.

———. "Na krawędzi pustki." *Teksty* 4 (46) (1979): 85–101.

Podraza-Kwiatkowska, Maria. "Polish Literature in the Epoch of Symbolism: Młoda Polska." In *Symbolism in Poland: Collected Essays*, edited by J. Patrice Marandel. Detroit: Detroit Institute of the Arts, 1984.

———. *Somnambulicy + Dekadenci—Herosi*. Cracow: Wydawnictwo Literackie, 1985.

Puzyna, Konstanty. "My, umarli." In *Półmrok*, 102–14. Warsaw: Państwowy Instytut Wydawniczy, 1982.

Puzyna, Konstanty, Tadeusz Różewicz, Andrzej Wajda. "Rozmowy: O *Umarłej klasie*." *Dialog* 2 (1977): 135–42.

Le Théâtre en Pologne/The Theatre in Poland 1, 1981. Special Issue, "Kantor—*Wielopole, Wielopole*."

Wyka, Kazimierz. *Tanatos i Polska, czyli O Jacku Malczewskim*. Cracow: Wydawnictwo Literackie, 1971.

Henry Monnier's Self-Portrait as *Monsieur Prudhomme* (1871)

HENRY MONNIER AND THE ÉROTIKON THÉÂTRON:
THE PORNOGRAPHY OF REALISM

Annoyed at the growing bourgeois domination of French cultural life during the Second Empire, a group of irreverent young writers and artists in the early 1860s established a private puppet theatre for invited guests (perhaps inspired by the marionette shows recently produced in the Tuileries Gardens), where they could stage libertine works composed specially for the occasion by members of their circle. The plays were outrageous farces and licentious comedies written in direct defiance of middle-class notions of morality and propriety.

The Érotikon was set up in the entrance hall of the house belonging to Amadée Rolland, the financial backer of the enterprise, at 54 rue de la Santé in the Batignolles district of Paris, hence the venture became known as the Théâtre Érotique de la rue de la Santé. The artistic director, architect, scene painter, and creative force behind the Érotikon was Louis Lemercier de Neuville (known affectionately to his close friends as Lemerdier), who was later to become celebrated as a puppeteer and creator of the Théâtre des Pupazzi, as well as the author of *Histoire anecdotique des marionettes modernes* (1892) and *Souvenirs d'un montreur de marionettes* (1911).

The stage devised by Lemercier for the Érotikon was 16 feet deep and equipped with complicated machinery and thirty-eight painted sets. The eight wooden puppets had hand-carved heads executed by Demarsy, an actor at the Théâtre de la Porte Saint-Martin. The mistresses of the theatre administration made the twelve costumes. All the dialogue for each play was read by the author himself, and the marionettes were worked by Lemercier and Jean Duboys, the co-director and one of the house playwrights.

The gala opening night took place on May 27, 1862, and the select audience included such well-known novelists and poets as Jules Champfleury, Paul Féval, Louis Duranty, Théodore de Banville, and the twenty-two-year-old Alphonse Daudet, as well as a few trustworthy journalists and several actors and actresses from the boulevard theatres and even the Odéon. After the theatrical program, consisting of a prologue entitled Érotikon Théâtron and six plays of varied genres and lengths, there was an elegant supper party provided for the guests, which lasted until two o'clock in the morning.[1]

The highlight of the evening's performances was undoubtedly *The Tart and the Student* (*La Grisette et l'étudiant*) by the celebrated satirist, artist, and playwright, Henry Monnier, then in his 60s, the creator of the immensely popular nineteenth-century cartoon figure, Monsieur Joseph Prudhomme. The embodiment of prosperous bourgeois pomposity, with a swelling paunch and a platitude for every occasion, Monsieur Prudhomme was a French cousin of Mr. Pickwick and a direct ancestor of Jarry's Père Ubu. Throughout his career, Monnier recorded Monsieur Prudhomme's life and sayings and sketched his imposing exterior.

The Érotikon offered Monnier an opportunity to provide stronger fare than his usual audiences would tolerate and to pursue to its logical end certain fundamental tendencies of his art. Frightened at his own daring, Monnier, with an almost Prudhommesque sense of discretion, denied the authorship of *The Tart and the Student* even while he was reading all three roles—student, tart, and eavesdropping Monsieur

—The Drama Review: TDR 25, no. 1 (T89) (March 1981): 17–24.

Henry Monnier's Érotikon Théâtron (circa 1860)

Prudhomme—and later opposed publication. The play did come out in a special limited edition in Brussels (probably in 1866) as *L'Enfer de Joseph Prudhomme*, along with another of the author's salacious works, *The Two Dykes* (*Les Deux gougnottes*), accompanied by a frontispiece by Monnier and Monsieur Prudhomme's ornate signature.

Henry Monnier (1799–1877) began his career during the Restoration and July Monarchy as a book illustrator and caricaturist, giving a vivid and faithful picture of French middle-class life in his albums and series of lithographs such as *Moeurs administratives* and *Rencontres parisiennes*. He excelled at vignettes of clerks and lawyers, portrayed the simple-minded joys of bourgeois family life, and was a pioneer in the depiction of the special Parisian type of "loose woman" known as the grisette. So called because of the gray costumes they once wore, the grisettes were poor shopgirls and milliner's assistants who, to supplement their meager salaries, became the mistresses of students or artists, officers or rich older men.

A gifted mimic, entertainer, and raconteur, Monnier often acted out the little scenes that he had sketched, playing all the roles himself. Urged by his friends who had been delighted by his private performances in their salons, Monnier began to write down his sketches, publishing his first collection of dramatic dialogue in 1830 as *Scènes populaires dessinées à la plume*. In the preface, the author insists that he is only the editor of his characters' actions and gestures and has simply recorded what he has overheard. Fascinated by the ordinary banality and stupidity of the petty bourgeois world that he chronicles, Monnier presents scrupulous transcriptions, remaining absolutely faithful to everyday reality, without any artistic heightening or stylization. Théophile Gautier praised Monnier for creating the theatrical equivalent of the daguerreotype or stenographic report, but precisely for that reason his best plays were thought to be undramatic and unplayable according to the critical opinion of the time. Therefore Monnier's highly original dramatic scenes had to be adapted by professional men of the theatre to make them conform to the standards of the Scribean vaudeville with its tricky plotting and clever couplets.

Monnier was a total realist long before the movement existed, and his careful reproduction of moronic banal chatter anticipates Ionesco (who, in fact, mentions Monnier in *Notes and Counternotes* as a forerunner to the Romanian playwright Caragiale). To give a more complete and faithful picture of the characters whom he had already drawn in words and images, Monnier himself went on the professional stage and tried his hand as an actor. When in 1831 at the Théâtre du Vaudeville he played five different roles in the comedy *La Famille improvisée* (by Ouvert, Brazier, and Oupeuty), Monnier was the theatrical sensation of the season. But as a self-taught actor with an unconventional approach, Monnier in the long run was not able to succeed in the French theatre, then dominated by artificial declamatory techniques of acting, although he did appear at the Odéon in 1852 as Monsieur Prudhomme in his own play, *Grandeur et decadence de Monsieur Joseph Prudhomme*.[2]

Monnier's contemporaries were fascinated by his creation. Balzac had various unrealized theatrical projects to use Prudhomme as the hero of a comedy; Baudelaire called him "a monstrously true type"; and Daumier did one of his best series of lithographs on the subject of Prudhomme as the quintessential smug bourgeois.

Before his participation in the Érotikon Théâtron, Monnier had frequently treated the theme of the tart and the student in both his graphics and his writings. *Les Grisettes* is the title of a series of lithographs produced by Monnier in the period 1827–29,[3] and in the first edition of *Scènes populaires* of 1830, the short dialogue between the artist Charles and his mistress, the shopgirl Fanny, called *The Street Girl* (*La Petite fille*), tells exactly the same story as *The Tart and the Student*, even including many of the same lines, but without the sexual episodes or Monsieur Prudhomme's interruptions. Freed of all constraints of propriety and censorship, Monnier was able for the first time to develop in full honesty the sketch he had begun some thirty years earlier, now showing it as it would actually have occurred and in the language the characters would really have used. Realism is here pushed to the point of obscenity; a scrupulously observed and stenographically recorded account of the tart's visit to the student inevitably leads to pornography. For the Érotikon Monnier produced his most faithful and successful portrait of the grisette, sensual, vulgar, charming, tender, generous, quick to be hurt and equally quick to forgive and laugh.

NOTES

1. For the history of the Érotikon, see Gilbert Signaux, "Préface," *Le Théâtre Érotique du XIXe siècle* (Paris: Les Classiques Interdits, 1979), 7–12. The volume contains *La Grisette et l'Étudiant*, 13–27.
2. For details of Monnier's life and career, see Anne-Marie Meininger, "Préface," *Scenes populaires: Les Bas-fonds de la société* (Paris: Gallimard, 1984), 7–37, and Patricia Mainardi, "Henry Monnier: The Comedy of Modern Life," *Exhibition Catalog* (New York: Art Gallery of the Graduate Center, the City University of New York, 2005), 4–5.
3. On the origins of the grisette, see Jerrold Seigel, *Bohemian Paris* (New York: Elisabeth Sifton Books/Penguin Books, 1986), 39–42, and Hanna Manchin, "The Grisette as the Female Bohemian," http://www.mtholyoke.edu/courses/rschwart/hist255-s01/grisette/manchin.htm (June 21, 2006).

Henry Monnier's Érotikon Théâtron (circa 1860)

Martin E. Segal Center Production of *The Tart and the Student*
at the Art Gallery of the Graduate Center, City University of New York (2005)

THE TART AND THE STUDENT

A Play in One Act
by
Henry Monnier

THE STUDENT (Hippolyte)
THE TART (Fanny)
THE VOICE OF MONSIEUR PRUDHOMME

The action takes place in Paris, in a furnished room, on the rue de la Harpe, in 1830 at the earliest, in 1840 at the latest.

STUDENT (*reading a letter*): ". . . Tuesday, at twelve noon, I'll be at your place, if anything a little before rather than after. Love me always the way I love you. Be very good and very sensible, and not too awfully naughty. If we feel like it, we'll do something crazy . . ." (*Speaking.*) Ten past eleven . . . She won't come. (*Reading.*) ". . . Tuesday, at twelve noon . . ." (*Speaking.*) She's not late . . . Put her chair here . . . Eleven thirty! (*Rereading.*) ". . . I'll be at your place if anything a little before rather than after. . . . " (*Speaking.*) Quarter of twelve! . . . (*A knock is heard at the door.*) Who's there?

A LILTING VOICE: Me!

STUDENT (*pretending not to recognize her*): You? Who are you?

THE SAME LILTING VOICE: Me!!

(*He opens the door. Enter the* TART, *red as a lobster that's just climbed six flights.*)

TART: Greetings, doggie. How are you doing? . . . Good gracious, you really are up high! I'm all out of breath. . . . And that concierge of yours who keeps asking me where I'm going, you know what I mean? . . . She makes me keep repeating it so as to get me flustered. . . . Well, I really can't stand that old hunchback! . . . Going to give me a kiss? . . . Let me take off my hat.

STUDENT (*with all the eagerness of a man who's getting horny*): Give it to me, my angel.

TART (*taking off her hat*): There . . . Do you love me, kitty cat? . . . Come give me a kiss.

STUDENT (*holding her in his arms*): I do . . .

TART (*pressing her little mug against her lover's lips*): We're going to behave ourselves, mind what I say!

– *Translated by Daniel Gerould, New York, 1981.*

STUDENT (*who is getting hornier than ever, sticking his tongue in her mouth*): Sure . . .

TART: Ah! not like that, kitty cat, not like that. . . . Ah! you're a nasty boy! . . . Not with your tongue, no, honestly, not with your tongue. . . . Guess what I've got under my shawl. . . .

STUDENT (*who is too horny to guess anything whatsoever*): Suspenders you embroidered for me?

TART (*who, for an instant, has gotten free from her lover and his tonguings, and who flits about the room like a canary*): No. . . . In a jar?

STUDENT: Suspenders . . . in a jar?

TART (*roaring with laughter*): Don't be silly! Those are fruit preserves in the jar, mama sent it to me for winter. . . . You like fruit preserves, don't you, great big tom cat? We'll eat them.

STUDENT (*who's only interested in screwing the* TART): Sure . . .

TART (*stopping in front of the fireplace*): Say! Where's your clock?

STUDENT: At the shop being repaired.

TART: And the glass shade too, I suppose? . . . It's at the pawnshop!

STUDENT: I'm afraid so.

TART (*pouting*): Ah! yes, I know. . . . That was for the other day, with your Madame Whatchamacallit, when you went to Meudon and two-timed me. . . . (*Spontaneously.*) I had some money actually, 25 francs. . . . I'd have lent it to you!

STUDENT (*who has succeeded in pulling her onto a chair*): Don't be silly, now! . . .

TART: Kiss me quick, naughty thing. . . Kiss me! . . . (*He gives her a prolonged tonguing.*) No . . . not like that, doggie, not like that . . . honestly! . . . . Try again. . . . No silly business, kitty cat! . . . honestly! . . . (*He squeezes her ass amorously.*) I don't want any of that . . . no! . . . Get to work! . . . (*He paws her breasts.*) No . . . leave me alone . . . I tell you . . . I'm here to see that you work . . . I'm going to sit next to you . . . (*She jumps up on the chair next to his.*) That's the way . . . be nice and polite . . . Haven't seen you for ages. . . . Kiss me, horrid baddy . . . kiss me better than that. . . . Now just tell me, has that Madame of yours as much of a bust as I've got? . . . .

STUDENT (*with his hands full*): Are you kidding?!

TART (*throwing her shoulders back to make her breasts stick out more*): I'm sure hers don't stand up like mine. . . . You know, you won't find them like that every day of the week, kitty cat! No! . . . Your madamey-dadamy may be better dressed, but she hasn't got my body. . . . Just look at my tits, see how nice and plump they are . . .

(*She pushes them up to the opening in her bodice.*) Do you like my boobs? . . . (*He diddles them with his finger and his tongue.*) Oh! No . . . no touching, monsieur! . . . I want to preserve them for the future. . . . No, honestly . . . Ah! . . . No... kitty cat . . . no . . . Get to work . . . Ah! . . . nasty boy! . . .

STUDENT (*pulling her on his knees, and lifting up her dress*): But I am working.

TART (*defending herself halfheartedly*): I didn't mean that kind of work . . . I want you to be sensible. . . . (*He spreads her thighs.*) Come on! . . . Come on! where are you going like that? . . . What are you fishing for in there? . . . Ah! what a nasty boy you are! what a nasty boy you are! . . . I don't want any of that, no I don't . . . I know you: once you've done it, you'll send me packing . . . No . . . honestly! No . . . I tell you . . . kitty cat . . . No! . . . No!!!! not like that . . . it pulls my tummy. . . (*He keeps jacking her off.*) Leave my button alone . . . my little bitty button . . . All right! . . . Ah! . . . yes! . . . (*In a scarcely audible whisper.*) Get to work . . .

STUDENT (*using his prick instead of his finger*): I'll work later. . .

TART (*who is beginning to blank out*): No . . . kitty cat . . . I know what you did the other time . . . No! Oh! no! . . . Why do I always have to give in to you? . . . Yes . . . You want to do it . . . Ah! . . .

STUDENT (*pushing his point*): Yes . . .

TART: On the bed, doggie . . . on the bed . . . it's more comfortable doing it on the bed . . . (*He carries her over to the bed, and begins the attack with a certain frenzy.*) Wait . . . wait till I pull my dress up underneath . . . do you want to tear all my things? . . . There . . . now I'm ready . . . Go ahead . . . Not that way, though! You're heading in the wrong direction. . . . Let me guide it in . . . There now! . . . Wait, my big baby . . . Oh! . . . wait! . . . Let's do it a long time, a long, long time; right, little puppy dog? . . . Now you're in . . . can you feel me?

STUDENT (*moving his loins vigorously*): Yes, I feel you . . .

TART (*starting to come, and unable to hold back her sighs of bliss, which sound like the grunts of a baker's assistant beating the dough*): Huh! . . . huh! . . . huh! . . . It's so good! . . . I'm coming! . . . Keep going! . . . Huh! . . . Ah! it's so good. . . .

STUDENT (*starting to come, but more silently*): Dearest angel! . . . I love you! . . .

TART (*answering the thrusts of her lover's prick with corresponding thrusts of her ass*): You'll . . . love . . . me. . . al . . . ways, won't . . . you? . . .

STUDENT (*who hasn't yet shot his bolt*): Of course I will! . . .

TART (*at the height of her orgasm, yelling*) Go on! . . . go on! . . . go on! . . . big baby . . . not right away . . . not yet. . . . Ah! it's coming. . . . You're drenching me. . . . Ah! I'm coming, my god, I'm coming! . . . I can feel it in the roots of my hair! . . . Ah! . . . yes! . . . kill me! . . . Ah! kill me . . . Ah! kill me!

VOICE OF MONSIEUR PRUDHOMME: No assassinations in this house, if you please! . . . You! over there, have you about finished your acts of moral depravity? . . .

TART (*still flailing about*): What's that noise over there, next door?

VOICE OF MONSIEUR PRUDHOMME: You are going to drive me to regrettable assaults on my own person . . .

(*The two lovers, who haven't quite finished yet, do not breathe a word, the bed alone speaks for them, eloquently.*)

TART (*in the last convulsions of bliss*): What's that noise over there, next door?

STUDENT (*still grinding away, out of a sense of duty, since he's not as stiff and horny as before*): Some old idiot!

TART (*who is still as hot and horny as ever*): We do it so nice! . . . I'd like to start all over again. . . . Wouldn't you, kitty cat?

STUDENT (*using his finger, to give his prick a breather*): You bet I would . . .

TART (*who is for serious screwing, and not any halfway measures*): Not like that! . . . Polyte, my Lilyte, take your hand off it, take your hand off it. . . . No! I don't want to do it that way. . . . Take your hand off it . . . honestly!

VOICE OF MONSIEUR PRUDHOMME: Hippolyte, take your hand off it!

STUDENT (*to* MONSIEUR PRUDHOMME): Why don't you mind your own goddamn business! . . .

VOICE OF MONSIEUR PRUDHOMME: Very well, Monsieur. . . . You're driving me out of my own bed. . . . I leave the field to you. . . . I am going to finish my siesta in an adjacent room, while you complete your lewd and filthy practices in yours. . . .

STUDENT: Well, that imbecile finally left. . . . What were we talking about before?

TART (*who does not let her subject of interest get out of sight or hand*): We were saying, kitty cat, that we were up to no good. . . . I'd like to give you a big hug. . . . Show me your pretty little kisser . . . (*Caressing his balls and tickling his virile member.*) I want to see if you're in a fit state. (*Noticing that he's got a hardon.*) Yes, you're in a fit state, nasty boy! . . . (*Admiringly, and hoping to seize the opportunity.*) It's stiffer than it was just a few minutes ago. . . . And hard! You'd think it was made of steel! How come a great big awful thing like that doesn't rip your tummy up when it goes in! . . . (*She grabs hold of it voraciously and slips it in.*) Wait, doggie, wait. . . . There, now it's in nice and snug. . . . Go ahead! . . . Ah! . . . mama! . . . Ah! mama! . . . mama! . . .

STUDENT (*who is getting his off more quietly, but just as thoroughly*): Ah! Dearest angel! dearest angel!

Monsieur Prudhomme and the Two Lovers,
Martin E. Segal Center Production of *The Tart and the Student*
at the Art Gallery of the Graduate Center, City University of New York (2005)

TART (*swimming in a sea of bliss*): Oh! Do it! do it! .... But just keep on doing it! ... Drive it home, big baby ... drive It home! ... But just shove it in all the way! ... Ah! I can feel every bit of you! ... Ah! mama, mama, it's so good! ... You do it so nice, sweetheart, so nice. ... Are you having as good a time as I am? ... Talk to me, honestly ... Ah! it's so good! ... Tell me you really love me ... but, there, that's it!

STUDENT (*banging away all the time*): I do. ...

TART (*rotating her buttocks*): Tell me yourself. ...

STUDENT (*banging away all the time*): I do. ...

TART (*rotating her buttocks*): Tell me yourself. ...

STUDENT: I really do love you.

TART (*imploring*): Give me your tongue ... your dear sweet little tonguey-tongue-tongue ... (*Imperiously.*) Your tongue! your tongue! Ah! tom cat of mine ... Ah! ah! ... ah! ...

STUDENT: Chickie, my chickie! ...

TART (*half-unconscious*): Your chickie, yes. ... Your sweet little chick ... your ... your ... sweet ... chick. ...

STUDENT: Yes. ...

TART (*using her legs like a nutcracker*): Can you feel how I'm squeezing it? . . . Go to the bottom . . . right to the very bottom. . . . Drive it home, big baby . . . drive it home . . . You'll tell me when it's going to come . . .

STUDENT (*speeding up his thrusts*): Yes . . .

TART (*begging*): Not without me! not without me! . . . Together! . . . come . . . we'll come together . . . all right . . . together! . . . Oh! . . . mama! . . . mama! it's so good! . . . Kill me! . . . kill me! . . . kill me! . . . Oh!

STUDENT (*who has shot his wad*): Yes . . .

TART (*contracting her feet and hands*): Ah! . . . ah! . . . ah! I really came . . . yes! . . . What about you, kitty cat! . . . What about you?

STUDENT (*pulling out his dick*): I did too . . .

TART (*reproachfully*): Ah! You're pulling it out! . . . Why didn't you leave it inside me? . . . I wouldn't have eaten it up, you know! . . . Stay a little longer like before . . . there . . . tummy against tummy. . . Finished already! . . . Ah! that's stupid! . . . It ought to last a whole lifetime. . . .

(*Silence. . . . The two lovers, still interlaced, peck at each other tenderly a bit longer, but without moving their loins. The tart energetically squeezes the student against her breast, sighing and shuddering due to the final tremors of her orgasm; it wouldn't take much to get her started all over again, even now, her hand, skillfully gliding underneath her lover's balls, prepares to tickle them and reawaken the sleeping sperm within; but the student, who has only two shots to his bow, pulls away brusquely from this invitation, jumping out of the bed to the floor.*)

STUDENT: Didn't I tell you I had to go out?

TART (*astounded*): No. . . . See what a nasty man you are. . . . Once you've done it, you send me packing! . . . It's always the same old story. . . .

STUDENT: But since I've got to go out?

TART (*still in bed, and dissolving in tears*): Boo hoo! Boo hoo! . . . Boo hoo!

STUDENT (*annoyed*): Ah! If you're going to start crying, we're going to have a really wonderful time.

TART (*still crying*): And I was so counting on our going out together! . . . Boo hoo! Boo hoo!

STUDENT (*showing impatience*): But since I tell you that I have to do something for my mother!
TART: So your mother's going to be coming here?

STUDENT: Didn't I tell you so?

TART: You told me that the last time. . . . Ah! I'm not at all happy . . . no . . . I have the worst luck. . . . It's like the dress you promised me. . . .

STUDENT: You'll get it! . . .

TART (*jumping down from the bed*): When? . . . In a month of Sundays, I suppose?

STUDENT (*going to his desk*): Look, there it is, take your dress! . . . (*He tosses her a 25 franc piece with an angry gesture.*)

TART (*bursting out with a cry of anguish*): That's not how I wanted it! . . . That's not how . . . Ah! My god! . . . my god! (*She sobs and faints away.*)

STUDENT (*running to her*): Come now! What! Now you're going to get sick! Fanny! Fanny! . . . Poor sweet pussycat . . . say something to me . . . Fanny! Fanny! . . . I beg you! . . . (*He takes her in his arms, and caresses her tenderly.*) You're crying! . . . Stop it! That's naughty! . . . Won't you dry those awful tears as quickly as you can!

TART (*laughing on one side of her face and still crying on the other*): No! I'm not crying anymore . . . I'm laughing. . . . Look! . . . and you cried too. . . . Kiss me, and don't be a bad boy any more, kitty cat. . . . I don't hold it against you any more, but not the least little bit!

THE END

NOTE

The first performance of this translation of *The Tart and the Student* took place on December 12, 2005, as part of the Monnier exhibition, "The Comedy of Modern Life," curated by Patricia Mainardi at the Art Gallery of the Graduate Center, City University of New York, which ran from December 13, 2005, to January 21, 2006. The puppet play was directed by Amy Trompetter and performed by three students from Barnard College: Katherine Coon (Monsieur Prudhomme), Colleen Lucey (The Student), and Lydia Brunner (The Tart).

Ubu Roi, woodcut by Alfred Jarry (1896)

TYRANNY AND COMEDY

Comedy thrives on tyranny. Here is a proposition that can lead in a number of different directions. As a matter of theatre history, we know that farces and light comedies have flourished on the stage under totalitarian regimes and brutal military occupations. Comedy, in such a context, is nothing more than a shallow escape or, perhaps, a tool of manipulation on the part of the authorities. If, on the other hand, we examine the psychology of the innumerable jokes directed at dictators by the victims suffering unjustly at their hands, even in the depths of secret prisons and concentration camps, the comic spirit under tyranny emerges as a positive force, necessary for survival and, indeed, liberating and heroic. Systematic repression induces laughter as a healthy outburst. And provided we define tyranny in the broadest sense, it is surprising how many of the traditional targets of comedy, since its earliest days, have been tyrants. Consider, for example, the *senex* of Roman drama, the pedants and doctors of commedia dell'arte, and all the despotic parents and jealous husbands peopling the stage since the time of Molière and the English Restoration dramatists. Comedy characteristically relishes and ridicules tyrants.

Among possible approaches to the topic, I have chosen to single out one striking phenomenon: the comic portrayal in drama of the all-powerful political tyrant wielding the apparatus of mass oppression and ruthlessly crushing the human rights of others on a vast scale. By using such a peculiarly modern and troublesome test case for standard comic theory, I should like to push back certain supposedly fixed boundaries of comedy and to reformulate some of its laws.[1] Can savage tyranny, with its reign of terror and death, be treated as comical? Can even the indiscriminate victimization of the guiltless be laughable?

Traditional theories say no. According to Plato in the *Philebus*, the object of ridicule must not have the power to harm, or else fear will prevent laughter.[2] In "Notes on the Comic," W. H. Auden finds that Hitler is no fit subject for humor, declaring that we cannot consider comic what we hate.[3] On these grounds, the comic despot who is both hateful and powerful becomes an impossibility. And yet the evidence will show that in actual fact the loathsome dictator is by his very nature grotesquely ludicrous, and the terrible plight of the tyrannized may well be equally preposterous. The arbitrary exercise of absolute power by a deranged tyrant can be a source of comic pleasure to an audience—and comic, not in spite of the arbitrariness, but precisely because of it. The ridiculous and the terrifying coalesce.

In an unusual transformation of an older comic pattern, the clever rogue swindling his gullible victims becomes the twentieth-century tyrant using the totalitarian state to defraud his citizens of their freedom. The modern era of tyrannies (which, according to the French historian Elie Halévy, began in August 1914, when the coercive state first gained total control over man's daily life and thought)[4] has made it possible for the traditional comic relationship of duper and duped to exist on a new scale and in a new dimension—those of the nation and of public life—which had previously been reserved for serious drama. Comic scoundrels like Volpone and Mosca now become heads of state and usurp dictatorial powers; their foolish prey is the masses of people who, out of stupidity and servility, actively collaborate in their own enslavement. The frequent blows and beatings of ancient farce grow magnified and multiplied into large-scale torture and killing.

—*Comedy: New Perspectives*, ed. Maurice Charney (New York: New York Literary Forum, 1978).

During the period between world wars in which Hitler, Mussolini, and Stalin rose to power and turned Europe into a madhouse, a handful of farsighted playwrights, obsessed with a similar vision and themselves witnesses and victims of dictatorship, dramatized the absurd spectacle of tyranny in a number of intensely theatrical works for the stage. Among the most brilliant of these plays about comic tyrants are *Gyubal Wahazar* (1921) and *The Cuttlefish* (1922) by the Polish avant-gardist Stanisław Ignacy Witkiewicz; Jules Romains's *Dr. Knock* (1923); Ernst Toller's *Wotan Unbound* (1923); *Angelica* (1928/29) by the Italian exile Leo Ferrero; *The Naked King* (1933), *The Shadow* (1940), and *The Dragon* (1941) by the Russian children's author Evgenii Shvarts; and Bertolt Brecht's *The Resistible Rise of Arturo Ui* (1941). Here are the principal examples upon which to base any theories concerning comedy and political tyranny.[5]

But it is a mistake to think that the subject is an exclusively twentieth-century one.[6] The Renaissance, another spectacular era of tyrannies, was also productive of comic dictators, as witness Herod the Great, an ever-popular figure of ridicule and loathing since the late Middle Ages, and Shakespeare's Richard III, the prototype for subsequent upstart rogues cheating and killing their way to the top of the political ladder. Writing in 1523 of the German princes of his day, Martin Luther commented that God Almighty must have driven such rulers mad, observing that tyrants "are usually the greatest fools or the worst scoundrels in the world"[7]—a view shared by all the playwrights here under consideration. Already in Luther's formulation we can start to perceive one of the prime reasons why tyranny naturally lends itself to the comic sense of existence: buffoons, swindlers, and demented charlatans, no matter what the scope of their folly and vice, cannot be treated seriously or accorded tragic dignity.

In nineteenth-century czarist Russia, where stagnant institutional despotism prevailed, the small cogs in the machinery of tyranny—themselves both the victims and perpetrators of the oppressive system—become richly comic figures in the works of Nikolai Gogol and Alexander Sukhovo-Kobylin. Fear of sudden arrest and imprisonment, confession to uncommitted crimes, universal mistrust and suspicion in the face of swarms of spies and informers, and gradually deepening terror are all transformed, through the comic vision of these Russian masters, into the preposterous events of a farcical nightmare. In France, at the end of the century, Alfred Jarry's *Ubu Roi* made it possible for audiences to enjoy the excesses and outrages of arbitrary power and even to identify with the moronic barbarian who commits such atrocities with slobbish zest.

Herod, Shakespeare, the Russians, and Jarry provide antecedents to the comic portrayal of the dictator in the Hitler years. Since then, in contemporary theatre, we have become familiarized with the comic dimensions of tyranny as reflected by the bizarre shifts in power between Pozzo and Lucky in *Waiting for Godot* and the thundering herds of conformists in *Rhinoceros*, as well as in dozens of other works. As a recognizable theme in dramatic literature, comic despots and despotism are well established, even classic, and I have briefly sketched the scope and ancestry of the topic. Now it is time to enunciate laws and working principles governing the comic treatment of tyranny.

Metamorphosis is the modus operandi of dictatorship: human nature and human society are remade. Tyranny systematically transforms its subjects into automatons; the tyrant himself is an immense puppet. Here Henri Bergson's basic postulate—that laughter results when the mechanical is encrusted on the living—finds a perfect illustration, but the process of mechanization is carried out on such a vast scale as to be both ludicrous and terrifying. Instead of one rigid eccentric quarantined by laughter in the midst of a healthy, living society, as envisaged by the French philosopher, the comedy of tyranny presents a single all-powerful maniac who forces the entire world to conform to his monstrous notions. The Bergsonian "transformation of a person into a thing" applies to everyone in the realm, for the dictator regards human beings solely as objects.

In Witkiewicz's *Gyubal Wahazar, or Along the Cliffs of the Absurd*—"A Non-Euclidean Drama in Four Acts"[8]—the absolute dictator, Wahazar, is transforming all the women in the sixth-dimensional continuum over which he rules either into Mechanical Mothers or androgynous Masculettes. Although he beats and abuses his subjects with savage glee, his Onlyness—as Wahazar is called—considers himself a martyr and benefactor to mankind, regimenting human beings only in order to restore them to the homogeneous happiness of the primitive tribe and of the anthill and wasp's nest.[9] At the same time, the dictator's private scientist, the sinister Dr. Rypmann, is conducting strange experiments involving "the fission of psychic atoms" and will soon be able to fabricate new Wahazars out of hyenas, jackals, or even bedbugs. Thus his Onlyness, who has imagined that he is the sole deity, can be mechanically reproduced. In fact, his subjects refer to Wahazar as an old puppet, and large Gyubal dolls have started to appear on the market, while in Albania lesser tyrants are already imitating his Onlyness.[10] When Wahazar is finally assassinated by Morbidetto, head of the secret police, the tyrant's glands are cut out and transplanted still warm into a senile old man who then becomes Wahazar II.[11]

Comic proliferation and reduplication overtake not only the tyrant's automated subjects but also the tyrant. The metamorphosis into brutes and beasts, traditional to comedy, itself undergoes a transformation in the machine age; as science and technology become the tools of the tyrant, a system of mechanical indoctrination can forge herds of identical, docile fools ready to be manipulated like marionettes.

Jules Romains's *Dr. Knock* likewise is a drama of tyranny that explores the remarkable power of pseudo-science allied to technology in bringing the masses into total submission. Ostensibly a satire on medicine—a traditional subject for French farce since the Middle Ages—Romains's comedy shows a small-time con man availing himself of all the modern techniques of mass production and advertising in order to create an infallible propaganda machine and achieve absolute power over others. Although it still has one foot firmly planted in the festive world of old-fashioned farce, *Dr. Knock* is perhaps the most prophetic of all plays about the growth and operation of the totalitarian corporate state because it reveals the tyrant's extraordinary ability to galvanize and transform the community by giving the people a purpose in life, no matter how bogus that purpose may be.

Using only the simplest materials and devices of farce, Romains has written a universal parable about tyranny, without secret police, killing, or any sort of violence. Yet by the end of this seemingly lighthearted comedy, the free, open, nineteenth-century countryside and village of Acts I and II have become transformed into the white, sterile, regimented world of totalitarian dictatorship that anticipates the anti-utopias of Zamyatin's *We* and Huxley's *Brave New World*. Through Dr. Knock's hypnotic genius, everyone in the small town has been made to imagine that he is sick and has been transformed into a patient and then put to bed in the local hotel, now metamorphosed into a hospital. The subjective mania of Molière's "*le malade imaginaire*" has been artificially imposed on an entire population for manipulative purposes, thereby satisfying the deepest needs of both the tyrant and the tyrannized. Rendered mentally ill, a human society becomes refashioned as a smoothly functioning machine.

Gyubal Wahazar at the National Theatre, Warsaw, directed by Wanda Laskowska, closed by the censor after the dress rehearsal on February 11, 1968

The final revelation of the nature of the new community—the "redeemed society" in Northrop Frye's *Mythos of Spring*[12]—comes at the very end of the play after night has fallen. Instead of the usual hymeneal celebration preparatory to the consummation of the marriage that serves as the traditional denouement of comedy, the collective rectal temperature-taking at precisely 10:00 p.m. by all of Dr. Knock's several hundred patients becomes the appropriate ritual in honor of the new "medical existence"—a perfect image of the synthetic, asexual, and technologically efficient civilization ushered in by totalitarianism.[13]

In another parable play that demonstrates exactly how the dictator comes to power, Brecht's *The Resistible Rise of Arturo Ui*, blind greed, masked as capitalist ideology, is revealed as the motive force driving human beings to submit to tyranny. The tyrant is exposed as a simple bandit whose field of operations has been extended to the public arena. In discussing his own "great historical gangster play," Brecht stresses that comedy is the most effective way to destroy the dangerous respect commonly felt for great tyrants.

> The petty rogue whom the rulers permit to become a rogue on the grand scale can occupy a special position in roguery, but not in our attitude to history. Anyway there is truth in the principle that comedy is less likely than tragedy to fail to take human suffering seriously enough.[14]

In other words, comedy—rather than tragedy or melodrama, both of which magnify evil and render it exceptional—is the best antidote to the tyrant's pretenses to grandeur because the comic spirit revels in universal pettiness and vulgar complicity, reducing the mighty dictator to a properly banal, everyday plane. "It is this reverence for killers that has to be done away with," Brecht writes, "whatever applies to small situations must be made to apply to big ones."[15] Through the device of microscopic reduction, Brecht in *Arturo Ui* shrinks Hitler and Nazism to a bloodthirsty Chicago gangster and a protection racket called the Cauliflower Trust, just as Romains in *Dr. Knock* even more drastically contracts the figure of the modern demagogue to a farcical quack doctor in a tiny provincial village. On these reduced stages, we can perceive step by step, as in the numbered pictures of a cartoon, how Knock and Ui gradually seize possession of a community and gain complete control of the minds and bodies of its inhabitants through the spreading of terror.

While maintaining exactly the same equation between small and large that Brecht demands, Jarry in *Ubu Roi* works by expansion rather than contraction. Père Ubu is blown up out of all proportion and assumes a rank perfectly unbefitting to his character. In Jarry's monstrous farce we are shown how a crude nobody—the personification of bourgeois stupidity and mediocrity—can become a great actor on the world-historical stage, on which, in the company of kings and emperors, he commands armies and determines the destiny of nations by robbing, plundering, and slaughtering along with the best of them. All of human history is a bloody farce. Ubu's elevation to the realm of a Shakespearian monarch proves that anyone—a hyena, a jackal, or even a bedbug—can become transformed into a powerful dictator.

As a moralist, Brecht would have us believe that the tyrant-rogue is discredited through the process of comic deflation. Certainly, through inflation, Père Ubu, the contemptible clown with unlimited power, the gigantic guignolesque marionette with base appetites, elicits our sympathy and gives us comic pleasure when he abuses others as well as when he himself is abused. In *Le Symbolisme au théâtre*, Jacques Robichez suggests that Ubu appeals to all that is most trivial and gross within us: "he demands the complicity of our least avowable instincts."[16]

In "Thoughts on Dictatorship," Leo Ferrero, who fled from Mussolini's Italy to France in 1928, comes to similar conclusions about the rise of fascism, finding the reverence for tyrants to lie deep in human nature:

> The popularity of dictators and our admiration for them can be explained by the life of the instinct, by our love for ourselves. We identify with them. . . . The dictator is only the projection on another person of the desire to find ourselves in an imaginary situation where this frenetic love of self could be satisfied.[17]

In Ferrero's satirical drama, *Angelica*, the inhabitants of the Fascist City of Masks are all the old commedia dell'arte characters who seek new roles under the totalitarian regime; Arlequin, Scaramouche, Pantalon, Pulcinella, and Tartaglia eventually find positions of security, wealth, and power through successful accommodation to dictatorship. Only the hero and heroine appear to stand apart from this world of corruption, for they are Orlando and Angelica, the chivalrous knight and his lady from Ariosto's heroic Renaissance epic, *Orlando Furioso*. But love and honor can no longer survive in a modern dictatorship, and no one—especially not the beautiful Angelica—can tolerate Orlando's gauche and naïve insistence on fighting for freedom.

In the commedia world of masks, the populace grows accustomed to tyranny and learns to live comfortably in slavery, resisting and resenting any attempts to restore its lost liberty. The tyrant Regent—an elegantly dressed poet and playwright with sense of style and theatrical spectacle—is about to violate liberty in the person of Angelica on the eve of her marriage, according to the ancient *droit du seigneur* (as used by Beaumarchais in *The Marriage of Figaro*, a domestic variant of tyrant comedy). The people approve of the Regent's staging of the event as he approaches on a purple carpet, illumined by colored spotlights and flaming torches; and Angelica—the perfidious ideal of freedom—actually wishes to be raped. Although Orlando succeeds in provoking a revolution and temporarily brings back a republican form of government, the Regent, as he is being deposed, explains to the noble-minded hero that the fundamental stupidity, pettiness, and envy of the commedia citizens make them willing to follow any imposing strongman. Democracy proves to be chaos, tyranny is soon restored, and Orlando is betrayed and shot by Angelica. Describing what life is like under the Regent's dictatorship, one of the masks declares:

> There are no laws any more. It is the regime of the arbitrary. Spies, police, agents, traitors abound.

Such a quintessential perception corresponds to John Locke's concise definition: "Wherever law ends, tyranny begins."[18] And herein lies the crucial issue—under dictatorship the comic results from the very fact that all normal laws are suspended and the arbitrary reigns. As in the wildest farce, every restraint is gone. The famous scene in Jarry's play in which Ubu takes the Nobles, Magistrates, and Financiers and one after the other dispatches them "down the trap door" shows how total capriciousness combined with absolute power can create comedy.[19] Senseless cruelty and pandemic injustice, in becoming the norm, become preposterous; if whole classes of people can be arrested and liquidated for no reason, the world is a madhouse. Ubu's disembraining machine is used on friend and foe alike. We are in the realm of pure nonsense.

In *The Other Kingdom*, a study of life in the concentration camps, that ultimate form of tyranny, the French author David Rousset sees Ubu as the reigning spirit and god of the camps and speaks of

> . . . the fascinating discovery of humor, not so much as a projection of the personality, but as an objective pattern of the universe. . . . Ubu and Kafka cease to be literary fantasies and become component elements of the living world. The discovery of this humor enabled many of us to survive.[20]

TERROR AND COMEDY

The arbitrary arrest of a single individual in an essentially ordered and just world is an outrage, arousing feelings of pity and indignation. If, however, millions of people are unjustly arrested—as happened under Stalin—and then those who arrested them are themselves arrested by agents who will later be arrested, the arbitrariness becomes all-inclusive, self-propelling, and grotesquely laughable. In this absurd and frightening realm of the totally arbitrary, there is neither freedom nor necessity, and thus tragedy is an impossibility. Any realistic portrayal of such a world in drama is ruled out because life under tyranny lacks known probabilities and produces no sense of reality; and it is for these reasons that the playwrights under consideration go for their models to farce and to fable.

Tyrannical power is so arbitrary in its sudden shifts that those who arrogantly wield it at one moment are unexpectedly struck down by it at the next. The tyrant invariably rewards his own loyal henchmen by killing them; Ui has his lieutenant Ernesto Roma (Ernst Röhm) gunned down, and Gyubal Wahazar personally shoots Baron Oskar von den Binden-Gnumben, his commander of the guard, who has just dutifully beaten a crowd of defenseless prisoners. From such turns of the wheel of blind fortune, represented by the dictator's capricious will, a bizarre sort of justice may even be seen to emerge in the form of a crude punitive nemesis that levels all to the same base destiny. Regardless of deserts, everyone goes "down the trap door." Even the tyrant himself is subject to the vicissitudes of arbitrary power and feels constantly threatened by the terrors of arrest, imprisonment, and execution. Pursuing the insane logic of his own absolute authority, Wahazar declares: "I can condemn myself to death if I feel like it—if I become convinced that I'm wrong." After putting all his followers—including the secret police chief—in an underground dungeon, his Onlyness unexpectedly finds that he has been imprisoned along with them by some mysterious higher power of arbitrariness. Witkiewicz's "They"—those higher, faceless oppressors who control all our destinies, even those of dictators—are utterly inscrutable and unpredictable.

The anonymous, institutional tyranny of the state and its organs represents a subject for comedy of even greater scope than the tyranny of the individual. Particular despots may come and go, but the despotic state continues triumphant. In czarist Russia, for example, tyranny was deeply entrenched, and its inflexible bureaucracy and ubiquitous police agents gave rise to a rich literature of comic dread in the face of arbitrary power.

Fear of arrest by the authorities for crimes real or imaginary haunts the imaginations of Gogol's abject, petty-minded cheats and swindlers. In his great comic novel, *Dead Souls*, the enigmatic hero, Chichikov, travels about Russia buying up "dead souls" (serfs who are no longer living but still remain on the tax lists), causing the

Evgenii Shvarts's *Naked King*, by Polish illustrator and stage designer, Daniel Mróz (1965)

officials he meets to wonder "whether he was the sort of man who was to be seized and detained as an undesirable character, or whether he was the sort of person who might seize and detain them all himself as undesirable characters."[21] This ambiguous state of apprehension and uncertainty is the inevitable result of the ever-changing winds of arbitrariness in the unstable world of tyranny. In *The Inspector General*, Gogol's masterpiece for the stage, Khlestakov, the penniless clerk from St. Petersburg, waits fearfully in his provincial hotel room, expecting to be arrested for debts by the town officials, while at the same time the corrupt town officials gather nervously at the Mayor's, expecting to be arrested by Khlestakov—whom they imagine to be the dreaded inspector general. At the end of the play, the "real" inspector general—that higher power of absolute authority always waiting in the wings—is announced, literally petrifying in a frozen tableau all the petty tyrants for what is the most spectacular coup de théâtre in Russian drama.

Gogol's successor in the art of grotesque comedy, Sukhovo-Kobylin, brought to perfection the comic terrors of police interrogation in *The Death of Tarelkin*, which the author—who spent seven nightmarish years in and out of Russian courts and jails on charges of murdering his mistress—calls a "comedy-farce." Here the itch to arrest and the conviction that everyone is a traitor engaged in heinous conspiracies reach such colossal proportions that the madness threatens to engulf all of Russia. The last half of Sukhovo-Kobylin's comedy-farce takes place in a gloomy, dimly lit police station, where loutish rogues in police uniforms conduct their investigations with the aid of broomsticks and a specially devised human beating machine constructed out of their moronic subordinates. Guilt by association is the fundamental principle of justice, innocent landowners and merchants are sent off to "the secret chamber," and terrified victims name as their accomplices "all Petersburg and all Moscow" and readily confess to being vampires and werewolves who have sucked the blood of their neighbors. The interrogators and torturers grow so enchanted with their work that they declare:

> Everything belongs to us now. We'll demand all of Russia! . . . There aren't any people here—just monsters . . . All they deserve is Siberia and chains . . . That's why we have to establish a rule of subjecting everyone to arrest! . . . The machinery will operate by itself.[22]

In *The Death of Tarelkin*, the reign of institutional terror is presented by the means of the techniques of nineteenth-century comedy-vaudeville, which Sukhovo-Kobylin knew and admired from his visits to Paris.[23] "Because of its humorous character," the author explains in a note, "the play should be performed in a lively, gay, loud manner—*avec entrain*.[24] The Russian equivalent of Père Ubu's disembraining machine and trapdoor for disposing of unwanted social classes, Sukhovo-Kobylin's police-station state functions automatically, generating its own savage energy.

HUMAN NATURE AND TYRANNY

A later Soviet satirist in the same tradition, Evgenii Shvarts (who survived all the Stalin years by writing children's literature) had an excellent vantage point from which to observe how the machinery of tyranny operates and maintains itself in power; and the worst traits of human nature, which are brought out by dictatorship, become the subject of his mockery in a series of brilliantly allusive fairy-tale plays. Shvarts's parables can apply to any totalitarian regime, but for reasons of prudence in the USSR it was always argued by Shvarts's defenders that they are directed only against fascism; for example, in *The Naked King*, the tyrant's anti-Semitism, book burning, and threats of sterilization may be seen as direct references to Nazi Germany, but of course the absurd cult of personality, the intellectual dishonesty, and the servile, creaking bureaucracy that characterize the court all strike closer to home.[25] Written in the style of a slapstick comedy and music-hall revue, *The Naked King* renders hilarious the stupidity and cruelty of a highly personalized dictatorship and suggests that it can be destroyed quickly once the truth about the king's nakedness is publicly acknowledged.

Unfortunately, human beings prefer lies, and the stubborn persistence of tyranny becomes the theme of Shvarts's later dramatic fable, *The Dragon*, whose hero, Lancelot—like Ferrero's Orlando—is an idealistic knight-errant fighting for the freedom of docile slaves who do not wish to be free. Over the years of accommodation to the Dragon's totalitarian regime, the inhabitants of Shvarts's fairy-tale kingdom have grown so accustomed to all forms of moral corruption that they accept bribery, spying, informing, and even killing as normal, everyday occurrences. To these deformed human beings it seems only natural that a young girl should be sacrificed yearly to the tyrant—much as Angelica is to be offered up to the Regent. After all, the townspeople reason, the Dragon is quite nice—a sentimental middle-aged gentleman, slightly deaf in one ear, who smiles frequently and "drops by like an old friend." And besides, he wards off all other dragons who might oppress them.

Evil in *The Dragon* is perfectly banal, existing solely because of the lethargy of those who endure it. When Lancelot challenges the passive citizens to resist and accuses them of collaboration—"But it turns out that you, my friends, are bandits too"—the populace turns against its savior as a troublemaker. A typical response is: "I was taught to be what I am."[26]

Debunking legends of dragons and heroes who are supernaturally powerful, Shvarts shows that tyranny persists even after the tyrant is killed, often in a more insidious form, because despotism lives in the hearts of the tyrannized. Once Lancelot has slain the Dragon, the sickness of conformity turns out to be so deeply rooted that the system automatically continues; and the Mayor, who now becomes dictator, proves still more dangerous because he masquerades under slogans about democracy and freedom. Cowardice, a traditional comic vice, is given a new dimension: the collective guilt of complicity and the moral cowardice of capitulation are attributed to an entire people. Adaptation to the group, which in Bergson's theory is the proper corrective to folly, becomes under tyranny the mark of the greatest fools and scoundrels. At the end of *The Dragon*, Lancelot concludes that it will be a long, hard struggle to bring freedom to such human beings: "The Dragon has to be killed in each and every one of them"—a perception only slightly less melancholy than Orlando's dying recognition that the commedia masks do not wish to be saved from their own degeneracy.

Shvarts's third great parable, *The Shadow* (written when Stalin and Hitler were allies), presents a bleaker picture of a "mad, unhappy world" in which even the fairy-tale princess, like Angelica, is herself a corrupt betrayer of the naïve, honest hero. Those in power are predatory monsters and cannibals, afraid of everything and everyone, including themselves, and unwilling to forgive the scholar-hero for "being such a good man." In this universe of total distrust, false appearances are all that matters. "Smile, we're being watched" becomes the only expression of gaiety, and the executioner's block has been set up "in the pink drawing room, beside a statue of Cupid, and disguised with forget-me-nots."[27] The corruption lies so deep in human nature that the hero discovers that the tyrant is his very shadow and alter ego and that he must go to his death in order to live.

Melodrama—the alternate mode for the dramatization of tyranny—separates its characters into hateful villains and pitiable, innocent victims. Comedy, with its stress on mankind's universal participation in folly and vice, would appear to be the most suitable tool to kill the dragon in each and every one of us—or at least to expose the beast. It is for this reason that in the tyrant plays under consideration (written by firsthand witnesses of the European dictators), the element of pathos—an easy response to evoke when dealing with victims—is deliberately eliminated. In Chaplin's *The Great Dictator* (1941), on the other hand, despite the film's many brilliant moments, the comedy of the tyrant is severely flawed by the sentimental melodrama of the Jewish ghetto and the hero's optimistic belief in the goodness of the people and their ability to triumph. Chaplin's portrayal of dictatorship lacks any sense of terror, based, as it is, less on fundamental human flaws common to all than on the aberrations of a few lunatics. Brecht, who left the Jews out of *Arturo Ui* for good reasons, insists that "the comic element must not preclude horror."[28] In the comic depiction of tyranny, terror is an essential ingredient, but pathos sounds a false note.

A case in point is Shakespeare's prototypical tyrant play, *Richard III*, in which the comic scenes tracing Richard's rise to power through diabolical manipulation are founded upon the complicity of his victims. Crude comic justice emerges as Richard sends down the trapdoor all those who have abetted him in his many crimes and are thus equally guilty of murder and perjury. Even Anne, knowing the tyrant's crimes against her family, is culpable for accepting Richard against her better judgment; and, in fact, upon their meeting by the hearse of Henry VI, she curses herself if she should ever marry such a monster. Concentrating on the tyrant and his accomplices and not on his innocent victims, Shakespeare omits any presentation of the murder of the little princes (who are tainted only through the sins of their father), whereas the melodramatized stage and film versions by Colley Cibber and Laurence Olivier exploit the scene for its pathos.

The comic workings of higher arbitrariness in *Richard III* can be seen most fully in the scenes with Hastings, who first gloats over the unjust deaths of his enemies, Rivers, Grey, and Vaughan, and then smugly imagines that he stands high in the tyrant's favor. Asked by Richard what punishment those plotting against him deserve, the obsequious Hastings replies death, of course, thus dooming himself to be led off to instant execution. The tyrant's henchman gets his proper reward in a suitably ironic fashion.

The farce of Richard's rise to power is, to be sure, only a part of a much larger, serious drama of redemption for England. The comedy occurs primarily in Act III, where, in a series of mordantly funny episodes, Buckingham and Richard use every totalitarian trick to "persuade" the Mayor and Citizens of London to accept Richard as legitimate king. All the modern techniques of political violence, rabble-rousing, and propaganda are there: smears against rivals, trumped-up charges about dangerous associates, elimination of potential enemies, false promises and false laments for betrayed friends, accusations against the dead, predated death sentences, staged rallies (what Halévy calls "organized enthusiasm"),[29] provoked crises and fabricated states of alert (Gloucester and Buckingham appear "in rotten armor, marvelous ill-fitting" and pretend to drive off imaginary attackers), and feigned piety and reluctance to rule (Richard enters with "two right reverend Fathers," reading the Holy Book).[30] In all these stunts it is apparent that Richard can "counterfeit the deep tragedian" and is a master at manipulating reality and appearance through the equivocal and misleading use of language. To lull suspicion, the dictator knows how to feign geniality (as in Richard's good-humored inquiry about strawberries); to terrify, he can simulate a towering rage (as in his accusations against Hastings). All is fraudulent, for the tyrant is in essence an actor.

It is no wonder that Brecht sent his Arturo Ui to school to study with Shakespeare's Richard III, whose methods of eliminating opposition become a model for the Chicago gangster. "Doesn't he make you think of Richard the Third?" Brecht asks in the prologue;[31] and later, in order to play his role impressively, Ui takes lessons in speech and deportment with an old-fashioned Shakespearian actor. In actual fact, Hitler may have taken similar lessons, and the entire comparison between the Führer and Richard III is a natural one, as witness the following entry for July 20, 1935, from the diary of Harry Kessler, the "Red Count":

> Breukner [one of Hitler's adjutants] ... said, "Man alive, have you still not noticed that the Fuehrer is nuts?" Hitler always allows the murder of people with whom he is on friendly terms to be "wrested" from him. He tears his hair like a Wagnerian hero, makes a show of despair ("I really cannot permit that"), and finally "concedes" what he decided a week ago. "Richard III," I commented. "Much worse," replied Breuning, because the theatrical, sentimentally romantic, Wagnerian element enters into it.[32]

Untitled drawing by Mrożek (1965) showing the cooperative hierarchy
by which the tyrant is raised aloft and the resulting precariousness of his position

As the triad Hitler/Ui/Richard III reveals, the tyrant is a multiple sham, a parody of an authentic ruler (usurping his place) and a parody of an actor putting on a show (counterfeiting the tragedian). A comedian and clown by nature, the dictator must constantly perform before an audience. Put on the stage by a dramatist, such a ludicrous figure becomes theatre-in-the-theatre, a parody of parodies. And here is why the playwrights who portray tyrants find inspiration in commedia, Shakespeare, gangster films, fairy tales with ogres, and Punch-and-Judy shows.

TYRANNY AND THEATRICAL SPECTACLE

Tyranny is theatre, and totalitarian regimes consist of ceremonies and rituals centering around the dictator and manipulated by him. In *The Arena of Ants*, a novel about German prisoners of war in America, James Schevill observes that "the Nazis were conquering Europe by theatrical spectacles, illusions, as much as the reality of industrial and military power. Masks are as necessary in politics as on the operatic stage."[33] Arturo Ui must learn to wear the mask of the tyrant; during the course of the play, particularly in the scene with the old Shakespearian actor, we see the man become the mask and watch Ui grow transfigured as he assumes what Hannah Arendt calls the dictator's "aura of impenetrable mystery."[34] Dr. Knock (especially as played by Louis Jouvet) wears an unfathomable mask of gravity from the start, never once letting on through the slightest gesture that the medical existence might be a common swindle and thereby convincing his patients that they are sick by the sheer force of his superb performance. In the film version of *Dr. Knock*, Jouvet transformed even the washing of his hands into an awesome and intimidating ritual, expressive of the doctor's absolute knowledge and power over others.

The tyrant's mastery of spectacle is a principal source of his power. "Do you know why people thought I was a great statesman?" Ferrero's Regent asks Orlando. "Because I had cannons fired when I received the bankers who brought me money." Wahazar concocts special court rites that are a bizarre mixture of quack medicine, pseudo-science, modern technology, and mystical belief. The dictator must offer his people a new religion of which he is the sole deity: a lonely, preposterous, terrifying, and sometimes pitiable ham actor. "I alone rule everything and I'm responsible for everything, and answer only to myself," his Onlyness screams. Megalomania and paranoia are the two poles between which the dictator oscillates.

THE RHETORIC OF TYRANNY

As an upstart, a nobody, arising out of nothing, with no warrant to rule, the modern tyrant must invent himself and his realm through his ability to devise names and symbols. Above all, the tyrant is the creation of his own perverted rhetoric. Diderot was the first to comment on the linguistic impact of totalitarianism: "Tyranny imprints a character of baseness on all kinds of productions; even language is not protected from its influence."[35] The tyrant's language is a grotesque debasement of normal speech, constantly approaching utter nonsense; for the playwright, this *rodomontade* becomes the key to the character's dramatic vitality. The dictator abuses words as he abuses his subjects; his repeated distortions have a hypnotic and almost magical power. The tyrant's torturing of language is his most extreme form of action, expressing his total personality. Ubu's invented insults and misshapen curses and profanity are the motive force behind his aggression and his ascent to power. In his first appearance as the dictator Hynkel haranguing the masses in absurd mock German, Chaplin captures the essential linguistic madness of the tyrant. Gyubal Wahazar perpetually froths at the mouth and flies into hysterical rages that, like Hitler's, seem self-consciously staged performances. Witkiewicz's note, explaining how the frothing is to be done, furthers the impression that we are witnessing an act: "It's very easy to do by first stuffing one's mouth full of soda tablets or Piperazina flakes from Klawy's drugstore." Deliberately playing the buffoon, Richard III speaks a double-talk full of ironic wordplay and quibbles that say the opposite of what he intends. But as he begins to lose military and political control of the situation in Act IV, Richard no longer simply feigns anger—he actually flies into a screaming fit against the messenger who brings bad news as well as against his own subordinates.

The ancestor of all ranting dictators who froth at the mouth in frenzied rages is, of course, Herod the Great in the Christian mystery plays. Much as we enjoy seeing Chaplin as the Great Dictator raving insanely, so medieval audiences evidently delighted in the spectacle of Great Herod and other tyrant figures in the cycles (Pharaoh, Caesar,

Hyrcan IV in *The Cuttlefish*, the first postwar production of Witkiewicz at Cricot II, Cracow, directed by Tadeusz Kantor (1956)

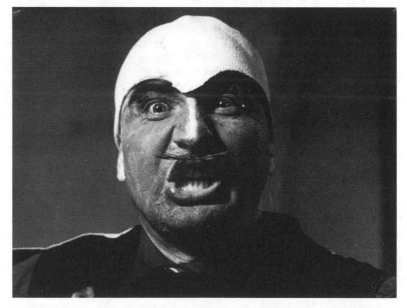

Hyrcan IV in the Warsaw Sigma Student Theatre production of *The Cuttlefish* (1966)

Augustus, and Pilate) blustering in comic fury. The medieval stage despot struts about the stage, swears, and speaks incomprehensible French;[36] he despises the multitude that he abuses, and his repeated calls for silence (addressed to the audience) suggest that he was hooted and jeered.[37] Much like his modern counterparts in drama, Herod accuses everyone of being a traitor and threatens to beat and break the bones of all his subjects, especially his own knights and retainers. There is every reason to believe that derisive laughter was the audience's response to such a base and clownish figure. In his essay on "The Comic in the Cycles," Arnold Williams points out that even the reactions of the brutish soldiers sent out by Herod to kill the Innocents were often comic: "In one cycle they enjoy the task, in another they feel it beneath them to kill babies and fight women. . . . It seems likely that the attack of the women was sometimes played for laughs."[38] In particular, the portrayal of Herod in the Wakefield cycle reveals all the possibilities for comedy inherent in the tyrant. Cruel and violent, stupid and cowardly, the Wakefield Master's Herod is a medieval Ubu who brags of his omnipotence over all creation, yet constantly gives way to impotent rage. This great dictator is an ignorant, mean, malicious monster who rages directly against the audience and menaces them with all the might of his great power.

For, despite his vain boasting, the medieval despot has, in fact, the full weight of authority, human and divine, to support his claims. The modern Herods, on the other hand, have no such sanctions and must fabricate the myth of their own omnipotence. The power of language to forge totalitarian myths and concepts is illustrated in Witkiewicz's *The Cuttlefish, or The Hyrcanian Worldview*.[39] A total fraud in a world of total fraud, the tyrant-hero is a synthetic superman—"a very clever, but ordinary bandit" surrounded by a "depraved band of madmen and drunkards"—who proclaims himself ruler of the artificial kingdom of Hyrcania and calls himself Hyrcan IV. Without a name or hereditary title of his own, the would-be dictator must first invent a country and then a worldview to justify its existence. Wearing a helmet with a red plume and a purple robe that comes down to the floor, Hyrcan talks impressively and carries a huge sword; but beneath these trappings, he is an ordinary twentieth-century man in a dark business suit. The petty modern tyrant must impose himself on the world through theatrical illusion and gesture.

Improvising his realm and his values as he goes, Hyrcan plans to rule over the inert masses—whom he despises as stupid cattle—by means of what he calls Hyrcanian desires. When challenged to explain the meaning of such a nonsensical phrase, the self-created despot reveals the true nature of totalitarian might: the power of the word to create the thing. "Once I give it definition, this empty sound will become a concept," the strongman declares. But Hyrcanian desires (daydreams of self-aggrandizement, as it turns out) cause Hyrcan to have a tantrum when he learns that his mother is a whore and that he may well be the illegitimate son of a Jewish banker. Deeply humiliated, the racist demagogue abruptly leaves the stage, muttering ominous threats; he is soon murdered by an anarchist artist who proclaims himself Hyrcan V and promises a government based on pure nonsense. The same fabrication of myth plays a major role in the tyrant's rise in Toller's *Wotan Unbound*. The hero, an anti-Semitic barber named Wotan, is a compulsive reader of Romantic literature who writes grandiose memoirs while in prison; at first a tool of financial and military interests, Wotan by the end of the play becomes transformed into a true dictator who screams maniacally that his book alone will save Europe.[40]

TYRANNY AFTER WORLD WAR II

With the deaths of Hitler, Mussolini, and Stalin (and their lesser confreres, such as Franco and Salazar), tyranny did not disappear from the earth, nor has the race of tyrants died out. After all, Idi Amin demonstrated better than any imaginable fictional character my central thesis that frightening despots are inherently preposterous. But in recent times tyranny has undergone a drastic demythification. For the most part, contemporary despotism is less colorful and spectacular than regularized and systematized. Tyranny has grown year by year more impersonal, more normal, and more efficient—and, therefore, even more dangerous.

Since the end of World War II and the vogue of the absurd, we have had many comic parables and savage farces about totalitarian systems and the tyranny of the state. One thinks of Ionesco's *The Lesson* and *Rhinoceros* as well as Armand Gatti's *Le Crapaud-Buffle*, and *The Tot Family* by the Hungarian István Örkény. Of playwrights in the second half of the twentieth century, none has devoted more attention to the quiet, everyday workings of tyranny and its effects on the average tyrannized citizen than the Polish writer, Sławomir Mrożek. Instead of flamboyant dictators, Mrożek presents the small victims of oppression who eagerly seek to justify their own submission to the power of power. In a whole series of parable plays—some short and some long—Mrożek lays bare the mechanism of tyranny as it operates in ideologies and institutions, in bureaucracies and social classes.

An early Mrożek one-act drama, *Striptease* (1961),[41] effectively illustrates the invisible tyranny that is the object of the playwright's ironic and detached scrutiny. Two official-looking gentlemen wearing dark suits and carrying briefcases unexpectedly find themselves trapped in an impersonal room into which a gigantic hand protrudes and forces them to remove their clothes. One protests and argues eloquently; the other talks of inner freedom—but all to no avail. Regardless of their philosophical positions, both are compelled to submit to arbitrary power and strip off their own clothes and dignity before going to their destruction. The tyrant is absent from *Striptease*; only a symbol is necessary to keep the system operating. In *Emigrants* (1975), in which the two characters are complementary figures in a theorem, AA observes: "When there's only one authority we're all equal . . . In a dictatorship we're all the same."[42] Mrożek's parables are dedicated to demonstrating how tyranny strips supposedly civilized human beings of their pretenses and reduces them to a common denominator where certain universal laws hold sway.

In a trilogy of one-act plays, *Serenade, Philosopher Fox,* and *Fox Hunt* (1977),[43] Mrożek makes his tyrants a rooster and a fox from an animal fable. The third section, *Fox Hunt*, is a richly allusive political parable about the shifting tides of power and the fate of those caught in the crosscurrents. In a new egalitarian regime, all the people—and not simply the king and nobles—have the right to hunt; in fact, everyone is required to go hunting, even Uncle, a sick old man in a wheelchair who does not know how to shoot and would prefer to stay home. The result of such "democratic" hunting on a mass scale is that there are no more wild animals left in the forest, except for one last fox desperately trying to save his hide. This fox—a clever farmyard bandit—has, therefore, brought with him into the woods a rooster—a petty henhouse tyrant—to serve as a decoy, hoping to convince the hunters that domestic animals would make good prey. The hunters are ready for the chase and urge the dogs on, the latter being bureaucrats with briefcases who keep careful count of the exact number of times they bark. Suddenly, in a surprising

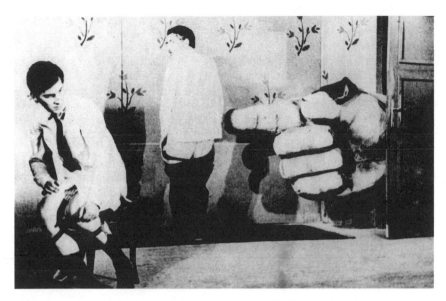

Mrożek's *Striptease*, Teatr im. Al. Węgierki, Białystok (1962)
Directed by Krystyna Meissner

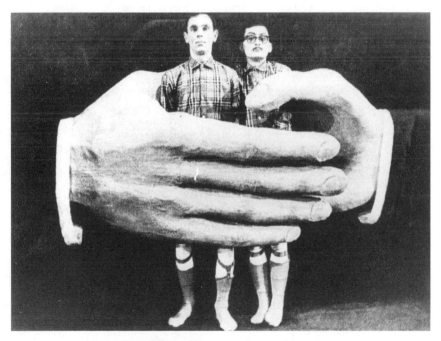

Mrożek's *Striptease*, Stary Teatr/Teatr Kameralny, Cracow (1962)
Directed by Lidia Zamkow-Słomczyńska

coup d'état denouement (already used to good effect in *Tango*), the terrifying howling of a pack of wolves can be heard offstage—evidently, not all wild animals are extinct. As the wolves draw closer and closer, the hunters rush for home in panic, and Uncle, abandoned by all, fires his shotgun twice wildly, accidentally killing both the fox and the rooster who had concealed themselves in a tree.

In the sharp twists of *Fox Hunt*, we see the comic laws of tyranny in operation. The higher power of arbitrariness blindly levels differences between greater and lesser figures in the hierarchy of oppression. Often cunning is helpless when confronted by brute force; wolves can replace hunters and even the feeblest are momentarily dangerous with gun in hand.

Comedy has no limits. The most monstrous tyranny of the twentieth century has been assimilated within its bounds. The Ubuesque follies and vices of dictatorship represent a subject of enormous importance for our age. Not only because tyranny has in the recent past been so widespread and wreaked such havoc on our fragile civilization. Not only as a warning of what may still come to pass if we are not vigilant. Not only as a picture of what prevails elsewhere, in other countries. But primarily because tyranny reflects in exaggerated form all that is wrong with the modern state. This view that despotism is the essence of all contemporary government finds eloquent expression in the words of Paul Valéry:

> Hence, the (political) mind, which under all circumstances is the opponent of man—contesting his liberty, his complexity, and his versatility—attains, in a dictatorial regime, to the fullness of its development. . . . Dictatorship merely completes the system of pressures and obligations of which modern man is the more or less conscious victim, even in the politically freest countries.[44]

The mirror and model of what already exists around us, tyranny, when viewed as a comic phenomenon, discloses follies and vices to which we are all subject; and the tyrant expresses our delusions, dreams, and fantasies of power. The little Jewish barber and Hynkel are identical twins in Chaplin's *Great Dictator*. The tyrant is our puppet, our inseparable shadow from whom we can never free ourselves entirely. Comedy offers no cure, but through laughter calls attention to the inescapable situation.

NOTES

1. In the discussion that follows, I am not concerned with the dramatic genre, comedy, but only with the comic treatment of tyrants wherever this occurs, even in plays that as a whole would be classified as tragicomedy, history, or some form of serious drama. Likewise, I do not attempt to distinguish between farce and comedy or between satire and comedy. Because the subject of tyranny and comedy is a complex one, I have here attempted only to explore the basic relationships between the two.
2. Plato, *Philebus*, in *Theories of Comedy*, ed. Paul Lauter (New York: Doubleday Anchor, 1964), 7–8.
3. W. H. Auden, "Notes on the Comic," in *Comedy: Meaning and Form*, ed. Robert W. Corrigan (San Francisco: Chandler. 1965), 62.
4. Elie Halévy, *The Era of Tyrannies*, trans. R. K. Webb (New York: New York Univ. Press, 1966), 266.
5. As might be expected, there is also a literature of comic dictators in Spanish that I have not been able to explore. For example, Ramón del Valle-Inclán, in both his plays and his novels, portrays hateful and ludicrous tyrants. Gabriel García Márquez's novel, *The Autumn of the Patriarch*, is a modern example of the genre.
6. Actually, the beginnings of the topic could be traced to the ancient world. Aristophanes, in *The Knights* and other comedies, ridicules the tyrannical demagogue Cleon, using many of the same techniques as the modern portrayers of dictators.
7. Quoted in Oscar Jászi and John D. Lewis, *Against the Tyrant* (Glencoe, IL: The Free Press, 1957), 44.
8. In Stanisław Ignacy Witkiewicz, *Seven Plays*, ed. and trans. Daniel Gerould (New York: Martin E. Segal Theatre Center Publications, 2004). Subsequent quotations come from this edition.
9. Wahazar dreams of the perfect totalitarian state, which, in Hannah Arendt's words, will come Into being when "all men have become One Man." *The Origins of Totalitarianism* (New York: Harcourt, Brace & World, 1966), 477.
10. The chain reaction that Wahazar sets off in Albania bears out Paul Valéry's contention, made in 1934, that "dictatorship at present is contagious, just as, in the past, freedom was." *Collected Works*, trans. Denise Folliot and Jackson Matthews (New York: Pantheon, 1962), 10:245.
11. When Gyubal dies and is replaced by an inferior dictator, his victims lament that life has "lost its last remaining charm."
12. Northrop Frye, *Anatomy of Criticism* (Princeton: Princeton Univ. Press, 1957), 185.
13. Jules Romains, *Knock, ou le triomphe de la médecine* (Paris: Gallimard, 1947), 165. The ironic sense of this passage is lost in the English translations that I have seen, because the translators fail to indicate that French hospitals use rectal, not oral thermometers.
14. Bertolt Brecht, *Collected Plays*, trans. Ralph Manheim (New York: Vintage, 1976), 6:457.
15. Ibid.
16. Jacques Robichez, *Le Symbolisme au théâtre* (Paris: L'Arche, 1957), 360.
17. Leo Ferrero, *Angelica* (Paris: Editions Rieder, 1934). Both the play and the essay which accompanies it were originally written in French. Subsequent quotations are taken from this edition, and the translations are mine. Ferrero was killed in an automobile accident during a visit to the United States in 1933 when he was 30; *Angelica* was later staged by the Pitoëffs in Paris in 1936, and it was first performed in Italy in 1948 with Marcello Mastroianni and Giulietta Masina.
18. Quoted in Jászi, *Against the Tyrant*, 102.
19. Alfred Jarry, *Ubu Roi* (Paris: Fasquelle, n.d.), III, ii.
20. David Rousset, *The Other Kingdom*, trans. Ramon Guthrie (New York: Reynal and Hitchcock, 1947), 172.
21. Nikolai Gogol, *Dead Souls*, trans. David Magarshack (Baltimore: Penguin, 1961), 206.
22. *The Trilogy of Alexander Sukhovo-Kobylin*, trans. Harold B. Segel (London: Harwood Academic Publishers, 1995), 243, 260, 244, 243, 253.

23. Harold Segel gives valuable information about Sukhovo-Kobylin's use of French comic techniques in the introduction to his translation. Ibid., xliii-xlv.

24. Ibid., 263.

25. In contrast, Brecht's *Arturo Ui* is so closely tied historically to the facts of Hitler's life that its resonance as a parable is limited. It applies to the Führer, but not to Stalin; it looks to the past, not to the present or future; and its approach to tyranny is retrospective rather than prophetic. For these reasons, it was safely presented in the Soviet Union (in an outstanding 1963 production at the Leningrad Gorky Theatre, directed by Erwin Axer with Evgenii Lebedev as Arturo Ui) without encountering the many difficulties that Shvarts's plays normally experienced or the outright censorship that kept *Rhinoceros* off the Soviet stage until the 1980s because Ionesco refused to say the play specifically targeted the Nazis.

26. Yevgeny Schwartz, *The Dragon*, trans. Max Hayward and Harold Shukman, in *Three Soviet Plays*, ed. Michael Glenny (Baltimore: Penguin, 1966), 151, 211, 215.

27. *The Shadow*, in *Twentieth-Century Russian Plays*, trans. F. D. Reeve (New York: Norton, 1963), 434, 409, 444–45.

28. Brecht, *Collected Plays*, 6:453.

29. Halévy, *The Era of Tyrannies*, p. 266.

30. *Richard III*, III, v and vi.

31. Brecht, *Collected Plays*, 6:198. Richard's courtship of Anne is overtly parodied in Ui's scene with Dullfeet's widow, but this is the least important analogue between Shakespeare's play and *Arturo Ui*.

32. Harry Kessler, *In the Twenties*, trans. Charles Kessler (New York: Holt, Rinehart and Winston, 1971), 470–71.

33. James Schevill, *The Arena of Ants* (Providence: Copper Beech Press, 1977), 176.

34. Arendt, *The Origins of Totalitarianism*, 373.

35. Quoted in Jászi, *Against the Tyrant*, 105.

36. *The Wakefield Mystery Plays*, ed. Martial Rose (New York: Norton, 1961), 172.

37. A tyrant play originally produced at the New York Shakespeare Festival in 1977 with Estelle Parsons and revived briefly in 1990 on Broadway at the Helen Hayes Theatre, *Miss Margarida's Way*, by the Brazilian playwright Roberto Athayde, attempts to provoke a similar kind of response. The play's only performer, a dictatorial and abusive schoolteacher, uses the audience as her class and the supposed object of her tyranny. Whereas Ubu Roi, based on a hated teacher from Jarry's childhood, becomes all tyrants, in *Miss Margarida's Way*, the concept of tyranny is reduced to a hated teacher. The idea is good, but the execution faulty. Miss Margarida has no mask or aura of mystery; her words inspire no fear and transform no one; her rhetoric degenerates quickly into commonplace obscenity, rather than becoming shaped into the imposing comic rant and invective necessary for the despot if he is to subdue others and convince them of his mission.

38. Arnold Williams, "The Comic in the Cycles," *Medieval Drama*, Stratford-Upon- Avon Studies, vol. 16 (London: Edward Arnold, 1973), 121.

39. *The Cuttlefish*, in Witkiewicz, *Seven Plays*.

40. For information about Toller's play as well as for other ideas on Hitler in film and drama, I am indebted to Alvin Goldfarb's essay, "Adolf Hitler as Portrayed in Theatre and Film During His Lifetime," *The Journal of Popular Culture* 13, no. 1 (1979): 55–66.

41. Sławomir Mrożek, *Striptease*, trans. Lola Gruenthal, in *The Mrożek Reader*, ed. Daniel Gerould (New York: Grove Press, 2004).

42. Sławomir Mrożek, *Emigrants*, trans. Henry Beissel, in *The Mrożek Reader*, 377.

43. Sławomir Mrożek, *Serenade, Philosopher Fox*, and *Fox Hunt*, trans. Jacek Laskowski, in *The Mrożek Reader*.

44. Valéry, *Collected Works*, 10:238, 244.

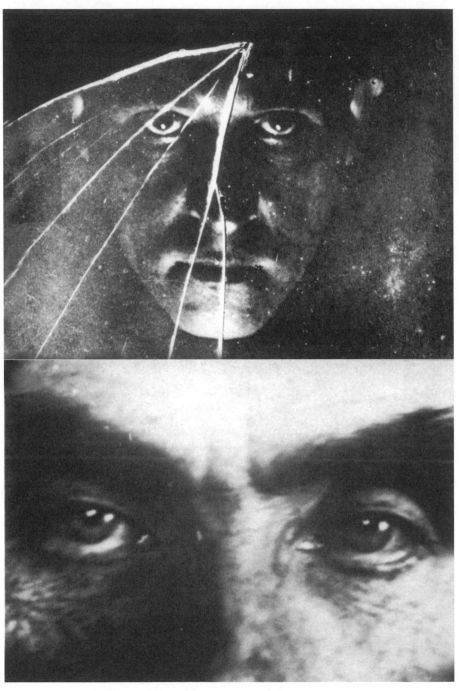

Above: Stanisław Ignacy Witkiewicz (Witkacy), Self-Portrait, Zakopane, before 1914
Below: Stanisław Witkiewicz Senior, Photo taken by his son Witkacy in Lovran, 1913

WITKACY:

AN ALBUM OF PHOTOS — A BUNDLE OF LETTERS

Playwright, painter, aesthetician, philosopher, Stanisław Ignacy Witkiewicz (1885–1939) was also a pioneering photographer. Exhibitions of his works in Poland, Western Europe, and the United States have acquainted large audiences with this hitherto little known aspect of his creative genius. *Presences Polonaises*, shown at the Centre Georges Pompidou from June 23 to September 26, 1983, was in large part a tribute to Witkacy (the artist's pen name by which he was known to friends and admirers), and over 150 of his photographs were on display. in 1998, a major exhibition at the Robert Miller Gallery in New York introduced his photography to American audiences.

Witkacy created his own private theatre with a camera. He produced a long series of photographic portraits of himself and his many alter egos, his family and friends, and his surroundings. Whether he composes the picture or is himself the subject of the composition, Witkacy is the artist-director probing the limits of self, discovering new identities, relishing the lying masks, yet penetrating to the unfathomable individual beneath.

As a boy Witkacy learned from his father (an important turn-of-the-century artistic personality and cultural critic) the value of photography in the development of his creative work; he was encouraged to pose and play in front of the camera. He began his career as a photographer in 1899–1900 by taking many pictures of locomotives; a quarter of a century later he would write one of his best plays, *The Crazy Locomotive*, on this childhood theme. Next he photographed the natural surroundings of his mountain hometown, Zakopane, in the south of Poland, and then came to what would be his true subject, the human face.

Witkacy's photographic portraits and autoportraits are psychic studies, revelations of the inner man, showing the inevitable gulf between people and the existential incommunicability of feelings. Witkacy was obsessed with faces ("mugs" he called them), particularly the eyes; in his plays features are described in precise detail. In his photographs before 1914 the face often fills the entire picture and is both the foreground and the background.

Two sides of the individual are given prominence in Witkacy's photographic portraits. There are the social masks and camouflage of the theatricalized photos; in this world of lies and the absurd, where one plays endless roles in a comedy, there is no abiding self, only play, theatre, inauthenticity. From the disintegration of the self, schizophrenic doubles and deceptive personalities arise. Witkacy's series of "faces" and staged paratheatrical scenes—actually photographed by his friend Józef Głogowski—are the flamboyant expression of this outer drama.

The other side of Witkacy's photographic exploration of the psyche is the anxiety, dread, and terror of the individual in the face of existence—the suffering that lies behind the mask. Here the eyes are the conduit to the inner man or woman. In many of his photographic auto-Witkacies, the artist caught the look of incipient madness in his own haunted eyes. He kept photographing himself throughout his life, keeping various albums and collections arranged by kind, also photographing his own paintings and

—Performing Arts Journal 7, no. 3 (PAJ 21) (1983): 59–75.

keeping them in albums. Totally rejected by the art and theatre establishment of his day, Witkacy created his own museum in his home and staged his own mini-dramas with his camera.

Witkacy's letters give another portrait of the artist engaged in battle with existence, trying somehow to survive. These letters, quite without any literary affectation, seem written out of desperate need and give a picture of someone immensely vulnerable, full of insecurities and fears. Offered here is a representative sampling of letters to parents, friends, editor, artistic collaborators, wife, and admired master. A protean self, constantly dissolving into nothingness, Witkacy adopts a variety of tones of voice (the verbal equivalent of his "faces") depending on the recipient of the letter. With his friends, he is ironic and sarcastically self-depreciating; with the German philosopher, Cornelius—like Witkacy a painter as well as a thinker little recognized by his compatriots—he is almost abjectly servile and admiring, finding a father and hero he can worship. To his wife, in some 1600 letters and cards written from 1922 to 1939, he is flamboyant in his self-revelations, often using the same symbols he put on his paintings and pastel portraits to indicate what drugs he has been using and how long he had kept from smoking and drinking. And beyond the grimaces and poses of these letters, there is the naked self, full of horror at his own botched life, poverty, and loneliness and isolation, and clearly foreseeing his own suicide, which he committed on September 18, 1939.

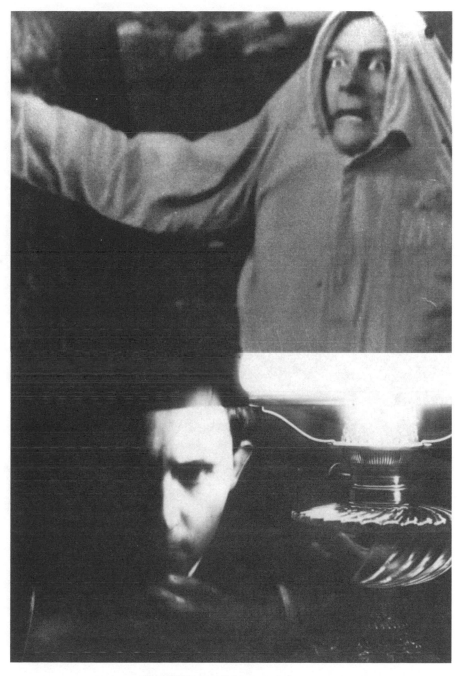

Above: Witkacy in Zakopane, circa 1930

Below: Witkacy in Zakopane, circa 1913

Above, left: Witkacy in Zakopane, circa 1930

Above, right: Witkiewicz Senior, photo taken by his son Witkacy in Lovran, 1913

Below: Witkacy and his wife Jadwiga née Unrug in Zakopane, circa 1920s

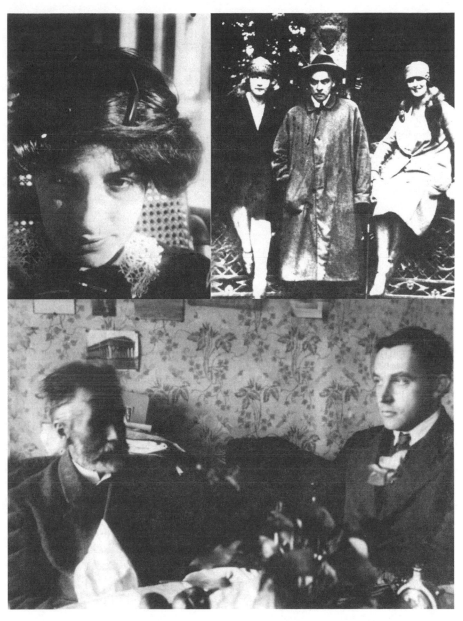

Above, left: Jadwiga Janczewska, Witkacy's fiancée in Zakopane, 1913

Above, right: Witkacy with members of his metaphysical harem in Zakopane, circa 1930

Below: Witkacy with his father in Lovran, circa 1910

Karol Beaurain (1867–1927), Freudian psychiatrist who spent summers in Zakopane. In 1913 he befriended Witkacy and began his psychoanalysis. The letter was written aboard the steamship Orsova *on which Witkacy (after the suicide of his fiancée) sailed with his friend the anthropologist Bronisław Malinowski on their way to Australia via Ceylon.*

Herr Doctor Karol Beaurain Esquire   R.M.S. *Orsova*
Director, Medical Institute   [early June 1914]

Szlazk
Schlesien
Austria
Osterreich
Europe

My Dear and Highly Esteemed Doctor:

I did not come to see you, Doctor, because each moment spent in Poland dealt frightful blows to my pride. It was either death or New Guinea. At this point it's easy to say that. Death and thoughts tending in that direction are no different whether I'm in Zakopane or on the Red Sea. I want to make it to Colombo. Each moment is unbearable torture. I am worthless. As a human being I have lost all credit. As an artist I have ruined myself. Now I have taken on myself the task of effecting a cure by means of a trip. That's what was needed to finish me off completely. All the beauty that I'm seeing acts as the most frightful poison. Why isn't she seeing this, why did I destroy her and the most beautiful love that has ever existed? I'm not idealizing it now that she's dead. I was not able to esteem myself. Because I was worthless. I love only her and I hate only myself. Death must come sooner or later, because it is not possible to endure such hideous suffering for long.

So I bid farewell to you, Dear Doctor, and I kiss your wife's hand and thank you both for everything.

                                                    S. Witkiewicz

My self-portrait and my drawing of you will always be yours for the asking.

– All letters translated by Daniel Gerould, New York, 1983.

Emil Breiter (1886–1943), writer and literary critic, member of the editorial staff of the influential journal, Skamander, *in which Witkacy published "Introduction to Pure Form in the Theatre" in 1920.*

To Emil Breiter   1919(?)

Dear Emil:

You're a real stinker for never writing to me; but I won't say any more about it. You're on the board of *Skamander* and I'm addressing you in your official capacity. The articles and Part II of my theory of the theatre which I have sent to *Skamander* are, given the total confusion existing in the field of art theory, simply *revelations*. I'm very modest and far from being a megalomaniac, but I can vouch for what I'm saying, with only this reservation: the relativity of values in these matters. Almost nothing is written about painting and whatever appears on the subject goes unread because it is mostly nonsense. Literary journals ought to reserve a special column (even if it has to be in small print) for painters who are able to express their thoughts on the subject. Art is one and indivisible and often theory in one field supports another field. I'd like to know whether *Skamander* will publish those pieces or not. There's no way of getting a letter out of Lechoń [the editor of *Skamander*]. If the answer is no, help me to get them published somewhere else. If the answer is yes, there's no terrible hurry and I'd very much like to belong exclusively to *Skamander* and have my own column and associates; at such an advanced age isolation is becoming a bit oppressive. I'd like to have my writing judged for what it is; it's ridiculous for me to be my own promoter. The polemical nature of my writing is unavoidable and contains nothing personal, as you can see from my quarrel with Chwistek whom I treat quite decently despite his gross unfairness toward me. [Bertrand] Russell writes about Bergson, so I *must* write about Chwistek, having no worthier opponent. As for your theory of "classicalization," I am quite classical enough, that is to say, in essence deeply serious in my thinking without false pomposity or willingness to compromise my principles. Your objection about what the Mummy said to Plasfodor is beside the point. What I am concerned with are *formal* values about which no one has the slightest Idea.

In any case, I want to mogulize my energies, that is, start to earn more money, since my financial situation is very difficult.

Please look into my requests. They are pressing ones at the moment. In a year's time none of this will do us any good. Right now I am working exclusively on pure philosophy and what I'm doing might be of some value.

Warmest greetings,
Witkacy

Love to your wife. My address: Cracow, 13 Krupnicza Street c/o Żeleńskis.

[Added on the margin of the page.] Don't show me any *merciful* understanding, but judge me objectively. I beg you.

Kazimiera Żuławska (1883–1971), translator from French and Spanish, mountain climber, wife of novelist and playwright Jerzy Żuławski. Reviewing one of Witkacy's exhibitions, she called him "a painter of great talent, even of genius."

To Kazimiera Żuławska   May 23, 1922
Toruń

Dear Mrs. Kazia:

Thanks a lot for your letter. Unfortunately right now I can't even dream about visiting you. Jasiński sent you the libretto [for my operetta *Miss Tootli-Pootli*]—did you get it? It's too bad I can't meet Mr. Popławski [the composer] personally. Losing one's violin is a terrible thing. My life is complicated and exhausting, but recently it's improved a bit. However, artistically nothing works out right. I've been refused space for my exhibition and I still don't know whether any of my plays will be staged in Cracow this season. I think I'll croak before too long, and not even in the proverbial ditch. I've written a one-act play called *The Cuttlefish, or The Hyrcanian Worldview*. I'm painting in a more highly finished manner.

Tymon is impossible as usual, but one forgives him a lot. My "new" friend, Mr. Zan, Is here with me. What a pity he can't seduce you. He's a real devil. Bronio [Malinowskl] is coming to Poland for the summer. No word from Edward [Zytecki]; I don't know whether he got the copy of *The Water Hen* that I sent him. I have the feeling that I'm totally abandoned and that nothing will ever come of any of my plans for the theatre. I'm renouncing all my ambitions and shutting myself up in a broken-down imitation-ivory tower in Zakopane. Please write to me from time to time, so the umbilical cord between us won't be cut.
        I kiss your metaphysical navel. I embrace Mr. Popławski's lost violin. I have ghastly nightmares.

Yours,

Witkacy

Jadwiga Unrug (1893–1968), granddaughter of the painter Juliusz Kossak. She met Witkacy in Zakopane in the summer of 1922, and they were married on April 30, 1923. By 1925 they agreed to live apart in an experiment in free marriage. From her apartment in Warsaw, Jadwiga promoted Witkacy's career, reading and preparing his manuscripts for publication. Witkacy wrote Jadwiga almost daily. After his death, she worked to preserve and disseminate his works.

To Jadwiga Unrug   Zakopane
                                                      March 25, 1923

Nina:

I haven't yet stopped smoking, but I'm not drinking and have no intention of starting again. The Gucio business ended amicably. But I must point out (in strictest confidence) that as a result of it I am so disgusted with honor and affairs of honor that I totally approve of Karol's idea to have honor abolished by the Senate.

I am painting a large painting and portrait of Mrs. L. (a funny little hen). In addition to that I must write you a few of the things we were talking about, but I don't know whether to go to the very end.

When you were here I thought very little about the real side of our life. Now rather black thoughts, relatively speaking, are coming to me and I must express them. But please don't think that they are the remnants of a state of confusion. In general I always take what is said and what is written at face value and don't you go looking in me for false bottoms and hidden drawers.

1. My hotel brings in almost no income and at times there's a real shortage of cash. As long as the hotel is in operation, which isn't completely certain, there'll always be room and board.

2. I have to make clear in advance that I cannot give up my essential work in order to raise our standard of living. I can do whatever I'm capable of in addition to the essential line, but if my paintings and plays do not prove successful, I won't exhibit inessential things for commercial purposes and I can only limit myself to portrait painting, to which I cannot give my whole being and reach eventual perfection.

3. I count on the success of *Hellcat*, which is to be premièred in the middle of April. [. . .]

4. I can hang a sign on the street advertising my portrait painting—that's as far as I'll go. I could write articles for the papers, but the entire press has boycotted me so far. My book on the theatre [. . .] will earn me a fantastic number of implacable enemies. I cannot count on any friends being won over by the book because of the incredible stupidity of the great majority of "theatre professionals."

5. Any sign of dissatisfaction with me on your part given these difficult conditions might prove to be beyond my endurance. I am writing this not to scare you away from me, but only so you'll see clearly the whole danger of the situation. In certain matters I must be "firm as a rock" and that's where my whole value lies.

I kiss you my poor Nineczka and wish you happiness with me wholeheartedly.

Your Staś

To Jadwiga Unrug   Zakopane
                                                 March 30, 1923

Dear Nineczka:

[. . .] Please stop writing and talking for good and all about uncertainty on my part. For you I am "resigned" to everything, and if I write all that, it is only to avoid in the future any misunderstandings that could destroy good relations between us.

I would like the judgments of other people not to have an effect on you in relation to me and not to call forth the application of various "methods." If I detect a "method" in your way of dealing with me it can only result in a twisting on my part which will take away my freedom in relation to you and destroy what I consider *the most precious in relation to someone, that is, the possibility to be oneself and not the exercising of control by any method.*

I am not a diplomat, and now wearing a mask (which preoccupied me 13 years ago) is torture for me. [. . .]

One must spare oneself unnecessary disappointments. We are both psychic sadists and physical masochists. One has to watch out for that. I can handle my sadism and it will even do me good. [. . .]

Don't think any more about uncertainties and consider me as your husband with a capital "H." [. . .]

Love and kisses. I miss you a lot.

Your Witkacy

To Jadwiga Unrug   Zakopane
                                                                July 20, 1926
NP₂ [2 days of no smoking]

Dearest Nineczka:

        I have no idea why the postcard I sent you from Zakopane made such an
impression on you, since I haven't been drinking since Wednesday and I have no
intention of starting again. I haven't smoked for two days and I feel awful. My life is a
total fiasco. I live through the days with tightly clenched teeth, writing, rewriting, taking
walks (what for?), and talking. Absolutely for no purpose. What for? I'm growing more
and more serious about committing suicide, because the shape my life is taking disgusts
me profoundly, and yet I don't see any possibility of creating any other shape for it: all of
it leads to sinking into worse and worse material poverty. Of course I don't treat any of it
the least bit seriously and am working enthusiastically on a new novel. Undoubtedly I'm
suffering a temporary setback due to NP [no smoking]. *Durchhalten.*
        But I have rotten luck. Yesterday when I was taking a pee in the woods and
looking absentmindedly at the landscape, a horse fly bit me on the prick. It swelled up
like a balloon and I thought it was going to fall off. But iodine and [Dr.] Staroniewicz
saved this priceless gadget for the benefit of future generations. Now It's just red, but it
still may fall off. If it does, I'll send it to you preserved in formaldehyde. [. . .]
        With all my love,

                                                                    Yours,
                                                                    W

P.S. Best to the family.
        Both clocks show 9:30 p.m. as I write these words—highly significant.
        I eat little, but well. I'll fast on Fridays.
        But it's all pretty piss poor.

To Jadwiga Unrug   Zakopane
                                                                March 12, 1929
                                          NP$_{9m}$ NHer$_4$P [no tea drinking]

    Oh Nineczka. You know I never ran out on you spiritually. Except when you put me on the chain physically. But even then I would hate the Queen of Sheba and every one of "my women" if I had to be duty-bound by her. Freedom is all that counts. And yet I wouldn't have endured so much with any woman as with you—six years is something infernal. I love you not because it's on paper, but really, but I cannot force myself to do certain things, on a desert island it would really be just the same and I would be forced to hate you. So it's time to forget accusations that I have a roving eye. Burdening my conscience and guilt without guilt is for me frightful. When you write that you're crying it wrings my guts but what am I to do? Damn it all, I can't feel something that I don't feel. I think that we must get out of this trap or what will the rest of our lives be like? Remember, I go on loving you, when you yourself send me out into the world of people. I can't write about it any more. [. . .]

To Jadwiga Unrug   Zakopane
                                                                 May 13, 1927
NP$_3$

My dearest Nineczka:

    Thank you very much for your letter and the news. The more I think about the latest experiments in our married life, the more convinced I become that a fundamental reform has to take place according to the precepts of my theory, since otherwise the results may be deplorable on both sides. If we follow my plan, we still have a chance to preserve what is most important in our marriage, which is our devotion to each other. I'm working on another article. I long for you psychically (and even more psycho-physically, but not erotically), but I shudder at the thought of the chain that my neck is still aching from.

    Oh, if only you'd try to understand what the true value of our relationship can be in the future instead of destroying what is most important in it, all for the sake of a fiction—because for you there's no question of passion, only an illusion of ownership. Of course I'm quite unhappy about it, and so far at the point we've reached there's only moral and physical disaster, the loss of any desire for life and creativity, and *hatred*.

                                                          Your true husband

I sent the book to your Father.
Thanks a lot for the proofs.
Total poverty. I keep borrowing 5 złotys at a time.

To Jadwiga Unrug   [Zakopane]
                                                                October 8, 1937

D.N. [Dearest Nineczka],

    Cornelius arrived yesterday. An incredibly nice guy. But there are atrocious revelations besides real life ones: he accepts occultism—a defeat for me (don't tell anyone about this). Around October 18 we'll be in Warsaw. Could we put him up in my room? The sofa—a mattress, I can sleep on the floor, wherever you want (in bed with you)—provided he can stay with us. Rent a sofa? Think about that. I beg you. Warm kisses. You are unique in your family.

                                                                      Your St.

My Nineczko—if you arrange this you'll be a second Cleopatra. Warm kisses.

                                                                      Your St.

Running low on the moolah. But what I'll earn in Warsaw is yours—my little monster.

To Jadwiga Unrug   Zakopane
                                                                    May 3, 1938

Dearest Nineczka:

You have no idea how I'm longing for you and how I need spiritual help from you. [. . .] What I'd give to be able to be assured of 200 zlotys on a regular basis. There's no news from Nowy Sącz—all the portraits were done for a down payment, the remainder was to have been sent after the first. My state is not good—we'll talk about it all, it's not worth writing any more. It's terribly difficult for me to rise above all this and I have a strong premonition that it's all coming to an end. Certain negative sides of my nature have indirectly made me recognize this and I have strongly doubted whether I will succeed in adequately constructing the final era of my life or whether it will all end tragically. You can perhaps help me with this if you so desire. In my relationship to you I have been in the wrong too—in fact I have been in the wrong with everyone and everything, including life itself. And now it's extremely difficult to start all over again. My cold is better, but the weather is lousy. [. . .]
    Love and kisses. My attachment to you is great and so is my belief in your compassion for me, which serves to justify my further life.

                                                                      Your Staś

To Jadwiga Unrug   Zakopane
July 11, 1938

Dearest Nineczka,

[. . .] Reading your letter, I felt tears well up in my eyes. Your goodness touched me so, but if someone really saw my state, you would not be astonished at anything and you would give me complete freedom of action. I am constantly suffering and I have no hope of improvement. Therefore I beg you—give up trying to save me and if I dig my way out it will be a miracle. I don't have anything within me on which to find support. [. . .] Therefore don't have any expectations as far as I am concerned, and if something comes of it, it will be a surprise. I won't write on this subject any more. Think how much horror I shall avoid if I leave this world in time. That will be the only sensible thing to do. So don't insist on my holding out, I'm doing what I can, but I cannot promise that I will go on living in constant suffering.

Love and kisses,
with great devotion.

Witkacy

Marceli Popławski (1882–1948), Polish composer and music director at Teatr Nowy in Toruń. Witkacy attempted to interest Popławski in producing his anti-colonial African "Operetta in Three Acts in Pure Form," Miss Tootli-Pootli (written in 1920, but not published until 1974 and first performed in 1975).

To Kazimiera Żuławska   Zakopane
In Toruń   February 6, 1924

Dear Mrs. Kazia and You, Oh, Marceli!

The Szpakiewiczes were here and he promised to put on one of my plays in the Spring. It will be either *Gyubal Wahazar* or *The Madman and the Nun* on a double bill with *The New Deliverance*. Could you eventually lend the latter to him (it's in numbers 3 and 4 of *Zwrotnica* [*The Switch*])? I'm wallowing in pessimism and covered with snow. You can't see the fences. For the past two days we've been cut off from Cracow. I've stopped developing philosophically. I've been doing portraits for money and I made $24. Yesterday I finished the first draft of a play in three acts and four scenes (Act II has two scenes), entitled *A Normal Person*.

I've got a feeling I'm sinking Into the abyss. I may have an exhibition in Warsaw in March.

Irreproachable family life.

More and more enemies. Fewer and fewer friends. I'd like to see you both very much (especially you and Marceli).

My sense of humor has deserted me.

My projects for the near future are seven plays and about 100 paintings.

I kiss your navels with lips twisted in moral pain. I expect the worst, that is to say, physical pain, blindness, fire and idiocy.

Your faithful

Witkacy

Please write me a lovely long letter.

Mother and Nina send their greetings.

Edmund Wierciński (1889–1955), actor with the Reduta, educator, and from 1927 director of the Teatr Nowy, Poznań, where he staged Witkacy's Metaphysics of a Two-Headed Calf in 1928.

To Edmund Wierciński   August 26, 1927

Dear Mr. Wierciński:

Thank you for your letter and for not taking my behavior as a sign of ill will. I consider Poznań as a most unfortunate location for an experimental theatre, but there's nothing to be done on that score. It should have been established in Warsaw. As far as Polish authors are concerned, there aren't many who count. [. . .] As for foreign playwrights, Strindberg's *Ghost Sonata* (there's a very good translation by Stanisław Alberti). I'm not well acquainted with foreign literature. But in German there's Ivan Goll, Hasenclever, Kaiser, Unruh, Bronnen, Paul Kornfeld (Vienna). In English there's Synge (Irish) (very interesting, Tauchnitz edition). I've got one thing by Goll and one by Synge in translation, but not authorized—I'll send them to you. [...] I don't know O'Neill (American), but they say his plays are excellent. Of the French, there's *Ubu Roi*, I've forgotten the name of the author, and there's Pellerin's *Têtes de rechanges* (Masques, Société des Spectacles Gaston Baty, 15, Avenue Montaigne). It would be wonderful if it were finally possible to give a staging of Miciński's *Basilissa Teophano*, even a condensed version using curtains instead of scenery. I'm sure you know all these plays (Ribemont-Dessaignes's *L'Empereur de Chine*) (Synge's collection contains 6 plays). As for my plays, I'd recommend as a trial presenting what was given at the Maly Theatre: *The Madman and the Nun* and *The New Deliverance* (one act) for one evening or *The Pragmatists* and *The Cuttlefish* for one evening. Or *The Water Hen*, *Gyubal Wahazar*, (4 acts, three settings) and *Pentemychos*, *In a Small Country House* of the full-length plays. I can't provide you with manuscripts because I'm a member of ZAD and they're with my agent Rechtleben. Write to him at Leszno 52 (the Agency). That's all for now. Perhaps I'll have better luck with you than with the others; Modrzejewska was my godmother, but I didn't inherit anything from her.

In the meantime I remain very truly yours and wish you and your entire company all the best. Special greetings to Murcia and Felcia.

S. I. Witkiewicz

Did you and your wife simply leave the Reduta, or had you had enough?

Hans Cornelius (1863–1947), German philosopher and professor in Munich, whose work Witkacy had admired since his youth and with whom he corresponded from 1935-1939, writing over 100 letters and cards. Unable to afford a trip to Germany, Witkacy invited Cornelius, whom he regarded as his master and father confessor, to Zakopane in 1937.

To Hans Cornelius   July 26, 1935

Dear Sir and Honored Herr Professor:

I was truly happy to get your letter and photograph. But in retrospect I was horrified that you sent such treasures by regular mail, and not registered. If the package had been lost, I wouldn't have known anything about it and might have thought that you left my letter unanswered.

I have read both your monographs. Such a concise formulation of your philosophy is quite wonderful, and the course of your life most interesting, showing a striking similarity to my own. I totally agree with your social ideas and I eagerly await their full exposition in print. There's yet another similarity between us; like you, I was devoid of musical ability, until I was seven years old I hated music, and even prevented my mother, who graduated from the Conservatory, from taking up that art. Smeared with holy oil during a very serious illness—something not in the least funny—I became, psychically and physically, a totally different child. I started to like music and due to practicing developed my ear (which before had been hopelessly unmusical) to the point that I could write down the notes if something was played for me. With the coming of the war my passion for music (whose musicality I grasped in formal terms) died out. I mention this because these occurrences are psychologically arresting—I think that Weismann cites such an instance. My later life as well was marked off by misfortune (one of the greatest)—my fiancée committed suicide in 1914. (I have now been married for twelve years, without children fortunately, since the responsibility for them would have driven me crazy.) After that incident, I went to Australia with the friend of my youth, Malinowski (at present professor of sociology at London University—his book, *The Sexual Life of Savages*, published in German by Grethlein in Leipzig, it's even dedicated to me), and from there during the war to Russia (I was a Russian subject, and the Australian press recognize me as a supporter of the coalition). There in Russia in a regiment of the guard (quite by chance!) I spent the war and observed the entire course of the revolution from close up; it was a splendid show, especially since the Pawlowski regiment in which I served started the first revolution. In 1918 I returned to Poland and I have been working here ever since almost without a break, but in very modest circumstances, since I wish to be free and uncompromising in my work. But enough about personal matters.

I am thankful beyond words for your kindness to a disciple scarcely known to you and for sending your photographic likeness. I am waiting for a particular moment of inspiration to make a sketch from both your photographic portraits; I shall send it to you immediately. In the meantime I am sending you a Polish-German dictionary, deeply touched that you wish to learn my difficult language. I am somewhat pained that I cannot express my thoughts to you accurately. I've decided to make something like a "piano transcription" of my monadology—which is the completion of my *Hauptwerk*—which I will translate into German and, if you will agree, send it to you in typescript. I have here in the vicinity of Zakopane a few friends and enemies (in the theoretical sense of the word, something that Lipps could not understand), with whom I can discuss things. These are figures from the "official" circle of Polish philosophy: Professor Ingarden from Lwów (a pupil of Husserl—a phenomenologist), Professor Szuman (a psychologist from Cracow University), Assistant Professor Metalmann from the same University. Kotarbiński (a reist, not unlike "late" Brentano), a Professor at Warsaw University, with whom I'm engaged in a controversy (he has received from me 250 pages of a critique of his reism), is somewhat further off in Silesia. And so you can see that now I am not completely isolated, which has been the curse of my life. Three of the above mentioned are going to make critiques of my *Hauptwerk*.

Once more I thank you from the bottom of my heart for your extraordinary kindness which together with your picture (so very important for me!) not only allows me to honor you and be grateful for your very existence, but also—if you will give your permission—to love you from afar. I am now waging war with Whitehead, about whom I am planning to write a critical piece (it's already begun). Please accept, dear sir and honored Herr Professor, the expression of my deepest respect and love.

Your unworthy disciple,
S. Witkiewicz

SOURCES

Czartoryska, Urszula. "Laboratorium 'psychologi nieeuklidesowej' czyli o fotografiach Witkacego." *Odra*, March 1980, 55–61.

———. "Le Photographie." In *S. I. Witkiewicz; Génie multiple de Pologne*. Lausanne: L'Age d'Homme, 1981.

Degler, Janusz. *Witkacego Portret Wielokrotny. Szkice i materialy do biografii (1918–1939)*. Warsaw: Państwowy Instytut Wydawniczy, 2009.

Franczak, Ewa and Stefan Okołowicz. "Le Portrait multiple de Witkacy." In *Cahier Witkiewicz* no. 4, Actes du colloque de Bruxelles, Novembre 1981. Translated and edited by Alain van Crugten. Lausanne: L'Age d'Homme, 1982.

Muzeum Pomorza Środkowego w Słupsku. *Witkacy i Przyjaciele w Fotografii Władysława Jana Grabskiego*. Słupsk: Zamek Książąt Pomorskich, 1999.

Skwara, Marta. *Szczecińskie Witkacjana*. Szczecin: Książnica Pomorska, 1999.

Witkacy. Metaphysical Portraits: Photographs by Stanisław Ignacy Witkiewicz. Edited by Urszula Czartoryska and Stefan Okołowicz. NY: Robert Miller Gallery, 1999.

Witkiewicz, Jan Stanisław. *Witkacy i Witkiewiczowie*. Bern: Wydawnictwo Pocublice, 1982.

Witkiewicz, Stanisław Ignacy. *Listy do Bronisława Malinowskiego*. Edited by Tomasz Jodełka-Burzecki and introduction by Edward C. Martinek. Warsaw: Państwowy Instytut Wydawniczy, 1981.

———. *Listy do żony (1923–27)*, Vol. I. Edited by Janusz Degler and Anna Micińska. Warsaw: Państwowy Instytut Wydawniczy, 2005.

———. *Listy do żony (1928–31)*, Vol. II. Edited by Janusz Degler and Anna Micińska. Warsaw: Państwowy Instytut Wydawniczy, 2007.

———. *Przeciw Nicości: Fotografie Stanisława Ignacego Witkiewicza*. Edited by Ewa Franczak and Stefan Okołowicz. Cracow: Wydawnictwo Literackie, 1986.

———. *Wiersze i rysunki*. Edited by Anna Micińska and Urszula Kenar. Cracow: Wydawnictwo Literackie, 1977.

Witkiewiczowa, Jadwiga. "Wspomnienia o Stanisławie Ignacym Witkiewiczu." In *Spotkanie z Witkacym*. Edited by Janusz Degler. Jelenia Góra: Teatr im. Cypriana Norwida, 1979.

Żakiewicz, Anna. *Witkacy (1885-1939)*. Warsaw: Edipresse, 2006.

Żuławski, Juliusz. *Z domu*. Warsaw: Państwowy Instytut Wydawniczy, 1978.

Caricature of Villiers de l'Isle-Adam by André Gill

VILLIERS DE L'ISLE-ADAM AND SCIENCE FICTION

Count Jean Marie Mathias Philippe Auguste Villiers de l'Isle-Adam (1828–89), an impoverished French aristocrat and disabused late Romantic living in an age of positivism and technology, is best known for his grandiose Symbolist drama, *Axël*. But he was also the author of many fantastic and macabre stories (collectively titled *Cruel Tales*), several of which can be considered science fiction in that they provide a supposedly scientific basis for imaginary inventions, and also of a full-fledged science fiction novel, *The Future Eve*, about the fabrication of an ideal female android. Largely a cult figure until the late twentieth century, Villiers has been rediscovered by new generations of readers as a result of the popularity of fantastic literature and its intensive study by modern scholars who no longer regard it as marginal and out of the mainstream.

Acclaimed by some as Villiers's masterpiece (the author himself called it his *Don Quixote* that would make his name and avenge his neglect at the hands of the critics), *The Future Eve* has been reprinted in France in every decade since the 1950s and is available in several different English translations.[1] It is now possible to place this major work within the science fiction tradition and to appreciate its originality.

Written between 1877 and 1879, appearing in periodical form in 1880, and published in final version in 1886, this strange and fascinating novel is remarkably contemporary in its sardonic tone and skeptical sensibility, despite its slow pace and ornate, overblown manner of presentation. Viewed as a total structure, *The Future Eve* conforms to a familiar science fiction pattern in stories of man-made creatures: that of the creator who loses control of his creation—in this case, happily so, since the android acquires a soul from contact with mystical powers from beyond. But philosophical discourse, not plot, dominates the novel, and Villiers ironically twists the basic story of the creation of the android, renders it equivocal, and adds layer upon layer of parodic dimension in his exploration of what for him is of prime importance: the problem of how we perceive the material world and how we represent it, given the newly discovered technical means of recording, reproduction, and duplication. Epistemological questions about the limits of our ability to know reality come to obsess the twin protagonists of the novel, representing opposite sides of the human psyche: the rationalistic and the spiritual. Since illusion ultimately proves to be indistinguishable from reality, the solution to the dilemma proposed by Villiers in *The Future Eve* through his two alter egos is to will one's own superior illusion and impose it on the world as a subjective reality, with the aid of modern technological artifice. Such radical solipsism can be sustained on Earth only briefly; because the Ideal cannot co-exist with reality, death becomes the sole realm where the dualities of spirit and matter are to be resolved.

As the novel opens, Lord Celian Ewald—a wealthy, handsome, twenty-seven-year-old English nobleman—is ready to blow his brains out because Miss Alicia Clary, the beautiful actress he loves, has a crass, banal soul that fills him with revulsion and destroys his desire. Enamored of the Absolute and the Infinite, Lord Ewald is appalled to discover that the body of a Venus de Milo can be inhabited by a foolish materialistic bourgeoise who typifies the soulless mechanical world of the nineteenth century. This degenerate age does not repress commonplace sexuality, but denies fulfillment to longings for the transcendent. Aspiring to the religious and moral beliefs of an earlier time, a fastidious idealist and aesthete like Lord Ewald feels himself an alien in a culture given over to commerce and rationalism, and seeks a way out—to another world—through suicide.

–*Science-Fiction Studies* 11, no. 3 (November 1984): 318–323.

In New York with his attractive but vacuous fiancée, the English nobleman pays a farewell visit to his old friend, Thomas Alva Edison, at the inventor's home in Menlo Park, New Jersey. Learning of the young man's desperate decision, the "Wizard of Menlo Park" offers to provide Lord Ewald with an android that will be an exact replica of Miss Alicia Clary but without her offensively vulgar soul. Spokesman for scientific pragmatism, the American inventor sets out to demonstrate the superiority of artifice over nature and the necessity of illusion in the face of an unknowable external reality.

Inclusion of the historical Edison in the framework of fantasy was Villiers's masterstroke. It gave the novel topicality when it first appeared. The inventor had moved to Menlo Park only in 1876, and the following year was made a member of the French Legion of Honor. Recent inventions, such as the telephone, microphone, and phonograph, figure prominently in *The Future Eve*; and since the principles upon which the android is constructed are possible extensions of what has already been discovered, the author is able to give a scientific rationale for the creation of such a marvelous being and induce belief in his readers that perhaps it could someday be realized. For this purpose, the novel has been projected a few years into the future; we are told that Edison is forty-two, making the time of the action 1889. Inventions still to come—the loudspeaker and the cinema (in color and with sound!)—are included among Edison's accomplishments and described in detail.[2]

It is sometimes said (by Maxim Jakubowski in *Anatomy of Wonder*, for example) that Villiers in *The Future Eve* was a follower and imitator of Jules Verne.[3] But if Villiers has a French precursor, it is rather his friend Charles Cros (1842–88), bohemian poet and inventor, who in 1869 wrote treatises on the means of communication with the planets and on color photography, and in the spring of 1877 submitted a description of a phonograph to the Academy of Sciences. For his conception of Edison, the author of *The Future Eve* may have drawn upon Cros and his bizarre tale, *The Science of Love* (1874).

In any case, the inclusion of the historical Edison results in a curious mixture of fact and fiction that gives the novel its modern sensibility and disturbing resonances. Combining facetious jokes, erudite digressions, satire, sarcasm, farsighted predictions, and long Wagnerian arias (Villiers was an early French pilgrim to Bayreuth), *The Future Eve* presents a grotesque and prophetic picture of a commercial culture of mechanical duplication, deceptive publicity, and manipulated appearances. The tone is at one and the same time playful, operatic, and ironic. (In *Against Nature*, Joris-Karl Huysmans, one of Villiers's first admirers and disciples, refers to his "savage raillery, cruel jeering, and gloomy jesting" and likens it to Swift's black rage against humanity.)[4]

The crux of the matter lies in Villiers's ambivalent attitude towards Edison, his technological feats and showmanship, and at the same time in the extremely ambiguous role that both the "Wizard of Menlo Park" and his magical "science" play in the novel. Edison, the apostle of reason, the very embodiment of the new, becomes the agent for reinstating the Ideal, as he himself re-enacts the old religious and cultural mythologies in modern scientific guise. The rationalistic worldview which has killed the Absolute now offers to manufacture a perfect replica as a substitute. This is the paradox at the heart of *The Future Eve* and of Villiers's attitude to science.

Doubly dedicated to both dreamers and deriders, *The Future Eve* maintains an unresolved duality in all its aspects. Edison's perfect android, showing the superiority of artifice over nature, is praised to the point of mockery, and Lord Ewald's lofty Ideal of womanhood, which makes him prefer his own imaginings to any living human being, emerges as an extreme form of narcissism and autoeroticism. As an aristocratic poet,

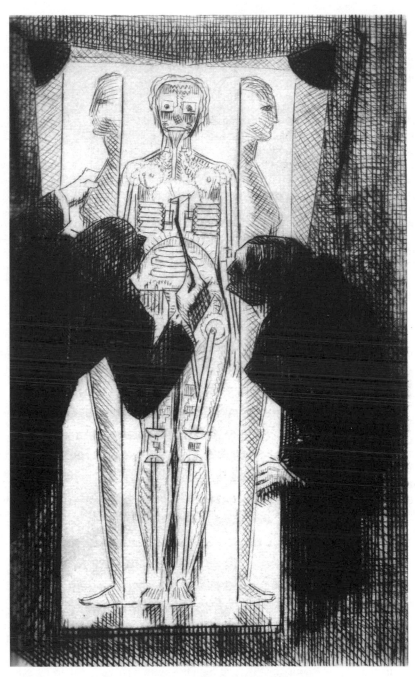

Illustration by Raphael Drouart for *L' Éve future* (1925),
The android's insides

Villiers is filled with hatred for a scientific-technological age that worships progress and material success, and yet at the same time he is fascinated by its machines which can copy and forge with such skill that in a world of impoverished nature and cheapened feelings, he is tempted to choose the reign of artfully calculated illusion over that of vulgar reality.[5]

In his *Cruel Tales*, Villiers portrays an inauthentic world in which illusion and artifice are replacing life; genuine emotion no longer exists or has been driven inward to the realm of solitude and silence. But publicly everything can be brilliantly staged and given striking shape by simulated words and gestures. The theatre and the theatricalization of life become images of this process for Villiers, an ardent playgoer and playwright, who recognized the centrality of the Parisian stage (with its newly-acquired technical means of dazzling illusion) for French social life in the second half of the nineteenth century and saw its broad metaphoric implications.

"I hope that there will soon be four or five hundred theatres in every capital, where the ordinary events of life are acted far better than in reality, so that nobody will take much trouble any more over living for himself," Villiers declares in one tale, "Sentimentalism," where the suggestion is made that whenever we feel a strong emotion we should hire an actor to express it for us.[6] In another story, "The Glory Machine," canned applause is produced in the theatre by newly perfected automata. In other tales, advertising slogans are projected into the sky (where heavenly signs and portents once appeared), and a device is patented for chemical analysis of the final sighs of the dying. What was formerly the expression of the supernatural will or the individual soul is now subject to recording and duplication. Since the reality of the phenomenal world is an illusion, each human being is imprisoned within his or her own consciousness and lonely dreams; the only communication possible with others is via a limited number of programmed words and gestures which can be better produced by duplicating machines, actors, or automata.

Accordingly, it is not inappropriate that *The Future Eve* opens with Edison alone in study, lamenting that it was not possible to record great "noises of the past" or to recapture for an audio-archive "lost sounds" such as the sound of the trumpet at Jericho, the Sermon on the Mount, and the Tidings brought to Mary. He then thinks how it would have been possible to verify the supernatural happenings in the Bible if photographs could have been made, for example, of the Deluge taken from the top of Mount Ararat, or the crossing of the Red Sea (with subsequent issuing of postcards). These seemingly irrelevant and jocose reflections actually establish Edison's (and Villiers's) primary concern in the novel: the retention, recording, and reproduction of a "reality" that will always remain uncertain and problematic.

The method by which the android's speech is produced is an instance of the novel's concern with the ingenuities of dubbing and doubling. All the words pronounced by the new Eve are those of her model, Alicia Clary, as she recited the works of the greatest poets—recorded, recombined, and played back on a golden phonograph in the android's chest. When Lord Ewald objects that his ideal love will have only a limited number of possible responses, Edison points out that "real" conversation is infinitely more restricted in its narrow circle of clichés.

The novel's recurring theme of replication is carried one step further by the author in that the old gods, myths, and beliefs—seemingly vanquished by science—are repeated in new technological modes; even the great poetic works—the Bible, *Paradise Lost*, and *Faust*—become synthesized and replayed. Science is mythologized.

Returning from exile, the occult, otherworldly, and transcendent infiltrate the stronghold of materialism, where they are reanimated and reinstated. Brandishing a perpetual cigar and offering his friend lights from strange electrical devices, Edison is a modern Prometheus attempting to bring humankind freedom. He is also a daring rival of God the Father, proclaiming *fiat lux* with electricity and creating the new Eve in his underground laboratory, which is "our lost Eden, rediscovered," in America; formerly it was a cave used as burial grounds of Algonquin tribes. In this Avernus to which the questing heroes must descend in a special electrical elevator, there is an "artificial paradise" with counterfeit vegetation, breezes, flowers, and birds—some with human voices and laughter—featuring a recorded nightingale's song and a mechanical hummingbird which can recite all of *Hamlet*. Here the influence of Verne's *Journey to the Center of the Earth* (1864) is discernible, as well as the example of the bizarre inventions designed for King Ludwig of Bavaria.[7]

Legendary and epic analogues abound, but it is the Faustian theme (so prominent in fantastic literature) that is the most fully deployed after the fundamental biblical and Promethean motifs. In the second section of the novel, entitled "The Pact," Lord Ewald, in pursuit of the Absolute; enters into a demonic bargain with Edison, even though he knows the experiment to be mortally dangerous. But the "Wizard of Menlo Park" is a white magician, a compassionate modern devil, whose mocking laugh contains all human sorrows. Edison's creation of the android, Lord Ewald senses, is a "violent shriek of despair," expressing his love for humanity. The heavens are vacant; "on this stellar speck, lost in a corner of the boundless abyss," Edison is a rebellious angel using the old forbidden knowledge to fashion solace for man. "Since our gods and our aspirations are no longer anything but *scientific*, why shouldn't our loves be so too?" asks the American inventor.

Daughter of the Zeus-like Edison's mind, the magneto-electric android (named Hadaly) is the Ideal made material, corresponding to Lord Ewald's deepest desires, a radiant priestess and envoy from a land beyond, recalling her lover to heaven. "Photosculpted" on the body of Alicia Clary, the copy will be more like the model than the original itself, because reality is mediocre and ever-changing, whereas the android has the eternal beauty of the dream. The young English lord—who despises the woman he loves because she is a sphinx without an enigma, merely ordinary mortal exuding animal spirits—is anti-human and therefore rabidly anti-woman. The novel's misogyny is part of its ideological thesis (the triumph of thought over matter) and based on hatred of life and of the life-giving. It is significant that Lord Ewald first experiences true passion for his fiancée in what he imagines to be his last interview with Alicia Clary, but what is in fact his initial meeting with the android, who is "a superlative machine for creating visions" and a consummate actress capable of playing many different women. In her he finds his own soul reduplicated.

Villiers's future Eve would seem to anticipate the Dadaist bachelor machines and mechanical brides, if it were not for the fact that she is utterly chaste and serves to neutralize any low and degrading desires that her lover might have had for the original living model. The only women whom Lord Ewald can accept are martyrs and consolers, and it is essential that the android will remain an eternal virgin. In this, the future Eve resembles the second Eve, Mary. In all the detailed technical discussion of the construction and functioning of the android, there is never any mention of sexual organs. The novel is concerned with reproduction as replication by artificial (that is to say, artful and artistic) means, but turns its back on reproduction as procreation, which is natural

Illustration by Raphael Drouart for *L' É ve future* (1925),
The android is shipped to England by Lord Ewald in a black ebony coffin

and life-continuing. *The Future Eve* moves relentlessly towards renunciation of all that is earthly—and finally of life itself.

Through telepathic communication and psychic current from a mysterious being, the android acquires a supernatural essence. "A soul which is unknown to me has passed over my work," Edison is forced to admit. The secret voice of Sowana, a consoling woman who has suffered greatly and become a spiritual medium of thought transmission, has guided the "Wizard of Menlo Park" and now directs the android on her transcendent journey. Edison, who starts the novel as a ruthless and pragmatic technician, is revealed to be a creative artist and the director of a *theatrum mundi* controlled by higher powers,

Since the ability of mind to rise above matter and of consciousness to mold reality is transient, and perhaps itself an illusion, Lord Ewald's desire for union with the Absolute can be accomplished only in death. Thus the novel moves to an ironically tragic denouement. Resolving to live in happy isolation with Hadaly on his ancestral estate, the young lord has his android bride shipped to England in a large crate—after she has first climbed into the black ebony coffin, lined with black satin, in which she travels (ominously recalling tales of vampires), and then been disconnected. Edison packs the instruction manual in the coffin, telling Lord Ewald how his new Eve is to be activated by manipulating the rings on her fingers, to be fed on special pills, and to have her joints oiled once a month with an extract of roses.[8]

During the crossing of the Atlantic on the liner *Wonderful*, a storm strikes and fire breaks out in the hold—the Promethean flame now turned destructive. Despite the young lord's superhuman efforts to reach his love, the android is immolated as on a funeral pyre; and when the ship goes down, she sinks back into the non-being of the waters. The natural elements express their fury after being downgraded in favor of the artificial; the deluge has come again, in vengeance for Edison's challenge of the deity. The despairing English nobleman is forcibly saved against his will, whereas the real Alicia Clary, coincidentally on the same voyage, drowns when her lifeboat overturns. From his castle in England, Lord Ewald telegraphs Edison a few final words before committing suicide (as he had originally intended at the start of the novel). *The Future Eve* ends with a Wagnerian *Liebestod* in which love is linked to death; only suicide enables one to rise superior to a detestable world where life is inherently vile. (The poet Paul Verlaine called the catastrophe devastating in that a soul is forever annihilated and Edison, its creator, crushed. Noting that when Villiers died in 1889 [the year the novel takes place], the real Edison was in Paris, Verlaine wonders if the American inventor was aware that he was the hero of such a splendid symbolic work.)

Epic in its ambitions, Villiers's novel has been called the French *Faust*. In the chapter on "Robots and Humans" in his theoretical study *Futurology and the Fantastic*, Stanisław Lem makes a somewhat less favorable estimate. He judges *The Future Eve* as proto-science fiction, touchingly anachronistic in its naïve technical descriptions of the mechanism of the android (lacking even any indication of how her sight functions) and inept in its inadequately justified attribution of a soul to Hadaly, but farsighted in its satiric analysis of linguistic clichés, which anticipates the plays of Ionesco.[9] The Soviet scholar, Nadezhda Rykova, on the other hand, considers *The Future Eve* as a science fiction utopian fantasy which by the end—given Villiers's belief in the power of the dream—becomes transformed into a fairy tale, but nonetheless remains prophetic in its exploration of the motif of the automaton that acquires independent existence and free will. Here the Russian writer sees a bond between Villiers's work and modern science fiction; indeed, she compares it to Lem's *Solaris*, where the heroine created by powers unknown to man has more than a little in common with the android Hadaly.[10] Soviet writers looked upon the decadent aristocrat with unexpected favor in part because he was one of the very few established French authors who welcomed the Commune sympathetically.

Musicians have been drawn to Villiers's work. *The Future Eve* was one of Maurice Ravel's favorite books, along with Huysmans's *Against Nature*, and he hoped to write an opera about a female android. The American composer Glenn Branca calls his Ninth Symphony "L'Ève Future" because it contains sung portions of Villiers's text. It seems likely that sooner or later *The Future Eve* will become an opera or perhaps a film.

NOTES

1. *L'Ève future* first appeared in English in an abridged and adapted version by Florence Crewe Jones as *The Future Eve*, published in *Argosy-All-Story* in December 18, 1926–January 22, 1927. The first complete English version, in book form, was *The Eve of the Future*, translated by Marilyn Gaddis Rose (Lawrence, KS: Coronado Press, 1981). The following year a new English version appeared, *Tomorrow's Eve*, translated and introduced by Robert Martin Adams (Urbana, IL: University of Illinois Press, 1982). Citations from the novel are from Adams's translation, since my essay was originally a review article of *Tomorrow's Eve*. Adams's translation also appears as *The Future Eve* in *The Decadent Reader: Fiction, Fantasy and Perversion from Fin-de-Siècle France*, ed Asti Hustvedt (New York: Zone, 1998).
2. For a discussion of Edison's creation of the android, see Jacques Noiray, "*L'Ève Future*. I. L'Andréide. Ses Origines, Son Fonctionnement," *Le Romancier et la Machine: L'Image de la machine dans le roman français (1850–1900). II Jules Verne—Villiers de l'Isle-Adam* (Paris: Jose Corti, 1982), 277–312.
3. Maxim Jakubowski in *An Anatomy of Wonder: A Critical Guide to Science Fiction*, ed. Neil Barron (New York: Bowker, 1987), 408.
4. Joris-Karl Huysmans, *Against Nature*, anonymous translation (New York: Dover, 1989), Chapter 14.
5. See Jean Pierrot, *L'Imaginaire décadent (1800–1900)* (Paris: Presse Universitaires de France), 97–98, 207–8, 214. Pierrot points out Villiers's ambivalence toward the machine. The creation of material simulacra allows the human imagination to create its own universe. Edison's technology enables artificial settings to replace natural landscape and bring about the triumph of illusion. Artifice is superior to nature.
6. Villiers de l'Isle-Adam, *Contes cruels. Nouveaux Contes cruels*, ed. P.-G. Castex (Paris: Garnier, 1968), 155.
7. Pierrot, *L'Imaginaire décadent*, 208.
8. Noiray, *Le Romancier et la Machine*, 352–57.
9. Stanisław Lem, *Fantastyka i Futurologia* (Cracow: Wydawnictwo Literackie, 1970), 46–47, 50–51.
10. N. I. Rykova, "Vilye de Lil'-Adam i ego rasskazy," in *Les Contes Cruels et autres histoire* (Moscow: Progress, 1966), 14–15.

Drawing by Franciszek Starowieyski for Janusz Majewski's film *Lokis* (1970)

EASTERN EUROPEAN BEAR HUGS:
CINEMA, THEATRE, OPERA

The Russian film *Bear's Kiss* (2002), written and directed by Sergei Bodrov with music by Giya Kancheli, is a polyglot, international production involving a half dozen European countries and eleven production companies.[1] Bodrov's film is a twenty-first century version of the stories about a man-bear that are found in the folklore and mythology of many nations, but seem particularly indigenous to Eastern Europe.

It is this cultural aspect of *Bear's Kiss* as an archetypal animal-groom narrative that interests me. The major source for modern treatments of inter-species love between bear and human is Prosper Mérimée's nineteenth-century fantastic tale set in Lithuania, "Lokis," which, as we shall see, has repeatedly been adapted for the theatre and cinema in Russia and Eastern Europe.

Although not directly inspired by Mérimée, Bodrov's *Bear's Kiss* is a contemporary variant on the archetype of the animal fiancé. In this myth or legend the beast appears in the form of a bear, who embodies raw power, sexuality, and pagan magic beyond civilization and outside established religion. In traditional retellings of the story, such as the fairy tale of Beauty and the Beast, the heroine's anxieties about her future husband's animalistic side are overcome by her love and devotion, which restore the beast to human shape. The young girl undergoes rites of initiation that successfully bring the wildness of nature into the orbit of social constraint.

In *Bear's Kiss* Bodrov has created an updated version of the man-bear myth for an age that honors youth culture, animal rights, ecology, and animistic reverence for nature. Lola, a young traveling circus acrobat deserted by her mother, tends an orphan bear cub sold to the circus after its mother was shot in the ancient forests of Siberia by native hunters. Girl and bear, lonely, alienated, and longing for a lost homeland, grow up together and fall in love. The story, seen from Lola's point of view, is one of transformation; love awakens both the human within the animal and the animal within the human. The true nature of the man-bear, stifled in captivity, is waiting to be released. The film is suffused with nostalgia for the woods and respect for the grandeur and beauty of the unfettered animal.

When Lola lets the bear out of the cage, the creature becomes metamorphosed into a very handsome naked young man, who is able to shape-shift back and forth between human and ursine form. The metamorphosis of Misha into his human incarnation is always instantaneous and complete; the process of transformation is not shown. We never see the painful intermediary and grotesque moments when the human strives to realize itself in the animal or when the animal starts to manifest itself in the human. Both bear and natural man are wholly beautiful and noble.

As the Fortunato Circus travels throughout Western Europe in its motorized caravan, the lovers wander the picturesque streets of Germany and Spain. Danger arises not from the man-bear but from the ugly debased society that cannot accept such an animal-human idyll. Even in anthropoid form Misha is chased by dogs and tormented by punks. When the repulsive sideshow entrepreneur sexually assaults Lola, Misha comes to her rescue and kills the rapist. To save Misha from the Spanish police who plan to shoot him, Lola smuggles her bear out of town in a truck and drives him back to his homeland. Having killed a human, the man-bear reverts to all bear and is released by Lola into the wilderness from which he had been stolen. The final images of the film

Rebecka Liljeberg (Lola) and Sergei Bodrov, Jr. (Misha) in the poster
for *Bear's Kiss*, directed by Sergei Bodrov (2002)

show Misha as a wild creature, bounding through the woods and streams followed by
Lola. Bodrov's fairy tale is framed by the primeval forest, a pure realm out of which the
man-bear comes and to which he returns. The last frame shows two bears loping off into
the forest—a larger bear accompanied by a smaller one. Lola too has been transformed.

Bear's Kiss is, for the most part, in English, with occasional Swedish, Italian,
Spanish, and Russian; like the producers of the film, the cast is multinational. The
Swedish actress Rebecka Liljeberg plays Lola, and Bodrov's son (who was killed in an
earthquake and avalanche while filming in Ossetia the following year) is the human
Misha. Four different multinational bears—Seryozha, Ilya, Gosha, and Vorchun—play the
ursine Misha at various ages. Since the story is about performers in a traveling circus, a
notoriously multicultural enterprise, the babble of accents and tongues and the use of
English as a lingua franca seem quite natural. The fable itself is composite, consciously
echoing other films, such as *Beauty and the Beast*, *La Strada*, and *Born Free*. It is in part
the story of a wild animal kept in captivity and finally released back into the wild, in part
the story of a love affair between a human and an animal, and in part the story of the
metamorphosis of a bear into a human, and back again. The petty human jealousies and
sordid affairs of the Felliniesque circus performers constitute a large part of the film,
serving as a contrast to the innocence and beauty of the bear's world.

The love between human and beast celebrated in *Bear's Kiss* has no dangerous underside. Lola's loss of virginity takes place discreetly in the dark with Misha in his human incarnation. There is never any question of violence being done to the girl by the bear, but rather what we witness is the brutal violation of nature by so-called civilization. Bodrov's film is the story of a bear's gentle kisses. There is no wedding and no monstrous offspring.

II.

"Lokis" (1869) is Prosper Mérimée's seminal nineteenth-century novella about the legendary "Son of a Bear." Set in the wilds of primeval Lithuania where the atavistic and fantastic have persisted into modern times, it is a violent but veiled and ambiguous tale concerning the rape of a woman by a bear and the birth of a child—half-human and half-ursine—who will commit an atrocious murder, despite himself, unless his pending marriage can be stopped. The mystery of the past must be unraveled if a new tragedy is to be averted. The tale's fantastic premise of the human child born of a bear is based on Slavic folk tales, such as "Ivanko the Bear's Son" (in Afanasyev's *Russian Fairy Tales*). "Lokis" takes place at Count Mikhail Szemioth's castle in Samogitia, a remote and ancient region of western Lithuania, as the Count is preparing to marry. An episode that happened forty years earlier proves decisive. We learn that two days after her wedding Count Kazimir's bride accompanied her husband on a hunting expedition. Separated from the group, she was carried off and mauled by a bear before the beast could be shot. Finding herself pregnant and left mentally unbalanced by the violent episode, the Countess was horrified by the child she gave birth to. Grown into a handsome introspective young man, Count Mikhail is full of deep anxieties about his own nature. On his wedding night he kills his bride and escapes into the forest.

Mérimée's tale is told obliquely by the pedantic German Professor and Pastor, Wittembach, a clergyman from Königsberg (working on a Biblical translation) who visits the young Count Mikhail at the time of his marriage. The tale is inseparable from the medium of its telling. The rational and erudite Professor is incapable of grasping the danger hidden in the ancient forest; despite his knowledge of languages, he fails to read correctly the signs given him by the Doctor, who tends the crazed old Countess locked up in the castle, and he is unable to stop the tragedy.

The reader must be more perceptive than the Professor in interpreting the wealth of details that he observes and notes down. There is a gradual accumulation of small hints, uncanny incidents, and disquieting events: the Count's propensity for tree climbing, his crushing embrace, the terror that he inspires in dogs, his sudden accesses of savage violence, his mother's madness, the mysterious remarks of a witch-like old woman with a snake whom he meets in the forest.

In Mérimée's narrative the pain and fear of transformation experienced by the Count are palpable. The hero is tormented by his biological monstrosity. The signs— squeezing his fiancée too hard, climbing down the tree outside his bedroom window, growing excitement at the sight of blood—are evident to the reader and a cause for alarm. Nature and culture are at war. Although he is gentle, reserved, and cultivated, the Count is driven by another self, buried deep within him that thirsts for blood. He must drink it from the neck of his bride. The forest, mysterious and menacing, contains elemental forces beyond our comprehension. A beast lurks within all of us.

"Lokis" is an outgrowth of Mérimée's interest in the Slavic world. An early French

"The Bear's Allurements," a sixteenth-century woodcut
from Olaf Magnus's *Historia de gentibus septentrionalibus*

translator of Pushkin and Gogol, Mérimée was responsible for first introducing Russian literature in France, although he only began learning Russian when he was almost fifty and never visited Russia. An expert archaeologist and linguist, he was fascinated by exotic foreign cultures and "primitive" peoples; he sought out the violence lurking in primitive man, in the primordial instincts of civilized man, and in the dark recesses of human mind. He knew that there were Russian tales of women who were violated by bears giving birth to half-human, half-ursine monsters, and he was aware of the training school for bears in Smorgony, Lithuania.

Appearing the year before his death after more than twenty years of silence as a fiction writer, "Lokis" is Mérimée's next to last story and, in the opinion of some, his masterpiece. Not originally intended for publication because the author felt it was too scabrous, the tale was written as a society entertainment and risqué joke to be read aloud to the Empress Eugénie and her ladies of honor at one of their readings of fantastic tales. Mérimée's fears of scandal proved unfounded; no one was offended because his listeners failed to comprehend. The signs were so ambiguous that it never occurred to the court ladies that the Count was descended from a bear, nor did it to the initial readers of the story in the *Revue des Deux Mondes*, who were sure that the pregnant mother's terrors had been passed on to her child in the womb and that the Count was driven to murder by his nervous disposition.

Mérimée had been translating some fantastic tales by his friend Ivan Turgenev, and he wished to try his hand at something similar with an Eastern European atmosphere and setting. Concerned to give his horror story as much basis in reality as possible, he consulted doctors to see if the union of a bear and a human could actually produce a child. Even though the postulate of the tale rested on an impossibility, Mérimée took pains to make the setting and material circumstances seem exactly observed and precisely

Title page of Anatoly Lunacharsky's *Bear's Wedding*

rendered. The fantastic had to be presented in a matter-of-fact fashion. For authentic details of daily life in Polish Lithuania, Mérimée turned to Mickiewicz's *Pan Tadeusz* (which he read in French) and *La Pologne captive et ses trois poètes* by Charles Edmond (Edmund Chojecki), a Polish émigré living in Paris, the author of French melodramas and comedies, and a friend of Mérimée's.

He began studying Lithuanian grammar, and hoped to check the accuracy of his descriptions with a native of the region (whom he never found). It was Turgenev who provided the local color and suggested that Mérimée use the Lithuanian word for bear as his title.

On October 9, 1868, Mérimée wrote to Turgenev, summarizing his new tale with which he needed help on the local color, "A lady meets a bear who rapes her. She has a child, a very handsome boy, a bit hairy, quite strong, who is well brought up, but who is always somewhat bizarre. This gentleman has not lost his virginity, reads books on metaphysics and is in love with a little flirt who is all white and rosy . . . he does not realize what kind of feelings she inspires in him; is it physical or Platonic? He gets married and eats her."

Even though Mérimée in his final version toned down explicit indications of the bear's fathering the Count, "Lokis" is a bizarre and disturbing tale of abnormality and monstrosity deeply rooted in human nature.

Scene from Lunacharsky's *Bear's Wedding* at the Maly Theatre, Moscow, 1924,
showing the tracking down of the Count after his murder of Joulka

It is not surprising that "Lokis" became adapted for the stage as a vampire thriller. The first dramatization of Mérimée's tale was made by Charles Esquier (1874–1931), a minor French playwright and screenwriter, author of comedies, operettas, and dramas for the Grand Guignol in the early 1900s. His *Lokis*, a drama in two acts, was premièred on November 25, 1906 at the Théâtre des Funambules.[2]

Esquier follows Mérimée closely in the general outline of the plot, but concentrates on the mounting revelations rendering inevitable the horrible murder at the end of the play. The drama has been stripped to its essentials: there are only seven characters, two short acts, and a single setting. The hints that there is a wild animal lurking within the Count are highlighted from the very beginning, and throughout we hear the cries of the crazy Countess: "Lokis! Lokis! Kill the beast!" Joulka, the bride to be, becomes increasingly terrified of her future husband, and the Count himself, realizing the terrible force of his base instincts, tries to struggle against the temptations of blood lust and implores his fiancée to help him overcome the temptation. The final scene of violence is presented directly onstage in the traditions of the Grand Guignol.

He takes her in his arms and bites her neck, with his back to the public. She falls with an agonizing cry, the Count crouched over her, continuing to bite her neck; he gets up after a rather long time, during which the madwoman's shrieking stops; he looks at her terrified, after having regained his self-control. He is wild looking, staggers . . . seeming to wake up, he reflects for a moment, looks at his blood-stained hands and recoils in horror; like a man acting resolutely, he takes down a hunting rifle and leaps out the window.

As the Professor and Doctor discover the viciously massacred bride, a gunshot is heard offstage. The Count has killed himself. The madwoman howls, "Lokis! Lokis!" Long before Bram Stoker's novel *Dracula* (1897) was adapted for the stage (1924), Esquier transformed Count Mikhail into a Grand Guignol vampire preying on a young woman for blood.

III.

In the summer of 1922 the Soviet Commissar of Education, Anatoly Lunacharsky, wrote his version of *Lokis*, called *The Bear's Wedding*, "A Melodrama in Nine Scenes on a Theme from Mérimée." The play was premièred at the Maly Theatre in April 1924 and proved so successful with audiences that it played throughout the USSR in provincial theatres and remained in the Maly repertory until 1930. But despite its strong popular appeal, Lunacharsky's melodrama was attacked by Soviet critics as decadent, bourgeois, and old fashioned.

Had the learned and urbane Commissar of Education simply written *The Bear's Wedding* as a commercial venture to make money and provide his wife, the actress Natalia Rozenel', with a choice role as the flighty, luxury-loving Joulka? In fact, Lunacharsky, as a theorist of theatre, had for many years promoted melodrama as the genre best suited to convey new revolutionary ideas to mass Soviet audiences. A long resident in Paris steeped in French literature and culture, the Commissar of Education was well acquainted with Mérimée and might even have seen, read, or heard of the stage version of "Lokis."

Moreover, Mérimée's work was unusually popular in the Soviet theatre in the early 1920s because of the author's anticlericalism, aesthetic non-conformity, and sharp social critique. In 1923 the Musical Studio of the Moscow Art Theatre did a version of Bizet's *Carmen*, called *Carmencita and the Soldier*, that, under the slogan of "Back to Mérimée," stripped away the false trappings of the nineteenth-century opera libretto in order to recover the elemental passions of the original. A number of Russian theatres staged plays from *The Theatre of Clara Gazul*, and *The Jaquerie* was given its world première at the Workshop of the Experimental Heroic Theatre.

To give the story mass appeal, Lunacharsky turned Mérimée's subtle and ambiguous tale into a sensational horror melodrama with a didactic social theme and a clear Marxist message. At the same time to make his *Bear's Wedding* a serious literary work, Lunacharsky displayed his erudition by developing at great length the local color and cultural and intellectual background touched on in Mérimée's tale, resulting in a long, overblown drama with six different settings, a large cast, and extended disquisitions on social conditions.

The last of his line, Count Mikhail is an aristocratic oppressor of the people, driven by bestial instinct and erotic blood lust. With his death the peasants will be freed from feudal enslavement. Abandoning Mérimée's fantastic postulate of a bear's fathering a half-human child, Lunacharsky makes Count Mikhail a predatory vampire sucking the blood of the peasants and raping their women. He is a class monster, not a biological one. His psychopathic criminal behavior is the consequence of his hereditary position of social privilege. For centuries his ancestors have built their lives of luxury on the bones of serfdom. Now the people rise up against the cruel autocratic system and overthrow the Count.

The bear who mauled his mother behaved only naturally, but the crazy old Countess claims that she was raped by her husband and denies that the Count Mikhail is her son. He is inclined to derangement and violence due to prenatal influence and corrupt genes.

The Doctor, a former peasant who has risen in the world due to his determined pursuit of education, has become a radical critic of the decadent aristocratic society, which, he says, is doomed to extinction and must be exterminated. The time of reckoning

A "friendly caricature" based on Ivan Krylov's fable, showing a bear beating Lunacharsky with a copy of his play, by Kukryniksy (collective pseudonym of three Soviet artists who always worked together: Mikhail Kupriianov, Porfirii Krylov, and Nikolai Sokolov)

has come. At the folkloristic wedding celebrations, which Lunacharsky reconstitutes with an eye to ethnographic accuracy, the servants and peasants are compelled to pay their respects to their master and his bride in a variety of rituals. The Gypsy Fortuneteller predicts that the bride will not long survive, and the Doctor urges the people to revolt. Four peasants appear in bear disguises to provide entertainment, but the Count spurns their efforts.

The murder of Joulka takes place offstage, and the audience only learns of it after the fact through Wittembach's narration. The Count flees to the woods hoping to become one with nature, but his divided self can find no peace even in the forest and he returns to his castle, intending to commit suicide. The huntsmen, manor serfs, and peasants pursue the Count and hunt him down like a wild animal. Mariya, Joulka's seventeen-year-old sister, who tries to be the Count's guardian angel, attempts to save him, but when the Count attacks the Doctor, Mariya shoots and kills the troubled aristocrat, who cannot resist his worse instincts but who in a gesture of generosity has signed over his property to the peasants. "The beast is killed, the land is yours," the Doctor explains. The peasants cheer.

At the Maly Theatre *The Bear's Wedding* was powerfully staged by Konstantin Eggert, who kept Lunacharsky's melodrama within the conventions of the horror genre, while at the same time using expressionistic stylization in the sets, costumes, make-up, lighting, and acting. The atmosphere was murky, often pitch-dark. All the spectacular theatrical effects of traditional melodrama were present in Eggert's *Bear's Wedding*: large scale crowd scenes, a wedding in the castle at night, grotesque musicians, gypsy dances and songs, popular merry-making with bonfires, and finally a frenzied hunt for the villain.

It is hardly surprising that such a successful drama would be adapted for cinema. The Mezhrabpom-Rus film studio—a semi-private production firm, in which Eggert had a financial interest, that specialized in big-budget entertainment films—saw the commercial possibilities of Lunacharsky's play. *The Bear's Wedding* was filmed in 1925 with a screenplay by Grigorii Grebner and Anatoly Lunacharsky, and co-directed by the veteran filmmaker Vladimir Gardin and Konstantin Eggert who also starred as the Count. (Vsevolod Pudovkin was at first Eggert's assistant before moving to another project.) When it was released in January 26, 1926, *The Bear's Wedding* proved to be a sensational box-office hit, one of most popular of all Soviet films. Released at same time as Eisenstein's *Battleship Potemkin*, it drew twice as many spectators when both were shown in Moscow. Eggert acquired a following for his portrayal of the Count as a believable and sympathetic ursine vampire.

Both a theorist and practitioner of cinema, Lunacharsky wrote a book and many articles on film, created a number of screenplays, and appeared in several films, in which he played himself. The Commissar of Education defended plot, fast action, and romance, declaring, "Our films must be just as attractive and just as entertaining as bourgeois films. The melodramatic form is the best for cinema." The antithesis of what a Soviet film should be, *The Bear's Wedding* was banned in the countryside for peasant audiences and attacked in the press as an example of New Economic Policy commercialism, designed to appeal to readers of fantasy novels published by NEP firms.

Foreign films, particularly American, were immensely popular with Soviet audiences from 1925 to 1928. *The Bear's Wedding* imitated Western models and had all the stock horror film elements: dark forests, murky castles, a human beast, hereditary insanity, storms, and a dungeon. It was successfully exported to fifty countries (but banned in Germany). Released in May, 1927, in New York, as *The Legend of the Bear's Wedding*, it was the first film shown at the new Fifty-Fifth Street Cinema (just east of Seventh Avenue) dedicated to the art of film. Mérimée was not credited in the film, nor was his contribution recognized outside of France, where there were accusations of theft.

Like the decadent pre-revolutionary films of Yakov Protazanov (with whom Gardin had worked), *The Bear's Wedding* exploited obsessive love, wild depravity, and tragic mayhem. In the Prologue (directed by Gardin and photographed by Eisenstein's cinematographer Eduard Tisse) we see Adelina, the young the bride of Count Kazimir Szemioth, several days after her marriage before the corpse of her supposed lover who has been killed by her jealous husband; then she is abducted by a bear and goes mad. Some twenty-five years later, young Count Mikhail returns home. On his desolate estate, the handsome young count roams the forest, wearing a bearskin, and attacks a young peasant girl, biting her neck. The village women are terrorized. Cursed by his insane mother's traumatic experience, the deranged nobleman has seizures that transform him into a bear on the prowl.

Franciszek Starowieyski's poster for Janusz Majewski's *Lokis* (1970)

Drawing, by Starowieyski, from Majewski's *Lokis*, showing what happened to the old Countess

When the count falls in love with the innocent Joulka, the Doctor, who tends the crazy mother and knows the family's shocking history, advises him not to marry. But the wedding takes place, followed by a lavish, sexually charged celebration, which grows more and more sinister as the night progresses. Tension mounts as a dancing bear appears and blood-colored burgundy in the bride's mouth arouses the Count's base instincts. Close-ups of Eggert's face show his uncontrollable animal passions. In a frightening and gruesome scene, the mad Count savagely mutilates his bride with his teeth in the wedding bed. Overcome by anguish for his crime, the Count tries to flee the vengeful mob of villagers. He is shot by the sister of the bride, and the villagers set fire to his castle. The violent denouement was the most powerful and memorable section of the film.[3]

IV.

In his *Lokis* (1970), which was billed as a horror film, the Polish director Janusz Majewski gives a subtle, nuanced reading of the "Son of a Bear" legend, refusing either to endorse or deny the interpretation that the Count is the child of an animal rape. Since everything is a matter of perception, the question is: Who is doing the seeing? Majewski emphasizes the shortcomings of the civilized rational observer from the West, Pastor Wittembach, a member of the Königsberg Bible Society and a prurient, repressed figure who upon contact with a mysterious world he cannot fathom is ready to believe any kind of atavistic regression on the part of his host. Played by Edmund Fetting as a creepy psychopath and peeping Tom in reflecting glasses, Wittembach becomes the focus of the drama's ironies and an unreliable narrator. Swearing him to secrecy, the Doctor shows the Professor a series of drawings in the library that depict the various events connected with the Countess's encounter with the bear; these pictures, he explains, were done by an Italian artist who had been engaged by the Count's father and are not shown to guests. The Polish graphic artist Franciszek Starowieyski, who also designed posters for the film, created these drawings. The artist's wife, Ewa Starowieyska, designed the costumes, and Wojciech Kilar wrote the music. The Count, played by Józef Duriasz, is afraid of his own wild instinctive urges, effectively illustrated by the episode in which he bare-handedly captures a hawk. The film skillfully evokes in striking visual detail the atmosphere of the place and time.

Majewski moves the story ahead in time slightly to the turn of the century 1900. The film begins and ends in the train that brings Pastor Wittembach to Samogitia from Königsberg and then takes him home. He has come from a smug rational civilization; telephone poles indicate that light is being brought to the wilds of Samogitia. The film ends quite differently than Mérimée's novella. The Doctor says that Joulka is not dead but has only fainted; the Count will be back. The ambiguity of the tale has grown—is it only the repressed Professor who thinks that the Count is the son of the bear?[4]

V.

Commissioned by the Vilnius Festival, the two-act opera, *Lokys*, by the Lithuanian composer Bronius Kutavičius (born 1932) was premièred on June 25, 2000, at the National Opera and Ballet Theatre. As a grand opera of elemental passions and violent deeds, Mérimée's perverse and ironic tale returned to its place of origin: the landscape and language of Lithuania. Kutavičius's musical drama was steeped in an atmosphere of ancient mystery in which the legend of the man-bear had originally arisen.

Projection of a dissected hand on a bear-skin on the wall,
above the pathway on which Julija is killed; wedding guests gathered on either side,
Bronius Kutavičius's opera *Lokys*, the Lithuanian National Opera and Ballet Theatre (2000)

What for Mérimée had been an outlandish setting, full of exotic people and primitive superstition, was for Kutavičius native soil, and he was able, through his music, to evoke the pagan roots of the story and the ancient deities of the forest. The composer sought to go back to the pre-Christian Baltic past and revive its dark myths. With a libretto by US based Lithuanian writer Aušra Marija Sluckaite-Jurašiene and directed by Jonas Jurašas,[5] with stage design by the sculptor Mindaugas Navakas, *Lokys* has a primordial structure and a world view encompassing both the natural and social worlds. Kutavičius's Baltic minimalism has its sources in archaic Lithuanian folk music, particularly in the *sutartines* (polyphonic folk songs), an ancient form of Lithuanian counterpoint singing. In 1974 he performed with the Lithuanian Musical Folklore Theatre, an ethnographic ensemble directed by Povilas Mataitis, which was engaged in cultural and anthropological reconstructions of Lithuanian rituals of the eighteenth and nineteenth centuries. Kutavičius's first major vocal work, his theatrical oratorio, *Last Pagan Rites* (1978), aimed to return music to ritual.

Explaining that he had long dreamed of writing a traditional opera with a chorus, orchestra and ballet, Kutavičius said that in *Lokys* he was less interested in the conflict between civilization and paganism than in the themes of love and fate typical of Romantic opera. The composer combined different musical idioms with the Lithuanian tribal style to create a work that mixed different musical epochs and cultures.

Mérimée's narrative was modified and new characters added to heighten the conflicts and make the visual and vocal effect more powerful. Discarding Mérimée's techniques of innuendo, inference, and fleetingly glimpsed horror, Kutavičius makes

Folk-singer Veronika Povilioniene as the One-eyed Fortune Teller, with the Mute Servant Franciškus, Bronius Kutavičius's opera *Lokys*, the Lithuanian National Opera and Ballet Theatre (2000)

Lokys a stark drama of fatality and nemesis in which violence and suffering are not masked, but foregrounded.

The stage was bare and ominous, the floor marked in black and white squares. Images illustrating the dialogue and action were projected on a huge bear skin hanging in the background: dissected human bodies were shown while the Professor sang of phobias; mushrooms and an owl were displayed as these were mentioned.

Two worlds, the real and the unreal, are contrasted; the Count, Julija, and One-Eyed Old Woman belong to the mythological world, whereas the Doctor, Professor, and the Marshall inhabit the inconsequential real world.

Kutavičius has added a new character, Franciškus, the mute servant (an archetypal figure from nineteenth-century melodrama) who lost his speech when he rescued the Countess from the bear that had attacked her and now must communicate solely in sign language. There is also the Count's Double (a distinct vocal part), with whom the Count talks about his attraction to the woods and his desire for blood as he shaves his hairy breast and stares at himself in the mirror.

The One-Eyed Gypsy Fortuneteller, whom the Count meets at the crossroads in the forest, tells him that if he goes to the left, he will become king of the animals, but that if he goes to the right, it will bring Julija misfortune. While visiting Julija at her aunt's, the Count sucks blood from his fiancée's foot which she cut on a broken wine glass.

In Act II, during the Wedding, the crazed Countess seeking revenge attacks with a knife the bear skin hanging on the wall. During the dancing and revelry, the Count drinks wine from Julija's blood-stained slipper. The One-Eyed Gypsy Fortuneteller appears with her smoking kettle and ashes used for divination. After the offstage murder, the Doctor in his wheelchair enters bearing Julija's mutilated corpse. The mad Countess enters with a shotgun and kills her son as he claws at the bear hide and brings it down on top of him. The chorus plays a major role in *Lokys*. At the beginning the chorus and orchestra plunge the audience into a gloomy atmosphere with a pagan curse and chant which engulf the stage. It is the forest spirit that dominates the Count with an ominous rhythm. At climactic moments this chant breaks in: in the forest scene in Act I and wedding scene in Act II. But the cursing spirit disappears in the epilogue, in which there is first a prayer paraphrase, and then a coda consisting of the final words of Mérimée's tale read in French.

VIDEO AND CD SOURCES

Bodrov, *Bear's Kiss*. DVD available in Russian, Spanish, and other European versions.

Kutavičius, *Lokys*. The Choir and Orchestra of the Lithuanian National Opera and Ballet Theatre. Martynas Staškus, conductor. 2 CDs. Ondine ODE 1021-2D, Helsinki, 2002.

Majewski, *Lokis*. Filmy Polskie videoteka 92, Agencja Producentów Filmowych.

I wish to thank Veronika Janatjeva of the Lithuanian National Opera and Ballet Theatre for providing me with production photographs and information about the staging of *Lokys*, Lenny Borger for discovering material about Le Théâtre des Funambules, and Mary Keelan for locating resources on foreign screenings of *The Bear's Wedding*.

NOTES

1. *Bear's Kiss* was shown on January 30, 2003, at the Walter Reade Theatre as part of the Film Society of Lincoln Center's program—"Soviet Sounds: Russian and Soviet Composers in the Cinema."
2. The Théâtre des Funambules had been established in the former Théâtre Bodinière (at 18 rue Saint-Lazare) by a former Grand Guignol actor Désiré Gouget, who played the role of the Count. The Funambules lasted only three months, and *Lokis* was one of the only two plays produced there.
3. Lunacharsky's wife Natalia Rozenel' appeared in the film, as she already had in the play, but she changed roles from the vain and shallow Joulka (who was marrying the Count to advance her social ambitions and attend balls in Paris) to her more complex younger sister Mariya (who was in love with the Count). The popular actress Vera Malinovskaya played Joulka.
4. Walerian Borowczyk's erotic French film *La Bête* (*The Beast*) of 1975 could be considered a degenerate variation on the same theme, in which we see in graphic detail the mating of the woman and the beast. Because of its pornographic nature, which leads in quite a different direction, I have not included Borowczyk's film in my discussion.
5. In the Soviet era Jurašas had run the innovative Drama Theatre of Kaunas from 1968 to 1971 when he was forced to emigrate for his refusal to conform. For twenty years he worked abroad, in the United States, Canada, Germany, and Japan, before being able to return to the Drama Theatre.

King Candaules by Jean-Léon Gérôme (1859)

CANDAULES AND THE USES OF MYTH

In order to explain a change of dynasties in his *History of the Persian Wars*, Herodotus tells the story of Candaules, king of ancient Lydia and descendant of Hercules, who grows obsessed with his wife's beauty and insists on showing her naked to his servant, Gyges. Despite his objections, Gyges is secretly smuggled into the royal bedroom to watch the queen undress. But the plan miscarries and has, in Herodotus' words, "strange consequences." The queen discovers Gyges and offers him the choice of being killed or killing the king and replacing him as her husband. Gyges chooses life and murder; he gains possession of both Candaules' wife, Nyssia, and his kingdom.

In the second book of *The Republic*, Plato alludes to Gyges as a shepherd who discovers a magic ring that makes its wearer invisible. This may be an earlier version of the legend in which the servant consciously plots to overthrow Candaules by using the ring to seduce his wife.

These are the principal sources on which a number of later stories, poems, plays, operas, and ballets about Candaules have been based. My play *Candaules, Commissioner* is the latest in this series, and the first American play on the subject.[1] Both in writing the play and in working on productions, I have had occasion to think about the dramatic possibilities of this legend and about the use of such myths in the American theatre.

American playwrights face special problems in utilizing Greek mythology; not only is there little historical precedent in American drama for how to handle myth, but there is also the prior question of why choose such an obsolete mode in the first place. Direct use of Greek mythology is not an American tradition, and it is doubtful if it will ever become one.[2] In the nineteenth century there were virtually no American plays for the stage on Greek themes. In the twentieth century the classical heritage, which was never very strong in the new world, grew progressively weaker. Democratic, enlightenment ideals foster the replacement of archaic, aristocratic legends by a study of the common man and his problems, as witness the dramatic theories of Diderot, Rousseau, Beaumarchais, and Arthur Miller. American drama, like American literature and culture, has sought a native tradition unencumbered by restrictive European conventions.

Moreover, the dominant modes of modern American drama had until the 1960s been realism and Naturalism, which exclude the undisguised utilization of myth; and modern departures from the realistic in the American theatre towards the fantastic, absurd, and grotesque show no tendency to return to the known and prescribed patterns of classical mythology. If, in works like Lowell's *Benito Cereno*, Hivnor's *Assault on Charles Sumner*, Sackler's *Great White Hope*, Kopit's *Indians*, and Shepard's *Buried Child*, there is discernible a trend towards a new legendary drama, it is based on the American past and built out of the native heritage of American history, literature, and folklore. The mythic heroes are representative of the new world, not the old.

The few American plays whose plots and characters come from the traditional Greek myths are either poetic dramas like Jeffers's *Medea* and *The Cretan Women* and MacLeish's *Herakles*, which remain essentially poetry written by poets, or experiments in adaptation, like O'Neill's *Mourning Becomes Electra* and Williams's *Orpheus Descending*, in which the mythic fable is transposed to a specifically American setting, and the legendary heroes are morphed into American types. In this second category of

—*Modern Drama* 12, no. 3 (December 1969): 270–278.

Katja Rivera as Nyssia in *Candaules, Commissioner*,
directed by Brian Katz at Custom Made Theatre, San Francisco (2006)

American drama on Greek themes, even the names of the characters are usually changed, so as to be consistent with their speech, surroundings, and occupations. Only the titles of the plays call attention to their classical antecedents.

For the American dramatist the problem necessitating such transpositions is largely one of tone and style. As soon as the name of Oedipus or Agamemnon appears at the top of the page, the American playwright finds that there is no viable idiom in which to write the dialogue. A colloquial American style produces comic parody, and a high tone leads to stilted, unnatural speech.

In contrast, Giraudoux, Cocteau, Sartre, and Anouilh are the heirs of a long French tradition of Greek myth on the stage. No matter how contemporary the idiom, a universalizing neutral tone of voice whereby the speaker can be Antigone and the scene Argos has been available to the French dramatist interested in mythology. At least until quite recently French education and literary history prepared actors and audience to accept as quite normal the appearance of classical kings, queens, and even gods in the modern theatre.[3] Lacking this tradition and style, the American dramatist who for one reason or another is obsessed with Greek myth quite naturally reduces and disguises the heroes and their origins and Americanizes their speech, names and clothes. O'Neill's Agamemnon becomes Ezra Mannon; Williams's Orpheus appears as Val Xavier. The process is essentially the democratic one of minimizing class distinctions.

In my play *Candaules, Commissioner* I transposed a Greek legend into the present, but I found that I did not have to change the names of the characters. On the contrary, it seemed desirable to keep them. The retention of the traditional names offered me the inevitability and solidity of the original fable and also opened the possibility for ironic parallels between past and present.

The fact that the old names "work" in the new context indicates that there is something special about the Candaules legend. At least in America it is not a well-known myth and has the advantages, as well as the disadvantages, of unfamiliarity. The outlines of the characters have not yet been filled in, and the names do not have such built-in resonance as to drown out the words they speak, but rather serve to enrich them. The story of Candaules and Gyges is a minor, off-beat myth, derived not from the poets Homer and Hesiod and their tales of the Greek gods and heroes, but from a chronicler, Herodotus, and a philosopher, Plato; it is based on what was then recent Near Eastern history. Candaules and Gyges are historical figures who evidently lived in the eighth century BC, and the legend, as elaborated by Herodotus and Plato, is a poetic version of how a young opportunist gained power by seducing the king's wife and overthrowing the regime. Secular and unheroic, the legend lies halfway between history and myth.

The intertwined themes are sex and politics, not on the grandiose archetypal scale of *Agamemnon* or *Oedipus*, but in a very contemporary sense: a bedroom comedy and a palace coup. The dimensions of the Candaules story are smaller and more human than those of the vintage myths. No inflation is necessary to blow up the contemporary substance to fill the mythic outlines. The linking of perverse eroticism and sudden revolution is familiar and intelligible to us. Open as to genre, the myth falls into the pattern of the foolish wise man whose own cleverness brings about his downfall.[4] The legend invites a grotesque, bizarre treatment, rather than any straining for the tragic. Even the supernatural (present only in Plato) does not involve the gods but is simple magic used for self-advancement.

An air of mystery nevertheless surrounds the myth. Despite the comic clarity of the fable and its neat reversal, the characters and their relationships are ambiguous. The fatuously doting husband, the outraged wife, and the ambitious servant may seem to be types who lend themselves to farce because of their instant characterization, but the strangeness of the central action—the exposure of the naked queen and the revolution it provokes—calls into question their initial identities. The motives for and reactions to the key event give rise to speculation and make possible widely varied explanations—psychological, sociological, and philosophical. The three characters are caught forever in a closed circle of love, friendship, and power, and the fascination for writers who have dealt with the story lies in finding a solution to the puzzle. Although the materials and structure are given, possibilities for new interpretations constantly open as the myth is recreated by different ages and civilizations.

Herodotus presents the story with concision, simplicity, and only the barest motivation; as an expert chronicler, he makes the overthrow of an empire follow excitingly and convincingly from an act of voyeurism. Plato, in contrast, uses Gyges' ring as a metaphoric illustration in the philosophical debate between Socrates and Thrasymachus as to whether man would be moral without fear of punishment. As far as we know, none of the great Greek tragedians ever treated the subject, but a papyrus fragment discovered in 1950 indicates that there was a fourth-century Hellenistic tragedy about Candaules. The sixteen lines that could be reconstructed are from a speech by the Lydian queen in which she recounts how she has seen Gyges in her bedroom the night before and announces that she has summoned him to appear before her.[5]

There are many mentions of Candaules and Gyges in ancient writers, who often allude to the stories in Herodotus and Plato, but the tale is not retold until the early Renaissance when it becomes a moralistic biography in Boccaccio's *The Fates of Illustrious Men* (*De Casibus illustrium virorum*) and a ribald joke in Hans Sachs's *The Naked Queen from Lydia* (1538).

In modern times it is chiefly the French who have been intrigued by the erotic piquancy of the legend. La Fontaine touches on the myth briefly in one of his *Contes et nouvelles en vers* (1674), treating it as a comic anecdote or *fabliau*. It appears as one of Fontenelle's *New Dialogues of the Dead* (1683), where Candaules discusses with Gyges whether it is worth dying for a woman's honor (they decide it isn't), and it becomes the pedagogic "Gyges' Ring" in Fénélon's *Collection of Fables for the Instruction of the Duke of Bourgogne* (1690).

Nineteenth-century France gave the legend its most enthusiastic reception. In *Le Roi Candaule* (1844), Théophile Gautier turns the short myth into a long erotic Eastern tale, full of picturesque detail and sensuous description. Gautier's Candaules is a refined artist who wishes to share his appreciation of beauty with others. Inspired by Gautier, *Tsar Candaules*, a sumptuous Asiatic grand ballet in four acts and six scenes, was created for the Imperial Ballet in St. Petersburg by Marius Petipa in 1868. A record-breaking success because of its lavish costumes and décor,[6] the ballet was frequently revived and danced by Vaslav Nijinsky in 1908 and by George Balanchine (in a minor role as a satyr) in 1922.

In 1873 Meilhac and Halévy, playwrights who wrote the libretti for Offenbach and Bizet, created a clever theatre-in-the-theatre one-act comedy showing the spectators in the foyer of a theatre where they have come to see the scandalous *Le Roi Candaule* by Meilhac and Halévy. Different bourgeois spectators discuss the play and explain how the story of Candaules and Gyges reflects their own marital situations. The comedy was adapted in English by W.S. Gilbert as *The Realm of Joy*.

In his *Le Roi Candaule* (1901), André Gide follows Gautier in depicting Candaules as an aesthete, but he is a perverse one who must force his happiness and good fortune on his servant in order to experience them himself. In his attempt to make a generous gesture which will enable him to transcend his own limits, Gide's Candaules remains trapped in his own egotism and arouses only the hatred of the poor man whom he imagines he befriends. Gide's *Le Roi Candaule* was first performed at the Théâtre de l'Oeuvre in 1906, with Lugné-Poe as the King and then presented in German at the Volkstheatre in Vienna in 1906. Gide hoped to have it made into an opera by Henry Février, a composer known for his version of Maeterlinck's *Monna Vanna*.

In 1903 Hugo Hofmannsthal sketched an outline for a tragedy on the subject that he never wrote. The Austrian composer Alexander Zemlinsky, while in exile in the United States, proposed his work in progress *Der König Kandaules* (based on Gide) to the Metropolitan Opera in 1938, but it was turned down as too daring a subject. Zemlinsky's opera was completed in 1989 by Anthony Beaumont and had its world première in 1996 at the Hamburg Opera. It was revived in 2004 in Nancy in a dynamic and stylish modern-dress production.

In 1920 Maurice Donnay, known for his version of *Lysistrata*, wrote a comic operetta,[7] *Le Roi Candaule*, in which the theme of vicarious experience is treated on a farcical level. The aging king can revive his flagging sexual powers only by an act of transferred voyeurism; Candaules hopes to overcome his own impotence by seeing his wife naked through the eyes of his younger friend, but at the crucial moment he falls from the tree where he is watching and misses the unveiling.

Perhaps the most famous of all later versions of the legend is, however, German, not French. Friedrich Hebbel, in his philosophical tragedy *Gyges und Sein Ring* (1854), presents Candaules as a noble and far-sighted king in conflict with his age. His revolutionary innovations in manners and morals collide with the people's wishes, and his own over-civilized decadent nature contributes to his undoing. Hebbel's Gyges is a romantic adolescent who grows up in the woods, ignorant of women. When he first sees the queen, he suddenly loses his innocence and becomes a man. He falls so violently in love that he kills his friend and protector, although he has terrible feelings of guilt; as king, he continues Candaules' radical new programs and ideas.

For me what emerges from all these different versions of the legend (not all of which I knew at the time that I wrote *Candaules, Commissioner*) is a certain cluster of ideas and themes that are relevant to our own age, country, and predicament. The rich, successful representative of authority and the establishment, Candaules, is figuratively and perhaps literally impotent. He suffers from an abnormal desire to share what he thinks is his great happiness and good life with his inferior whom he hopes to make his friend. Candaules' display of his wife naked is his attempt to put Gyges in his place and then vicariously to put himself in Gyges' place so as to enjoy his own generosity. But the playful substitutions and reversals of position become deadly serious, since the king's patronizing liberality produces violent resentment, not gratitude. And the enigmatic Gyges, who may be an unwilling killer consumed with guilt, or who may be a cold schemer waiting for his chance, ends by adopting the role as well as the station of his former master.

In the theatre, however, the story of Candaules and Gyges must provide action, not simply ideas. In their efforts to philosophize the content of the legend, both Hebbel and Gide illustrate the difficulties of dramatizing the myth as a full-length serious drama. It becomes overblown and static. The theatrical strength of the legend as given by Herodotus lies in its economy, dynamism, and formal perfection. There are no side issues, and events happen rapidly, Candaules forces Gyges to agree to his plan, the viewing takes place, and the empire topples.

The legend, with its three necessary and sufficient characters, can only become cluttered and padded by the addition of invented figures. As in a chess problem, the limited cast is integral to the nature of the myth. To realize the full theatrical potential, a play based upon it should be short and restricted to Herodotus' inevitable triad of characters.

I have come to these conclusions about the myth only gradually, and the actual way I came to write *Candaules, Commissioner* was quite different. As a student I had read Herodotus and become fascinated by the mysterious eroticism and symmetry of the legend. The series of confrontations between master and servant, husband and wife, queen and future king, seemed an invitation and a challenge to do a dramatization. In 1958 I attempted to set the legend in ancient Lydia, with characters conceived historically and motivated psychologically. I soon discovered that although it was possible to write an ingenious scenario, it was impossible to write dialogue. To come to life and produce human speech, the myth would have to be transposed to the present and rooted in some kind of reality, and at that point I had no deeper personal involvement than a desire to explore the abstract geometric dimensions of the legend's theatricality. I abandoned the play.

In the meantime I wrote a verse play based on the Alcestis theme in which the characters' names were changed and the setting and action radically modernized. The result was still abstractly "universal," but the difficulty I had finding a proper idiom and style convinced me that the only way of handling myth was through the discovery of an obsessive and necessary transposition to the present. Unless the myth got under one's skin to such an extent that it became actual, there was no reason and no way to write

Jay Martin as Candaules and Perry Aliado as Gyges in *Candaules, Commissioner*
Directed by Brian Katz at the Custom Made Theatre, San Francisco (2006)

an American play on a classical theme. The legendary play is not a ready-made genre in America, as it had been in France, and the technique of creating a timeless, placeless world in which to explore the human condition will not work for us, or at least for me. In order to utilize classical mythology in American drama, it must be given a cultural milieu and physical concreteness. In other words, it must be treated more or less realistically. The impetus for my returning to the story of Candaules and Gyges came from misguided American foreign policy and my own personal experiences ten years earlier.

In 1964 my reading and brooding about the war in Vietnam revived memories and feelings about being an American soldier in Southeast Asia during the Korean War. As a private first-class in an army education center in Okinawa, I was in a peaceful enough niche among "decent" American civilians who thought they were doing good. Being a lowly functionary in a colonial occupation force, I was both servant and master, depending on whether I looked up or down the scale of servitude, and I was thus able to experience the effects of good will toward one's inferiors from both sides.

Our efforts to improve the natives' lot in Vietnam brought all this back to me. I saw myself again being chauffeured over dusty, bumpy dirt roads by an Asian driver; I would try to strike up a friendly, "democratic" conversation as I sat in the back seat and stared at the back of his head. This image gave me the transposition for the Candaules legend, which had been lying dormant somewhere in my mind. There was Candaules, High Commissioner of Economic Assistance to Lydia—a small Asian country where a civil war has been raging for seventeen years—riding over winding roads and expounding to his native chauffeur Gyges on the superior way of life that he and western civilization were bringing in the form of paved roads, a higher standard of living, and opportunities for advancement. It was an easy step from there to Candaules' desire to share a glimpse of his beautiful wife's bare flesh with his servant, who must of course desire to possess everything his master has. This Candaules is a well-intentioned, humane bureaucrat, an expert in the rice economy, interested in feeding people, and a part of the whole liberal machinery that wages wars.

My own experience of the colonial mentality and what I read in the newspapers about Vietnam gave me the reality necessary for the incidents and dialogue. Americans abroad who help their "inferiors" provided the proper class structure and authoritarian hierarchy for a legend about a king and his servant who usurps the power.

The new play bore no relation to the one I had started six years before; I was no longer primarily concerned with psychological motivation but theatrical movement and politics. Once I had a firm base in reality, with Gyges as native chauffeur and Candaules as government official, the theatrical elements—clothes, car, journey—began to collaborate with the natural directions of the myth. Their relative positions in the car defined the relationship of Candaules and Gyges, as did their costume and speech. And then the chauffeur's uniform and the diplomat's formal dress became a part of the subsequent focus on clothes and nakedness, so central to the myth.

The trip through the outskirts of Sardis in the limousine brings into the play a fourth character who never actually appears but who is essential to the dynamics of the transposed myth: the people or chorus. Candaules and Gyges drive past a cafe where people are eating ice cream by the edge of a hole made by a terrorist bomb, they see a crowd of "happy peasants" waving flags, they hear a group of war orphans thumping on the fenders of the car, and they are finally stopped by an angry mob who beat on the car windows menacingly and peer in at the commissioner.

Riot and revolution are a constant threat; Candaules and Nyssia are afraid of what the people may do and always aware of their presence. Gyges is the visible representative of the unseen hordes. To both Candaules and Nyssia he is the "typical Lydian," the embodiment of their hopes and fears. Their anxious comments, patronizing or contemptuous, create an invisible chorus of ragged victims of the war who finally revolt; although I saw no necessity for showing them on the stage, two productions (The Stanford Repertory Theatre and L'Aquarium at the École Normale Supérieure in Paris) used black-robed property men to make sounds and gestures for the crowd.

In the last scene a full-scale revolution topples the colonial empire. Nyssia and Candaules report on the progress of the disorders. The explosion of a plastic bomb at a children's movie (according to Nyssia, thrown by Gyges at her instigation) leads to a wave of arrests and the rounding up of students in special detention camps. This repressive action in turn sets off rioting in the streets, causing more police brutality and violence. Candaules claims that the occupiers themselves have engineered a coup in order to get rid of the ruling clique and replace it with another more easily manageable; due to the bombing, the uprising has gone out of control and spread throughout the entire structure of society. In keeping with the legend, Gyges' role remains enigmatic.

At the École Normale Supérieure, where Maoist slogans lined the walls and a blackboard in the dressing room urged the actors to continue the class war to the end, Gyges was played as a guerilla fighter who waited the right moment to arouse the people to open revolt against imperialism. This production was not anti-war, but pro-revolution; the chorus of peasants chanted "NLF will win," and Gyges throwing the bomb became the turning point in arousing the masses to action. Candaules' treatment of the people, seen in his treatment of his servant, brought Gyges and the audience (which was to be revolutionized) to a full consciousness of the necessity for rebellion.

On the other hand, at the Stanford Repertory Theatre the play was interpreted as a critique of the American dream, in which Gyges, played by a young black actor, at first almost believed. The naïve and innocent servant is caught between his master's patronizing liberalism and his mistress's compulsive fear and guilt. They fight among themselves for possession of Gyges' soul, and he is passively molded by their competition. Racked by indecision and conflicting loyalties, his slave mentality makes him the inheritor of a portion of his superior's ideology. This Gyges clearly did not throw the bomb, nor could he ever; it is only Nyssia's sick imagination which suggests the idea. Gyges reacts with astonishment to her revelation and only reluctantly cooperates in the burning of Candaules, whereas the revolutionary French Gyges gleefully doused his master with gasoline and invited the audience to enjoy the lighting of the matches.

In terms of the myth, the question of whether or not Gyges throws the bomb and actively foments the revolution is a rephrasing of the following problem: Did Gyges seek to win the kingdom by guile, as Plato's allusions seem to suggest, or was he an unwilling victim forced to act as he did, as in Herodotus' account? In the production by L'Aquarium, Gyges was in the driver's seat figuratively, as well as literally from the beginning. The radical younger generation saw Candaules and Nyssia from the activist point of view and relished their destruction. At Stanford the audience experienced the bankruptcy of the illusions and dreams of the middle-aged couple. The impact of their lives on Gyges was shattering, but only at the very end of the play did it force him to act and then very unwillingly, as he assumed the mantle of his master whom he still could not help but imitate.

The richness and resonance inherent in the myth carry over into the drama.

Katja Rivera as Nyssia, Perry Aliado as Gyges, and Jay Martin as Candaules in
Candaules, Commissioner, directed by Brian Katz at Custom Made Theatre, San Francisco (2006)

Candaules and Gyges are the eternal master and servant; they can mirror the American liberal and the subservient black shaking off the chains of servitude and coming out of his stupor, or they can reflect the benevolent imperialist and the revolutionary out to subvert him. One of the advantages of myth, even when realistically particularized, is its implication that the situation is not just one of the moment, but can happen anywhere and is repeated over and over again in human history.

Postscript. Thanks to *The English Patient*—both novel and film in which Herodotus' tale is read aloud and becomes an incitement to the hero's fatal love—Candaules, Nyssia, and Gyges have now been made familiar to millions of readers and viewers. Once again it is demonstrated that this exotic and cryptic Near Eastern legend is a profound source of insight about the ties of eros and violence in an age of war. When my play was revived in San Francisco in 2006, *Candaules, Commissioner* seemed to have been written expressly to comment on the current war in progress.

NOTES

1. *Candaules, Commissioner* first appeared in *First Stage* 4, no. 3 (Fall 1965) and was reprinted in *Drama and Revolution*, ed. Bernard Dukore (New York: Holt, Rinehart and Winston, 1971). In the 1960s and 1970s it was performed by the Actors Workshop of San Francisco as a radio play and on the stage by the Theatre Company of Boston; the Bread Loaf School of English; the Stanford Repertory Company in Palo Alto, California; L'Aquarium at the École Normale Supérieure, Paris; the Chelsea Theatre and Mercer-Hansberry Theatre in New York; the Nordmark Landestheater Schleswig-Holstein, Germany; and in a 2006 revival by the Custom Made Theatre in San Francisco.

  When I asserted that *Candaules, Commissioner* was the first American play on the subject, I was unaware of Thomas Joseph Morgan's *Gyges: A Tragedy in One Act* (Chicago: Indigo Press, 1952).

2. Writing in the mid-1960s, when Jack Richardson's *Prodigal*, based on *Agamemnon*, was the only instance of new Greek-inspired drama being staged, I was unable to foresee the resurgence of interest in Greek mythological themes that would occur among American playwrights starting in the 1980s, with Lee Breuer's *Gospel at Colonus* serving as a major catalyst. The appeal and relevance of Greek myth that I felt was shared by many others, resulting in the establishment of a viable tradition of American myth-based drama that is flourishing in the twenty-first century. Some of the playwrights who have contributed to this trend are Oscar Mandel, Charles Mee, John Jesurun, Karen Hartman, Ellen McLaughlin, Sarah Ruhl, Caridad Svich, and Susan Yankowitz. The reasons for this return to myth are many and complex, but all testify to the power of the mythology itself and of its representation in Greek theatre. What these myths have to say about war, tyrannical abuses of authority, and displacement and suffering of war's victims remains prophetic and of urgent applicability.

3. To what extent is this tradition still alive in France? Have French playwrights and French-language writers since 1968 continued to mine this once rich vein of dramatic inspiration? It is likely that while American playwrights have discovered the many uses of Greek myth, French authors have turned away from what is for them an overexploited convention.

4. Georges Polti locates the plot as one of "murderous adultery," the fifteenth of his *Thirty-Six Dramatic Situations* (Boston: The Writer, 1944). Others find that Herodotus has given the Asiatic fairy-tale the simplicity, inevitability, and unities of Attic tragedy. See Kirby Flower Smith, "The Literary Tradition of Gyges and Candaules," *American Journal of Philology* 41, no. 1 (1920): 35–36.

5. Edgar Lobel, "A Greek Historical Drama," *Proceedings of the British Academy* 35 (1950): 1–12.

6. Candaules and Gyges made their entrance in a golden chariot drawn by two white horses, followed by Queen Nyssia atop an elaborately decorated elephant and a procession of 200 Lydians.

7. The music for Donnay's opera was written by Alfred Bruneau, known for his many collaborations with Zola.

Acknowledgements

Of the many editors who have encouraged my work, I particularly wish to express my gratitude to Jeanine Plottel *(New York Literary Forum)*, Mel Gordon, Michael Kirby, and Richard Schechner *(TDR)*, Bonnie Marranca and Gautam Dasgupta *(PAJ, Performing Arts Journal; A Journal of Performance and Art)*, Joel Schechter, Erika Munk and Elinor Fuchs *(yale/theater)*, Jill Levenson and Ruby Cohn *(Modern Drama)*, Darko Suvin *(Science-Fiction Studies)*, and Henry Salerno *(Drama and Theatre)*, who first published *Candaules Commissioner* and the earliest English translations of Witkiewicz.

The twenty-eight essays (sometimes with an accompanying play or theoretical text) appeared in the following fifteen journals or conference proceedings: *Assaph, Cahier Witkiewicz: Colloque de Bruxelles, Contemporary Russian and Polish Drama: Theatre Perspectives, Comparative Literature, Modern Drama, New York Literary Forum, PAJ, , Pamiętnik Teatralny, Sacred Theatre, Science-Fiction Studies, Slavic and East European Performance, Theatre Three, TDR, World Literature Today, yale/theatre (Theater)*. The source of each essay is acknowledged at the bottom of its first page.

The articles and translations in this collection previously appeared in the following publications:

"Imaginary Invalids: A Theatre of Simulated Patients," *Theater* 19, no. 1 (Fall/Winter 1987): 6–18.

"Margueritte and *Pierrot Assassin of His Wife*" and "Eulogy for Pierrot," *The Drama Review: TDR* 23, no. 1 (March 1979): 103–112.

"Sologub and the Theatre," *The Drama Review: TDR* 21, no. 4 (December 1977): 79–84.

"Russian Drama and Polish Theatre in the Communist Era: The Case of Mayakovsky," *Contemporary Russian and Polish Drama, Theatre Perspectives*, no. 2 (1982): 28–32.

"Enter Fortinbras: Shakespeare's Strongman in Modern Eastern European Theatre," *Assaph: Studies in the Theatre* 1, section c, no. 1 (1984): 5–27.

"Fregoli, Witkiewicz, and Quick Change," *Theatre Three* 3 (Fall 1987): 47–60.

"Shaw's Criticism of Ibsen," *Comparative Literature* 15, no. 2 (Spring 1963): 130–145.

"The Apocalyptic Mode and the Terror of History: Turn-of-the-Century Russian and Polish Millenarian Drama," *Theater* 29, no. 3 (Winter 1999): 47–70.

"Valerii Briusov: Russian Symbolist," *Performing Arts Journal* 3, no. 3 (Winter 1979): 85–91.

"Historical Simluation and Popular Entertainment: The *Potemkin* Mutiny from Reconstructed Newsreel to Black Sea Stunt Men," *TDR* 33, no. 2 (Summer 1989): 161–184.

"Andrzej Bursa" and "Count Cagliostro's Animals," *PAJ: A Journal of Performance and Art* 27, no. 2 (PAJ 80) (2005): 99–113.

"Laocoön at the Frontier, or The Limit of Limits," *Modern Drama* 29, no. 1 (March 1986): 23–40.

"Tadeusz Kantor (1915–1990): A Visual Artist Works Magic on the Polish Stage," *Performing Arts Journal* 4, no. 3 (1980): 27–38.

"Jerzy Grotowski's Theatrical and Paratheatrical Activities as Cosmic Drama: Roots and Continuities in the Polish Romantic Tradition," *World Literature Today* 54, no. 3 (Summer 1980): 381–383.

"Gorky, Melodrama, and the Development of Early Soviet Drama," *yale/theatre* 7, no. 2 (Winter 1976): 33–44.

"Contexts for *Vatzlav*: Mrożek and the Eighteenth Century," *Modern Drama* 26, no. 1 (March 1984): 21–40.

"Witkacy's Doubles," *Colloque de Bruxelles: Cahier Witkiewicz*, no. 4 (Lausanne: L'Age d'Homme, 1982), 129–145.

"Lunacharsky on Melodrama" and "What Kind of Melodrama Do We Need?," *Slavic and East European Performance* 14, no. 3 (Fall 1994): 57–64.

"Pictorial Citation: Witkacy and Selous's Shakespeare," *Pamiętnik Teatralny* (1980): 529–540.

"Oscar Méténier and *Comédie Rosse*: From the Théâtre Libre to the Grand Guignol," "Meat-Ticket," and "Little Bugger," *The Drama Review: TDR* 28, no. 1 (T101) (Spring 1984): 15–28.

"Lunacharsky on Revolutionary Laughter" and "We Are Going to Laugh," *Slavic and East European Performance* 26, no. 1 (Winter 2006): 58–66.

"Iconographic Images in the Theatre of Tadeusz Kantor," *Sacred Theatre*, ed. Daniel Gerould, Bettina Knapp, and Jane House (New York: 1989).

"Henry Monnier and the Érotikon Théâtron: The Pornography of Realism" and "The Tart and the Student," *The Drama Review: TDR* 25, no. 1 (T89) (March 1981): 17–24.

"Tyranny and Comedy," *Comedy: New Perspectives*, ed. Maurice Charney (New York: New York Literary Forum, 1978).

"Witkacy: An Album of Photos—A Bundle of Letters," *Performing Arts Journal* 7, no. 3 (PAJ 21) (1983): 59–75.

"Villiers de l'Isle-Adam and Science Fiction," *Science-Fiction Studies* 11, no. 3 (November 1984): 318–323.

"Eastern European Bear Hugs: Cinema, Theatre, Opera," *Slavic and East European Performance* 25, no. 1 (Winter 2005): 48–71.

"Candaules and the Uses of Myth," *Modern Drama* 12, no. 3 (December 1969): 270–278.

Also by Daniel Gerould—Books, Essays, Translations, Plays.

"*The Cherry Orchard* as a Comedy," *Journal of General Education*, II:2 (April 1958): 109 122. Reprinted in *The Making of Drama: Idea and Performance*, ed. by Norman M. Small, 379 92. Boston: Holbrook Press, 1972.

"*Saint Joan* in Paris," *The Shaw Review*, VII:1 (Jan. 1964): 11 23. Reprinted in *Saint Joan: Fifty Years After, 1923/24-1973/74*, ed. by Stanley Weintraub, 201 19. Baton Rouge: Louisiana *State University Press, 1973*.

"Eisenstein's 'Wiseman and Montage of Attractions,'" *Drama and Theatre*, IX:1 (Fall 1970): 8–9.

Sergei Eisenstein, "Montage of Attractions for the Production of A. N. Ostrovsky's *Enough Stupidity in Every Wise Man*," [translation] Drama & Theatre, IX: 1 (Fall 1970): 10–13.

"Candaules, Commissioner," *First Stage*, IV:3 (Fall 1965): 150 67. Reprinted in *Drama and Revolution*, ed. by Bernard F. Dukore. N.Y.: Holt, Rinehart and Winston, 1971. German edition, trans, by Peter M. Ladiges. Berlin: Verlag Johannes Hertel, 1970.

"Explosion," *Drama and Theatre*, IX:3 (Spring 1971): 169 176. Reprinted in James Schevill, *Break Out! In search of new theatrical environments*, 134 57. Chicago: Swallow Press, 1973.

"Eisenstein's Wiseman," *The Drama Review*, XVIII:1 (T 61, March 1974): 71 76.

Twentieth Century Polish Avant Garde Drama: Plays, Scenarios, Documents, trans. and ed. Ithaca: Cornell University Press, 1977.

"Russian Formalist Theories of Melodrama," *Journal of American Culture*, 1:1 (Spring 1978): 152 68. Reprinted in *Imitations of Life: A Reader on Film & Television Melodrama*, ed. by Marcia Landy, 118 34. Detroit: Wayne State University Press, 1991.

"Andrei Bely: Russian Symbolist," *Performing Arts Journal,* 3:2 (Fall 1978): 25 29.

Melodrama, ed. with an introduction and contributions. New York Literary Forum, Vol. 7, 1980.

Witkacy: A Study of Stanisław Ignacy Witkiewicz as an Imaginative Writer. Seattle: University of Washington Press, 1981. Polish edition in 1981.

American Melodrama, ed. with an introduction. New York: Performing Arts Journal Publications, 1982.

"Madame Rachilde: Man of Letters," *Performing Arts Journal*, 7:1 (1983): 117 22.

Madame Rachilde, "The Crystal Spider" [translation] *Performing Arts Journal*, 7:1 (1983): 123 129.

Gallant and Libertine: Eighteenth Century French Divertissements and Parades, ed. and trans. with an introduction. New York: *Performing Arts Journal* Publications, 1983.

"Experiences as a Cultural Mediator," in *Amerikastudien/American Studies (Amst)* 32 (1985): 13–17.

Doubles, Demons, and Dreamers: An International Collection of Symbolist Drama, ed. with an introduction and 8 translations. New York: Performing Arts Journal Publications, 1985.

"The Coming of the Barbarians," in *The Play and Its Critics: Essays for Eric Bentley*, ed. by Michael Bertin, 269 304. New York: University Press of America, 1986:

"Corpse, Ghost, Seance: Translating Witkacy," *LMDA Review*, I:2 (Summer 1988): 2 5.

"Eisenstein's Wise Man," *Eisenstein at Ninety*, ed. Ian Christie and David Elliott, 88-100. Oxford: Museum of Modern Art, 1988.

"Introduction," in Stanisława Przybyszewska, *The Danton Case & Thermidor: Two Plays*, trans. by Boleslaw Taborski, 1–18. Evanston: Northwestern University Press, 1989:

"Concepts of Authority, Power and Freedom in the Life and Works of Witkacy," in *Poland Between the Wars*: 1918 1939, ed. by Timothy Wiles, 270 79. Bloomington: Indiana: University Polish Studies Center, 1989.

"Terror, the Modern State and the Dramatic Imagination," in *Terrorism and Modern Drama*, ed. by John Orr and Dragan Klaić, 15 47. Edinburgh: Edinburgh University Press, 1990.

"Representations of Melodramatic Performance," in *Browning Institute Studies*, 18, ed. by Adrienne Auslander Munich, 55 71. New York: The Browning Institute, 1990.

Guillotine: Its Legend and Lore. New York: Blast Books, 1992. Japanese and Polish editions.

"Foreword: Zygmunt Hübner, Man of the Theater," in Zygmunt Hübner, *Theater & Politics*, trans. by Jadwiga Kosicka (Evanston: Northwestern University Press, 1992), vii–xvi.

The Witkiewicz Reader, ed., trans., and with an introduction. Evanston: Northwestern University Press, 1992. British edition: London, Quartet Books, 1993.

"Melodrama and Revolution," in *Melodrama: Stage Picture Screen*, ed. by Jacky Bratton, Jim Cook, and Christine Gledhill, 185 98. British Film Institute, 1994.

"Seismograf der Zeiten: Avantgardeschauspiel in der Zwischenkriegszeit von 1918 bis 1939 am Beispiel Osteuropas und der Sowjetunion," in *Europa, Europa: Das Jahrhundert der Avantgarde in Mittel und Osteuropa*, Vol. 2, curated by Ryszard Stanislawski and Cristoph Brockhaus (Kunst und Ausstellungshalle der Bundesrepublick Deutschland, 1994): 113 127.

"The Pitoeffs' Chekhov," in J. Douglas Clayton, ed. *Chekhov Then and Now: The Reception of Chekhov in World Culture*, 31-40. New York: Peter Lang, 1997:

"Prosper Mérimée," *Dictionary of Literary Biography*, Vol. 192, *French Dramatists, 1789-1914*, ed. Barbara T. Cooper, 244-55. Detroit: Gale Group, 1998.

Stanisław Ignacy Witkiewicz, *Country House*, translated and with an introduction. Luxembourg: Harwood Academic Publishers, 1998.

Bruno Jasieński, *The Mannequins' Ball*, translated and with an introduction. Luxembourg: Harwood Academic Publishers, 2000.

Theatre/Theory/Theatre: The Major Critical Texts from Aristotle and Zeami to Soyinka and Havel, ed. with introductions. N.Y.: Applause, 2000.

Yurii Olesha, *The Conspiracy of Feelings* and Konstanty Ildefons Gałczyński, *The Little Theatre of the Green Goose*, ed. and trans. London: Routledge, 2001.

Stanisław Ignacy Witkiewicz, *Mr. Price, or Tropical Madness. Metaphysics of a Two-headed Calf*, ed. and trans. London: Routledge, 2001.

"Landscapes of the Unseen: Turn-of-the-Century Symbolism from Paris to Petersburg" in *Land/Scape/Theater*, ed. Elinor Fuchs and Una Chaudhuri303-2l. Ann Arbor: University of Michigan Press, 2002,

The Mrożek Reader, ed. and with an introduction by Daniel Gerould. New York: Grove/Atlantic, 2004.

Stanisław Ignacy Witkiewicz, *Seven Plays*, trans. and ed. with an introduction. N.Y.: Martin E. Segal Theatre Center Publications, 2004.

"In Praise of the Anthologist's Craft," *PAJ: A Journal of Performance and Art* 85 (Vol. 29, no. 1), January 2007, 113-25.

"Encounters," in *Theatre Journal* 59, no. 3 (October 2007): 349–52.

"Foreword," *roMANIAAfter 2000: Five New Romanian Plays*. Edited by Savianna Stanescu and Daniel Gerould, vii-xiv. N.Y.: Martin E. Segal Theatre Center Publications, 2007.

"Playwriting as a Woman: Prosper Mérimée and *The Theatre of Clara Gazul*," *PAJ: A Journal of Performance and Art* (30: 1), January 2008, 120-9.

Prosper Mérimée, "Heaven and Hell: A Comedy" [translation], *PAJ: A Journal of Performance and Art* (30: 1), January 2008, 129-40.

Stanisław Ignacy Witkiewicz, *Maciej Korbowa and Bellatrix*, translated and ed. with an introduction. Ashby-de-la-Zouch, Leicestershire, England InkerMen Press, 2009.

"Foreword: 'A Seismograph of the Times.' The Czech Tradition in Modern Drama." *Czech Plays: Seven New Works*. Edited Marcy Arlin, Gwynn MacDonald, and Daniel Gerould, ix-xix. N.Y.: Martin E. Segal Theatre Center Publications, 2009.

"The Symbolist Legacy to Present-Day Arts," *PAJ: A Journal of Performance and Art* 91 (Vol. 31, no. 1), January 2009, 80-90.

In Collaboration:

"The Drama of the Unseen" (with Jadwiga Kosicka), *The Occult in Language and Literature,* The New York Literary Forum, Vol. 4, 1980: 3 42.

A Life of Solitude. Stanisława Przybyszewska: A Biographical Study with Selected Letters, trans. and ed. (with Jadwiga Kosicka). Evanston: Northwestern University Press, 1989.

Vassily Aksyonov, *Your Murderer: An Anti-Alcoholic Comedy*, ed. and trans (with Jadwiga Kosicka). Amsterdam: Harwood, 2000.

Pixérécourt: Four Melodramas, trans. and ed. (with Marvin Carlson.) N.Y.: Martin E. Segal Theatre Center Publications, 2000.

A Maeterlinck Reader: Plays, Poems, Short Fiction, Aphorisms, and Essays, ed. and trans. (with David Willinger). Belgian Francophone Library., Vol. 24. N.Y.: Peter Lang, 2011.

Biographical Note:

Daniel Gerould is the Lucille Lortel Distinguished Professor of Theatre and Comparative Literature at the Graduate Center, City University of New York, and director of publications and academic affairs at the Martin E. Segal Theatre Center. He has a B.A. (1946), an M.A. in English Literature (1949), and a Ph.D. (1959) in Comparative Literature from the University of Chicago, and a Diplôme in French Literature from the Sorbonne (1955). Before coming to the Graduate Center he taught at the University of Arkansas (1949-51), the University of Chicago (1955-59), and San Francisco State University (1959-1968), where he established and headed the Department of World and Comparative Literature. He visited Poland in 1965 on a travel grant from the U.S. Office of Education International Studies Project with California State Colleges, developed an interest in Polish theatre, and then taught for two years at Warsaw University as a Fulbright Lecturer (1968-70). He was an exchange scholar in the Faculty Research Program with the Soviet Union at Moscow State University in 1967.

He is the editor of the journal *Slavic and East European Performance: Drama—Theatre--Film* (since 1981) and of the twelve-volume Routledge/ Harwood Polish and Eastern European Theatre Archive (1996-2002). He has translated twenty-one plays by Stanisław Ignacy Witkiewicz (Witkacy), and written extensively about Witkiewicz and twentieth-century avant garde drama and theatre. His play *Candaules Commissioner* has been performed in France, Germany, and America. For his translations from Polish he has received numerous awards, including prizes from the Polish International Theatre Institute, Los Angeles Drama Critics, Polish Authors Agency, Jurzykowski Foundation, American Association of Teachers of Slavic and East European Languages, American Council of Polish Cultural Clubs, and Marian Kister. He is recipient of the City University of New York Award for Excellence in Teaching (Graduate Center) and was honored by TWB, Theater Without Borders, as as a *Groundbreaker* in international theatre exchanges. Daniel Gerould, an avid jazz collector, is married to Polish scholar and translator Jadwiga Kosicka, with whom he frequently collaborates.

Picture Credits:

The pictures in Quick Change *are reproduced courtesy of the following journals in which the articles originally appeared, as well as private collections, museums, theatres, photographers, and artists.*

Assaph Magazine: 60, 68, 71, 73

New York Literary Forum:
Gyubal Wahazar: photographer, W. Prażuch, 356
Criccot II, *The Cuttlefish*, photographer, K. Jarochowski, 360, 362
Białystok *Striptease*, photographer, J. W. Brzoza, 364
Cracow *Striptease*, photographer, W. Plewiński, 364
as well as 131, 133, 352

Contemporary Russian and Polish Drama: 49, 50, 54, 55

yale/theater: 110, 123, 124

Modern Drama: 241, 245, 248

PAJ: 168, 199, 20-212, 370, 373-75

TDR: 24, 27, 141, 147, 149, 152, 157, 336, 339

Colloque de Bruxelles: 254

Theatre Three: 82, 84

Slavic and East European Performance: 314, 316, 400, 402, 404-8

Pamiętnik Teatralny, Lech Sokół, and Warsaw University Library: 278, 282-89

Frank Hentschker, portrait xiv

Lenny Borger collection, *Dr. Knock*, 6

Mel Gordon collection, *Spiegelmensch*, A. Baranowsky, Altes Theater, Leipzig.
        Photograph by Selma Genthe, 263

SIMULATIONS, Clinical demonstration, 9

Martin E. Segal Theatre Center, *Erotikon* Puppet Play, Photographer: A. Poyo, 340, 345

Bibliothek des allgemeinen und praktischen Wissens. Bd. 5 (1905), *Abriß der Weltliteratur,* Seite 85, Maxim Gorky, 222

Alma Law collection, Akimov, *Hamlet,* Two *Orphans,* 63, 231

Hennry Monnier, Art Gallery of the Graduate Center, CUNY, *Self-Portrait as Monsieur Prudhomme* 1871; special thanks to Jane House, 354

St. Petersburg Public Charitable Foundation of the Friends of the Dostoevsky Museum, Yuri Brusovani, Dostoevsky's *The Double,* 264

Alexandrinsky Theatre, St. Petersburg, Valerii Fokin, *The Double,* photo by Valentin Krasikov

National Museum in Warsaw, 256, 257 Double Self-Portrait as *Dr. Jekyll* and Mr. *Hyde* Tomasz Dąbrowa/Muzeum Narodowe w Warszawie

Tadeusz Kantor and the Cricoteka, Cracow, 196

The Grotowski Institute, Wrocław, 216

Tymon Terlecki collection, Martin E. Segal Theatre Center, CUNY Graduate Center, Miciński, *Potcmkin,* 119

Stanisław Ignacy Witkiewlcz. Lost Paintings and Drawings before 1914 from the original photographs in the collection of Konstanty Puzyna. Warsaw: Auriga, 1985, 269

Daniel Gerould collection, Oscar Méténier, 293

Agnieszka Wójtowicz, Grotowski's Opole Productions, *Mystery Bouffe,* 52

Chudak, No. 11, 1929, Lunacharsky laughing, 318

Lithuanian National Opera and Ballet Theatre, 412, 413

Custom Made Theatre, San Francisco, 422, 425

Index

The Martin E. Segal Theatre Center (MESTC), is a non-profit center for theatre, dance and film affiliated with CUNY's Ph.D. Program in Theatre. The Center's mission is to bridge the gap between academia and the professional performing arts communities both within the United States and internationally. By providing an open environment for the development of educational, community-driven, and professional projects in the performing arts, MESTC is a home to theatre scholars, students, playwrights, actors, dancers, directors, dramaturgs, and performing arts managers from the local and international theatre communities.

Through diverse programming—staged readings, theatre events, panel discussions, lectures, conferences, film screenings, dance—and a number of publications, MESTC enables artists, academics, visiting scholars and performing arts professionals to participate actively in the advancement and appreciation of the entire range of theatrical experience. The Center presents staged readings to further the development of new and classic plays, lecture series, televised seminars featuring professional and academic luminaries, and arts in education programs, and maintains its long-standing visiting scholars-from-abroad program. In addition, the Center publishes a series of highly-regarded academic journals, as well as books, including plays in translation, written, translated and edited by leading scholars.

www.theSegalCenter.org

Ph.D. Program in Theatre, The Graduate Center, CUNY, is one of the leading doctoral theatre programs in the United States. Faculty includes distinguished professors, holders of endowed chairs, and internationally recognized scholars. The program trains future scholars and teachers in all the disciplines of theatre research. Faculty members edit MESTC publications, working closely with the doctoral students in theatre who perform a variety of editorial functions and learn the skills involved in the creation of books and journals.   **www.web.gc.cuny.edu/theatre**

The MESTC Publication Wing produces both journals and individual volumes. Journals include *Slavic and Eastern European Performance* (SEEP), *The Journal of American Drama and Theatre* (JADT), and *Western European Stages* (WES). Books include *Four Melodramas by Pixérécourt* (edited by Daniel Gerould and Marvin Carlson—both Distinguished Professors of Theatre at the CUNY Graduate Center), *Contemporary Theatre in Egypt*, *The Heirs of Molière* (edited and translated by Marvin Carlson), *Seven Plays by Stanisław Ignacy Witkiewicz* (edited and translated by Daniel Gerould), *The Arab Oedipus: Four Plays* (edited by Marvin Carlson), *Theatre Research Resources in New York City* (edited by Jessica Brater, Senior Editor Marvin Carlson), and *Comedy: A Bibliography of Critical Studies in English on the Theory and Practice of Comedy in Drama, Theatre and Performance* (edited by Meghan Duffy, Senior Editor Daniel Gerould).

New publications include: *BAiT-Buenos Aires in Translation: Four Plays* (edited and translated by Jean Graham-Jones), *roMANIA AFTER 2000: Five New Romanian Plays* (edited by Saviana Stanescu and Daniel Gerould), *Four Plays from North Africa* (edited by Marvin Carlson), *Barcelona Plays: A Collection of New Plays by Catalan Playwrights* (edited and translated by Marion Peter Holt and Sharon G. Feldman), *Josep M. Benet i Jornet: Two Plays* (translated by Marion Peter Holt), *I Am a Mistake: Seven Works for the Theatre by Jan Fabre* (edited and foreword by Frank Hentschker), *Czech Plays: Seven New Works* (edited by Marcy Arlin, Gwynn MacDonald and Daniel Gerould), *Playwrights before the Fall* (edited by Daniel Gerould), *Timbre4*, (edited and translated by Jean Graham-Jones), *Jan Fabre: THE SERVANT OF BEAUTY, 7 monologues for the theatre by Jan Fabre* (edited and foreword by Frank Hentschker).

www.theSegalCenter.org